BOLT ACTION RIFLES

by Frank de Haas

EDITED BY JOHN T. AMBER
EDITOR OF GUN DIGEST

DIGEST BOOKS, INCORPORATED, NORTHFIELD, ILLINOIS

THE COVERS

Two versions of the Sturm Ruger
& Co. M77 bolt action rifle
appear on the front cover.
The full-length rifle is the
newly-introduced M77RT Round
Top which accepts standard scope
mount bases; the action
pictured is Ruger's standard M77.
The back cover exhibits
four views of the Weatherby Mark V
rifle and action, illustrating
some of the features that are
unique with this popular action.

ISBN 0-695-80220-8   Library of Congress Catalog Card #73-16310-5

Contents

Introduction

AS the title implies, this book is about centerfire turnbolt rifle actions. The action is the heart of any gun, and to most gun enthusiasts it is the most interesting part. The action, the mechanical part of the gun, usually is patented or patentable. It is the part which largely distinguishes one make and model of rifle from another of the same type. Great arms designers like Peter Paul Mauser and James Paris Lee were not actually "gun" designers, they were "action" designers.

The turnbolt action is about the simplest and strongest mechanical arrangement ever devised to lock a cartridge in a chamber. In its simplest form this action consists of a tube-like receiver to which the barrel is attached, and a bolt with a handle which locks inside the receiver when the handle is turned down. From this principle the modern sophisticated centerfire turnbolt rifle action has evolved; by one designer putting a firing pin and spring inside the bolt and a trigger in the receiver to fire the rifle, another putting an extractor on the bolt to extract the fired case, another attaching a magazine to the action to make the gun a repeater, still another adding extra locking lugs to make the action stronger, etc., etc. In this book the reader will find described all sorts of actions from the simplest and cheapest to the most up-to-date and expensive.

This book was no spur of the moment undertaking. During the years I was doing a lot of remodeling and conversion work on high powered bolt action rifles I often wished for a book such as this; a book solely devoted to centerfire turnbolt actions. Since no such book was available, and with the germ of an idea already in the back of my mind, I began collecting rifles and actions to study. Since I had no desire to own a bolt action rifle collection, nor did I have room for such a collection, I merely collected the actions. Many were the rifles I bought or traded, that I stripped, discarding everything except the action. In time I was literally able to sit in the middle of my den, spread all of the actions around me on the floor, and study and compare them at my leisure. With the actions available, and an extensive library of gun books on the shelves in my den, I had all sorts of material for a book at my fingertips. This, plus my own past first hand experience of having worked on many of the same actions, it was natural and inevitable that I should attempt to compile this information between the covers of a book.

This book is intended for everyone interested in centerfire turnbolt actions and rifles, which would include amateur and professional gunsmiths, firearms designers, arms students, experimenters, collectors, varmint and big game hunters, and those target shooters who use bolt action rifles. However, I had mostly in mind the countless amateur and part-time gunsmiths scattered throughout this continent and all future gun fixers who have yet to discover the joys of gun tinkering or who have not yet been born. I must point out, however, that I did not intend this to be a gunsmithing book, but rather one that gives detailed information on the various turnbolt rifle actions that have been, or still are available today. I've tried to include a bit of history about each of the principal actions, how they are made, of what they are made, how they function, how they are marked, their specifications, etc. The gunsmithing information I have included is not of the "how-to-do-it" nature, but rather I've tried to answer the many "what-can-be-done?" questions. In discussing the various actions I've tried not to get too technical, but rather to be as practical as possible in my comments and suggestions.

I don't claim to know everything about the turnbolt actions covered in this book, nor are all such actions included herein. All of the most common military turnbolt actions are covered, as well as nearly all of the commercial turnbolt actions, both domestic and foreign, which have been or still are available today as separate actions or as barreled-action units. Also covered are a few actions which have never been available separately or as barreled-action units, but which have been widely used by gunsmiths for building custom sporting rifles. Also, more actions and rifles are covered than are named in the chapter titles since there are often several different makes and models of rifles based on the same action. Some of these extra rifles are listed in the index.

Readers who want additional information on the actions and rifles covered in this book, or want information on some of the centerfire turnbolt actions and rifles not included should check my bibliography.

I don't know why, but many gun enthusiasts are interested in dimensional specifications of actions. I have included figures obtained by me mostly so the reader can compare one action with another. For the most part, the figures were taken from the one or two representative actions of each model in my collection, but this does not necessarily mean that all actions of the same make and model will weigh and measure exactly the same. In most cases the weight includes the guard screw (stock) bushings, magazine (if the action has a detachable one), cartridge clip (if the action requires the use of a clip) and, in some cases, includes some dirt and grease hidden in the crevices of the action. In some cases I did not have certain actions at hand and obtained the weights and measurements from the manufacturer. These figures were usually qualified as being "approximate only." The reader, therefore, should bear this in mind when using the dimensional specification charts. F d H

Acknowledgements

A special "thank you" goes to the following persons who have helped me more than they know in preparing this book: My son Mark, who made the barrel shank drawings and helped me with the photographic work; Ronald Van't Hof, who was my man Friday; Gilbert Blum and William Johnson, who loaned me many of the rifles illustrated in this book.

I am also grateful to the following individuals and firms for their technical and material assistance, and for loans of rifles and actions: Elmer Bogh, George Burgers, Bob Brownell, Burdette Beers, Jim Carlson, George L. Casswell, Raymond De Jong, Lloyd Dolphin, Ellwood Epps, Albert Hancock, Lambert Hollinga, Harold Langenhorst, Dean Miller, Gene Miller, Arlo Neumann, Boyd Robeson, Arnie Te Stroete, Gordon Tritz, Floyd Van Kley, Tom Willroth, Sr., Paul Vander Woude, Peter Ver Mulm, Otto Wolhowe, E.C. Bishop & Sons Inc., Maynard Buehler Inc., Champlin Arms Co., Reinhart Fajen Inc., Firearms International Corp., Interarms Ltd., J.L. Galef & Son Inc., Ranger Arms Co., Remington Arms Co., Savage Arms Corp., Smith & Wesson Inc., Sturm-Ruger Inc., Tradewinds Inc., Stoeger Arms Corp., Waffen-Frankonia., Weatherby's Inc., and Winchester-Western.

Frank de Haas

About the Author

Frank de Haas has never considered himself a professional gunsmith, only as an advanced amateur. As a part-time gunsmith his "gunshop" has been a corner of a plumbing shop and a room in the basement of his home. His most expensive piece of equipment is a 36″ lathe which he bought new in 1940 for about $150. In these modest surroundings he has done much gunsmithing for fun and some for profit—rechambering, rebarreling, restocking and remodeling all sorts of firearms. Since the early 1960s he has devoted most of his time to writing about guns. He now does gunsmithing only as a hobby. He writes simply and directly, mostly from first-hand practical experience, about the guns he knows best. In this book he reveals a wide knowledge of centerfire turnbolt rifles and actions. He has been a Contributing Editor for *The American Rifleman* since 1959. This is his second book, the first being SINGLE SHOT RIFLES AND ACTIONS, published in 1969. He resides with his wife in Orange City, Iowa.

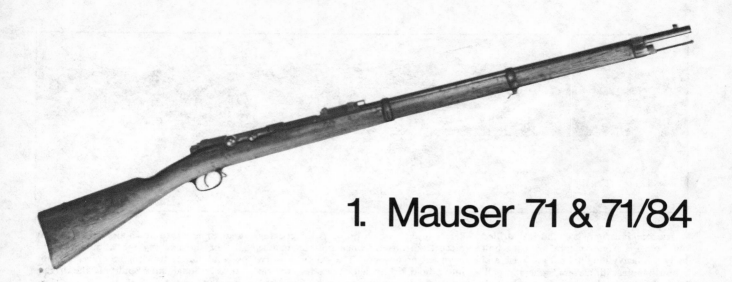

1. Mauser 71 & 71/84

IF THERE WERE a Hall Of Fame for firearms designers and inventors the accomplishments of German born Peter Paul Mauser would certainly be displayed most prominently, because he, like our own John M. Browning, was one of the world's foremost creators of firearms mechanisms.

The Model 71 was the first successful rifle designed and produced by Paul Mauser, but this achievement did not come easy, and it was coupled with a personal disaster which would have stopped many a man not as hardy as Paul Mauser. Its success signaled the start of a long career of firearms development which ultimately led to the Model 98 Mauser action system, unquestionably the best military turnbolt action ever designed.

It was natural that Paul Mauser (1838-1914) became a gunmaker; his father and 6 older brothers were also gunmakers. After some schooling, and an apprenticeship in the gunmaking trade, he began to show an interest in gun designing while working in a government arms factory in Oberndorf, Germany.

Wilhelm Mauser (1834-1882), Paul's brother, 4 years older, was also interested in firearms development work, and they worked together until his death. Paul, however, had the brains and hands for the mechanical details, while Wilhelm handled the business end. Together they developed the M71, obtained a contract and set up a factory to produce them.

Paul and Wilhelm probably began working together in the mid-1860s. Their first efforts were focused on improving the Dreyse needle rifle, at that time a widely used breech-loading military arm. Its firing mechanism had a long needle-like firing pin which had to penetrate the paper cartridge case and powder charge to detonate the primer, positioned at the base of the bullet. Their initial improvement changed the action to cock on the uplift of the bolt handle. About the same time, they converted the action to use a metallic cartridge, its primer located in the case head. It appears the Mauser brothers also worked over the Chassepot action in a similar manner, but failed to sell their ideas to modernize these rifles.

The Mausers then, about 1867, built some rifles on actions of their own design incorporating these new features, but again they failed to sell their new rifle design. However, an American arms salesman, Samuel Norris, representing Remington, heard of their rifle and thought it showed promise.

Norris negotiated a partnership with the Mausers, and evidently thought enough of the Mauser action to have it patented in the United States. This patent, No.78,-603, was granted to him and the Mausers on June 2, 1868. This action, known as the Mauser-Norris, was the first patented design bearing Paul Mauser's name.

Meanwhile, the Mauser brothers continued working to design and develop a rifle action which would interest someone, Remington having failed to take up the patented rifle. Discarding many of the Mauser-Norris features, they built another rifle with several important aspects. The new rifles were given to the Prussian army for testing. After these tests a few changes were suggested. The Mauser brothers made the necessary changes, following which the Prussian commission tested the new rifles and found them good. The new rifle was officially adopted in 1871, and the Mauser brothers received a contract. They were in business at last! (The Mauser-Norris, or the Mauser M67/69, as it is also known, and a second Mauser rifle, known as the Interim Model, are extremely rare. Only a few test rifles were made, and fewer exist today.)

The M71 and their next rifle, the M71/84, were made in large numbers, and are still common today. I will limit my detailed discussion in this chapter to these two models.

The Model 71 Mauser

With the Prussian contract in hand, the Mauser brothers set up a small temporary shop in Oberndorf, then moved to larger quarters in 1872. In 1874 the new factory was destroyed by fire, but they promptly rebuilt and resumed production of the M71. Not long after they were given a new contract to make 100,000 M71s. They granted licenses and received royalties from other armsmaking firms, which also began producing 71s in large numbers. M71s were made in various German government arsenals at Amberg, Danzig, Erfurt and Spandau, and in the great Austrian arms center at Steyr. While the M71 became the standard shoulder arm for the entire German empire, the Steyr factory built thousands of them for China, Japan and other countries. All in all, huge quantities were made from 1872 to 1884 and, though they were more or less obsolete by the latter date, many were not retired from service until years later.

The M71 Mauser was made in several styles. Foremost was the M71 rifle with a barrel 33.5″ long, 53″ over-all and weighing about 10 pounds. The M71 Jaeger rifle has a 29.45″ barrel, is 48.75″ over-all and weighs about 9 pounds. The M71 short rifle weighs about 8.5 pounds and has a 20.5″ barrel.

The M71 Carbine has a 20″ barrel, is about 39.5″ over-all, and weighs about 7.5 pounds. All were chambered for the 11mm Mauser cartridge.

The M71 Mauser Action

The receiver, a one-piece iron or steel casting or forging, is bored lengthwise to accept the bolt; the front end, about 1″ long, is threaded to take the barrel shank. Beginning behind the ring, part of the top and right side of the receiver is milled away, leaving a loading port about 3.12″ long. The receiver bridge behind the loading port is slotted to allow passage of the bolt handle and bolt guide rib. Behind the bridge the receiver is milled down to form a tang.

Illustrated above: The M71/84 Mauser rifle.

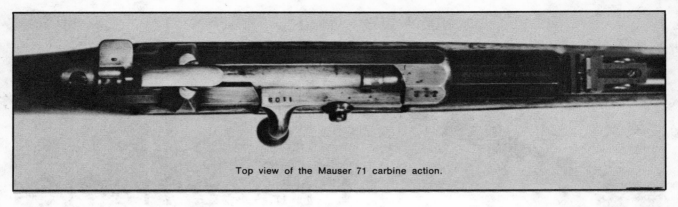

Top view of the Mauser 71 carbine action.

The steel bolt body is cylindrical, drilled out from the front. Integral with the bolt body is a heavy longitudinal guide rib and a bolt handle with a round grasping ball. With the bolt in the receiver and the bolt handle turned down, the rear end of this rib lies in front of the right receiver bridge wall, locking the bolt in the receiver.

The M71 bolt has a separate head which does not rotate with the bolt when the handle is raised or lowered. The rear end of the bolt head fits partly into the front of the bolt, and is drawn back with the bolt by a collar which fits into a notch cut under the front part of the bolt rib. The face of the bolt head is not recessed for the cartridge rim. The one-piece extractor spring is fitted into the left side of the bolt head, its rear end held in place by the bolt body.

The one-piece firing pin, and the coil mainspring which surrounds it, fits inside the bolt through the front end. The mainspring is compressed between the step-down in the rear of the bolt and the collar on the front of the firing pin. The firing pin extends through the rear of the bolt, through the heavy cocking piece, and all are held in place by the firing pin nut which threads on the rear end of the firing pin. A deep notch in the rear end of the bolt, and a matching projection on the front of the cocking piece, cause the cocking piece to be pushed back when the bolt handle is raised to cock the action. A heavy rib on top of the cocking piece extends forward into the slot in the re-

ceiver bridge, which prevents the cocking piece from turning when the bolt handle is raised or lowered. The safety is fitted into a hole, drilled lengthwise into the rib on the cocking piece, and is held in place by a cross pin. When the action is cocked and closed, the safety, when swung to the right, cams the cocking piece back slightly off of the sear and locks it there, at the same time locking the bolt so it cannot be opened.

On opening the bolt the front end of the bolt rib, contacting an inclined surface on the rear of the receiver ring, forces the bolt back to provide the initial extraction power. Conversely, the rear end of the rib, its locking surface, and the top corner of the right receiver bridge wall are similarly rounded or angled so that, on closing the bolt and lowering the bolt handle, the bolt is forced forward to seat the cartridge in the chamber. A heavy washer, held on the bolt rib with a screw, acts as the bolt stop when the bolt is opened—then the washer contacts the semi-circular cuts in the top edges of the receiver bridge walls.

The sear is attached to a long spring member by a pin, the spring being attached to the solid bottom of the receiver with a screw. The trigger, also attached to the end of this spring, pivots on a pin. The sear projects upwards through a hole in the receiver, contacting the bottom of the cocking piece when the action is operated. The trigger has three small humps where it contacts the receiver. On pulling the trigger back, the first hump causes the

sear to be pulled down almost all the way off of the cocking piece, but after the second hump touches the receiver only an additional short pull on the trigger moves the sear free of the cocking piece to fire the rifle. This is the standard military double stage trigger let-off. The third hump on the trigger is provided to move the sear all the way down, when the trigger is pulled back all the way, so the bolt can be withdrawn from the receiver, but only after the bolt stop screw and washer are loosened.

The M71 has a one-piece walnut butt-stock and fore-end. A long narrow plate is inletted into the bottom of the stock under the action. Two sturdy screws—one through the receiver tang and stock threads into this plate, the other, through the front end of this plate and stock, threads into the receiver—hold the action in the stock. These two screws, the rear end of the receiver tang and an upright projection on the front end of the trigger guard plate all tend to prevent setback of the action in the stock from the recoil of firing the rifle. The trigger guard bow is screwed to the plate to protect the trigger. Barrel bands around the barrel and fore-end hold the fore-end against the barrel.

The M71 has a simple yet reliable action, well made and convenient to operate. It is not an overly strong action but it is considered safe for firing smokeless powder ammunition as now loaded by Canadian Industries, Ltd., described at the end of this chapter.

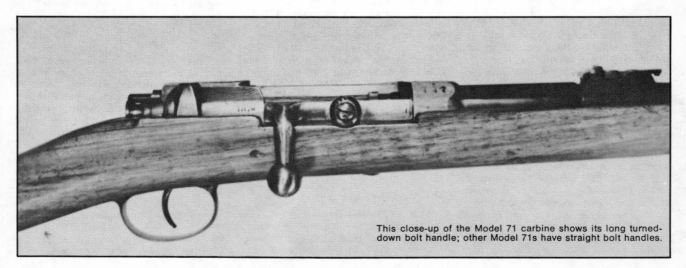

This close-up of the Model 71 carbine shows its long turned-down bolt handle; other Model 71s have straight bolt handles.

Take-Down and Assembly

To remove the bolt, raise the bolt handle and pull the bolt back as far as it will go. Turn out the bolt stop washer screw and remove washer. While pulling back on the trigger, pull the bolt assembly from the receiver.

To disassemble the bolt, first turn the cocking piece one-quarter turn counterclockwise so that the cocking piece is forward. Pull the bolt head from the bolt, then pull the extractor from the bolt head. Rest the firing pin tip on a hard surface and press down on the cocking piece so the firing pin nut can be unscrewed from the firing pin. The firing pin and mainspring can then be pulled from the bolt and the parts separated. Drive out the safety pin to remove the safety. Reassemble in reverse order.

To remove the barrel and action from the stock, first unscrew the ramrod and pull it from the fore-end, then remove the barrel bands. Turn out the tang screw and the front trigger guard plate screw, then lift the barrel and action from the stock. The trigger assembly can then be removed by turning out the trigger/sear spring screw. Reassemble in reverse order. The barrel is threaded tightly into the receiver (right hand threads) and is not easily removed.

M71/84 Mauser Rifles

Wilhelm Mauser died in 1882, but even before this Paul Mauser was working alone on further development of the M71 action. By this time most military nations began to see the wisdom of adopting a repeating rifle for their armed forces. Paul Mauser began working on a repeating mechanism for the M71 in the late 1870s, and it was pretty well perfected by 1881, when he demonstrated it before German officials. The conversion, on which he obtained a patent, was effected by installing a magazine tube in the fore-end under the barrel and providing a carrier in the bottom of the receiver to lift the cartridge from the magazine to the receiver opening. The demonstration was successful and Mauser soon obtained contracts to make these repeating rifles—designated the M71/84. The M71/84 rifles were not converted M71s, but were entirely a new manufacture.

The M71/84 Mauser rifle has a 30.5″ barrel, is 51″ over-all and weighs about 10.2 pounds. Chambered for the 11mm Mauser cartridge, the tubular magazine has a capacity of 9 rounds. It was the official German shoulder arm from 1884 to 1888, at which time Germany adopted the Model 88 Commission rifle chambered for the 8mm cartridge. Although a great many of the M71/84s were made during these 4 years, probably not enough were made to entirely replace the M71 rifles then in use in Germany.

The M71/84 Action

To say that the M71/84 Mauser action is a M71 with a cartridge carrier added

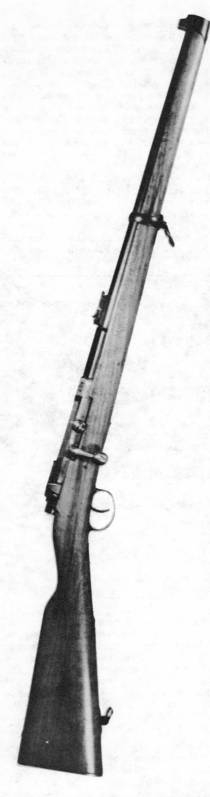

The Model 71 Mauser carbine. Chambered for the 11mm (.43 caliber) Mauser cartridge, this carbine has a 20″ barrel, is 39.25″ overall and weighs about 7.6 pounds. The model designation, stamped on the left side of the receiver, is "K. MOD. 71." The date (year) of manufacture is stamped on the right side of the receiver. On the top flat over the breech end of the barrel is stamped the makers name, on this one: "GEBR MAUSER & Cº OBERNDORF."

Tom Willroth coll.

is an over-simplification. Adding a carrier and making the action a repeater required considerable changing of the receiver, plus adding parts such as the carrier, cartridge stop, ejector, cut-off and some means to cause the carrier to tip up and down when the bolt is operated. Adding these parts also necessitated changing other parts, such as the trigger mechanism. I will enumerate and briefly describe all of these changes.

1. Receiver: The receiver of the M71/84 is similar in profile to the M71 receiver but, instead of being round with a solid bottom, it is made with a heavy rectangular box underneath it, which is in turn milled and machined to accept the various parts of the repeating mechanism, leaving an opening in the boltway through which the cartridges may pass. The rear part of this box acts as a recoil-lug surface transmitting the recoil to the stock.

2. Carrier: The heavy cartridge carrier (often called the "lifter") with its U-shaped trough is fitted into the box below the receiver; it is held in place by, and pivots on, a heavy pin through the rear of the box. A large-headed lock screw holds this pin in place. The carrier is tipped up and down by a cam fitted into recesses cut into the left side of the carrier and receiver-box wall. This cam pivots on a stud which is part of the magazine cutoff lever, which in turn pivots on a stud set into a hole on the left, outside of the receiver.

The cutoff is held in place and is provided two-position tension by a spring screwed to the receiver. A checkered thumb-piece on top of the cutoff lever projects above the stock line and allows the cutoff to be moved. When the cutoff is tipped back the cam is raised so its upper, rounded end projects into the ejector raceway. When moved or tipped forward, the cutoff lowers the carrier cam within the carrier box so it is out of contact with the ejector.

3. Ejector: To actuate the carrier, that is, to tip it up and down, an ejector rib is incorporated with the bolt assembly. It is as long as the entire bolt and is attached to it by a spring clamp on its front end, engaging a groove in the bolt head. There is a small lug under the ejector which fits into a hole in the bolt head and another lug on the cocking piece which fits in a groove in the rear part of the ejector—this helps align these parts and holds the ejector in place. A raceway is milled into the inside left receiver wall for the ejector and, besides its other functions, helps guide the bolt and prevents it from binding. The main function of this long ejector, however, is to activate the carrier and to eject the fired cases from the action. There is a recess groove milled in the outside bottom edge of this rib and, when the cutoff is tipped back to bring the carrier cam up, the end of a cam is brought up into this groove. Thus, when the bolt is opened and the end of the groove contacts the cam, the carrier is tipped up. It is tipped down again when the bolt is fully closed and the rear end of the groove pushes the cam, tipping the carrier down once more,

to pick up a new cartridge from the tubular magazine.

Functioning as the ejector, the front end of this rib projects through a groove cut into the recessed bolt face. It is made to have some longitudinal movement on the bolt. As the bolt is opened and the rib strikes the carrier cam, the bolt moves slightly farther back than the ejector to tip the cartridge case to the right and out of the action. When the cutoff is tipped back to disengage the carrier cam from the ejector, a stud on the front inside of the cutoff spring, projecting through a hole in the ejector raceway, contacts the end of the ejector groove instead of the cam, halting the ejector as before to eject the case.

4. Cartridge stop: Part of the repeating system is the cartridge stop built into the

kept the firing pin nut from turning.

8. Minor changes: Other changes were made in the M71/84. A cross-pin through the bolt rib prevents the bolt stop screw from being turned out completely, which done by making a separate sear lever pivoted on a pin at the rear of the carrier box. A coil spring, set in a hole in the sear lever, gives it tension. The sear and the trigger, fitted to the rear end of the sear lever, are held in place by pins just as in the M71. The trigger has the same double-stage pull.

7. Safety: The safety was improved in two ways. First, instead of using a cross-pin as in the M71 action, the safety and the firing pin nut were so made that the nut held the safety in place. Secondly, by having a coil spring around the safety stem to push the safety back, the safety also

Take-Down and Assembly

Make sure the chamber and magazine are empty. To remove the bolt proceed as follows: If the cutoff button is not in the forward position, open the bolt and pull it back to raise the carrier, then push the cutoff forward. Loosen the bolt stop screw several turns or as far as it will go without resistance. (Note: there is a cross pin through the bolt rib which prevents the complete removal of the bolt stop screw. If it is necessary to remove this screw then the cross-pin must first be driven out.) Open the bolt and pull it back. Tip the rifle far over to the right, making sure the bolt stop washer is against the head of the bolt stop screw, then move the cutoff lever back about 1/8″ to raise the cutoff spring slightly. The bolt can

Left side of the M71/84 Mauser action, opened.

left side of the carrier box. It is a lever, pivoted on a pin set in a groove in the side of the box and given tension by a spring which also places the carrier under tension. There is a projection on the front end of the cartridge stop which extends inside the box just ahead of the carrier, and is activated to release a cartridge from the magazine when the carrier is tipped down, and holding back the cartridges when the carrier is up.

5. Magazine: To complete the repeating system a magazine tube is fitted into the fore-end, with its rear end extending into a hole in the front of the carrier box. The front end of the magazine tube has a thread-on cap, while a long thin magazine spring and plug follower completes the magazine. A cross-key between the front end of the magazine tube and the barrel prevents the tube from sliding forward from the recoil of the rifle.

6. Trigger: Because of the carrier box on the M71/84 receiver, a different trigger arrangement had to be designed. This was

prevents possible loss of the screw and stop washer when the bolt is removed. The extractor is positioned on the top, right-hand side of the bolt head instead of on the left as in the M71 action. The trigger guard bow is made as an integral part of the trigger guard plate, and a screw through the inside bottom of the stock holds the trigger guard in the stock when the two guard screws are removed.

In practically every other respect the M71/84 action is about the same as the M71 action. The extractor, bolt body, firing pin, mainspring, bolt head, bolt handle and bolt stop are all similar to the Model 71. The locking system is the same, and so are the extractor camming and bolt camming features.

Minor design and construction changes were made in the 71 and 71/84 Mausers when they were in production, but these changes are of little importance and I have not thoroughly examined enough of these rifles to describe them in detail.

then be pulled from the receiver. To replace the bolt the cutoff must be forward.

To disassemble the bolt: Lift up the rear end of the ejector and remove it from the bolt. Turn the bolt head one-quarter turn in either direction and pull it from the bolt body. The extractor can then be lifted from the bolt head. Now, rest the firing pin tip on the workbench, and while pressing down on the safety with the thumb of the hand grasping the bolt, unscrew the firing pin nut.

After the nut is removed, the firing pin and mainspring can be removed from the bolt and the safety removed from the cocking piece. Reassemble in reverse order.

To remove the barrel and action from the stock: Remove the small screw from the left side of the muzzle barrel band and drive out the cross-key to the left. Slide the muzzle band off the barrel. Also, remove the other barrel band or bands. Pull out the magazine tube about 1″. Turn out the front and rear trigger guard screws; the barrel and action can now be lifted

1. Receiver (side view)
2. Trigger
3. Sear
4. Sear holder
5. Sear holder spring
6. Sear holder pin
7. Sear pin
8. Trigger pin
9. Cutoff
10. Cutoff spring
11. Cutoff spring screw
12. Carrier cam
13. Carrier (lifter)
14. Carrier pin
15. Carrier pin lock screw
16. Center trigger
    guard screw
17. Cartridge stop
18. Cartridge stop pin
19. Cartridge stop/
    carrier spring
20. Cartridge stop/carrier
    spring screw
21. Trigger guard
22. Front trigger guard screw
23. Rear trigger guard screw
24. Bolt
25. Bolt head
26. Ejector
27. Extractor
28. Bolt stop washer
29. Bolt stop washer screw
30. Firing pin
31. Mainspring
32. Cocking piece
33. Firing pin nut
34. Safety
35. Safety spring
Not shown:
    Bolt stop screw pin

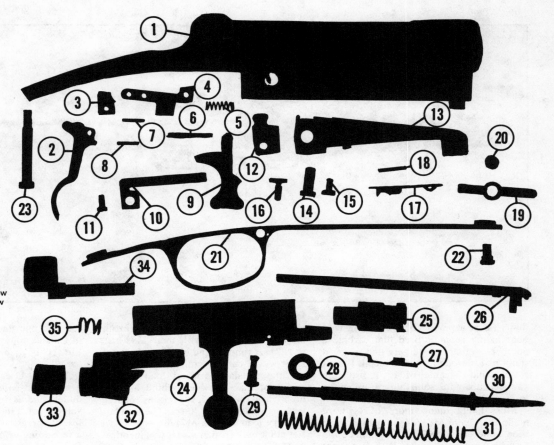

Mauser 71/84

Dimensional Specifications

Weight (Approx.)	3.5 lbs.
Receiver length	10.5"
Receiver ring dia.	1.290"
Bolt dia.	.735"
Striker travel	.565"
Bolt travel	3.385"
Bolt face recess: Depth	.085"
Dia.	.595"

General Specifications

Type	Turnbolt repeater.
Receiver	One-piece machined steel forging. Slotted bridge.
Bolt	Two-piece with separate non-rotating bolt head. Rib on bolt body forms the only locking lug, engages in front of receiver bridge wall.
Ignition	One-piece firing pin powered by coil mainspring. Cocks on opening of the bolt.
Magazine	Tubular magazine in fore-end. Cartridges transported from magazine to chamber by carrier (lifter).
Bolt stop	Screw and washer on the bolt body stop bolt as the washer contacts groove on receiver bridge.
Trigger	Non-adjustable, two-stage military type.
Safety	Swinging wing-type built into cocking piece. Locks striker and bolt when swung right.
Extractor	One-piece spring type fitted into bolt head.
Magazine cutoff	Lever type disengages carrier when pushed forward.
Ejector	Sliding type fitted to bolt.

from the stock. Turn out the center guard screw and the trigger guard can be removed. Reassemble in reverse order.

To disassemble the rest of the action, first turn out the cutoff spring screw and remove the cutoff spring. Lift out the cutoff. Turn out the carrier pin lock screw and lift out the carrier pin. Remove the carrier and carrier cam from the bottom of the action. Drive out the sear holder pin to remove the sear and trigger assembly. Reassemble in reverse order.

M71 and 71/84 Markings

Both the M71 and M71/84 Mauser rifles are easily identified by the stampings on the left side of the receiver. **I G Mod. 71** is stamped on the 71 and **I G Mod. 71/84** on the M71/84. The name of the manufacturer, such as Spandau, Amberg, et al., is usually stamped on the top flat of the breech end of the barrel on both models, along with a crown. The date (year) of manufacture is usually stamped on the right wall of the receiver bridge. Both models are serial numbered, with the numbers stamped on the receiver ring, breech end of the barrel and bolt, with the last two digits of that number stamped on most of the other parts.

Various German proof marks are stamped on the barrel, receiver and bolt, as well as various inspector's marks. A small number "11" stamped over the chamber indicates caliber 11mm.

Comments

The first Mauser rifle I ever owned was a Model 71/84, and with it came several boxes of fresh commercial ammunition. It was a carbine, in excellent condition, with a very nice light colored walnut stock. At that time I lived a long way from any boar hunting, but I often swung and snapped

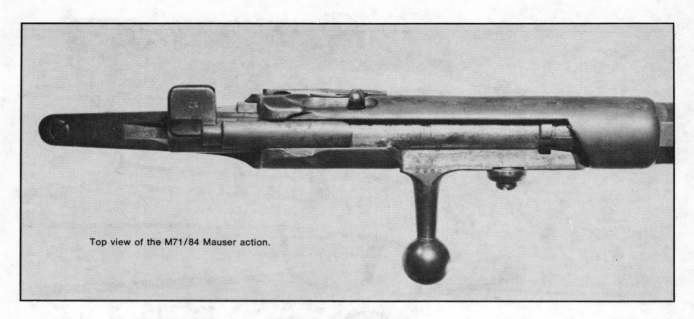

Top view of the M71/84 Mauser action.

that rifle at a picture of a charging wild boar in my room. I fired that carbine a number of times at targets and enjoyed shooting it despite its heavy recoil. I don't recall what became of it; I probably swapped it off for something more suited to my hunting needs.

Most likely many more M71s were made than were M71/84s, but both have been quite common in the U.S. since the turn of the century. After WW II a great many more were imported and sold; as late as 1967 one firm still offered M71/84s in very good condition for less than $15. These are the only large caliber military bolt action rifles for which ammunition is still being loaded and available today. Some of them were sporterized, but by and large they were mostly used "as issued" for fun shooting, deer hunting and the like.

11mm Mauser Cartridge

The 11.15x60R (.43") Mauser cart-ridge, also designed by the Mauser brothers, was introduced with their M71 rifle in 1871. A rimmed and bottle-necked cartridge with a case 60mm long, for military use the standard original load was 77 grains of black powder behind a round nosed lead bullet of 385 grains. Muzzle velocity was about 1440 fps. The standard military load for the M71/84 rifle had a flat point bullet, otherwise it was identical.

The 11mm Mauser cartridge is practically the same as such other 11mm military loads developed during the 1870s as the .43 Spanish, 11mm French Gras, 11mm Belgian Comblain and others. Like many cartridges developed for Mauser rifles, the 11mm Mauser round became popular for sporting use in "as issued" M71 and M71/84 rifles and carbines, in remodeled military rifles, and in some sporting rifles specially chambered for it. Because of the many M71 and M71/84 Mauser rifles sold in the U.S. and Canada by Francis Bannerman & Son, both Remington and Winchester loaded ammunition

for it at one time. It is still being loaded in Canada today by Canadian Industries, Ltd. (C-I-L), but as a smokeless powder load.

The C-I-L catalog lists it as the ".43 Mauser." It is loaded with a 385-gr. lead bullet, and is listed as having a muzzle velocity of 1360 fps, delivering 1580 ft. lbs. of energy. At 200 yards the bullet has a remaining velocity of 1030 fps and 910 ft. lbs. of energy.

Sighted-in to strike dead center at 100 yards the bullets will strike about 2" high at 50 yards, 3.5" low at 125 yards and 24" low at 200 yards. This cartridge has ample power to take many big game species at ranges up to about 150 yards or so.

This cartridge is well adapted to reloading with black or smokeless powder, but the latter loads should be no heavier than the C-I-L. factory loads.

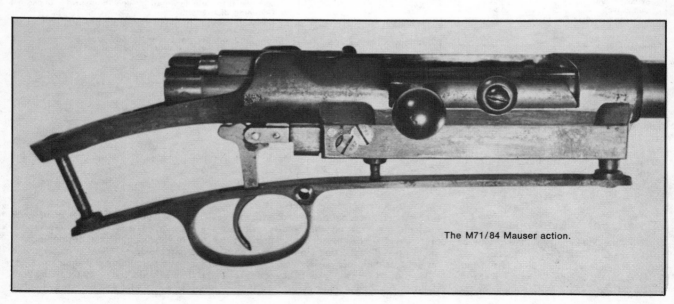

The M71/84 Mauser action.

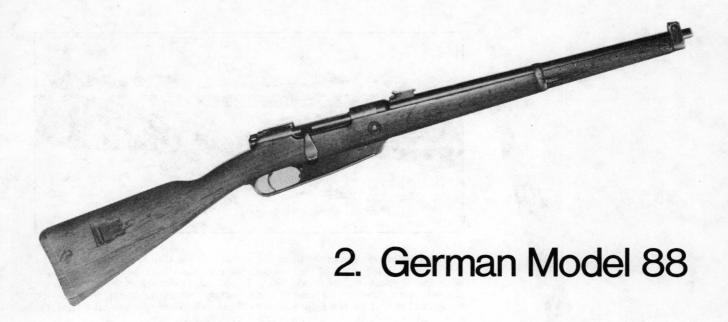

2. German Model 88

THE GERMAN MODEL 88 rifle, adopted in 1888 and correctly known as the German Commission Model 88, was the official German military rifle until succeeded by the famous Model 98 Mauser in 1898. The M71 Mauser single shot and the M71/84 Mauser repeater, both in 11mm caliber, preceded the M88 as the official German military shoulder arms.

The 88 rifle was developed by a group of men, headquartering in Spandau, Germany, who formed the German Military Rifle Testing Commission, thus its unusual name. Although it has some features taken from earlier Mauser and Mannlicher rifles, it is neither a "Mauser" nor a "Mannlicher." A well-planned and thought out rifle, the main features of the receiver and bolt are still being used today on modern Mannlicher-Schoenauer sporting rifles.

Developed with the M88 rifle was Germany's first small caliber smokeless military cartridge. It was a bottle-necked, rimless cartridge of 8mm caliber, and the forerunner of the world famous 8x57mm Mauser cartridge.

Vast quantities of M88 Commission rifles and carbines were made in various German government arsenals. These rifles were usually marked "GEW.88" stamped on the left side of the receiver. "GEW" is an abbreviation of the German word *Gewehr* meaning rifle. The rifles had a 29.1″ barrel, the carbines with a 17.62″ barrel; the receivers were usually marked "KAR.88." "KAR." is an abbreviation for *Karabiner*, meaning carbine. Both the rifle and carbine were made with a barrel jacket, a thin-walled steel tube covering the entire length of the barrel. The jacket is large enough to leave an air space between the jacket and barrel. The carbine has a turned down spoon shaped bolt handle, while the rifle has a straight bolt handle with a round grasping ball. A great many of these arms were also made in plants in Austria, including the great Steyr works.

As these rifles became obsolete many of them turned up in the United States. During the 1920s and '30s the M88 Carbine was especially common, many of them used "as issued" for hunting big game.

Action Construction

The receiver is milled from a one-piece steel forging. The receiver ring is round except for a very small projection underneath which forms the recoil lug. The small recoil lug required that a square-stemmed cross-bolt be used in the stock—the recoil lug engaging a groove milled into the cross-bolt. A longer projection at the bottom rear of the receiver ring forms the cartridge guide. The front of the receiver is threaded on the outside for the barrel jacket collar, and on the inside for the barrel shank. The breech end of the barrel abuts against two semi-circular shoulders milled inside the receiver ring; these shoulders partially ring the bolt head. To the rear of these shoulders, the inside of the receiver is milled out to receive the locking lugs of the bolt.

The rear part of the receiver, commonly called the bridge, is slotted on top so that the bolt handle can pass through it when opening and closing the action. A simple bolt stop is positioned on the left side of the receiver bridge and hinged there by a pin through a stud on the receiver. Tension is provided to the bolt stop by a small coil spring.

The bolt assembly is comprised of the bolt body with its integral handle, bolt head assembly and firing mechanism. The bolt body is a cylindrical, hollow tube drilled from front to rear. The opposed dual locking lugs are on the extreme forward end of the bolt body and engage matching recesses in the receiver when the bolt is closed.

The left (or top) locking lug has a narrow slot cut through it. This allows the bolt to pass over a finger on the end of the bolt stop—this finger activates the ejector when the bolt is opened. The right (or bottom) locking lug is solid with its top front corner beveled to match a similar bevel machined on the top shoulder inside the receiver ring. This provides the initial extraction camming power on opening the bolt.

The separate bolt head is made to fit closely on and inside the front end of the bolt body. A small lug on the stem of the bolt head fits in a matching circular recess cut inside the bolt body to hold the two parts together, except when the bolt head is rotated to a certain position. The small spring extractor is mortised into a groove in the right side of the bolt head. The extractor easily snaps over the cartridge rim when the bolt is closed on a cartridge singly loaded into the chamber, or on a cartridge that is chambered from the magazine ahead of the extractor. A lug on the left of the bolt head matches the left locking lug on the bolt and contains the very small ejector. On some bolt heads, the ejector is held in place by a small screw, while on others friction alone holds it in place when the bolt head is disassembled from the bolt body. The end of the ejector protrudes through a hole in the face of the bolt head recess. The face of the bolt head is recessed for the cartridge head. On some bolt heads, the rim of the recess covers about 75% of the circumference of the cartridge head. On others, the rim is not cut away at all—except for the extractor cut. The bolt head does not rotate with the bolt. It is prevented from doing so by the flattened end of the firing pin fitted into its slotted stem.

The rear end of the bolt has a hole that is smaller than the main hole through the bolt body. The mainspring is compressed between the shoulder formed by the smaller hole and the shoulder on the front of the firing pin.

Illustrated above: M88 (Kar. 88) German Commission carbine.

13

Close up of the M88 German Commission carbine action.

The threaded rear end of the firing pin extends through the center of the cocking piece and is retained there by the firing pin nut. A flat spot on the rear of the unthreaded part of the firing pin matches a flat surface inside the cocking piece and prevents the firing pin from turning. A notch in the front of the firing pin nut engages the rear end of the safety when it is turned tight—to prevent the nut from coming loose. The rear, flared part of the firing pin nut has a narrow flange extending into the cocking cam raceway of the receiver and a wide flange, the size of the locking lug raceway, extending to the left. Their purpose is to deflect powder gases away from the shooter's face—in the event of a ruptured primer or case head.

The rear end of the bolt body has a deep cam notch to engage the cam on the front of the cocking piece. When the bolt handle is lifted, the cocking piece is cammed back about .370"—the remaining cocking motion is done on closing the bolt. Essentially, the M88 is a "cock-on-opening" action, since the greatest amount of cocking is done when the bolt is opened. This action can be uncocked without snapping by closing the bolt while holding the trigger back. *This should only be done on an empty chamber.*

The wing safety fits into a hole bored longitudinally in the top part of the cocking piece. It is held in place by the firing pin nut. A small coil spring around the safety stems holds the safety back against the firing pin nut to prevent the nut from turning, yet allows the safety to be pushed forward so the nut can be unscrewed. It also provides tension to the safety so it will remain in the position to which it is rotated.

Rotating the safety to the "up" or "right" position, its forward end engages a notch cut into the rear of the bolt body, camming the cocking piece back slightly so it is free of the main sear and, at the same time, locking the bolt so it cannot be opened. Since the safety, safety spring, cocking piece, firing pin nut and firing pin are assembled as a unit, they all move as a unit when the action is cocked and fired.

The trigger assembly is a simple one composed of a trigger, sear housing, sear trigger spring, trigger pin, sear pin and sear housing pin. The sear housing pin holds the assembly to the receiver. The

trigger is the double-stage type. The first part of the trigger pull, quite long and light, nearly disengages the sear from the cocking piece. A shorter, but heavier, final pull disengages the sear from the cocking piece.

The trigger guard/magazine is machined and formed as a single unit. A long screw, through a hole in the rear of the trigger guard, threads into the tang of the receiver. A shorter screw, through a hole in the front of the guard, threads into a round stud, silver soldered to the barrel jacket. Both hold the action and barrel in the stock.

The trigger guard bow opening is long —the bow itself is very thick and wide. The magazine box, more or less a walled shell, extends below the stock line, forward of the guard bow, housing the various magazine parts which hold and guide the cartridge clip. It is essential that a clip be used in this action, since it is the clip that holds the cartridges in position in the magazine. I will go into more detail later.

A catch, which pivots on a screw and is given tension by a small coil spring, is positioned in the rear of the magazine. This catch has a hook on its upper end to engage and hold the loaded clip down. A button on the lower end of the catch protrudes inside the guard bow, and can be depressed to release the loaded clip. The follower arm, positioned in the front of the magazine on a screw, is given tension by a heavy coil spring and plunger, located in a hole in the heavy front part of the magazine. The rear underside of the magazine is open to allow the empty clip to fall out. The remainder of the magazine opening is closed by a flat piece of steel, held in place by a screw.

The clip is a U-shaped piece of spring steel which holds 5 cartridges. The top and bottom of the clip are identical. The edges of the side walls are curved inward to hold the cartridges and to form guide or retainer lips when the loaded clip is in the action. Ridges inside the rear of the clip match the extractor groove in the cartridge head. When loading the cartridges into the clip they must be inserted with their heads engaged behind these ridges. The ridges thus hold the cartridges securely in the clip and the rifle's recoil cannot dislodge the cartridges forward from the clip. This clip form is of some

German M88 (Gew. 88) Commission rifle.

Front view of the M88 bolt, minus the bolt head, clearly showing the groove inside the bolt body, the lug on the bolt head stem that engages and holds the bolt head in place, and the dual bolt locking lugs.

advantage when soft point ammunition is used, as it will keep the bullet point from being battered—by striking the front of the magazine from recoil.

The loaded clip is inserted into the top of the opened action and pushed down against the tension of the follower arm until engaged by the clip catch. Since the top and bottom of the clip are identical, it isn't possible to insert the clip incorrectly. As each cartridge is fed out of the clip, the follower arm raises the remaining cartridges in the clip—the clip remaining stationary. A fully or partially loaded clip can be released from the top of the opened action by depressing the clip catch. When all the cartridges have been fed from the clip, it will drop from the magazine of its own weight.

Military M88s are usually serial numbered. The full number is stamped on the receiver, barrel, barrel jacket and bolt. Other parts of the action may also be stamped with the same number or with part of that number. If all the numbers match, this indicates that all the parts are original. The date (year) of the rifle's manufacture is usually stamped on the receiver ring. Commercial sporting rifles based on this action usually follow the serial numbering practice used on military arms, though they are not always stamped with the date of manufacture. Military rifles seldom have the caliber designation stamped on them. On sporting rifles, the caliber is usually stamped on the barrel, but it may be underneath the barrel, requiring the removal of the stock to see it.

Strong and Weak Points

The German M88 actions are well made, all the parts are of steel, machined

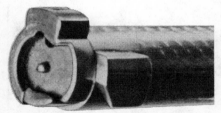

Position of the bolt and bolt head when the bolt is locked in the receiver. The angled corner on the right (bottom) locking lug provides initial camming power for extraction—it moves past a matching surface in the locking lug recess in the receiver ring. On closing the action the reverse motion of the angled surfaces starts rotation of the bolt to the locked position.

and finished to close tolerances and properly heat treated. The outside of the bolt body, the inside of the receiver and all the contacting surfaces of the firing mechanism within the bolt and receiver carry a very fine finish, resulting in exceptionally smooth and easy opening and closing of the bolt. Despite the slotted receiver bridge, there is little sloppiness of the bolt in the receiver, even when the bolt is open. Feeding of the cartridges from the magazine is smooth and reliable, and there is ample extraction camming power. The bolt stop is quite rugged, the safety positive. Although the bolt head is a separate part of the bolt, and the front end of the bolt is hollowed out to accept it, there seems to be ample metal at the front to adequately support the dual locking lugs.

This action, however, has more weak and undesirable features than strong ones. The weakest part is the very small extractor. Not only is it weak and delicate, but it can be lost easily when the bolt is taken apart. The ejector is small and delicate also.

The separate bolt head can be readily disassembled and can easily be lost —

Two types of bolt heads used in M88 Commission rifles. Top: Bolt head with the wide extractor hook and undercut recess rim. When feeding from the magazine into the chamber, the cartridge head moves upward with the extractor hook engaging the cartridge. If the bolt is closed but not rotated and locked, the cartridge will be extracted and ejected on opening the bolt. Bottom: This is, perhaps, the earlier type of bolt head with the narrow extractor and a full-recess rim. The cartridge is pushed into the chamber ahead of the extractor but the extractor hook cannot engage the cartridge head unless the bolt is fully closed and locked. With this bolt head it is possible to "double load" the rifle. Unless the bolt is rotated and locked the cartridge will not be extracted.

another undesirable design feature. The bolt can be assembled in the action minus the bolt head, and it is possible to fire a cartridge in the rifle with the bolt head missing with unpredictable consequences.

The worst feature is the need for a special clip to hold the cartridges in the magazine. When the M88 rifle was used as a military weapon, with the ammunition supplied in clips, these clips were then expendable. However, when these rifles were used as sporting arms, the sporting ammunition was not furnished in clips, and their easy loss became a problem. A small device known as a "clip-saver" was developed to prevent the clips from dropping from the magazine. It was a small, sliding spring cover slipped over the rounded edges of the bottom of the magazine. Covering the hole in the magazine held the empty clip in the magazine. Commercial sporting rifles made on this action often had a hinged magazine hole cover serving the same purpose.

Another undesirable feature is the mass of metal attached to the striker, resulting in rather slow lock time. This mass includes the heavy striker, massive cocking piece, striker nut, safety and safety spring.

No provision is made to allow powder gases to escape harmlessly from the action in the event of a pierced primer or ruptured case head. There are no gas escape vents in the bolt or receiver ring.

Minor design faults include the forward position of the bolt handle, inconveniently placed for rapid bolt operation. The split bridge design prevents installing a conventional receiver sight and also places some limitations on the choice of scope mounts which can be used. The magazine box extending below the stock line is also a nuisance in carrying the rifle. Although not an action fault, the barrel jacket is not a desirable feature.

Take-Down and Assembly

Open the bolt and, while depressing the bolt stop, withdraw the bolt from the receiver. Disassemble the bolt as follows: Press the safety forward and unscrew the striker nut. Remove the cocking piece from the firing pin. Holding the bolt in the left hand, firmly grasp the bolt head with the fingers of the right hand and turn the bolt head ¼-turn clockwise. Bolt head, firing pin and mainspring can now be pulled out of the bolt. The extractor is removed from the bolt head by raising the hooked end and sliding it forward. The ejector can be removed by pushing it back with a drift punch. Reassemble the bolt parts in reverse order, as follows: Lay the bolt on a table with the lugs to the right and the bolt handle toward you. Place the bolt head on the firing pin with the ejector lug aligned with the flat spot on the rear of the firing pin. Slip the mainspring over the firing pin. Now, grasp the bolt with the left hand and, with the bolt handle pointing toward you, insert mainspring, firing pin and bolt head into the front of the bolt. With the ejector lug pointing away from you, or opposite the bolt handle, push the bolt head into the bolt as far as it will go; then turn the bolt head ¼-turn counterclockwise so the ejector lug is aligned with the left locking lug. Place the cocking piece over the rear end of the firing pin, with the safety lug in line with the bolt handle. Insert the safety and spring into place with the safety wing to the left and, while depressing the safety, turn on the striker nut until the rear end of the firing pin is flush with the end of the nut.

Remove the barrel, action, and magazine assembly from the stock by removing the front and rear guard screws from the bottom of the magazine/guard. Remove the bolt stop by driving out the bolt stop pin from the bottom. Remove the trigger assembly by driving out the trigger sear pin. Depress the follower arm and insert a wire or brad into the hole exposed at

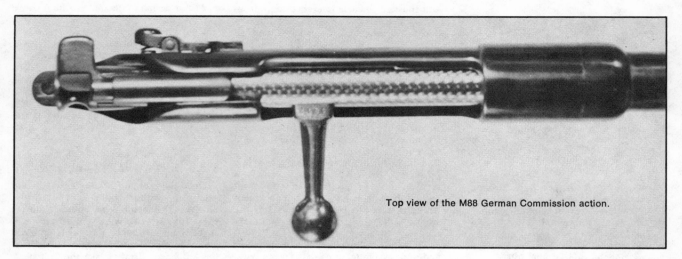

Top view of the M88 German Commission action.

the end of the follower plunger. Then remove the follower screw to remove the follower. Remove the magazine plate screw and slide out the magazine plate. Remove the clip catch screw and remove the catch and spring. Pull out the wire or brad from the follower plunger to remove the plunger and spring. Reassemble in reverse order. Do not unscrew the barrel jacket or barrel from the receiver unless you have the proper tools available.

Remodeling

As soon as the M88 rifle had been adopted, German and other European gunmakers began making sporting rifles on this action. The practice continued long after the M88 was dropped in favor of the far better M98 Mauser.

At first, these sporting rifles were generally chambered for the 8mm cartridge originally designed for this action. This round was originally known as the 7.9mm, and later on as the 7.9x57mm or 8x57mm Mauser, or simply as the 8mm Mauser. Its commercial designation was 8x57J, the "J" meaning Infanterie.* This cartridge was loaded with a bullet of .318"

diameter to match the normal bore (.311") and groove (.320") diameters of the military barrel. Therefore, the correct ammunition to use in the military M88 rifles and carbines is the 8x57J, loaded at present by Norma. The sporting rifles were also chambered for the 6.5x57mm, 7x57-mm, 8x56mm, 9x57mm and other cartridges, all of them originally factory loaded to breech pressures of less than 45,000 psi. That was considered maximum safe working pressure for this action.

The clip of the M88 will accept and handle any rimless cartridge having the standard .30-06 head size and those that are no more than about 3.250" long. Cartridges feed in a straight line into the chamber and even those as short as the .35 Remington will function very nicely. In past years I have seen several M88 carbines rebarreled to .35 Remington, and their owners liked them very much for hunting deer. I have also seen some rebarreled with a M98 Mauser 8mm barrel so that commercially loaded U.S. 8mm Mauser hunting ammunition could be safely used. U.S.-loaded 8mm Mauser cartridges show a breech pressure of less than 40,000 psi and, therefore, are quite

safe for these old actions if the new barrel fitted has a groove diameter matching the .323" diameter bullet used in these cartridges. In fitting the M98 barrel to this action it is necessary to turn and thread a new shank.

When the German gunmakers used the M88 action for a sporting rifle they seldom used the barrel jacket. The front guard screw was threaded into a nut inletted into the barrel channel in the fore-end. When using the military action without the barrel jacket, the collar on the jacket can be used to cover the threads on the front of the receiver. For looks only, the new barrel should have a shoulder like any sporting rifle barrel, as shown in the drawing of the barrel shank specifications. German gunsmiths installed some double-set trigger mechanisms in these actions, and I see no great problem involved in installing those made for the M98 Mauser in the M88 action.

The German gunmakers also used the basic M88 action, but minus the magazine, for making up many fine, light-

*The literal rendition of this letter "J" in English translation or terminology has been the cause of much confusion. In fact, the "J" in German printing stands for "I," not our "J."

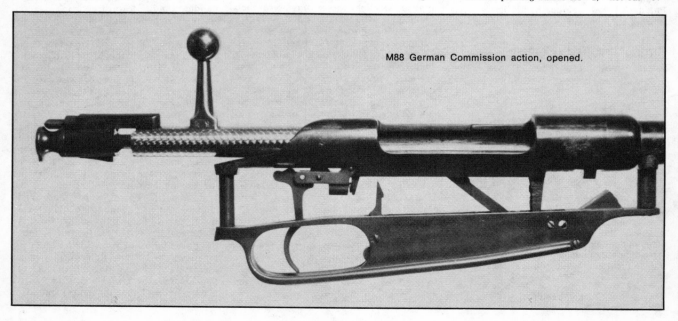

M88 German Commission action, opened.

Parts Legend

1. Receiver (side view)
2. Barrel
3. Barrel jacket
4. Cartridge clip
5. Bolt stop
6. Bolt stop spring
7. Bolt stop pin
8. Bolt
9. Bolt head
10. Extractor
11. Ejector
12. Mainspring
13. Firing pin
14. Firing pin nut
15. Cocking piece
16. Sear
17. Sear pin
18. Sear lever
19. Sear lever pin
20. Sear lever spring
21. Trigger
22. Trigger pin
23. Trigger guard/
    magazine box
24. Rear guard screw
25. Rear guard screw sleeve
    (stock bushing)
26. Front guard screw
27. Safety
28. Safety spring
29. Magazine box plate
30. Magazine box plate screw
31. Magazine follower
32. Magazine follower screw
33. Magazine follower plunger
34. Magazine follower
    plunger spring
35. Cartridge clip latch
36. Cartridge clip latch spring
37. Cartridge clip latch screw

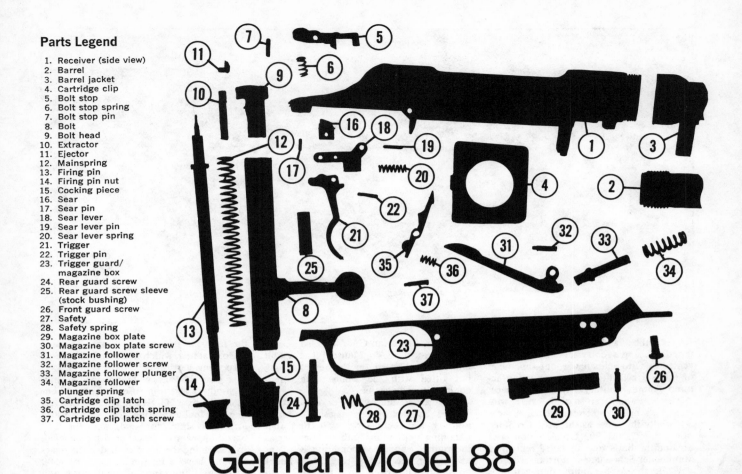

German Model 88

Dimensional Specifications

Weight	3 lbs.
Length	9.625"
Receiver ring dia.	1.300"
Bolt body dia.	.700"
Bolt travel	4.585"
Striker travel	.575"
Guard screw spacing	9.093"
Magazine well.	
Width: front	.480"
rear	.540"
Length:	3.415"
Bolt face recess:	
Depth	.112"
Dia.	.500"

General Specifications

Type	Turnbolt repeater.
Receiver	One-piece machine steel forging. Slotted bridge.
Bolt	Two-piece with dual-opposed locking lugs on forward part of body. Separate, non-rotating bolt head.
Ignition	One-piece firing pin, coil mainspring, cocking piece and firing pin nut. Cocks on opening bolt.
Magazine	Single column, non-detachable box magazine. 5-shot capacity. Special clip needed.
Trigger	Non-adjustable, double-stage military type.
Safety	Rotary wing type safety built into bolt sleeve. 180° swing from left to right, locking striker and bolt when in the "up" or right side positions.
Extractor	Machined, one-piece spring type built into bolt head.
Bolt Stop	Separate, hinged to the rear left of receiver. Stops bolt travel by contacting left locking lug.
Ejector	Plunger type, built into the bolt head, activated by an integral finger on bolt stop.

weight single shot target/hunting rifles. I once owned and used a rifle of this type chambered for the 5.6x52R (.22 Savage Hi-Power) cartridge. The receivers of these rifles have a solid bottom and the action is almost always fitted with a fine double-set trigger. The barrels are usually partially octagonal, fully octagonal or ribbed, and fitted with sporting sights. When the .219 Zipper cartridge was introduced in 1937, I made up a single shot varmint rifle on the military M88 action. I left off all the magazine parts, filled the magazine well opening in the receiver with an aluminum block and used a Krag trigger guard. The bolt face was easily opened to accept the rimmed .219 case. It was one of my first successful varmint

rifles, and it dropped many a crow in the Iowa farm country where I lived.

Comments

Thus far I have referred to the action under discussion as the German Model 88 Commission action since it was the first of this type and design to be adopted. Actually, the action is partly Mannlicher design, partly Paul Mauser's, with some ideas thrown in by the German Testing Commission—whose job it was to find, develop if necessary, and test the new action which was to be adopted. The magazine was entirely the invention of Ferdinand Ritter von Mannlicher, an Austrian arms inventor. It seems likely that Mann-

licher may have had a hand in designing the receiver and bolt, although the two-piece design of the bolt, the firing mechanism, safety, trigger and the slotted receiver were all Mauser patents. The forward dual-opposed locking lug system had been used previously on some other rifles, a design feature that is neither Mannlicher nor Mauser. Credit must be given to the testing commission for arranging all of these features in a single action that turned out so well. Later on, the great Steyr arms factory in Austria, the firm that manufactured most of the many rifles von Mannlicher invented, produced other military and sporting rifles based essentially on the same action. These included the M92 and M93 Roumanian rifles in

M88 German Commission action.

6.5mm caliber and the M95 Dutch Infantry rifle. Using a rotary spool magazine invented by Otto Schoenauer, one-time head of the Steyr factory, they also manufactured 6.5mm military rifles for Greece.

The bolt and receiver of this rifle, with minor changes and improvements, was essentially the same as the M88 Commission rifle. The M1903 Greek action later became the basis for the world renowned Mannlicher-Schoenauer sporting rifle.

While the M88 Commission action is not generally referred to as a "Mannlicher" action, other similar actions are, including those with the Schoenauer magazine. Some authorities have flatly stated that the Mannlicher-Schoenauer action has a receiver and bolt invented by von Mannlicher and the magazine invented by Schoenauer—but can the receiver and bolt be Mannlicher when the bolt and receiver of its parent action, the M88, was admittedly based largely on Mauser features and those of the Commission? Incidentally, the Hungarian G98/40 (also known as the Model 98/40 Mauser) has a bolt and receiver based on the same design, but fitted with the Mauser staggered-column box magazine.

M88 rifles and carbines are getting scarcer as each year passes. Beginning military arms collectors will find that obtaining either or both of these arms in original, very good condition is not as easy as it was 20 years ago. Amateur gunsmiths, however, will find it much easier to obtain them, since there are still a lot of them around in a condition suitable for gunsmithing purposes—those in less than good condition, having been previously reworked or missing some parts. Speaking of parts, parts houses have long been out of bolt heads and extractors for the M88. So, unless you can make these parts, be certain they are not missing from the gun you plan to buy.

In gathering information on the M88 I discovered two unusual items. I found the first one in the 1902 Sears, Roebuck & Co. catalog, which listed and illustrated a sporting version of this rifle at $24. It was described as a Mannlicher 6-shot, high-power sporting rifle in 8mm caliber as made by C.G. Haenel in Suhl, Germany. It had a sporting stock with a pistol grip and short fore-end, and the 25″ barrel appears to be covered by a jacket. In describing the 8mm cartridge the Sears catalog shows a maximum range of 4500 yards, a killing range of 3000 yards, and a point-blank range of 300 yards! The other item was Golden State Arms advertisement in a 1958 issue of *the American Rifleman* which still listed surplus M88 rifles at $9.95 each. These two items give us some idea of the time spread that these have been on the American market, indicate that a lot of them must have been made, and that there must still be a lot of them in this country.

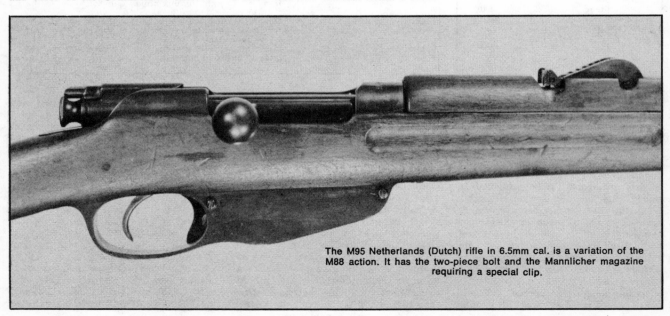

The M95 Netherlands (Dutch) rifle in 6.5mm cal. is a variation of the M88 action. It has the two-piece bolt and the Mannlicher magazine requiring a special clip.

3. The First Mauser Smokeless Powder Actions Models 88, 89, 90 & 91

PAUL MAUSER must surely have been disappointed when his native country adopted the Model 88 Commission rifle in 1888. Although the M88 action contained a number of original Mauser design features, it was not a "Mauser." The Mauser features used in the M88 were those of the black powder M71/84 including the non-rotating separate bolt head, ejector, trigger and firing mechanism.

While Germany was considering adoption of the M88, Paul Mauser was busy designing a new action. He tried to improve and strengthen his M71/84 action, and at the same time eliminating the special clip needed to hold the cartridges in the M88 magazine, a poor feature.

Experimental M88

This action was an improved version of the M71/84 Mauser with high receiver walls, double locking lugs engaging recesses in the receiver bridge, and a 9-shot single column box magazine. It was chambered for a new Mauser cartridge, the 7.65mm, a smokeless powder load. Mauser entered this rifle in the Belgian rifle trials but was not successful in selling it—it remained an experimental model.

Failing with the experimental M88, Paul Mauser designed an entirely new action. A far departure from any of his earlier types, it was the forerunner of the justly famed Model 1898 Mauser. This new and vastly improved action introduced the Mauser locking system for the first time. The one-piece bolt, bored from the rear, had dual-opposed locking lugs on the forward end. The rifle, chambered for the 7.65mm Mauser cartridge, was adopted by Belgium in 1889 and became known as the Model 1889 Belgian Mauser.

The M89 was the first highly successful Mauser action designed for a powerful, smokeless powder, rimless military cartridge. It was also the first Mauser action designed to load the magazine with a

charger (more commonly referred to as a stripper clip). This action set the general pattern for other Mauser turnbolt rifle actions which followed, with changes and improvements that made Mauser actions a standard the world over.

M89 Mauser Rifles

The first Belgian M89s were made in the large Fabrique Nationale (FN) plant in Herstal, Belgium. Originally there were three versions: a rifle with a 30.67″ barrel, a carbine with a 21.65″ barrel and a shorter carbine with a 15.75″ barrel. All of these (plus a carbine to be introduced in 1916) were made with a barrel jacket—essentially like the one used on the M88 Commission rifle. This jacket was a thin-walled steel tube covering the barrel. The rear of the tube threaded on to the front of the receiver ring, with a bushing at its opposite end to center the barrel muzzle. The FN plant made some 275,000 of these rifles and carbines from 1889 to about 1925. A great many more were made in the Belgian government arsenal in Liege. Many were also made in Birmingham, England, at a plant set up and operated by Belgian refugees. Oddly enough, an American firm (Hopkins & Allen of Norwich, Conn.) obtained a contract and made many of these rifles for Belgium a few years before World War 1.

Some versions of the Belgian Mauser made after the introduction of the 1890 Turkish and 1891 Argentine Mausers will often have minor improvements found on these later rifles. These improvements will be pointed out in the detailed discussion which follows.

The last version of the M89 Belgian Mauser, the M89/36, does not have the barrel jacket. None of the M89 Belgian rifles were made by the Mauser plant in Germany. Some of the late M89/36 Belgian rifles were made by Ancetab Pieper in Herstal,

and were so marked.

Model 1890 Turkish Rifle

During the development of the M89, Mauser had a contract to make the M87 rifle for Turkey, one based on the M71/84 action. A clause in the contract provided Turkey with the benefit of any improvements made to the Mauser actions. After more than 200,000 M87s were made, Turkey insisted that the rest of the contract be filled with rifles based on the Model 89 action. Thus Mauser made upward of 280,000 of these M89 rifles (some of which may have been carbines). Designated the Model 1890 Turkish, these rifles had a 29.13″ stepped barrel, without barrel jacket, but with a short wooden handguard to cover the top rear of the barrel. The only noticeable change made in the action was a buttress thread used to thread the bolt sleeve in the bolt. These rifles were chambered for the 7.65mm Mauser cartridge, as were the Belgian rifles and carbines. The M90 Turkish rifles are very uncommon today.

Model 1891 Argentine

In 1891, Argentina adopted a Mauser rifle based on the M89 action. It was designated the Model 1891 Argentine Mauser. The M91 was made with a 29.13″ barrel and chambered for the 7.65mm cartridge, a popular military cartridge by this time. M91s had no barrel jacket, but a wooden handguard covered part of the breech end of the barrel. An M91 carbine version had a 17.63″ barrel. The principal supplier of these rifles and carbines was Ludwig Loewe & Co., Berlin, who made 180,000 rifles and 30,000 carbines. DWM, of Germany, also made a quantity of the

---

Illustrated above: M91 Argentine carbine, caliber 7.65mm Mauser. Barrel is 17.63″ long, length 37″ overall, weight about 7.2 lbs.

Argentine rifles. Peru, Columbia, Bolivia and Ecuador also adopted the M91 as their military arm.

M91 Spanish Mauser

In 1891 Spain became interested in these new smokeless powder rifles and, mostly for trial purposes, bought about 1800 of them in caliber 7.65mm. Known as the Spanish Model 91, it was essentially the same as the Turkish M90. Few were made and therefore the M91 Spanish rifle is very scarce today. Spain did adopt the carbine version, almost the same as the

M91 Mauser bolt face.

M91 Argentine carbine, and since more of these were made, the carbine is more common than the Spanish M91 rifle.

The Spanish M91 Mauser action differs from the Turkish M90 in that it has a small spring built into the right locking lug on the bolt to prevent double loading. The Belgian M89, Turkish M90 and Argentine M91 actions were made without this feature. It is possible, therefore, to double load those rifles unless the bolt is fully closed and locked when chambering a cartridge.

Normally, in these rifles, the cartridge is pushed into the chamber by the bolt, and not until the bolt is turned down and locked does the extractor slip over the cartridge rim. Therefore, if a cartridge is chambered, and the bolt is not fully closed, on withdrawing the bolt the cartridge will be left in the chamber. Then, on closing the bolt again it would pick up another cartridge and its bullet would strike the cartridge already in the chamber. This is not only annoying, but could discharge the chambered cartridge should the pointed bullet strike the primer hard enough. The bolt head recess of the Spanish M91 is so undercut that, on pushing a cartridge from the magazine, the cartridge head slides directly into the bolt face recess, under the extractor hook. Held there under tension by a small spring in the right lug, if the bolt is not fully closed, the cartridge will be extracted and ejected when the bolt is drawn back.

The Actions

As already noted, except for minor differences the M89 Belgian, M90 Turkish, M91 Argentine and M91 Spanish Mauser actions are essentially alike. I suspect, therefore, that practically all action parts are more or less interchangeable. At any rate, all of them were made for the 7.65mm Mauser cartridge. Since the M91 Argentine rifles and actions appear to be the most common, I have chosen this action to describe in detail. The description following applies to the other actions as well—except for the few differences already mentioned or to be noted later on.

The one-piece receiver is a machined steel forging. The recoil lug, integral with the receiver, is located about 1.00″ back from the front edge of the receiver. The front part of the receiver ring is round. The bottom of the receiver, from the recoil lug to the rear of the magazine, is flat. The magazine well opening is milled in the center of this flat area. The receiver ring is threaded inside to accept the barrel shank. The barrel has a short shoulder that butts against the front of the receiver when the barrel is tightened. The M89 Belgian rifles with the barrel jackets have about 9/32″ of the front outside of the receiver threaded for the barrel jacket collar.

The receiver is the same width from receiver ring to bridge, making the left side of the receiver ring, side wall and bridge a smooth, rounded surface. The front part (about ½″) of the bridge is the same diameter as the receiver ring. A rectangular notch, milled into this part, forms the charger guideways. The rest of the bridge is milled thinner to reduce weight. The receiver ends in a tang about 2.3″ long.

The one-piece machined bolt has dual-opposed locking lugs on its forward end. These engage matching recesses in the receiver ring and hold the bolt locked against the barrel when the action is closed. The right (or bottom) locking lug is solid, while the left (or top) locking lug is slotted to allow the ejector to pass.

The bolt face is recessed to a depth of about .120″. Except for a shallow notch in the bottom of the bolt face, the narrow extractor and ejector slots, the cartridge head is surrounded by a ring of steel when the bolt is closed.

The extractor is a thin piece of spring steel about 1.460″ long with a small hook on its front end to engage the cartridge rim. It is fitted into a slot and dovetail mortise, cut lengthwise in the head of the bolt body. Held in place in its recess by the dovetail mortise, the extractor is prevented from moving forward by a lip under its forward end, engaging a cut in the bolt head. On closing the bolt with a cartridge in the chamber the extractor snaps easily over the cartridge rim.

There is a small stud (pin) pressed into a hole in the right receiver ring locking recess. When the bolt is fully closed, this stud coincides with the hook end of the extractor. Its purpose is to support the end of the extractor and prevent it from springing too far should powder gases escape in the extractor area. Thus, with the bolt closed and locked, the extractor hook becomes part of the supporting rim around the cartridge head.

M91 Argentine Mauser rifle, caliber 7.65mm Mauser. This rifle has a 29.1″ barrel, length 48.6″ overall, weight about 8.8 lbs.

M91 Argentine Mauser action.

The bolt handle, an integral part of the bolt body, has a short square base, a slender round shank and a round ball grasping handle. On most of the rifles the bolt handle is straight, while on the carbines it is generally bent down. Primary extraction power is achieved on opening the bolt—the base of the bolt handle contacts and moves over an inclined surface on the left rear edge of the receiver bridge.

The bolt body is drilled from the rear to accept the firing mechanism. The coil mainspring is compressed over the stem of the firing pin, between the shoulder on the firing pin and the forward, threaded shank of the bolt sleeve. The rear end of the firing pin extends through the bolt sleeve and is held in place by the cocking piece, threaded to the firing pin. The unit is retained in position by the bolt sleeve, being threaded into the rear of the bolt body. A small rib on the firing pin and a matching groove in the bolt sleeve, through which the firing pin moves, pre-

vents the firing pin from turning in the cocking piece. This rib is of such length that in assembling the firing pin parts, the cocking piece is turned on just far enough for correct firing pin tip protrusion when the cocking piece is threaded against the rib.

There are two notches at the rear of the bolt into which the cam or sear of the cocking piece can fall. A deep notch coincides with the cam on the cocking piece when the bolt is fully closed and locked, allowing the firing pin to move forward under mainspring tension for proper firing pin protrusion and ignition. On raising the bolt handle, the inclined surface of this deep notch moves the cocking piece, firing pin, and firing pin tip back within the bolt face. When the bolt handle is fully raised the cam on the cocking piece falls in the shallow notch. In this second position, the firing pin tip is still within the bolt face and prevents easy turning of the bolt sleeve when the bolt is drawn back.

The rifle cannot be fired unless the bolt is closed enough to allow the cocking piece to fall within the deep notch; in which case, the locking lugs are engaged in the receiver and lock the bolt closed.

No provision is made to block the sear when the bolt is not fully locked. The action is cocked on the bolt's final closing motion — the sear engages the cocking piece and holds it back when the bolt is closed. The firing pin can be lowered, without snapping the action, by holding the trigger back as the action is closed.

The wing-type safety is fitted lengthwise into a hole at the top of the bolt sleeve. A small spring-loaded plunger in the safety wing engages a shallow groove in the bolt sleeve, holding the safety in place; shallow detents at either end of the groove provide the "off" and "on" safety positions. Swung to the left, the safety is disengaged, allowing the action to be operated. When the action is closed and the firing pin cocked, swinging the safety to

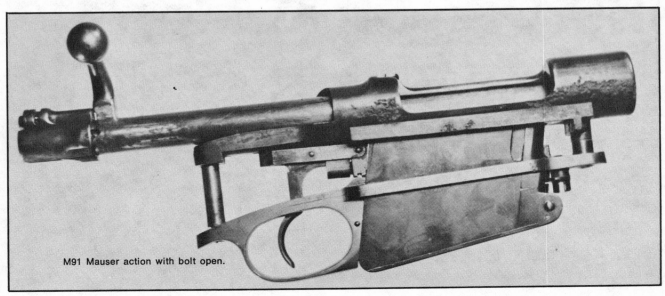

M91 Mauser action with bolt open.

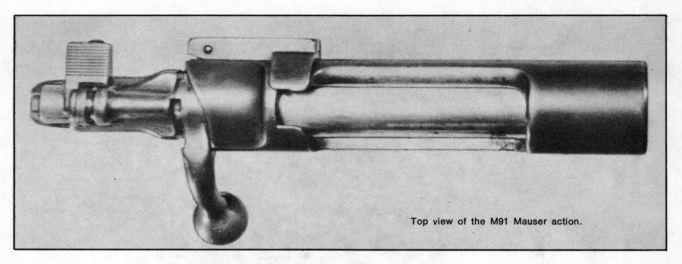

Top view of the M91 Mauser action.

the vertical or to the far right position locks the bolt closed, so it cannot be opened, and holds the cocking piece from contact with the sear. The safety can also be swung to the right, when the firing pin is uncocked, to lock the bolt.

The sturdy box-like bolt stop is hinged to the rear left side of the receiver on a stud and pin. A projection on the bolt stop extends through a hole in the receiver and, on opening the bolt its travel is stopped when the left locking lug contacts this projection. Swinging the bolt stop outward manually allows the bolt to be removed. The thin ejector extends into the receiver through a narrow slot. It is housed in the bolt stop and pivots on the bolt stop pin. The bolt stop is tensioned by a sturdy flat spring, mortised in the bolt stop housing and bearing against the top surface of the square bolt stop stud. This spring keeps the bolt stop closed and against the receiver. The small flat ejector spring, dovetailed inside the bolt stop housing, contacts the ejector to keep it against the bolt body. A small screw, through the rear end of the bolt stop

spring, holds it and the ejector spring in place.

The bolt stop is made with a long lip curving upward at its forward end. The end of this lip extends slightly past the left edge of the clip charger guideway. The end of the bolt stop lip holds the special stripper clip in place. The lip, of course, is also the means by which the bolt stop can be swung outwards so the bolt can be removed.

The sear is attached to the underside of the receiver and pivots on a small pin. Tension is provided by a coil spring within the sear. The trigger is of the double-pull type and is pivoted to the sear on a pin.

The trigger guard is combined with the magazine plate through which the detachable box magazine enters. Two guard screws, one on each end of the trigger guard, thread into the recoil lug and tang, holding the action securely in the stock.

The single column, 5-shot box magazine is extremely well made, with thin sides of spring steel. The top edges of the sides are bent inward slightly to hold the

cartridges in place, but can spring outward when cartridges are inserted. The jointed-V follower pivots at the bottom front corner of the magazine box on a screw. This screw also holds the bottom plate of the magazine in place along with a pin (riveted in place and not easily removed) at the rear of the box. Two leaf springs, grooved in place, one each in the bottom plate and lower follower arm, tension the follower to raise cartridges in the magazine. The magazine is guided, and precisely positioned in the action, by a hole in the trigger guard and the guide extension at the bottom of the receiver where the sear is pivoted. A spring-loaded latch, in the front of the trigger guard bow, holds the magazine in place. The magazine, not intended to be quickly detachable, can be removed, however, by depressing the latch with a pointed tool or bullet point, through the trigger guard bow, and down pulling on the magazine. On the M91 Argentine Mausers, the magazine is fastened in front by a coin-slotted, lipped stud. It is riveted into the trigger guard with the lip of the stud engaging a

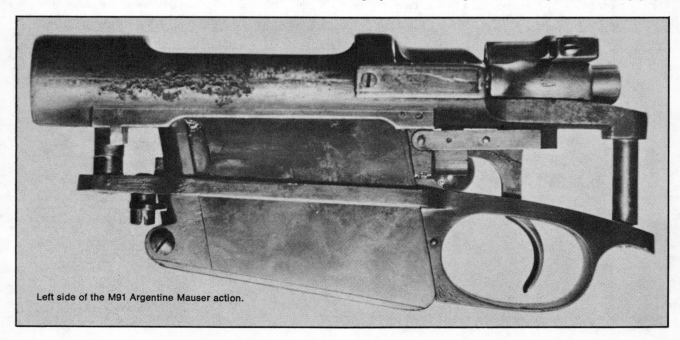

Left side of the M91 Argentine Mauser action.

Parts Legend

1. Receiver (side view)
2. Bolt stop
3. Bolt stop spring
4. Bolt stop spring screw
5. Bolt stop pin
6. Ejector spring
7. Ejector
8. Bolt
9. Bolt sleeve
10. Mainspring
11. Firing pin
12. Cocking piece
13. Safety
14. Extractor
15. Sear
16. Sear spring
17. Sear pin
18. Trigger
19. Trigger pin
20. Magazine latch
21. Magazine latch spring
22. Magazine latch pin
23. Magazine lock stud
24. Trigger guard
25. Rear guard screw
26. Rear guard screw sleeve (stock bushing)
27. Front guard screw
28. Safety plunger
29. Safety plunger spring
30. Safety plunger cap screw
31. Magazine box
32. Magazine plate
33. Magazine plate follower arm screw
34. Magazine follower arm
35. Magazine follower arm spring
36. Magazine follower
37. Magazine follower pin
38. Magazine follower spring

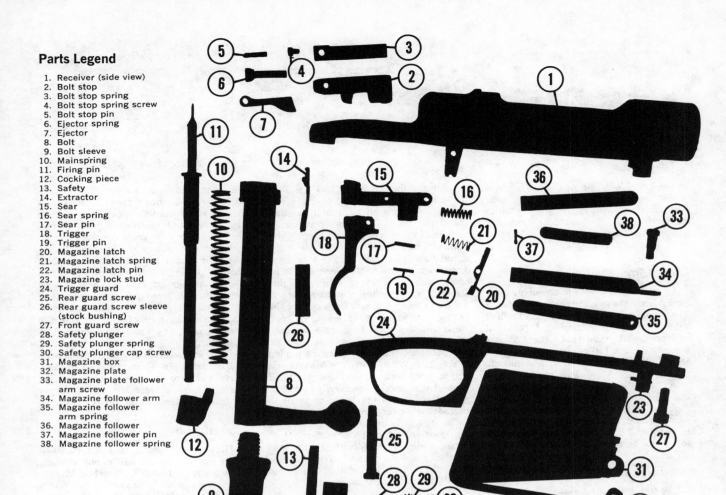

Mauser M-91

Dimensional Specifications

Weight	2.75 lbs.
Length	8.312"
Receiver ring dia.	1.300"
Bolt body dia.	.700"
Bolt travel	4.100"
Striker travel	1.00"
Guard screw spacing	7.062"
Magazine well:	
Width	.475"
Length	3.110"
Box magazine opening:	
Width	3.65"
Length	3.100"
Bolt face recess:	
Depth	.120"
Dia.	.475"

General Specifications

Type	Turnbolt repeater.
Receiver	One-piece machined steel forging, unslotted bridge. Clip charger guideways in bridge.
Bolt	One-piece, dual-opposed forward locking lugs.
Ignition	One-piece firing pin, cocking piece and coil mainspring. Cocks on closing bolt.
Magazine	Single-column detachable box magazine. 5-shot capacity.
Trigger	Non-adjustable double-stage military type.
Safety	Rotary wing-type built into bolt sleeve. 180° swing, left to right, locks both striker and bolt when "up" or at far-right (horizontal) position.
Extractor	One-piece spring type built into bolt head. Extractor rotates with bolt.
Bolt Stop	Separate, hinged at the left rear of receiver. Stops rearward travel of bolt by contacting left locking lug.
Ejector	Swinging type, positioned in bolt stop housing.
Magazine cutoff	None provided.

slot at the front of the magazine.

The magazine is normally loaded while it is in the action. With the bolt open, the magazine can be loaded through the top of the action, by either using a stripper clip or loaded singly by pressing the cartridges directly into the magazine. The magazine could be removed from the action, loaded, and reinserted into the action, but removing the magazine is not easily done without a tool to depress the magazine catch.

All of the Belgian and German M89, 90 and 91 Mauser rifles and carbines I've seen were superbly made and finished. There were no short cuts, crude stampings or soft alloys used in their manufacture. All of the action parts are precisely machined and well finished. I would assume that such vital parts of the action as the receiver, bolt, extractor, firing pin, etc. were made of the best steels available and suitable for these parts, and that they

were properly heat treated.

Markings

The serial number, or a part of that number, is stamped on all major parts of these actions. If these numbers match, it can be assumed that all the parts are original. Some parts are proof marked as well. The model designation and the name of the manufacturer is usually stamped

A M91 Argentine Mauser rifle sporterized by the author.

on the left side of the receiver. The crest of the government for whom these arms were made was usually stamped on top of the receiver ring, but in many cases this identification was ground off before the arms were sold as surplus.

The 7.65mm Cartridge

All of these arms were chambered for the 7.65mm Mauser cartridge, very popular in years past. It was and is an excellent military and sporting cartridge. It is loaded by Norma today and called the 7.65 Argentine. With a 150-gr. semi-pointed soft point bullet it has an advertised muzzle velocity of 2920 fps. This places it in a power velocity class between the .308 Win. and .30-06. Therefore, if you have one of these rifles with an excellent bore and want to use it, I'd suggest using its present caliber. The 7.65 cartridge is well designed, and it can be handloaded easily.

Action Strength and Safety

I would judge these actions to be as strong and safe as any other pre-98 Mauser action—the M93 and M95. These actions have no "safety" or "third" locking lug. No provision is made to vent escaping powder gases harmlessly from the action, in the event of a case or primer failure. However, the deeply recessed bolt head and narrow extractor slot actually provide more cartridge head support and coverage than does any of the later Mauser actions — including the Model 98. Nevertheless, though these actions may have been proofed at much higher pressures, when converting to other calibers by rechambering, reboring or rebarreling, I would limit the cartridge choice to those developing less than 45,000 psi. The magazine, bolt head and extractor, as well as the chamber and bore, impose other limitations on the choice of cartridges suitable for this action, which largely limits any conversion to rebarreling only. By rebarreling, the M89, 90 and 91 Mauser actions would be suitable for the following cartridges, none requiring any action changes to be made: .250-3000 Savage, .257 Roberts, 6.5mm Mauser, 7mm Mauser, .300 Savage and .35 Remington.

Gunsmithing Tips

The receivers of the M89, 90 and 91 Mausers are of the same general size, length and contour as the M93, 94, 95 and 96 Mausers; any scope mount suitable for the latter group can be used on the former.

Receiver sights made for the M98 are correct for the M89, 90 and 91. When mounting a scope low and over the bore, it is necessary to alter the bolt handle to clear the scope. The same procedure is followed when altering any other bolt handle. I recommend cutting off the original handle and electrically welding on a new one. Maynard Buehler makes a low scope safety for these actions. I don't know of any practical way to rework the action to make the bolt cock on opening, nor a way to alter the magazine to be flush with the stock. I can only suggest, if you use one of these actions, that you accept these limitations, including the long striker fall. When using the M89 Belgian action fitted with a barrel sleeve, I would discard the jacket. However, you can use the collar from this jacket to cover up the threads on the receiver ring by turning the collar on tightly and dressing it flush with the front end of the receiver. Several different styles of semi-inletted and semi-finished sporter stocks are available from E.C. Bishop & Sons, Reinhart Fajen, Inc., of Warsaw, Mo., and others.

Take-Down and Assembly

To disassemble the Model 89, 90 or 91 Mauser action proceed as follows: Remove the bolt by swinging the bolt stop to the left and pulling the bolt to the rear. To remove the firing mechanism from the bolt, pull the cocking piece back slightly with a small tool and unscrew the bolt sleeve from the bolt. Grasp the bolt sleeve firmly in one hand, and, resting the firing pin tip on a hard surface, push the bolt sleeve down to compress the mainspring. Then unscrew the cocking piece from the firing pin.

Remove the safety by unscrewing the plug screw in the safety wing. Remove the spring and plunger, then pull out the safety. Reassemble in reverse order.

Remove the extractor by inserting a small screwdriver under the extractor hook, pushing the hook outward, and at the same time prying the extractor forward until the lip on the extractor clears its recess. Reassemble in reverse order.

Remove the magazine by unlocking the forward magazine lock stud and depressing the magazine latch in the trigger guard with a pointed tool. Pull out the magazine. Disassemble the magazine by removing the exposed magazine follower pivot screw, allowing the magazine plate to swing down and remove the follower. Do not attempt to remove the bottom plate entirely — the small pin hinge is riveted in place. To reassemble the magazine, insert the follower and partially insert the follower screw. Swing the bottom plate into place and turn the screw tight.

To remove the receiver, barrel and trigger guard from the stock, first remove the barrel bands, then both guard screws and lift these parts from the wood.

Remove the sear and trigger by driving out their retaining pins. Remove the bolt stop by driving out its pin. Bolt stop and ejector springs are held by the bolt stop spring screw; remove it and drive each spring rearward from the bolt stop housing. The ejector comes out of the bolt stop without removing the springs by pulling if forward.

Remove the magazine latch by driving out the latch pin. Reassemble all of these parts in reverse order. *Do not* unscrew the barrel from the receiver unless proper tools are available to do this correctly.

Conclusion

Here are some questions I've been asked many times about these rifles and actions: How many of the M89, 90 and 91 Mauser rifles were made? Answer: All told, a great many. I don't have any exact figures, but if the known quantities given in the first part of this chapter are totaled, there must have been over a half-million of the M89s made for Belgium, and about the same number of the M90s and 91s made for Turkey and Argentina combined.

Do you consider these actions as being suitable for cartridges like the .22-250, .243, 6mm, .308 and .358? Answer: No, I do not. These are all modern high-intensity cartridges, and should be restricted to stronger and safer actions. I don't mean to imply that a Model 91 Argentine action, for example, would blow up if properly barreled in any one of these calibers. However, in case of a serious primer or case head rupture, with a high intensity cartridge, this action does not offer the shooter the same protection from escaping powder gases and brass particles that a safer action like the M98 Mauser would. In other words, the action may be *strong* enough, but is it *safe* enough? I know that many gunsmiths do not agree with me on this point, but I prefer to err on the side of safety.

Is it practicable to build a rifle based on one of these actions? Answer: Yes, as a hobby, if you can fit a low-cost barrel to the action and do all the work yourself. No, if you have to hire most or all of the work done, or do the work yourself and expect to sell the rifle at a profit. It is practicable to sporterize or remodel only if you start with a rifle having an excellent bore and don't change its present caliber.

4. Mauser M92, 93, 94 & 95

AFTER SEVERAL YEARS of use by their armies the Model 1889 (Belgian), 1890 (Turkish) and 1891 (Argentine) Mauser rifles, all essentially the same action, began to show some design and construction faults: The small spring extractor, with its narrow hook, proved unreliable; the magazine charger clip and clip guide, on the receiver bridge, proved faulty; the detachable box magazines were often lost and, because the magazine projected below the stock line, the rifles were not always easily carried. The trigger could be pulled regardless of the position of the bolt; the threaded connection between striker rod and cocking piece often presented an assembly problem; the action had too many parts and needed simplifying. Double loading was possible — that is, unless the bolt was fully closed and locked after chambering each cartridge, the bolt could be opened without extracting and ejecting the chambered cartridge and the next round would jam behind it on reclosing the bolt.

Paul Mauser, hoping to gain new arms contracts, set to work to improve, strengthen and simplify this action. This effort led to the development of the Model 1892 Mauser (a few of which were made for Spain) and, shortly thereafter, to the Model 1893 Mauser — destined to become a world-wide favorite.

In the transitional M92, Paul Mauser introduced the long, non-rotating extractor attached to the bolt body with a collar. This extractor prevented double loading, since the cartridge head could slip behind the extractor hook when pushed out of the magazine. The cartridge was extracted and ejected on opening the bolt, even if the bolt had not been fully closed. The magazine box was made part of the trigger guard, so it could not be detached and lost, but it was still a single-column affair projecting below the stock line. A pin was provided at the front of the sear, projecting into the receiver and matching a notch milled in the bolt body, so that the trigger

could not be pulled unless the bolt was fully closed and locked. The magazine clip-charger and charger guide were improved, eliminating the need for the bolt stop to hold the clip in place. Instead of threads, the cocking piece and firing pin had interrupted lugs so these parts could not be assembled incorrectly. A thin bolt guide-rib, milled in the center of the left locking lug raceway over which the slotted locking lug passed as the bolt was operated, helped to prevent the bolt from binding as it opened and closed. Introduced with the M92 Spanish rifle was the now famous 7mm Mauser (7x57mm) cartridge.

Although the M1892 Spanish rifle was an improvement over its predecessors, it had a short life. The same was true for the test Model 92/93 Spanish Navy carbine in 7.65mm caliber, only a few hundred being made. Apparently Mauser was dissatisfied with the single-column magazine arrangement in the rifles, for in 1893 he introduced the flush, staggered-column box magazine.

The new rifle, with its new magazine, was entered in the Spanish trials, where it was a huge success. It was promptly and enthusiastically adopted by Spain and designated the Spanish Model 93. Apart from having the new magazine trigger guard combination, and the receiver altered to accept this magazine, the rest of the action was essentially the same as the M92. The M93 safety, however, was simplified by eliminating the spring and plunger.

Model 93 and 95 Actions

The receiver of the M93 Mauser is a machined, one-piece steel forging. The bottom is flat for most of its length. The recoil lug, about ¼″ back from the forward edge of the receiver ring, is about .225″ deep and 1.086″ wide. The barrel has 12 threads per inch (V-type, 55°). The barrel is flat at the breech and is made with a shoulder to butt against the

front of the flat receiver ring, rather than against a collar inside the receiver ring. The receiver is the same width throughout, thus the left side of the receiver ring, wall and bridge is an evenly rounded surface. The front part of the receiver bridge is of the same radius as the receiver ring and a clip-charger guideway is milled into this area. Behind the clip-loading guideway, the receiver bridge is machined to a smaller diameter to reduce weight. The receiver ends in a tang about 2.5″ long.

The one-piece bolt has dual-opposed locking lugs on its forward end, these engaging shoulders milled in the receiver ring which securely hold the bolt against the barrel breech when the bolt is closed. The right (or bottom) lug is solid; the larger left (or top) lug, being slotted, allows the ejector to pass. The left locking lug raceway in the receiver is milled to leave a long ridge or rib of metal down its center, matching the ejector slot in the locking lug. This rib acts as a guide and helps to keep the bolt from binding as it is opened or closed.

The bolt face is partly recessed to enclose about two-thirds of the cartridge head extractor rim. The left locking lug extends ahead of the bolt face and forms part of the cartridge rim recess. The recess is about .060″ deep, slightly deeper than the thickness of the 7mm Mauser cartridge extractor rim.

The long spring extractor is attached to the outside of the bolt by a collar which fits into a groove in the bolt body. Hooks at the ends of the collar engage in a mortise, cut into the inside of the extractor, holding the extractor against the bolt. A lip machined inside the front of the extractor engages a groove cut partly around the bolt head to prevent longitudinal movement of the extractor on the bolt. The extractor's beveled hook extends over

---

Illustrated above: The 7mm Spanish Model 93 Mauser Short Rifle, 21.75″ barrel, 41.3″ over-all, weight about 8.3 pounds.

the bolt face rim recess far enough to engage the extractor rim on the cartridge, thus holding it against the extended left locking lug for proper extraction and ejection of the cartridge, or fired case. The extractor does not rotate on the cartridge head as the bolt is opened, but only moves back and forth with the bolt.

All M93 and M95 bolts, including the variant M94 and M96 Swedish Mausers, have part of the cartridge rim recess cut away, permitting the cartridge rim to rise and slip under the extractor hook as it emerges from the magazine. The extractor hook is made to hold the cartridge head in place within the bolt head. The extractor will hold it there until the cartridge or case is ejected when the bolt is opened. This feature prevents double-loading, since the extractor engages each cartridge as it leaves the magazine and will extract and eject it when the bolt is opened — even though the bolt was not entirely closed or locked. Most of these rifles permit the bolt to close on a cartridge singly loaded into the chamber ahead of the extractor, but not all. A few require some extra force to close and lock the bolt on a cartridge in the chamber — the extractor hook does not easily snap over the case rim.

The bolt handle, at the extreme rear of the bolt, is forged as an integral part. The shank of the handle ends in a round grasping ball. On most M93 and M95 rifles the shank is straight, the bolt handle sticks straight out or horizontal. On some short rifles or carbines the shank is bent down to bring the grasping ball closer to the stock. At the left rear of the receiver bridge a rearward slope forms a camming surface against which the bolt handle's square base moves as the bolt is opened. This provides initial camming power to the extractor.

The bolt sleeve threads into the rear of the bolt body. The coil mainspring slips

Model 93 Spanish Mauser action.

over the firing pin and is compressed between the bolt sleeve and a shoulder at the front of the firing pin. The rear end of the firing pin extends through the bolt sleeve and is held to the cocking piece by a series of interrupted lugs. The rear part of the firing pin is milled flat on two sides to match a hole through the bolt sleeve. This prevents the firing pin from rotating and coming loose from the cocking piece. A cam on the cocking piece extends through a slot in the bolt sleeve and slides in a groove cut into the receiver tang. The cam catches the rear end of the bolt or sear, depending on whether action is cocked or uncocked. The rear of the bolt is notched in two places. The front end of the cocking cam can engage either a deep notch, when the bolt is closed so the firing pin tip can reach the primer, or a shallower notch when the bolt handle is raised or the bolt opened. The purpose of the shallow notch is to retain the firing pin tip within the face of the bolt, and to prevent the bolt sleeve from being easily turned out of position when the bolt is opened. The firing pin is cocked on the closing

motion of the bolt.

The wing safety has a round stem which fits lengthwise into a hole at the top of the bolt sleeve. It is held in place by the wing overlapping a lip on the bolt sleeve. A notch in the right side of this lip allows the safety to be removed, but not while the striker head is in place. Swung to the far left the safety is disengaged. It is then in the "off" or "fire" position. Swung upright to the intermediate position, the safety locks the striker back and the bolt can be opened and closed. Swung to the far right to the "on" or "safe" position, the safety locks the striker back and the bolt closed. When the safety is either up or to the right, it draws and holds the cocking piece off the sear — the sear will still be in position ready to engage the cocking piece when the safety is moved to the "fire" position. With the safety upright, this offers a safe way to unload the magazine, chambering and ejecting cartridges with the bolt. No bolt sleeve lock is provided, therefore, the slightest touch against the bolt sleeve or safety, when the bolt is open, could cause it to rotate

Model 93 Spanish Mauser action open.

Left side view of Model 93 Spanish Mauser action, cocked, with wing safety upright.

counter-clockwise and twist out of alignment with the receiver, prohibiting closure of the bolt.

Most M93 and M95 Mausers, including the German-made Chilean Mausers, had no provision to divert or vent powder gases harmlessly out of the action in the event a primer or case head ruptured. In such cases, then, these actions will permit gases to enter the bolt through the firing pin hole, rush back along the striker and mainspring and spray them, and some oil picked up along the way, at the shooter's face. Gases escaping past the unrecessed part of the bolt face will be directed backward, down the left locking lug raceway, toward the shooter's face despite the bolt stop lug and flared bolt sleeve. Some M93 Spanish Mausers, notably the ones made in Spain by Industrias de Cataluna, have a single gas escape vent hole in the bolt near the rear bottom edge of the left locking lug, matching an oblong hole in the receiver ring. These vented actions are safer but the one small hole is not likely to vent all the escaping gas from a serious case head rupture and some may still be directed to the shooter's face.

The bolt stop is attached and hinged to the left of the receiver bridge by a pointed screw passing through the bolt stop and an integral square lug on the receiver. A stud, on the end of the bolt stop, protrudes through a hole into the locking lug raceway and halts the rearward travel of the bolt when it contacts the locking lug. This stud is slotted for the ejector, housed partially within the bolt stop, and held in place by the bolt stop screw. A double-leaf flat spring, mortised into the bolt stop housing, holds the bolt stop against the receiver and keeps the ejector pivoted against the bolt body.

The sear is attached to, and pivots on a pin through a stud on the bottom of the receiver. The trigger pivots on a pin in the sear to the rear of center. The top of the trigger, which bears against the receiver, has two humps which provide the double-stage let-off. The sear and trigger are tensioned by a coil spring between the front of the sear and receiver. Just ahead of the trigger spring, a pin pressed into the sear projects through a hole into the receiver. There is a single, narrow groove cut into the bolt body that aligns with the point of the pin *only* when the bolt is completely closed, otherwise the bolt body prevents the sear being released. There is also a flat spot on the bottom of the bolt which positions over the pin when the bolt handle is raised, and when the bolt is closed until the cocking cam contacts the sear. This allows the trigger to be pulled back, lowering the firing pin as the bolt is closed.

The cartridge guide lips are milled integral with the magazine well opening in the receiver. These guide lips, one at each side of the magazine well, hold the staggered column of cartridges in the magazine until pushed forward from the magazine by the bolt, and they guide the bullet point into the chamber.

The magazine box and trigger guard are of one-piece, machined steel construction, with the open top of the magazine box matching the magazine well in the receiver. The receiver and barrel are held securely in the stock via two heavy guard screws going through the front and rear ends of the magazine/guard. The front guard screw threads into the recoil lug, the rear screw into the end of the tang. Many post-1898 rifles have lock screws to prevent the guard screws from turning. The magazine/guard is securely held in alignment with the receiver by a stud collar toward the front overlapping a matching stud extending from the bottom of the recoil lug.

A longitudinal rib, to the left on the top of the milled steel follower, causes the cartridges to be staggered in the magazine. A W-shaped follower spring, held by undercuts in the bottom of the follower and inside the floorplate, provides the upward pressure to the follower. The detachable magazine floorplate is held in position by lips at both ends engaging recesses cut into the magazine/guard. A spring loaded plunger, at the rear of the magazine box, acts as the floorplate catch to lock it forward. Depressing this catch with a pointed tool through the hole in the rear of the floorplate allows the plate to move back, and carry the follower and follower spring with it free of the action.

Model 93 or 95?

For all practical purposes the M93 and M95 Mauser actions can be considered the same. In fact, an early Mauser catalog describing them makes no distinction. They are listed under the sub-heading MAUSER MODEL 93-95 with a single description. There are, however, variations by which one may determine their correct designation, or identify them positively by markings on these actions. If an action is marked "Model 1893" or "Model 1895," as in the case of the Chilean M95, there is no question about the correct designation.

When first made, the M93 bolt had two slight bolt face projections forming a small

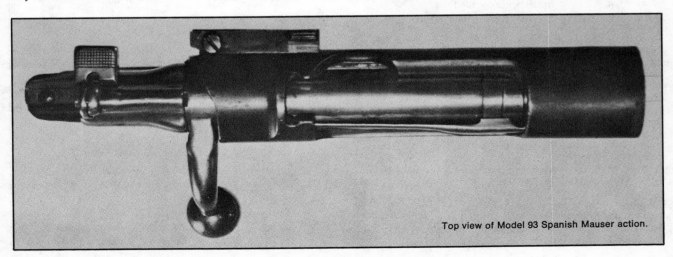

Top view of Model 93 Spanish Mauser action.

flat spot under the bolt, clearly shown elsewhere in this chapter. The tang and the rear of the receiver, as well as the loading ramp, were cut accordingly to allow passage of the bolt. These small projections permitted more of the bolt head surface to contact the cartridge heads when feeding them from the magazine into the chamber. Later on, however, this feature was dropped—it was found to be unnecessary for proper feeding—and the bolt was then made round. Actions having this later type round bolt head, and otherwise unmarked, can be either M93s or M95s. M93 bolts with flat bottom bolt heads are not interchangeable in receivers made for the round headed bolts.

The M95 Chilean Action

The M95 Chilean action is almost identical in every detail to the regular M95 Spanish action, except that it has a third, or safety, locking lug. This lug, about .175″ high, .125″ wide and .540″ long, is located on the right side of the tang just behind the bolt handle root. This lug does not contact the bolt handle, but is designed to leave a visible gap between it and the bolt handle. Its purpose is not to help hold the bolt locked in the receiver, but to act as a safety measure. That is, if the forward dual-locking lugs should fail when the rifle is fired, the small safety lug behind the bolt handle would halt or retard the rearward movement of the bolt. In such an extremely rare event the safety lug would afford some protection to the shooter by preventing the bolt from striking his head. It is in this respect only that the M95 Chilean action is somewhat safer than the other pre-98 actions. In my opinion, however, this feature does not make the action any more suitable for high intensity cartridges.

Other Variations

Earlier in this chapter the M93 Spanish action, made in Spain by Industrias de Guerra, was mentioned as having a gas escape vent in the bolt and receiver. This particular action further differs from the usual M93 and M95 in that the magazine/guard has a hinged floorplate. The floorplate is hinged at the front on a pin and is held closed by a small spring-loaded latch—fitted into a hole at the upper front of the trigger guard bow. Pushing the small plunger of this latch to the left, with a bullet tip or pointed tool, releases the floorplate so it, along with the follower and follower spring, can be swung down to empty the magazine. On others of the same make a different latch was used. A release lever similar to that used on the Japanese Type 38 caliber 6.5mm rifle is located inside the front curve of the trigger guard bow, and depressing the button releases the floorplate.

Another distinct variation is found on M93 Turkish rifles in 7.65mm caliber. This action has a magazine cutoff — a thumb-operated lever, pivoted on the right side of the receiver. When the cutoff is engaged, it forces the cartridges in the magazine down so the bolt can be closed

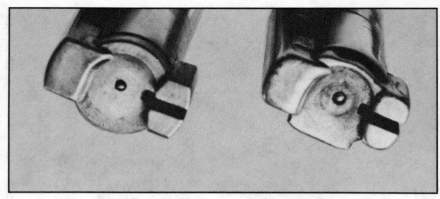
Faces of the M95 (left) and M93 (right) Mauser bolts. Note the flat spot on the bottom of the Model 93 bolt.

without picking up a cartridge. To lower a full magazine of cartridges, a deeper floorplate was used on this rifle.

Most M93 Spanish Mausers were made with a magazine follower, square at the rear, which blocked the foreward movement of the bolt when the magazine was empty. This feature prevented "blind loading" of the rifle. After ejecting the last case, the bolt will not close, indicating an empty magazine. Other military rifles based on the M93 action, like the M94 Brazilian and the M95 Chilean, had the follower sloped at the rear so the bolt would close when the magazine was empty.

Some M93s and M95s have a deep thumb notch cut into the left receiver wall just ahead of the bridge—an aid in loading the rifle from a stripper clip. The notch is frequently as deep as that found on the M98 action. On others, the thumb notch will be very shallow, just the top edge of the locking lug raceway cut away and rounded. Another type, like the M95 Chilean Mauser, shows no left wall cut at all.

Model 93 and 95 Rifles

I will list here a few of the variant rifles and carbines based on M93 and M95 Mauser actions. Foremost were the M93 Spanish rifle with 29.06″ barrel, weight about 9 pounds; the M93 Spanish short rifle with a 21.75″ barrel, weight about 8.3 pounds, and the M95 Spanish carbine with a 17.56″ barrel, weight about 7.5 pounds. Many of these Spanish rifles and carbines were made in Germany—Ludwig Loewe & Company, Berlin made about 250,000, the Mauser firm made 30,000. A great many of these arms were made at the Fabrica de Armas arsenal in Oviedo, Spain, and a huge number of the short rifles were produced by Industrias de Guerra de Cataluna arsenal, also in Spain. The Spanish arsenals made these rifles for many years and I have seen some dated after WW I.

Perhaps, the next most common rifle using this action is the M95 Chilean. It carries a 29.06″ barrel and weighs about 9 pounds. Like the Spanish M93s and M95s, it is chambered for the 7mm Mauser cartridge.

Century Arms has Chilean M95 Mausers with "OVS" over the serial number (left side of the receiver ring). These were originally sold to Orange Free State, Africa, but a portion were not paid for or

Bottom of the M95 bolt (right) as compared with the M93 bolt (left). Note gas escape vent near M93 bolt head.

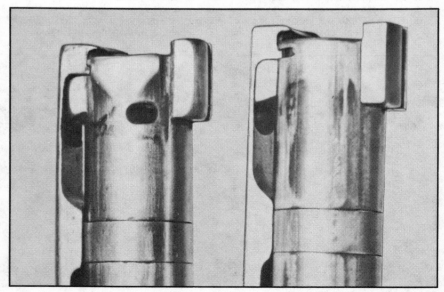

were refused — for what ever reason. These were then engraved (?) with the Chilean coat of arms on top of the receiver ring and sold to Chile.

Rarer, and not as well known, are the M93 Turkish caliber 7.65mm rifle with a 29.06″ barrel, the Brazilian M94 in 7mm caliber with 29.06″ barrel and the Orange Free State M95, which is similar to the Brazilian M94. Other countries which also adopted the M95 Mauser were Mexico, Uruguay and Persia (Iran).

The Mauser firm made over 200,000 of the Turkish M93 rifles. Ludwig Loewe & Company (Germany) and Fabrique Nationale (FN) of Belgium produced rifles for Brazil.

M94 and M96 Swedish Mausers

By the time Spain had adopted the M93

Safety lug (arrow) on the Chilean M95 action is located on the tang just behind the bolt handle base. The lug is about .175″ high, .125″ wide and .540″ long. It does not (and should not) contact the base of the bolt handle.

Mauser in 1893, Paul Mauser was making further changes to improve it and obtain contracts from other countries. In 1894, Sweden adopted a carbine with these improvements, designated the Model 94 Swedish Mauser Carbine. The new cartridge introduced with this carbine was the 6.5 x 55mm, which eventually became famous for its long range accuracy, both as a military and target round.

The Swedish government ordered 12,185 of these carbines, during 1894 and 1895, to be made by Mauser Werke in Germany. Later, the M94 carbines were made by Carl Gustafs Stads Gevarsfaktori (the Swedish government arsenal) in Eskilstuna, Sweden.

Being made for a different cartridge, having a slightly larger body and head diameter than the 7mm, the M94 Swedish action differed from the M93 and M95 actions in that the cocking piece had an upright projection at the end, the top checkered. The true purpose of this feature is not known, but most likely it was meant to uncock the action manually: that is, a

way to hold the cocking piece so that, on pulling the trigger, the striker could be lowered or uncocked. It is almost impossible to cock the striker by pulling the checkered projection. Hence, its purpose must have been to uncock the action rather than to cock it, if it had any purpose at all.

Just ahead of this checkered projection there is a notch which allows the safety to be swung over when the striker is down. Like most other bolt actions, when the M94 firing pin is forward and the bolt closed the firing pin tip protrudes from the face of the bolt. If the safety is swung over to the right, engaging this extra notch in the cocking piece, the firing pin is pulled back within the bolt and locked there. It may have been that this feature, plus the checkered projection on the cocking piece, allowed the soldier to uncock a loaded rifle (with a cartridge chambered) and then engage the safety; thereafter, an accidental blow to the cocking piece would not discharge the rifle. With the safety engaged on the uncocked action, the bolt is locked closed.

In 1896, Sweden adopted a rifle called the Model 96 Swedish Mauser, based on the M94 action, but made with an important additional feature. The early M94 Swedish action only had a shallow cut for the thumb in the left receiver wall, and this was found to have insufficient thumb clearance when charging the magazine with a stripper clip. On the M96, the thumb notch was made much deeper, extending through the left locking lug raceway. Therefore, to prevent the left locking lug from striking the edges of this notch as the bolt was operated, and to keep the bolt from binding, the bolt body was made with a narrow guide rib which passed through a matching groove cut inside the receiver bridge.

In addition to the deep thumb notch and guide rib, the M96 bolt had more gas

escape holes. One small hole was located behind the extractor collar, directing any escaping gases to the left and into the lug raceway. A second hole is forward of the extractor collar, visible when the bolt is locked, just behind the receiver ring above the extractor. Another smaller hole was bored through the front of the extractor under the extractor hook. The gas escape holes made these Swedish actions safer than any of the other pre-98 Mausers.

The M96 Swedish Mauser retained the checkered projection and the uncocked safety notch features of the M94 Swedish action. All M94s made after the introduction of the M96 were made with the deep thumb notch, guide rib and gas escape holes. Since few early M94 Swedish carbines were made, they are very scarce and seldom encountered, therefore, M94 and M96 actions usually seen are alike in practically every detail. The only noticeable difference is that the M94 bolt handle is bent down, while on the M96 it sticks straight out to the side. The M94 and M96 actions are like the M93 and M95 actions in most other respects.

Besides the M94 Swedish carbine, the Mauser plant at Oberndorf (Germany) made many of the M96 Swedish rifles. In 1899, for example, they were given a contract to make 45,000 M96 rifles.

A great many more of both the M94s and M96s were made in Sweden by the Carl Gustafs firm, and they continued to produce them for many years — I have seen them dated as late as the early 1940s.

In 1938, Sweden adopted a shorter barreled version of the M96 rifle, namely the M38 Swedish Short Rifle. In 1941, they introduced the Model 41 Sniper Rifle, simply a M96 rifle selected for accuracy and with a high, side-mounted telescope fitted to the receiver. The actions of both the M38 rifle and the M41 were the same as the M96, except for the turned-down bolt handle of the M41.

M94 and M96 Swedish actions are readily identified by the checkered projecting lug on the cocking piece. The early M94s will not have the guide rib on the bolt, but all M94s will have the bent bolt handle.

Markings

Mauser actions made in Germany are stamped on the receiver thus:

MAUSER/OBERNDORF

Those made in Sweden are stamped on the receiver ring with a date (year) as follows:

CARL GUSTAFS STADSGEVARSFAKTORI

Both the German and Swedish made actions will have their major parts numbered, and only if all the numbers of the action match can it be considered original. The full serial number is on the receiver, and the smaller parts usually carry only the last two or three digits of the entire number. This numbering practice was gen-

M94 Swedish Mauser bolt face.

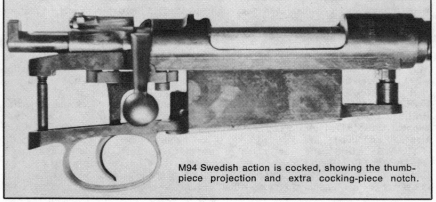

M94 Swedish action is cocked, showing the thumb-piece projection and extra cocking-piece notch.

erally followed by all makers of the M93 and M95 actions.

Interarmco (now Interarms) of Alexandria, Va., imported many M94 and M96 Swedish Mausers into the U.S. after WW II. For some reason the receiver of most M94s imported by them were remarked with

INTERARMCO G33/50.

Of course, the G33/50 is an incorrect model designation for these rifles.

Take-Down and Assembly

The following procedures apply to all models described in this chapter. To remove the bolt, raise the bolt handle, draw the bolt back, swing out the bolt stop and pull the bolt from the receiver. To remove the firing mechanism from the bolt, first close the bolt and place the safety in its upright position, then remove the bolt from the receiver. Unscrew (counterclockwise) the bolt sleeve from the bolt. Place the firing pin tip on a hard surface and, firmly grasping the bolt sleeve, push it down; turn the cocking piece one-quarter turn in either direction and lift it off the firing pin. The striker and mainspring can now be removed. Swing the safety to the right and pull it from the bolt sleeve. Remove the extractor on the M93 by turning it to the top of the bolt and push it forward, off the bolt. Remove the extractor on the others by turning it to the

bottom of the bolt before pushing it forward, which releases it from the collar. The collar can be spread apart to remove it from the bolt body but *do not remove it* unless absolutely necessary. Reassemble the bolt in reverse order.

Remove the magazine floorplate by depressing the floorplate catch with a pointed tool, moving it to the rear until it is released. Slip the follower spring off the follower and the floorplate. To remove the action from the stock take out front and rear guard screws, lift the barrel and action from the stock and then pull out the magazine/guard. Drive out the sear pin and remove sear, trigger and trigger spring from the receiver. Drive out trigger pin to remove the trigger from the sear. Turn out the bolt stop screw and remove bolt stop from the receiver. Pull the ejector forward and out of the bolt stop housing. Hold the bolt stop housing in a vise by its lug and, using a drift punch, drive the bolt stop spring forward until the end of it snaps inside the housing. Insert a sharp narrow screwdriver blade between the end of the spring and the housing and pry it back until it is free. Reassemble these parts in reverse order.

The barrel is threaded (right-hand) very tightly into the receiver and should not be removed unless necessary, and then *only* if proper tools are available.

Evaluation

The M93 and M95 Mauser actions (in-

cluding the M95 Chilean) made in Germany by Loewe in Berlin and by Mauser in Obendorf, show the highest quality of workmanship. They are extremely well made and finished. All the parts show careful machining and polishing. Without question, they were made of the finest and most suitable steels for the various parts. These were properly heat-treated and tempered for maximum strength and safety the action design allowed. On most of these actions the receiver and magazine/guard parts were finished a rich blue, while the bolt and all attached parts were left bright. The same praise would certainly apply to the German-made M94 and M96 Swedish actions.

As a general rule, the Spanish M93 and M95 actions made in the Oviedo and Industrias de Guerra arsenals are not as well machined or finished as their German counterparts. It is assumed that the Spanish actions conformed to the same general specifications as the German actions, and it is probable that similar steels and heat treating methods were also used in their manufacture. Since this is likely, the Spanish-made actions should be as strong and as safe as the German ones—though the latter actions are always preferred.

Of all pre-98 Mauser actions, the Swedish-made M94s and M96s are considered the best. Some experts believe that the Swedes used a better steel for their bolts and receivers. This may well be true for the high quality of "Swedish steel" is well known. Their actions were also as well

Top view, M94 Swedish action showing the bolt stop, clip-charger guideway, extractor, bolt guide rib (under extractor), exposed gas vent hole and checkered cocking-piece thumbpiece projection.

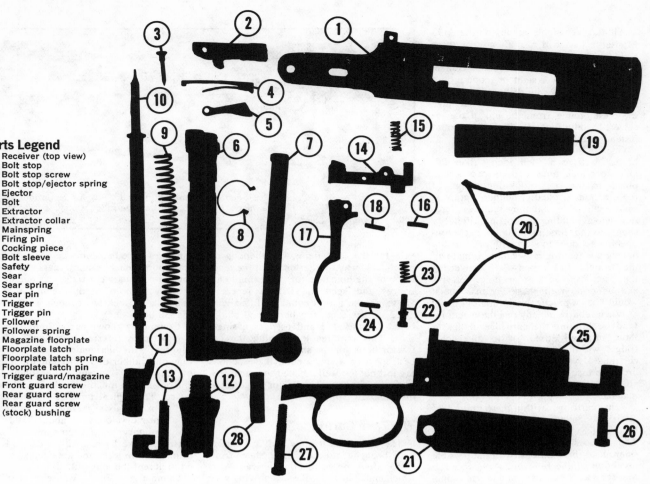

Parts Legend
1. Receiver (top view)
2. Bolt stop
3. Bolt stop screw
4. Bolt stop/ejector spring
5. Ejector
6. Bolt
7. Extractor
8. Extractor collar
9. Mainspring
10. Firing pin
11. Cocking piece
12. Bolt sleeve
13. Safety
14. Sear
15. Sear spring
16. Sear pin
17. Trigger
18. Trigger pin
19. Follower
20. Follower spring
21. Magazine floorplate
22. Floorplate latch
23. Floorplate latch spring
24. Floorplate latch pin
25. Trigger guard/magazine
26. Front guard screw
27. Rear guard screw
28. Rear guard screw
   (stock) bushing

Mauser Models 93 & 95

Dimensional Specifications
Model 93 & 95 Mauser
Weight ....2 lbs., 10 oz.
Length ....8.375"
Receiver ring dia. ....1.300"
Bolt body dia. ....700"
Bolt travel ....4.275"
Striker travel ....1.00"
Guard screw spacing ....7.625"
Magazine well width:
    Front ....550"
    Rear ....507"
Magazine length ....3.125"
Bolt face recess:
    Depth ....055"
    Dia. ....485"
Models 94 & 96 Swedish Mauser
Bolt face recess (partial):
    Depth ....062"
    Dia. ....487"
Magazine length ....3.235"*
Receiver well opening
    Rear ....595"*
    Front ....4.84"
*Widest spot, about 1" from the rear of well. Other specifications are about like those of the M93 & M95 actions.

General Specifications
Type	Turnbolt repeater.
Receiver	One-piece machined steel forging, unslotted bridge. Clip-charger guideway in bridge.
Bolt	One-piece, dual-opposed locking lugs forward.
Ignition	One-piece firing pin, coil mainspring and cocking piece. Cocks on closing the bolt.
Magazine	Staggered column nondetachable box type. 5-shot capacity. Detachable floorplate. One Spanish-made M93 has hinged floorplate.
Trigger	Non-adjustable, double-stage military type.
Safety	Rotary wing type built into bolt sleeve. 180° swing from left to right, locks striker when "up," locks striker and bolt when at right.
Extractor	One-piece, non-rotating, spring steel. Attached to the bolt by a collar.
Bolt stop	Separate, hinged at left rear of receiver. Stops rearward bolt travel by contacting left locking lug.
Ejector	Swinging type, positioned in bolt stop housing.

made and finished as the German actions. The Swedish-made actions were proofed with load developing up to 66,000 psi breech pressure. I don't think Swedish actions are actually stronger than any of the other M93 or M95 Mauser actions, but they are safer because of the gas-venting holes.

The firing pin can be lowered to the uncocked position on all of these actions by pushing the opened bolt forward and holding the trigger back while turning the bolt closed. Of course, this should only be done on an empty chamber.

Remodeling and Rebarreling

Any of these actions can be used to build a sporting rifle with a minimum of remodeling required. If a scope is to be mounted low over the receiver, the bolt handle must be altered to clear the scope. I recommend cutting off the original bolt handle and electrically welding a new

forged one to the bolt body. Alter the bolt on the M95 Chilean, so that the base of the bolt clears the safety lug on the receiver just as the original bolt did. Otherwise, the problem of altering the bolt handle, or welding on a new one, requires no more work than the M98 Mauser.

Commercially made low safeties are available for these rifles, eliminating alteration of the original. Attachments to eliminate the double-stage trigger pull are made, but it's a much better idea to install a commercially made adjustable, single-stage trigger mechanism in these actions if you dislike the military pull.

All receiver sights made for the M98 Mauser action will also fit any of these actions. Most scope mounts made for the small ring M98 can be used. Of course, installing a receiver sight or scope mount requires that holes be drilled and tapped in the receiver. For actions which have the crest ground from the top of the receiver, I would suggest using a side mount instead of a top mount for the scope.

One of the main objections to pre-98 Mauser actions is their long striker fall and slow lock time. Most shooters also object to the cock-on-closing design of these actions. Actually, neither feature is so objectionable that they require alteration when building a sporting rifle. My suggestion to those insisting on a cock-on-opening action is to start with one already having this feature, rather than going to all the trouble and expense of converting these actions to cock on opening. Yes, this can be done with these actions, but it would not be practicable to attempt it.

When rebarreling any one these actions, I advise limiting the cartridge choice to those originally used, or to other cartridges within the following limits: Any cartridge developing less than 45,000 psi breech pressure, of .30-06 head size, with an over-all length less than that of the magazine.

Some cartridges within these limits are: .250-3000 Savage, .257 Roberts, 6.5x57 Mauser, 6.5x55mm, 7x57mm, .300 Savage, 7.65 Mauser and .35 Remington. I consider all of these actions, with the possible exception of the M94 and M96 Swedish Mauser actions, as having marginal strength and safety for the .308 Win. (7.62mm NATO) cartridge. I would not recommend any of these actions for the .22-250, .220 Swift, .225 Win., .243, .244 or 6mm Rem., .284 Win. and .358 Win.

What about the .222, .222 Magnum and .223 Rem. cartridges? I believe these actions would be sufficiently strong and

M93 Spanish action with hinged floorplate magazine box as made by Industries de Guerra de Cataluna arsenal.

safe for the .222 Rem., but there is no practicable way to alter or adapt the magazine or the bolt face for these small cartridges and keep the rifle a repeater. However, the action could be fitted with a .22 caliber centerfire barrel and chambered for the .222 and used as a single shot. This requires lengthening the extractor hook for the smaller cartridge. At best, even as a single shot, these actions are just not too well adapted for cartridges having a head size smaller or larger than the standard .30-06 size.

The 7mm Cartridge

The first "war trophy" M93 Mausers were brought into the United States from Cuba after the Spanish American War, which ended in 1898. Besides proving very effective militarily, the 7mm was soon established as an excellent sporting cartridge for big game hunting. Almost as soon as the M98 Mauser rifle was introduced and sporting rifles were made on its action, the 7mm caliber was one of its most popular chamberings.

By the turn of the century, these sport-ing rifles were becoming known to American sportsmen. For many years afterward, the 7mm Mauser cartridge was one of the most "written up" of all foreign cartridges and received nearly as much wordage as the .30-06.

Commonly known as the 7mm Mauser, it is correctly referred to as the 7x57mm Mauser. This designates a case 57mm long and caliber of 7mm (bullet diameter of .284″). It is a rimless bottle-necked cartridge, with much of its long bullet exposed. The typical military round had a 173-gr. round-nosed jacketed bullet driven at a muzzle velocity of about 2300 fps. Most military rifles chambered for this cartridge have barrels with a rifling twist of one turn in 8.8″, and are deeply throated to accept the long bullet.

Commercial 7mm Mauser cartridges loaded in the United States have a 175-gr. soft point bullet with a muzzle velocity of around 2490 fps. It is loaded to approximately the same over-all length, using a bullet that matches the military chamber and rifling perfectly. Ballistically this 7mm load is comparable to the .308 Winchester (180-gr. Power Point).

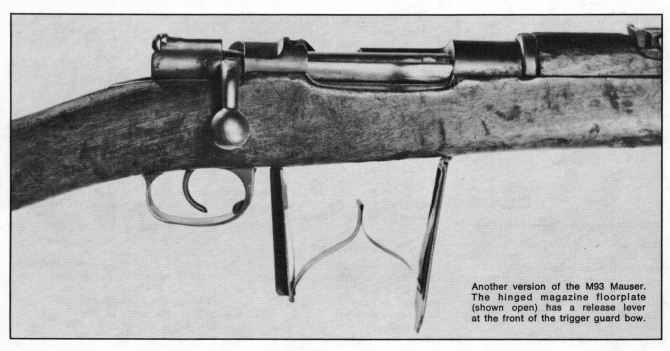

Another version of the M93 Mauser. The hinged magazine floorplate (shown open) has a release lever at the front of the trigger guard bow.

M96 Swedish rifle, 29.1″ barrel chambered for the 6.5x55mm Mauser cartridge, 49.5″ overall, weight about 9 pounds.

At 300 yds.	7mm	.308
Remaining velocity	1680	1680
Remaining energy	1100	1130
Mid-range trajectory	9.5″	8.9″

I included the figures and comparison above for two reasons: First, for hunting game like deer, antelope, black bear, sheep, goats, caribou and elk, the U.S. commercially loaded 7mm cartridge is equal to many of our popular cartridges; secondly, if you have an M93 or M95 rifle in 7mm caliber with an excellent bore, why not use the rifle as it is?

If you dislike the "stepped" barrel it can be lathe-turned or filed down to a straight taper, but I see no reason to fit a different caliber barrel to the action simply because

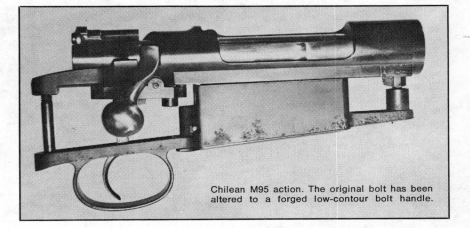

Chilean M95 action. The original bolt has been altered to a forged low-contour bolt handle.

the 7mm cartridge was developed over 75 years ago.

Norma-Precision, South Lansing, N.Y., imports Norma brand ammunition offering the 7mm Mauser cartridge loaded with three different bullet weights. Their 175-gr. soft point load delivers the same ballistics as the U.S. 7mm load. The Norma 150-gr. soft point semi-pointed boat-tail bullet has a muzzle velocity of 2756 fps, a remaining velocity of 2133 at 300 yards. Their 110-gr. soft point semi-pointed load has a muzzle velocity of 3067 fps and at 300 yards 2277 fps. The 7mm cartridge has always been favored for its mild recoil,* and the Norma 150-gr. load should especially appeal to the recoil-sensitive deer hunter. The 110-gr. load, designed for varmint shooting, should prove satisfactory for the purpose.

The 7mm Mauser has always been a handloader's dream cartridge. It is even more so today because there is such a wide range of domestic—and foreign—bullets available in this caliber. In military rifles the best accuracy will usually be obtained with heavier bullets, those ranging from 139 to 175 grains. Some of the lighter bullets may give fine accuracy if seated very shallowly in the caseneck, for a minimum of jump from case to rifling.

*Other things being equal — stock form, rifle weight, MV and ME and the rest — the 7x57mm has no more or no less recoil than any other caliber.

The 6.5 x 55mm Cartridge

If I have praised the 7mm Mauser cartridge, then I should extol the 6.5x55mm Mauser cartridge as well since it, too, is a renowned performer. It is, in the opinion of many experts, the finest 6.5mm cartridge ever developed. It first proved to be an excellent military cartridge, and later on a better sporting and target cartridge. As a target cartridge, it established some enviable records. Its present high esteem is reflected by the fact that it is offered as one chambering for the Remington 40XB target rifle. Therefore, if you have an M94, M96 or M41 Swedish rifle with an excellent bore, it would be plumb foolish to rebarrel it in another caliber.

The 6.5x55mm, also loaded by Norma, is available from many dealers handling the brand. At present, it may be had with either 139- or 156-gr. soft point bullets. Both loads are excellent for hunting most species of North American big game. According to modern notions muzzle velocity is not impressive compared to the .264 Magnum. However, at long ranges 6.5x 55mm ballistics become very impressive if we can believe the figures put out by Norma and Winchester. Judging a cartridge on the basis of these figures, we may then wonder why Winchester bothered to develop the .264 Magnum, or Remington the 6.5 Magnum.

Like the 7mm, the heavier-bullet loads perform best in the deep-throated 6.5x 55mm militarily chambered barrels.

This is a good cartridge for the reloader, and I suggest using new Norma cases rather than forming them from .30-06 brass—the 6.5x55mm case head is slightly larger in diameter. For varmint shooting, I consider the 6.5mm cartridge less desirable than the 7mm. Your Swedish Mauser may prove accurate with light bulleted handloads, but the only way to find out is to try it.

Conclusion

The Swedish rifles discussed in this chapter were never plentiful. From time to time during the 1950s, some dealers in military surplus offered M94 carbines for

A fine custom made sporter based on the M94 Swedish Mauser action. A 1903 Springfield 4-groove barrel is fitted to the action, rechambered to .308. A new bolt handle, Buehler safety and Weaver detachable side mount carrying a K-4 scope were also fitted. The figured walnut stock has skip-line checkering.

about $30. M96 rifles were offered less frequently, and were usually priced a bit higher. Some M38s were offered, as were the actions, in the late 1950s. Sales apparently were good—for these items were seldom listed after 1960. Surprisingly, however, in 1967 and 1968 a couple of firms offered the M41 Swedish sniper rifle complete with scope and mount for about $70. While all the Swedish Mauser rifles are becoming more scarce, it usually is not too difficult to pick one up from dealers handling used firearms.

As for the M93s, they appear to be more common than ever before. Since the military surplus market boom began after WW II, it seems that more of the various M93 carbines and rifles have been offered, as well as M93 actions, than any other foreign arm. I expect this condition to exist for a few years yet, though the supply will diminish eventually. M95 Mausers, especially M95 Chilean rifles, are much more scarce today.

Left side of the M94 Swedish action, showing the thumb-slotted receiver wall. The first stop on the bolt allows the trigger to be pulled, uncocking the firing pin as the bolt is closed and locked.

M94 Swedish carbine, 6.5x55mm cal., 17.38" barrel, 37.4" over-all, weight about 7.3 pounds.

5. Mauser Model 98

THROUGH STUDY of other rifle actions and his own development work, Paul Mauser gained considerable insight into precisely what features were necessary and desirable in a military rifle. He knew that each of his succeeding designs was better than the preceding one, so he problably felt that the Model 96 action was still short of perfection. It's interesting that there was a lapse of two years between the introduction of the M96 Swedish Mauser and the advent of the M98, while most other successful Mauser designs were only a year apart.

There was indeed a great advance from the basic M71 black powder action to the next important change, the smokeless powder cartridge M81 action. The latter introduced dual-opposed forward locking lugs and the one-piece bolt drilled from the rear. The next major and important design changes were in the M92 action, which introduced the non-rotating extractor, and in the M93 with its flush staggered-column, nondetachable box magazine. All of this design activity by Mauser on his bolt action system culminated in the design and the perfection of the inside collar in the receiver ring, the third, or safety lug on the bolt, and the improved firing mechanism of the M98.

This achievement was crowned when Germany, his native country, adopted the Model 98 Mauser rifle. Although Mauser continued to invent other arms, some of which were outstanding, it is the M98 action for which he is best known. Paul Mauser died in May, 1914, just at the start of WW I, a conflict that would see his M98 pitted against a variety of inferior rifles.

The Action

The one-piece receiver is machined from a steel forging. The recoil lug, an integral part of the receiver, is located about 1.43" behind the front edge of the receiver. It is about 1.1" wide and .25" in depth, ample in area to secure the action in a reasonably hard wood stock if properly bedded and tightened in place. Behind the recoil lug the bottom of the receiver is flat, including the tang.

The receiver ring is threaded inside to accept the barrel shank. The threads are of common V-type, but with a 55° angle rather than the standard American 60° angle. The barrel breech is flat, with the chamber edge slightly rounded. Inside the receiver ring there is a collar against which the breech end of the barrel abuts. This collar extends entirely around the inside of the receiver ring except for an extractor cut. It forms a ring that closely surrounds the bolt head when the bolt is closed. The rear of this collar, beveled toward the chamber, forms a wide funnel which sometimes helps to guide the cartridges into the chamber.

This collar strengthens the receiver ring and, except for the extractor cut, provides a good seal around the bolt head. Normally, the barrel shank is made to butt tightly against this collar so that the shoulder of the barrel need not nor should contact the front edge of the receiver.

The magazine well of the M98 action is milled from the bottom of the receiver, between the bridge and ring, leaving lips at either side of the upper edge to hold the cartridges in place. The front of the well is milled to form a shallow "U" ramp to guide the cartridges into the chamber. The right side of the receiver opening is cut very low, leaving little more than the side rail of the magazine well. The left side of the receiver opening has a wall extending about two-thirds of the way up the receiver ring which is milled for the left locking lug raceway. However, the rear of this left wall, close to the bridge, is cut as low as the right side to form a thumb recess to aid loading the magazine from a charger clip. The only really weak point in the action results from this notch —more on this later.

The top front of the bridge is slotted for the charger clip. The top of the bridge behind the charger clip slot is milled thin-ner to remove excess metal. The rear of the receiver ends in a tang, grooved to accept the cocking piece cam.

The bolt is a solid steel machined forging, with an integral bolt handle. Dual-opposed locking lugs are on the front end. The right (bottom) lug is solid. The left (top) is slotted to allow the ejector to pass through. The bridge and the left receiver wall are milled inside to pass the bolt and lugs. The receiver ring is milled inside to form supporting shoulders for the locking lugs to engage when the bolt is closed. These lugs hold the bolt securely against the barrel breech.

A recess in the bolt face leaves a shallow rim about two-thirds of the way around the bolt head, partially supporting the cartridge head. The left side of this rim (opposite the extractor), through which the ejector slot passes, is made higher and undercut so the extractor pressure will securely hold the cartridge, or the fired case, while the bolt is being opened. This prevents the case from dropping down and supports it until the ejector flips it out.

The long spring-steel extractor is attached to the bolt by a collar which fits a groove cut into the bolt body. A lip under the extractor, behind the extractor hook, engages a narrow groove in the bolt head in front of the locking lugs, preventing longitudinal movement of the extractor on the bolt. The front of the extractor lip, and the groove into which it fits, is slightly undercut to prevent the extractor hook from moving outward or from slipping over a cartridge rim when force is required to extract a tight cartridge or case from the chamber.

The M98 bolt has a third or safety lug located at the rear of the bolt slightly forward of the bolt handle, and in line with the right locking lug. A recess is milled in the receiver below the bridge in which the

---

Illustrated above: Original M98 Mauser rifle.

Standard M98 military action.

lug moves when the bolt is closed. The recess is milled with enough tolerance so the lug will not contact the receiver—it is not intended to help hold the bolt in the locked position but acts only as a safety lug in the event the front locking lugs or receiver ring should fail. The bolt, at top, has a center guide rib about 2.2″ long and .235″ wide. When the bolt is closed, this rib rotates under the rear part of the extractor. The underside of the bridge is grooved to allow passage of the rib.

The top forward corner of the square base of the bolt handle is slightly beveled, the rear surface of the receiver bridge inclined to the rear. On opening, the bolt is cammed rearward by the bolt handle base which moves along this inclined surface. This movement provides the initial extraction camming power. This inclined surface also aids in starting rotation of the bolt when it is closed. In addition, inclines on the approaches of the locking shoulders in the locking lug recesses in the receiver ring, along with a slightly beveled corner on each locking lug, provide the power to force the bolt forward the last 5/32nds of an inch as the bolt is rotated 90° to lock it. The bolt handle shank usually has a slight taper and ends in a round grasping ball. On most early military Mauser rifles the bolt handle shank is straight, at a right angle to the long axis of the action. On most short rifles and carbines, the bolt handle shank is bent down to place the ball nearer to the stock.

The rear of the bolt body behind the bolt handle (about .60″) is made larger (.78″) than the main body of the bolt (.70″). This provides extra metal for the firing and safety mechanism. The bolt is bored from the rear to accept the firing pin and mainspring, and has buttress threads to hold the bolt sleeve. The rear half of the firing pin is flat on two sides and extends through a matching hole in the bolt sleeve. The rear of the firing pin and cocking piece are machined with three evenly-spaced interrupted lugs to afford

a solid and precise quarter-turn fastening between these parts. The coil mainspring is compressed between the bolt sleeve and the flange on the firing pin, and is retained by the cocking piece.

Most M98 type actions made after 1901 were made with a safety firing pin. These firing pins have two lugs forward of the mainspring flange matching similar depressions forged inside the bolt. The purpose of this feature is to block the fall of the firing pin should it break before the bolt is fully locked. For example, if the firing pin broke while closing the bolt on feeding a live cartridge into the chamber, it could not strike the primer because the firing pin safety lugs would strike the shoulders within the bolt and block its fall.

The cocking piece cam fits into the rear of the bolt sleeve. The cam extends down into the tang groove and forward into a deep notch cut into the thick rear end of the bolt. This notch is inclined to one side so that on raising the bolt handle the cocking piece and the firing pin are forced back about .350″—enough so the sear drops in front of the cocking piece sear surface. Then, on the final closing motion, the bolt moves forward while the sear holds the cocking piece back, cocking the action fully. Although the M98 action is normally referred to as a "cock-on-opening" action, about one-third of the cocking motion is accomplished as the bolt is closed.

The bolt-sleeve lock fits into a hole in the left side of the bolt sleeve. It is given forward tension by a coil spring and is positioned by a small stud on the body of the lock within a groove in the bolt sleeve. As the bolt is turned to unlock it, the safety notch cut in the rear of the bolt is rotated in line with the bolt-sleeve lock, allowing them to engage. This securely locks the bolt sleeve and prevents it from turning on the bolt until it is locked again, when the bolt is closed and the bolt-sleeve lock is pushed back into the bolt sleeve by the rear edge of the bridge.

The wing safety is positioned in a hole,

lengthwise, in the top of the bolt sleeve. The wing part of the safety is notched and fits over a collar on the bolt sleeve, which prevents the safety from falling out. This collar is notched on its far right side to permit the safety to be removed from the bolt sleeve, but only when the cocking piece is removed first. With the action assembled, and the safety swung to the right, the mainspring tension on the cocking piece holds the safety in place. The stem of the safety extends forward through the front of the bolt sleeve to intersect the rear of the bolt body. The end of this stem is notched and engages in the notch in the bolt only when the safety is swung to the far right or "safe" position. In this position both the striker (firing pin and cocking piece) and the bolt are locked.

Swung to the left or "off" position, the safety is disengaged. Swung upright, in its intermediate position, only the striker is locked back, allowing the bolt to be operated to safely unload the magazine by running the cartridges through the chamber. When the safety is swung from the left to the upright position or beyond, it engages behind the cocking piece and draws it back clear of the sear. When it is released, the sear will be in position in front of the cocking piece, holding it cocked.

The bolt has two large oblong vents through which powder gases can escape in the event of a pierced primer or ruptured case head. These two holes are located in the front part of the bolt, one on either side of the extractor collar and near the small part of the firing pin. When the action is closed these vents align with the left locking lug raceway, thus directing any escaping gases backward. Much of the escaping gases would exit at the thumb slot. If any gases pass into the bridge raceway the bolt would block much of it, while the wide, bolt sleeve flange effectively deflects the remainder away from the shooter's face. This flange is as wide as the rear part of the receiver.

The bolt stop, positioned at the left rear

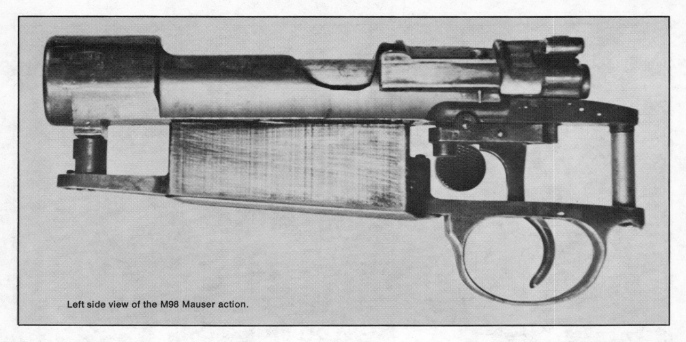
Left side view of the M98 Mauser action.

of the receiver, is held in place by, and pivots on, a pointed screw which passes through the bolt stop and a slotted square stud integral with the receiver. A projection on the bolt stop projects through a hole in the receiver bridge, placing it in the path of the left locking lug. This halts the rearward motion of the bolt when it is drawn back. The flat ejector is held inside the bolt stop and pivots on the bolt stop screw. The ejector protrudes through a slot in the receiver. A two-leaf spring, mortised into the bolt stop, provides tension to the bolt stop to hold it against the receiver, and to keep the ejector riding against the bolt so it will be in position to eject the cartridge or case.

The sear is hinged, via a pin and a stud under the rear of the receiver. A coil spring, recessed at the front of the sear, tensions the sear and trigger. The trigger is hinged to the sear by a pin. The top of the trigger is made with two humps to provide the two-stage trigger pull.

The trigger guard and the magazine box are machined from a single piece of steel. Although the trigger guard is combined with the magazine box, it is usually called the trigger guard—or simply the guard. The guard bow is quite heavy and the same width as the guard tang above it. The magazine box, open at the bottom, is closed by a milled detachable floorplate. The floorplate is held in place by lips at either end fitting grooves cut into the guard and retained by a spring-loaded plunger at the rear of the magazine box, and engaging in a hole in the stud on the rear of the plate. Depressing the plunger through the hole in the rear of the floorplate allows it to be moved to the rear and released.

The magazine follower is made with a rib on its upper left side, forcing the cartridges to form a staggered column in the magazine. The rear end of the follower rib is square. When the magazine is empty and the bolt is opened, the follower rises into the path of the bolt and prevents it from being closed. This informs the

shooter that the magazine is empty. The ends of the W-shaped flat magazine spring fit shallow mortises cut into the bottom of the follower and inside the floorplate.

Heavy guard screws pass through holes at each end of the trigger guard and thread into the recoil lug and tang of the receiver. A large stud on the front end of the guard, through which the guard screw passes, is recessed to fit over a smaller stud on the bottom of the recoil lug. This stud aligns the receiver and the trigger guard magazine box. A sleeve in the rear guard screw hole of the stock correctly spaces the rear of the guard and receiver.

Most M98 military actions use two small screws to lock the guard screws. The heads of the guard screws are notched, and the lock screws are positioned just in front of them to prevent their turning. The lock screws are also notched. If they are turned so the notch aligns with the guard screws, the latter can be turned out without removing the lock screws.

Operation

The action is opened by grasping the bolt handle, rotating it upward 90° and pulling back as far as it will go. The striker is partially cocked when the bolt handle is raised. If the cartridges are in a charger clip, insert either end of the clip into the charger guideway of the receiver bridge and, with the fingers under the action and thumb on the topmost cartridge, shove the cartridges down into the magazine. Cartridges can be singly loaded into an empty or partially empty magazine, by laying the cartridge in the open action and pressing it into the magazine with the tip of the thumb. To close the action, grasp the bolt handle and push the bolt forward. As the bolt moves forward it pushes the top cartridge in the magazine into the chamber. The cartridge head slides under the extractor hook on the final forward movement of the bolt.

During the final forward movement of

the bolt, and on rotating the bolt clockwise to the locked position, the sear engages the cocking piece to hold it back as the locking lugs pull the bolt fully forward to lock and seat the cartridge in the chamber. The rifle can now be fired by pulling the trigger, releasing the firing pin under mainspring tension, or the action can be made "safe" by swinging the safety to the right. Cartridges can be extracted and ejected safely by swinging the safety to its intermediate or upright position and opening and closing the bolt.

The firing pin can be lowered without snapping it by merely swinging the safety to the left, or fire position, raising the bolt handle, and then holding the trigger back as the bolt is rotated down to its locked position. *This should only be done with an empty chamber.*

Take-Down and Assembly

Check the chamber and magazine—to be certain the rifle is unloaded. Close the bolt and place the safety in the upright position. Now raise the bolt handle, swing the bolt stop to the left, and draw the bolt from the receiver.

To disassemble the bolt proceed as follows: Depress the bolt sleeve lock plunger, then unscrew the bolt sleeve and firing mechanism from the bolt; place the firing pin tip on a hard surface and, firmly grasping the bolt sleeve, press the bolt sleeve down; turn the cocking piece one-quarter turn in either direction, and lift it off the firing pin. Firing pin and mainspring can now be separated. Swing the safety to the right and pull it out of the bolt sleeve. Depress the bolt sleeve lock plunger and rotate it counterclockwise until it is released; pull it and the spring from the bolt sleeve. Remove the extractor by lifting the front (hook end) away from the bolt so that it can be turned to the bottom of the bolt; the extractor can now be removed by pushing it forward. Reassemble in reverse order.

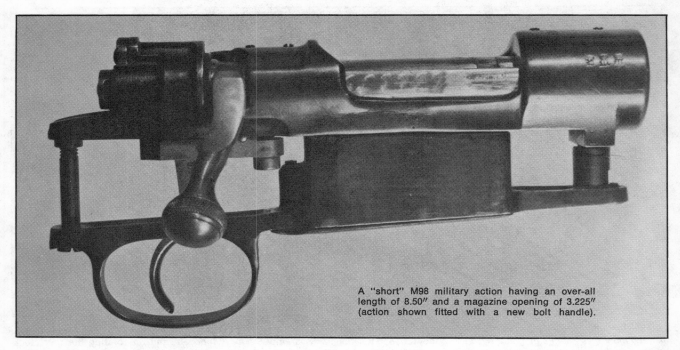

A "short" M98 military action having an over-all length of 8.50″ and a magazine opening of 3.225″ (action shown fitted with a new bolt handle).

To remove the bolt stop turn the bolt-stop screw out, and lift it from the receiver. Pull the ejector forward out of the bolt stop. Place the bolt stop in a vise and, using a drift punch, drive the spring forward until its end slips down. Now insert a small screwdriver between the end of the spring and the bolt sleeve, and pry the spring forward. In reassembling the spring into the bolt stop, the end of the spring must be raised over the edge of the bolt stop when it is being driven into place.

To remove the barrel and action from the military stock, first remove the upper and lower barrel bands from the fore-end, then remove the two guard screws from the bottom of the trigger guard. The barrel, action, and magazine can now be lifted out of the stock.

Remove the floorplate by depressing the floorplate plunger with a pointed tool (or pointed bullet tip) put through the hole in the rear of the plate, then slide the plate to the rear. The magazine follower and its spring will come out with the plate. The three parts can be separated by sliding the plate and follower off the ends of the spring. Remove the floorplate plunger by driving out the crosspin from the rear of the magazine box. Remove the trigger and sear by driving out the trigger and sear pins. Reassemble in reverse order.

Large and Small Ring Actions

Model 98 actions with a receiver ring about 1.410″ in diameter are commonly called "large ring" Mausers. Most M98 sporting and military rifles made up to the end of WW II are based on this large ring action. Most of the commercial M98-type actions made after WW II, like the FN, are also of the large ring type.

The "small ring" Mauser actions have a receiver ring diameter of about 1.300″. A lot of the early M98 carbines, like the 98a, were based on the small ring action.

The most notable later carbine using this action was the lightweight Czech Model 33/40.

The difference between the large and small ring actions is readily discernible by sight or touch, and there is no need to use a caliper to identify them. On the small ring action the left side of the receiver is straight, including part of the bridge, the wall and ring. However, on the large ring action this surface has a notable jump where the receiver wall merges with the ring, which can be seen and felt.

Because the large ring action has a thicker wall of metal surrounding the sides and top of the barrel shank and locking lug recess areas, it naturally is stronger than the small ring action. Just how much stronger is difficult to say. However, German gunmakers considered the small ring action strong enough for the most powerful 8mm military or sporting cartridge. Generally, the large ring actions are preferred and recommended for use with belted magnum and larger rimless cartridges like the .30-06 and 8mm. The small ring actions are preferred for lightweight sporters using small rimless cartridges like the 7mm and 6mms.

Steel and Heat Treatment

In our study of Mauser actions preceding the M98, we noted that Paul Mauser made each successive action better, stronger and safer than the preceding model through better design. It is generally agreed by experts that the M98 Mauser obtains its strength from its design rather than by the use of specially formulated or alloyed steels, or by some special heat treatment. It is not known just exactly what kind of steels were used to make the various parts, or the details of the heat treatments, but there is no doubt that whatever steels and heat treatments were used, they were entirely adequate to make the

Top view of the M98 action.

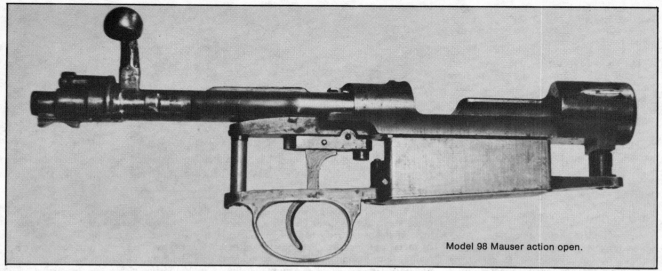

Model 98 Mauser action open.

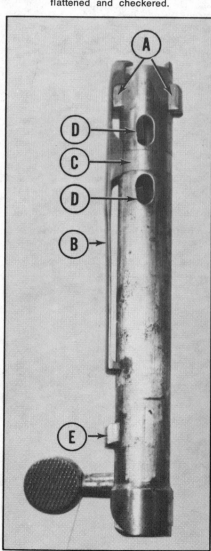

An underside view of the M98 Mauser bolt shows the dual-opposed locking lugs (A), extractor (B), extractor collar (C), dual oblong vent holes (D), and safety lug (E). This 98a carbine bolt has a bent down handle with the underside of the grasping ball flattened and checkered.

M98 the world's most successful military turnbolt action.

It is believed that the M98 receivers were made of tough quality low-carbon steel. After machining, the only heat treatment the receiver got was carburizing (case hardening). This resulted in a hard outside surface to resist wear and rust, but left the core relatively soft for strength.

Receivers of the pre-WW I era, especially the small ring type, tend to be somewhat softer than those manufactured in the 1920s, 30s and early 40s. I have observed that receivers made late in the WW II period, or those dated "44" and "45," are sometimes either very soft or hard, mostly the latter. The normal range of hardness for a good receiver seems to be about 35C Rockwell.

Model 98 bolts and some of the other working parts of the action were evidently made of medium- or high-carbon steel, so that these parts could be made much harder.

There seems to be no evidence to indicate that any re-heat treatment of a soft M98 receiver will improve it or make it stronger. It is inadvisable, therefore, to have this done.

This brings up a question I'm often asked: "How do I go about selecting a good original Mauser 98 military action on which to build my own custom rifle?"

My suggestions are: Buy the action, or a complete rifle from which the action is to be taken, from a reputable dealer who will refund your money, if for any reason, you are not satisfied with the action or rifle they sell. Avoid those dated before 1920 and those dated after 1943. Finally, if possible to do so, pick one that was made by one of the better plants. For example, you can hardly go wrong in picking an action made in the 1930s having such names (or code letters) as Mauser, DWM, FN or Brno (VZ-24) stamped on the receiver. After getting one of these actions there is no point in having the receiver tested for hardness; whether it is somewhat harder than 35C Rockwell, or considerably softer, the action is still good.

One final word of caution about very soft receivers: If you have an M98 rifle

and you want to use the action for building a rifle—if of pre-1920 manufacture, or if the rifle shows evidence of having been used a great deal—it would be a very good idea to test fire it, preferably with several full service rounds. After each firing, if the bolt handle can only be raised with difficulty this may indicate locking lug set-back in the receiver ring. This is usually a sign that the receiver is very soft, and that the locking lugs have hammered depressions into the locking shoulders. The result is that when the bolt is opened the locking lugs must pass from the depressions to the higher undamaged part of the locking shoulders, forcing the bolt forward in so doing. The total set-back may be only a couple of thousandths of an inch, but even so, on opening the bolt the fired cartridge must be forced forward into the chamber the same amount. Such a receiver should not be re-used. This condition is not easily corrected and it indicates, possibly, a very soft receiver.

The "Short" Mauser Action

The regular or standard M98 action made for the 8mm Mauser cartridge, whether large or small ring type, is 8.75″ in length. Various countries using the 7x57mm cartridge as their official military round adopted M98 action rifles that were, in some cases, slightly shorter than the regular 8mm Mauser action. The short Mexican M98 action was once the best known of the short actions. It is 8.50″ in over-all length. Today these Mexican actions, either small or large ring type, are scarce. However, during the past few years other short M98 actions have appeared on the surplus market, chiefly the Model 24 Yugoslav.

Here are the dimensional specifications of the short M98 action and the regular length 8mm action:

Model 98 Mauser Action Data

	Short	Regular
Weight	43 oz.	45 oz.
Length over-all	8.50″	8.75″
Bolt travel	4.40″	4.570″
Bolt body length	6.175″	6.375″

Guard screw spacing	7.625"	7.825"
Magazine length	3.225"	3.320"

All other specifications are about the same for both actions.

The short M98 actions have long had, and still have, a great appeal to shooters and gunsmiths wanting to build lightweight sporting rifles for cartridges like the .220 Swift, .257 Roberts, .243 and .308 Winchester. When reading about short actions the word "short" seems to have a magical appeal and shooters will go to almost any length to get such an action— only to find out later, as shown in the above table, that the short action is not as short or as light as they expected.

Strong and Weak Features

Without question the M98 Mauser is the best, strongest and most foolproof military turnbolt action ever made. It has many outstanding features which have been little improved upon in modern bolt actions, but like all actions, including the latest designs, the M98 Mauser has its faults and weak points. I shall list the various good and poor features as I see them—based on 30 years of experience in using, remodeling, rebarreling and building many rifles on these actions.

As I see it, the only major weak point in the M98 military action is the thumb notch in the left receiver side rail. I have seen a number of these actions with the left receiver rail cracked at this point. I have cracked one myself inletting it into a stock, another when I accidentally dropped it on a cement floor. Once I dropped a barreled action on the cement floor and the entire rear part of the receiver broke off at the thumb notch. Although the entire length of the right rail has no more metal in it than the thinnest part of the left rail at the thumb notch, it seems to be stronger and resists cracking when subjected to strain—much better than the left

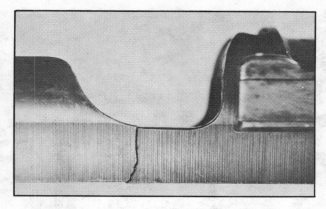

A cracked Model 98 receiver. The crack is located in the left receiver rail where the thumb slot is cut. This usually happens only with late WW II receivers, which were not always properly heat treated, and occurring only if the rifle or receiver is dropped on a hard floor.

rail. This is probably due to the heat treatment given the receiver in which a thin area of metal between two larger masses of metal becomes harder, and thus more brittle, than a similar thin area not close to a larger mass. Another example is the receiver bridge; although the entire receiver has been given the same heat treatment or undergone the same hardening treatment, the thin receiver bridge is always much harder to drill or tap than the much thicker receiver ring.

Commercial M98 type receivers made without the thumb notch are naturally much stiffer and more rigid than the notched military receivers, so they're usually preferred for sporting and target rifles. Some gunsmiths stiffen the military receiver by filling the thumb notch with a piece of pre-shaped steel and welding it in place.

Although the 98 action is a very safe one, I believe it would be even safer by having one or two gas vent holes in the left side of the receiver ring and wall opposite the vent holes in the bolt, as in the 03A3 Springfield.

Not a weakness or a fault, but to me a nuisance, is that the bolt cannot (without a great deal of force) be closed on a car-

tridge that has been dropped into the chamber because the extractor will not slip over the cartridge rim. However, this minor nuisance can be corrected by careful alteration — shortening the extractor hook and increasing the forward slope is all that is needed.

It must be remembered that Paul Mauser designed this action solely for military use, and from this standpoint all other features of this action are outstanding. These include the inside collar in the receiver ring, the safety lug on the rear of the bolt, a very rugged extractor which will not let go of a cartridge rim when the bolt is opened, the simple and positive ignition system, the sturdy and reliable safety and bolt stop, and the fine unbeatable magazine system.

Despite the "militaryness" of this action, German and British gunsmiths soon found that it met all the requirements of sportsmen who desired a repeating magazine rifle for hunting large game. The M98 action was sometimes used "as issued." Even at the peak of European bolt action sporting rifle development, the foreign sportsman demanded little more than the basic action, or at most only a lower profile of the bolt handle, and more con-

The 8mm military cartridges were supplied in stripper-clips. To load the rifle the bolt is opened, the loaded clip inserted into the clip-charger guideway slot in the receiver bridge and the cartridges pushed down into the magazine. The empty clip falls away when the bolt is closed, which feeds the top cartridge in the magazine into the chamber. Single cartridges can also be inserted into the partially empty or empty magazine by opening the bolt, dropping the cartridge in the receiver opening, and pressing it into the magazine with the thumb.

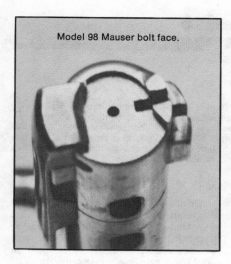

Model 98 Mauser bolt face.

The M98a carbines have a special hinged muzzle cover. Rifles were stacked with the cap closed to protect the bore from the weather. By opening the spring loaded cap the bore could be cleaned from the muzzle. A hole in the cover, smaller than the bore, prevents wear and damage to the muzzle from the steel Mauser cleaning rod. The cover must be removed to fire the rifle. The projection on the rear of the cover blocks the view beyond the front sight. The 98a's rugged front sight has a forward hook to engage the muzzle cover. To remove the cover, close the cap, push down and turn 90° counterclockwise.

venient floorplate release and, for the Germans, a double-set trigger mechanism. American hunters, shooters and gunsmiths, however, demanded more from this action; in time it was found to be more adaptable and easier to remodel than any other military bolt action. So much so that it has been universally adopted by most amateur and professional gunsmiths as their first-choice military bolt action on which to build a rifle.

The M98 action is popular in the U.S. for several reasons, but primarily because it is readily available, especially since 1945. American shooters first became familiar with this action in fair numbers after WW I when the first souvenir rifles appeared. Commercial Mauser sporters had been imported since about 1910. However, it was not until after WW II that M98 military rifles and actions appeared in great numbers. Since that time countless thousands of these rifles and actions have reached the American market. Shortly after WW II commercial M98 actions began to appear, beginning with the Belgian-made FN and followed by others made in Yugoslavia, Sweden, West Germany, Spain and Japan.

At present there must certainly be far more M98-type actions and rifles in the U.S. than any other centerfire turnbolt design, and perhaps more than all these other actions combined.

The M98 Breeching

I have previously described the M98 breeching system which centers around the collar or ring inside the receiver. The flat breech face of the barrel butts against this collar and the head of the bolt is

recessed within the collar, touching the barrel when the bolt is locked. There are other breech systems that are much more simple and equally as strong and safe, but few of them offer the one advantage that has contributed to the unmatched popularity of this action — a feature seldom discussed.

Many people have said to me, "There are several firms making and offering low-cost turned, threaded and chambered barrels in various calibers and weights for the M98 action. Why don't they offer similar barrels for other actions like the 03 Springfield and 1917 Enfield, as well?" The answer is that there is no single military or commercial high power bolt action that is as numerous or as popular, so low in cost, strong, safe and suitable for a variety of cartridges as is the M98 Mauser

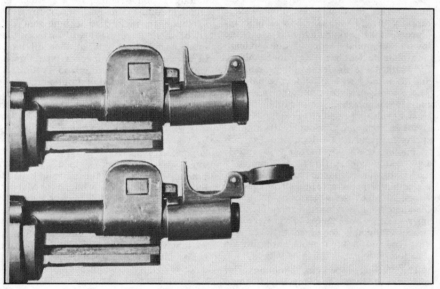

—and to which a barrel can be fitted so easily.

I cannot go into the detailed procedures of fitting and headspacing a barrel here. Suffice it to say that it is far easier to properly fit a barrel to the M98 than it is to fit one to most of the other military bolt actions, especially those not made to accommodate a flat-breech-end barrel. It is, however, possible and practicable to manufacture barrels for the M98 action to close enough tolerances so that a knowledgeable amateur gunsmith should be able to fit it properly to his action without the use of a metal lathe or chambering reamer. This would be very difficult, if not impossible, with an 03 Springfield or similar action. The reader should not get the impression from what has been said that fitting a barrel to the M98 action is a snap and simply requires turning it up tightly. This is not the case.

Gunsmithing the M98

To begin with, it is only practicable to use a military M98 action for building a rifle if you can do all or at least most of

the remodeling work yourself. For example, if you have an action which cost you nothing, and hired the remodeling work done to equal the commercial FN Supreme Mauser action, then it probably would have been advisable to buy the commercial action in the first place. On the other hand, if you can do the remodeling yourself there is no military action quite as ideal as the M98 on which to build a rifle.

The standard M98 military action made for the 8mm Mauser cartridge has a magazine length opening of approximately 3.320″ and, therefore, is best suited to cartridges loaded to a slightly shorter overall length. The bolt face recess and extractor are correct for any centerfire cartridge of .30-60 head size. Therefore, without modifying the magazine, bolt head or extractor, the standard M98 military action will handle such cartridges as these: .243, .244, 6mm Remington, .257 Roberts, 7mm Mauser, .284, .308, 8mm Mauser, .358 and wildcats based on these cases. The unaltered actions will usually handle shorter cartridges quite well, such as the .22-250, .225, .220 Swift and .250-3000. However, for perfect feeding it usually is necessary to install a filler block in the rear of the magazine and use a shorter follower for the shorter cartridges.

Lengthening the magazine is not too difficult. This makes the M98 action suitable for cartridges slightly longer than the 8mm Mauser. By thinning the rear and front magazine walls and altering the loading ramp, or by moving the front magazine wall forward and altering the loading ramp accordingly, it can handle most .30-06 or .270 length cartridges. Then, by opening up the bolt face recess and shortening the extractor hook, the action can handle such short belted-magnum cartridges as the .264 to .458. Opening up the magazine and altering the loading ramp enough for such longer magnum cartridges as the .300 H&H Magnum is not recom-

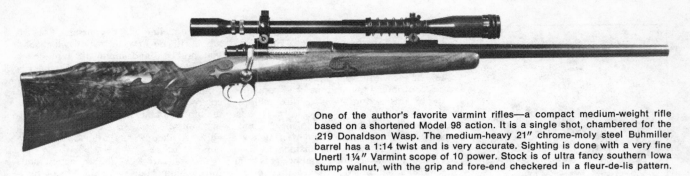

One of the author's favorite varmint rifles—a compact medium-weight rifle based on a shortened Model 98 action. It is a single shot, chambered for the .219 Donaldson Wasp. The medium-heavy 21″ chrome-moly steel Buhmiller barrel has a 1:14 twist and is very accurate. Sighting is done with a very fine Unertl 1¼″ Varmint scope of 10 power. Stock is of ultra fancy southern Iowa stump walnut, with the grip and fore-end checkered in a fleur-de-lis pattern.

mended since this greatly weakens the receiver where it supports the lower locking lug.

Remodeling the M98 military action is made easier by a number of accessories offered especially for it. There are trigger shoes available for the trigger, trigger attachments to change the double-stage military trigger to a single-stage pull, replacement safeties which will clear the lowest mounted scopes, quick-release floorplate devices, set trigger mechanisms, fully adjustable single-stage trigger mechanisms with or without slide type safeties. There are more scope mounts made for the M98 action than for any other, and at least a half-dozen receiver sights. If this is not enough, you can buy a stiffer mainspring to speed up the lock time (as well as making the action harder to operate). Last, but not least, threaded, chambered and finish-turned barrels are available in a number of popular calibers from several firms. Most of the accessories are easily installed by following the manufacturers instructions, but unless you have the proper equipment for barrel fitting, I suggest you let a competent gunsmith do that job.

If a hunting scope is to be mounted low and over the bore—the only way it should be mounted—then the main alteration will be to the bolt handle so it will clear the eye-piece of the scope. The bolt handle can be forged to a low profile, or the original bolt handle cut off and it or a new bolt handle welded on in the low profile position. I prefer the latter, using an electric weld to attach the new handle. There are several gunsmithing books available which give detailed instructions on altering bolt handles, drilling and tapping the receiver for sights and scope mounts, installing barrels and altering the magazine, etc. If you want to do this work, and don't know how, get these books and find out. They include *The Modern Gunsmith* by

W. J. Howe, *Modern Gunsmithing* by Clyde Baker and *Gunsmithing* by Roy Dunlap.

M98 Barrel Thread

Model 98 rifles have been made over a long period of time, in a number of countries and by many different firms. It is, therefore, natural to assume that not all of them were made with *exactly* the same barrel thread. What they all have in common is a Whitworth type thread with a metric pitch. This is a 55° V-thread, usually with rounded bottom and crest. The metric pitch is very close to 12 threads per inch. The drawing of the barrel shank specifications indicates the thread diameter is 1.100″, the length of the shank .625″, with a pitch of 12 threads per inch. The American standard V-thread has a 60° angle and it has long been a customary practice of American gunsmiths to use the 60° thread in fitting new barrels to Mauser actions, a practice that's perfectly acceptable. Barrelmakers producing threaded and chambered M98 replacement barrels must of necessity cut a minimum thread, so that the barrels will fit in practically every M98 action—this is also all right since a slightly loose thread fit is permissible. The important thing for the amateur to understand is that the barrel must be turned in and "set up" very tightly. The flat breech end of the barrel should contact the collar inside the receiver rather than having the shoulder of the barrel contact the front of the receiver. The custom gunsmith, in threading a barrel for the M98, will cut the threads on the barrel to fit the individual action, and can achieve as tight a fit as he wishes—even with a 60° thread cutter.

Besides a fairly snug thread fit, the ideal fit is also to have both the breech end and the barrel shoulder contact the receiver, but with the breech end contacting the collar much more firmly.

M98 Military Rifles

This book is chiefly concerned with the actions of various centerfire turnbolt rifles and what can be done with them rather than with the original rifles. There were so many different military rifles based on the M98 action that to describe them all is beyond the scope of this book. For information on these many rifles, refer to our bibliography. The most informative of these titles are *Mauser Bolt Rifles* by L. Olson, *Mauser Rifles & Pistols* by Smith and *Small Arms of the World* by Smith.

A number of firms in Germany turned out huge quantities of M98 military rifles and it is estimated that several million had been made by the end of WW I in 1918. They were made by several commercial arms firms including Mauser, Sauer, Haenel and DWM. DWM made a million alone. The German government arsenals in Danzig, Erfurt, Spandau and Amberg also made vast quantities.

In the years following WW I there was only limited production of the M98, but in the mid-1930s, when Hitler began rattling his saber, production again went into high gear. This time many more firms got into the act, including some in German occupied countries. No one knows how many million M98s were made from this time until the defeat of Germany in 1945, but the quantity was immense.

The principal M98 arm of the pre-1918 period was the rifle with a 29.13″ barrel. The main carbine version of that period was the 98a with a 23.62″ barrel. The most common M98 developed after WW I, and the principal shoulder arm used during the WW II period, was the M98k with a 23.62″ barrel. There were other variations, too numerous to mention, plus several custom variations of sniper's rifles used during both wars. The M98k carbine was developed in the mid-1920s and it eventually became the most frequently produced German military shoulder arm.

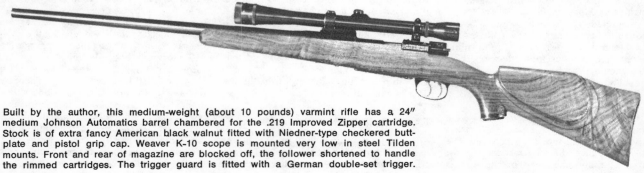

Built by the author, this medium-weight (about 10 pounds) varmint rifle has a 24″ medium Johnson Automatics barrel chambered for the .219 Improved Zipper cartridge. Stock is of extra fancy American black walnut fitted with Niedner-type checkered buttplate and pistol grip cap. Weaver K-10 scope is mounted very low in steel Tilden mounts. Front and rear of magazine are blocked off, the follower shortened to handle the rimmed cartridges. The trigger guard is fitted with a German double-set trigger.

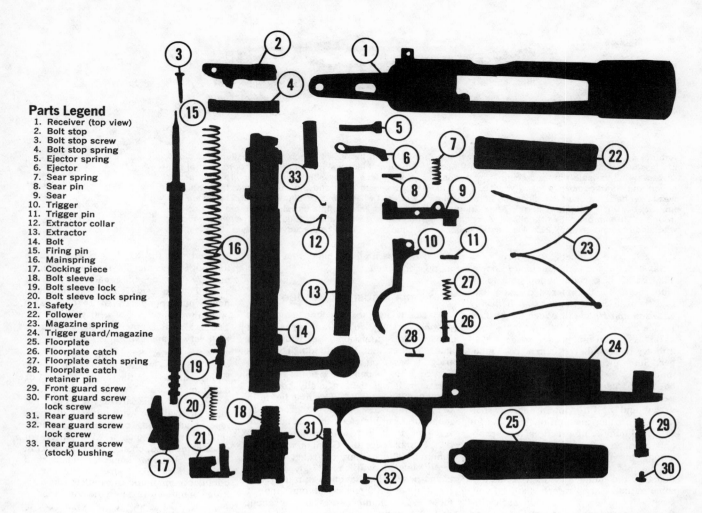

Parts Legend

1. Receiver (top view)
2. Bolt stop
3. Bolt stop screw
4. Bolt stop spring
5. Ejector spring
6. Ejector
7. Sear spring
8. Sear pin
9. Sear
10. Trigger
11. Trigger pin
12. Extractor collar
13. Extractor
14. Bolt
15. Firing pin
16. Mainspring
17. Cocking piece
18. Bolt sleeve
19. Bolt sleeve lock
20. Bolt sleeve lock spring
21. Safety
22. Follower
23. Magazine spring
24. Trigger guard/magazine
25. Floorplate
26. Floorplate catch
27. Floorplate catch spring
28. Floorplate catch retainer pin
29. Front guard screw
30. Front guard screw lock screw
31. Rear guard screw
32. Rear guard screw lock screw
33. Rear guard screw (stock) bushing

Mauser Model 98

Dimensional Specifications

Weight	45 oz.
Length	8.75"
Receiver ring dia.	
Large ring	1.410"
Small ring	1.300"
Bolt body dia.	.700"
Bolt travel	4.570"
Striker travel	.535"
Guard-screw spacing	7.825"
Magazine-well opening	
Length	3.320"
Rear width	.620"
Front width	.490"
Bolt face partial recess:	
Depth	.045"
Dia.	.480"

General Specifications

Type	Turnbolt repeater.
Receiver	One-piece machined steel forging, unslotted bridge. Stripper-clip guide milled in bridge.
Bolt	One-piece, with dual-opposed locking lugs forward. A third lug on the bottom of the bolt acts as the safety lug.
Ignition	One-piece firing pin, coil mainspring and cocking piece. Cocks mainly on opening of bolt.
Magazine	Staggered column, nondetachable box magazine, 5-shot capacity. Detachable floorplate.
Trigger	Non-adjustable, double-stage military type pull.
Safety	Rotary wing-type safety built into bolt sleeve. 180° swing from left to right, locking striker only when in upright position; locks both bolt and striker when at right.
Extractor	One-piece, nonrotating, long Mauser spring type attached to the bolt by a collar.
Bolt stop	Separate, hinged to the left rear of receiver, stops bolt by contacting left locking lug.
Ejector	Swinging type, located in bolt stop housing.

Markings

As previously mentioned, the many variations of the M98 military rifles were carried out by a number of different arms making plants in Germany, and later on in different plants in a number of other countries. In the period prior to the 1920s it was standard practice for each plant to stamp its name on the receiver ring, along with the year in which the rifle was made. The left receiver wall was usually stamped to indicate the model of the arm, such as "M/98," "GEW. 98" or "KAR. 98." Sometimes the name and address of the maker was stamped on the side of the receiver. The maker's insignia or the crest (coat of arms) of the country for which the rifle was made, was also sometimes stamped on the receiver ring.

In the 1930s a number-code system was inaugurated. Each of the producers of this rifle was given a code numeral which was stamped on the receiver ring, along with the date (year) of manufacture. Around 1940 this number code was largely replaced by a letter code; for example, the letters "byf" stamped on the receiver meant that the rifle was made by the Mauser Werke plant in Oberndorf. Earlier, when the number code was in use, the Mauser firm had the code number "42." During WW II usually only the last two digits of the year were stamped on the receiver, like "41" instead of "1941." During 1944 many manufacturers merely stamped one "4" on the receiver. Many of

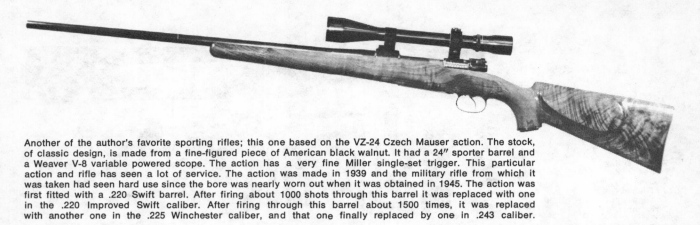

Another of the author's favorite sporting rifles; this one based on the VZ-24 Czech Mauser action. The stock, of classic design, is made from a fine-figured piece of American black walnut. It had a 24″ sporter barrel and a Weaver V-8 variable powered scope. The action has a very fine Miller single-set trigger. This particular action and rifle has seen a lot of service. The action was made in 1939 and the military rifle from which it was taken had seen hard use since the bore was nearly worn out when it was obtained in 1945. The action was first fitted with a .220 Swift barrel. After firing about 1000 shots through this barrel it was replaced with one in the .220 Improved Swift caliber. After firing through this barrel about 1500 times, it was replaced with another one in the .225 Winchester caliber, and that one finally replaced by one in .243 caliber.

the early code numbers never have been unraveled, but the code letters are known. The list of these codes is too long to include here, but the interested reader can find them listed in *Mauser Bolt Rifles* by L. Olson and *Hatcher's Notebook* by J. S. Hatcher.

It was normal practice to prove all M98 military rifles and give them a serial number. Such proof marks, the number of marks and their location on the receiver, barrel and perhaps on some other parts, varied; since these proof marks are so varied and of little importance, I shall make no further mention of them. As for the serial numbering practices, there probably was no universal system employed among the many manufacturers during the entire period they were made, except that they did number them. It seems that some manufacturers merely stamped consecutively higher numbers on each rifle they made, and when the number reached a certain point they started over again. Thus there may be more than one rifle made by the same or a different manufacturer having the same serial number. Later on each manufacturer was assigned a letter to be added to the serial number, for example 7436d, so that production figures could be kept secret. Regardless of the system or systems used, the serial number itself is not important since the date and manufacturer's name, or code, are stamped on the receiver. Generally, the full serial number is stamped on the side of the receiver ring and barrel, and either the complete number, or the last two digits of it is stamped on most of the other parts of the action. If all the numbers are the same on a given rifle or action, this indicates that all the parts are original with that rifle or action. That the numbers match may be of some importance to the owner of an M98, but having matching numbers on an action

which is to be used for building a rifle is of no consequence.

The 8mm Mauser Cartridge

Germany adopted the 8mm smokeless powder cartridge in 1888 along with the Model 88 Commission rifle, with which Paul Mauser had little to do. This cartridge is based on a rimless, bottle-necked case and was loaded with a bullet of .318″ diameter. It was then officially known as the 7.9x57I or 8x57I*. The first figure in the cartridge designated the groove dimensions in millimeters, the second figure is the length of the case in millimeters, and the "I" stands for the German word "Infanterie." This military cartridge was normally loaded with a 227-gr. jacketed round-nose bullet having a muzzle velocity of about 2100 feet per second (fps) at an average chamber pressure of about 45,500 pounds per square inch (psi).

When the M98 was adopted by Germany in 1898, it was also chambered for the 8x57I cartridge. The Germans soon wanted better ballistics from this cartridge, so about 1905 they adopted a new spitzer (pointed) bullet for the 8x57mm case, with a new diameter of .323″. This cartridge was designated 7.9x57IS or 8x57IS. This new bullet weighed 154 grains and in the new cartridge it was driven to a muzzle velocity of 2870 fps at a breech pressure of about 49,800 psi. When this larger bullet was adopted it became necessary to enlarge the rifle bore accordingly. This was done by increasing the groove diameter only, from .320″ to .324″. M98 rifles already made for the "I" cartridge were then rebarreled and chambered for the "IS" cartridge. Later on, a heavier spitzer bullet with a boat-tail base was

*Common U.S.-English usage shows the "I" in print as a "J," but this is incorrect.

adopted and the 8x57 case loaded with this bullet became the standard German military cartridge designated as the 8x 57sS. This bullet weighed 198 grains and had a muzzle velocity of 2476 fps at a breech pressure level of nearly 50,000 psi. The 8x57sS is a potent military cartridge with very impressive ballistics.

In the United States, the sporting version of the German 8mm cartridge is known simply as the 8mm Mauser or 8x57mm Mauser. Most U.S. ammunition makers loaded this cartridge years ago and made it available with several different types and weights of bullets. However, since there was such a wide variety of rifles being used, chambered for the 8mm Mauser cartridge, some of which had actions of marginal strength or barrels bored too small for the bullets, the cartridge manufacturers became concerned.

In due time, the 8mm Mauser cartridge loaded in the U.S. evolved into a single bulleted loading which developed only mild breech pressures so that it could be fired in most 8mm Mauser rifles. Therefore, as loaded today by Federal, Winchester, Remington and Peters, it has a 170-gr. jacketed soft-point bullet giving a muzzle velocity of about 2500 to 2570 fps at a pressure level of about 34,000 psi. Gauged by modern standards, or compared to a cartridge like the .30-06 with the 180-gr. bullet, the U.S. loaded 8mm Mauser cartridge appears outdated. This is not the case, however, for these 8mm Mauser cartridges are equal to the .30-40 and .303 British for taking most species of North American big game animals.

The 8mm Mauser cartridge is very responsive to handloading, and the careful handloader having a sound M98 military or sporterized rifle can reload the case to nearly equal the .30-06 in performance.

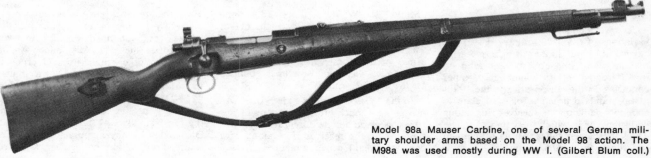

Model 98a Mauser Carbine, one of several German military shoulder arms based on the Model 98 action. The M98a was used mostly during WW I. (Gilbert Blum coll.)

6. 8mm Siamese Mauser

IN HIS excellent book *Mauser Bolt Rifles*, Ludwig E. Olson describes so many different models, variations and styles of Mauser turnbolt rifles that scanning the index never ceases to amaze and baffle me. Many of these are described in some detail, but the one listed as "8-mm Mauser, Siam," (on page 126 in my copy of this book) has but one short paragraph, another short note about the 8mm rimmed cartridge it fired, and that's all. This is understandable for these rifles have been extremely scarce, and Mr. Olson probably never had a good chance to examine a specimen and take it apart. I never thought I'd have a chance either, but suddenly their "extremely scarce" status has changed, via the military surplus arms market.

I first saw the 8mm Siamese rifles and actions advertised in the June 1, 1970, issue of *Shotgun News*. Hunter's Lodge, 200 S. Union St., Alexandria, Va. 22313, a member firm of the Interarms group, offered them as "M98 actions for rimmed cartridges," and as "Sleek M98 actions designed exclusively for rimmed cartridges. Bolt face and magazine will accommodate such popular calibers as .45-70, .444 Marlin, .303 British and 7.62 Russian." They were priced at $20 each or, in lots of 10, at $12 each.

Farther down in the ad complete rifles were described as "Cal. 8mm x 52R M98 Thai rifles (Japanese manufacture). Model 45/46." These rifles were priced at $15 each in lots of 10. Selling the actions and rifles in lots of ten makes me believe they had a considerable number for sale and might result in the rifle and action becoming well known.

I ordered one action and the invoice from Hunter's Lodge listed it as "RT M-98 Mauser Action." I have no idea what the "RT" means. Thus, the action and the rifle are given several different designations, such as: 8mm Siamese Mauser (the one I use), M98 Thai (Thailand), and Model 45/46. The southeast Asian country of Thailand was formerly known as Siam, hence the use of both names.

I have found but little history of the 8mm Siamese Mauser rifle, and not much of anything about the rifle itself.

Apparently most of these rifles were made in a Japanese arsenal—at least the actions, marked with three interlocking circles, are Japanese made. An item in the September 1955 issue of the *American Rifleman* mentions that some of these rifles were made in the Siamese government arsenal in Bangkok, Thailand, but I have no facts to prove this. Without much doubt, all of these actions and rifles that Hunter's Lodge had for sale are of Japanese origin. I have no idea as to when or how many were made nor how long they were in service in Siam or Thailand, as the case may be. By the 1960s the Thai army was fairly well equipped with the most modern arms, with the 8mm Siamese Mauser rifles being sold as obsolete surplus arms sometime before the 1960s. The rifle is somewhat similar to the old German M98 Mauser. The stock has a semi-pistol grip, a finger grooved fore-end that extends to within about 5″ of the muzzle. It has a half-length wooden handguard held in front by the middle barrel band with the front sling swivel attached thereto. The rear sling swivel is screwed to the bottom center of the buttstock. The front and rear sights are typically M98 Mauser, with the graduation markings in unusual Siamese numerals. If the rifle is complete, its most identifiable feature would be the sliding breech cover which is not connected to the bolt and must be moved manually. Another distinctive feature is the Japanese Arisaka-type tangs to strengthen the grip area of the stock.

Action Markings

The 8mm Siamese action I have shows several distinct markings. The Siamese crest, or coat of arms, is stamped on the top forward part of the receiver bridge. This crest is round and about ⅜″ in diameter. A line of five Siamese numerals or letters is stamped on the receiver bridge below the crest, and another line stamped across the bridge. Although I have been unable to get these lines deciphered or translated, they probably refer to the date of manufacture and model designation. The Japanese arsenal proof mark, three interlocking circles, is stamped on the left receiver wall. Arabic numbers are stamped on various parts of the action, but those which are apparently the serial numbers are stamped on the flat bottom of the receiver ring and on the left side of the front tang of the trigger guard.

The Action

The 8mm Siamese is a copy of Paul Mauser's M98 turnbolt action with certain modifications and additional features that make it one of the most distinctive and unusual forms of the basic M98. The modifications are essentially those needed to handle the 8x52R Siamese cartridge; the additions which are of Japanese influence, include the detachable tangs and the sliding breech cover.

By carefully comparing the 8mm Siamese specifications with those of other M98 Mauser actions covered in this book, and by studying the photographs of this action and the others, it is easily seen that this is a peculiar variation of the Model 98 Mauser.

First, let's see what this 8mm Siamese action has in common with the regular M98 military action made for the 8mm Mauser cartridge. The receiver is of the same general pattern and configuration, it is the large ring type and has the regular collar inside the ring, slotted only on the right for the extractor. It has the clip-charger guide slot in the bridge and the

---

Illustrated above: The right side view of the Japanese-made 8mm Siamese Mauser action minus the tangs and sliding breech cover.

Siamese Mauser action open, tangs in place and breech cover slid forward.

deep thumb cut in the left receiver wall. The receiver will accept a standard length M98 bolt, though the receiver is only 8.50", or .250" shorter than the standard M98. The receiver is flat on the bottom and has the integral recoil lug like all other M98 actions.

Except for the bolt face and cartridge head recess, the bolt and firing mechanism are an exact copy of the M98 bolt. The straight bolt handle has a pear-shaped grasping ball. The bolt has dual-opposed forward locking lugs with the left (top) lug slotted for the ejector, a third rear safety lug, a guide rib, and twin gas-vent holes. The extractor is the same except that the hook is a bit narrower. The bolt sleeve, bolt sleeve lock, safety, firing pin, mainspring and firing pin head are enough like the standard M98 parts that they are almost, but not quite, interchangeable.

The bolt stop and ejector are of the standard M98 pattern except that the ejector spring is riveted to the bolt stop spring. The sear is also standard, but the trigger stem is cocked back a bit to bring the fingerpiece to a more rearward position.

In addition to these similarities, the Siamese action has the same functional features as the standard M98, including cock-on-opening, safety operation, extractor camming, etc. Also, everything is dis- and reassembled in the same way.

The differences between the two actions are:

1. The breech cover. The Siamese action is fitted with a very neat spring-steel breech cover which slides to the rear to cover the loading and ejection port, and forward to expose the port. On each side of the receiver there is a narrow raised integral guide-rail over which the sides of the cover engage and slide. This is unlike the Japanese Arisaka receivers which are grooved for a sliding cover. On the right side of the Siamese Mauser breech cover there is riveted a hooked catch which engages notches in the side of the receiver ring and bridge to hold the cover either open or closed, and by which the cover can be slid back and forth. It is entirely independent of the bolt; it must be moved manually by grasping the hooked catch and pulling it outward. The cover can be removed by sliding it forward off of the receiver. The bolt can be operated and the rifle fired with the cover in any position, but it must be open to eject a fired case or to load the magazine.

2. Receiver shroud. The front end of the receiver has a shroud or collar extending about ⅛" forward as on the Polish Radom M98 Mauser. The purpose of this collar is to hold the rear of the handguard in place.

3. Barrel shank threads. The receiver is threaded to receive a barrel shank about .990" in diameter with 14 V threads per inch. The regular M98 actions have a pitch of 12 threads per inch and usually for a thread diameter of 1.10". The Siamese barrel is made with a shoulder large enough to abut and "set-up" against the front face of the receiver rather than having the breech face of the barrel butt against the inside receiver collar, as in the regular M98 action.

4. Left receiver wall. The 8mm Siamese receiver ring is slightly larger in diameter than the large ring M98 action, but unlike the latter, there is no "step" between the left side wall and the receiver ring. This means that the left receiver wall is much thicker in the Siamese receiver, and the reason that it is so made is because of the breech cover guide rails. The average M98 Mauser left side wall is about .155" thick, while the Siamese Mauser is about .200" thick.

5. Bolt face. The recessed bolt head will accept a cartridge rim no larger than about .564". There are no lips extending forward on the left side of the rim recess as in the regular M98 Mauser action. The rim recess is cut away at the bottom to allow the cartridge rim to slip under the extractor hook on feeding a cartridge from the chamber, which prevents double loading.

6. Extractor hook. It is narrower than the extractor, being only about .300" wide.

7. Tangs. Separate upper and lower tang extensions on the 8mm Siamese action extend rearward about 3" and are inletted into the top and bottom of the grip of the stock. They are milled at the front end to fit closely against the rounded end of the integral receiver tang and trigger guard, and are held in place by the rear guard screw. The tangs, connected at the rear by a screw, are almost exactly the same as those used on the Type 38 Japanese Arisaka 6.5mm rifles and carbines. They are used to strengthen the grip area of the stock.

8. Magazine. The combined trigger guard/magazine is of one-piece milled steel construction like the regular M98 Mauser. The front and rear ends of the magazine box, however, are slanted forward at a sharp angle. This slanted magazine box permits easy loading of the larger-rimmed 8mm Siamese cartridge, the slope preventing their rims from catching on each other. Each cartridge pushed into the magazine moves to the rear so that the next cartridge inserted over it will have its rim ahead of the cartridge rim below. To gain adequate magazine capacity, the rear of the magazine box was made about ¼" deeper than the regular M98 8mm Mauser. The floorplate of the Siamese action is not hinged, but is quickly detachable via a latch built into the forward part of the trigger guard bow. Due to the slanted magazine box, the trigger guard bow is positioned back farther than the regular M98 and for this reason the trigger shank is bent back as mentioned earlier.

Incidentally, the front and rear guard screws of the Siamese action have the same thread pitch as the regular M98 Mauser guard screws, but the Siamese screws are slightly larger in diameter. However, regular M98 Mauser guard screws can be used in the Siamese action, but not conversely.

The 8mm Siamese Cartridge

Generally referred to as the 8x52Rmm Siamese, this is a rimmed, bottle-necked cartridge normally loaded with a 181-gr. pointed, jacketed bullet. Not much is known about it—when it was adopted or who developed it. It's probably merely a

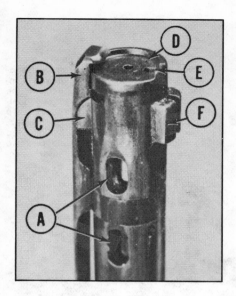

Bolt head of the Siamese action, showing: A) twin gas-vent holes; B) extractor; C) right (bottom) locking lug; D) undercut cartridge head recess; E) ejector slot, and F) slotted left (top) locking lug. The bolt also has the regular M98 Mauser short guide rib and the rear safety locking lug (not shown).

ballistically improved version of the older 8x50R Siamese Type 45 cartridge; a little longer case, a pointed bullet and more powder.

Fred A. Datig in his book *Cartridges For Collectors* designated this cartridge as the 8x52R Siamese Type 66—so does George C. Nonte in his book *Home Guide To Cartridge Conversions*. I don't know what the "Type 66" means. Regardless, if you have the Siamese Mauser rifle and want to shoot it, there is very little chance that you will ever find any factory loaded ammunition for it. If you are a handloader, Nonte suggests the following: make cases from new .45-70 brass, trim to 2.04" and turn the rim to .560" diameter. Full length resize in a .33 WFC die, size down the neck and push the shoulder back in an 8mm die until the case will chamber, then fire-form. Use .323" bullets.

Comments

The 8mm Siamese Mauser action I received was in very good condition. Very well made and finished, it was as smooth in operation as any military M98 Mauser I've ever handled. I have no way of knowing the kind of steel used in making the receiver and bolt, nor do I know what heat treatment was given these parts. If I might guess, I'd say that if the arsenal in Japan that made the Siamese Mauser actions also made Arisaka actions, the same steel and heat treatment were used for both. I know that a file test for hardness is none too reliable, but it can be used to compare the hardness of such parts as rifle bolt heads. To do some comparing I took a file to the locking lugs of a couple of M98 German Mauser bolts, but could not get a good bite. This is normal, for most M98 bolts are very hard. Then I tried the file on the Siamese bolt and I could cut both locking lugs and the front edge of the

bolt. Next, I got out two each of the Japanese Type 38 and 99 Arisaka bolts and, with the same filing effort, cut all four of them. Because the M98 Mauser bolt has smaller locking lugs than the Arisaka it is probably a good idea that they are made very hard. I don't think they have to be made as hard as they are for strength alone so I see no reason why the softer bolt in the Siamese action wouldn't be just as strong. However, to be on the safe side, the Siamese Mauser action should be limited to cartridges that do not develop much over 45,000 psi breech pressure.

The 8mm Siamese cartridge (8x52R) has a rim diameter of .561" and is about 2.925" over-all. You'll recall that the ad I read called this action suitable for the .45-70, .444 Marlin, et al. I checked a number of cartridges in this action, and here's what I found.

.45-70. The .45-70 rim is .608" wide,

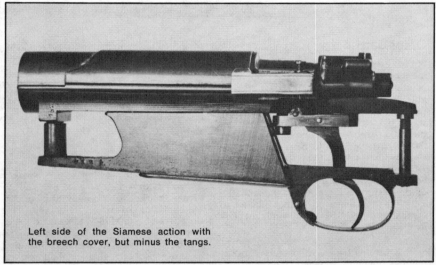

Left side of the Siamese action with the breech cover, but minus the tangs.

too big for the .565" diameter recess in the bolt face. The front of the magazine well (cartridge guide lips) is also slightly too narrow to pass the .45-70 rim. The unaltered magazine will accept and hold .45-70 cartridges, but the bottom or last cartridge is not tipped high enough in front for it to feed correctly. To use .45-70 cartridges, the bolt face recess must be opened up to about .610" and the front of the magazine well widened—not difficult to do. The latter job will most likely end the feed problem of the last cartridge. With these modifications this is a good action for the .45-70 cartridge.

.444 Marlin I don't think the use of this action is going to be too successful with the .444 Marlin cartridge. The .444 rim diameter is only about .514", and the 8mm Siamese bolt face recess is too large for the too short extractor to hold this cartridge in place for proper ejection. Also, the magazine will not retain the first cartridge inserted into it; similarly, if the magazine is loaded with more than one cartridge, the last cartridge will pop out after the other cartridges have been fed. This last problem can be corrected by rebuilding the follower, but I know of no

practicable way to reduce the bolt face recess. Therefore, if you want to use this action for the .444 Marlin I'd suggest you solve the bolt face recess and magazine problem before going to the trouble and expense of fitting a .444 barrel to the action.

.303 British The .303 British cartridge is normally loaded to an over-all length of 3.075" and it will just enter the 8mm Siamese magazine, with little length-room to spare. It has a rim diameter of .540", and it fits the bolt face recess OK, although for better ejection of the fired cases the extractor hook should be a trifle longer. As with the .444 Marlin cartridge, the .303 British case rim is a bit too small for the rear width of the magazine well, and in order for the magazine to retain the first cartridge inserted into the magazine, or the last cartridge after the others have been fed, the right side of the fol-

lower ridge (left side of the follower) should be built up slightly. This can be done by sweating (soft soldering) a thin piece of sheet steel onto it. The .303 British cartridge does not fit this action perfectly, but it comes very close, and with the modifications to the extractor hook and follower, the Siamese Mauser action should prove to be ideal for this cartridge. This action would also be suitable for the .303 British Improved and for the most wildcat cartridges based on this case.

7.62mm Russian This is the old Russian military cartridge with rimmed case, and is *not* to be confused with the more modern 7.62x39mm Russian or the 7.62mm NATO cartridges. The 7.62mm Russian case has a rim of .564" and is loaded to an over-all length of just over 3.00"—just short enough to fit in the magazine of the 8mm Siamese action. The several samples of this cartridge which I have in my collection fit perfectly. Norma has loaded this cartridge for several years and it is a good round for big game hunting. If you want to build a .30 caliber rifle on this action, then the 7.62mm Russian is a good cartridge to choose.

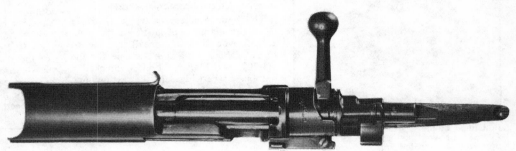

Top view of the Siamese action with breech cover closed. Breech cover is independent of the bolt and must be moved manually by grasping the small hook at the right rear of the cover, pulling it out slightly then moving the cover. The spring snap hook locks the cover in either position. The cover can be completely removed by sliding it forward off of the receiver. Below—Action with breech cover open.

Other Cartridges

I'm surprised Hunter's Lodge did not mention the .30-40 Krag or the .348 Winchester cartridges, as both are quite suitable for the Siamese Mauser action. In fact, the .30-40 cartridge with a rim diameter of .545″ fits this action better than the .303 British. My opnion is that the .30-40 cartridge would be a much better choice than either the .303 British or 7.62mm Russian. Many wildcats have been developed on the .30-40 case—the 6mm Krag, .25 Krag, .35 Krag and the .30-40 Krag Improved. If not loaded to the extreme, any of them would be OK in this action.

The .348 Winchester is also well suited to this action. Its rim diameter of .610″ requires the bolt face recess to be enlarged, but other than that the .348 functions perfectly in this action. There are also some very fine wildcats based on this case—.30/.348 Improved, .35/.348 Improved, .40/.348 Improved, .44/.348 and .450 Alaskan.

Finally, after building up the left side of the follower to move its ridge slightly to the right, the 8mm Siamese action would be a good choice for the wildcat .458 American. This is a short .45 caliber cartridge based on a shortened (2.00″) belted magnum case. However, I cannot recommend this action for use with any other belted magnum cartridge.

Gunsmithing

At this writing the 8mm Siamese Mauser action is just too new on the surplus market for anybody to have done any building of rifles on it. However, since it is a basic M98 Mauser action, most gunsmithing work that has to be done, or can be done, on a regular M98 for sporting rifle use can also be done on this oddball Siamese Mauser. For example, the bolt handle can be altered as usual by heating the shank and bending it down, or forging it in bolt handle bending blocks, or by cutting off the handle and welding it or a new bolt handle into the new position. Low scope safeties made for the M98 Mauser can also be fitted to this action.

Several commercial M98 adjustable single stage trigger mechanisms will also fit, though on some it would be a good idea to heat and bend the finger-piece of the trigger back so it will position better in the trigger guard bow.

The breech cover can be removed and discarded, its guide rails ground off level with the receiver, and almost any top scope mounts made for the M98 Mauser can be fitted to the receiver. A receiver sight for the M98 Mauser will also fit this action. The breech cover can be retained and used with a receiver sight but, if this is done, the hook on the breech cover catch should be made longer. The breech cover cannot be used if top receiver scope mounts are used.

I imagine most of these actions will be used to build rifles in the larger calibers to take big game at short to moderate ranges. For this use, a long eye-relief scope like the Leupold M8-2 mounted on the barrel would be very practical—with the scope so mounted the breech cover can be retained and used.

Stocking the 8mm Siamese action rifle is going to be the biggest problem for the amateur gunsmith, but if he can make a stock from a blank for any other centerfire turnbolt rifle, he'll be able to manage this one. I don't know how many of these actions and rifles Hunter's Lodge had for sale, but I'd imagine there were more than just a few hundred. In this case, if enough owners of these actions request it, no doubt Reinhart Fajen Inc., and some other stockmaking firms will make semi-inletted stocks available for it. In stocking the rifle the separate tangs can be discarded.

This chapter may look a little bare, not having all of the usual detailed pictures, parts lists and other specifications. However, except for the hinged magazine floorplate and floorplate latch, the component parts of the 8mm Siamese Mauser are essentially the same as the M98 Mauser military action—covered in the preceding chapter.

General Specifications
Japanese-made Siamese (Thailand) Mauser

Weight (complete with breech cover and tangs)	46 oz.
Total length (with tangs)	11.60″
Receiver length	8.50″
Receiver ring dia.	1.410″
Bolt body dia.	.700″
Bolt travel	4.425″
Striker travel	.450″
Magazine opening (length)	3.00″
Receiver magazine-well width:	
Rear	.645″
Front	.560″
Bolt face recess:	
Dia.	.565″
Depth	.055″
Guard screw spacing	7.60″
Guard screw thread	¼ x22
Barrel shank and thread:	
Pitch (approx.)	14 V per inch
Length	.515″
Dia. (approx.)	.990″

7. French Military Turnbolts

THE FIRST important metallic cartridge shoulder arm adopted by France was the Model 1874 Gras single shot rifle—developed by General Basile Gras (1836-1901) of the French Army. This turnbolt arm evolved from the bolt action breechloading Model 1866 Chassepot needle-fire rifle, so called because the firing pin was needle-like to penetrate the self-consuming paper or linen cartridge and strike the priming mixture positioned at the base of the bullet. The Gras rifle was chambered for the 11x59R French Gras centerfire cartridge, developed and adopted with the Gras rifle in 1874. Usually called the 11mm Gras, this cartridge is very similar to, but not interchangeable with, such other .43 caliber cartridges of the same period as the 11mm Mauser, 11mm Murata and 11mm Werndl. The Gras rifles (there were three principal versions having barrels of different lengths) were widely used in countries other than France.

Unlike some other 11mm foreign military arms, Gras rifles never were commonplace in the United States. Even before the Model 1874 Gras rifle was officially adopted, France converted many of her older M1866 Chassepot needle-fire rifles to the Gras system to handle an 11mm self-contained cartridge.

The Gras rifle had a very simple action. The bolt was locked in the receiver by the heavy base of the bolt handle engaging in front of the receiver bridge. The extractor was fitted in the separate bolt head. The action cocked by lifting the bolt handle. There were two notches under the cocking piece and a checkered thumbpiece depression on top that positioned the striker at "half-cock." It had no safety. The stock was of one-piece construction. Gras rifles, of value only to military arms collectors, are quite scarce today in original and very good condition.

The Kropatschek Rifle

After the single shot Gras was in production for a few years, there was a growing demand for a repeating rifle. An Austrian inventor named Alfred Kropatschek worked out a method to make the Gras rifle into a repeater. France adopted his system about 1878, and it became known as the Model 1878 Gras-Kropatschek. The repeating mechanism consisted of a Henry-type tubular magazine in the fore-end, under the barrel, and a pivoting cartridge carrier positioned under an opening in the bottom of the receiver. The magazine was loaded by pushing the cartridges into it through the opened action. On closing the bolt, the carrier would tip down, allowing one cartridge to move back onto the carrier platform. On opening the action the bolt would tip the carrier up, placing the nose of the cartridge in line with the chamber. On closing the bolt, the cartridge would be pushed into the chamber and the carrier depressed again to pick up another round. Gras-Kropatschek rifles were used largely by the French Navy. Like the Gras rifle, the Gras-Kropatschek rifles had a one-piece stock. They are of little value to either the shooter or amateur gunsmith, but since they are quite rare they are prized by arms collectors.

The Lebel Rifle

The original Gras rifle and the Gras-Kropatschek repeater were soon obsoleted by improved rifle and cartridge designs. In France, a commission was set up to develop a new rifle and cartridge. Headed by General Tramond of the French Army, Colonel Nicolas Lebel was one of the other leading men on this board. The result of their efforts was the adoption of a new rifle and cartridge in 1886.

Actually, the new rifle was merely an improvement of the Gras-Kropatschek rifle. The cartridge, however, was really new; it was the first relatively small-bore smokeless powder cartridge to be adopted by any world power. Lebel is credited with being largely responsible for developing this cartridge, and on this account it was named after him. He probably had a hand in the design improvements of the rifle, too (some sources refer to the "Lebel System"), but the rifle bore his name largely because of the cartridge. At any rate, the cartridge is now universally known as the 8mm Lebel, and the rifle as the French 8mm Model 1886 Lebel, or variations thereof.

Actually, the Lebel action is a major "beef-up" job on the Gras-Kropatschek. The changes consisted mainly of providing a box-like receiver to house the action parts, incorporating dual-opposed locking lugs on the bolt head, and making the receiver accordingly. This made the action much stronger to handle the more powerful 8mm Lebel cartridge.

The Lebel receiver is a long box-like housing. The barrel is threaded into the top front of this housing. The separate fore-end containing the magazine tube is attached to the barrel by two bands and a hook at the rear of the magazine tube—engaging a recess in the front of the receiver. The separate buttstock is attached to the rear of the receiver by two tang screws. One of these screws connects the separate lower tang to the upper tang (an integral part of the receiver) while the second screw passes through a plate inletted into the bottom of the stock grip and threads into the upper tang.

Illustrated above: French Model 1886/93 Lebel rifle chambered for the 8mm Lebel cartridge, has two-piece stock and a tubular magazine under the barrel in the fore-end.

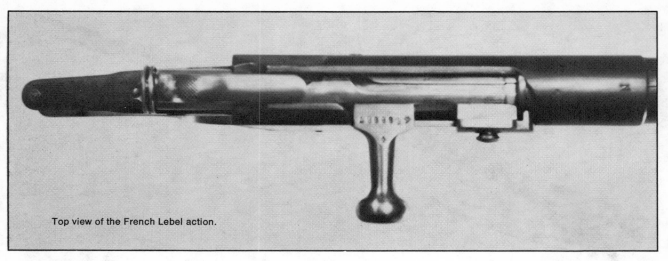

Top view of the French Lebel action.

The top of the receiver is bored and milled to accept the bolt assembly and provide one opening for loading and another below the bolt for the carrier. The bolt handle and its heavy rectangular base are integral parts of the bolt, positioned about midway on the bolt body. The receiver bridge is slotted to allow passage of the bolt handle.

When the bolt is locked, the heavy bolt handle base becomes the safety lug ahead of, but not contacting, the right wall of the bridge. At the front of the bolt body, in line with the bolt handle base, is another heavy rectangular lug. The separate bolt head has a stem which fits into the front of the bolt body. A heavy stud screw, threaded into this forward lug and extending into a hole in the stem of the bolt head, holds the head to the body so it can rotate with the bolt.

The locking lugs are positioned on the forward end of the bolt head. When the bolt is locked the locking lugs are horizontal—just as the Russian Model 1891 Moisin-Nagant. The left (lower) locking lug contacts the cartridge carrier to tip it up and halt the rearward travel of the

bolt when the bolt is opened. The extractor is mortised into the bolt head. The face of the bolt head is recessed for the cartridge rim.

The firing mechanism—firing pin, mainspring, cocking piece and firing-pin button—is essentially like that in the Berthier action to be described later.

The feeding and trigger mechanisms of the Lebel rifle are not attached to the receiver, but rather to the carrier plate which closes the bottom of the receiver. The trigger guard, combined with the lower tang, is attached to this plate with a screw. The entire assembly is held in the receiver by a lip at the front of the carrier plate engaging in a groove in the receiver and by one screw through the rear of the receiver.

The sear is pivoted and attached to the upright projection on the carrier plate on the pivot axis of the magazine cutoff lever. The trigger pivots on the sear via a pin. A V-type spring compressed between the sear and the carrier plate tensions the sear.

The cartridge carrier is also held in place, and pivots on, the axis of the maga-

zine cutoff lever. The carrier is tensioned to keep it either in the up or down position by a lever and a flat spring. The front end of this pivoting lever also functions as the cartridge stop at the magazine tube opening. The carrier is tipped up when the bolt is opened by the lower locking lug contacting a lug on the rear of the carrier. It is tipped down when the bolt is closed (and locked) by the base of the bolt handle depressing a lever linked to the carrier.

The checkered round button of the L-shaped magazine cutoff extends to the bottom rear edge of the receiver housing. Swinging this button forward disengages the carrier-depressing lever so that the carrier remains in the tipped-up position when the action is operated. The rifle can then be conveniently loaded and used as a single shot while cartridges in the magazine are held in reserve.

The M86 Lebel action (as well as the rifle) underwent some changes to improve it; the result was designated the Model 1886/93—presumably, the changes were adopted in 1893. The M86 receiver was made with a long forward extension into

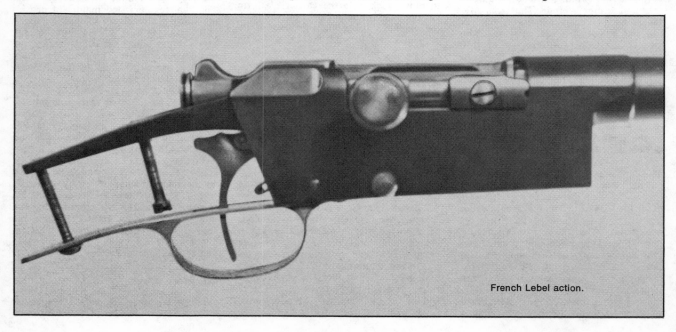

French Lebel action.

50

Parts Legend
Lebel M 86/93

1. Receiver
2. Bolt body
3. Bolt head
4. Bolt head connecting screw
5. Firing pin
6. Mainspring
7. Cocking piece
8. Firing pin button
9. Extractor
10. Bolt head connector
11. Tang plate
12. Tang plate screw
13. Front tang screw
14. Trigger guard
15. Rear tang screw
16. Front guard screw
17. Carrier plate screw
18. Carrier (bottom) plate
19. Magazine cutoff spring screw
20. Magazine cutoff spring
21. Carrier lever spring
22. Carrier lever spring screw
23. Carrier lever (cartridge stop)
24. Cartridge carrier
25. Cartridge depressor lever
26. Magazine cutoff lever
27. Sear
28. Sear spring
29. Sear spring retainer screw
30. Trigger
31. Trigger pin
32. Ejector screw (threaded through left receiver wall)

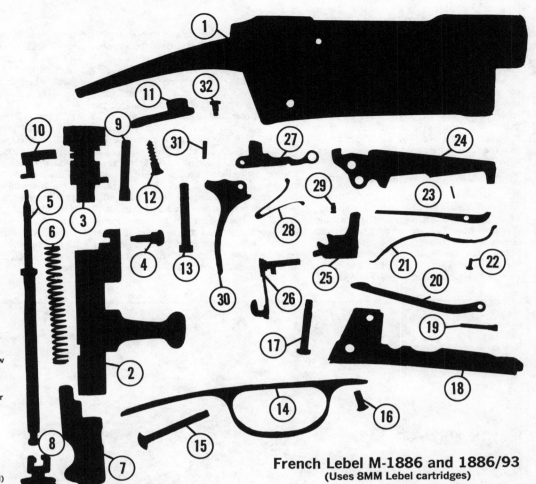

French Lebel M-1886 and 1886/93
(Uses 8MM Lebel cartridges)

Dimensional Specifications

Weight (approx.)	56 oz.
Receiver length:	
Model 1886	12.5″
Model 86/93	10.5″
Receiver width	1.250″
Bolt dia.	.720″
Bolt travel	3.850″
Striker travel	.550″
Bolt face recess:	
Dia.	.635″
Depth	.0722″

General Specifications

Type	Turnbolt repeater.
Receiver	One-piece machined steel forging with integral upper tang. Slotted bridge. Lower tang/trigger guard separate part fastened to receiver with screw. Made for two-piece stock.
Bolt	Two-piece with dual-opposed locking lugs on separate bolt head. Base of bolt handle is safety lug.
Ignition	One-piece firing pin powered by coil mainspring. Cocks on opening bolt.
Magazine	Tubular magazine in fore-end loaded through opened action. 8-shot capacity for rifle.
Trigger	Non-adjustable, double-stage military pull.
Safety	None provided.
Extractor	One-piece spring type mortised into the bolt head.
Magazine cutoff	Lever type positioned at rear right side of receiver.
Bolt stop	No separate bolt stop; see text.
Ejector	Stud screw threaded into left receiver wall.

which the barrel was threaded. This extension, called the barrel reinforce, accounts for the extra length of this receiver when compared to the M86/93 receiver as shown in the specification chart. The bolt head to bolt body junction on the M86/93 was strengthened by the addition of a separate collar and lug between these two parts. The latter action was also made safer by having a small gas vent hole in the bolt head, plus other minor changes. These various improvements made the M86/93 action considerably stronger and more reliable than the M86. M86/93 rifles are usually marked to indicate the 1893 changes by **Modele 86/93** or **M 93** stamped on the left side of the receiver.

The caliber designation was not stamped on the Lebel rifles. They were serial numbered, however, with the full number usually stamped on the bolt handle base, barrel breech, receiver and carrier plate —the last two digits of this number were stamped on some of the other important parts. Various inspector's, arsenal and proof marks are stamped on the breech end of the barrel, receiver and bolt. Date of manufacture (year) is usually stamped on the breech end of the barrel, as well.

Lebel Models

There were three principal models of the Lebel: 1) the 1886 rifle has a 31.4″ barrel, is 51.3″ over-all and weighs about 9.3 pounds; 2) the 1886/93 rifle has the same specifications as the 1886, but has the improved action; and 3) the 1886/93 R35 carbine has a 17.7″ barrel, is about 37.65″ over-all and weighs about 7.84 pounds. The carbine is merely a modification of the Model 1886/93 rifle— shorter barrel, fore-end and magazine tube hold only three cartridges, and different sights. It is one of the shoulder arms used by the French army during WW II, indicating the reluctance of France to discard old rifles.

Lebel rifles were not very satisfactory militarily; the tubular magazine could not be loaded quickly and it could be dangerous if loaded with spitzer-point bulleted ammunition.

Quite to my surprise, on taking apart the Lebel rifle (illustrated) I found the entire rifle well made. The action parts were very nicely finished, fitted and polished. In fact, parts like the springs, levers, sear and some bolt parts were flawlessly polished. While the design of the action and rifle can be criticized, quality workmanship is evident, especially in the action.

All true French Lebel rifles are much more common in the United States than are the French Gras and Gras-Kropatschek rifles. The Lebel rifles are of more value and interest to the collector than to anyone else since they are about hopeless for remodeling into a sporter.

Take-Down and Assembly/Lebel

To remove the bolt, raise bolt handle and pull the bolt back about halfway. Turn the large-headed screw out of the forward bolt lug, turn the bolt head one-quarter turn clockwise and, while holding the bolt head, pull the bolt from the receiver. The bolt head can then be removed. Reassemble in reverse order.

then lifting the front of the fore-end away from the barrel until it is free. Reassemble in reverse order.

Disassemble the trigger and carrier mechanism as follows: remove the screw from the right side of the carrier plate which aligns with the bottom leaf of the trigger spring and, using pliers, pinch the spring together, pull it to the right and remove. Remove the screw from the left front of the carrier plate and remove the magazine cutoff spring and carrier lever spring; with the magazine cutoff button straight down, lift it out. The cartridge carrier, sear and carrier lever (cartridge stop) can now be removed and separated. Drive out the trigger pin to remove trigger from sear. Turn out carrier lever spring srew to separate it from the carrier lever. Remove trigger guard front screw and drive guard rearward to separate it it from the carrier plate. Reassemble in

arate part of the action; 3) the two-piece stock was replaced by a one-piece design; 4) relocating the dual-opposed locking lugs on the bolt head so that they are vertical when the bolt is locked, and the receiver machined accordingly.

A carbine form of the new design was adopted in 1890, chambered for the 8mm Lebel cartridge. In time, various rifles and carbines were developed around the Berthier action, these becoming the standard French shoulder weapon in both World Wars. By far the most common French military rifle, it is one of the few foreign arms that appeared on the surplus market after both wars. Remington made several thousand "Lebels" for France during WW I which were never delivered; these were the first ones offered on the U.S. market. Now, over 25 years after the end of WW II, Berthier rifles are still being sold.

French Lebel action open.

To disassemble the bolt, remove the extractor by raising the hook end with a screwdriver, then drive the extractor to the rear. To remove the firing mechanism from the bolt, first rotate the cocking piece counterclockwise so it falls against the bolt body. Turn the firing pin button so its slot aligns with the notch in the rear of the thumbpiece on the cocking piece. Grasp the bolt and cocking piece firmly and, placing the firing pin tip on a hard surface, press down on the bolt until the firing pin button clears the cocking piece and can be slipped off to one side. The firing pin and mainspring can now be removed. Reassemble in reverse order.

To remove the carrier plate assembly, remove the rear tang screw and the carrier plate screw from the left side of the receiver and, grasping the trigger guard bow, pull the assembly out of the receiver. The buttstock can now be removed by turning out the front tang screw. Take off the fore-end by removing the two barrel bands, depressing the magazine follower with a finger from inside the receiver, and

reverse order.

Lebel rifles, as well as the Berthier and MAS rifles described later, have two types of screws. The main screws that are removed for field stripping (bolt head, trigger guard, magazine housing and carrier plate screws) are slotted so they can be removed with a screwdriver or similar tool. Practically all other screws are unslotted and require special two-pronged screwdrivers to remove them.

The Berthier Rifle

The Lebel design was soon superseded by another, and similar, turnbolt system. M. Berthier, a Frenchman and an officer of the Algerian Railway Company, adapted a Mannlicher-type magazine to the Lebel 8mm rifle, eliminating the unsatisfactory tubular magazine. The main changes were as follows: 1) the "housing" type receiver was made more like a conventional receiver; 2) cartridge-carrier mechanism and tubular magazine were replaced by a single-column magazine under the receiver, making it largely a sep-

The Berthier rifles and carbines have long been known as "8mm Lebel" rifles, perhaps because they're chambered for the 8mm Lebel cartridge, but the correct designation is "Berthier." In any case, the French rifle discussed here has a single-column Mannlicher-type magazine.

Since it has been available for such a long time, and because they have always been low-priced, Berthiers are about the only French military rifle in some demand for remodeling and sporterizing. In the 1930s Stoeger offered a sporter stock for it, and both Fajen and Bishop still do today. Although most firearms experts and gun writers dismiss this action as being wholly unsatisfactory for a hunting rifle, the fact is that many of them have been remodeled in years past and, I expect, many more will be reworked in the future.

The Berthier Action

The receiver is machined from a one-piece steel forging. The barrel is securely threaded into the receiver. The V-type

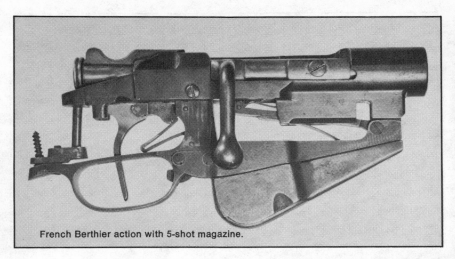

French Berthier action with 5-shot magazine.

Bolt head of the Berthier bolt showing: (A) dual-opposed locking lugs, (B) ejector slot, (C) extractor and (D) bolt guide lug and screw.

threads are right hand. The barrel breech is slightly coned and part of its circumference is beveled for the extractor. The receiver bridge is slotted to allow passage of the bolt handle. The right wall of the receiver is partially cut away for loading and allows the bolt to be turned down to the locked position. Raceways are milled inside the left and right walls of the receiver for passage of the locking lugs. The raceways end abruptly inside the bridge. The magazine well opening is milled from the bottom of the receiver to allow insertion of the clip and cartridges. The cartridge loading ramp begins at a point about midway in this opening, narrowing toward the front and sloping upward to guide the cartridges into the chamber.

There is no recoil lug as such, but a slotted lug under the receiver ring is fitted with a cross pin to engage the front end of the magazine wall. Two flat surfaces at the rear tang junction take up most of the recoil, but other parts of the receiver and trigger guard also absorb some recoil and prevent the action from moving back in the stock.

The magazine shell is attached to the trigger guard by two screws. The follower assembly (follower arm, follower plate, two flat springs and a screw) is positioned by and pivots on, a screw in the front of the shell. The front part of the trigger guard provides a housing in which the clip latch and trigger are fastened—a single V-spring tensions both parts. The top of this housing extends into the bottom of the receiver and is attached by a screw passing through the receiver and the housing. The receiver and the magazine/trigger guard are held together in the stock by this screw, the hook on the front of the magazine shell engaging the receiver and the two guard screws which connect the rear of the trigger guard to the receiver.

The trigger let-off is the usual double-stage type. The Berthier trigger, like that of most other French military rifles, is practically straight and extends into the guard bow like a peg or stick.

There were several variations in the Berthier magazines—all required a clip. The cartridges are first placed in the clip, then the clip and cartridges are inserted into the magazine through the top of the

Berthier action open.

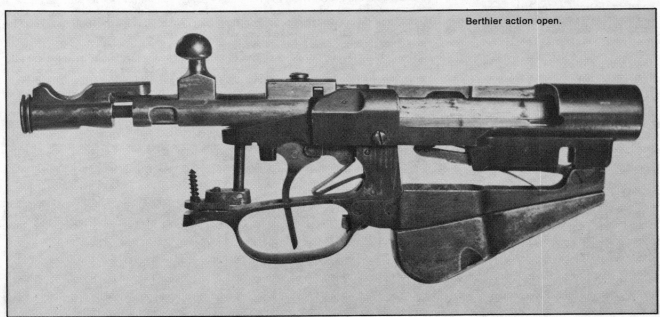

open action. When fully inserted, the clip latch holds the clip and cartridges down against the pressure of the follower. After the last cartridge is fed from the clip, the clip drops free from the bottom of the magazine.

Most early Berthier rifles had a 3-shot magazine capacity, with the rear bottom part of the magazine open for the empty clip to drop free. Later, the magazine was modified to hold a clip of 5 cartridges. This extended the magazine-well below the trigger guard. The bottom shell or cover of this magazine has a hinged cover plate to block the clip opening and retain the clip within the action after the last cartridge is fed from it. The cover plate can be opened, allowing the clip to fall out. Many Berthiers were made for the 5-shot clip, while many 3-shot rifles were later converted to the 5-shot system.

The bolt assembly, rather complex, has a separate head, with dual-opposed locking lugs at the front; neither lug is slotted. The simple hook spring-extractor is dovetailed into a slot cut into the bolt head. The bolt face, recessed for the cartridge rim, is cut only for the extractor and ejector.

The bolt handle has a heavy rectangular base which appears to be an integral part of the bolt body. When the bolt is locked, this heavy base is in front of the receiver bridge and becomes the safety lug. On the front of the bolt body, in line with the bolt handle base, is a heavy lug which acts as a bolt guide. This lug extends forward of the bolt body and is notched to engage over a small lug on the bolt head when it is in place. In addition, there is a large-headed screw threaded through this lug and into a hole in the bolt head. The notch, lug and screw hold the bolt head in place, preventing it from rotating on the bolt body.

The bolt body is drilled from the front to accept the coil mainspring and the one-piece firing pin. When the bolt head is in place the mainspring is compressed between a shoulder on the firing pin and a collar in the rear of the bolt body.

The heavy cocking piece fits over the back end of the firing pin, which projects from the bolt body. The firing pin is anchored within the cocking piece by a double hooked button fitted in the rear of the cocking piece and engaging notches on the end of the firing pin. On top of the cocking piece there is a heavy lug which

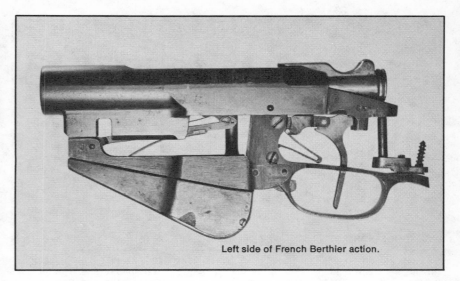

Left side of French Berthier action.

fits the slot in the receiver bridge. Below this lug is a cocking cam matching a notch in the bolt body. The action is cocked on lifting the bolt handle.

The Berthier action has no safety, no magazine cutoff, nor any separate bolt stop. The bolt stops when the locking lugs contact the ends of the lug raceways in the bridge. The ejector is merely a small projection on top of the housing on the trigger guard which protrudes into a groove in the bolt body and head.

Operation

To load, raise the bolt handle and pull the bolt back. Insert a fully- or partially-loaded clip into the opened action, pressing the cartridges down until the clip latch has engaged the clip. Pushing the bolt forward moves the top cartridge out of the clip into the chamber, allowing the follower to raise the next cartridge in the clip against the bolt. Turning the bolt handle down locks the cartridge in the chamber and the action is cocked. Pulling the trigger releases the firing mechanism, discharging the cartridge. On raising the bolt handle the striker is cocked and the fired case is cammed back when the front of the bolt guide rib moves over the inclined surface of the receiver ring. Pulling the bolt back draws the case from the chamber, ejecting it up and to the right. When the last cartridge is fed from the

clip, the clip is free to drop of its own weight, either falling from the magazine or when the hinged cover plate is opened. To unload a full- or partially-loaded clip, open the bolt and slightly depress the cartridges and clip while pressing the clip latch in the trigger guard. Releasing the pressure on the cartridges allows the clip to rise and be pulled from the action.

Take-Down and Assembly

To remove the bolt, raise the bolt handle and pull the bolt about halfway back. With a large screwdriver remove the large-headed screw from the bolt guide rib lug. Move the bolt until the bolt head can be turned free from the bolt body, then pull the bolt to the rear and lift out the bolt head. Reassemble in reverse order.

To disassemble the firing mechanism, remove the bolt from the action and rotate the cocking piece counterclockwise so it falls against the bolt body. Turn the firing pin button so its slot aligns with the notch in the thumbpiece on the cocking piece. Grasp the bolt and cocking piece firmly and, placing the firing pin tip on a hard surface, press down on the bolt until the firing pin button clears the cocking piece and can be slipped off. The firing pin and mainspring can then be pulled from the bolt. Reassemble in reverse order.

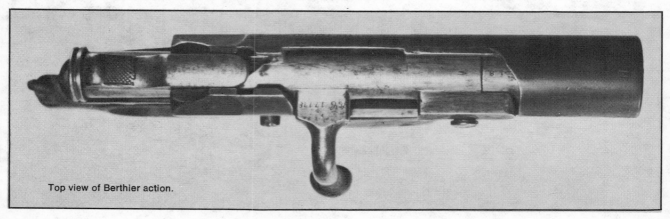

Top view of Berthier action.

French Model 1916 Berthier rifle chambered for the 8mm Lebel cartridge.

To remove barrel and action from the stock, remove the barrel bands from the fore-end. Remove the screw from the right of the receiver bridge and the screw from the rear of the trigger guard, grasp the trigger guard and pull it out of the stock. Remove the tang screw and lift the action and barrel from the stock. All other parts can then be removed by turning out various screws and driving pins from the receiver and magazine units. Reassemble in reverse order. The barrel should not be unthreaded from the receiver unless absolutely necessary and then only if the proper tools are available.

Comments

The French Berthier rifles (there are many models and variations) were rugged and serviceable military weapons and their long use has proved this. The action is strong and safe enough for the 8mm Lebel cartridge. The rifles, provided the bore is in excellent condition, are generally quite accurate. Feeding, ignition, extraction and ejection are positive and reliable.

All action parts are well made, generally well-finished and smooth. No doubt good steels were used in the manufacture and heat-treated where needed. All in all, Berthier rifles are good.

However, the Berthier action has a number of faults and undesirable features, especially so in view of reworking the Berthier rifle into a sporter. The worst feature is that a special clip must be used to fire the rifle as a repeater. Requiring the bolt to be separated before it can be removed is also bad. The lack of a safety may also be highly undesirable to some shooters. The 5-shot magazine projecting so far below the stock is never liked, and the belly of the 3-shot magazine is often disliked.

Very little can be done to improve the Berthier action. It can be gunsmithed to the extent of replacing the bolt handle with a flat Mannlicher-type, the trigger pull improved by honing the sear surfaces and the metal parts given a better polish, but that's about all. There is no other common cartridge for which the rifle can be rechambered, and rebarreling is not practical. The issue barrel has a very pleasing contour after the original sights are removed. Despite its many undesirable aspects, and that little can be done to change them, the 3-shot Berthier can be made into a nice sporter by fitting a new stock, better sights and a new bolt handle, as on the sporter illustrated. Except for polishing and rebluing, I don't recommend any further remodeling.

Berthier Markings

Usually the place of manufacture and the model designation are stamped on the left side of the receiver, like:

St Etienne Mle 1892.

Since many Berthiers were "transformed" to another model at a later date, the original model designation may not always be correct. The serial number is stamped at the base of the bolt handle and breech end of the barrel. The date of manufacture (year) is usually stamped on the breech end of the barrel as well, along with an assortment of inspector's, arsenal and proof marks. Sometimes there are two dates stamped on the barrel; the earliest date probably indicating when the rifle was made originally and the later date perhaps showing the year of "transformation." The letters **MAC, MAS** or **MAT** are often stamped on the barrel. These indicate the French arsenal where the rifle or barrel was made, or where it was rebuilt or transformed. In each case the letters **MA** stand for "Manufacture d'Armes," and the last letter—**C, S** or **T** —indicates the arsenal located at Chatellerault, St. Etienne or Tulle.

The 8mm Lebel Cartridge

This cartridge was the first relatively small-bore smokeless powder rifle cartridge to be adopted by a world power. In doing so, France led other countries by about two years. The 8mm Lebel cartridge is based on a rimmed, bottle-necked case, with the case body having a double taper. Although originally loaded with a full-jacketed flat-nosed bullet, for use in the tubular magazine Lebel rifle, in 1898 it became the first military cartridge loaded with a spitzer-point boat-tail bullet.

During WW I, Remington contracted with France to make both rifles and ammunition. As a result of contract cancellations after the war, a great many of these rifles remained in the United States and were sold on the commercial market. Remington then loaded sporting ammunition for these rifles until about 1964. Remington loaded 8mm Lebel sporting ammo with a 170-gr. soft point bullet to a muzzle velocity of 2640 fps. At 200 yards the velocity is 1960 fps, remaining energy 1450 ft. lbs., while midrange trajectory over this range is 3.4″. This compares favorably with such more popular cartridges as .30-40, .303 British, .300 Savage and 8mm Mauser. Regardless of what I said about the French rifles chambered for the 8mm Lebel cartridge (to my knowledge no other rifles were so chambered), it is a good load.

The number of models, variations and transformations of rifles and carbines based on the Berthier action are too many to list here. Starting with the very old Gras action, we have seen how France used this basic turnbolt system with various types of magazines of Kropatschek, Lebel and Berthier designs. This brings us to the last version, a turnbolt action fitted with a Mauser type staggered-column magazine. These rifles (there are about three different variations) are known as the French Model 1934.

The Model 1934 French Rifle

I have to backtrack a bit here. In 1929, France developed a modern rimless military cartridge for light machine gun use— it was difficult to make or adapt any machine gun to handle the rimmed 8mm Lebel cartridge. The new cartridge, a rim-

Parts Legend
8MM BERTHIER

1. Receiver
2. Sear
3. Trigger
4. Sear screw
5. Trigger pin
6. Trigger spring roll pin
7. Trigger spring
8. Trigger spring roll
9. Clip latch
10. Clip latch screw
11. Bolt body
12. Bolt head
13. Bolt head connecting screw
14. Firing pin
15. Mainspring
16. Cocking piece
17. Firing pin button
18. Extractor
19. Tang plate
20. Tang plate screw
21. Tang screw
22. Trigger guard
23. Rear trigger guard screw
24. Front trigger guard screw
25. Magazine shell
26. Upper magazine shell screw
27. Lower magazine shell screw
28. Magazine extension cover
29. Magazine extension cover screw
30. Magazine cover plate
31. Magazine cover plate screw
32. Magazine cover plate spring
33. Follower plate
34. Follower plate screw
35. Follower plate spring
36. Follower arm
37. Follower arm screw
38. Follower arm spring
39. Follower arm spring platform

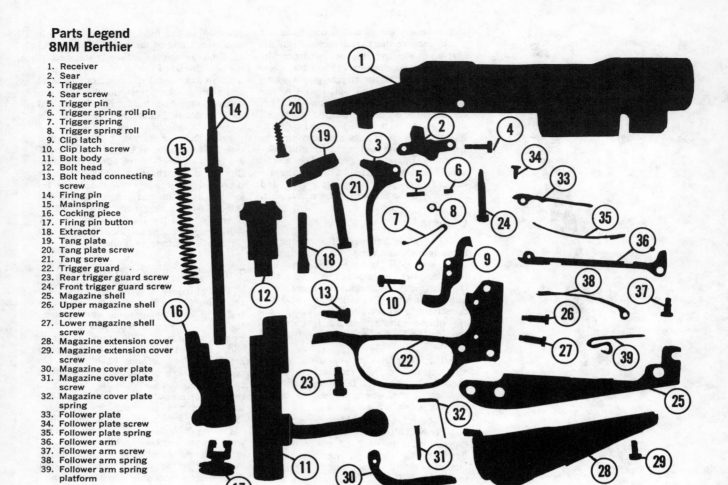

French Berthier Model 1890 (and later)
(Uses 8MM Lebel cartridges)

Dimensional Specifications

Weight (5-shot model)	51 oz.
Receiver length	8.50"
Receiver ring dia.	1.265"
Bolt dia.	.720"
Bolt travel	4.450"
Striker travel	.50"
Magazine well opening:	
Length	3.065"
Width, rear	.695"
Width, front	.395"
Bolt face recess:	
Dia.	.635"
Depth	.072"

General Specifications

Type	Turnbolt repeater.
Receiver	One-piece machined steel forging, slotted bridge. One-piece stock.
Bolt	Two-piece, dual-opposed forward locking lugs on separate bolt head. Base of the bolt handle is safety lug.
Ignition	One-piece firing pin powered by coil mainspring. Cocks on opening bolt.
Magazine	Single column non-detachable box magazine. Special clip required. Three- or 5-shot capacity.
Trigger	Non-adjustable, double-stage military pull.
Safety	None provided.
Extractor	One-piece spring type mortised into bolt head.
Magazine cutoff	None provided.
Bolt stop	No separate bolt stop; see text.
Ejector	Stud type, made as integral part of trigger.

less, bottle-necked case loaded with a 7.5mm bullet, is known as the 7.5mm French M1929C, 7.5x54mm French MAS or as the 7.5mm MAS. It was almost impossible to use the old 8mm Lebel cartridge in anything but a tubular or single-column magazine and, since the prospects for continued peace looked poor, the French officials decided to adapt the Model 1907/15 rifle (a Berthier variation) to this new cartridge.

This was done by fitting the old receiver with a box magazine wide enough to hold a staggered-column of five 7.5mm

cartridges. The bottom of the magazine box has a detachable floorplate which fits in place and is held closed by a spring-loaded plunger—like the M98 Mauser. The magazine well opening in the receiver was milled so integral cartridge guide lips remain—also like the Mauser system. A follower, with a rib on one side and set on a W-shaped follower spring, completed the magazine. Notches were then milled in the front of the receiver bridge slot to accept a stripper clip—so the magazine could be loaded quickly. Other necessary things were done with the action to handle

the 7.5mm cartridge. The barrel and action were set into a one-piece stock, and the result was the Model 1934—the year in which it was adopted.

The outside appearance of the M34 is not too unlike the 3-shot Berthier, except that it does not have quite as much belly. At best, the new rifle was only a makeshift stop-gap affair, practically obsolete before it was made. Probably not too many M34s were made—they are rare in the U.S., hence of considerable interest to the collector, but of little worth for remodeling.

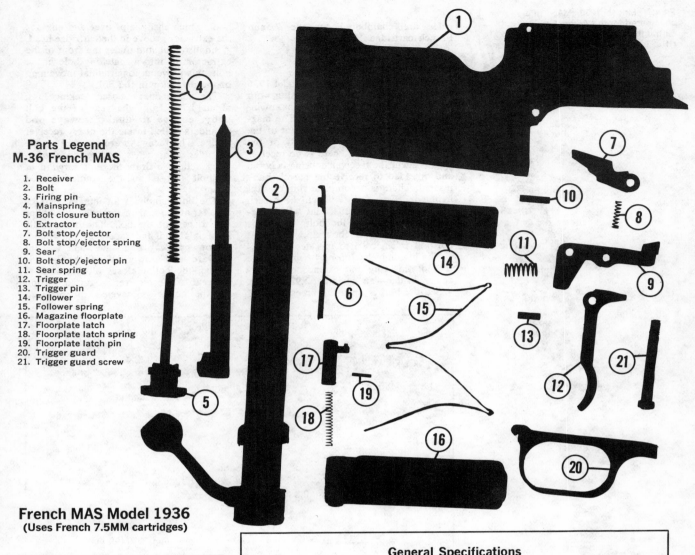

Parts Legend
M-36 French MAS

1. Receiver
2. Bolt
3. Firing pin
4. Mainspring
5. Bolt closure button
6. Extractor
7. Bolt stop/ejector
8. Bolt stop/ejector spring
9. Sear
10. Bolt stop/ejector pin
11. Sear spring
12. Trigger
13. Trigger pin
14. Follower
15. Follower spring
16. Magazine floorplate
17. Floorplate latch
18. Floorplate latch spring
19. Floorplate latch pin
20. Trigger guard
21. Trigger guard screw

French MAS Model 1936
(Uses French 7.5MM cartridges)

Dimensional Specifications

Weight	51 oz.
Receiver length	7.75″
Receiver width	1.385″
Bolt dia.	.800″
Bolt travel	3.485″
Striker travel	.550″
Magazine well opening:	
Length	3.10″
Width (average)	.650″
Bolt face recess:	
Dia.	.485″
Depth	.090″

General Specifications

Type	Turnbolt repeater.
Receiver	One-piece, machined steel forging with integral magazine box. Non-slotted bridge. Two-piece stock.
Bolt	One-piece, with dual-opposed locking lugs at rear. No safety lug.
Ignition	One-piece hollow striker powered by coil mainspring. Cocks on opening bolt.
Magazine	Staggered-column box magazine made integral with receiver. 5-shot capacity. Quick detachable floorplate.
Trigger	Non-adjustable double-stage military pull.
Safety	None provided.
Extractor	One-piece flat spring extractor mortised into bolt.
Magazine cutoff	None provided.
Bolt stop	Pivoting type engages in groove at bottom of bolt.
Ejector	Pivoting type integral with bolt stop.

The MAS Model 1936

A year or so after the 7.5mm French cartridge was introduced, French ordnance began to develop a new shoulder arm for it. Discarding all previous turnbolt rifle designs, they devised an entirely new action system in 1932, and that rifle is the MAS M-1932. A limited number of M32s were made for testing, and after four years (with a number of modifications) the final version was approved and adopted as the MAS Model 1936. The development work was done in France's largest arms making city, St. Etienne, by the Manufacture d'Armes St. Etienne, of

which "MAS" is an abbreviation. It was the latest and the best military bolt action rifle adopted and made by France.

The MAS M36 rifle weighs about 8.25 pounds, has a 22.6″ round, stepped barrel and is 49.13″ overall. The buttstock, held in place by a single screw, is very short. The distance from buttplate to trigger is only 12.62″. A separate fore-end (extending to within 5″ of the muzzle) and the full-length wooden handguard are held to the barrel by two bands. A metal hook, attached to the rear of the fore-end, engages in a recess at the front of the receiver and holds the fore-end assembly against the receiver. The M36 is fitted

with a skewer-type bayonet carried reversed in a tube within the fore-end under the barrel. The leather carrying sling is attached to the left side of the rifle on a bar on the buttstock and on a loop on the middle barrel band. The aperture rear sight, mounted on the receiver bridge, is adjustable for elevation only—from 200 to 1200 meters.

The only variation of this rifle is the paratroop model, designated the MAS Model 1936 CR39 rifle. This model has a folding aluminum stock, hinged just forward of the trigger. When unlatched, it can be swung under and to the left of the fore-end. It weighs about 8 pounds. Both

French Model 1936 MAS rifle chambered for the 7.5mm French cartridge. Like the Lebel, this rifle has a two-piece stock.

rifles are chambered for the 7.5mm French cartridge.

The M-1936 Action

The receiver of the French Model 1936 rifle is a box-like affair, or housing, with the entire magazine box made as an integral part of the steel forging. The magazine housing extends to the front of the receiver and is hollow forward of the front magazine wall. There is no receiver ring as such; the receiver housing is bored and threaded to receive the barrel shank instead. There is a complete ring of steel in the receiver against which the breech end of the barrel butts, and which surrounds the head of the bolt when it is closed. The ring is about ¼" wide and the bolt is enclosed to this depth.

The loading/ejection port begins at the rear of this ring and extends to the receiver bridge—an opening 2.925" long. When the bolt is open the breech end of

hook which easily slips over and engages the extractor groove in the cartridge head. A small round stud under the front of the extractor fits into a matching hole in the bolt; this prevents longitudinal movement of the extractor in the bolt.

The solid, dual-opposed locking lugs, about 1.75" from the rear of the bolt body, engage in dual raceways and shoulders milled inside the heavy receiver bridge. The raceways are inclined on the shoulder approaches and provide camming action to draw the bolt forward as the bolt is closed and the handle is turned down.

The bolt handle is an integral part of a collar at the rear of the bolt—the collar is also part of the bolt. The bolt handle stem is round and tapers to the round, hollow grasping ball—the stem is bent forward and down. When the bolt is closed, the collar closes all openings at the rear of the receiver. A raised portion on the collar is beveled to match a

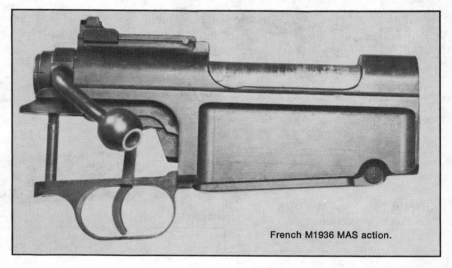

French M1936 MAS action.

the barrel and the chamber are clearly visible. The right side of the ejection port is cut down to the level of the cartridge guide lip of the magazine well, while the left side is cut slightly below the level of the top of the bolt, leaving a wall about ½" high. A thumb notch is cut into the rear of this left wall to aid in stripping cartridges from a clip when loading the rifle. Because the bolt diameter is quite large, the loading/ejection port is also, but this is not at all objectionable.

The receiver bridge, about 2.60" long, is unslotted. An integral raised strip is milled on top of the bridge to form a housing for the rear sight components. At the front of the receiver bridge is the clip-charger guide.

The one-piece bolt, very rugged, is also quite large in diameter; .800" as compared to the Mauser and Springfield .700" and the Mark V Weatherby .840". The front of the bolt is recessed for the cartridge head. The only break in the recess is the narrow ejector slot and the cut for the extractor, about .320" wide. The extractor, made of spring steel, and about 2.80" long, is mortised and dovetailed into the bolt body. It has a sturdy beveled

similar surface on the left rear of the receiver, and provides the initial extraction power on raising the bolt handle. On moving the bolt forward to close the action, these surfaces impart initial turning motion to the bolt.

The bolt is drilled from the rear to accept the one-piece hollow firing pin. The collar at the rear of the bolt is milled to accept the bolt closure button. This button has two lugs, and the inside of the collar is milled leaving shoulders and recesses so the button is locked in place when it is rotated after insertion. There is a rod projecting forward out of the bolt button and the small coil mainspring is compressed over this rod as it extends into the hollow firing pin.

The rear underside of the bolt body, just forward of the bolt collar, is milled to form a cocking cam surface. The cocking cam on the rear of the firing pin fits into this notch. The cocking cam extends below the bolt body into a groove cut into the receiver, and has a notch to engage the sear. On raising the bolt handle, the firing pin is forced back until the cocking cam slips onto a flat spot on the end of the camming surface. On closing the bolt, the sear engages the cocking cam and holds the firing pin back as the bolt is fully closed and locked.

The sear is positioned in a groove below the receiver bridge and is held in place by, and pivots on a pin. Tension is provided by a stiff coil spring. A projection on the rear of the sear protrudes through a hole in the receiver to engage the cocking cam of the firing pin. The trigger is pivoted on a pin in the sear.

The combination bolt stop/ejector fits partially inside the sear, partially over the trigger, and pivots on the pin with the trigger. The front of the bolt stop/ejector projects upward through a hole in the receiver and is provided upward tension by a small coil spring between it and the sear. A narrow inclined groove is cut into the bottom of the bolt, extending into the bolt face recess for the narrow ejector. A wider groove is cut beside it for the bolt stop, but this groove ends abruptly about ¼" from the head of the bolt. The bolt stop is released (to remove the bolt) by pulling the trigger back as far as it will go. The bolt stop/ejector, riding in the grooves, also acts as a bolt guide when the bolt is operated and prevents the bolt from turning as it is drawn back.

Two gas vent holes in the front of the bolt-stop groove effectively take care of any gases that enter the firing pin hole by venting them rearward through the thumb notch in the left receiver wall. If this is not enough, there is another hole, in about the center of the bolt, to vent any gases getting back this far into the magazine. The firing pin, bolt and bolt button are constructed to make gas escape impossible through the rear of the bolt. There is no danger of the firing pin or button ever being blown out of the bolt.

The trigger guard bow is a separate part

and a hook at the front engages a groove in the rear wall of the magazine box. The buttstock is clamped between the trigger guard bow and receiver by the guard screw threading into the receiver tang. The rear of the magazine housing is hollowed out slightly, and the tenon on the front of the buttstock fits into this hollow to help secure the stock to the receiver and prevent it from splitting.

As mentioned before, the four walls of the magazine box are an integral part of the receiver housing. The walls are quite thick (about .090") and reinforced in spots. A machined, hollow floorplate fits in the bottom of the magazine box. It is held in place by a lip at the rear of the plate engaging in a groove in the magazine box and by a push-button latch on the front engaging in a groove at the front of the right magazine wall. A conventional steel follower and W-shaped follower spring are used. The ends of the spring are mortised into the follower and floorplate.

Operation

The MAS M36 rifle operates like most other staggered-column box magazine bolt action rifles. The bolt handle is raised and drawn back to open the action. With the bolt open, the magazine is loaded by pressing single cartridges directly into the magazine or placing a loaded stripper clip in the clip-charger and pressing the cartridges into the magazine. The bolt is then pushed forward, feeding the topmost cartridge from the magazine into the chamber. Turning the bolt handle down locks the cartridge in the chamber. The action is left cocked when the bolt handle is turned down, and pulling the trigger will release the firing pin to discharge the cartridge. The rifle can-

not be fired unless the bolt handle is nearly all the way down and the bolt locked. On opening the bolt the fired case will be extracted and ejected from the action—the cycle can then be repeated. The rear of the follower is beveled and does not prevent the bolt from closing when the magazine is empty. The magazine can be unloaded by removing the floorplate. There is no safety, but the bolt handle fully raised makes an effective safety.

Take-Down and Assembly

Make sure the chamber and magazine are empty. Remove the buttstock by turning out the trigger guard screw. Pull the trigger guard from the stock and away from the receiver and pull the stock back and down from the receiver. Remove the fore-end and handguard by turning the cross screw out of the front barrel band and pulling the band forward. Turn out the screw from the middle barrel band and remove it, then lift off the fore-end and handguard. Reassemble in reverse order.

Remove the bolt by raising the bolt handle and drawing the bolt to the rear as far as it will go; pull the trigger back all the way and then remove the bolt. To disassemble the bolt, grasp it in the left hand and, with the right thumb, depress the bolt button and turn it clockwise ¼-turn or until it snaps out. The bolt button, mainspring and firing pin can then be removed from the bolt. Reassemble as follows: insert the firing pin in the bolt with the cocking cam lug resting on the flat spot of the cocking cam. Insert the mainspring and bolt button, aligning the left index mark on the bolt button with the index mark on the bolt. Press the but-

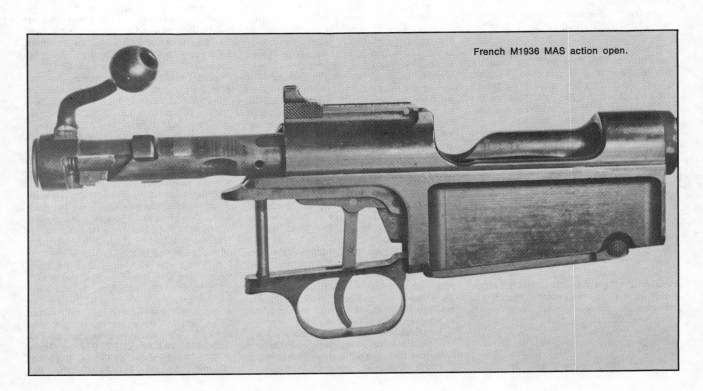

French M1936 MAS action open.

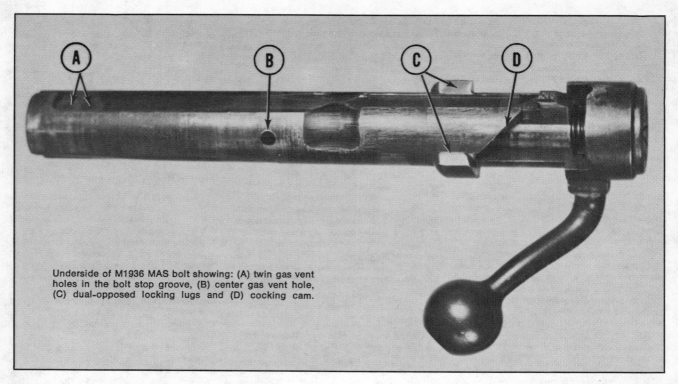

Underside of M1936 MAS bolt showing: (A) twin gas vent holes in the bolt stop groove, (B) center gas vent hole, (C) dual-opposed locking lugs and (D) cocking cam.

ton all the way into the bolt or until it can be rotated counterclockwise ¼-turn.

The extractor can be removed using a screwdriver and lifting its front end up, away from the bolt, until the extractor can be pulled forward and out of the bolt. Reassemble in reverse order.

Depress the button on the right front of the floorplate and pull it, along with the spring and follower, from the magazine box. The follower and floorplate can then be pulled off the ends of the follower spring. In reassembling, the narrow end of the follower spring goes into the follower. To remove the floorplate latch and spring, drive the small latch retainer pin from the floorplate.

Remove the trigger assembly by driving out the sear pin, then pull down on the rear of the sear until it is free of the receiver. The trigger pin can then be driven out to separate trigger, bolt stop/ejector and bolt stop/ejector spring from the sear. Reassemble in reverse order.

The barrel is threaded (right-hand threads) tightly into the receiver and it should not be removed unless necessary, and then only if you have the proper tools.

Markings

The French MAS Model 1936 rifles are boldly marked with the designation **MAS M^{LE} 1936** stamped on the left side of the receiver. The serial number is stamped below the designation marking, as well as on the floorplate and on the stem of the bolt handle. Various French proof marks and inspector's marks are stamped on the receiver ring and breech end of the barrel.

Comments

I have gone to some length describing the MAS Model 1936 rifle and action because I think this action is most interesting and unusual. To be sure, this action has some faults, but it also has some excellent features worthy of comment and consideration.

It appears to be a very strong action. The two locking lugs are solid and massive. There is a lot of metal in the receiver bridge to support the lugs when the bolt is locked and there is no chance that these supporting shoulders will fail. Though the left side wall of the receiver has a thumb notch, there is ample metal connecting the receiver bridge and ring. The receiver is strengthened further by the ridge of metal along each side and by the heavy walled integral magazine. There is little chance of the receiver parting in the middle even though the locking lugs are at the rear of the bolt. I cannot see how the receiver could "stretch," and the very heavy bolt is certainly not going to compress when firing the rifle. For many years, the prevailing opinion has been that only a bolt action with at least two forward locking lugs is worth considering. If we consider the success of the fine Schultz & Larsen action, the new Remington Model 788, the Steyr-Mannlicher SL and others with locking lugs at the rear of the bolt, then I can see nothing wrong with the MAS design. The MAS design also results in a shorter bolt travel (the reader may want to compare the action specifications in this book), and this may aid in speed of operation. An important result of this design is that the cartridges do not span any gap between the magazine and chamber, the resultant feeding being more positive and reliable.

I believe the MAS M36 is also a very safe action because the front of the bolt is surrounded by a solid ring of steel when the bolt is locked, the bolt face nearly contacts the barrel, and the rim of the cartridge is almost fully enclosed; the rear of the bolt is entirely closed so that gases can't escape.

The bolt of the MAS is relatively short and the long receiver bridge gives considerable support, resulting in little "play" or looseness of the bolt when the action is open. On the few rifles I have examined and handled, bolt operation was easy and smooth. I noticed too, that the actions were generally very well made and finished. I especially like the extractor of this action. It is simple and strong—modern designers of turnbolt actions might do well to copy it. I certainly would consider it better than some puny modern rifle extractors like those of the Remington M700 and Weatherby actions.

As for the magazine box being made as part of the receiver, I have not decided whether I like this or not. The same goes for the two-piece stock design imposed by the "housing" type receiver. However, I have always admired the Model 99 Savage rifle with its exposed receiver and I do not believe I'd mind the exposed MAS M36 receiver on a sporting rifle. To my way of thinking, this receiver has rather nice lines, including those where the buttstock contacts the receiver. I like the magazine floorplate and the way it is released, although I'd rather have the floorplate fitted so it would be flush with the bottom of the magazine box.

I found the box magazine to be a marvel the way it will accept and feed a wide variety of cartridges. It will only handle cartridges about 3.0″ in over-all length, but many cartridges fall within these limits. For example, it will feed perfectly such cartridges as the .22-250, .250-3000, .243, 6mm, .257 Roberts, 7mm, .284, .308, .35 Rem. and .358. If loaded carefully, it could also handle the .225

and .220 Swift cartridges. Cartridges with larger rims that would also function are the .219 Zipper, .25-35, .30-30, .30-40 and .303 British. If this isn't enough, I also found that the magazine would take fatter rimmed cartridges like the .444 Marlin and .45-70, though the cartridge lips at the front half of the magazine well must be widened a bit. I believe it would also handle short wildcat cartridges based on the belted magnum case.

The MAS M36 is an astonishingly simple action with a minimum of parts—fewer than any other high powered turn-bolt repeater of which I am aware. For example, this action has 12 less component parts than the M98 Mauser, which has fewer parts than the 03 Springfield. The entire M36 bolt assembly consists of just five parts; bolt, extractor, firing pin, mainspring and bolt button. An action that has few parts is not always an indication it is good, but like any piece of machinery, fewer parts lessen the chance for breakdown.

This action has no safety and that may be a strike against it—depending on one's viewpoint. I can't see how a safety could be incorporated in the bolt to lock both the bolt and firing pin, but a simple safety could be built into the trigger guard to lock the trigger.

venient to operate and is out of the way of the trigger finger.

7.5mm MAS and Rechambering

As previously mentioned, the 7.5mm French MAS (7.5x54mm) cartridge was introduced in 1929. It is a rimless bottle-necked cartridge nearly identical in appearance and ballistics to the .308 Winchester or 7.62mm NATO cartridges. The 7.5 indicates the caliber and bore diameter, which is .295″, and 54 indicates a case length of 2.12″. The over-all length of the cartridge is about 3.00″. The standard military ball loading drives the 139-gr. jacketed pointed bullet of .307″ diameter at a muzzle velocity of 2674 fps.

The above figures for the bore and bullet diameter show that the cartridge is very close to being a .30 caliber like our .308 and .30-06 which have a normal bore size of .300″, and normally use .308″ bullets. The groove diameter of the 7.5mm MAS barrel runs about .3075″ to .3085″, and has a rifling twist of one turn in 10″. In handloading this cartridge, regular .308″ jacketed bullets can be used.

The 7.5mm MAS cartridge was loaded only for military use and was Berdan primed. No Boxer primed cases are available. The problem presented to the hand-

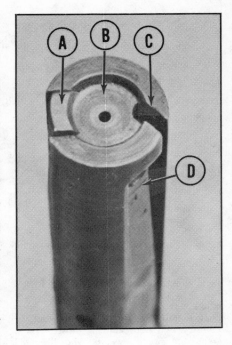

Bolt head of the M1936 MAS showing: (A) extractor, (B) cartridge head recess, (C) ejector slot and (D) bolt stop notch.

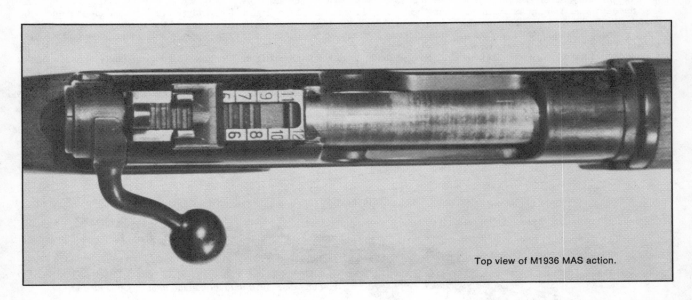

Top view of M1936 MAS action.

There is one thing I do not like about this action—the bolt handle. To keep the action and the rifle as compact as possible, the trigger and trigger guard were positioned well under the receiver bridge. Since the base of the bolt handle must be on the rear end of the bolt due to the bolt design, in order to keep the grasping ball from bruising the shooter's finger it had to be arched forward. I haven't found this bolt handle placement to be awkward or inconvenient when operating this action, but I don't like the looks of it. So far, I'm still not used to the looks of the forward bent bolt handles on the 600 Remington and 800 Mossberg rifles, but like the MAS M36, one should not mind the looks of the handle if the bolt is con-

loader is that the 7.5mm case is an odd size, having a head diameter of about .481″ compared to the .470″ for the .30-06 case. It is possible to make the 7.5mm cases from Norma 7.62mm Russian brass, but this requires that the rim be removed, an extractor groove cut and the case fire-formed. Naturally, if the 7.5mm case is some .011″ larger in diameter at the head than the .30-06 case, so is the 7.5mm chamber. This restricts rechambering to cartridges like the .300 Savage, .308 or 7.65mm Mauser unless the barrel is set back about .750″. This is also more or less out of the question because the very narrow shoulder on the barrel would be entirely removed, leaving no secure butting surface between barrel and receiver.

Thus, if you want to fire the M36 MAS rifle you will be limited to using 7.5mm MAS military ammunition, reloading the Berdan primed military cases, making the cases from 7.62mm Russian brass, or rebarreling to another caliber.

Sporterizing

Since the end of WW II, military surplus arms dealers have imported and offered for sale many different bolt action rifles. Most abundant of these have been the many models of the Mausers, Lee-Enfields and Carcanos. From time to time, French Lebels and Berthiers have been offered and, at this writing, I note that Berthiers are still listed. MAS M36 rifles

A remodeled and restocked French M1892 Berthier rifle. These rifles are chambered for the 8mm Lebel cartridge and for this reason are usually mistakenly called "Lebel" rifles.

seem to have been more scarce for I have not seen them advertised for sale very often in the last 25 years. There are, however, a sprinkling of them throughout the country, and I suspect that most of them were sent home by GIs who liberated them from the German Occupation Forces in France.

Though I have never remodeled this rifle, and probably never will, if I had one in the days when I did much remodeling and rifle building, I probably would have approached the job with great enthusiasm. This is what I would have done: I'd replace the barrel with one 22″ of sporter-weight chambered for .257 Roberts or 7mm Mauser; fit a tapered fore-end of the Model 99 Savage rifle pattern; remove the military rear sight and base

from the receiver and install a Lyman or Redfield receiver sight and a ramp front sight on the barrel, or mount a scope on the receiver using a Buehler blank base. I'd weld a strap to the front of the trigger guard to move it about 1″ farther to the rear and make a similar tang extension on the receiver for the guard screw; the trigger would be altered, positioning it to the rear in the relocated trigger guard. A crossbolt safety in the rear of the trigger guard would lock the trigger and a new buttstock with a capped pistol grip and panels forward of the grip like the Model 99 Savage stock. With the trigger, trigger guard and grip located farther back on the action, I would then bend the bolt handle down, and shorten its stem to place the grasping ball within easy reach. Fin-

ally, I'd polish and blue the metal parts, jewel the bolt and checker the grip and fore-end.

In my search for information about the MAS M36, I came across an item written by a well-known gun authority stating that Manufacture d'Armes had made a sporting rifle on the M36 action. According to him these were made in 7x57mm, 8x60mm Magnum and 10.75x68mm. The last two cartridges are longer than the magazine opening of the military action, therefore, the sporter action must have had a longer box. A safety was also provided in the trigger guard. Apparently very few of the MAS M36 Sporters were made, for I have never seen one, or even a photo of one, so I have no idea whether it resembles my proposed sporter or not.

French Model 1916 Berthier carbine in 8mm Lebel caliber.

8. The Lee-Enfield

THE BRITISH Lee-Enfield rifle had a long and colorful history; one which includes two world wars and many smaller wars and conflicts covering wide areas and many countries over the face of the earth. The "Lee" of Lee-Enfield is James Paris Lee, a Scottish-born American firearms designer who invented the Lee turn-bolt magazine firearm in 1879. A book could be written about the life and work of this inventor; it would be an interesting challenge for some biographer. "Enfield" derives from the Royal Small Arms Factory at Enfield Lock in England, a great arms manufacturing plant where, for many years, most military development work was done on arms later adopted by Great Britain.

Many articles have been written about Lee and his turnbolt rifle that was the forerunner of the British Lee-Enfield. The reader need only check the bibliography at the back of this book to find a few of the articles published in *American Rifleman*. In addition, there is an excellent book on Lee-Enfields—*The Lee-Enfield Rifle* by Major E.G.B. Reynolds—must reading for anyone interested in these arms. Because of this wealth of background material I won't go deeply into the history and development of this famous military rifle. I will limit my main discussion to the two Lee-Enfield actions used during two World Wars: The No. 1 Mark III of WW I and the No. 4 Mark I of WW II.

A very brief historical outline of the Lee-Enfield, however, is in order. After Lee patented his vertical magazine turn-bolt action in 1879 he was not immediately successful in getting the rifles made and sold. He tried to interest the U.S. Navy in the design, but it was not until the Remington Arms Co. of Ilion, N.Y., bought the manufacturing rights that the Lee rifle had any worthwhile backing. Known as the Remington-Lee rifle, a few were sold to the Navy for experimental purposes in 1881. Remington tried in vain

to interest the U.S. Army in the same rifle. Meanwhile, Remington also tried to interest foreign countries in the new rifle (some samples were made for China and Japan, among others) and did sell some to Cuba and Spain. At about this time (1883) England became interested in adopting a magazine rifle, and the Lee rifles submitted came out best in their 1887 trials. This brought Lee his first real taste of fame. The Remington firm then began making Remington-Lee sporting rifles for a variety of cartridges, eventually including the 6mm Lee, .30-30, .30-40, .303 British, .35 Remington, .45-70 and others. Remington made these rifles until about 1906.

After England's initial acceptance, the Lee system was somewhat modified with development and manufacturing done at Enfield. The first British Lee rifle was the Lee-Metford Magazine Rifle Mark I, the design sealed in December, 1888. Various improvements and modifications followed with the first true Lee-Enfield being introduced late in 1895.*

This was followed by other changes, modifications and mark designations every few years or so until the Mark III was adopted in 1916 and the Short Magazine Lee-Enfield (SMLE) No. I Mark III.

The Rifles

The No. 5 Mark I carbine weighs about 8.9 pounds, has a 25.2″ barrel and is 44.8″ over-all. It has a full length fore-end and the rear sight is mounted on the barrel.

The No. 4 Mark I rifle, about 8.6 pounds, has a 25.2″ barrel and is 44.4″ over-all. Its fore-end extends nearly to the muzzle, and the rear sight is mounted on the receiver bridge. It was adopted in 1941.

The No. 5 Mark I carbine weighs about 7.2 pounds, has a 20.5″ barrel and is 39.1″ over-all. Often called the "Jungle Carbine," it has a short sporter-type fore-end and a funnel-like flash hider on the muz-

zle, but is otherwise like the No. 4 rifle. It was introduced in 1944. All Lee-Enfields were discontinued in 1954.

The No. 1 Mk III Action

The Lee-Enfield receiver (called the "body" in England) is a one-piece steel forging which required a great many machine operations before it was finished. It is more complex than the usual centerfire turnbolt action because of the two-piece stock design; the separate buttstock is attached to the rear of the receiver (called the "butt socket") by a through-bolt. The receiver forging was made with a large mass of metal on its rear which was milled and threaded to accept the buttstock tenon and the through-bolt. This is a very secure and rugged stock fastening.

The front end of the receiver has right hand threads of the common V-type. A heavy collar is left inside the rear of the receiver ring against which the flat breech end of the barrel butts. The barrel is also made with a reinforced shoulder which butts against the front of the receiver, making a rigid barrel-to-receiver joint. A slot cut through the right side of the collar (and a matching beveled notch in the breech face of the barrel) admits the extractor hook. The collar closely surrounds the front of the bolt head and provides a good seal at the breech. Neither the face of the barrel (chamber), nor the bolt head is recessed for the cartridge head. Since the cartridge rim is nearly the same diameter as the bolt head, the head is so

---

* These first official Lee-design rifles had barrels cut with Metford's segmental, shallow-land rifling. The Cordite powder then used was highly corrosive, soon ruining the Metford barrels. Enfield rifling — essentially similar to today's standard rifling, and a Metford design too, in fact—offered much deeper, and somewhat wider, lands to the hot powder gases. Barrel life was considerably extended.

Illustrated above: British SMLE Mark III rifle, which later became the No. 1 Mark III.

well sealed that a recess is not needed.

The center of the receiver is bored and milled to accept the two-piece bolt. The receiver bridge is slotted to allow passage of the right locking lug/guide rib and the extractor lug on the bolt head.

The heavy left wall of the receiver is slightly lower than the top of the receiver ring line. A shallow thumb notch is cut into it to aid in loading the rifle from the top through the opened action. The right wall is milled much lower than the left, providing ample opening for loading and ejection.

The receiver bridge is slotted through. It is, however, bridged over by the narrow clip-charger guide bridge over the middle of the receiver, connecting the high left wall with the low right wall. It appears that this clip-charger bridge was made from a separate piece of metal, then afterward forged to become integral with the receiver. The top front of this bridge is grooved to accept the .303 British stripper clip.

The two-piece bolt has a separate bolt head threaded into the front of the bolt body. The small hooked extractor fits in a slot through a lug on the bolt head, and is held in place by, and pivots on, a screw through the underside of the lug. A small but sturdy flat V-spring tensions the extractor. The extractor easily snaps over the rim of a cartridge placed in the chamber.

The bolt has dual-opposed locking lugs located slightly to the rear of its center. The left (bottom) locking lug engages in a recess milled into the left wall of the receiver bridge. The long guide rib on the right (top) of the bolt is also the right locking lug—it engages forward of the receiver bridge wall, on the right. Both lugs are solid and the rear locking surface of each is slightly angled to cam the bolt forward as it rotates to the fully locked position. In addition, the front surface of the left lug is also angled to match the surface in its locking recess. This provides the initial extraction power when the bolt handle is raised. The bolt handle, at the extreme rear end of the bolt, has a tapered square-to-round stem that ends in a round grasping ball. When the bolt is closed and locked, the bolt handle lies against the

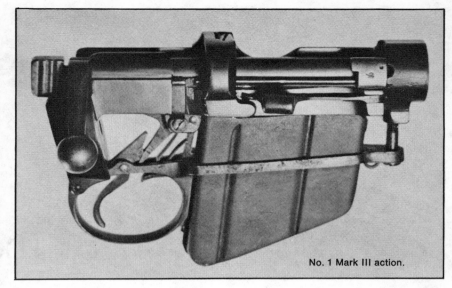

No. 1 Mark III action.

butt socket of the receiver, with the grasping ball only slightly away from the side of the rifle. There is no auxiliary locking lug on the bolt.

The bolt head does not turn with the bolt. As the bolt is fully closed, the threads of the bolt head draw it against the front of the bolt—so the thrust of firing is not placed on the threads. The large lug on the bolt head housing the extractor also acts as the bolt stop when it contacts the receiver bridge wall as the bolt is opened. A lip under the outside edge of the extractor lug fits over a groove cut into the top edge of the right receiver wall and this keeps the bolt head from turning as the bolt is operated. This groove ends short of the receiver bridge wall. When the bolt is fully open the extractor lug can be pulled up and rotated into a slot in the receiver bridge—the bolt can then be removed. A small spring retainer, provided in the right side of the receiver extractor-lug groove, engages with the lip under the extractor lug when the bolt is fully drawn back. It prevents the bolt head from turning under normal operation of the bolt, yet allows the bolt head to be rotated manually to remove the bolt from the action.

The firing mechanism consists of a one-

piece firing pin, coil mainspring and cocking piece. The bolt is drilled from the front, with the mainspring compressed between a collar on the front of the firing pin and a rear shoulder in the bolt body. The rear end of the firing pin is threaded into the cocking piece. A screw at the rear of the cocking piece prevents the firing pin from turning. Forward travel of the firing pin is stopped when the collar on the firing pin contacts the back of the bolt head, not by the cocking piece contacting the rear of the bolt.

An arm or tongue on the bottom of the cocking piece extends forward under the bolt body, into a raceway milled in the receiver where it engages the sear and safety projecting into this raceway. The action cocks on closing the bolt, the sear engaging the front of the cocking piece arm and holding it back as the bolt is closed. The head of the cocking piece may be round and knurled, or flat and notched. There is also a half-cock notch (called "half-bent" notch in England) on the arm of the cocking piece; by firmly grasping the cocking piece it can be lowered from the cocked position or drawn back from the fired position to engage the sear in this intermediate position. This locks the bolt

Top view of the No. 1 Mark III action showing cutoff pulled out; the bolt will pick up cartridges from the magazine as the bolt is operated.

Left side view of the No. 1
Mark III Lee-Enfield action.

and the sear. To fire the rifle in this half-cock position, the cocking piece must be manually pulled back to full cock. Originally designed as a safety measure, the half-cock notch serves no useful purpose. There is also a small stud or cam on top of the cocking piece arm which engages a notch cut in the rear of the bolt body. On raising the bolt handle with the action closed and the striker down, the notch engages the stud and pushes the cocking piece and firing pin back. The purpose of this arrangement is to prevent the firing pin from going fully forward unless the bolt is locked. In other words, the Lee-Enfield action cannot be fired unless the bolt handle is nearly all the way down and the action locked.

The safety is at the left rear side of the receiver. A flattened integral stud on the safety projects into the cocking piece raceway. Two shallow notches cut into the left bottom edge of the cocking piece arm can engage the safety when it is swung back. These notches are so spaced that one or the other is opposite the safety when the rifle is cocked or uncocked. When the action is cocked, the safety locks both the striker and bolt; when uncocked it locks the bolt and pulls the firing-pin tip within

the bolt head so that a blow on the cocking piece cannot discharge the rifle.

The bolt is locked by a small part threaded on the stem of the safety. The thread is multi-threaded and left hand. Part of this bolt lock extends through the receiver wall to engage in a groove cut into the rear of the bolt body. As the safety is swung back, the threads force the bolt lock toward the right to engage a groove in the bolt and lock it. A spring bracket screwed to the receiver holds the safety in place. (In England and perhaps elsewhere, the part which I call the "safety"—the part which actually locks the striker—is called the "locking bolt," and the part I call the "bolt lock," which actually locks the bolt, is called the "safety catch.")

The sear, an L-shaped piece of metal, is held in place by, and pivots on, a screw under the receiver. This screw also holds the bolt-head release spring. It is under tension from a flat V-spring positioned between the sear and magazine catch which also supplies tension to these parts. The trigger pivots on a pin in the trigger guard. The curved trigger is grooved; its top part, which contacts the sear, has two humps which provide the common double-

stage military pull.

The detachable staggered-column box magazine, of 10-round capacity, is made from heavy-gauge sheet metal. The follower has a raised rib on its left side which causes the cartridges to lie staggered in the magazine. The follower is tensioned by a W-shaped spring. Curved lips at the front and rear of the magazine opening hold the cartridges in the magazine.

The magazine box, positioned in the milled-out bottom of the receiver by the trigger guard/magazine plate, is held up by the magazine latch. Partial cartridge-guide lips, milled into both sides of the magazine well, hold and guide the cartridges into the chamber as they are fed out of the magazine by the bolt. The magazine can be single loaded whether in or out of the rifle, or it can be loaded with a stripper clip while in the rifle.

The No. 1 SMLE action has a cartridge cutoff, a flat triangular piece of metal positioned in a slot milled in the right receiver wall. It pivots on a screw through the bottom front edge of the receiver. Pushed in (engaged) the cutoff slides over the cartridges in the magazine, so the bolt can be closed without picking up a cartridge. This allows single-round loading, holding the cartridges in the magazine in reserve. Pulled out, the cutoff is inoperative, letting the bolt pick up the top-most cartridge in the magazine as it is closed.

The ejector is merely a small stud screw threaded into the left receiver wall. When the bolt is opened, the extracted case or cartridge slides along the inside wall of the receiver until its head strikes the end of the ejector screw—the bolt nearly all the way open. This tips the case to the right, out of the action.

A gas-escape hole in the bolt head vents any powder gases which might enter the firing-pin hole in the case of a pierced primer. It vents the gases upward along the edge of the left receiver wall. There is another small oblong gas-escape hole in the left side of the receiver ring, in line with the space occupied by the cartridge rim between the face of the bolt and barrel. There is also a notch cut into the rear of the receiver ring, just ahead of the ex-

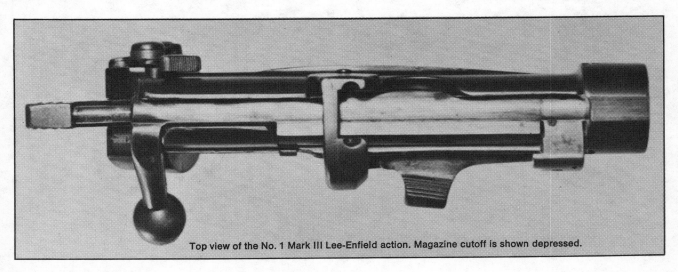

Top view of the No. 1 Mark III Lee-Enfield action. Magazine cutoff is shown depressed.

British Lee-Enfield No. 5 Mark I Jungle Carbine.

tractor lug on the bolt head; this space, and the oblong hole opposite it, should expel any gases escaping from a ruptured case head.

A new system of model designation was introduced in May, 1926. The SMLE Mark III became the No. 1 Rifle, Mark III. The Pattern 1914 Rifle (known in the U.S. as the 1917 Enfield) became the No. 3 Rifle. The No. 4 Rifle, Mark I, was a development of the SMLE Mark VI.

The No. 1 Lee-Enfield (also known as the SMLE, for Short Magazine Lee-Enfield), introduced shortly after 1900, underwent many changes before the No. 4 Lee-Enfields were introduced about 1939. We are not concerned here with the many minor changes in the action since it remained structurally the same. Officially, as each change was adopted, the model designation was changed, beginning with Mark I and continuing to Mark VI and including such asterisk or "starred" (*) designations as the Mark I*, etc., etc. The No. 1 action itself remained substantially the same for over 30 years and, since it was made in large quantities, it is the most common one encountered today.

The No. 4 Lee-Enfield Action

Little development was done on the Lee-Enfield rifle after WW I since the rifle and action had proved reliable during that conflict. Nor was there much need to make many additional rifles—at least not until WW II loomed into sight. However, it had been previously found that the rifle could be simplified and improved, and the action made somewhat stronger. The development work done accordingly was toward making the rifle more accurate, simpler and stronger. For example, it was found that the rifle gave better accuracy with an aperture sight mounted on the receiver, and that there was no real need for the magazine cutoff. Thus, in the late 1930s, when the British again needed rifles, they adopted the Mark VI, a simplified and improved version that became the No. 4 Lee-Enfield.

Here are some of the changes adopted:

1) The cutoff was eliminated, the machining for it omitted. This left the right receiver wall stronger than before, simplified and stiffened the action, left more metal in the right wall to support the right locking lug.

2) The bridge was made a bit higher so that a leaf aperture sight could be mounted.

3) The front of the bridge was also made a bit higher, so that a connecting strip of metal joining these projections formed a much smaller and neater clip-charger guide bridge.

4) The thumb notch in the left receiver wall was made shallower, further strengthening the receiver.

5) The bolt head was altered, as well as the method by which it was guided and retained. The extractor lug was made smaller and, instead of engaging over the edge of the right receiver wall, it moved in a groove cut inside the wall. On early No. 4 actions a plunger type bolt head release, fitting in a mortise cut into the receiver, could be depressed to release the bolt head. Later, this release was omitted; instead, a notch cut out of the bolt head groove in the front of the right receiver wall allowed the bolt head to be rotated at this point for removal of the bolt from the action. With this change the rifle became the No. 4 Mark 1*.

6) The safety shape was changed and a new safety spring used, eliminating the safety washer.

7) The left side of the bolt head was made flat to allow a greater amount of powder gases to escape out of the bolt head hole and past the receiver wall. The gas-escape hole in the left of the receiver was enlarged and made round.

In addition to the above, a groove was milled in the right locking lug/guide rib to make the bolt lighter. There are a number of changes in the configuration of the receiver which were the result of eliminating or simplifying the machining operations:

On late No. 4s the trigger was pivoted in the receiver instead of in the trigger guard. The No. 4 actions in which the trigger was pivoted in a bracket brazed on to the butt socket became the Mark 1/2. Later, when the brazed-on bracket was eliminated and the trigger pivoted directly to the butt socket, the designation was changed to Mark 1/3.

The No. 5 Lee-Enfield Jungle Carbine has the same action as the No. 4.

Take-Down and Assembly

Make certain the rifle is unloaded. Remove the magazine by lifting up magazine latch in the trigger guard and pull magazine out of action.

Disassemble magazine by depressing the

No. 1 Mark III Lee-Enfield action open, shown with stock bolt.

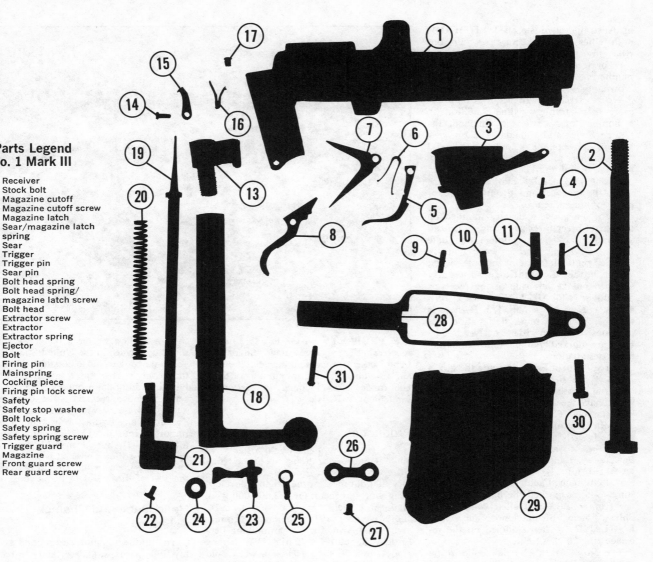

Parts Legend
No. 1 Mark III

1. Receiver
2. Stock bolt
3. Magazine cutoff
4. Magazine cutoff screw
5. Magazine latch
6. Sear/magazine latch spring
7. Sear
8. Trigger
9. Trigger pin
10. Sear pin
11. Bolt head spring
12. Bolt head spring/ magazine latch screw
13. Bolt head
14. Extractor screw
15. Extractor
16. Extractor spring
17. Ejector
18. Bolt
19. Firing pin
20. Mainspring
21. Cocking piece
22. Firing pin lock screw
23. Safety
24. Safety stop washer
25. Bolt lock
26. Safety spring
27. Safety spring screw
28. Trigger guard
29. Magazine
30. Front guard screw
31. Rear guard screw

rear of the follower until its front end slips out of magazine box, then gently lift follower and follower spring out. Reassemble in reverse order.

Remove bolt from the No. 1 Mark III by raising bolt handle and pulling the bolt back as far as it will go; then rotate bolt head by lifting up on the extractor lug, and the bolt can be pulled from the action. To remove bolt from the early No. 4 rifle, first tip up rear sight, depress bolt head release and open bolt as far as it will go; now rotate bolt head counterclockwise and pull the bolt from receiver. On the late No. 4, open bolt and pull it back about ½", or until the bolt head can be rotated, then pull bolt from the receiver.

To disassemble the bolt unscrew bolt head, remove extractor screw, then pull out extractor spring. Turn out firing-pin lock screw from the cocking piece. Using the special tool shown, insert it into the front of bolt and, while pressing the firing pin down with this tool, unscrew firing pin from cocking piece. Reassemble in reverse order.

Remove the safety mechanism by turning out safety-spring screw and lifting safety-spring and safety parts from receiver. If the bolt lock is removed from the

safety, it must be re-aligned on the threads so that it will fit the hole in receiver with safety in forward (FIRE) position.

Remove buttstock by opening buttplate trap, removing felt wad that covers stock bolt head; use a large, long-bladed screwdriver to unscrew stock bolt. Remove trigger guard/magazine plate by removing rear and front trigger-guard screws, then lift it out of fore-end. Remove muzzle cap and barrel bands, then gently pull fore-end away from barrel and action.

On the No. 1 Mark III turn out magazine cutoff screw and remove cutoff. Drive out magazine-catch pin and remove catch and spring. Turn out bolt-head release-spring screw and remove release spring and sear. Reassemble in reverse order.

On the No. 4, turn out magazine-catch screw and remove bolt-head release stop, bolt head release, bolt-head release spring, magazine catch and spring. Drive out sear pin and remove sear. Drive out trigger pin and remove trigger. Reassemble in reverse order.

Markings

The No. 1 Mark III & III*: After assembly each rifle was proved by firing two

proof loads, these developed about 25% more breech pressure than the normal load. After inspection, if nothing was wrong with the rifle, British proof marks were stamped on the breech end of the barrel, receiver ring, bolt head and bolt body. The serial number was usually stamped on the barrel breech, receiver and stem of the bolt handle. The rest of the markings, stamped on the right side of the butt socket, include a proof mark, manufacturer, date and model designation as follows: A crown with the letters **G.R.** was stamped on top. Below this the name or initials of the manufacturer was stamped; such as **ENFIELD** (for the Royal Small Arms Factory at Enfield Lock, Middlesex, England), **B.S.A.Co.** (Birmingham Small Arms Co., Birmingham, England) or **L.S.A.Co.** (London Small Arms Co., of London); below this and over the model designation would be the date (year) the rifle was made, as follows:

S^{HT}L.E.
III (or III*)

The letters "S^{HT}L.E." mean "Short Lee-Enfield." The No. 1 rifles made in India were stamped **ISHAPORE**, those made in Australia were stamped **LITHGOW**, both cities in those countries. Various rifle parts also are stamped with inspector's or viewer's marks, which may be a number, a letter or both, often with a crown.

No. 4 Rifles were all made under more-or-less trying wartime conditions in a number of factories in England, the United States and Canada. The marking systems so were many and varied and I can't list them all. To begin with, most No. 4s were proof marked, serial numbered and dated, generally marked with the model designation and the name and/or place of manufacture.

Proof marks were usually stamped on the barrel breech, receiver ring, bolt head and bolt body. Serial number and date (year) of manufacture were usually stamped on the left side of the butt socket.

The model designation was usually stamped on the left side of the receiver, as follows: N° **4 MK I**, N° **4 MK I***, N° **4 MK 1/2**, or N° **4 MK 1/3**. If there is a "(T)" after the mark designation this indicates the sniper rifle. The No. 5 Carbines are marked **"No. 5"**, followed by the mark designation.

Three firms in England made the No. 4 rifles. These firms were assigned blocks of serial numbers so that no two rifles would have the same number. The number was stamped (or sometimes etched) on the left side of the butt socket. Rifles marked with a **FY** or **ROF(F)** were from the Royal Ordnance Factory at Fazakerley, Lancashire, while those with an **M, RM** or **ROF(M)** came from the Royal Ordnance Factory at Maltby, Yorkshire. Those marked **B, 85B** or **M 47** are from a BSA-controlled company in Shirley, near Birmingham. The word **ENGLAND** is often stamped on the receiver ring of these rifles.

The No. 4 Mark I* rifles made in the Long Branch arsenal near Toronto, Canada, were marked **LONG BRANCH** on the left side of the receiver. Rifles made in the U.S. by the Savage Arms Company (in the former J. Stevens Arms Co. plant in Chicopee Falls, Mass.) were stamped

Lee-Enfield No. 4 Mark I action.

U.S. PROPERTY on the left side of the receiver. (They were made under the Lend-Lease arrangement between the U.S. and England.) The serial number of these U.S.-made rifles includes the letter **C,** for Chicopee Falls.

Production

A great many Lee-Enfield rifles were made. Hundreds of thousands of the No. 1 rifles were made at Enfield Lock, the factory that did most of the original development work on them. Over 2,000,000 were made at Enfield between August, 1914, and November, 1918. The large Birmingham Small Arms firm began making Lee-Enfields about 1903. During WW I, they made some 7000 to 10,000 a week, and during WW II they made about 1,250,000 of the No. 4 rifles. The factories in Australia made over 640,000 Lee-Enfields. Over 1,000,000 No. 4 rifles, including about 1000 sniper rifles, were made in the Long Branch arsenal in Canada. More

than a million of the No. 4s were also made by Savage in the United States. This accounts for around 6,000,000 rifles, but that's only part of the total production. I have no additional production figures, nor serial number records, so I can't even guess how many were made in all. Nor do I have any figures on how many were imported into the U.S. as surplus arms after WW II, but it probably runs into hundreds of thousands. At least there are enough of them in the United States and the rest of the world to last a long time.

Headspace and Chamber Tolerances

To cut down manufacturing and assembly time, perhaps, and certainly to reduce maintenance time later on when headspace corrections were needed, a new headspacing system was introduced with the No. 4 rifles. It was a simple system, made possible by the two-piece bolt with separate bolt head. It consisted of making

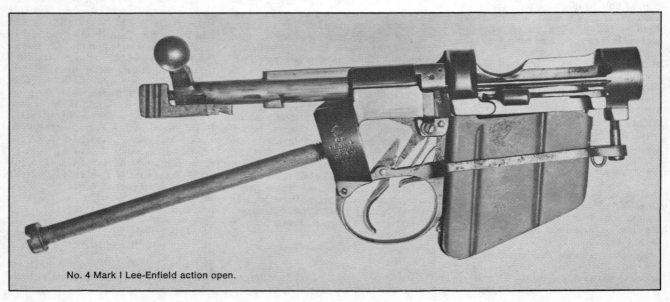

No. 4 Mark I Lee-Enfield action open.

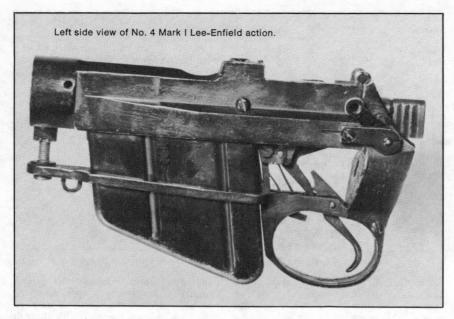
Left side view of No. 4 Mark I Lee-Enfield action.

Gunsmithing the Lee-Enfield

Both No. 1 and No. 4 rifles can be remodeled into fine sporting rifles for hunting big game. For most big game hunting, in my opinion, few cartridges are better than the .303 British. Underneath the wood handguard is a slim tapered barrel of the most pleasing contour, ideal in weight for a sporter. The action is reliable, strong and easy to operate, smoother, too, than many other military turnbolt actions. The action has a good safety and a low, well-positioned bolt handle. Shortening the barrel, installing the sights of your choice, remodeling the issue stock, or installing a new sporter stock and fore-end, is about all that is needed to turn these rifles into sporters. Other things can be done to make the Lee-Enfield into a deluxe sporter, but whether you want a plain or deluxe job, the "makings" are there.

I don't think, though, that it's practical to spend a lot of time and money to build a deluxe Lee-Enfield sporter for several reasons. First; it is much easier to remake the rifle or carbine into an open-sighted rough-and-ready, spare, second or loanout rifle. The No. 5 Carbine, usually called the "Jungle Carbine," is such a rifle as is. It is perhaps the best choice of any military rifle to use pretty much as issued for hunting. The buttstock is rather short for many shooters, and the comb is very low, but putting on a low-cost Fajen or Bishop buttstock will correct these problems—and all you need is a large and long screwdriver to install it. A new fore-end is as easy to install, but the issue fore-end on the No. 5 is acceptable the way it is.

Because it has a longer barrel, the No. 1 rifle makes a better looking sporter. I suggest shortening the barrel to 22 or 24 inches, then installing such open sights as the Williams Guide rear sight, and a bead or blade front sight mounted on the Williams sweat-on or screw-on ramp base. If you'd rather have a receiver sight I'd recommend the Williams Foolproof sight. For the No. 4 Lee-Enfield, I suggest the Redfield adaptor bracket and their receiver sight, since no drilling and tapping is required.

After the barrel has been shortened and the sights installed the No. 1 or No. 4 sporter can be completed by installing a new sporter stock and fore-end. They are furnished by several stock firms. To im-

the bolt heads of different lengths to obtain and maintain proper headspace; in the .303 Lee-Enfield rifle this is the space between the face of the bolt head and the barrel face.

The bolt heads, made in 4 different lengths, were numbered from "0" to "3." No. 0 head was the shortest; No. 1 was .003" longer than No. 0; No. 2 was .003" longer than the No. 1, and the No. 3 was .003" longer than the No. 2 head. During factory assembly, a bolt head was fitted which gave normal headspace of .064" to .074". These figures represent minimum and maximum allowable headspace. If, after much use, headspace increased, a new bolt head could be installed to decrease headspace by .003", .006", etc. Bolt heads of the No. 4 rifles were marked with the qualifying number on the extractor lug.

To the consternation of many handloaders, No. 4 rifles were often found to have overly large chambers—that is, longer than need be to accept commercial .303 British cartridges. These wartime chambers were purposely made large so that the rifles would function properly even with dirty, corroded or slightly damaged ammunition. While most Lee-Enfield military rifles have "maximum" chambers, most No. 4 rifles (as well as the No.

5 carbines) seem to have chambers much larger than normal maximum, so large that the fired cases show pronounced body enlargement, with body splits not uncommon. Manufacturing tolerances for both rifles and ammunition were generous during the war, which in no way affected the rifle for military use, or even for sporting use. A large chamber, however, is not desirable in a target rifle, so it was a problem for many handloaders, since their cases seldom lasted over two or three reloadings before they'd separate.

Case separation is generally caused by over-working the brass, by repeated full-length resizing. Shooters often blame excessive headspace for case separation (and it may be partly to blame in some rifles) but even in a rifle with minimum or zero headspace, too-frequent full length resizing is the real cause of case separation. The Lee-Enfield reloader should A) get a full length sizing die tailored to his rifle's chamber; RCBS can supply these if several fired cases are sent to them. B) Resize the case just enough to let it enter the chamber with a touch of effort. C) Neck size only, assuming that cases so-worked will enter the chamber without undue force. Other than this, the only positive solution is to set the barrel back and rechamber it, or install a new barrel with a normal chamber.

Top view of the No. 4 Mark I action.

prove the looks of the rifle, the metal can be polished bright and then reblued. A lot of these rifles have Parkerized metal. If you like this matt surface but dislike the color, the parts can be reblued without doing any polishing. To remove the Parkerized finish it will have to be polished off. Some No. 4 rifles have a dark, painted-on finish, which can be removed with coarse emery cloth in the first step in making the metal smooth.

Altered 5-shot magazines for the Lee-Enfield are available from several firms handling military surplus goods, or the regular 10-shot magazine can be cut down. Cut off the bottom part of the magazine, which projects below the stock, and weld or silver solder on a new bottom plate made from a piece of heavy sheet metal.

To make the receiver a bit trimmer, the clip-charger guide bridge can be cut off entirely. This will not weaken the action to any noticeable extent. The magazine cutoff on the No. 1 actions should be discarded.

Lee-Enfields are not ideally suited for use with a scope sight. However, a hunting scope can be mounted on No. 4 and No. 5 rifles with one of the several commercial scope mounts from Weaver, Williams, Buehler, Redfield and S&K. The S&K is the easiest to install since no drilling and tapping are required. The Williams is a side mount, as is the Buehler. The Buehler places the scope slightly off-

The No. 4 (left) and No. 1 Mark III (right) Lee-Enfield bolt heads.

set to the left. The Redfield mount is for their long eye-relief scope, designed for mounting on the barrel ahead of the action. This seems to be the only mount suitable for the No. 1 Lee-Enfield.

I have often been asked about the feasibility of restocking the Lee-Enfield with a one-piece stock. A couple of my friends stocked their Lee-Enfields in this manner, but after I saw the work involved my advice is—*don't attempt it!* On one rifle, the owner cut away practically all of the metal butt socket, relocated the trigger, installed a Mauser M98 type magazine box, then inletted the reworked barreled action into a stock blank. The final result was satisfactory, but certainly not worth all the work. The other owner only cut away the sides of the metal butt socket and then inletted the barreled action into a stock blank. He retained the original trigger guard and magazine. The final result was not very satisfactory because the sides of the stock over the action were so thin as to leave the stock very weak at this point. The Ellwood Epps shop in Clinton, Ontario, does this one-piece stock conversion.

Rechambering and Rebarreling

Lee-Enfield rifles offer no rechambering possibilities. There is the .303 British Improved cartridge, a blown-out, sharp-shouldered version of the standard .303, but rechambering the Lee-Enfield for it is not advisable. (The .303 British P-14 Enfield rifle, which has a stronger action than the Lee-Enfield, however, is suitable for this rechambering.)

I continually get letters from shooters who would like to build a .45-70 or some other bigbore caliber bolt action rifle, many of them wanting to know if the Lee-Enfield action would serve their purpose. Well, the forerunner of the Lee-Enfield, the Remington-Lee rifle, was made in

Lee-Enfield firing pin removal tool.

.125" 3" .218" .250" .406"

Below—British Lee-Enfield bolt showing: (A) bolt head; (B) extractor; (C) bolt head lug which houses the extractor and extractor spring; (D) bolt guide rib/locking lug; (E) cocking piece; (F) left locking lug and (G) gas vent hole in the bolt head.

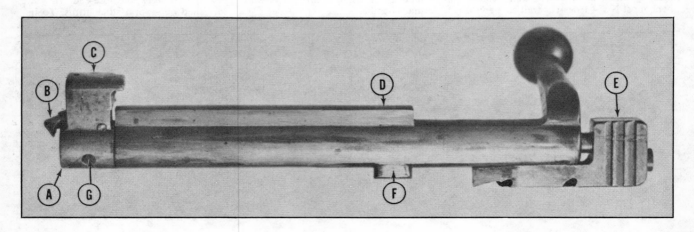

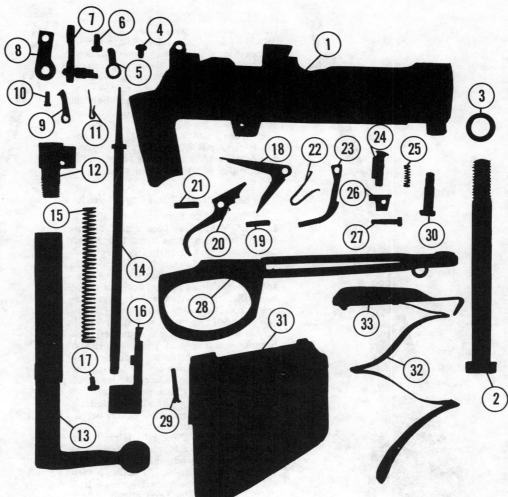

Parts Legend
No. 4 Mark I

1. Receiver
2. Stock bolt
3. Stock bolt washer
4. Ejector
5. Bolt lock
6. Safety spring screw
7. Safety
8. Safety spring
9. Extractor
10. Extractor screw
11. Extractor spring
12. Bolt head
13. Bolt
14. Firing pin
15. Mainspring
16. Cocking piece
17. Firing pin lock screw
18. Sear
19. Sear pin
20. Trigger
21. Trigger pin
22. Sear/magazine latch spring
23. Magazine latch
24. Bolt head release
25. Bolt head release spring
26. Bolt head release stop
27. Magazine latch screw
28. Trigger guard
29. Rear guard screw
30. Front guard screw
31. Magazine box
32. Follower spring
33. Follower

Dimensional Specifications

Weight
No. 1 ....49 oz.
No. 4 ....52 oz.
Over-all length ....7.50"
Receiver ring dia.
No. 1 ....1.270"
No. 4 ....1.305"
Bolt body dia. ....580"
Bolt travel ....3.575"
Striker travel ....775"
Bolt face (no recess) ....Flat

Below—All Lee-Enfield bolts have separate
bolt heads, the bolt head threading into the
bolt body. Shown here is a No. 4 bolt head,
unscrewed from the bolt body.

General Specifications

Type	Turnbolt repeater.
Receiver	One-piece machined steel forging with slotted main bridge. The forward part of the main bridge is built over to form a narrow bridge for the clip-charger guide.
Bolt	Two-piece, with separate non-rotating bolt head. Dual-opposed locking lugs on the rear of the bolt.
Ignition	One-piece firing pin powered by a coil mainspring. Cocks on closing bolt.
Magazine	Detachable, staggered-column, 10-round box.
Trigger	Non-adjustable double-stage military type pull.
Safety	Lever type at left rear of receiver, locks striker and bolt when swung back. Striker can also be placed in "half-cock" or "safe" position manually; see text.
Extractor	Non-rotating hook type positioned in bolt head; separate spring.
Magazine cutoff	Cutoff provided on No. 1 Mark III, none on No. 4 or 5.
Bolt stop	No separate bolt stop; extractor housing on bolt head acts as bolt stop. See text.
Ejector	Stud screw threaded into left receiver wall.
Stock fastening	Buttstock attached to receiver by a through-bolt.

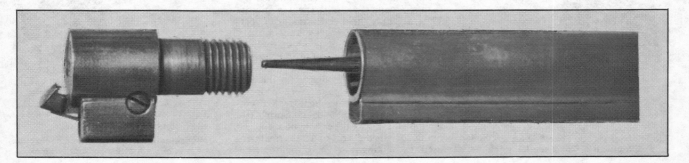

.45-70, and the No. 1 and No. 4 Lee-Enfield actions, with some alterations, could be adapted and rebarreled to handle this cartridge. With similar modifications the No. 4 action would also be suitable for the .444 Marlin cartridge. Whether this rebarreling would be practical or not is something else, much depending on how much of the work you can do yourself.

I strongly advise against using any Lee-Enfield action for rebarreling to any one of the wildcat cartridges based on the .303 British or .30-40 Krag case.

The Lee-Enfield for Target Work

In England, Canada and Australia the Lee-Enfield has long been used for competitive target shooting, a sport for which these rifles have been highly developed. Parker-Hale, Ltd., (Golden Hillcock Rd., Sparksbrook, Birmingham 11, England) still offers a line of target accessories for this rifle, including the best precision-made receiver sights. Since the 7.62mm NATO (.308) is now the standard military cartridge of these countries, and because the supply of good .303 British target ammunition is no longer plentiful, many target shooters are converting the No. 4 rifles to the 7.62mm. At least one firm in England (there may be others) offers a conversion kit, which includes a threaded and chambered 7.62mm barrel, magazine, extractor, ejector and clip-slot adaptor. In fact, if the rifle is used as a single shot, only a barrel is needed, and any competent barrelsmith can do the job. Only the No. 4 (or No. 5) action is suitable for 7.62mm rebarreling, since it is the strongest of the Lee-Enfields.

Comments

During the many years that rifle mechanisms have interested me, I've read and heard much praise and criticism of the Lee-Enfield action and rifle, with devotees and critics equally vehement. While I don't want to enter into this debate, I will make some comments.

Although the Lee turnbolt action system was of advanced design when James Paris Lee patented it in 1879, and when a modified version of it was adopted by Great Britain in 1888, it must be conceded that it was, along with the rimmed .303 British cartridge, outmoded by the Mauser system actions developed from 1893 to 1898. Regardless of this, the British, having made the choice, probably spent more time and money in experimenting and testing the Lee-Enfield rifle than any other country spent similarly. The fact that the Lee-Enfield rifle performed so well during its long military history proves without a doubt that the action is sound. Manufacturing specifications were quite rigid. The steel used in it was always the best available for the purpose. The various parts were properly machined, finished and heat-treated. Unlike the early Model 1903 Springfield actions, there was never any doubt about the quality of the steel and heat-treatment used in making the Lee-Enfield action.

No. 5 Mark I Lee-Enfield Jungle Carbine fitted with a Fajen sporter stock.

A remodeled No. 1 Mark III Lee-Enfield rifle. It is fitted with a Bishop sporter stock.

Generally, however, it is not material or manufacture that is criticized, but the design.

The two-piece stock design is often criticized, yet I think no other military bolt action rifle has a stronger buttstock attachment to the receiver. It is, perhaps, stronger than the Japanese Arisaka Type 99 rifle. The separate Lee-Enfield fore-end, though, has always given trouble. I believe, however, that if the butt socket had been designed with a front recess, so the rear of the fore-end could have been fitted inside it, and the barrel had been made a bit shorter and heavier from the start, bedding problems would have been largely eliminated.

The protruding sheet-metal magazine is also criticized. The British did not develop the Lee-Enfield for anything except military use, and I believe its magazine system is one of the best for military use. The magazine box was made rather light, but it was quickly detachable, and if it was damaged another one could be quickly inserted. For some military uses it probably was more convenient to carry extra loaded magazines than loose ammunition or ammunition in clips. Even though the magazine was detachable, for most military use it was left in place and loaded from the top through the action, either with clips or by pressing single cartridges into it. The large capacity was certainly desirable, and the fact that the magazine protruded below the bottom of the stock was of no disadvantage for military use since the point of balance of these rifles is forward of the magazine.

The Lee-Enfield action has more than ample strength for the .303 British cartridge. The two rear locking lugs are not only more than adequate to secure the bolt in the receiver, but keep the neces-sary bolt travel to a minimum. The threaded-in detachable bolt head is a good feature; it provided a good bolt stop, and a very convenient means to control headspace, as was done in the No. 4 rifles. The safety and trigger mechanisms are rugged and reliable. The extractor is good, but I believe it would have been a better design with a coil spring rather than a flat one since the extractor spring is about the only part subject to breakage. There was no need for the half-cock feature.* The action cocks on closing the bolt and is not liked by many shooters, but it's really not a drawback once a person gets used to its proper operation. This goes for the double-stage trigger pull as well.

The .303 British Cartridge

Like the Lee-Enfield rifles, the .303 British cartridge proved an excellent military round. The original military loading was with a 215-gr. bullet. The standard .303 British ball loading from 1910 used a 174-gr. pointed full-jacketed bullet at a muzzle velocity of 2440 fps.

Not long after its adoption in 1888, the .303 cartridge became a very popular sporting round. It was used throughout the British Empire on all kinds of game; tigers in India, small antelope to elephants in Africa, crocodiles to water buffalo in Australia, and deer to moose in Canada. Much of this shooting was done with the regular unmodified Lee-Enfield military rifle, but many double-barreled rifles chambered for it were the choice of more affluent sportsmen. Winchester chambered their Model 95 lever-action rifle for the .303 British cartridge, making the rifle popular in Canada.

For the most part, the only .303 British sporting loads available for many years were the 215-gr. soft point for use on thin-skinned animals and the 215-gr. full-metal cased bulleted load for thick-skinned game. Both had about 2010 fps muzzle velocity. Remington, Peters and Norma still furnish the 215-gr. soft point load, at 2180 fps, with remaining energy at 200 yards of some 1300 ft. lbs. Remington, Norma, Winchester and Federal also furnish a 180-gr. soft-point load, MV about 2540 fps, 200-yard energy 1750. Norma also loads the .303 British with a 130-gr. semi-pointed bullet at about 2790 fps, and a 150-gr. bullet at 2720. Depending on which load gives the best accuracy in an individual rifle, the 150- or 180-gr. loads would be best for such game as antelope or deer, while the 215-gr. SP would be better for such larger game as elk and moose. The .303 British cartridge is in the same power class as the .30-40 Krag and .300 Savage. It should not be confused with the smaller .303 Savage cartridge, nor is the .303 British inter-changeable with any other cartridge, although its case is nearly the same as the .30-40.

The .303 British cartridge is reloadable, though the Berdan primer used in many of them is a nuisance. It uses standard .303 (.311"-.312" diameter) bullets. Lee-Enfield barrels have a left-hand rifling twist of one turn in 10 inches; bore (land) diameter is .303", groove diameter about .314". Most barrels have 5 grooves, although some late-manufactured No. 4 rifles may have 2-groove barrels. The No. 4 rifles made by Savage usually have 6-groove barrels.

---

* Nevertheless Reynolds (*op cit.*) says that demands from field units brought the half-cock feature back; that its lack was considered dangerous.

A fine example of superb gunsmithing on the No. 4 British Lee-Enfield rifle. Ellwood Epps (now retired) of Clinton, Ontario, Canada, fitted this Lee-Enfield with a fancy one-piece stock and a Weaver K-4 scope with Weaver detachable side mount.

NOTES

9. Italian Carcano Actions

THE CARCANO bolt action rifle was adopted by Italy in 1891 as her official military shoulder arm. Adopted with it was the 6.5mm Carcano cartridge, one of the first small-caliber smokeless military cartridges to be used by a major military power. The Model 1891 Carcano rifle and its various versions, and the 6.5mm cartridge, were in continual production and use until Italy's defeat in WW II. No doubt several million of these Carcanos were made in this long period (about 54 years). Returning American servicemen brought many home as souvenirs, but this number was a mere drop of water in a tub compared to the countless thousands dumped on the U.S. military surplus arms market since the late 1940s.

The Carcano action was developed jointly by Lt. Col. Salvatore Carcano and Col. G. Parravicino, both employed in the Torino (Turin) Arms Factory in Turin, Italy. Perhaps most of these rifles and carbines were made in Terni, but they were also made in Turin, Brescia, and Gardone in government or privately owned arsenals. The action, a turnbolt repeater with dual front locking lugs on the bolt, was copied from the Model 89 Mauser, but made with a single column box magazine of Mannlicher design. As a result of the various names and places connected with these arms, they have been called the Parravicino-Carcano, but they're now generally called the Mannlicher-Carcano, Italian Carcano, or Terni.

Carcano Markings

Markings are many and varied, and specific models are not always marked alike. The model designation is never stamped on the rifle, nor are the words "Carcano" or "Italy." Some receivers are entirely unmarked.

The serial number, usually beginning with one or two letters, may be stamped on the breech end of the barrel, on the receiver, or on both. The serial number,

or any part of it, is seldom stamped on any other part of the rifle.

There is usually an assortment of inspector's and/or proof marks stamped on the barrel breech, receiver, and bolt. Often unclear, they're not really important.

The name of the manufacturer, and/or the city where the rifle was made, is usually stamped on the receiver ring or on the breech end of the barrel. The marking **TERNI** indicates manufacture there by the Italian Army small arms arsenal. The marking **RE TERNI** stands for *Regio Esercito Terni,* which means **ARMY, TERNI.** The marking "F.N.A. Brescia" stands for *Fabbrica Naziionale d'Armi* (National Arms Factory) in the city of Brescia. The marking **BERETTA GARDONE** means manufacture by P. Beretta Arms Factory in Gardone, V.T., Italy.

The year of manufacture of many Carcanos is often stamped on the receiver ring. On others the date of manufacture may be stamped on the barrel breech, such as **01** for 1901. Most rifles produced during the Fascist regime were also marked with a Roman numeral, such as **XVI,** indicating manufacture in the 16th year of the regime.

Many Italian rifles were re-marked; for example, some are found marked **SPECIAL-GUARD-BAVARIA;** others carry the letters **SA** within a rectangle, which means "Suomen Armeija" or "Finnish Army." The Finns obtained these rifles from Italy during WW II for defense against Russia. No doubt there are Carcano rifles and carbines with other markings unknown to me at this writing.

Various Carcano rifle and carbine models were produced. Since they're all based on the same action, I'll describe the principal models briefly.

The first model was the 1891 Carcano rifle, its 30.8″ barrel adapted for a knife bayonet. Next came the M1891 Carcano carbine with a folding bayonet permanently attached to its 17.5″ barrel, and the M1891 TS carbine with a 17.5″-plus bar-

rel and detachable knife bayonet. There was also the Model 41 rifle with a 27″ barrel. All of these were made only in 6.5mm caliber.

In 1938 Italy adopted a new cartridge of larger caliber—the 7.35mm Carcano. It was based on the same case as the 6.5mm Carcano cartridge but with the neck expanded to hold the larger 7.35mm bullet. The rifles chambered for this cartridge were the M38 short rifle with a 21.1″ barrel and detachable bayonet, and the M38 carbine with a 17.5″-plus barrel. Italy, however, soon became involved in WW II and could not make a complete change-over to the new caliber, so it was dropped in favor of the older 6.5mm. As a result, many M38 rifles and carbines made for the 7.35mm cartridge were re-barreled for the 6.5mm load.

W.H.B. Smith, in his *The Book of Rifles* says that some M38 rifles were made in 7.92mm caliber (8x57mm Mauser) for use by Germany during WW II.

The 6.5mm Carcano rifle barrels were made with progressive or gain twist rifling; that is, the rate of twist gradually increasing from breech to muzzle. At the breech the twist was about one turn in 19″, increasing to about one turn in 8″ at the muzzle.

The 7.35mm Carcano barrels were made with a uniform rate of twist, one turn in 10″.

The Carcano Action

The Carcano is a relatively simple turnbolt, 6-shot repeating action having some Mauser and Mannlicher features, plus others found only in this action. Despite wide criticism leveled against it, the Carcano is a well designed and rugged action for military use since, presumably, the Italians did not have any major trouble

Illustrated above: Model 38 Italian Carcano Short Rifle, caliber 7.35mm.

with it or they would have changed the design.

The Carcano receiver appears to have started as a forging which was then milled and machined to final dimensions. The round receiver ring is quite large in diameter (1.335"), with only a small projection underneath to form the recoil shoulder. The inside of the receiver ring, threaded to receive the barrel shank, has a thin collar left in its center against which the breech end of the barrel abuts. The barrel breech is flat except for a thin ring which fits inside the receiver collar and around the head of the bolt. The rear of the receiver ring is milled to form locking recesses for the bolt lugs. There is more than ample metal at this point to securely support both locking lugs. In the lower left side, in the locking lug recess, a shelf of metal is retained which has a forward sloping surface. The angle of this surface matches a beveled corner on the left (upper) locking lug; on opening the bolt this arrangement provides the initial extraction camming power; on closing the bolt rapidly it helps to start the closing rotation of the bolt. The receiver walls behind the receiver ring are smaller in diameter than the ring; on the left side of the receiver there is a definite step, as in the large ring 98 Mauser action.

The left receiver wall is much higher than the right, and the high left wall lacks a thumb notch. A long opening is milled in the bottom of the receiver for the magazine. The rear half of this opening is wide enough to accept the cartridge clip, while the front half is only slightly wider than the body of the cartridge. The front end of this opening is sloped towards the chamber to form a loading ramp to raise and guide the cartridge from the magazine to the chamber. Cartridge feeding into the chamber is positive and reliable.

The receiver bridge is split or slotted at the top to allow passage of the bolt handle. The receiver ends in a top tang about 2.5" long.

Italian Model 91 Mannlicher-Carcano action (shown with loaded clip in place).

The trigger mechanism is mounted below the receiver bridge and tang. The sear attaches to the receiver, pivoting on a pin crosswise through a hole in the bottom of the bridge. A projection (made separately, but more or less permanently pinned in place) on the rear of the sear projects upward through a hole in the tang into a groove which is milled out for the sear notch to engage the cocking piece when the bolt is closed. The sear is tensioned by a coil spring positioned between recessed holes in the front of the sear and receiver. The trigger, attached to the sear, pivots on a pin through the sear. The upper part of the trigger, which bears against the bottom of the receiver, has twin humps which produce the two stage pull.

The ejector is a collared pin positioned over and inside the sear spring and extending upward through a hole in the receiver. A long tapering groove is cut into the front half of the bolt body to allow the ejector to rise, as the bolt is opened, to contact the head of the cartridge or case and eject it from the action. This appears to be a very efficient, though simple, arrangement.

The bolt stop is equally as efficient and simple as the ejector. It is a bar extending upward through a hole in the bottom right side of the receiver which projects into the right locking lug raceway in the receiver bridge. The bolt stop is attached to an arm on the trigger. Pulling the trigger back moves the bolt stop down so the bolt can be removed.

The bolt and bolt handle appear to have been machined from a one-piece forging, although the latter may have been permanently attached to the bolt by other means. The bolt handle is near the center of the bolt and, when the action is closed and locked, the heavy rectangular base of the bolt handle is forward of the receiver bridge, acting as a safety lug should the forward locking lugs fail. The shank of the bolt handle, round and quite thin, ends in a round grasping ball. On the Carcano rifles the bolt handle sticks straight out, but is bent down on the carbine.

The dual-opposed front lockings lugs are quite large and solid; neither has any slots or holes. The bolt face is recessed for the cartridge rim, but the rim of the recess is cut away one-fourth of its diameter for the extractor hook. Another quarter is cut away beyond the bottom of the extractor hook to allow the cartridge head to slip under the extractor hook when fed into

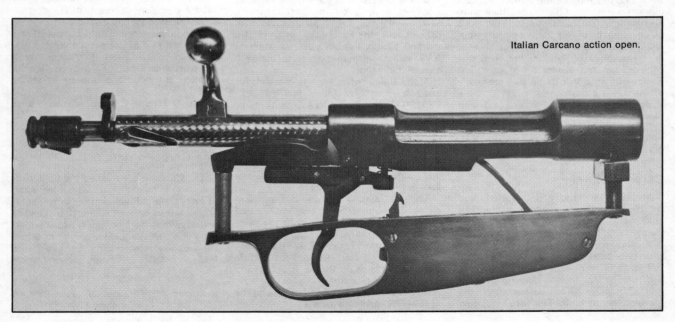
Italian Carcano action open.

Left side view of the Model 91 Italian Carcano action.

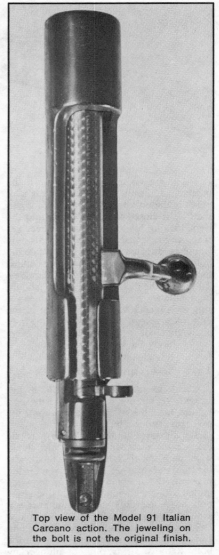
Top view of the Model 91 Italian Carcano action. The jeweling on the bolt is not the original finish.

the chamber from the magazine. This prevents double loading.

The one-piece spring steel extractor, about 2″ long, is mortised into the front of the bolt. A projection under the front end of the extractor fits in a slot in the bolt, preventing the extractor from pulling out. Cartridges normally slip under the extractor hook when being chambered from the magazine. Closing the bolt on a cartridge that is chambered ahead of the extractor (as in single loading the rifle by dropping a cartridge into the chamber) is difficult because the extractor hook is not made to slip easily over the cartridge rim.

The major parts of the firing mechanism are the firing pin, coil mainspring, firing pin nut, cocking piece and bolt sleeve. In addition, there is a spring and plunger in the cocking piece, the purpose of which is to prevent the firing pin nut from turning. The mainspring is compressed between a shoulder on the one-piece firing pin and the bolt sleeve which is backed by the cocking piece. All are retained on the firing pin by the firing pin nut, which threads on the rear of the firing pin. A flat spot on the firing pin matching a similar spot in the cocking piece prevents either part from turning on the other. A shoulder at the rear end of the firing pin prevents longitudinal movement of the firing pin in the cocking piece when the firing pin nut is fully tightened.

The bolt sleeve is usually defined as that part of the action which holds the firing mechanism in the bolt. In the Carcano action the bolt sleeve does this, but it also performs the function of a safety. A small lug on the front part of the bolt sleeve slides into a groove and notch cut into the rear of the bolt sleeve. When the action is cocked, the bolt sleeve is held forward by the lug engaging the notch, and heavy mainspring pressure holds it in this notch so that it rotates with the bolt. When the bolt is closed and the bolt handle down (it must be in this position or the rifle cannot be fired) part of the flange on the rear of the bolt sleeve is also engaged in a notch cut into the receiver tang. This keeps the bolt sleeve in place, and there is little chance of it being blown out even in the event of a severe primer rupture.

A deep cocking notch is cut into the rear of the bolt body, which the cocking cam on the cocking piece engages. The cocking cam, quite long, extends into the left locking lug raceway in the receiver bridge. When the striker is down, raising the bolt handle cocks the action.

To prepare the action for firing, the checkered safety wing on the bolt sleeve is positioned forward and to the right. To place the bolt sleeve (or safety—whatever you want to call it) in the "safe" position, it is pushed slightly forward and turned up. When this is done the bolt sleeve is partly released to move back against the cocking piece, relaxing the firing mechanism in the bolt. In this position the firing pin is held back, its tip held well within the bolt, so a blow on the cocking piece cannot fire the rifle. In this position the bolt is also locked, and cannot be opened.

To engage the safety it is necessary to grasp the bolt handle, while depressing and turning the safety (bolt sleeve), to prevent the bolt from opening. The bolt sleeve is under full mainspring tension and it is not easily operated. Moving the bolt sleeve on to "safe" calls for a strong thumb, but turning it again to the "fire" position is quite hard to do.

The action is securely held in the stock by two guard screws, these passing through holes in each end of the trigger guard/magazine, and thread into the tang and receiver ring. Stock bushings (or spacers) are used with each guard screw. The very small recoil shoulder on the receiver would be entirely inadequate to absorb the recoil if inletted directly into the stock. In the Carcano action recoil is taken up by a clever T-shaped stock bushing and spacer through which the front guard screw passes. The top of the "T" is a heavy metal bar about 1.20″ long and .40″ deep, its top grooved to fit the small lug on the receiver. With this T-bushing snugly bedded into the stock, and anchored between the trigger guard tang and the receiver by the guard screw, action set-back in the stock is hardly possible. In restocking this rifle I strongly suggest this T-bushing be used.

The trigger guard/magazine is made of a single piece of steel. The trigger guard bow is wide and heavy, the bow opening larger than needed. The thin-walled magazine box is an elongation of the guard bow bottom, thus extends well below the stock line. The single follower arm pivots on a pin through the lower front of the follower housing. It is given strong upward tension by a flat spring mortised in the follower housing. The follower housing closes the bottom front half of the magazine box and is in turn partly mortised in the magazine box and held in place by a screw. A special cartridge clip, holding up to 6 cartridges, must be used with the Carcano action if the rifle is to be shot as a repeater. The fully or partially loaded clip is inserted through the top of the open action, depressing the follower by the bottom cartridge. There is no top or bottom to the clip; it can be inserted either end first. When the clip is pressed down fully the spring-loaded magazine catch, located in the rear of the magazine box, engages it and holds it down. The bottom portion of the magazine box below the clip is open and when all the cartridges are fed out of the clip, it drops out. The fully or partly loaded clip can be released to pop up out of the open action by depressing the clip slightly and then depressing the magazine catch button in the front of the trigger guard.

Left—Model 91 Italian Carcano carbine, caliber 6.5mm. The barrel of this carbine has been increased to 18.50" by silver soldering a steel sleeve to the muzzle. Right—Italian Youth Carbine (minus the folding bayonet).

There are no gas-escape holes in the receiver, and only one small hole is provided in the bolt near the front end. When the bolt is closed this hole opens into the right locking lug raceway in the receiver ring. Any gases escaping through this hole would be directed backward alongside the bolt. This provision is sufficient unless the rifle is fired from the left shoulder. To make the action safer there should be a hole in the left side of the receiver ring to coincide with the under-cut in the bolt face recess. Without this hole any gases that got into the left lug raceway would surely be felt by the shooter.

Take-Down and Assembly

Check to make sure the rifle is unloaded. To remove the bolt raise the bolt handle, hold the trigger back and pull the bolt from the receiver.

To disassemble the bolt, first rotate the cocking piece one-quarter turn clockwise; with the thumbnail depress the firing pin nut plunger and unscrew firing pin nut; the cocking piece can now be pulled off the firing pin. Next, depress bolt sleeve (safety) slightly and rotate it a bit clockwise, allowing it to come back. Do this again and bolt sleeve, firing pin, and mainspring can be removed from the bolt. Remove firing pin nut plunger by driving out the cross pin. Remove extractor only if necessary. It is removed by raising the hooked end with a screwdriver until it can be moved forward. Since the stem of the extractor is usually wedged very tightly into the dovetail groove in the bolt, it may be necessary to drive the extractor forward with a pointed tool while the hook end is held up. Reassemble in reverse order.

To take the barrel and action from the stock remove barrel bands and the two guard screws. With barrel and action removed the sear, sear spring, ejector, bolt stop, and trigger can be removed by driving out the sear and trigger pin.

Pull trigger guard/magazine from the stock. Turn out clip latch screw, remove clip latch and spring. Turn out follower housing screw, drive the housing forward to remove it. Depress follower arm fully, insert a screwdriver blade in the slots in the sides of the housing to hold follower spring down, and remove follower pin and follower. Pull screwdriver out and follower spring can be removed. Reassemble in reverse order. Do not attempt to remove the barrel unless proper tools are available.

Carcano Action Strength

Many Carcano rifles may not be well-finished compared to M91 Mausers, but they're certainly finished better than most of the many Japanese Model 99 rifles I've seen, and far better than most WWII M98 Mausers. Carcano receivers are not always smoothly polished, and some concealed parts show no polish at all, but the bolts are generally well-machined and smooth. The receiver and bolt appear made of good steels and to be properly heat treated. Although the 6.5 and 7.35 Carcano military cartridges are only loaded to a maximum breech pressure of less than 38,000 psi, I believe Carcano actions are strong and safe enough to handle heavier loads. The 6.5 Mannlicher-Schoenauer cartridge is generally loaded to 40,000-45,000 psi and, in those 6.5 Carcano rifles rechambered for this cartridge, the actions seem to take these higher pressures in stride. However, in handloading Carcano cartridges I advise keeping loads moderate, not exceeding 40,000 psi.

The Carcano Clip

As noted before, a special clip must be used if the Carcanos are to function as repeaters. These clips, made of steel or brass, hold 6 rounds. Two crimped-in ridges, inside the back part of the clip, engage in the extractor groove of the cartridges to hold the rounds against the clip rear.

The receiver and the magazine box are milled out to accept the loaded clip, with shoulders left so it cannot move forward. This also holds the cartridges securely in the magazine so they cannot move forward from recoil. The ridges in the clip extend nearly to each end, allowing just enough room for cartridges to be inserted and removed (or fed out via the bolt) when the head of the cartridge is pressed against the curved lips of the clip. This is a good arrangement: the clip is easy to load; the fully loaded or partly loaded clip is easily inserted into the action (from the top with the bolt open); it is easily removed; feeding is in a straight line and reliable. The drawbacks are these: when the clip is emptied it drops out and is easily lost; without the clip the rifle can only be used as a single shot. Clips are still readily available at this writing, and both Italian 6.5mm and 7.35mm cartridges use the same clip.

Gunsmithing the Carcano

Carcano rifles are among the least desirable of all modern military bolt actions to remodel or sporterize, nor is the Carcano action a very good choice on which to build a rifle. I've already mentioned a couple of poor and undesirable features of the Carcano: the very awkward and hard-to-operate safety, and the necessity of using a clip. There are many more. The slotted receiver bridge prevents the installation of a regular receiver sight. No commercial replacement safety is made for this action, and there is no practical way the military safety can be altered to improve it. No replacement trigger is made for the action, although the military trigger can be improved. The box magazine extends below the stock and it isn't feasible to make it flush with the stock. The clip is too narrow to accept standard .30-06 head-size cartridges, so cartridge choice for rechambering or rebarreling is very limited. Until recently no commercial sporting loads were available, and now only the Norma 6.5mm Carcano cartridge is made as a sporting load. The military cases in both calibers use an odd-sized Berdan primer, not available to the handloader.

None of these objections has really bothered or stopped the enterprising amateur gunsmith from tackling them and working the rifle over into a sporter. Military loads in both calibers have been easily procurable, and it was common practice to pull the military bullets and seat the same weight (or lighter) soft point bullets. The 6.5 Carcano could be easily rechambered for the 6.5 Mannlicher-Schoenauer cartridge (the only readily available commercial cartridge with the Carcano head size), or the commercial cases of this cartridge resized or reformed into either the 6.5 or 7.35 Carcano cases. Now that Norma loads the 6.5 Carcano, the ammunition problem is largely solved, and 7.35 cases can be made from this brass by expanding the neck and trimming.

Rebarreling to another caliber, if the rifle is to remain a repeater, is also limited. The only popular U.S. cartridge I know of fitting the clip and action is the .35 Remington—the clip lips will have to be spread apart slightly, and the extractor hook honed down.

Even as a single shot, cartridge choice is limited because the bolt head and extractor are not easily adapted to cartridges with a rim smaller or larger than the .440"

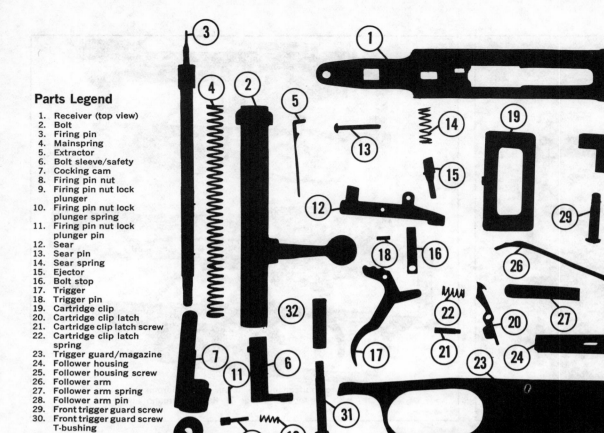

Parts Legend

1. Receiver (top view)
2. Bolt
3. Firing pin
4. Mainspring
5. Extractor
6. Bolt sleeve/safety
7. Cocking cam
8. Firing pin nut
9. Firing pin nut lock plunger
10. Firing pin nut lock plunger spring
11. Firing pin nut lock plunger pin
12. Sear
13. Sear pin
14. Sear spring
15. Ejector
16. Bolt stop
17. Trigger
18. Trigger pin
19. Cartridge clip
20. Cartridge clip latch
21. Cartridge clip latch screw
22. Cartridge clip latch spring
23. Trigger guard/magazine
24. Follower housing
25. Follower housing screw
26. Follower arm
27. Follower arm spring
28. Follower arm pin
29. Front trigger guard screw
30. Front trigger guard screw T-bushing
31. Rear trigger guard screw
32. Rear trigger guard screw (stock) bushing

Italian Carcano Model 91

Dimensional Specifications

Weight	45 oz.
Over-all length	8.625"
Receiver ring dia.	1.335"
Bolt body dia.	.680"
Bolt travel	4.140"
Striker travel	.540"
Guard screw spacing	7.84"
Magazine well opening	
Length	3.075"
Rear width	.565"
Front width	.455"
Bolt face recess	
Depth	.110"
Dia.	.450" (Approx.)

Specifications of the Italian Carcano Youth Carbine

Rifle:

Weight	3 lbs. 10 oz.
Over-all length	30"
Barrel length	14.375"

Action:

Weight	1 lb. 7 oz.
Length	6.75"
Bolt body dia.	.547"

General Specifications

Type	Turnbolt repeater.
Receiver	One-piece machined steel forging; slotted bridge.
Bolt	One-piece, with dual-opposed forward locking lugs. Base of the bolt handle serves as safety lug.
Ignition	One-piece firing pin and coil mainspring. Cocks on bolt opening.
Magazine	Single column, non-detachable 6-shot box magazine. Special clip is required to load and hold cartridges in magazine.
Trigger	Non-adjustable, double-stage military pull.
Safety	Combined with the bolt sleeve; 90° swing from right to up. When up, safety locks bolt and relaxes firing pin.
Extractor	One-piece spring type recessed in front of bolt.
Bolt stop	One-piece, connected to, and released by trigger. Stops bolt by contacting right (lower) locking lug.
Ejector	Plunger type located in receiver bottom.

to .460" range. The bolt face recess could be enlarged and the extractor hook dressed down to accept a .30-06 head-sized cartridge, but lengthening the extractor hook to accommodate, for instance, the .222 head-sized case would be difficult to do.

The only satisfactory remodeling of the Carcano carbine consists in starting with one having a good bore, then limit the work to putting on new sights, refinishing the metal, remodeling the issue stock or installing a new one. A good rear sight choice is the Williams Guide, adjustable for windage and elevation. This should be paired with a new front blade or bead sight mounted on the Williams Shorty ramp base.

Mounting a scope on Carcanos is not too practicable, since clip-loading the rifle requires an off-set mount. However, this can be done with the Williams side mount, using the regular rings. With the scope off-set, the open sights can also be used.

If the rifle is used as a single shot, the scope can be mounted low over the bore, using the Weaver detachable side mount and No. 5 base. Such mounting requires the bolt handle to be altered so it will clear the scope. This usually means that part of the top right portion of the receiver bridge must be cut away, and a new bolt handle with a very low profile welded on in place of the original.

Reinhart Fajen, Inc., Warsaw, Mo., makes several styles of sporter stocks for the Carcano rifles, including a Mannlicher (full length fore-end) design.

6.5 & 7.35 Carcano Cartridges

The 6.5 military round was normally loaded with a 162-gr. round-nosed, full-jacketed bullet, muzzle velocity about 2300 fps. It was a good military cartridge, comparing favorably with other 6.5 military loads.

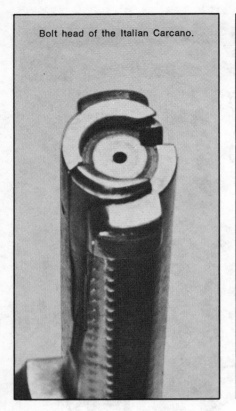

Bolt head of the Italian Carcano.

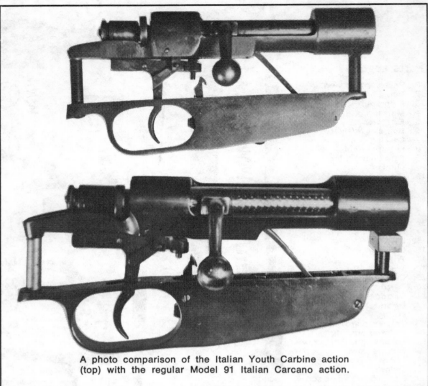

A photo comparison of the Italian Youth Carbine action (top) with the regular Model 91 Italian Carcano action.

The commercial Norma 6.5 Carcano is loaded with a 156-gr. soft-point, round-nosed bullet, 2000 fps muzzle velocity. Although this seems a very mild load it has ample power to take deer-sized game to about 200 yards. It could be hand-loaded safely to higher velocities with the same weight or lighter bullets. Because of the deep throat in the Carcano barrel, best results will be had with bullets of at least 130 grains. Poor accuracy may result with lighter bullets.

The usual 7.35 Carcano military cartridge carried a 128-gr. semi-pointed, full-jacketed bullet, its velocity about 2482 fps; normal bullet diameter is .298"-.300". Commercial loads in this caliber are not available, but Norma 6.5 Carcano cases can be expanded to form 7.35 cases. Hornady makes a good 128-gr. pointed SP bullet of .300" diameter for this cartridge. With suitable powder charges it can be driven up to about 2500 fps muzzle velocity, adequate for deer.

The Italian Youth Carbine

This title—the name it commonly goes by in English-speaking countries — describes one of the most unusual military arms of the WW II period. Mussolini and the Fascist Party leaders—aping the Nazis —wanted to start training Italian boys at an early age (probably at about 6) and a special small-sized arm was developed and manufactured for this purpose alone. The Youth Carbine is an almost identical but scaled-down version of the regular Model 91 Carbine with folding bayonet.

It is believed that about 30,000 of these small Carcano carbines were made between 1930 and 1940. American servicemen in Italy during the war took a number of these carbines home, but they're quite scarce today.

The IYCs are marked **F.N.A. BRESCIA** on the receiver for *Fabbrica Nazionale d'Armi.* Their serial number usually begins with a letter. The year date of manufacture is also stamped on the receiver, as well as the Roman numeral(s) indicating the Fascist regime year. On the carbine illustrated a rectangular stamping, atop the receiver ring, shows an insignia or crest with the Roman fasces.

The official Italian designation for the Youth Carbine is *Moschetto Regolomentare Ballila Modelo 1891 Ridutto.* Translated, this means "Ballila Regulation Musket Model 1891 Reduced." "Ballilo"

was the name of the Italian Fascist Youth Party.

The IYC was used for drill training only, since only blank ammunition was made for them, and the tip of the bayonet dulled. Some are smoothbored, others have a rifled bore of 6.5mm caliber. The blank cartridge is about the size of the .222 Remington, but has a longer neck ending in a folded crimp. The chambers are reamed minus any neck or throat; the neck of the blank cartridge is made small enough to enter directly into the bore, whether rifled or not. It is thought that perhaps IYCs with rifled barrels were made from discarded Model 91 Carcano barrels.

The action of the IYC is a regular little gem, and just over half the weight of the regular M91 and M38 Carcano actions. In every detail it is similar to the larger action. I don't believe it is made of good enough steel to be used with a modern bulleted cartridge, otherwise this miniature action would be just the right size for the .222 Remington.

The blank cartridges made for these carbines are extremely scarce, much more so than the carbines, and are prized collector items.

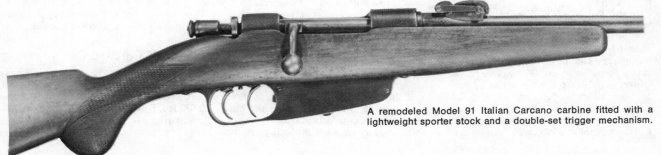

A remodeled Model 91 Italian Carcano carbine fitted with a lightweight sporter stock and a double-set trigger mechanism.

10. The Russian Mosin-Nagant

RUSSIA WAS NOT the first nation to adopt a smokeless powder cartridge for military use, but they were ahead of the United States by one year; they adopted the 7.62mm Russian cartridge in 1891, while the U.S. adopted the .30 Gov't. (.30-40 Krag) cartridge in 1892. The cartridges were similar; both were based on a rimmed bottle-necked case, were of the same caliber (bullet diameter .308″), and loaded with round-nosed full metal-jacketed bullets. The 7.62mm Russian cartridge has a larger body diameter than the .30-40 Krag round, thus the Russian cartridge was the more powerful of the two. While the .30-40 cartridge was not much improved during the brief time the Krag-Jorgensen rifle was the official U.S. military shoulder arm, the 7.62mm Russian cartridge was improved from time to time and loaded with a great variety of bullets to adapt it to various military needs. Improvements began as early as 1908 when the Russians adopted the 150-gr. spitzer bullet and loaded it to equal the ballistics and range of other military cartridges in use at that time.

As was the usual practice of most nations when major changes in a shoulder arm and cartridge were considered, the Russians, about 1883, appointed a committee to advertise for, study, test and make recommendations for the adoption of a new rifle and cartridge. After a few years of study two rifles remained under consideration. One was designed by a Belgian inventor and arms manufacturer named Emile Nagant; the other was designed by Sergey Ivanovitch Mosin, a Russian military man connected with the arsenal in Tula, Russia. After much study, experimentation and testing, the committee decided to use the Mosin bolt and receiver design and couple it with the Nagant-designed magazine. The final result was the Model 1891 Russian rifle, later to be known as the Model 91 Mosin-Nagant.

In 1891, and even later, Russia lacked adequate facilities to make the new rifle in sufficient quantities. As a result the first M91 rifles were made at an arsenal in Chatellerault, France.

Russia eventually began producing the rifles, but they apparently could not make enough to meet their army needs, so large contracts were placed abroad. Shortly before 1917, two U.S. firms made around 1,500,000 of these rifles. Remington Arms Company, in Bridgeport, Conn., made over 750,000 and New England Westinghouse, in Springfield, Mass., made the rest. Remington and Winchester loaded many thousands of rounds of 7.62mm military ammunition for Russia during this same period. Smith's *The Book of Rifles* states that the SIG firm in Switzerland and the Steyr arms factory in Austria also made M91 rifles at one time. These figures, plus the far greater quantity that Russian arsenals made in the intervening years, indicate that many millions of Mosin-Nagant rifles were made.

The Model 91 and the later Model 91/38 Russian rifle are plentiful today, as they have been since the 1920s. Before Remington and Westinghouse had completed their contracts with Russia, and with many thousands of the new Russian rifles still in the U.S., the October revolution in Russia came and the contracts were canceled. This resulted in no small financial crisis for the firms making the rifles and ammunition. The U.S. government softened the blow by buying a great quantity of these rifles (one book says 600,000), many of which were later shipped to Russia. The U.S. was also short of rifles at our entry into WW I, and over 280,000 of these government-purchased Russian rifles were used for training U.S. troops during the first part of the war. Eventually, this last bunch of M91s were sold to NRA members through the Director of Civilian Marksmanship for less than $3.50 each. Many of those made by Westinghouse were sold to private firms who resold them "as issued" or remodeled and converted to the .30-06 cartridge.

After WW II surplus arms dealers found more Russian rifles abroad and apparently imported a great many into the U.S. They were regularly offered for sale all through the 1950s and 1960s. Probably few Russian rifles were taken home by American servicemen during WW II, but veterans of the Korean conflict considered them prizes.

The M91 Mosin-Nagant rifle is still being used today by the Communist forces in Viet Nam. It seems that the preferred sniper rifle of the Viet Cong and North Viet Nam marksman is the M91 or M91/30 Sniper Rifle fitted with a short telescope sight, since a number of these rifles have been captured.

Mosin-Nagant Rifles

There are several rifle variations based on the M91 M-N action. I will briefly describe the principal ones. First, of course, is the M91 rifle with a 30.5″ barrel, weighing about 9.75 pounds. The first of these had sling swivels; later on swivels were omitted, and slots cut into the stock through which the sling could pass. Then there is the M91 Dragoon rifle, its barrel 28.8″ long and weighing about 8.75 pounds. The top of the receiver of M91 rifles is octagonal in shape and usually color case-hardened. Later models had a round receiver top, including the M91/30 standard rifle (28.7″ barrel, and about 8.75 pounds) and the Sniper's rifle—about the same except fitted with a telescope sight. Several types of mounts and scopes were used on these sniper rifles. The scopes are the short and low-powered hunting type, attached with high-bracket side mounts. The scopes usually had built-in windage and elevation adjustments, and usually with one or both of these adjustments also built into the mount. The mount base, attached to the side of the receiver, was designed to let the scope and mount bracket be easily detached. The

Illustrated above: Russian Model 1891 Mosin-Nagant rifle, caliber 7.62mm Russian.

Russian Model 1891 Mosin-Nagant action; late version with the rounded receiver ring.

Sniper rifle had a long bent-down bolt handle. Both M91/30s have a globe-protected front sight.

There were also three M-N carbine models. The Model 1910 has a 20″ barrel, weighs about 7.5 pounds, and has an unprotected blade front sight. The Model 1938 also has a 20″ barrel, weighs about 7.6 pounds, and M1910 blade front sight. The Model 1944 has a 20.4″ barrel, weighs about 8.9 pounds, and has a globe front sight. All M-N rifles and carbines have elevation-adjustable rear sights and are chambered for the 7.62mm Russian cartridge.

The Mosin-Nagant Action

An odd and unusual action, it has few features which can be said to have been copied from other actions. In fact, it has a number of features unique to it. In a way the action seems a fairly simple one, as indicated by its relatively few parts, but at the same time it has a complicated 3-piece bolt assembly. Its design and manufacture is complicated because it has to accommodate a rimmed cartridge. Many small and minor parts are eliminated in its design; there are no separate safety or bolt stop parts, and the number of trigger and bolt stop parts is four. Even the novel mazagine interrupter feature has only three parts, of which one is the ejector. Although the action is somewhat crude and is not easily operated, it is nonetheless quite reliable.

The Model 1891 actions with octagonal-topped receivers show much better workmanship throughout than do those with rounded receivers. This is especially true of the actions made by Remington and Westinghouse, doubtless because these plants were swarming with Russian inspectors (about 1500 of them, according to one report) to see that every part was made just so. The actions made in Russia, especially during the war years, are rather poorly finished.

The receiver is a one-piece steel forging machined to final shape. The inside of the receiver ring is bored and threaded to receive the barrel shank. The breech end of the barrel is flat except for an extractor hook recess, taking up about one-third of its face. Most receivers have an inside collar, against which the barrel abuts; this

ring is cut away, on the right for about one-third of its circumference, to make room for the extractor. Very late wartime receivers don't have this inside collar. The rear of the receiver ring is milled out to receive the dual locking lugs on the bolt head.

The recoil shoulder under the receiver ring is quite heavy but narrow, affording only about a ½″ x ⅜″ bearing surface against the stock. However, a crossbolt is used in most of the stocks of these rifles to reinforce the wood in the recoil shoulder area.

A portion of the bottom of the receiver, from the recoil shoulder back, is milled flat. The magazine-well recess in the bottom of the receiver is milled out to approximate the shape of the rimmed 7.62mm Russian cartridge, with a sort of tunnel or chute milled out in the narrower front half of the well to allow passage of the cartridge head as the cartridge is pushed into the chamber.

The receiver bridge is slotted to allow the passage of the bolt handle and the bolt-handle base rib or guide. The forward end of this slot is widened out a bit and grooved to form a clip-charger guideway. A special charger clip, made of steel and holding 5 cartridges, is normally used to load the magazine, but it can be loaded with single cartridges pressed into the open action with the thumb.

The bolt of the Mosin-Nagant rifle is rather a complicated affair, difficult to describe. To begin with, the bolt body proper is made up of three separate parts; the bolt head, the connecting sleeve and the bolt body.

The bolt head, about 1.50″ long, has two solid and opposed locking lugs on its forward end. The front edges of the lugs are rounded. When the bolt is in the locked position the lugs are horizontal, that is, to the left and right. This is the reverse of the Mauser locking lug system, where, when the bolt is locked, the lugs are vertical—one up and one down. Thus, when the M-N bolt is drawn back the upper (right) lug moves back through the slot in the receiver bridge, while the bottom (left) lug moves through the magazine well opening. On Mauser actions the left receiver wall is milled out for the left locking lug raceway, but on the M-N the left receiver wall is solid. This gives very

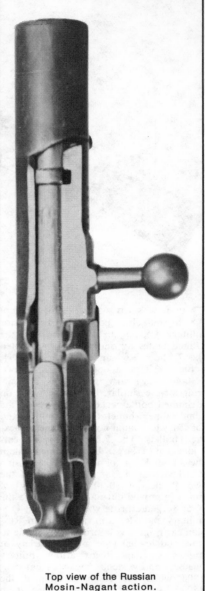

Top view of the Russian Mosin-Nagant action.

solid backing-up to the left lug, not unlike that afforded the bottom locking lug on the FN Mauser single shot benchrest action discussed in another chapter.

The face of the bolt is fully recessed for the cartridge rim except for the narrow extractor cut and ejector groove.

The extractor is a one-piece spring affair wedged in a slot and dovetailed in the bolt head. It cannot move longitudinally in the bolt head because of the abutment of the dovetail, and it cannot move backward as long as the bolt is completely assembled. The inside collar in the receiver ring is cut away over the extractor, giving the latter room to move outward when the bolt is closed on a cartridge, which always moves into the chamber ahead of the extractor hook.

The main bolt body is nearly 4″ long. Made integrally with it is a heavy guide rib, with the integral bolt handle posi-

Model 1891 Russian action open.

tioned near the rear of this rib. This places the bolt handle well forward, or about midway in the action. The bolt handle has a round stem and a round grasping ball, and projects straight out to the right of the action. The Mosin-Nagant sniper rifle has a long-stemmed bent down bolt handle. The heavy guide rib, extending almost from the receiver bridge to the receiver ring, has several functions. It guides and prevents the bolt from binding as it moves through the slot in the receiver bridge when the bolt is opened and closed. It also acts as a third safety lug when the bolt is closed by engaging forward of the receiver bridge, and this same bolt closing cams the bolt fully forward as the handle is turned down. On opening the bolt, initial camming power is provided by the forward end of the guide rib moving across a sloped surface on the receiver ring. The guide rib also links up with the bolt head and bolt connection sleeve, as will be pointed out later on.

The bolt body and the bolt head are aligned and connected by the bolt connecting sleeve. Each end of this sleeve is turned down to fit inside the bolt body and bolt head, leaving a ring about 7/32" thick separating body and head. A 6.5" long guide bar is an integral part of the bolt-connecting sleeve, and with the assembled bolt in the action, it lies in the bottom locking lug raceway. The bolt body, connecting sleeve and bolt head are held together as a unit, when the bolt is assembled in the action, by a lug on the connecting-sleeve collar engaging in a groove in the bolt-guide rib, and by a stud on the connecting-sleeve guide bar engaging in a groove in the bolt head. A stud on the bolt head engaging in a groove in the bolt-guide rib causes the bolt head to rotate with the bolt body. In raising and lowering the bolt handle the connecting sleeve does not rotate.

The bolt body is drilled and bored out from the front, leaving a step-down in the rear end. The coil mainspring is compressed against this step-down and against

the collar on the one-piece firing pin. The rear end of the firing pin threads into the heavy one-piece cocking piece. The firing pin is prevented from turning in the assembled bolt by the bolt connector sleeve, through which the flattened end of the firing pin passes. The cocking piece, although only of one-piece construction, is a product of many machining operations. It has a heavy guide rib which extends into the receiver bridge slot. A projecting cam on the cocking piece falls within a matching cam notch in the rear of the bolt body and, on raising the bolt handle, the cocking piece and firing pin are moved back to cock the action. The rectangular sear lug on the bottom of the cocking piece is loosely mortised in a notch in the rear end of the connecting-sleeve guide bar.

No provision is made to allow powder gases to escape harmlessly out of the bolt or action in the event of a pierced primer or ruptured case head. Gases escaping into the firing pin hole from a pierced primer would not likely get to the shooter's face but would probably dissipate through the joint of the bolt head and bolt connecting sleeve. In the case of a ruptured case head, especially if the break were in the upper half of the head, the gases would escape through the ejector groove and through the upper locking lug raceway, which would aim the gases directly toward the shooter's forehead. Late models, without the inside receiver collar to partly surround and enclose the bolt head, would afford even less protection. However, the occurrence of case head rupturing is extremely rare, and there is little chance of it happening with new ammunition.

The trigger is held to the receiver by a heavy pin running through integral lugs on the receiver. The sear, a one-piece flat-spring affair, is attached to the receiver by a heavy screw. The rear part of this spring sear extends through a hollow in the trigger, with a projection which extends through a hole in the receiver into the locking lug raceway. The trigger has

a single-stage pull, but when the action is cocked there is considerable slack in the trigger. Because the sear itself is a spring, and that spring quite heavy and short, the trigger pull is "spongy;" that is, the weight of pull seems to increase as one pulls the trigger through.

A groove milled lengthwise in the bottom of the connecting-sleeve guide bar (ending about 1" from the front end of the bar) is the raceway for both the sear and the stud on top of the trigger. The bolt is stopped by this stud contacting the end of the groove in the guide bar.

There is no separate safety mechanism on the Mosin-Nagant action, but there is a safety. The rear of the cocking piece ends in a good-sized knurled knob, and the cocked action can be made "safe" by grasping the cocking piece firmly, pulling it back slightly and rotating it counter-clockwise as far as it will go. This will hold the cocking piece and firing pin back, while locking the bolt at the same time. The safety is disengaged by reversing these movements. Considerable effort and a good grip is required to place the rifle in the "ON" and "OFF" safe positions.

The combination magazine/trigger guard is of one-piece steel construction. The vertical opening through the magazine is just wide and long enough for the 7.62mm Russian cartridge. The sides of the magazine have two step-downs; one near the back to match the cartridge rim, and one at about the shoulder of the cartridge, so that the opening is narrower in front to match similar step-downs milled in the receiver-well opening. A hinged cover closes the bottom of the magazine. It is hinged on a heavy rivet through the front of the magazine and closed by a spring catch screwed to the rear of the magazine.

The magazine follower assembly, hinged to the magazine cover (floorplate), is composed of the follower arm, follower plate hinged to the arm, a spring for each and a screw to attach the follower-arm spring to the cover. Pulling back on the end of the latch, which projects from a hole in the rear of the magazine cover, opens the cover to unload the magazine. Depressing the follower plate against the cover permits the entire follower assembly to be detached.

The action is held in the stock by two guard screws clamping the receiver to the magazine/trigger guard. The rear guard screw extends through the receiver tang and threads into the trigger guard bow; the front guard screw goes through the front of the magazine and threads into the recoil shoulder.

A novel feature of this action is the cartridge feed-interrupter and ejector system. The ejector, a flat piece of steel, fits into a narrow slot cut into the bottom left of the receiver, projecting inward. It then moves into a groove in the bolt head to hit the cartridge rim as the bolt is opened. The ejector is held in place and tensioned by the cartridge feed-interrupter, a bent piece of spring steel attached to the receiver by a screw. The front end of the interrupter projects into the top left of the rear part of the magazine, where it engages the second cartridge from the top in the magazine. Its main function is to prevent double loading. It does this by holding the second cartridge down freeing the top cartridge from any tension of the follower so it can be fed easily into the chamber; it frees the next cartridge only when the bolt is fully closed on the cartridge in the chamber, in which case the extractor hook has positively engaged the cartridge rim so it will be extracted when the bolt is opened again. When the bolt is closed and the handle turned down, the interrupter is pushed to the left, by a cut in the bolt body, to allow the top cartridge to rise. When the bolt handle is raised the interrupter again holds the second cartridge from the top down to repeat the cycle. The employment of the interrupter does much to eliminate feeding problems with rimmed cartridges.

Take-Down and Assembly

Make sure magazine and chamber are unloaded. Remove bolt by raising bolt handle, then pull it back while pulling the trigger back as far as it will go; the bolt can now be pulled free. The bolt can be put back into the receiver without pulling the trigger back.

Disassemble the bolt as follows: grasp bolt handle and, with the other hand, grasp the cocking piece; pull cocking piece back slightly, rotate it counterclockwise slightly and allow it to move forward; bolt head and bolt connecting sleeve can now be pulled forward off the bolt; rotate bolt head on bolt connecting sleeve until the two can be separated. Do not remove extractor unless necessary; to do this insert blade of a small screw driver under extractor hook to raise it above the edge of the bolt head, then drive extractor to the rear. Replace extractor by merely slipping it in place, then drive it forward until its rear end is flush with the bolt head.

Disassemble the firing mechanism by unscrewing firing pin from cocking piece —about 15 complete turns are required.

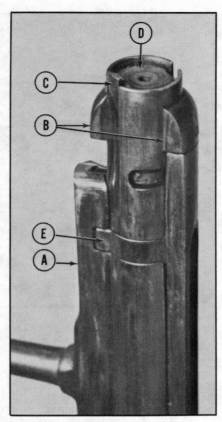

Underside view of the front end of the Russian Model 91 bolt showing: (A) bolt guide rib lug, (B) locking lugs, (C) extractor, (D) cartridge head recess and (E) bolt connecting sleeve.

The firing pin and mainspring can then be withdrawn from the bolt. Reassemble in reverse order, starting with cocking piece in the down or fired position. Turn the firing pin in until its end is flush with the cocking piece knob and index marks line up. Reassemble bolt head and connecting sleeve together, so the guide bar stud is engaged in the bolt head groove, then place these parts over the firing pin. Line up guide bar so it will slip over the sear on the cocking piece, and the stud on the bolt head so it will slip into the groove in the bolt guide rib until the three parts are against each other. Now grasp the bolt handle and cocking piece and, while pulling back on the cocking piece, rotate it clockwise until the end of the cocking cam falls into the shallow notch in the rear of the bolt.

As noted earlier, release the magazine cover by pulling back latch, swing cover down and press against follower. This releases the entire assembly from its hinge rivet. Remove follower-arm spring by turning out its screw. Remove follower-plate spring by pressing its end down, then swing it aside. Pushing out the two follower and follower-plate pins separates these parts. Reassemble in reverse order.

Turning out the two guard screws allows magazine/trigger guard to be pulled from the bottom of the stock; the barrel and action may be lifted from the top of the stock after removing the barrel bands. Re-move magazine-cover latch by turning out its screw; turn out magazine-interrupter screw, remove interrupter and lift out ejector. Turn out the sear screw, then push out trigger pin and trigger. The sear can now be removed. Reassemble in reverse order.

Comments

The various models of the Russian Mosin-Nagant rifle have proved very reliable military weapons—just consider the fact that they have been in use continuously since 1891, longer than almost any other military bolt action rifle. The M-N rifle may seem crude to most persons familiar with the various military bolt action rifles, and in my opinion the M-N action is a crude affair compared to the 98 Mauser action or to our own 1903 Springfield action. Nevertheless, the M-N action is still a good one, and the U.S.-made Russian rifles could hardly have been made any better. Remington probably never made other rifles before or since under so much supervision and such rigid inspections as they did these rifles. The M-N rifles made in Russia, especially those made during WW II, were not nearly so well made and finished, yet they were reliable military rifles. All were more than amply strong for the 7.62mm Russian cartridge.

For use on a sporting rifle the M-N action has a number of faults, yet many M91 rifles have been, and are still being, remodeled and sporterized today. Among the action's drawbacks and poor features, for use on a hunting rifle, are: the bolt handle is too far forward for easy and rapid manipulation. Putting the safety on and off is too hard; the projecting magazine often interferes with carrying the rifle; the trigger pull is poor, and the action is not well suited for a receiver sight or scope.

Little, if anything, can be done to remedy or correct these drawbacks. The bolt handle can be bent down or a new bolt handle made and attached to place the grasping ball lower and farther back. Nothing can be done to improve the safety, although it is possible to make and install a different type of safety, such as a cross-bolt type behind the trigger, through the stock or trigger guard. There is no practical way to change or eliminate the projecting magazine. Not much can be done to change or improve the trigger, except perhaps making the pull a bit lighter and smoother by honing the trigger and sear contacting surfaces. No commercial trigger or safety mechanism has ever been made for the Russian rifle.

Years ago two good receiver sights were made for the M-N action. One was the King "Little Giant," an adjustable peep sight which was mounted on the top arm of the cocking piece. The other was a Lyman with a swinging slide, similar to the one made for the Mannlicher-Schoenauer rifle which also has an action in which the bolt handle passes through a slotted bridge. There are no receiver sights made for the Russian action today.

Williams Gun Sight Co., Davison, Mich.,

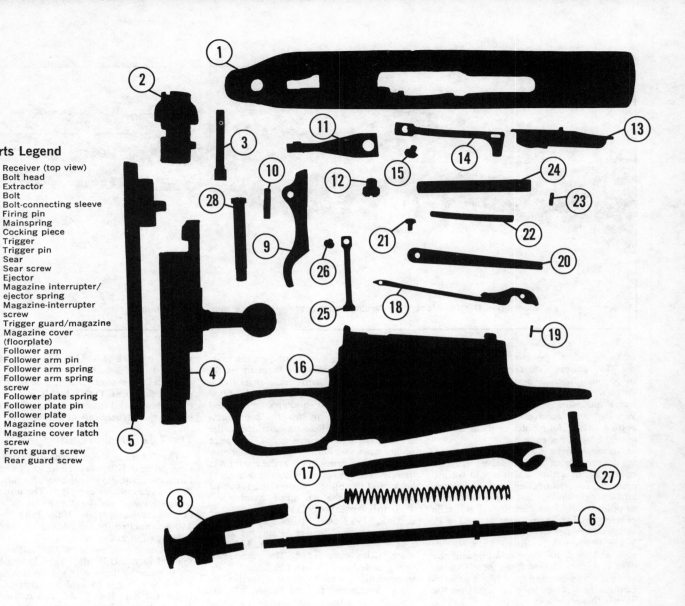

Parts Legend

1. Receiver (top view)
2. Bolt head
3. Extractor
4. Bolt
5. Bolt-connecting sleeve
6. Firing pin
7. Mainspring
8. Cocking piece
9. Trigger
10. Trigger pin
11. Sear
12. Sear screw
13. Ejector
14. Magazine interrupter/ejector spring
15. Magazine-interrupter screw
16. Trigger guard/magazine
17. Magazine cover (floorplate)
18. Follower arm
19. Follower arm pin
20. Follower arm spring
21. Follower arm spring screw
22. Follower plate spring
23. Follower plate pin
24. Follower plate
25. Magazine cover latch
26. Magazine cover latch screw
27. Front guard screw
28. Rear guard screw

Russian Mosin-Nagant

Dimensional Specifications

Weight	45 oz.
Overall length	8.87"
Receiver ring dia.	1.225"*
Bolt body dia.	.650"
Bolt travel	4.470"
Striker travel	.485"
Magazine opening: Length	3.140"
Bolt face recess:	
Depth	.060"
Dia.	.575"

*Approximate dimension for round receivers. Early receivers with octagonal top are about 1.230" wide across the flats.

General Specifications

Type	Turnbolt repeater.
Receiver	One-piece machined steel forging with slotted bridge. Stripper-clip charger guides milled in the bridge.
Bolt	Three-piece, with dual-opposed locking lugs on forward part of bolt head. Guide rib on bolt body acts as safety lug.
Ignition	Composed of one-piece firing pin, coil mainspring and cocking piece. Action cocks on opening.
Magazine	Single column, non-detachable box magazine of 5-shot capacity. Hinged and detachable magazine cover (floorplate). Magazine has cartridge-feed interrupter—see text.
Trigger	Non-adjustable single stage pull.
Safety	No separate safety, but cocked action can be placed in "safe" position by rotating cocking piece.
Extractor	One-piece rotating spring type dovetailed into bolt head.
Magazine cutoff	None.
Bolt stop	A stud on the trigger engaging in a groove in the bolt connecting sleeve.
Ejector	One-piece, recessed in the left receiver wall.

Close-up of Russian Model 1891 Mosin-Nagant action; early type with octagonal-topped receiver.

makes a side scope mount adaptable to the M-N action. This requires an off-set scope mounting, never very satisfactory. Another thing which may discourage scope mounting is that Remington and Westinghouse receivers are very hard; putting two to four holes in them for the mount base is not easy.

Although there is not a single outstanding feature about the Model 91 Russian rifle or on its action which would recommend it for remodeling into a sporter, amateur gunsmiths often overlook this, or point out that the "challenge" this rifle presents makes them want to tackle it. When these rifles were cheap and plentiful in the 1920s and 30s many were remodeled and used for deer hunting and the like. This work ranged from merely shortening the fore-end and barrel, and perhaps fitting a new set of hunting sights on the barrel, to super deluxe jobs, such as one that the famous stockmaker, the late Alvin Linden, once did.* Then, as now, sporter stocks are still made for this rifle today by Fajen and Bishop.

Because of the faults already mentioned, I hardly think it advisable to do any extensive remodeling of this rifle. About the only job I'd recommend would be to shorten the barrel to about 22", remove the original rear sight, install a Williams Guide rear sight and front sight on a ramp, and remodel the original military stock or fit the lowest priced Fajen or Bishop stock.

I certainly advise against rebarreling this action, whether to its original caliber or to any other caliber, since the action is neither worth it nor is there any other cartridge the action will handle better than the 7.62mm Russian. I am also against rechambering or reboring the barrel for another cartridge or caliber.

I have never heard of or read about a Mosin-Nagant rifle blowing up when used with military or commercial 7.62mm Russian ammunition. Years ago, however,

*The American Rifleman, Dec., 1927, and Jan., 1928. "The 7.62mm Russian Rifle . . ." by Alvin Linden.

when these rifles were a drug on the market some shops converted them to .30-06 caliber to make them more marketable and some of these rifles actually did blow up. In one case the shooter was reported killed. I do not know how the conversion from the 7.62mm Russian cartridge to the .30-06 cartridge was made, but they were booby traps and definitely very dangerous to fire. The chances are that the barrel was merely rechambered without setting it back, and the blow-ups were the result of case failure in the over-sized chamber.

At this writing (1971) sporterized and original M91 Russian rifles are still available from some dealers in surplus arms. I have noticed that both U.S. and U.S.S.R. made rifles were listed. The remodeled ones, called the "Finncub Sporter" by some dealers, were at times advertised as being chambered for the "7.62mm" cartridge. Advertising the caliber as such, instead of correctly listing the caliber as the "7.62mm Russian" is certainly misleading, and many amateur gunsmiths bought these rifles believing them chambered for the 7.62mm NATO or .308 cartridge, only to find out later that this was not so. Firing a .308 cartridge in the M91 rifle could be as disastrous as the M91 .30-06 booby traps. Therefore, if you want an M91 Mosin-Nagant rifle to shoot or remodel just make sure it has a good bore, that it has *not* been previously rechambered, and preferably made by Remington or Westinghouse, or one made before 1940.

Much information about gunsmithing and remodeling the M91 Russian rifles can be found in *The Modern Gunsmith* by Howe, *Modern Gunsmithing* by Baker and *How To Convert Military Rifles* by Williams Gun Sight Co.

Markings

On most Mosin-Nagant rifles the serial number is usually stamped only on the top of the bolt-guide rib. On most rifles made in Russia the date (year) of manufacture is usually stamped on top of the breech end of the barrel. Sometimes the

words **MADE IN U.S.S.R.** are also stamped on the receiver ring.

Model 91s made by Remington have the words **REMINGTON ARMORY,** date (year) and serial number stamped on the top of the breech end of the barrel.

The 7.62 Russian Cartridge

The 7.62mm Russian cartridge has a rimmed and bottle-necked case of fairly large capacity. Powerful and accurate, it is a proven military cartridge. The normal bulleted load used by the Russians and other countries (Model 1908 Ball) has a 150-gr. pointed bullet, driven at about 2850 fps muzzle velocity.

Because so many M-N 1891 rifles remained in the U.S. after WW I, and because many of them were sold to shooters, Remington began to load a sporting cartridge for it in the 1920s. This carried a 150-gr. Bronze Point expanding bullet at a velocity of about 2700 fps. Remington discontinued this cartridge about 1950. Since that time, however, a great many more Russian rifles were sold on the surplus arms market, and shooters began calling for this cartridge again. In response, Norma-Precision re-introduced the 7.62mm Russian cartridge in the mid-1960s. The Norma load has a 180-gr. semi-pointed, soft point boat-tail bullet, advertised muzzle velocity 2624 fps— against 2610 fps at the muzzle for Norma's .308 cartridge loaded with the same bullet. Of course, the Norma cases are reloadable. The obsolete Remington 7.62mm Russian load accounted for many head of big game on this continent in past years, and the Norma load should prove even more effective with its heavier .308" diameter bullet. The maximum established working pressure of this 7.62mm cartridge is about 45,000 psi. The Norma load is listed as producing about 42,000 psi against 49,000 psi given for the Norma .308 load mentioned above.

The .308 cartridge is interchangeable with the 7.62mm NATO cartridge, *but these cartridges are not interchangeable with the 7.62mm Russian cartridge.*

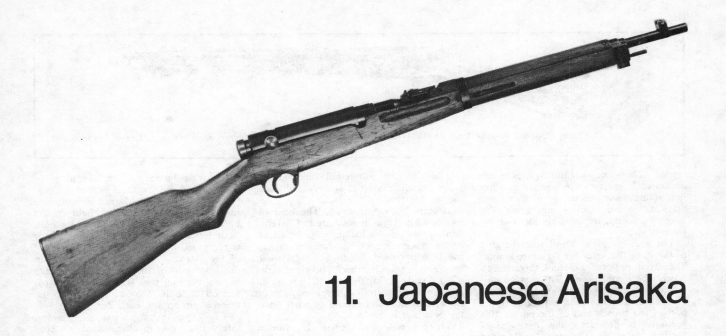

11. Japanese Arisaka

PRIOR TO WW II there were very few Japanese military rifles in the United States, apart from a small number of the older 11mm Japanese Murata rifles in various private and museum collections. Beginning with the bombing of Pearl Harbor on December 7, 1941, and ending with signing of the peace treaty on board the battleship Missouri in Tokyo Bay on September 2, 1945, our servicemen went through untold hardships in the Pacific area to win that peace. Perhaps because of these hardships, regulations regarding sending or taking home captured rifles for souvenirs were kept lenient, and largely overlooked by our military officers, so that by the end of the war Japanese rifles had become commonplace items.

Before and during the first part of the war not much was known about Japanese military rifles and cartridges. At that time gun writers generally scoffed at both the rifles and the cartridges, berating the rifles generally as junk and the 6.5mm cartridge as vastly inferior to our .30-06. This was unfortunate, since many servicemen reading these reports before they were inducted for duty in the Pacific area, didn't have the respect they should have had for their opponents' weapons. I could cite a couple of instances of this from among my own acquaintances, but suffice it to say they soon learned better, and it was not long before the "puny" 6.5mm Japanese cartridge, and later the 7.7mm cartridge, were rated among the world's best military cartridges.

It took somewhat longer, however, to establish the fact that the Japanese rifles firing these cartridges were also good. The Japanese knew this, of course, but it took some convincing to change the minds of some of our gun experts that the Japanese Arisaka rifles were good. The fact is, we discovered that the Type 38 and 99 Arisaka actions were perhaps the world's strongest and safest bolt actions, and that it is almost impossible to blow them up.

Development

Japan's first important breech-loading military shoulder arm was the Type 13 (1880) Murata chambered for the 11mm Murata cartridge. A single shot bolt action rifle, it was later modified and made as a repeater by installing a feed mechanism and a tubular magazine in the fore-end. Then, in 1887, Japan adopted an 8mm cartridge (8mm Japanese Murata) and used it in a further modification of the Murata rifle, again with a tubular magazine.

In Japan, as was done in many other countries, a commission was appointed to study, develop, test and adopt new military arms. In the late 1890s the superintendent of the Tokyo Arsenal, Col. Nari-aki Arisaka, headed such a commission, which in 1897 recommended the adoption of a 6.5mm cartridge and a new rifle to handle it. The rifle adopted was the Type 30 (1897), the cartridge a semi-rimmed bottlenecked smokeless powder one now commonly known as the 6.5mm Japanese. Although Col. Arisaka probably had little to do with the designing of either the cartridge or the rifle, his name is usually given to them, as well as to later versions. The Type 30 was a further development of the old Murata design, but with a staggered-column box magazine, a separate bolt head and a finger-hook safety. First made in about 1889, a still further development came around 1902 with the adoption of the Type 35 (1902) Arisaka rifle, of which only a limited number were made.

The Type 38 Arisaka

Having by this time perfected the 6.5mm cartridge, the commission, still under Col. Arisaka, continued looking for a better action. By 1905 they had found it. The rest of this chapter is about the Type 38 action, its modifications and the rifles built on it.

Before going into details of the action, I'll briefly describe the rifles and carbines based on this action the Japanese adopted in 1906, all of them chambered for the 6.5mm cartridge.

1. Type 38 (1905) Rifle. About 9.5 pounds, 31.25″ barrel, 50.25″ over-all. The standard Japanese infantry shoulder arm from 1906 to 1940.

2. Type 38 (1905) Short Rifle. About 8.5 pounds, 25.25″ barrel, 44.25″ over-all. Not many made.

3. Type 38 (1905) Carbine. About 7.75 pounds, 19″ barrel, 38″ over-all. The standard carbine.

4. Type 97 (1937) Sniper Rifle. Same as the Type 38 rifle but fitted with a short 2.5-power scope attached to the left side of the receiver; the detachable mount holds the scope off-set to the left to allow loading the magazine with a stripper clip. This model has a bent down bolt handle.

The above rifles have two-piece, pistol grip stocks. The bottom piece of the buttstock, a separate piece of wood, is glued to the top part. All have a one-piece cleaning rod in the fore-end and are made to accept a bayonet. All have sliding breech covers, and all but the sniper rifle have straight bolt handles.

5. Type 44 (1911) Cavalry Carbine. About 8.75 pounds, 19″ barrel, 38.25″ over-all. Straight bolt handle, sliding breech cover and a non-detachable folding bayonet.

6.5mm rifles and carbines of late manufacture usually have the bore and bolt face chrome plated.

The Type 38 Action

A modified Mauser design, the Type 38 action has several features distinctly of Mauser design, but a couple of others which were new and entirely Japanese de-

---

Illustrated above: 6.5mm Japanese Arisaka Type 38 (1905) carbine.

6.5mm Japanese Arisaka Type 44 (1911) Cavalry carbine, a folding bayonet recessed in the bottom of the fore-end.

signed. These new features make this action different from any other military bolt action made before or since. In some ways it is a crude action, not being very easy to operate, but it is simple and extremely strong.

The receiver is a round steel forging of the same diameter for its entire length. The front is bored out and threaded to accept the barrel shank. There is no collar inside the receiver ring as in the Model 98 Mauser action; instead, a collar forms part of the breech end of the barrel, this becoming a shroud for the front end of the bolt. More on this later. Ample sized locking shoulders are left in the rear of the receiver ring, in which the locking lugs on the bolt engage. The forward corners of these shoulders are beveled off to

The bolt and bolt handle are of one-piece construction. The straight bolt handle, at the rear of the bolt, has a large oval-shaped grasping knob. The base or root of the bolt handle is squared. The large dual-opposed front locking lugs lie ahead of the receiver locking shoulders when the bolt is closed, holding the cartridge securely in the chamber. The right (bottom) lug is solid, the left (top) lug is partly slotted in front to allow passage of the ejector, this slot extending partly into the bolt-face recess.

There is also an auxiliary lug (not a locking lug) just to the rear of the left (top) locking lug. This acts as an activator for the ejector, and as the bolt stop lug when it engages with the bolt stop when the bolt is opened. An inclined slot

or cartridge case will remain in place until forced out by the ejector.

The extractor, of Mauser design, is a long one-piece spring affair held on the bolt body by a collar around the bolt. Longitudinal movement of the extractor is prevented by a lip under the front part of the extractor engaging in a groove in the front end of the bolt. The extractor is non-rotating; that is, while it does rotate on the bolt, it does not rotate in the receiver or on the cartridge.

The Type 38 action has the simplest safety and firing mechanism of any centerfire bolt action known to me. Not counting the trigger, sear parts, receiver or bolt, the firing and safety mechanism consists of only three parts. This design has its virtues and drawbacks, as we shall

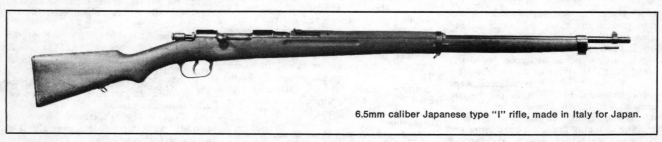

6.5mm caliber Japanese type "I" rifle, made in Italy for Japan.

form inclines, so that the final closing draws the bolt forcibly forward.

The top and right side of the receiver-center are milled away to form an opening, leaving the left receiver wall quite high. To the rear of this opening is the receiver bridge, of the same diameter as the receiver ring. Stripper-clip slots are milled into the front of the solid bridge. Raceways milled in the left receiver wall and in the right of the receiver ring and bridge allow passage of the locking lugs and extractor. The rear part of the bridge has an L-shaped slot milled from the top rear to the right front for passage of the bolt handle. The forward side of this slot, beginning at the corner, is angled slightly forward; this provides the initial camming power for extraction when the bolt is opened, and helps to rotate the bolt when it is closed smartly.

in the rear of this lug prevents the bolt hanging up on the ejector, and trips the ejector when the bolt is fully opened.

The bolt face is recessed to about the depth of the cartridge rim. Part of this rim recess is undercut to allow the cartridge head to move up and under the extractor hook when the cartridge is fed from the magazine, as in the Mauser 98 and Model 1903 Springfield actions. This prevents double loading, since any cartridge bolt-fed into the chamber from the magazine will be extracted and ejected upon opening the bolt, even though the bolt was not fully locked during this procedure. The lower left edge of the rim recess is slightly higher than the rest of the rim and is slightly undercut. This affords extra bearing surface for the cartridge rim, from the slight side pressure of the extractor, so that on opening the bolt the cartridge

see, but it is a very reliable and effective arrangement for a military rifle.

The bolt body is drilled from the rear to accept the one-piece hollow striker (call it the firing pin if you like) with its integral firing-pin tip in front and its cocking cam (sear) on the rear. The coil mainspring fits into the hollow part of the striker. The third part of the mechanism is the safety, although it has several other functions.

The safety is a large one-piece affair comprised of a cap to which is permanently attached a stem projecting forward from its hollow center. This stem extends into the hollow striker to compress the mainspring. The safety is held on the rear of the bolt by a lug inside of the cap engaging over a ridge on the outside rear of the bolt body. The safety can be quickly and easily removed from the bolt by pressing it forward and rotating it clock-

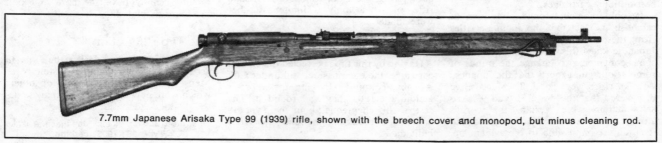

7.7mm Japanese Arisaka Type 99 (1939) rifle, shown with the breech cover and monopod, but minus cleaning rod.

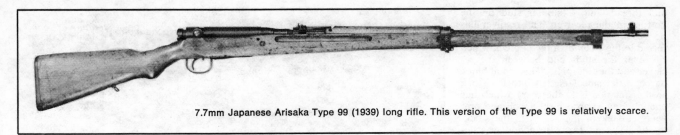

7.7mm Japanese Arisaka Type 99 (1939) long rifle. This version of the Type 99 is relatively scarce.

wise about ¼-turn. The safety is linked to the striker by a small stud on the safety stem engaging in a matching groove milled inside the striker. The safety is linked with the receiver when it is engaged by a small stud on the outside of the safety cap engaging in an L-shaped groove in the bottom rear of the receiver. In all, there is a complicated hook-up between safety, striker and bolt, and also with the receiver when the safety is engaged, certainly the result of someone's ingenuity. The lug on the outside of the safety cap, engaged in the groove in the receiver, prevents the safety from rotating when the bolt handle is raised or lowered. The rear surface of the cap-like safety is knurled in a circular pattern to prevent it twisting under thumb or palm pressure when it is engaged by

on the front of the sear projects upwards through another hole in the receiver, which prevents the trigger being pulled to release the striker, except when the bolt handle is straight up, the bolt then entirely un-locked, or when the bolt handle is fully lowered and fully locked. In these posi-tions two narrow grooves in the bolt body align with the pin. The sear spring is compressed over this pin between the sear and receiver. The trigger, which pivots in the sear on a rivet, has two humps where it contacts the bottom of the receiver and these humps provide the usual two-stage military trigger pull.

The striker can be lowered on closing the bolt as follows: push the bolt forward until the striker contacts the sear; pull the trigger to allow bolt and striker to be

in the groove provided for it in the bolt head.

An opening is milled into the bottom of the receiver for the magazine opening. Integral lips or cartridge-guide ribs at the top of the opening hold the cartridges in the magazine and guide them into the chamber. The magazine, a thin piece of sheet metal folded to form a box, is re-inforced at each end with a heavier piece of metal welded in place.

The milled steel trigger guard is com-bined with a magazine plate which has an opening to surround the bottom of the separate magazine box. A milled steel floorplate covers this opening. A lip on the front of the floorplate, engaging a groove in the trigger plate and a latch ar-rangement built into the front part of the

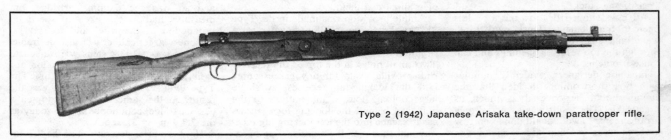

Type 2 (1942) Japanese Arisaka take-down paratrooper rifle.

pressing it forward and rotating it ⅛-turn clockwise, or disengaged by again pressing it forward and rotating it in the opposite direction. The safety can only be engaged when the striker is cocked, and when engaged it locks both the striker and the bolt. The outside edge of the safety cap is usually serrated and made with a small hump so located that it is up when the safety is engaged.

The trigger system follows the Mauser M93-96 design (later copied in the Pat-tern 14 and 1917 Enfield actions). It consists of a sear pivoted on a pin through a small lug on the bottom of the receiver. The sear projection on the rear of the sear protrudes through a hole in the re-ceiver and engages the cocking cam on the striker when the bolt is closed. The striker is thus cocked on the forward or closing motion of the bolt. A pin riveted

moved forward until the base of the bolt handle contacts the receiver; release the trigger; lower the bolt handle by striking it smartly with the palm of the hand. This should only be done on an empty chamber.

The bolt stop and ejector assembly is built into a long narrow integral housing which projects from the left of the receiver bridge. The bolt stop, of Mauser design, is held in this housing and pivots on a screw through the underside of the rear end of the housing. It is tensioned by a flat spring locked to the front end of the bolt stop. The ejector, positioned in a slot in the center of the housing, pivots on a separate screw, also turned in through the underside of the housing. There is no ejector spring. The ejector is activated by action of the auxiliary bolt-stop lug on the bolt which, on opening the bolt, pivots the front end of the ejector to the right,

trigger guard bow, holds the floorplate in place. Depressing the latch in the guard bow releases the floorplate.

The ends of the W-shaped magazine follower-spring fit into mortises cut into the bottom of the steel follower and floor-plate. The top surface of the follower has a rounded ridge on its left side which forces the cartridges to assume a staggered position when they are inserted into the magazine. The rear edge of the follower is square and, when the magazine is empty, the follower rises high enough to halt the forward motion of the bolt, in-dicating to the shooter that the magazine is empty.

The action is held in the stock by the two guard screws through the ends of the trigger guard and threading into the re-ceiver. The front guard screw passes through an integral stud on the floorplate

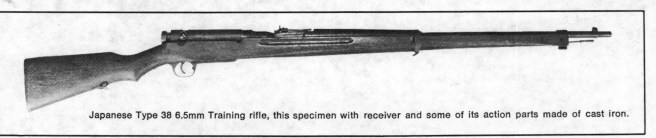

Japanese Type 38 6.5mm Training rifle, this specimen with receiver and some of its action parts made of cast iron.

and threads into a similar stud on the bottom of the receiver. The receiver has no recoil shoulder. The recoil is transferred to the stock by a recoil block which fits over the studs and between the receiver and the floorplate. This recoil block has one flat side (inletted into the stock so the flat side is to the rear) which has enough area to absorb the recoil and prevent set-back of the action in the stock.

The Type 38 Japanese action was designed to eliminate one of the major weak points found in most modern military bolt action rifles—the wrist or grip of the stock. In the Type 38 action strengthening the grip area was done with tangs connected to the receiver and trigger guard. The upper tang, made as a separate part, was milled and joined to the receiver to act as a solid extension to the receiver when the action is in the stock. The separate lower tang was also mated to the rear of the trigger guard. The rear guard screw passes first through the lower tang, then through the trigger guard and threads into a square stud in the receiver. The ends of the tangs are connected by a long screw through the top tang and stock which threads into the lower tang. The tangs extend well past the smallest part of the grip, greatly strengthening the weakest area of the stock.

All bolt action rifles are more or less open to the elements. Dust, mud, sand, water and sleet can get into the action through the top receiver openings and can cause problems.

Japanese designers, evidently familiar with this shortcoming, decided that the action should be covered as much as practicable. The result was a very simple arrangement. Two longitudinal narrow grooves were cut into the receiver, one high on the left receiver wall, the other on the low right receiver wall. A curved strip of spring-tempered sheet metal, its edges folded in, was made to fit over the receiver and slide in the grooves. The bolt handle

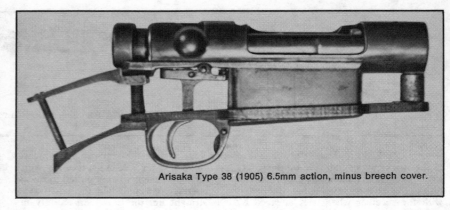

Arisaka Type 38 (1905) 6.5mm action, minus breech cover.

projected through a hole in the rear of this cover allowing the bolt handle to be raised and lowered. The bolt pulls the cover backward and forward with it as the action is opened and closed. This cover did effectively close the main receiver opening, but it still left a big opening around the base of the bolt handle where dirt could get in. The action was more difficult to operate with the cover in place than with the cover removed. Since many captured rifles were minus their breech covers, it seems that some Japanese soldiers discarded them.

Ample provision was made in the Type 38 Arisaka action to allow powder gases to escape harmlessly in the event of a ruptured case head or pierced primer. Two small holes in the top of the receiver ring provide vents for any gas escaping into the locking-lug recesses. A single large oblong hole in the bottom of the bolt, just behind the locking lugs, allows gas to escape into the left locking lug raceway and thence to the auxiliary lug opening in the top of this raceway, just to the rear of the receiver ring. Should any gas be directed rearward in this raceway, it would be deflected by the bolt stop lug, and if any got beyond this point, the

safety would deflect it from the shooter's face. Should a large volume of gas get inside the bolt through the firing-pin hole, all of it could not escape through the large vent in the bolt. It would expand into the inside of the hollow striker, but it would not reach the shooter because of the solid safety cap.

Type 99 Arisakas

In the late 1930s Japan was preparing for war. Type 38 Arisaka rifles were good, and so was the 6.5mm cartridge, but measures had to be taken to speed up production of the rifles and for several reasons a larger caliber was also desirable. Thus, in about 1938, steps were taken to modify the Type 38 (1905) action for easier, faster, less costly manufacture. The Type 99 (1939) Arisaka action was the result. At the same time they adopted a new cartridge, commonly known today as the 7.7 Jap or .31 Jap.

Here is a brief description of the 7.7mm caliber rifles and carbines based on the 99 action, or on further modifications of it.

1. Type 99 (1939) Long Rifle. About 9 pounds, 31.4" barrel, 50" over-all.

2. Type 99 (1939) Short Rifle. About

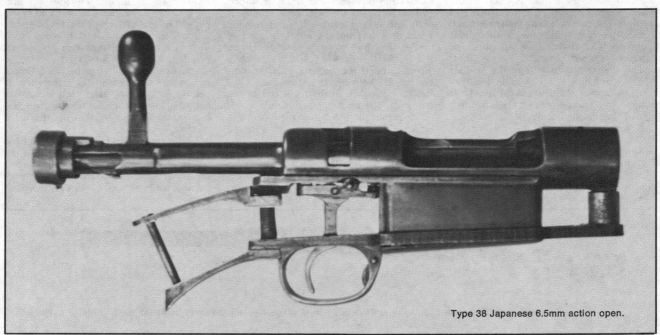

Type 38 Japanese 6.5mm action open.

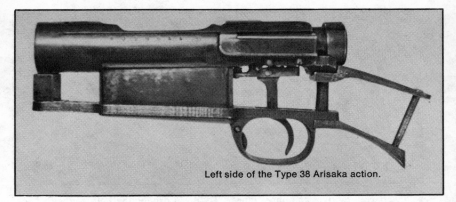
Left side of the Type 38 Arisaka action.

8.5 pounds, 25.75″ barrel, 44.25″ over-all. The standard Japanese infantry rifle used during WW II.

3. Type 99 (1939) Sniper Rifle, same as No. 2 above except fitted with a 2.5 power scope with a detachable off-set mount. Bent down bolt handle.

4. Type 99 (late version) Short Rifle, same as No. 2 above but more cheaply made. Identifying features are: wooden buttplate, fixed aperature rear sight, no model markings. See text for specific details of this and the Paratroop Rifles.

5. Type O Paratroop Rifle. About 8.75 pounds, 25.75″ barrel, 44.25″ over-all. Very rare model.

6. Type 2 (1942) Paratroop Rifle. About 9 pounds, 25.9″ barrel, 44.25″ over-all.

The main identifying features of all rifles based on the Type 99 action are the stamped trigger guard, hinged magazine floorplate, and lower tang extending below the pistol grip. Type 99 Long, Short and Type 2 Sniper rifles usually had chrome-plated bores and bolt faces, and all except the sniper model had straight bolt handles. Sliding breech covers were also standard.

The Type 99 Action

Just as the 1903A3 Springfield action was a modified version of the 1903 Springfield action to make it easier to manufacture, the Japanese 99 action bore the same relationship to the earlier Type 38 action. In neither case did this result in the action becoming less reliable nor weaker. Although the quality of the finish suffered, the modified Springfield and Arisaka actions were unaffected as far as military use was concerned.

The following are the most notable outward changes and modifications made in effecting the change over from the Type 38 (1905) 6.5mm action to the Type 99 (1939) 7.7mm action:

1. The separate recoil block was eliminated; the 99 receiver was made with an integral recoil lug of ample size, which was an improvement.

2. Instead of milling an L-slot in the receiver bridge for the bolt handle, most of the metal below this slot was cut away on the 99 receiver. This still left enough metal for a safety lug for the bolt handle in the event the front locking lugs should fail.

3. The integral bolt stop housing on the receiver was replaced by a copy of the Mauser bolt stop and ejector. The bolt stop, attached to a lug on the receiver, is held in place by a pointed screw turned in from the top, with the ejector pivoting on this same screw. The ejector is tensioned by a separate small spring wedged under the heavier bolt stop spring mortised in the bolt stop.

4. The auxiliary lug and the left (top) locking lug are milled entirely through for the ejector.

5. Sheet metal stampings were used for several parts on the 99 action. These include the upper tang, lower tang and trigger-guard bow, magazine floorplate and floorplate latch.

6. The magazine floorplate is hinged to the front of the magazine plate.

7. The 99 tangs were made longer to further strengthen the grip area of the stock. The non-detachable lower tang extends over the end of the pistol grip.

8. Generally, the safety cap of the 99 action had a shallow groove cut into its outside edge instead of having a hump. The outside edge was usually unserrated and sometimes the rear surface was not knurled or checkered.

9. Only a single gas port was made in the 99 receiver ring.

10. Barrel shank threads were changed; see barrel shank drawings.

11. Other minor changes were made in the 99 action to adapt it to the 7.7mm cartridge and to facilitate manufacture. The magazine box and well were made slightly longer and the magazine well made slightly wider. The cut for the extractor inside the receiver ring was generally milled entirely through to the front edge of the receiver and through the threads for the barrel shank. Some milling cuts in the striker were made from the outside and entirely through the striker wall, instead of making the cuts only in the inside. The outside of the extractor was made flat instead of rounded.

No changes were made in the breeching method. The bolt remained unchanged except as noted above and the same trigger and safety systems were used. As can be expected, 99 actions were not finished as well as 38 actions, with the quality of the outside finish getting worse each succeeding year. By 1944, shortly before the 99 Arisaka went into production, no attempt was made to smooth finish such parts as the trigger guard, floorplate, extractor and upper tang.

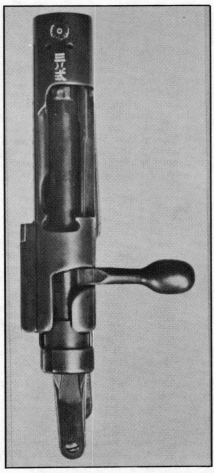
Top view of the Type 38 Arisaka action. Note twin gas-escape holes in the receiver ring, the Japanese Imperial seal and other Japanese markings on the receiver ring, the clip-charger slot in the receiver bridge, the L-shaped slot for the bolt handle, and the oval grasping ball on the straight bolt handle.

The 1945 Action

By 1944 Japan was sorely pressed in her efforts to manufacture enough small arms for the expected homeland defensive operations. Her "last ditch" rifle was the Type 99 (1944 or 1945) version. It was made as quickly and as cheaply as possible and still be usable for serious warfare. Outwardly, this hastily made rifle was the same as the regular 99 (1939) version except for its finish, buttplate and rear sight. Its rear sight was merely a sheet metal aperture affixed to the barrel, the buttplate a thin piece of wood fastened to the stock with a few brads. As for the rifle's finish, the word "rough" best describes it. On several of these rifles I've owned and examined, the receivers were not too bad, but the bolts appeared to be rough undersized forgings with only enough machining done to make them work. Safeties were unfinished, with the stem roughly welded to the cap (this same type of safety was also used on the regular 99 (1939) versions of late manufacture. Although these rifles were fully suitable for service, they were crude. No effort was made to mark the receiver for type, but the Imperial seal was usually stamped on them.

Take-Down and Assembly

First make sure the chamber and magazine are empty.

Type 38: Raise bolt handle, pull it back as far as it will go, then swing bolt stop to the left until bolt can be fully withdrawn. The bolt can be replaced by pushing it forward in the receiver. In replacing a bolt with a sliding breech cover, the cover must be aligned with the grooves in the receiver at the same time the bolt is inserted.

To remove the firing mechanism grasp the bolt with one hand and, with the palm of the other hand, depress the safety as far as it will go, then turn it clockwise about ¼-turn or until it is released. Safety and striker can then be removed from the bolt and the mainspring removed from the striker. Reassemble by inserting mainspring in the striker, inserting the striker in the bolt with the cocking cam positioned in the shallow cam notch, then insert the safety by starting it with the hump positioned slightly clockwise of the bolt handle. Pushing the safety forward as far as it will go and then turn it counterclockwise as far as it will go. When assembled, the lug on the bottom of the safety must align with the cocking cam otherwise the bolt cannot be inserted into the receiver.

Remove extractor by turning it on the bolt so it covers the gas vent and then push it forward. Replace in reverse order. Do not remove extractor collar unless absolutely necessary.

Remove the magazine floorplate, follower and follower spring by depressing the floorplate latch in the trigger guard bow.

To remove barrel and receiver from the stock, first remove barrel bands and turn out the two guard screws and the tang

Type 99 (1939) Japanese 7.7mm Arisaka action, minus breech cover.

screw. The barrel, receiver and upper tang can then be lifted from the top of the stock and the lower tang, trigger guard and magazine box can be removed from the bottom of the stock. Remove magazine latch by driving out its pin, then remove latch plunger and spring.

Remove trigger and sear by driving out sear pin. The trigger pin is riveted in, but can be driven out with a drift punch if necessary.

Remove bolt stop by turning it out, and pulling out the rear screw under the bolt stop housing. Turn out ejector screw to remove ejector. Remove bolt stop spring by swinging its rear end down ¼-turn and lifting it out.

Reassemble all above units in reverse order. In reassembling the bolt stop, first replace ejector and bolt stop, then replace the spring by swinging it in place.

Type 99 take-down: follow same procedures as described for the Type 38 rifle and action except for the following: to remove magazine floorplate, drive hinge pin out; to remove floorplate latch, turn latch screw out; remove bolt stop by removing its screw; the ejector can then be pulled forward out of the bolt-stop housing; the bolt-stop spring is removed by driving it forward out of the housing and the ejector spring is removed along with it.

To aid in driving the bolt-stop spring forward, a small screwdriver should be inserted under the rear of the spring so it can be held up while driving it forward until freed from the bolt stop.

In reassembling bolt stop spring, first place ejector spring under it, then drive both forward until caught. Then insert screwdriver under rear end of the bolt stop spring to hold it up so the spring can be driven fully in place.

The barrels of these rifles are threaded tightly into the receiver (right-hand threads). Do not attempt to remove the barrel unless you have the proper tools to do so.

Action Strength

By now almost every gun buff interested in military bolt action rifles, or in just the actions, knows that the 38 and 99 Japanese Arisaka actions are strong. Many articles have been written about the strength and safety of these actions, and many blow-up tests have been conducted since the late 1940s when someone discovered that all Japanese rifles were not junk. P.O. Ackley, in his book *Handbook For Shooters & Reloaders* Volume II, describes tests he conducted on various military bolt actions, and the Japanese actions

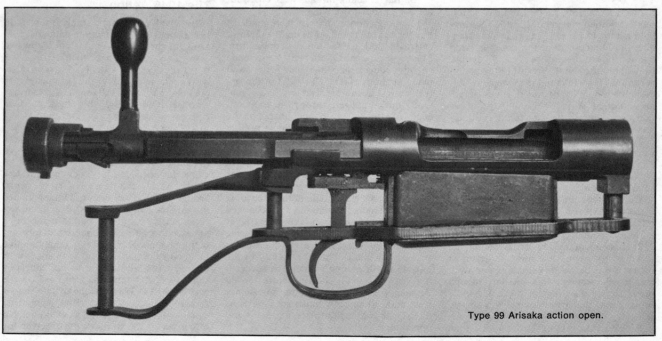
Type 99 Arisaka action open.

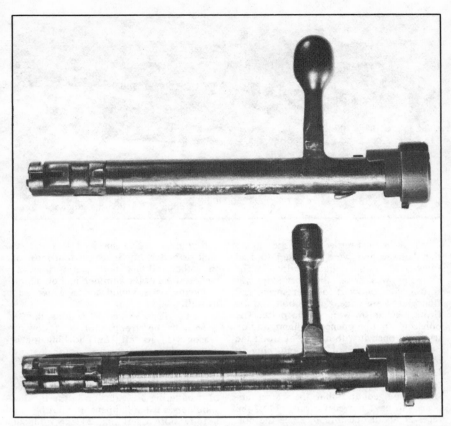

were still going strong after most of the others had failed. This book is recommended reading for anyone interested in action blow-up tests.

Of all the material I've read about the strength of Arisaka actions, the most astonishing report of the toughness of a Type 38 Japanese action and rifle appeared on page 52 in the May, 1959 issue of *The American Rifleman*. This describes a Type 38 6.5mm Arisaka which was rechambered to accept the .30-06 cartridge. The 6.5mm barrel was NOT rebored, only the chamber was enlarged. The fellow who did the rechambering accomplished it by grinding down the pilot of a .30-06 reamer so it would enter the bore. After rechambering he test fired it. Nothing much happened, so he used the rifle on a hunting trip and killed a deer with it. Because the rifle kicked so hard he took it to a reputable gunsmith who discovered what the owner had done with it and what he was shooting in it. Because the rifle was still intact after firing a number of .30-06 cartridges, the gunsmith sent the rifle to the NRA. The NRA staff then fired some more .30-06 rounds through it, and it seems incredible that neither the barrel

Above—Bolt from the Type 38 Arisaka. Below—Bolt from the late Type 99 (1945) Arisaka. Note smaller, cylindrical-shaped grasping ball on this bolt, compared to the larger oval-shaped ball on the Type 38 bolt.

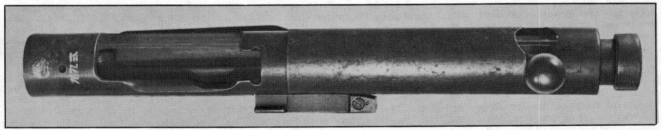

Top view of the Japanese Type 99 action. The action shown with breech cover and bolt open.

Receiver ring markings on the Type 38 Japanese action (left), and on the Type 99 (right). When the Japanese Imperial seal is entirely intact (not partially or entirely ground away) it means that the rifles were captured. Surrendered Japanese rifles generally have the seal ground off.

nor the action burst, for just imagine firing .308″ bullets through a .264″ groove diameter barrel! If one were to deliberately plan a torture test or blow-up test on the 6.5mm Japanese rifle one could hardly think of a better scheme, even though it is a little crazy. That this particular rifle did not burst, or even appear to be strained by this abuse, certainly proves that the bolt, receiver and barrel were made of the best heat-treated steels. It also shows that the breeching and locking system is excellent.

About 10 years before the above incident was reported on, a friend and I put another Japanese rifle through a torture test with the sole intention of firing it until it blew up or could no longer be fired. For this test we used the worst specimen of this rifle which was ever carted home by a returning GI, a Type 99 rifle in 7.7mm caliber. This particular rifle was such a crude specimen that initially we thought it to be a Japanese training rifle. I rechambered it for the .30-06 cartridge, and purposely cut the chamber fully .010″ deeper than normal.

For the test, I loaded a couple of cartridges of each of the following loads in military .30-06 cases.

No. 1. Case full of 3031 powder with a 180-gr. jacketed bullet. (44 grains of this powder with this bullet is normally a maximum load).

No. 2. Case full of 4198 powder with a 180-gr. jacketed bullet. (38 grs. of this powder with this bullet is considered maximum).

No. 3. Case full of 2400 powder with the 180-gr. jacketed bullet. (This powder is never recommended for the .30-06 with this bullet, but a charge of 25 grains would be near or above maximum).

It was dusk when we made the tests. The rifle was tied to an automobile tire and wheel, pointed towards a dirt bank and fired with a long cord tied to the trigger.

We did not expect much to happen on firing both No. 1 cartridges except flattened primers, and that is about all that happened. This was just a good "proof" load. We did, however, expect something to happen to the rifle when the No. 2 loads were fired, but aside from the rifle bucking in its hitch, the primer pockets expanding, the web splitting, and the case heads spreading to a snug fit in the bolt-face recess, nothing unusual happened. We could see a little spurt of flame coming out of the vent hole, but that was about all.

When we fired one cartridge of the No. 3 load, things happened! We noticed streaks of flame coming out all around the action, most of it concentrated around the top and right side of the receiver ring and from the bottom of the action, as the rifle bucked and bellowed from the shock.

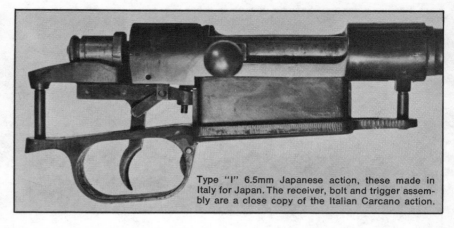

Type "I" 6.5mm Japanese action, these made in Italy for Japan. The receiver, bolt and trigger assembly are a close copy of the Italian Carcano action.

When the dust settled, we rushed to see the damage and were surprised to find the barrel, receiver and bolt intact. The extractor was gone, the bolt stop was sprung, the follower, follower spring and floorplate were gone, but the bolt and the firing mechanism were still in place. The bolt could not be opened by hand, and on trying to open it with a stick of wood the bolt handle broke off. On returning to my shop for closer examination, it was found that the right side of the receiver over the full length extractor cut was slightly bulged and that the barrel appeared to have moved forward out of the receiver about one thread. Since the bolt could not be opened we unscrewed the barrel from the receiver, after which the bolt was easily removed. The head of the case seemed to have melted over the bolt face, for it was practically welded in place. After knocking off the case and turning the barrel back into the receiver, the rifle was still in a condition to be fired! In fact, later on another shooter fitted this same barrel to a good 99 action and found that the chamber had not expanded at all. This experience thoroughly convinced us that the Japanese Arisaka actions are extremely strong. A large ring Model 98 Mauser

action might have survived this test as well or better, but I suspect that most of the other military bolt action rifles, as well as some of the commercial bolt action centerfire rifles, would not have stood up as well.

Of the Type 38 and 99 actions, the 38 is perhaps the stronger for the following reasons: 1) its left (top) locking lug is only partly slotted for the ejector, leaving it with a solid rear face to contact the locking shoulder in the receiver. The lug is not only stronger but there is less chance of it battering a depression in the locking shoulder as often happens in rifles having a fully slotted left lug; 2) the mill cut for the extractor in the receiver ring is no longer than needed. In the last test described above, it is to be noted that the receiver ring bulged along this cut, which in the Type 99 receiver extends all the way through the ring; 3) the barrel shank threads are coarser and, in my opinion, afford a stronger joint between the barrel and receiver than achieved by the use of finer threads. It is also possible that a better steel and heat-treatment was used in making Type 38 actions, but I'm not sure about this. It is usually assumed that any rifle made during desperate wartime

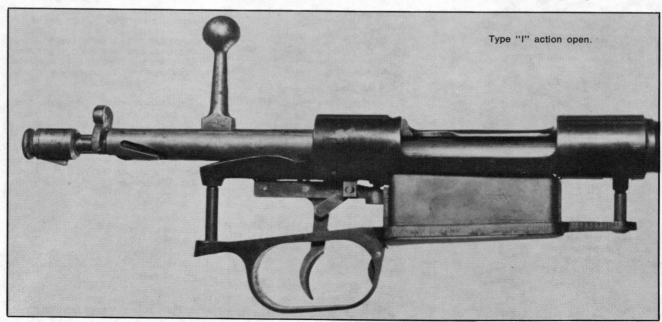

Type "I" action open.

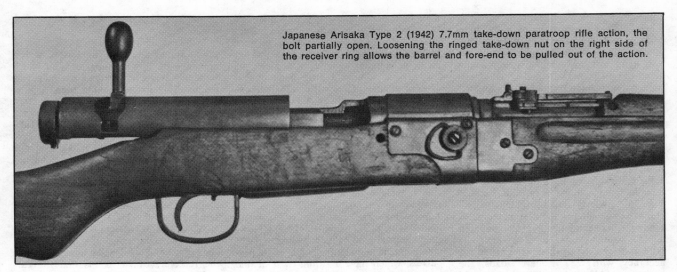

Japanese Arisaka Type 2 (1942) 7.7mm take-down paratroop rifle action, the bolt partially open. Loosening the ringed take-down nut on the right side of the receiver ring allows the barrel and fore-end to be pulled out of the action.

conditions might have inferior steel and/or improper heat-treatment compared to rifles made under ideal conditions, but nothing of this nature seems to have affected the late Type 99 version we tested.

As for the breeching system used in these rifles, I am not sure it has much effect on the over-all strength and safety of the action. This "system" is one in which the bolt head fits closely within a recess in the breech end of the barrel. This breeching system produces the same results as achieved in the M98 Mauser, in which a ring of steel is placed around most of the bolt head.

The weak points in both systems are the wide extractor cut in this ring of steel, and the undercut in the bolt-face recess. As far as strength and safety are concerned, I don't believe this breeching method is much superior to the 03 Springfield breech system. There is no question that the 98 Mauser and Arisaka breeching would be far stronger and safer if there was no undercut in the bolt-face recess, and if a flush-type narrow extractor were used so the wide extractor slot could be eliminated. When an action blows up it is usually the result of a faulty cartridge—when the

head of the cartridge splits open to let large amounts of powder gases escape to the rear. In this event, I fail to see where the 98 Mauser or Arisaka breechings are any better than the 1903 Springfield breeching. In the two previously mentioned Arisaka torture tests, none of the cartridge cases used were faulty. I wonder what would have happened with the 6.5mm Arisaka rifle chambered for the .30-06 cartridge if the head of one of the cartridges had cracked or split open when fired, rather than expanding evenly. I think the results would have been different. A good 03 Springfield action with its funnel breeching will withstand considerable abuse from overloads heavy enough to cause head expansion, but if the head of the case splits with such a load then the situation is different. So that I am not entirely misunderstood, I do prefer the Mauser M98 breeching method over that of the Arisaka, and I prefer either over the Springfield.

Rechambering

Type 38, 6.5mm caliber: During WW II much erroneous information circulated about "that small caliber Jap rifle." Beside

the early belief that neither the cartridge nor rifle was any good, many believed that they were of ".25 caliber." Among the uninformed there is still the belief that the 6.5mm Arisaka rifle is suitable for rechambering to some good American .25-caliber cartridge. Let me correct this if I can.

First, the Type 38 is a true 6.5mm, or the decimal equivalent of .256″ caliber. In this instance, it means "bore" size. Normally the 6.5mm Japanese cartridge is loaded with a .264″ bullet, which is the normal bullet diameter for all 6.5mm caliber rifles. Generally, however, most of the 6.5mm Arisaka barrels have a bore (or land) diameter larger than .256″, and a groove diameter larger than .264″, and this can vary from one barrel to another. Most 6.5mm Arisaka barrels I have checked show a bore diameter of about .257″ to .258″, and a groove diameter of at least .266″ or more.

Before Norma made the 6.5mm Japanese cartridge commercially available, it was common practice to rechamber the 6.5mm Arisaka rifle or carbine to the .257 Roberts case necked up to hold a 6.5mm or .264″ bullet. This cartridge is usually

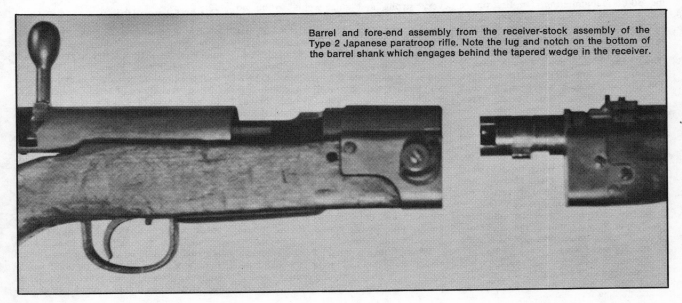

Barrel and fore-end assembly from the receiver-stock assembly of the Type 2 Japanese paratroop rifle. Note the lug and notch on the bottom of the barrel shank which engages behind the tapered wedge in the receiver.

considered to be a wildcat although it is essentially the same as the old 6.5x57mm Mauser cartridge. The .257 Roberts case is a perfect fit in the magazine, bolt face and extractor, and rechambering would clean out all traces of the original chamber. At any rate, the 6.5/.257 Roberts cartridge has to be handloaded.

I am often asked "Can the 6.5 Jap rifle be chambered for the standard .257 Roberts cartridge?" The answer is "Yes," and standard .257 Roberts factory ammunition can be fired in the rifle if it has been rechambered for the 6.5/.257 Roberts cartridge. But, the chances are that accuracy will be very poor because the .257 Roberts bullet of .257" diameter is too small for the 6.5mm bore. In many 6.5 Arisaka rifles I've rechambered a .257" bullet would drop through the bore and, when such rifles were tested for accuracy with .257 Roberts loads, the bullets would keyhole and accuracy would be terrible. However, where the .257" bullet would not drop through the clean bore, then such a rifle might give fair accuracy with the .257 Roberts 117-gr. bulleted load.

Japanese 6.5mm military ammunition has always been scarce, and the cases cannot be reloaded since there are no primers available which will fit. In a pinch, it is possible to make 6.5 Japanese cases from .220 Swift brass, but this is not recommended. Now that Norma commercial 6.5 Japanese ammunition and cases are available, there is no longer any practical reason to have the Arisaka 6.5mm rifle rechambered, or to attempt to reload the original military cases, or to make the cases from other brass. The Norma 6.5 Japanese case is just as reloadable as any other.

Type 99, 7.7mm caliber: here again we have the same situation. It no longer makes sense to rechamber the 7.7mm Arisaka rifle since Norma also loads this cartridge. Before Norma loaded this cartridge, it was common practice to rechamber 7.7mm Arisaka to .30-06 caliber. While these usually gave excellent hunting accuracy, there were two drawbacks against the .30-06 rechambering. The first one, a minor one, was the too-short magazine, and for it to handle the longer .30-06 cartridge properly it had to be lengthened about .20". The second reason was that the rear part of the 7.7mm chamber was already too large for the .30-06 cartridge head, and in some already over-sized wartime manufactured rifles this part of the chamber was often so large as to cause a dangerous condition with .30-06 ammunition. Because of this, most concerned gunsmiths advised against this rechambering unless the barrel was set back enough to remove the over-sized portion. When this was done in connection with the rechambering, then it was also more practical to rechamber for the .300 Savage or .308 NATO since these two cartridges fitted the magazine. Of course, any rechambering is hardly practical since the introduction of Norma 7.7mm Japanese loads.

During the Korean war many Type 99s were rechambered for the .30-06 cartridge and issued to troops of the Republic of Korea. The rechambering was done by U.S. Ordnance units stationed near Tokyo, Japan. I don't know how these rifles were rechambered—whether the barrel was set back or not, or how the magazine was lengthened, because I have been unable to examine one. These rifles can be identified by the marking **Cal. .30 U.S.** stamped on the left side of the receiver ring.

The 7.7mm designation is the metric equivalent of .303", and both figures indicate bore (land diameter) size. The 7.7mm Arisaka barrels usually have a groove diameter of .312", but since these barrels vary a great deal, bore and groove diameters are often .001" to .002" more. The 7.7mm Japanese cartridge is normally loaded with a .311" diameter bullet. However, regular .30-caliber bullets (.308" diameter) also perform well in 7.7mm barrels, which have a rifling twist of one turn in 9.75".

Rebarreling

Type 38 and 99 actions are not very popular for rebarreling. For various rea-

so the bolt head fits snugly in the breech cone.

Either action is well suited for rebarreling to almost any semi-rimmed or rimless cartridge of .30-06 head size, and which measures less over-all than the magazine length. This would include such popular cartridges as the .22-250, .225 Winchester, .243, 6mm, .250 Savage, 257 Roberts, .284, .300 Savage, .308 and .358. Incidentally, at the time of this writing I note that one firm intends to make available turned, threaded and chambered barrels in various calibers for these actions. If this comes about it will be good news for many amateur gunsmiths. The firm is Sanders Custom Gun Service, 2358 Tyler Lane, Louisville, Ky. 40205.

When the 38 action is rebarreled for any of these cartridges it will usually be necessary to widen the magazine well in the receiver, which means that the cartridge guide lips must be filed down a bit. This does not usually have to be done when the 99 action is rebarreled for these cartridges. With both actions it is usually necessary to alter the feed ramp a bit by filing or grinding it slightly wider and

An action from one of several different Type 38 military training rifles. This one, with breech cover, is an example of one of the better-made actions, having a regular bolt with full-sized forward locking lugs and regular extractor. However, it has a cast iron receiver, trigger parts and trigger guard. A distinctive feature of these actions is that the tangs are made integral with the receiver and trigger guard.

sons these actions are not highly regarded by most shooters as ones on which to build custom rifles. The fact that they are very strong and safe seems to be no recommendation in their favor. The main reason why few are rebarreled is that many gunsmiths try to avoid them, or refuse to work on them because of the odd barrel threads and the extra work required to duplicate the breeching. Generally the amateur gunsmith is the only one willing to tackle the job and often he can get closer to duplicating the odd thread pitch of the Type 99 barrel shank on his small non-quick-change-gearbox lathe than can the professional gunsmith with his big quick-change-gearbox lathe. For the 38 action, the barrel has to have a pitch of 14 threads per inch, and the 99 actions need 17 threads per inch, both V type. Actually, the 99 barrel has a pitch of 16.93 TPI, but 17 is as close as you can get without having special metric thread gears for the lathe.

When fitting a barrel to these actions always duplicate as closely as possible the breeching of the original barrel, and if possible, do this to even closer tolerances

lower at the rear. Afterward the ramp should be highly polished.

Other Gunsmithing

The wood in issue Arisaka stocks is of poor quality, and I think you will find it is a waste of time to try to remodel one or to refinish it. Fajen and Bishop, as well as some other stockmakers, can furnish several styles of semi-finished stocks for either type of Arisaka rifle. The stocks are not inletted for the tangs since it is common practice to discard them. The upper tang is discarded entirely. On the 38 action the lower tang is cut off about ½" to the rear of the rear guard screw hole and the end of this short piece rounded or filed flat. With the 99, the tang is cut off just to the rear of the guard screw hole. I see no objection in retaining the tangs on the 38 action if you want to go to the bother of inletting them.

The large oval shaped bolt-handle knob is unsightly. Whether a low-mounted scope is to be used on the rifle or not I would suggest attaching a new bolt handle. When this is done on the 38 that part of the receiver behind the bolt handle will have to be filed away on top or entirely removed leaving it like the 99 receiver. Unless you are a skilled welder I advise having a competent gunsmith or a good welder put on the new bolt handle.

I advise against attempting to change either action to cock on the uplift of the bolt handle. It is a difficult job, and presents a number of problems not usually foreseen.

If you dislike the safety arrangement, there is a commercial side safety available that is not difficult to install. These are made by Doc Line Co., 18440 John R., Detroit, Mich., 48203.

It is often possible to improve the trigger pull by careful honing of the various contacting surfaces, but it is not wise to eliminate entirely the first stage of the pull. If you dislike both trigger and safety, install the Timney trigger with the combined side safety.

The 6.5mm Japanese Cartridge

Japan adopted this cartridge in 1897. It is a semi-rimmed bottlenecked case

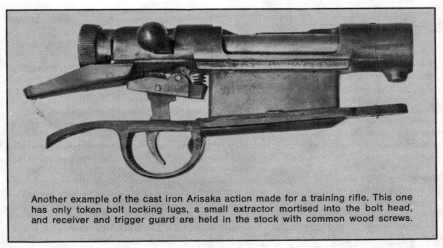

Another example of the cast iron Arisaka action made for a training rifle. This one has only token bolt locking lugs, a small extractor mortised into the bolt head, and receiver and trigger guard are held in the stock with common wood screws.

primed with a Berdan primer of a size never made available to reloaders. The "6.5mm" represents bore size, or the same as .256 caliber. It is normally loaded with a .263 or .264″ diameter bullet. The standard Japanese military ball loading was a 139-gr. spitzer bullet its muzzle velocity about 2500 fps. Sporting ammunition in this caliber is imported by Norma Precision, South Lansing, N.Y. 14882 and is available through many Norma dealers. Norma offers two 6.5 loads, one with a 139-gr. semi-pointed, soft-point, boat-tail bullet, the other using a 156-gr. soft-point 139-gr. spitzer bullet, its muzzle velocity the 139-gr. bullet is listed by Norma as 2428 fps, the remaining energy at 200 yards 1401 foot pounds. This is a better cartridge and load for hunting such game as deer and antelope than the best commercial load for the .243, 6mm, .250 Savage or .257 Roberts. For this purpose, I would also consider it better than the .30-30 and .32 Special. The other Norma 6.5mm load has a 156-gr. bullet at a muzzle velocity of 2067 fps, and at 200 yards remaining energy is 992 foot pounds. This

would be a better choice than the 139-gr. for hunting in wooded or brushy country.

The 7.7mm Japanese Cartridge

Adopted by Japan in 1939, the 7.7mm cartridge has a rimless bottlenecked case. The standard military ball load has a 183-gr. pointed bullet with a muzzle velocity of about 2300 fps. Norma has two loads for this cartridge; one with a 130-gr. soft-point semi-pointed bullet, the other with a 180-gr. soft-point semi-pointed boat-tail bullet. The 130-gr. load, muzzle velocity 2950 fps, shows 1581 foot pounds energy at 200 yards. The 180-gr. load, muzzle velocity 2493 fps, has at 200 yards a remaining energy of 1765 foot pounds. This last load would be suitable for taking most species of North American big game and, according to these figures, it is slightly more powerful than the .30-40 Krag and .300 Savage, which have long been considered good big game calibers.

Summary

For remodeling into a sporting rifle, or using its action to build a rifle, Arisaka rifles are far down on the popularity list of rifles having a non-detachable staggered-column magazine. Until Norma ammunition became available in the Japanese calibers, the Arisaka rifles were not seriously considered for gunsmithing because of the ammunition problem. Some of their unpopularity is undoubtedly due to the early unfavorable publicity given them during and shortly after WW II. However, I believe the main reason why they have not been used more frequently, or are not now being considered for remodeling, is because the action is not easy to operate.

I have not remodeled many Arisaka rifles, and I can think of only two occasions when I built a complete rifle on this action. I have, however, rechambered many of the 6.5s to the 6.5/.257 Roberts and converted many 7.7s to the .30-06 and .300 Savage calibers. Some of these rifles are still being used by their owners for hunting deer. The amateur gunsmith is cautioned to be on his guard against Japanese training rifles, which are unsuitable for any gunsmithing. These training

rifles are discussed at the end of this chapter.

The Arisaka Paratroop Rifle

This chapter would not be complete without illustrations and descriptions of 3 other types of Japanese military weapons used before and during WW II: the take-down paratroop models, the Type "I" rifle and the various training rifles.

The first of the take-down paratroop rifles is generally designated as the Type 0 Paratroop Rifle. This particular model is quite rare, and I have never examined one closely. Probably developed around 1940, it is based on the Type 99 Arisaka action. Chambered for the 7.7mm Japanese cartridge, it was made so the barrel and fore-end assembly could be separated from the buttstock and action assembly, with the take-down effected by an interrupted-thread joint between barrel and receiver. It also featured a detachable bolt handle. It has a 25.75″ barrel, weighs about 8.75 pounds and is 44.25″ over-all. In original and very good condition they're a desirable item for any military arms collection.

The second take-down paratroop rifle is the Type 2, developed in 1942 to replace the Type 0. Type 2 rifles also used the 7.7mm cartridge, weigh 9 pounds, and their 25.90″ barrel make over-all length 44.25″. It has a cleaning rod under the barrel and it will accept the regular Japanese bayonet.

The action of the Type 2 is also a modification of the basic 99 action, having the same bolt and magazine parts.

The Type 2 take-down system uses a wedge, through the massive front part of the receiver, to hold the slip-fit barrel in place. The barrel shank is round and smooth except for the solid lug underneath it. The front of the receiver is bored and milled to accept the lugged barrel shank. Under the front part of the receiver, and made integral with it, is a heavy mass of steel through which is milled a rectangular hole for the take-down wedge. It is so positioned that the wedge engages forward of the barrel lug. A ringed screw on the wedge threads into the side of the receiver and, with the barrel and wedge in place, this screw is turned to draw the wedge and barrel tightly into the receiver. When turned in the opposite direction, it allows the wedge and barrel to be removed. It is a simple and effective take-down system for a military bolt action rifle.

There is also a matching shaped block of metal attached to the breech end of the barrel to butt against the receiver when the rifle is assembled. The front tang of the trigger guard is fitted into a milled recess in the bottom of the receiver and held in place with a screw. The extra metal in the receiver and on the barrel adds over a half-pound to the weight of this rifle compared to the regular Type 99 Short Rifle.

The take-down system of the Type 2 appears rugged enough and, with the wedge drawn tight it is probably anchored as securely in the receiver as is the bolt in the receiver.

6.5mm Arisaka Type 38
Parts Legend

1. Receiver (top view)
2. Upper tang
3. Bolt
4. Extractor
5. Extractor collar
6. Firing pin
7. Mainspring
8. Cocking piece/safety
9. Breech cover
10. Sear
11. Sear pin
12. Sear spring
13. Trigger
14. Trigger pin
15. Bolt stop
16. Bolt stop spring
17. Bolt stop screw
18. Ejector
19. Ejector screw
20. Trigger guard
21. Floorplate
22. Floorplate latch
23. Floorplate latch pin
24. Floorplate latch plunger
25. Floorplate latch plunger spring
26. Magazine box
27. Follower spring
28. Follower
29. Front trigger guard screw
30. Recoil block
31. Lower tang
32. Rear trigger guard screw (stock) bushing
34. Tang screw

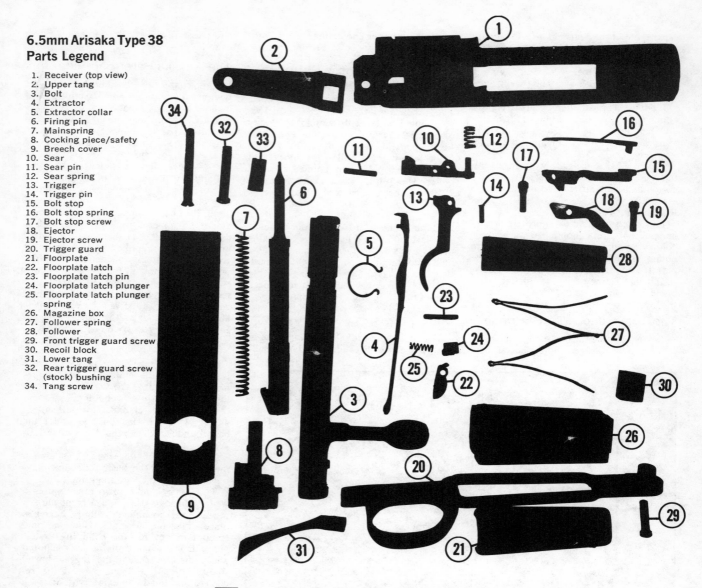

Type 38 Arisaka

Since Type 2 rifles are not very common they would be worth much more as a collector's arm if left "as issued" rather than remodeled into a sporter, so I advise against this latter course.

Type I Japanese Rifles

One of the unusual Japanese military shoulder arms is the Type I rifle. Very little is known about its history except that it is a hybrid, made in Italy for Japan. It has features of the Italian M91 Carcano rifle and the Type 38 Arisaka. Chambered for the 6.5mm Japanese cartridge, they were made by the Pietro Beretta firm in Gardone, Italy, perhaps even by other Italian firms. I don't know when or how many were made.

The Type I rifle has a 30.5″ barrel, weighs about 9 pounds and is 49.75″ overall. The barrel and sights are similar to those on the regular 38 Arisaka rifle. A half-length wooden handguard covers part

---

Type 38 and 99 Arisaka
(Type 38 uses 6.5mm and Type 99 uses 7.7mm Japanese cartridges)

General Specifications

Type	Turnbolt repeater.
Receiver	One-piece machined steel forging. Clip-charger guide milled in non-slotted bridge. Upper tang is a separate part of receiver.
Bolt	One-piece, with dual-opposed forward locking lugs. Bolt handle base acts as safety lug.
Ignition	Composed of one-piece hollow striker, coil mainspring and safety. Striker cocks on closing the bolt.
Magazine	Staggered-column non-detachable 5-shot box magazine. Quick-detachable floorplate on the Type 38, hinged floorplate on the Type 99.
Trigger	Non-adjustable, double-stage military pull.
Safety	Locks both striker and bolt when engaged. (See text)
Extractor	One-piece, non-rotating Mauser-type attached to the bolt with a collar.
Magazine cut-off	None provided.
Bolt stop	Mauser-type bolt stop attached to left rear of receiver bridge. Stops rearward movement of bolt by contacting auxiliary lug on the bolt.
Ejector	Lever type housed within the bolt stop.

7.7mm Arisaka Type 99
Parts Legend

1. Receiver (top view)
2. Upper tang
3. Bolt stop
4. Bolt-stop spring
5. Bolt-stop screw
6. Ejector
7. Ejector spring
8. Sear
9. Sear pin
10. Sear spring
11. Trigger
12. Trigger pin
13. Bolt
14. Extractor
15. Extractor collar
16. Firing pin
17. Mainspring
18. Cocking piece/safety
19. Breech cover
20. Trigger guard
21. Floorplate
22. Floorplate hinge pin
23. Floorplate latch
24. Floorplate latch spring
25. Floorplate latch retainer
    screw
26. Magazine box
27. Follower spring
28. Follower
29. Front trigger guard screw
30. Front trigger guard screw
    (stock) bushing
31. Rear trigger guard screw
32. Tang screw (stock)
    bushing
33. Tang screw
    bushing
34. Rear guard screw (stock)

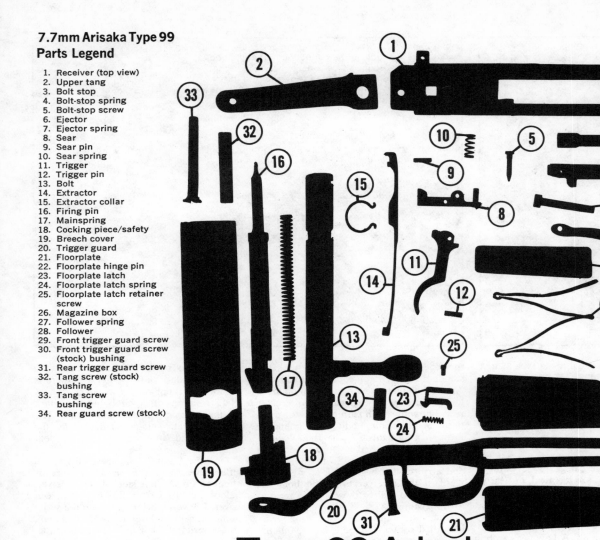

Type 99 Arisaka

of the barrel. It has a cleaning rod in the fore-end under the barrel and the rifle accepts the regular Arisaka bayonet. The barrel bands, and the method by which they are held in place with spring clips, the grasping grooves in the fore-end and the sling swivels, are patterned after the Type 38 rifle stock. No tangs are employed.

The receiver, bolt and trigger mechanism are near copies of the Italian M91 Carcano action, and the Mauser type staggered-column magazine is a close copy of that of the Type 38 action. The trigger guard bow is large, like that on the Carcano action. The bolt, firing mechanism, trigger mechanism, safety, extractor, bolt stop and ejector are practically identical to the same parts in the M91 Carcano action, though they are not interchangeable. The receiver differs from the Carcano in that its magazine well is wider, with cartridge guide lips milled in to handle cartridges from the staggered-column magazine. The front of the slotted bridge is grooved to accept a stripper clip. The trigger guard, magazine box, floorplate, floorplate latch, follower and follower spring are nearly identical to these parts in the Type 38 action. Type I action specs follow:

Dimensional Specifications

	Type 38 6.5mm	Type 99 7.7mm
Weight	48 oz	48 oz.
Over-all (not incl. tang)	4.73″	4.73″
Receiver ring dia.	1.335″	1.345″
Bolt body dia.	.700″	.703″
Bolt travel	4.415″	4.425″
Striker travel	5.60″	5.60″
Guard screw spacing	6.93″	6.93″
Magazine well opening:		
Length	3.120″	3.210″
Width	.600″	.640″
Bolt face recess:		
Dia.	.495″	.485″
Depth	.055″	.060″

Weight	42 oz.
Magazine well opening:	
Length	3.125″
Width, front	.550″
Width, rear	.540″

Receiver length, receiver ring diameter, bolt diameter, bolt travel and striker travel are about the same as in the M91 Carcano action. See the chapter on the M91 Carcano for more details.

The Type I would be more desirable for remodeling into a sporting rifle than the M91 Carcano, but less desirable than the Type 38. Of the thousands of military rifles I've seen, only two were Type I rifles, so I doubt if many are around. At any rate, if anyone wants to remodel or convert this rifle that's his business, but I think it would be better to sell or trade it to a military arms collector and use an M98 Mauser, which are plentiful.

Japanese Training Rifles

Illustrated here is a Type 38 Training Rifle, one of several variations of training or drill rifles the Japanese made. Outwardly, none of them appear to be much different from the regular Type 38, but outward appearances are deceiving. No discussion of Japanese military rifles would be complete without mention of them. The reader should be warned, however, that these rifles are *positively dangerous if fired with live ammunition*.

Although I've only been able to examine 4 of these rifles in the past, all were essentially alike in appearance except for bolt and receiver details. There probably are others that are different from the ones I

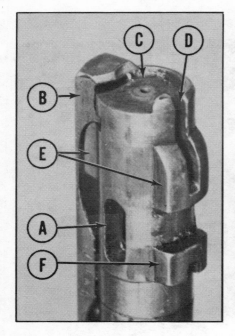

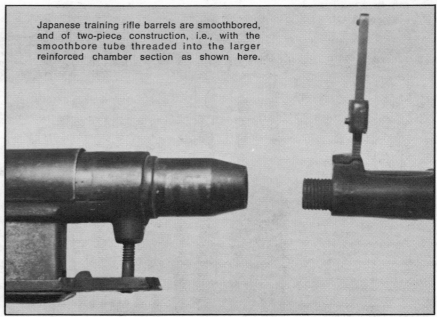

Japanese training rifle barrels are smoothbored, and of two-piece construction, i.e., with the smoothbore tube threaded into the larger reinforced chamber section as shown here.

Underside view of the Japanese Type 38 bolt head (6.5mm) showing: (A) gas vent hole, (B) extractor, (C) bolt-face recess with undercut, (D) ejector slot, (E) locking lugs and (F) bolt-stop lug. The Type 99 bolt is the same except that the extractor slot is milled entirely through the bolt stock and locking lugs.

have seen, but I believe they can all be classed in the same category. Outwardly, these training rifles are identical, or nearly so, to the regular Type 38 infantry rifle. They are approximately the same weight, length and size, and are stocked in the same manner and usually have sights similar to the Type 38. A bayonet can be attached to them, and often they're complete with a cleaning rod under the barrel. All have smoothbored barrels and are chambered for the 6.5mm Japanese blank or training cartridge. The barrel may be a worn out one salvaged from a regular Type 38 rifle and then bored out smooth, or merely a piece of tubing screwed into the heavier (reinforced) breech end of the barrel.

Most 6.5mm training rifles have a cast or forged iron receiver, the upper tang integral with it. Often the outside finish of these receivers is very rough. Some have a receiver made of steel tubing with the rear tang welded on. Practically all have the receiver grooved for the sliding breech cover, and a couple of them I examined had these covers. All have a rough cast trigger guard with an integral lower tang. Instead of a rear guard screw, these actions usually employed a tang screw connecting the two tangs. On one rifle I examined, only the barrel bands held the barrel and action in the stock and two wood screws held the trigger guard and magazine in place.

I have seen three different types of bolts and receivers in these training rifles. One had a standard pattern bolt with dual-opposed locking lugs which engaged in

the receiver ring, and was fitted with the standard long, non-rotating extractor. Another had a bolt with thin dual-opposed locking lugs which engaged in the receiver ring, but with a thin spring extractor mortised in the bolt body and extending through a slot through the right locking lug. The last one had no forward locking lugs, the extractor fitted in the bolt head, and a rib on the bolt which engaged forward of the receiver bridge to hold the action closed. All of these bolts appeared to be castings.

These training rifles can usually be identified by their smooth bores, but the surest method is to remove the barrel and action from the stock, and if the tang is integral with the receiver, or welded in place, then you know for certain that it is a training rifle. Regardless of the type of bolt it has, these rifles should never be fired with bulleted ammunition or the action used for building a rifle.

Markings

Regular issue Japanese military bolt action rifles in calibers 6.5 and 7.7mm have the Japanese imperial seal stamped on the top forward part of the receiver. This seal is round, up to about 7/16″ in diameter, and resembles a sunflower or daisy blossom with 16 petals. It is often referred to as the "rising sun" or "chrysanthemum" marking. On many Japanese rifles this seal has been partly or entirely ground away, indicating these particular rifles were surrendered. Rifles with the seal untouched were generally captured arms.

Below the imperial seal are stamped the Japanese characters indicating the type and year designation of the rifle. These markings are illustrated separately, with each character identified. The imperial seal is not found on Japanese training rifles, but a few are marked with Japanese

characters to indicate they are for use with blank cartridges only. Sometimes there is another marking on the receiver ring of these training rifles, probably the mark of the arsenal which made them. The Type 99 (late version) rifle carries the imperial seal, but has no type or year markings.

On all 6.5 and 7.7 Japanese bolt action rifles I've seen, the serial number is stamped on the left side of the receiver, below the groove for the sliding breech cover. I have no information on the serial numbering procedures followed in Japan, so the serial number in itself means little. The Type 38 action pictured in this chapter has a serial number well over 5,000,000, which may be some indication as to the number of these rifles produced.

One or more various small markings often precede or follow the serial number marking. These marks may be arsenal identification marks and/or arsenal proof marks. On Type 38 actions part of the serial number is usually stamped on the underside of the bolt handle base, and on some of the other parts as well, such as the trigger and trigger guard.

Conclusion

A great many of the Japanese rifles were brought into the United States by GIs after WW II, and many more were imported and sold by dealers in military surplus arms, so the total number now in the U.S. must be great. Many of them will remain souvenirs and many of the better specimens and the rarer ones are in collections or will be obtained for this purpose. I suspect, however, most of them have already been remodeled, or will be remodeled in future years. I predict also that there will be little decline in interest in the Type 38 and 99 rifles for a number of years to come as new corps of amateur gunsmiths seek out rifles to remodel.

12. Greek M1903 Mannlicher-Schoenauer

To MOST RIFLEMEN, the name Mannlicher-Schoenauer brings to mind a sleek little sporting rifle having a slim fore-end that extends to the muzzle of its short barrel. It is in the "elite" class of bolt action sporting rifles, and it's gained worldwide recognition and fame. Its popularity does not seem to decrease despite the great many other bolt action rifles it has had to compete against since it was first introduced many years ago. It all started with the Greek Model 1903 M-S military rifle, for the M-S sporting rifle is basically a sporterized version of the military rifle.

The M-S action was developed in the Austrian Arms Factory at Steyr in 1900, the name deriving from those of Ferdinand Ritter von Mannlicher and Otto Schoenauer. Mannlicher, born in Mainz, Germany, in 1848, became one of the world's leading military arms designers. He died in Austria in 1904. He is most noted for his development of the cliploading magazine system, "straight-pull" rifle actions, and automatic rifles and pistols, for which he obtained many U.S. and foreign patents. Most military arms produced by the great Austrian Arms Factory, often called the Great Steyr Works, from the mid-1880s on, were of Mannlicher design. Otto Schoenauer, a native Austrian, was the director of the Austrian Arms factory for a number of years. His main claim to fame is the rotary-type magazine used in the M-S rifle.

Although he was not the first inventor of the rotary-spool magazine system, Otto Schoenauer began working with that idea before 1885; it was first combined with a turnbolt .43 caliber rifle of Mannlicher design in 1887. A year later it was adapted to a Mannlicher straight-pull rifle. In the United States Arthur Savage was working on his lever action rifle fitted with a rotary-spool magazine, which he perfected by 1893 and on which he obtained patents. He became famous for his efforts which resulted in the Model 99 Savage rifle, still being made today.

The Schoenauer spool magazine, however, was not fully perfected until about 1900, when it was first successfully combined with a small-caliber turnbolt rifle. It is believed that Portugal obtained a few of the Model 1900 M-S military rifles. This rifle, with minor modifications, was adopted by Greece in 1903, and designated the Model 1903 Greek Mannlicher-Schoenauer rifle. It was produced in large numbers by the factory of which Schoenauer was the director. Mannlicher supplied most of the action designs.

At this point, I must backtrack a bit. In an earlier chapter I described the German Model 88 Commission action. Designed by a group of men, who borrowed some features from an earlier Mauser action and used the Mannlicher patented clip-loading single-column magazine system. Adopted by Germany in 1888, the only thing about this action which was "Mannlicher" was the magazine.

The Austrian Arms Factory in Steyr was one of the firms which contracted to make the M88 rifles for Germany. Because of the magazine, and because Mannlicher was also associated with the firm, and perhaps because they made some sporting rifles based on this action, the 88 rifles were often referred to as "Mannlicher" rifles.

When the Steyr factory developed the M-S rifle in 1900, they freely borrowed and copied the basic receiver and bolt features of the 88 action, fitting it with the Schoenauer rotary-spool magazine. This was an expedient thing to do since it was a smooth and very reliable turnbolt system and they were already making the 88 rifle. No doubt Mannlicher had a hand in modifying and adapting the 88 receiver for the Schoenauer magazine, but designing it so it could be readily detached from the rifle for cleaning. He was also responsible for the several changes and improvements on the bolt. The basic action, nonetheless, was not his creation.

Regardless of the minor role that Mannlicher had in the development of the

Model 1903 Greek rifle, that rifle, as well as all future rifles based on this action, were, and are still, known as "Mannlicher-Schoenauer" actions.

Greece adopted the M-S rifle in 1903, and it was to remain their principle military shoulder arm until after WW II. Compared to many other military bolt action rifles, the M1903 and the later 1903/14 Greek rifles did not gain any spectacular recognition as military arms outside of Greece. The M-S action, however, gained worldwide acclaim and popularity when used in the Steyr-built sporting rifles. First made and introduced to European hunters in 1903 or 1904, its most distinctive feature was a very short barrel and a very slim fore-end that extended to the muzzle. It is this feature more than anything else that the name "Mannlicher" has been associated with, and to such an extent that even today any rifle similarly stocked is called a Mannlicher-stocked rifle.

There are two model designations and a carbine and rifle version of each designation of the Greek M-S arm. The 1903 Greek rifle (marked **STEYR 1903** on the receiver) is 43.3″ over-all, has a 28.5″ barrel and weighs about 8.3 pounds. The 1903 Greek carbine is 39.4″ over-all, has a 19.7″ barrel and weighs about 7.3 pounds. Both have a wooden handguard which extends from the receiver to the middle barrel band. The Model 1903/14 Greek rifle and carbine (marked **STEYR 1903/14** on the receiver) adopted in 1914 are almost the same as the 1903s except that the handguard extended from the receiver to the upper barrel band. All are chambered for the 6.5 M-S cartridge, and made so a bayonet can be attached to the muzzle.

The 1903 and 1903/14 Greek military rifles were rather late-comers on the U.S. surplus arms market, not generally of-

---

Illustrated above: Greek Model 1903/14 Mannlicher-Schoenauer military rifle.

fered for sale until about 1961. Carbines were first priced about $35 each, the rifles at about $30. M98 military Mausers were then selling for about the same prices. I thought the Greek M-S rifles a good value when compared with any other military surplus bolt action rifle then being offered, except that their bores were neglected and usually dark. However, they apparently sold well, for after a year or so they were no longer advertised. Evidently, however, many of them must have had bores and/or stocks in such poor shape that, shortly after the rifles were first offered, separate actions were also made available. Moderately priced ($10 to $15) the actions also apparently sold well, for they too were soon off the market. At any rate, for a short time the amateur gunsmith had the opportunity to purchase a genuine Mannlicher-Schoenauer rifle or action, an opportunity which may never again be presented.

The Greek Mannlicher-Schoenauer Action

The receiver is a heavy one-piece steel forging machined to accept the barrel, bolt, magazine and other parts. The front end of the receiver is bored and threaded to accept the barrel shank. Inside the receiver ring there is a collar against which the barrel abuts. This collar surrounds the bolt head except for a slot on the left side for the ejector. Underneath the round receiver ring there is a small stud projection, which is tapped for the front receiver screw. It is not large enough to transfer adequately the recoil to the stock, but on military rifles a separate recoil plate is inletted into the stock, just to the rear of the stud.

The top and right center of the receiver are cut out to gain access to the magazine opening. Much metal is left under the center of the receiver, enough metal for front and rear walls, and this is milled to accept the various magazine parts. The magazine well opening in the receiver is milled out on the left side of the receiver

Greek Model 1903 military Mannlicher-Schoenauer action.

bottom to allow passage of the cartridges from the magazine into the chamber.

The inside of the receiver proper is precisely bored and milled out for the bolt and its locking lugs. Recesses with angled approaches, cut into the rear of the receiver ring, leave locking shoulders to engage locking lugs. The angled slope on the forward corner of each shoulder draws the bolt forward as the bolt is rotated closed. The receiver bridge is slotted to allow passage of the bolt handle, and the front of this slot is grooved to accept a magazine-charger clip. The rear of the receiver ends in a tang into which the rear receiver screw threads.

The small one-piece bolt stop is attached to the left side of the receiver bridge, and pivots on a stud made integral with the receiver. A pin holds the bolt stop on the stud, and a coil spring in the rear of the bolt stop provides the tension. An extension on the front of the bolt stop, projecting through a hole in the receiver wall into the locking lug raceway, halts the bolt in its rearward motion as it contacts the ejector and bolt locking lug.

The bolt has a separate non-rotating bolt head. Mortised into the right side of the bolt head and its stem is a one-piece spring extractor—no stronger or weaker

than that of the 88 Commission action. Loosely mortised into the left side of the bolt head, so that it has some longitudinal movement, is the ejector. It is held in place by a small screw. The ejector extends back and overlaps the locking lug when the bolt handle is raised so that, on pulling the bolt back, the bolt stop pushes the ejector forward to eject the cartridge or fired case before the bolt is halted, when the ejector contacts the locking lug. This arrangement, and the ejector itself, is much better than the ejector system in the 88 action. The outside front edge of the ejector is beveled to move the bolt stop out of the way when the assembled bolt is inserted into the receiver.

The bolt-head face is not recessed for the cartridge head. Instead, the breeching system is so made that, when the bolt is locked closed, the flat face of the bolt head contacts the breech end of the barrel. The chamber is deep enough to let the cartridge head lie flush with the end of the barrel. Shallow grooves cut across the face of the barrel allow room for the ejector and extractor. A good arrangement, but it makes barrel fitting a bit more difficult than it is with the 88 action, which has a recessed bolt head.

The bolt body is drilled from the front

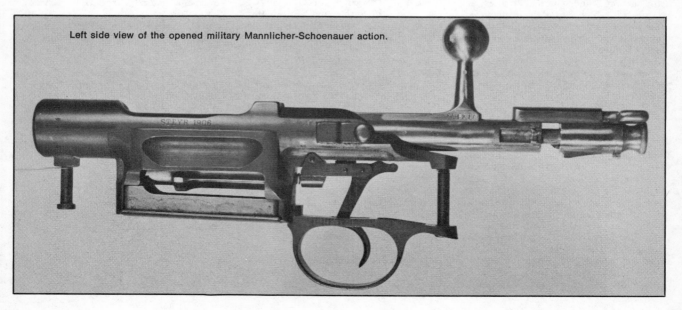

Left side view of the opened military Mannlicher-Schoenauer action.

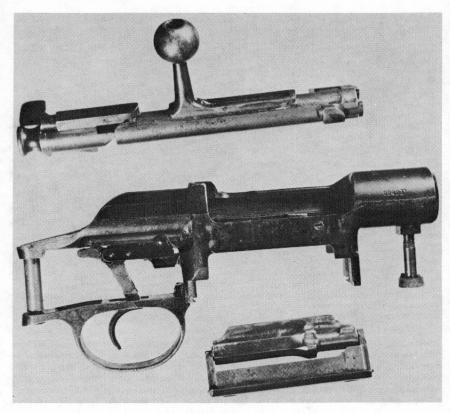

Main parts of the military M-S action, showing complete bolt assembly at top, receiver in the center, and detachable rotary magazine assembly at bottom.

depressing the bolt stop, something is amiss. This could prevent an extremely dangerous situation arising, since it is possible to fire the rifle with the bolt head missing.

The straight bolt handle, with its large hollow grasping ball, is an integral part of the bolt body. Also made integral with the bolt is the guide rib, which extends forward of, and becomes part of, the base or root of the bolt handle. This rib affords additional anchorage for the bolt handle, but also guides the bolt and prevents its binding. The rear of the rib, or the base of the bolt handle, is not high enough to contact the front of the receiver bridge, so apparently no effort was made to provide a positive safety lug arrangement. In the event the front locking lugs or receiver ring should fail, however, the bolt handle itself would prevent the bolt from being driven out of the receiver. The center of the guide rib is milled out to keep weight to a minimum.

The firing pin and mainspring are inserted through the front of the bolt, the mainspring being compressed over the firing pin stem between a shoulder on the front of the firing pin and a shoulder in the rear of the bolt body. The heavy cocking piece fits over the rear end of the firing pin, held there by the firing pin nut, which is secured to the firing pin with an interrupted lug arrangement. Flat surfaces on the rear of the firing pin, engaging a matching hole in the cocking piece, and the flattened front end of the firing pin, engaging a matched slot in the bolt head, prevent these parts from turning on the firing pin.

A cam projection on the cocking piece, matching a notch in the rear of the bolt body, cocks the firing mechanism when the bolt handle is lifted. This cocking action is easy because of the smoothness of the contacting metal surfaces. Since the firing pin nut, cocking piece, safety and safety spring are part of the firing mechanism, and are attached to the firing pin, lock time is a bit sluggish, but ignition is positive because of the weight of these parts.

to accept the firing pin, mainspring and bolt head. A small lug on the stem of the bolt head, and a matching longitudinal and circular groove inside the front of the bolt, hold these two parts together, allowing the bolt head to be removed and replaced when it is turned to a certain position. The dual-opposed locking lugs are on the extreme front end of the bolt body, both solid and quite large. The top front corner of the right (or bottom) locking lug is beveled to match a similar beveled surface left inside the locking-lug recess in the receiver ring. This provides the initial extraction camming power when the bolt handle is raised.

The front of the left locking lug has a circular groove cut across its face. The rear of the projection on the bolt stop, which projects into the locking lug raceway, has a ridge to match the groove in the left locking lug. Unless the ejector is in place or the bolt head and ejector not assembled on the bolt, the bolt cannot be inserted into the receiver unless the bolt stop is purposely depressed in doing so. Thus, the groove and hook arrangement on the locking lug and bolt stop serves as a warning that, unless the bolt can be inserted into the receiver *without* manually

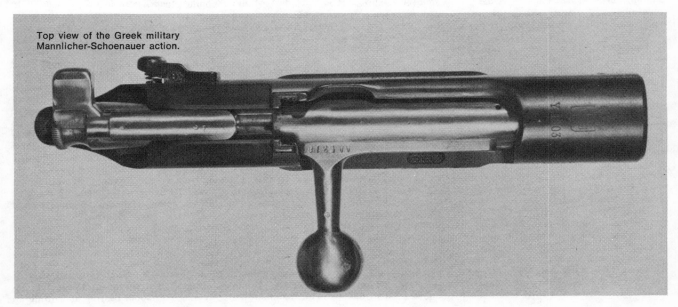

Top view of the Greek military Mannlicher-Schoenauer action.

The wing safety is positioned in a hole in the upper part of the cocking piece, and into an extension of the cocking piece which extends forward into the slot in the receiver bridge. It is tensioned by a short coil spring which fits over the stem of the safety. This keeps it pushed back against the firing pin nut, which holds the safety in place, and which in turn prevents the firing pin nut from being turned unless the safety is pushed forward. When the action is cocked, swinging the safety up and to the right locks both bolt and cocking piece. This is accomplished by the end of the safety stem engaging in a notch in the end of the bolt. With the action uncocked (striker forward), the safety can be depressed and swung over to the right to lock the bolt, but this is to allow the bolt to be disassembled easily, rather than to lock the bolt in the action.

One very small gas escape hole in the bolt is the only outlet should gas enter the firing pin hole. This hole, just forward of the mainspring shoulder on the firing pin, is exposed in the front of the receiver opening when the bolt is closed and locked.

The trigger assembly consists of trigger, trigger pin, sear, sear pin, sear lever, sear lever pin and sear lever spring, mounted under the receiver on the sear lever pin. The trigger has the usual two humps that provide the standard double-stage military pull.

The trigger guard bow, large and heavy, is held in place in the stock, along with the rear part of the receiver, by a tongue-and-groove arrangement with the receiver at the front, and by the rear receiver screw, which passes through the rear of the guard and stock, and threads into the receiver tang. The front of the receiver is held in the stock by a screw that runs through an escutcheon in the bottom of the stock.

The Schoenauer Magazine System

The most interesting feature of the Mannlicher-Schoenauer action is the box magazine, whose spring-tensioned rotary spool feeds cartridges into the path of the bolt.

The heart of the magazine is the spool, held in upright standards over a box-like trough, much like an old-fashioned chicken feeder. The spool has 5 shallow grooves that conform to the diameter and shape of the 6.5 M-S cartridges. The cartridges are not separated except for the first and last, which are divided by a wing that is actually the follower. A coil spring inside the spool provides the rotary power to feed the cartridges into the action. Bearings at the spring ends provide the means to anchor the spool to the standards and to keep the spool wound.

The floorplate is attached to the bottom of the box via a stud and spring clip, allowing the plate to rotate. The fore and aft magazine projecting walls under the receiver are milled out to accept the magazine box. Their inner ends are grooved for the ends of the floorplate so the magazine is locked in place when the floorplate is

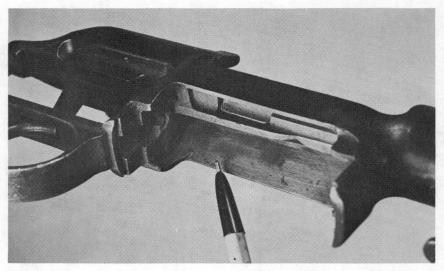

If the Greek M-S action is to be used for such cartridges as the .257 Roberts or 7mm Mauser (which have body diameters about .023″ larger than the 6.5mm M-S cartridge), some metal must be removed from the inside left of the magazine wall in receiver (shown by pencil point).

lengthwise with the action. A spring clip in the bottom of the magazine box, engaging a recess in the floorplate, locks the floorplate in its lengthwise position and, when depressed, allows it to be rotated.

The magazine well opening, in the left side of the receiver, slants slightly in that direction so that as the cartridges are fed into and out of the magazine, they are guided around the spool and magazine box. Circular cartridge guideways about ¼″ wide, built into the front and rear of the magazine opening in the receiver, and in the magazine box, hold the cartridges in a circle against the spool, allowing the cartridges to move around without much friction.

To allow insertion of cartridges into the magazine and to prevent them from coming out again, a cartridge stop was fitted into a milled cut in the underside of the right receiver wall. It is held in place, and pivots on, a screw through the front of the receiver wall. It is tensioned by a small coil spring. The rear part of the cartridge stop projects through a hole near the rear of the right side of the magazine-well opening, and a checkered projection protrudes through another opening in the top of the wall.

On loading a cartridge into the magazine and pressing it down with the thumb, the cartridge stop is depressed as the cartridge moves over it; when thumb pressure is removed the cartridge, forced up by the tension of the magazine spool, is halted by the bolt stop so that only part of the cartridge projects in the path of the bolt. The magazine can be fully loaded by inserting one cartridge at a time, or loaded by stripping cartridges from a charger clip. The loaded magazine can be quickly emptied by merely pressing down on the checkered projection on the bolt stop.

The Schoenauer magazine system is reliable in every way. It holds 5 cartridges in a space only slightly larger than needed for a staggered-column magazine. Feeding is positive and smooth, and there is

only one path for the cartridges to take as they are fed into the chamber. The spool prevents cartridges from moving forward as the rifle recoils. This prevents bullet point mutilation. Finally, the magazine box and spool can be easily removed for cleaning.

The Schoenauer magazine has disadvantages. It is much more costly to make than a staggered-column type because every part of the system has to be made for the specific cartridge for which the rifle is chambered. Once so made it is not readily adaptable to cartridges with different dimensions.

Take-Down and Assembly

Make sure chamber and magazine are empty. To remove bolt raise bolt handle and pull it back and out while depressing the bolt stop. To disassemble the bolt grasp the bolt body in one hand and, with the other rotate the cocking piece ¼-turn counterclockwise so it is against the bolt; depress safety and swing it to the right. Turn the firing pin nut ¼-turn counterclockwise and pull it free; swing the safety to the left, remove it from the cocking piece and the cocking piece off the firing pin; now grasp bolt head firmly (remember it is under tension of the mainspring), turn it counterclockwise until the ejector is in line with the guide rib and ease it forward. This will release firing pin and mainspring so they can be pulled forward out of the bolt. Remove ejector by turning out its screw and sliding it forward. Remove extractor by lifting its front end up with a screwdriver, then pull it forward. To avoid any chance of breaking the extractor, it should not be removed unless necessary. Reassemble in reverse order.

Using a bullet point or some other pointed tool depress the floorplate latch spring through the front hole in the floorplate. Turn it about ¼-turn and pull out magazine. Remove magazine spool by depressing rear spool bearing and lifting up

MANNLICHER-SCHOENAUER TRIGGERS
SINGLE AND DOUBLE-SET FOR RIFLES AND CARBINES

ADJUSTABLE SINGLE OR DOUBLE SET TRIGGERS

All models, both rifle and carbine, come with choice of regular single trigger or double set triggers. The single trigger is of the clean crisp shotgun type, that is, it is completely without creep, the pull being about 4½ lbs., and is the type most shooters are accustomed to. Below, it will be seen that the single trigger is provided with a regulating screw, permitting adjustment of pull.

The double set trigger represents a novelty to most American shooters, but once understood, has numerous advantages, particularly when used with a scope. In this type the front trigger alone always fires the gun, the rear trigger never does, its sole function being to "set" the front trigger thus making a "hair" trigger of it. If the rear trigger be ignored, the gun is fired by using the front trigger, tho the pull is somewhat heavier and less sharp than on the regular single trigger model. The reason for this will be clear from a study of the two illustrations, whereby it will be seen that the leverage exerted in the single trigger is several times as great as in the double set. To make a "hair" trigger of the front trigger, the rear trigger is pulled back until it clicks, and the front trigger is then "set" and a pressure of a few ounces fires it. This is perfect for long distance scope shots as the gun may be fired the instant the bead is on the target. If the trigger is "set" it can be *unset* without firing the gun or opening the bolt. To accomplish this the rear trigger is pulled first, and while pressure is on the rear trigger, the front trigger is pulled very lightly, and the gun is back to normal pull. This last "trick" should be practiced on an empty chamber until it is thoroughly understood. A small regulating screw is located between the triggers, permitting adjustment of from nothing to about three ounces.

DOUBLE TRIGGER MECHANISM

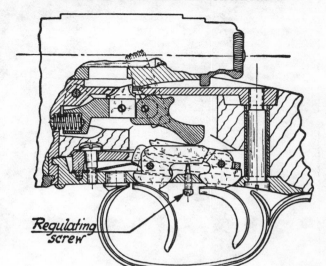

This illustration shows double set trigger unit complete with trigger lever. This entire unit can be replaced or used interchangeably with the single trigger mechanism shown at right.

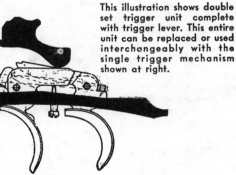

This is the new style single trigger mechanism (illustrated more fully below) which can be used to replace the double trigger unit if desired. This new style trigger is being furnished on all current Mannlicher-Schoenauers.

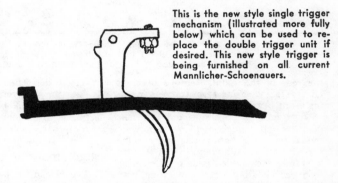

OLD SINGLE TRIGGER MECHANISM

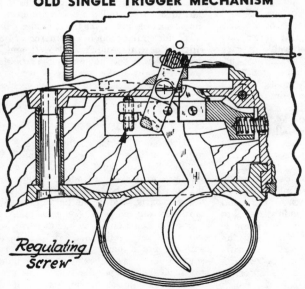

NEW SINGLE TRIGGER MECHANISM

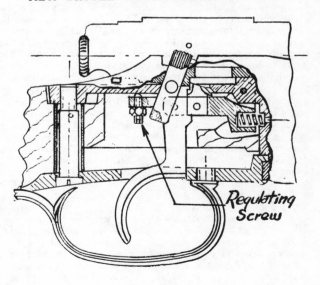

A page from the 1939 Stoeger's catalog showing the different trigger mechanisms available for the commercial M-S sporter at that time. (Courtesy Stoeger Arms Corp.)

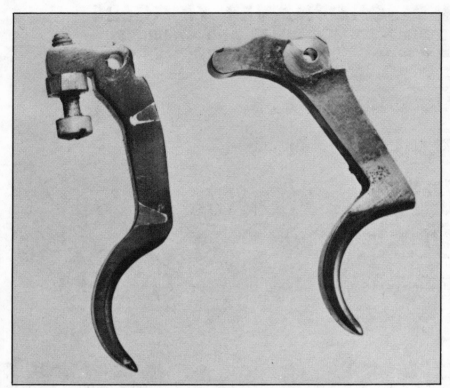

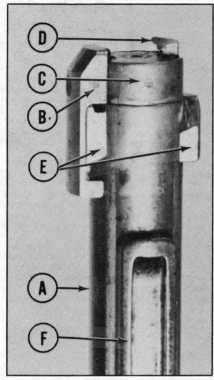

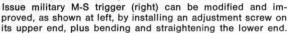

Issue military M-S trigger (right) can be modified and improved, as shown at left, by installing an adjustment screw on its upper end, plus bending and straightening the lower end.

Front end of the Greek M-S bolt showing: (A) bolt body, (B) ejector, (C) bolt head, (D) extractor, (E) locking lugs and (F) bolt guide rib.

the rear of the spool. Remove bearings and magazine spring from spool by rotating front bearing counterclockwise about ⅛-turn until it pops out and unwinds; bearings and spring assembly can now be pulled out. It is best not to remove the spring bearings, although this can be done by lifting the hooked ends of the spring from each bearing. The spool spring, with bearings attached, is reassembled by inserting it into the spool, rotating it until the small bearing projects through the spool; now depress the large bearing and turn it about one full turn counterclockwise until it falls into place and is locked into the spool. The assembled spool is then fitted in place by inserting the large bearing into its slot in the magazine box, and then depressing the rear bearing until it slips into place.

The floorplate can be removed by driving the spring clip off of the floorplate stud, which will release the floorplate and the spring catch. Reassemble in reverse order. The assembled magazine can then be inserted into the action and locked in place by turning the floorplate lengthwise with the action.

To remove barrel and action from the stock remove magazine and barrel bands; turn out rear receiver screw, lift rear of trigger guard out of the stock, slide it back and remove it; turn out front receiver screw and barreled action can be lifted out of the stock. Drive out (downward) bolt stop pin to remove bolt stop and spring. Turn out cartridge stop screw from right side of the receiver and work out the cartridge stop and spring. Drive out sear lever pin to remove trigger assembly. Drive out sear and trigger pins to remove sear and trigger. Reassemble in

reverse order. The barrel is screwed tightly into the receiver (right-hand threads) and it should not be removed unless the action is to be rebarreled, and then only if the proper tools are available.

Rechambering and Rebarreling

I've already pointed out some limitations of the M-S action and magazine, but there are more. There is just no way in which this action, made for the 6.5 M-S cartridge, can be altered to handle a cartridge whose over-all length is more than about 3.10", nor any practicable or easy way it can be made to handle any cartridge much shorter than about 2.875". The new cartridge, which must also be a rimless type, practically eliminates all modern cartridges except the .257 Roberts, .244 (or 6mm Remington) and the 7mm Mauser. While these three fall within the noted length limitations, they still pose a problem because the bodies of these cartridges are of larger diameter than the 6.5 M-S cartridge. This can be overcome, however, by widening the magazine well in the receiver and removing some metal from the cartridge-head guide surfaces in the receiver and magazine box. There is no commercial 6.5mm cartridge for which the 1903 (or 1903/14) Greek M-S rifle can be rechambered. It could be rechambered for the obsolete 6.5x57 Mauser, or to the wildcat 6.5/.257 Roberts, which two are about identical. However, since the 6.5 M-S is about as good as either one of these, there certainly is no point in rechambering for them. If the 6.5 M-S bore is in poor condition, it could be rebored and rechambered for the 7mm

Mauser cartridge. Since the .244 and 6mm cartridges develop higher breech pressures, which I consider a bit too high for this action, I feel that the only practicable rebarreling of the Greek M-S would be to its original caliber or, with the necessary action modification, to the .257 Roberts or 7mm Mauser.

I took the trouble one time to alter a Greek M-S action, rebarreling it to .308. The magazine is too short to handle this cartridge, so I installed a guide ring in the magazine box, much like the cartridge carrier guide in the modern commercial M-S rifle. At best, this didn't work well, and I decided that it was not worth the trouble and effort to make such a conversion again or to recommend that anyone else do it.

Good and Poor Features

To begin with, all of the Greek M-S military actions I've seen and handled, whether Steyr or Beretta made, were very well made in every detail. Undoubtedly the very best steels were used to make the various parts, and these parts properly hardened and tempered (or heat-treated) according to the task they had to perform. All parts are well fitted, finished and smooth. Some parts are polished very smooth, including the exterior of the bolt, magazine spool and the contacting surfaces of the various moving parts. All of this makes for a tight fitting yet smooth working action. Its smoothness of operation rivals that of our Krag. In fact, most of these military actions I've handled operated as easily and as smoothly as the action of any commercial M-S sporting

Parts Legend

1. Receiver (side view)
2. Bolt body
3. Firing pin
4. Mainspring
5. Cocking piece
6. Firing pin nut
7. Safety
8. Safety spring
9. Bolt head
10. Extractor
11. Ejector
12. Ejector screw
13. Sear lever
14. Sear
15. Sear pin
16. Sear lever spring
17. Sear lever pin
18. Trigger
19. Trigger pin
20. Cartridge stop
21. Cartridge stop screw
22. Cartridge stop spring
23. Magazine spool
24. Magazine spool wind-up spring
25. Magazine spool bearing, rear
26. Magazine spool bearing, front
27. Magazine spool box
28. Magazine floorplate
29. Floorplate latch
30. Floorplate retainer clip
31. Bolt stop
32. Bolt stop pin
33. Bolt stop spring
34. Trigger guard bow
35. Trigger guard screw
36. Trigger guard (stock) screw bushing
37. Receiver screw
38. Receiver screw stock escutcheon

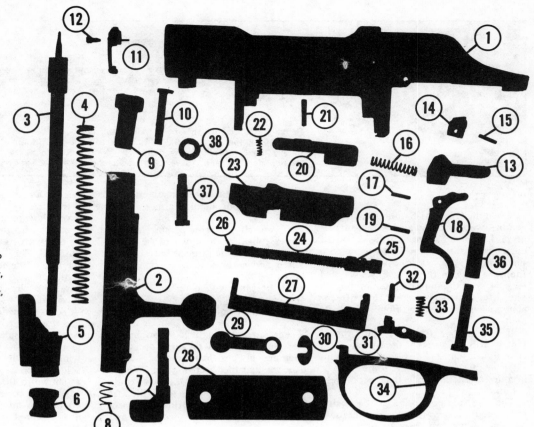

Greek 1903 Mannlicher-Schoenauer

(Uses 6.5 M-S cartridges)

Dimensional Specifications

Weight	48 oz.
Over-all	8.750"
Receiver ring dia.	1.290"
Bolt body dia.	.705"
Bolt travel	4.565"
Striker travel	.605"
Magazine opening (length)	3.075"
Bolt face	Flat, no recess.

General Specifications

Type	Turnbolt repeater.
Receiver	One-piece machined steel forging with slotted bridge. Stripper-clip charger guide milled in the bridge.
Bolt	Two-piece, with separate non-rotating bolt head. Dual-opposed locking lugs on front of bolt body. Bolt handle acts as safety lug.
Ignition	One-piece firing pin, coil spring powered. Cocks on opening bolt.
Magazine	Rotary spool, 5-shot capacity, detachable box-type.
Trigger	Non-adjustable, double-stage military pull.
Safety	Rotary wing-type built into cocking piece. 180° swing from left to right, locks striker and bolt when swung up or right.
Extractor	One-piece non-rotating spring extractor mortised in bolt head.
Magazine cutoff	None.
Bolt stop	Pivoting type, located at left rear of receiver.
Ejector	Sliding type fitted on bolt head, activated by bolt stop.

rifle made. It is this smoothness, plus the looks and feel of the sporting carbine, that most impresses the sportsman who handles this rifle for the first time.

I like the breeching system of this action, which is not too unlike the M98 Mauser breeching, and the bolt stop and ejector system, plus the fact that both locking lugs are solid. I also like the cartridge stop arrangement, which allows easy and convenient removal of cartridges from the magazine.

There are many things I don't like about the M-S action, some of which I consider poorly designed. I don't like the slotted bridge or the forward placement of the bolt handle, nor do I like the firing mechanism, with the heavy cocking piece and safety hung on the firing pin.

After almost 70 years of nearly continuous manufacture, the modern M-S action still has almost the same firing mechanism, and I should think that by

now it could have been improved.

I do not particularly dislike the separate bolt head, but the extractor is far from being the best. Of all its action parts, the bolt head and extractor are most often lost, and the extractor the part most often broken. Because of the separate bolt head design, the receiver ring and bolt travel are proportionally longer. Because of the long cocking piece, the receiver bridge is also quite long. The rotary spool magazine system requires longer space than would a

staggered-column box magazine holding a cartridge of the same length. Considering, however, the size and length of the 6.5 M-S cartridge, the M-S action seems unduly long and heavy.

Despite these criticisms, I still like this action very much. Just as many shooters complained when the Model 70 Winchester action was changed in 1964, I imagine that a similar reaction would occur if the modern Mannlicher-Schoenauer action were to be changed.

Regular sporter type rifle built around the Greek military M-S action. The action was fitted with a new barrel, a flat bolt handle and a 1903 Springfield trigger guard bow, and to this the Fajen stock was fitted. The Weaver K-6 scope is mounted in Weaver top-detachable rings on a Weaver 60 base attached to the receiver ring with two 8x40 screws.

Gunsmithing

When the Greek M-S military rifles and actions were first available as surplus arms, I obtained several of the actions. I did considerable experimental work with them, since little has been written about them in gunsmithing books. What I learned should interest those wanting to know the practical use of this rifle or action when remodeling or building a rifle on it.

If you have a complete and original Greek M-S rifle or carbine in excellent condition inside and out, you might consider the fact that they have some value as a collector's item, since they're not very common.

The M-S rifle or carbine can be readily remodeled into a very fine sporter, for it has one of the best-shaped and designed stocks of any military rifle. If you have the rifle, a standard type sporter can be made from it by discarding the handguard, removing the rear sight, cutting off the fore-end just to the rear of the middle barrel band, and shortening the barrel to 24″ or 22″. Or, if you want to make a typical Mannlicher carbine from either the rifle or carbine, shorten the barrel to 18″, fit a steel Mannlicher-type fore-end cap on the end of the fore-end and then trim the entire fore-end down. Install an open rear sight and a front sight of your choice on the barrel. Lastly, cut off the bolt handle and weld on a flat Mannlicher-type handle. I have made flat handles from the

shank of a small open-end wrench or a flat spoke from an old farm implement wheel.

If your rifle, carbine or barreled action has a ruined bore, it would be wiser, I think, to have the original barrel rechambered and rebored for the 7mm Mauser cartridge than to have the action rebarreled. It can then be remodeled as outlined above.

If you have only the action, or for some reason want to replace the original barrel, I suggest rebarreling it to its original caliber. But if you insist on a different caliber, then the only practical choices are the .257 Roberts and the 7mm Mauser. When rebarreled to either one of these two calibers about .005″ to .010″ has to be filed from the left side of the magazine-well opening in the receiver. Sometimes some metal also has to be removed from the circular cartridge guideways in the magazine box and receiver.

There is no receiver sight now made for this rifle, and it is most difficult to adapt any other receiver sight to fit it. If you want a hunting scope mounted you can choose one of such popular side mounts as the Echo, Pachmayr, Williams or Jaeger. Redfield now makes a mount for the commercial M-S rifle which can be adapted and fitted to the Greek M-S action. I've successfully mounted a scope on this action using the one-piece Weaver 60 base, attaching it with two 8x40 screws. In all cases, the receiver has to be tapped to attach the mount bases and a new bolt

handle attached to clear the scope.

In attaching a new bolt handle to achieve a very low profile, and so it will clear the eyepiece of a low-mounted scope, it may be necessary to weld it directly to the bolt guide rib. This will then require notching the side of the stock and cutting down the right side of the receiver bridge. In any case, the clip-charger humps should be filed down.

To my knowledge there is no commercial safety or trigger made for this action. I solved the safety problem when a scope is mounted low by cutting off most of the wing from the original safety and silver soldering on a L-shaped piece of flat steel, as shown in the illustration. The original trigger can be improved by fitting it with an adjustment screw, as shown. I have also replaced the original trigger with a 1903 Springfield trigger, modifying it as required. The original M-S trigger guard bow is unusually large and heavy, and on one rifle I replaced it with a 1903 Springfield guard. This not only improves the looks but, in combination with the Springfield trigger, the trigger and bow are placed farther to the rear and closer to the grip, making for better handling and feel.

A double-set trigger mechanism made for the M98 Mauser can be installed in the Greek M-S action. On one rifle I remodeled, I sawed off the bow, or loop part, from the guard, installed the trigger mechanism in the plate that was left, and then fitted a double-barrel shotgun guard to the plate and grip, nearly duplicating

Close-up of the above sporting rifle showing the altered safety wing, flat bolt handle, 1903 Springfield trigger and guard bow, and Weaver scope mount.

the original double trigger set-up of the commercial M-S rifle.

Conventional sporter and Mannlicher-styled stocks for the Greek M-S are available from Fajen and Bishop, as are the steel Mannlicher fore-end tips. Pressed horn buttplates and pistol grip caps of the type originally used on the sporting carbines are available from Brownell's, Inc., Montezuma, Iowa. The clevis type M-S front sling swivel is available from Stoeger.

When surplus Greek M-S rifles and actions were available in the early 1960s, amateur gunsmiths all over the U.S. and Canada expressed a great deal of interest in them. I know that many were rather disappointed in this action because of its limitations, while others bought a rifle or an action or two to lay away for the day they could build that "Mannlicher" rifle —that sleek little sporter they have seen in the Stoeger's catalog for many years but could never afford.

Additional Comments

I don't know how many Greek M-S military rifles and carbines were made, but the figure must surely be in the scores or hundreds of thousands. Of all the military and commercial centerfire turnbolt actions discussed in this book, I believe more separate manufacturing operations are required to make the Mannlicher-Schoenauer action than any of the others.

The 1903 and the 1903/14 Greek M-S rifles are serial numbered. The complete serial number is usually stamped on the receiver ring, on the bolt guide rib and on the breech end of the barrel, and with two or more digits of this number stamped on such other parts as the bolt head, cocking piece, firing pin, firing pin nut and safety. If all the numbers match, this indicates all of the numbered parts are original. The place and date (year) of manufacture are usually stamped on the left receiver wall, as for example; **STEYR 1914** or **BERETTA** and date. The model designation of the rifle is usually stamped on the receiver ring, as for example; **Y:1903/14.** A crown over a cross within a shield is also usually found stamped on the receiver ring.

The 6.5 M-S Cartridge

The 6.5 M-S cartridge was developed and introduced with the M-S military rifle in 1900, and adopted by Greece in 1903. It is a rimless, bottlenecked cartridge, loaded with a long round-nosed bullet. The 6.5 M-S case is slightly smaller at the head (.453″) than the .30-06 case (.473″ head dia.). As a military cartridge it was certainly as good as the 6.5mm Japanese and 6.5mm Italian-Carcano cartridges, but since Greece was such a small country the 6.5 M-S cartridge never became a noteworthy military cartridge. It did, however, become a worldwide favorite sporting cartridge in the famous M-S sporting carbine, and it has been successfully used for taking all species of big game, including elephant.

The 6.5 M-S is also known as the 6.5x54 or 6.5x53 M-S. The "6.5" indicates the caliber in millimeters or .256″—the approximate bore size of the barrel. The "53" or "54" (the latter figure is most generally used today) is the case length in millimeters. Bullets are usually of .264″ diameter to match the groove diameter of barrels made for this cartridge, which normally range from .266″ to .268″. M-S rifle barrels usually have a very fast rifling twist, one turn in 7.87″.

The 6.5 M-S Greek military cartridge was normally loaded with a 159-gr. full-jacketed round-nosed bullet, muzzle velocity about 2225 fps. Sporting loads, which were made in such countries as Austria, Germany, Great Britain, Canada and the U.S., were usually loaded with 150- to 160-gr. round-nosed expanding-type bullets. At present this cartridge is loaded in Canada (CIL, Dominion or Imperial brand) and by Norma-Precision in Sweden, and they're available in the U.S. through numerous dealers. The CIL 6.5 M-S cartridge is loaded with a 160-gr. soft point bullet at 2160 fps muzzle velocity. A few years ago Norma loaded this cartridge with 5 different types and weights of bullets, including one weighing only 77 grains and one of 139 grains with a full jacket, pointed nose and a boat-tail base. Now they offer only two loadings —the 139-gr. soft point, semi-pointed, boat-tail bullet and the 156-gr. soft point, round-nosed bullet.

Both loads function perfectly through the rotary magazine of the Greek M-S action. The Norma 139-gr. load develops 2575 fps muzzle velocity, with a remaining energy at 200 yards of 1591 foot pounds. Norma's 156-gr. load develops 2461 fps velocity, and at 200 yards its remaining energy is 1432 foot pounds. For such game as deer, antelope, sheep and black bear the 6.5 M-S is a better choice than the .243, 6mm, .250-3000, .257 Roberts or .30-30.

The handloader will want to use Norma cases because they accept Boxer primers. Since the 6.5 M-S chamber has a very deep throat for the long-bulleted factory load, and the M-S action and magazine are made specifically for such a load, the handloader will have the best results with long and heavy 6.5mm bullets.

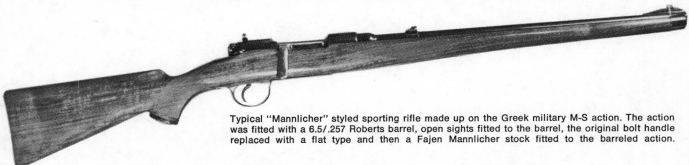

Typical "Mannlicher" styled sporting rifle made up on the Greek military M-S action. The action was fitted with a 6.5/.257 Roberts barrel, open sights fitted to the barrel, the original bolt handle replaced with a flat type and then a Fajen Mannlicher stock fitted to the barreled action.

Notes

13. German Model 98/40

IN THE CHAPTER on the German Model 88 Commission action, I mentioned that the receiver and bolt of the very popular Mannlicher-Schoenauer action evolved from the German Commission-designed Model 88 action, and that several other rifles, including the Model 98/40, have a similar receiver and bolt. In the M88 Commission rifle, we see how the German Testing Commission copied some features from the 71/84 Mauser rifle, used some of their own, and incorporated a Mannlicher-designed magazine to come up with a distinctive and smooth working action. With some minor bolt and receiver changes, and the fitting of the Schoenauer rotary-spool magazine, the Steyr firm headed by Ritter von Mannlicher produced the Mannlicher-Schoenauer action. This firm reintroduced the Mannlicher magazine to the action and made rifles with this action for the Netherlands—the Dutch Model 95 Mannlicher. This was followed by the Hungarian Model 1935, also with a Mannlicher single-column magazine. From this rifle the Hungarian Model 98/40 and the German G 98/40 action evolved—changing the Mannlicher magazine for the Mauser staggered-column flush magazine.

The German 98/40 (the G is usually dropped from the designation), as well as the Hungarian 98/40 (this rifle is more correctly designated as the Hungarian Model 43 — "43" because Hungary adopted it in 1943) were created because of Germany's dire need for military shoulder arms at the beginning of WW II. The Hungarian government arsenal in Budapest was tooled up to make the Mannlicher-magazined Model 1935 rifle, which, except for the magazine drawbacks, was a good rifle. Then by adapting the staggered-column Mauser magazine to it, and chambering it for the 8mm (8x57mm or 7.9x57mm) Mauser cartridge, the 98/40 was born. It is so designated because it has the basic M98 Mauser magazine and was adopted in 1940.

The German Model 98/40 Rifle

The German 98/40 rifle has a 23.6″ barrel, is 43.62″ over-all, and weighs about 8.9 pounds. It has a two-piece stock similar to the British Lee-Enfield rifle, with the fore-end attached to the barrel by the front guard screw and two barrel bands. The muzzle barrel band contains a bayonet stud so the regular M98 Mauser bayonet can be affixed. Unlike the 98K Mauser barrel, the G 98/40 (G stands for *Gewehr*, the German for rifle) barrel has no steps, but has a straight taper from the breech shoulder forward. The magazine holds 5 rounds.

Markings

The model designation of G 98/40 is stamped on the left receiver wall. The date (year) of manufacture, such as 41, which means 1941, is stamped on the top rear of the receiver ring. The factory code letters jhv are stamped on the top front of the receiver ring. The letters jhv are the code letters for the Metallwaren Waffen u Maschinenfabrik arsenal in Budapest, Hungary. The caliber (bore diameter), e.g., 7.91, is stamped on the barrel shoulder next to the receiver. The serial number is stamped on the breech end of the barrel, left side of the receiver ring, trigger guard, floorplate, buttstock socket and bolt, and with the last two digits of this number stamped on most of the other major parts.

The 98/40 Action

Although the Model 98/40 action closely follows the design features of the German 88 Commission action and some of the Mannlicher actions mentioned earlier, it has enough individual features to require a separate description. The receiver ring is about 1.735″ long. The loading port is about 3.2″ long with the higher left receiver wall made with a deep thumb notch like that in the M98 Mauser action. The receiver bridge is very long (about 2.25″) and split; that is, there is a slot milled through the top to allow passage of the bolt handle and guide rib. The front corners of this slot are grooved to accept the M98 Mauser stripper clip so the magazine can be quickly loaded. The bottom of the receiver is flat. The recoil lug, on the front of this flat, is about 1.60″ wide and 2.25″ deep. The magazine well is milled out of this flat, leaving an opening 3.30″ long and cartridge-guide lips to hold the cartridges in the magazine and to guide them into the chamber.

The magazine box is solidly constructed of sheet metal with reinforced ends, and the bottom of the receiver is milled to hold it securely in place. The rear wall of the magazine box also acts as a recoil lug and makes up for the small area of the main recoil lug on the front of the receiver. Recoil is mainly absorbed by the buttstock against the butt socket, while the rear of the magazine box and the recoil lug prevent the fore-end from moving forward.

Inside the receiver ring, there are two shoulders which the breech end of the barrel contacts. They are divided by cuts made to allow entrance of the extractor and ejector. The barrel is threaded tightly (right hand thread) into the receiver with the barrel made with a narrow shoulder to abut against the front of the receiver. A shallow groove cut across the face of the barrel provides room for the extractor and ejector to engage the cartridge rim. This breeching system is the same as used in the Greek Mannlicher-Schoenauer action.

The inside of the receiver is milled out to accept the bolt assembly. Locking lug raceways are milled nearly the length of the action and inside the receiver ring to form locking shoulders for the two locking lugs on the bolt. Slight inclines on the approaches of these shoulders cam the bolt forward as the bolt handle is lowered.

Illustrated above: German Model G98/40 rifle.

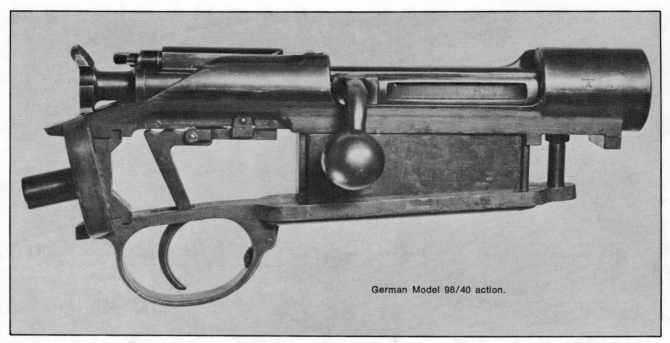

German Model 98/40 action.

The bolt is of two-piece design with a separate bolt head which fits into the front of the bolt body. The heavy hook extractor is mortised into the right side of the head, held in place and tensioned by a flat spring mortised in place behind it.

The extractor has a very wide hook, and is made so it cannot be pulled out from the front. It has ample movement so the hook can easily slip over the rim of a cartridge placed in the chamber ahead of the bolt. I believe this is even a better extractor than in the latest commercial Mannlicher-Schoenauer action. The ejector, almost an exact copy of the Mannlicher-Schoenauer ejector, is held in place by a small screw. The bottom corner of the extractor and ejector are rounded off so that, when the bolt pushes a cartridge from the magazine to the chamber, the rim of the cartridge slips under the extractor. This prevents double loading if the bolt is not fully locked before it is drawn back again. This is a good feature. The extractor is also made so that it holds the bolt head in place in the bolt and, on removing the bolt from the rifle, the bolt head cannot accidently fall out and be lost.

The bolt body has an integral guide rib along most of its length. The bent bolt handle is an integral part of this rib. This rib functions to guide and prevent the bolt from binding as it is operated. It also serves as the safety locking lug since it engages forward of the right receiver bridge wall when the bolt is closed. Its front end moves over an inclined surface on the rear of the receiver ring and provides the initial extractor camming power when the bolt is opened. The grasping ball on the bolt handle is flattened underneath and this flat surface is checkered.

The bolt body is drilled from the front to accept the coil mainspring and the one-piece firing pin. One side of the rear end of the firing pin is flattened to match a similar hole in the cocking piece through which the rear end of the firing pin

extends. This prevents the pin from turning. The firing pin nut threads onto the rear of the firing pin and holds the assembly together. The heavy cocking piece has a heavy rib which moves in a slot in the receiver bridge preventing it from turning when the bolt handle is raised and lowered. There is a small cam on the cocking piece which fits a matching shallow cam and notch in the rear of the bolt body. All this cam and notch do is hold the cocking piece and firing pin back unless the bolt handle is fully down and the action locked, thus preventing accidental firing unless the action is fully locked. When the bolt is open the cocking cam resting in the shallow notch prevents the cocking piece from turning.

The stem of the wing safety fits in a hole drilled lengthwise in the cocking piece rib. A coil spring over the stem holds the safety back against a notch in the firing pin nut and prevents the nut from turning. When the action is closed and cocked, swinging the safety to the right rotates the flattened end of the safety stem into a notch in the bolt. This locks both the bolt and cocking piece. The safety can also be swung to the right when the cocking piece is forward; this draws the firing pin tip within the face of the bolt and locks it back, as well as locking the bolt.

There is a thumb-piece on the firing pin nut by which the action can be manually cocked with the thumb, or the action can be uncocked (the firing pin lowered) by reversing the procedure. This provides a means to recock the action in case of a misfire. I do not know why the safety was made to lock the cocking piece and bolt when the action is uncocked. This feature is of doubtful value.

The 98/40 bolt stop is nearly identical to the one on the Greek Mannlicher-Schoenauer action. It is fitted on a stud on the left side of the receiver bridge, and is pivoted on a pin and tensioned by a coil spring. It projects through a hole into the

left locking lug raceway and stops the bolt on contacting the ejector which fits over the locking lug. Like the M-S action, there is a ridge-and-groove arrangement on the bolt stop and left locking lug, so that unless the ejector and/or bolt head are not assembled on the bolt, the bolt cannot be inserted into the receiver unless the bolt stop is depressed, but with the bolt head and ejector in place, the bolt can be inserted without depressing the bolt stop. Since this rifle could actually be fired without the bolt head, which would be very dangerous, the fact that the bolt cannot be inserted into the receiver without first depressing the bolt stop is a safety feature which reminds the shooter that the bolt is not fully assembled.

The trigger and sear mechanism is similar to that in the M-S rifle. The sear is pivoted on the bottom of the receiver on a pin. The trigger is pivoted on the rear end of the sear on a pin and has two humps which provide the double-stage pull. A projection in the rear of the sear extends through a hole in the cocking piece raceway in the receiver tang to contact the sear on the cocking piece, and holds it back when the action is closed. This action is cocked on the forward or closing motion of the bolt.

The sear and trigger are tensioned by a coil spring. A headed pin inside this spring, with its head resting on the front of the sear, projects into a hole in the receiver. There is a hole drilled into the rear edge of the bolt body, and when the bolt is fully closed and locked, this hole is aligned over the end of the sear safety pin so that, unless the bolt is fully locked the rifle cannot be fired. This arrangement is similar to that used in the M93 Mauser, Japanese Arisaka and 1917 Enfield. This extra safety device is of no value since the cocking piece will not let the firing pin protrude from the face of the bolt head unless the bolt handle is turned down completely. There is also a narrow groove in

Left side of the German Model 98/40 action open.

the bottom of the bolt which aligns with the sear safety pin when the bolt is forward, but with the bolt handle raised. This allows the trigger to be pulled to release the sear from the cocking piece so that it can follow the bolt forward. However, to lower the bolt handle afterward, the cocking piece has to be pulled back slightly.

Well constructed of sheet metal, the magazine box is held in place under the receiver by the trigger guard plate, with the plate attached to the action by a guard screw through each end, and threading into the receiver. A latch in the front of the large trigger bow holds the magazine floorplate in place. Depressing this latch allows the floorplate to be removed. One end of the W-shaped follower spring is mortised into the floorplate, while its other narrower end fits into the bottom of the milled steel follower. The rear end of the follower is square and, when the magazine is empty, it prevents the bolt from being closed, indicating to the shooter that the magazine is empty. This prevents blind loading. The magazine box, trigger guard plate and latch are not too unlike those of the Japanese 38 Arisaka action.

The method used to stock this rifle is quite different from any other stocking method used on military rifles known to me. It is most like that used on the British Lee-Enfield rifles; that is, with a two-piece stock; a separate buttstock and fore-end, with the buttstock attached to the action by a through bolt. From this point on, however, the Lee-Enfield and the G 98/40 stocking methods differ.

On the Lee-Enfield, the part of the action to which the buttstock is attached is an integral part of the receiver and called the butt socket. On the 98/40 action, the part which I will also call the butt socket is a separate part fitted between the rear end of the trigger guard and the receiver tang. The rear guard screw passes through this part to hold it in place. In addition, the top and bottom of this butt socket are milled out to fit closely over the tang end of the trigger guard to prevent it from pivoting. Hooks at the top and bottom of this part also engage in grooves in the tang and trigger guard and secure it to the action. In fact, it is so well attached to the action that it is almost an integral part. Two long oblong holes are milled through the inside of the butt socket so that tenons can be made on the fore-end and buttstock where they fit against it.

A heavy bolt threaded into a tenon on the butt socket is used to fasten the buttstock securely to the action. The fore-end, with tenons which extend halfway into the butt socket, is also held securely in place on the action by the trigger guard plate, magazine box, recoil lug and the front trigger guard screw. Even without the two barrel bands, the fore-end is secure.

While the buttstock attachment is no better than on the Lee-Enfield, the fore-end attachment method on the 98/40 is much superior to that of the Lee-Enfield. As I mentioned in the chapter on the Lee-Enfields, the British had a problem with the fore-ends of their rifles and I believe a lot of this could have been eliminated and the bedding problems easily corrected had the rear end of the fore-end been tenoned into the butt socket. The designers of the 1935 Hungarian rifle, from which the 98/40 was developed, probably knew about the fore-end problems of the Lee-Enfield and designed their fore-end and action so that it would be as secure as if the fore-end were part of the buttstock. It is believed that the designers went to the two-piece stock design for reasons of economy and to achieve a stronger buttstock. In doing this they developed perhaps the very best method and arrangement for fitting two-piece stocks.

Comments

All-in-all, the German Model 98/40 is a good action. It has its share of undesir-able features, but it also has some strong points. Manufactured from 1940 to 1945, those made early in this period show much better workmanship and finish than the ones toward the end. In early samples the bolt moves in the receiver as smoothly as the best Mannlicher-Schoenauer action. Although some experts dislike the separate bolt head feature, I don't think it is that bad. The extractor is probably more rugged than the extractor in the latest commercial Mannlicher-Schoenauer action. The forward placement of the bolt handle is not liked, but it is necessary in this type of action.

There is no need for the thumb-piece on the firing pin nut. The cock-on-closing feature is not generally liked, and without any extra trouble this action could just as well have been made to cock on the uplift of the bolt handle. The magazine floorplate release latch is neat, and although the floorplate is not hinged to the trigger guard, it is convenient for un-loading since it can be quickly removed.

Every part of the 98/40 action is made of steel—there are no stampings or alloy parts. There is little question that the finest steels were used in the manufacture of the major parts of this action, with the receiver and bolt parts properly heat treated. I believe this action entirely suit-able for almost any modern cartridge that is not too long for the magazine box; for if it was safe for the 8mm German mili-tary load it should also be safe for other cartridges developing breech pressures in the 50,000 psi range.

Gunsmithing

The 98/40 rifle and action offer a num-ber of remodeling, sporterizing and re-barreling possibilities. First, the 8mm Mauser cartridge for which this rifle is chambered is entirely satisfactory for big game hunting and, if the rifle you have has an excellent bore, it would be best to leave it in its present caliber. The 98/40 barrel has a very pleasing contour and taper, quite ideal for a sporter. To make a simple sporter, the original military sights can be removed and other sights installed. After removing the military rear sight the small square step on the barrel can be filed down to smooth out the shoulder contour. Good replacement sights for a hunting rifle made on the 98/40 would be the Williams Guide rear sight and a front sight mounted on the Williams ramp base. The barrel is not too long, but it can be shortened if desired.

The issue stock and fore-end can be remodeled if you want to keep expenses to a minimum. The main thing is to shorten the fore-end. It need not be any longer than about 14 inches.

For a more finished sporter you can get a semi-finished sporter stock and fore-end for the 98/40. There are no commercial receiver sights, triggers or safeties available for this rifle, although it is possible to install a double set trigger made for the M98 Mauser action in the 98/40.

There is no scope mount made especially for the 98/40, nor is this rifle well adapted for scope mounting. A side mount made, however, for a large ring M98 Mauser action can be used. Of course,

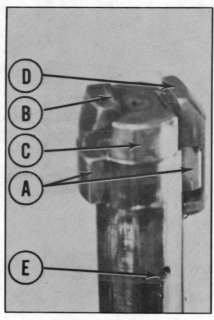

Model 98/40 bolt head showing: (A) dual locking lugs, (B) extractor, (C) bolt head, (D) ejector and (E) gas vent hole in the bolt body.

this will require that a new low-profile bolt handle be fitted to the bolt and the safety altered. Because of these limitations, it would be best to consign this rifle for open sight use only.

There are no rechambering possibilities for this rifle. While no one makes a threaded and chambered barrel available for this rifle, a different calibered barrel can be fitted to the action. By rebarreling, this action would be suitable for such cartridges as the .257 Roberts, 7mm Mauser, .308 and .358.

I see no practical way to change the action so it cocks on opening, or an easy way to lengthen the magazine to accept longer cartridges.

Take-Down and Assembly

Make sure the rifle is unloaded. To remove the bolt, raise the bolt handle and pull the bolt back while depressing the bolt stop. Disassemble the bolt by first removing the bolt head. This is done by turning the bolt head so the ejector is in line with the bolt rib. Using a cartridge, place its rim under the extractor hook, lift or tip the hook outward and pull the bolt head from the bolt. Turn out the ejector screw to remove the ejector. Remove the

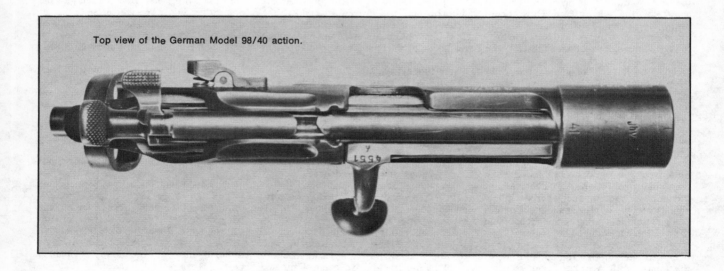

Top view of the German Model 98/40 action.

Parts Legend

1. Receiver
2. Butt socket
3. Stock bolt
4. Bolt stop
5. Bolt stop pin
6. Bolt stop spring
7. Bolt head
8. Extractor
9. Extractor spring
10. Ejector
11. Ejector screw
12. Bolt
13. Firing pin
14. Mainspring
15. Cocking piece
16. Firing pin nut
17. Safety
18. Safety spring
19. Trigger
20. Trigger pin
21. Sear
22. Sear pin
23. Sear spring
24. Sear safety pin
25. Magazine box
26. Follower
27. Follower spring
28. Trigger guard
29. Magazine floorplate
30. Floorplate catch
31. Floorplate catch pin
32. Floorplate catch spring
33. Rear guard screw
34. Front guard screw

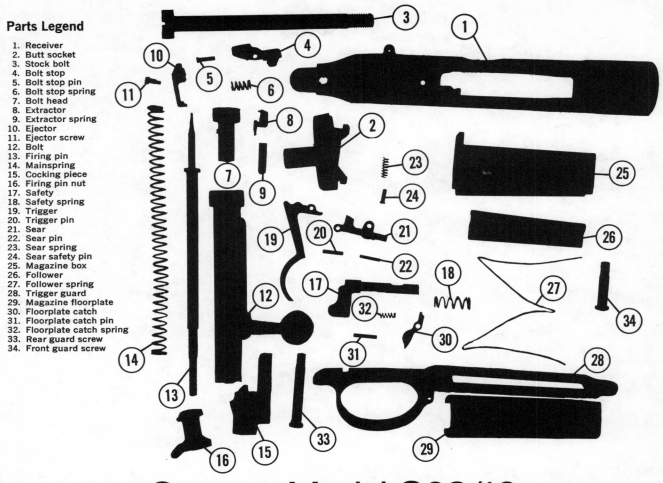

German Model G98/40

Dimensional Specifications	
Weight	56 oz.
Receiver length	9.312"
Receiver ring dia.	1.370"
Bolt dia.	.700"
Striker travel	.615"
Bolt travel	4.650"
Magazine length	3.30"
Magazine well width,	
rear	.595"
front	.525"
Guard screw spacing	7.062"

General Specifications

Type	Turnbolt repeater.
Receiver	One-piece machined steel forging. Slotted bridge with stripper-clip guides.
Bolt	Two-piece with separate non-rotating bolt head. Dual-opposed locking lugs forward. Bolt guide rib on bolt with its integral bolt handle acts as safety lug. Flat bolt face.
Ignition	One-piece firing pin powered by coil mainspring. Cocks on closing.
Magazine	Non-detachable staggered-column box type. Quick-detachable floorplate.
Bolt stop	Mannlicher type positioned on the left side of receiver bridge, stops bolt travel by contacting ejector over the left locking lug.
Trigger	Non-adjustable, double-stage military pull.
Safety	Wing-type built into the cocking piece, locks striker and bolt when swung to the right.
Extractor	Non-rotating, fitted into the bolt head. Uses separate flat spring.
Magazine cutoff	None provided.
Ejector	Sliding type attached to the left side of bolt head.

extractor by pushing down on the extractor spring with a tool so the extractor can be moved back and lifted out. Lift out the extractor spring. In reassembling the extractor, first insert the extractor spring in its slot with its round end to the rear, then push the extractor down until it slips in place.

Remove the firing mechanism by pressing the safety forward and unscrewing the firing pin nut from the firing pin, after which all the parts can be removed. Reassemble in reverse order, turning the firing pin nut on as far as it will go and then backing it off until the safety engages in its notch in the nut.

Remove the buttstock by first removing the buttplate; then, using a long screwdriver, turn out the stock bolt. Depress the floorplate latch and remove the floorplate, follower and spring. The follower and floorplate can then be slipped off of the spring. Remove barrel bands and trigger guard screws. Next, remove trigger guard from the fore-end and the fore-end from the barrel. The buttstock socket and the magazine box are also released at this time. Drive out the floorplate latch pin to remove the latch and spring. Drive out the sear pin to remove the sear and trigger mechanism.

Push the bolt stop pin out toward the bottom and remove the bolt stop and spring. Reassemble in reverse order. The narrow end of the follower spring fits into the follower.

The barrel is threaded very tightly into the receiver and cannot be easily removed, nor should it be removed unless necessary, and then only if the proper tools are available.

Notes

14. Spanish "Destroyer" Carbines

IN YEARS PAST and continuing today, many countries have developed and adopted short and light semi-auto and full-automatic sub-machine guns and machine pistols chambered for a common military and police pistol cartridge, e.g., the British Sten, American Model 50 Reising and German Schmeisser. Today, Spain has similar sub-machine guns, but back in the 1920s and continuing for a number of years thereafter, their standard police carbine was a bolt action repeater, known today as the Spanish Destroyer Military-Police Carbines.

I say "carbines" rather than "carbine" simply because there is more than one model or version of this weapon. I have only examined two of them, but I do know that at least two other versions were made. Probably several more variations exist than will be described here.

There is very little authoritive information available on these lightweight bolt action police carbines. They are given brief mention in W.H.B. Smith's *The Book of Rifles,* wherein they are listed as the Carbine Destroyer, Model of 1921. Smith says they were made in Eibar, Spain, and the one such carbine I have, so-marked, bears this out. Smith also says these carbines were commonly used in Spain by the police, and probably used in some South American countries for the same purpose.

I also found some information on them in the book/catalog put out by Golden States Arms in 1958 and entitled *World's Guns.* Two different specimens are illustrated and briefly described on page 135, with one listed as the Model 1921 Destroyer.

I have also picked up some dope from advertisements listing them for sale as war surplus. For example, on page 14 in the Nov., 1957, issue of *The American Rifleman,* Golden State listed the "Rare Spanish Military Police Carbine." Interarms Ltd. (formerly Interarmco) of Alexandria, Va., imported a quantity of these Spanish carbines and distributed them through their various surplus arms dealers, and at times I have seen them for sale by Service Armament Co., and Hunter's Lodge. One firm listed these carbines for sale as late as 1968. Generally, they sold for about $40 each.

In an article in *Shooting Times* (March, 1968), and in a follow-up article a couple of months later, author J. B. Wood describes a specimen of this carbine he obtained, and sheds some light on some other models. According to Mr. Wood, the original Destroyer carbines were manufactured by Gaztanaga y Compania of Eibar, Spain, and later made by Ayra Duria S.A., also in Eibar. The Destroyer carbine is still being made there and their principal agent is E. Alvarez-Garcillan of Madrid, Spain. From these sources of information I believe the two Destroyer carbines illustrated in this chapter represent the original Model 1921 Destroyer and the latest one still being made today.

1) I believe the gun pictured above represents the original 1921 Spanish Destroyer Carbine. It is a simple turnbolt, short-barreled rifle with a detachable box magazine (magazine is missing). It has a 20″ round tapered barrel with fixed open sights; an inverted-V front and a V rear. The walnut stock has a straight grip and a steel buttplate, the fore-end extending nearly to the muzzle and held in place by two barrel bands. The fore-end has finger grooves, and simple sling swivels are fitted to the butt and rear barrel band. The bolt, which has a smooth, rounded cocking piece, cocks on closing. The safety, in the front of the trigger guard bow, locks the trigger when it is engaged. The detachable box magazine, apparently of the staggered-column type like that of the Browning Hi-Power pistol, is listed as being of 7- or 10-shot capacity. The carbine illustrated, weight 5 pounds, is chambered for the 9mm Bergmann-Bayard pistol cartridge, and is stamped with various Spanish proofmarks. The word **EIBAR** in very small letters is also stamped on the barrel, while the letters **PAZ** within a shield are stamped on the receiver ring. A detailed description follows.

2) As shown in *World's Guns,* this Destroyer carbine has a checkered pistol grip stock and a half-length fore-end with a single barrel band. One sling swivel is attached to this band, the other is screwed into the butt. Chambered for the 9mm Bergmann-Bayard cartridge, it has a 7- or 10-shot detachable box magazine. The unusual feature of this one is that it has a tube mounted under the barrel which extends into the fore-end to hold spare cartridges. It is not a magazine tube, just a place to carry extra ammunition. The 20″ round barrel has fixed open sights. The action cocks on closing, and the bolt has a knurled cocking piece. The safety is on the rear right side of the receiver. This carbine looks more like a sporting arm with its checkered pistol grip and short fore-end but is still described as the Spanish Military Police Carbine.

3) This Destroyer, described in the March, 1968, issue of *Shooting Times,* is also more of a sporting arm than a military or police weapon. It has a straight-gripped stock with a very short fore-end. The front sling swivel is mounted on the barrel ahead of the fore-end, the rear swivel is screwed into the buttstock. The round tapered barrel has an inverted-V front sight and a military type elevation-adjustable folding-leaf rear sight. The 10-shot detachable box magazine is held in place by a latch mounted into the trigger guard plate, which is inletted flush in the stock. The action of this rifle, probably identical to the No. 4 carbine described below, is marked **DESTROYER CARBINE** on the receiver, plus the caliber designation of **9mm BERGMANN.** It is

Illustrated above: Spanish Model 1921 Police Carbine, a short and light bolt action carbine chambered for the 9mm Bergmann-Bayard pistol cartridge. This and similar arms are usually labeled "Destroyer" carbines.

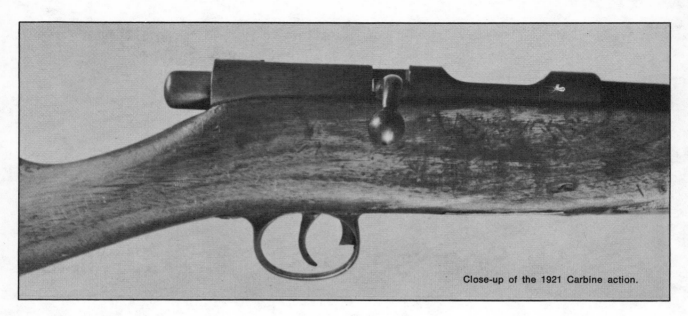

Close-up of the 1921 Carbine action.

very possible that this carbine is a sporter version of No. 4, or has been sporterized by someone. Except for the trigger guard, magazine latch and plate this carbine has an action identical to the carbine to be described next.

4) Shown on pages 120, 121 and 122 are views of the latest Destroyer carbine still made today. It appears to be brand new and shows evidence of modern manufacture, as the one-piece trigger guard and magazine housing appears to be an investment steel casting. This rifle has a military type stock with long fore-end and two barrel bands held on with wood screws. It has a pistol grip and the pressed steel buttplate is attached with a single wood screw. The simple sling swivels are fitted to the left side of the gun,

the rear one threaded into the fore-end through a hole in the rear barrel band. The barrel is fitted with sights as on the No. 3 rifle described above, the barrel 21.25″ long. It weighs about 6.3 pounds and is 39.75″ over-all. It has a receiver and bolt just like No. 3 carbine which I will describe in detail later on.

No doubt there are other distinctive versions of these Destroyer carbines, but the four of them just described have many things in common — they're all short-barreled, lightweight arms, all have a turnbolt action which cocks on closing, all have detachable box magazines, and all are chambered for a 9mm pistol cartridge. I have heard of one that was chambered for the .38 Super pistol cartridge and so stamped.

The Model 1921 Destroyer

As the illustrations show, the 1921 has a simple turnbolt action not too unlike the action of some low-cost American-made .410 bolt action shotguns. The Model 1921 action weighs about 2 pounds without magazine.

The receiver, a piece of thick-walled steel tubing is 7.125″ long and 1.125″ in diameter. The barrel threads into the front of the receiver. The magazine and loading-port opening is about 1.750″ long. An L-shaped slot is milled in the rear of the receiver for the bolt handle to pass and lock into.

The bolt, with its integral bolt handle, is of one-piece construction. The heavy square base of the bolt handle is the locking lug; when engaged in its slot in the

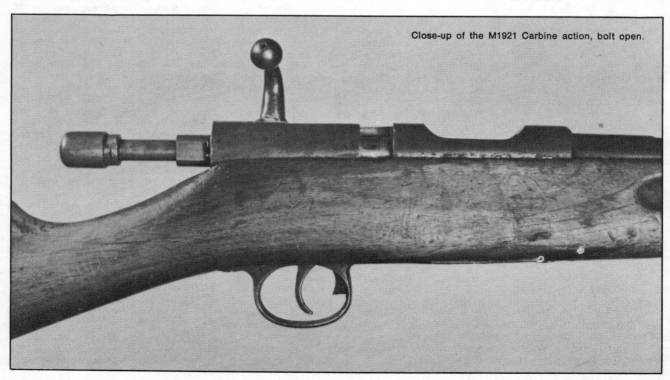

Close-up of the M1921 Carbine action, bolt open.

Spanish Destroyer action with stock removed.

ment to hold the magazine in place was probably attached to the magazine itself, for there is no evidence that such a catch was provided on the plate.

This action has no separate ejector. The firing pin is so made that it projects about ¼" out of the bolt face, thus it becomes the ejector when the bolt is opened.

The action is poorly and crudely made; the parts which don't show are hardly finished at all and are sloppily fitted. The action is amply strong for any 9mm pistol load, but that's about the only good thing I can say about it. Like many other very cheap Spanish-made guns of the 1920s, this carbine probably sported a fairly good outside finish when new. It was a rifle all right, but I don't believe it was a very reliable one.

The Latest Destroyer Action

This is the turnbolt action from the No. 4 Destroyer carbine described above. As the illustrations show, this version is better than the M1921 Destroyer, its action better designed, constructed and finished. It is also more compact, being only 6.375" long.

The receiver bears Spanish proofmarks and the circular **DESTROYER TRADE MARK** stamping. Chambered for the 9mm Parabellum (Luger) cartridge, it is so-marked on the left side of the receiver. This carbine has every appearance of being new, and is very well finished. All metal parts are well polished and nicely blued.

The receiver appears to be an investment casting as its sides and bottom are flat. The barrel is threaded into the receiver. It has a long unslotted bridge. The top loading port is amply big enough so that the rifle can be as easily loaded as a single shot.

The bolt, of modified Mauser design, has an integral bolt handle base with two opposed locking lugs about midway on its body. These lugs engage locking re-

receiver it locks the bolt in place. The bolt stop is a pointed, stepped notch milled in the bolt handle slot which contacts and engages a matching cut in the base of the bolt handle when the bolt is pulled back. To remove the bolt from the action after it has been pulled back it is only necessary to push the bolt slightly forward and turn the bolt handle up. The bolt face is recessed, and the one-piece spring extractor is dovetailed into the bolt.

The bolt, .575" diameter, is drilled from the rear to accept the long one-piece firing pin. The rear end of the bolt is turned much smaller than the front end and slotted; over this is fitted a short sleeve which functions as a cocking piece. The cocking piece sleeve is attached to the firing pin by a screw through the cocking piece, bolt and firing pin. The long, thin coil mainspring is compressed over the thinned rear end of the firing pin and held in the bolt by the round-ended cap, which is threaded over the rear end of the bolt; this cap is prevented from turning by a small setscrew.

The trigger mechanism is simple; a sear and trigger are hooked together and attached to the receiver with pins. Both have coil springs. A steel ball bearing under the sear spring, projecting into the boltway to contact the bolt, provides tension to hold the bolt handle up or down. The rear end of the sear projects through the receiver and, when the bolt is closed, holds the cocking sleeve back to cock the action. Striker travel is about 1".

The trigger guard is combined with a plate through which the magazine is positioned. Screws running through the ends of the guard hold barrel and action to the stock. The safety, fitted into a groove cut into the front part of the guard bow, pivots on a pin and is tensioned by a flat spring. The trigger has a hook which engages a matching hook on the safety when it is pivoted back.

The magazine was missing from my specimen of this carbine, but the hole in the trigger guard plate and the magazine well indicates it was of the staggered-column type. The latch or other arrange-

Top view of the M1921 Carbine action. The rectangle base portion of the bolt handle is the locking lug; when the bolt is closed it engages in a deep notch cut into the thick receiver wall, locking the bolt. The small undercut notch in the top rear of the receiver acts as the bolt stop, engaging a matching notch in the bolt handle base when the bolt is opened.

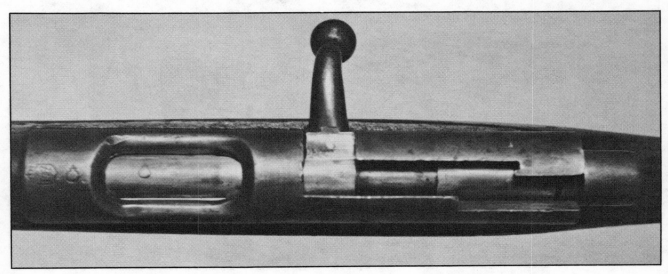

Above—Left side of the latest Destroyer action.

Below—Action of the latest Spanish Destroyer carbine showing it open.

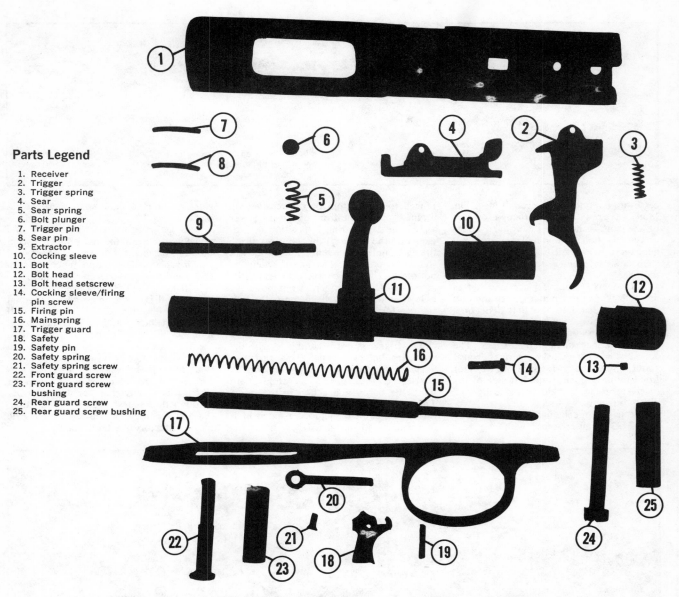

Parts Legend

1. Receiver
2. Trigger
3. Trigger spring
4. Sear
5. Sear spring
6. Bolt plunger
7. Trigger pin
8. Sear pin
9. Extractor
10. Cocking sleeve
11. Bolt
12. Bolt head
13. Bolt head setscrew
14. Cocking sleeve/firing pin screw
15. Firing pin
16. Mainspring
17. Trigger guard
18. Safety
19. Safety pin
20. Safety spring
21. Safety spring screw
22. Front guard screw
23. Front guard screw bushing
24. Rear guard screw
25. Rear guard screw bushing

Spanish Destroyer Carbine

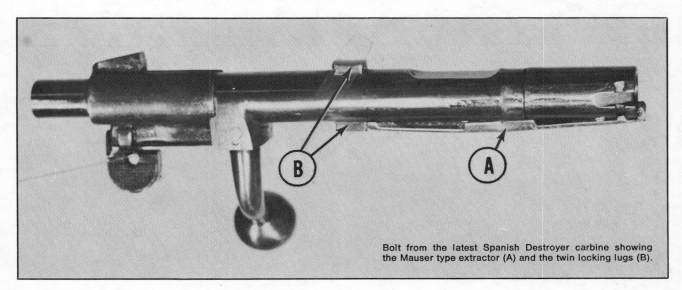

Bolt from the latest Spanish Destroyer carbine showing the Mauser type extractor (A) and the twin locking lugs (B).

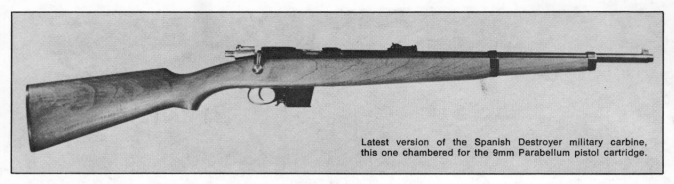

Latest version of the Spanish Destroyer military carbine, this one chambered for the 9mm Parabellum pistol cartridge.

cesses milled into the receiver bridge. The Mauser-type extractor, mounted on top of the bolt, is held in place by a collar around the bolt. The round grasping ball appears to be threaded on the bolt handle stem, and the stem in turn threaded into the base.

Bolt sleeve, cocking piece and safety are of M93 Mauser pattern, with the bolt sleeve threaded into the bolt. The one-piece firing pin is powered by a thin coil spring. When swung to the right the safety locks both the bolt and the striker. The action cocks on closing, striker travel about .780″. The spring-tensioned ejector fitted into a groove in the left side of the receiver bridge, is held in place by and pivots on a pin.

The trigger mechanism is also a modified M93 Mauser type, with the sear hinged to the bottom of the receiver on a pin. A pin on the front of the sear, over which the sear spring is positioned, projects into the boltway, this prevents firing the rifle unless the bolt is fully closed. Rearward bolt travel is halted when the bottom locking lug contacts the end of its raceway in the receiver. To remove the bolt after drawing it back, push the bolt slightly forward and turn the bolt handle down until the locking lug is out of its raceway.

The trigger guard is combined with the magazine holder or well. This part also appears to be an investment casting. A guard screw through each end of the guard holds the barrel and action in the stock. The magazine well extends well below the stock line; a spring-loaded latch built between it and the guard bow holds the single-column 6-shot box magazine in place.

This action is rather well finished and polished, with all the parts blued except the bolt, extractor, bolt sleeve, safety and cocking piece. The action functions well and is quite easy to operate. The magazine is well made and feeding is reliable. The trigger pull is poor, being quite long and rough. Inside, this carbine is not as well made as the nice outside appearance would indicate, but it is made far better than the M1921 Destroyer action. With its dual locking lugs and heavy receiver, this action could handle more powerful cartridges than the 9mm pistol cartridges for which it is usually chambered. The owner of this rifle has test fired it for functioning and accuracy and he reports the rifle was satisfactory on both counts.

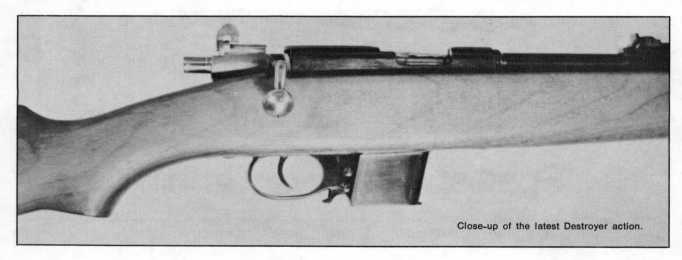

Close-up of the latest Destroyer action.

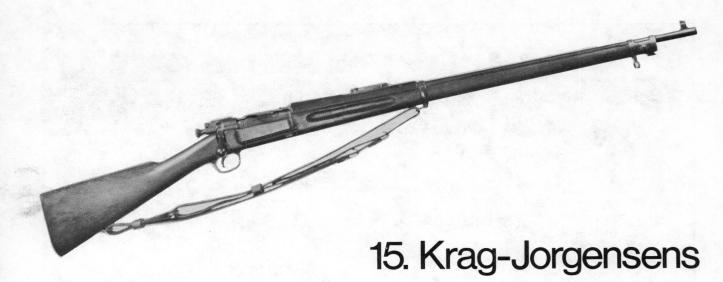

15. Krag-Jorgensens

U.S., DANISH and NORWEGIAN

THE CALIBER .45-70 single shot "trap-door" Springfield rifles and carbines had served the United States Army quite well from 1873, when the model was adopted. By the late 1880s, however, military men were discontented with it, and it was felt that a smokeless powder cartridge and a repeating rifle to handle it were needed. Some of the other world powers had already adopted these changes, including France (8mm in 1886), Germany (8mm in 1888), England (.303 in 1888) and Belgium (7.65mm in 1889). To work toward this change, boards of inquiry were appointed to look into the selection of a suitable new rifle and cartridge, to determine by test the best rifle to adopt and manufacture. In 1890 some 53 rifles were submitted (some were nearly alike or minor variations of the same action) for the tests.

Among the rifles submitted were the Lee Magazine system, Mauser (Belgian M1889), Swiss Rubin, French Berthier, German Commission M1888, Mannlicher, Savage and Krag-Jorgensen. Incidentally, the Savage was an early version of the M99, a lever action with rotary-spool magazine. As a result of these trials, the Krag-Jorgensen (with some modifications to be made) was adopted in 1892, with a royalty to the inventors.

This rifle was a joint invention of two Norwegians: Capt. Ole Hermann Johannes Krag and Erik Jorgensen.* Denmark had already adopted their design in 1889, but Norway waited to do so until 1894.

Adopted with the new rifle was a new .30-caliber cartridge. Using a rimmed, bottlenecked case it was the first U.S. military cartridge loaded with smokeless powder. Officially the ".30 Army" or ".30 Government" or, more popularly, the ".30-40 Krag." More on the cartridge later.

Although officially adopted in 1892, it was not until 1894 that Springfield Ar-

mory (Springfield, Mass.) was sufficiently tooled up to begin making the Krag. Meanwhile, and for several years after 1892, the old .45-70 Springfield continued in service use. In fact, not enough Krags had been made by 1898 to arm all of our soldiers who fought in Cuba during the Spanish-American War, and many of the old 73s were used in that short but costly conflict.

The Krag Rifles and Carbines

All U.S. Krag rifles and carbines are marked on the left side of the receiver roughly as follows:

U.S.

MODEL (year) SPRINGFIELD

ARMORY (serial number)

Only rifles were made at first, these the M1892. On this rifle the word **MODEL** was omitted from the receiver marking and they were stamped **1894**, indicating only the year they were made.* The M1892 (marked **1894**) has a 30″ barrel with a flat muzzle, a ramrod under the barrel, a square-toed stock, and is without a trapdoor in the buttplate. First deliveries were made in the fall of 1894.

A very few test M1892 carbines were also made. These had a 22″ barrel, were stocked nearly to the muzzle and had a ramrod. All military U.S. Krags were made without a pistol grip.

Some changes were made, and a Model 1896 rifle and carbine were brought out —and so-marked—in that year. The muzzle was crowned, the ramrod was eliminated, and a 3-piece sectional cleaning rod, to be stored in a hole in the buttstock through a trap in the steel buttplate, was furnished. The buttplate toe was rounded also.

The M1892 Krag rifles already in use in the field were returned to the armory

and converted to the M1896 pattern. To identify these converted models look for M1896 features on those pieces bearing the 1894 date.

The first real carbine production began in 1896. The M1896 carbine had a half-length fore-end with a barrel band to hold fore-end, hand guard and barrel together. The barrel band lay against the front end of the rear sight. These carbines had no ramrod or sling swivels, but were fitted with a so-called saddle ring on the left side of the stock.

The biggest changes to both Krags came with the M1898 rifles and carbines. The two most noticeable changes were the reversal of the magazine cutoff so that it was in the ON position when swung down by changing its spring, and eliminating the lip under the bolt-handle notch. Far more M1898 rifles were made than any others, nearly 263,000 of them. Only 5000 M1898 carbines were produced.

The M1899 Krag carbine had a fore-end about 2″ longer than the M1896 type, and used the same length handguard as the rifle. This placed the barrel band about 2″ ahead of the rear sight. The "saddle" ring was omitted, and some were made with a knurled, but unflared, cocking piece—commonly called a "headless" type.

A number of very minor changes were made in the Krag from 1894 on, but they are not important enough to be mentioned here. Various rear sights were also used, and these, as well as other changes, are covered thoroughly in other books.

Some unusual and now rare versions of the Krag were made. The Cadet rifle was similar to the regular M1896 but it lacked sling swivels and had a ramrod.

A few .22 rimfire Gallery Practice rifles were made at Springfield Armory in 1906. They were single shot rifles based on the M98 action, the barrels offset at the breech and made with an auxiliary ex-

---

*Director and Chief Armorer, respectively, of the Kongsberg arms factory.

---

*The unending search for U.S. Krags marked **Model 1892** has failed, so far, to turn up even one. Ed.

Illustrated above: U.S. Krag-Jorgensen Model 1898 rifle. (From the Ronald Van't Hof collection)

U.S. Krag-Jorgensen Model 98 action.

tractor. These .22 barrels were made under the watchful eye of famed barrel-maker Harry Pope. Some, at least, carry his name stamp.

After the 1903 Springfield rifles were in production most of the Krag rifles and carbines were sold to NRA members through the DCM at unbelievably low prices.* The carbines were far more desirable than the rifles, so many of the M98 Krag rifles were converted to the carbine style at the Benicia Arsenal. These were like the regular M99 carbine, but came with sling swivels and 03 Springfield front sights.

The Krag Action

As already mentioned, those changes made in the Krag action were minor, relatively unimportant. Since the M98 Krag was made in the largest numbers and is the model most likely to be seen today, I'll describe it.

The Krag has a very smooth-working, turnbolt action with a unique non-detachable but quick-loadable, horizontal magazine. It is probably the smoothest bolt action ever made in the United States, but it does have its faults, as we shall see.

The receiver was precisely machined from a one-piece steel forging. The barrel is threaded (square-type threads) into the front of the receiver. The barrel, made without a shoulder, has a flat breech end which butts against a collar machined inside the receiver ring. The round receiver ring has no recoil shoulder. The left wall of the receiver continues straight back

*Sometime in the mid-1930s, I learned that a "special" Krag was available from the Rock Island (Illinois) Arsenal. These were brand new rifles, the barrels 24″ long (not 22″, as had been the standard DCM carbine) fitted with a carbine stock, also new, and an 03 front sight. The price was $6.50, plus the usual packaging and shipping charges, against the $1.50 the 22″ barreled carbines had cost some years earlier.
I obtained two of these, kept them a while and traded them off. I wonder where they are now? Ed.

from the ring and, since it is not milled out for a locking lug raceway, it is very thick. The receiver bridge is slotted for the extractor and top part of the bolt sleeve, but naturally has no cuts for a stripper clip, since the magazine can only be loaded from the side. The receiver ends in a tang, rounded on top.

The one-piece smoothly machined and polished bolt has a single forward locking lug which engages a matching mortise milled in the bottom front of the receiver, just to the rear of the internal collar against which the barrel abuts. The rear surface of this mortise is partly inclined so that the locking lug can gain a purchase on it in closing the bolt to force it forward the last .150″ against the tension of the mainspring and/or a hard-to-chamber cartridge. When the bolt is locked the locking lug is at the bottom, but on the ¼-turn required to open the bolt, the lug is to the right.

On the center of the bolt body, 90° above the locking lug, there is a guide rib about 2.70″ long. As the bolt is opened and closed, this guide rib and attached long extractor, slides through the slot in the receiver bridge, helping to prevent any binding of the bolt movement. More importantly, however, the guide rib provides an auxiliary safety locking lug for the bolt; it engages forward of—but does not contact by a few thousandths of an inch—the front edge of the bridge.

The bolt handle, integral with the bolt, is on the extreme rear of the bolt body. Its base is square, its shank is straight, round, heavy and tapered, and it ends in a round grasping ball. It is positioned at a very low angle when the bolt is closed, and is still sufficiently low when fully raised to clear the eyepiece of a low mounted scope. The receiver tang is deeply notched to receive the square base of the bolt handle and, although there is normally considerable space between the rear of the handle base and the notch, this provides another safety lug to hold the

bolt in the receiver should the single forward locking lug and the guide rib fail. More on the Krag locking system later on.

The right rear of the receiver bridge is slightly angled. Primary extraction power is achieved on raising the bolt handle when its base slides along this surface.

The face of the bolt is recessed the depth of the .30-40 cartridge rim. The rim around this recess is quite thin, but when the bolt is closed, the head of the bolt fits snugly within the receiver ring collar. Thus the cartridge head and rim are fully enclosed and supported.

The firing mechanism is held in the bolt by a projection on the bolt sleeve which is milled to form a hook to engage over a raised semi-circular collar on the rear end of the bolt. This projection houses the rotary wing safety and, in a slot in its front part, the long extractor is held with a rivet driven in from the underside.

The striker rod, with its peened-on cocking piece, extends through the bolt sleeve; the coil mainspring is compressed over the striker rod against the front of the bolt sleeve and the separate firing pin. The firing pin fits over a groove on the front of the striker rod. When the striker is forward, a cocking cam on the bottom of the cocking piece extends forward into a deep notch cut into the rear of the bolt; on raising the bolt handle the cocking piece is forced back, cocking the action.

The safety consists of a wing-type lever to which a round stem is permanently pressed in place, and a small spring and plunger assembled in the wing before the stem and wing are joined. The stem of the safety extends through a hole in the upper part of the bolt sleeve with the plunger engaging a shallow groove cut into the bolt sleeve. Swung to the far left, the safety is in the OFF or FIRE position. When the striker is cocked, swinging the safety upright or to the far right position locks both striker and bolt. There is a wide notch cut into the top of the cocking piece to allow the safety to be engaged

Left side of the Model 98 Krag action.

(swung up, or to the right) when the striker is forward, locking the bolt closed. Whether cocked or uncocked, the bolt is locked closed when the safety is up, or to the right, by the flattened end of the safety stem engaging a notch in the rear of the bolt.

The extractor serves several functions besides its primary job of extracting fired cases or cartridges. The extractor, about 5″ long, is made of a rectangular bar of spring-tempered steel, and is attached to the bolt sleeve by a rivet. A narrow hook on the front of the extractor extends over the forward end of the bolt and through a matching notch in the receiver ring collar when the bolt is closed. The breech end of the barrel also has a shallow inclined notch for the entrance of the extractor hook, so that it can engage the case rim when the bolt is closed. Although the long extractor itself is spring-tempered and made to lie with tension against the bolt, an additional small extractor spring is fitted into the underside left front end of the extractor. It slides under a small shelf in the receiver and provides extra downward tension to the extractor for positive initial extraction.

The extractor also functions as a means of holding the bolt in the receiver and in removing the bolt from the receiver. When the bolt is fully opened, it can be removed from the receiver by merely raising up the extractor hook so the bolt handle can be turned open further, and then the bolt can be pulled out of the receiver. The long stem of the extractor, which fits snugly in the receiver bridge slot, also prevents the bolt binding in the receiver when the action is operated and adds to the smoothness of operation. There is also a small pin projecting from the top right front of the extractor and, when the bolt is fully opened, it engages a shallow notch in the receiver bridge. This small pin has enough tension to hold the bolt open when the muzzle is pointed down. This is helpful to the shooter using the rifle as a single

shot, as he can drop a cartridge directly into the chamber. This feature, retained in the 1903 Springfield by different means, was called the "bolt stop."

Actually, there is no separate bolt stop in the Krag action, that is, a part or parts to halt the rearward travel of the bolt. The Krag bolt is stopped in its rearward travel by the locking lug contacting the receiver bridge. This is a very simple and positive arrangement, but few actions other than the Krag can use this feature.

The ejector, a small lever positioned in a groove in the rear bottom of the receiver, pivots on a small pin. One end of the ejector is always above the inside bottom line, and there is a long L-shaped groove cut into the bottom of the bolt to allow passage over the protruding rear part of the ejector. The long groove in the bolt ends just short of the front end of the bolt and, when the bolt is fully opened, the ungrooved end of the bolt causes the ejector to tip up. This in turn, causes the cartridge case to tip up and be flipped upward out of the action.

The trigger assembly is composed of the trigger, sear, sear spring and trigger pin. The sear, with a cylindrical pivot surface on its front end, fits into a matching hole in the receiver. A projection on the rear of the sear passes through a hole in the receiver and engages the sear projection on the cocking piece cam when the action is operated.

The trigger is the standard double-stage military pull type, the first stage disengaging the sear about halfway off the cocking piece; the heavier second-stage pull moves it entirely off to release the striker. On being pulled, the trigger not only moves back but also swings downward, not too unlike the trigger on the military Mannlicher-Schoenauer action. This is why the curved part of the trigger appears so short; by the time the trigger is pulled back far enough to release the striker, the bottom end nearly touches the guard bow.

The trigger guard bow is a separate part milled from a steel forging. Two guard screws, passing through holes in the ends of the guard, thread into the bottom of the receiver at the rear of the magazine and tang. These two screws are more than ample to hold the rear part of the action in the stock, but some additional fastening is needed (a barrel band is employed on the military Krags) to hold the barrel and front of the action in the stock.

The Magazine

The Krag magazine is novel, clever, and somewhat complicated. The receiver forging was made deep enough so a hole could be milled through it to form a horizontal magazine well. The milling is complicated, the front and rear ends of the well slanting forward from right to left to compensate for over-lapping of the cartridge rims. Another long opening is milled into the left receiver wall to provide an opening to allow cartridges to enter the receiver.

A concaved cover, mortised and screwed in place, is positioned over the openings on the left side of the receiver; this forms a rounded curve for passage of the cartridges from the magazine well proper into the receiver-well opening. The rear part of this opening is only wide enough to allow part of the cartridge rim to project from it so it can be picked up by the bolt. About halfway forward, the opening widens so the rim can slip out into the receiver while being pushed into the chamber.

The rest of the magazine is fully as complicated. The follower arm consists of the arm itself, plus a movable follower plate pivoted on a pin at the rear of the arm. The front end of the follower arm has a round integral hinge pin which fits into a matching hole milled into the right front side of the receiver. The follower is powered by a flat spring which lies in a groove in the bottom edge of the magazine well, with its front end contacting a

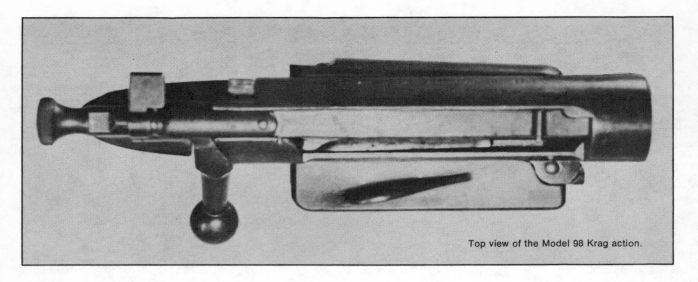

Top view of the Model 98 Krag action.

small lug on the follower arm hinge pin. Finally, to cover the right opening, and to allow loading the magazine through it, a box-like gate is hinged longitudinally to the bottom edge of the magazine well on a long hinge pin. The gate is powered by the follower spring, providing a lot of tension to the gate to keep it either closed or open. A sturdy hook in the forward bottom edge of the gate engages a matching cut in the follower arm so that, when the gate is swung open, the hook engages the follower arm and pulls it within the hollow gate, so cartridges can be dropped into the open magazine.

With cartridges in the magazine and the gate closed, the follower arm is released and the cartridges are pushed to the left and up around the curve into the magazine receiver-well opening. An upright projection on top of the gate serves as a thumb-piece so the magazine can be quickly and easily opened. The magazine can be loaded with the bolt open or closed, and cartridges can be added to a partially filled magazine. No skill or precautions need be exercised when loading; as long as the bullet is pointed forward, the cartridges can be just dropped into the open magazine.

The magazine cutoff is a lever on the rear left of the receiver. The round stem of the cutoff fits into a hole drilled lengthwise into the side of the receiver. The end of the hole exits in the top of the magazine-well opening. The end of this stem is flattened on one side, and when the cutoff is in the upright or ON position, the flattened end of the stem is level with the surrounding metal and does not interfere with cartridges moving through the magazine. When swung down, however, in the OFF position, the round end of the cutoff stem projects into the magazine well, preventing cartridge movement in the magazine and holding the top-most cartridge head within the magazine well so the bolt cannot pick it up when it is closed. The rifle can then be used and loaded as a single shot while keeping a reserve of cartridges in the magazine. The cutoff is tensioned to keep it in place in either the up or down positions.

Take-Down and Assembly

First make sure the rifle is unloaded. To remove the bolt open it fully and, while lifting up the front end of the extractor, turn or raise the bolt handle further until extractor swings to the right, then pull the bolt out. To remove the firing mechanism, grasp the bolt handle with one hand and, with the other hand, pull back on the cocking piece and rotate it counterclockwise until it is released from the bolt. With a firm grasp on the rear of the firing mechanism, and with the other hand grasping the firing pin, tilt the firing pin up or down. The firing pin, mainspring and striker rod can then be removed from the bolt sleeve. Place the safety in the upright position and, with the rear of the bolt sleeve resting on an edge of the workbench, give a sharp rap to the safety with a hammer handle and it will snap out. The safety plunger and spring cannot be removed. Remove the extractor by driving out the holding rivet from top to bottom with a drift punch. The auxiliary extractor spring can be driven out to the left, and the bolt stop pin can be driven out. These two parts, however, should remain in place unless it is absolutely necessary to remove them. Reassemble in reverse order.

To remove barrel and action from the stock, first remove barrel band (or bands), then remove the two trigger-guard screws; lift barrel, action and trigger guard from the stock.

To remove trigger and sear assembly pull the rear of the sear down as far as it will go; then tap the assembly to the left. Drive out the trigger pin from left to right to remove trigger from the sear.

The magazine cutoff is removed by inserting a small screwdriver blade under the cutoff plunger, depressing the plunger as far as it will go and then pulling the cutoff out. The cutoff plunger is peened in place. It and the spring should not be removed from the cutoff unless necessary; as it would be if this part is to be blued in hot-dip bluing salts. If it is necessary the plunger can be pulled and twisted out by gripping it with a pair of pliers.

To remove the magazine gate, hold the rear part of the gate and receiver in a padded vise or by some other means, the lip on the hinge pin pivoted up; the pin is then driven, or pulled forward, all the way out. On removal from the vise the gate can be lifted off and the follower spring lifted out. Swing the follower to the right and it can be pushed downward and removed. Do not remove the follower-arm plate unless necessary, and then only by driving out its pin. Remove the side-plate screw, lift up the rear of the plate and remove it. Pull out the ejector pin with the fingers and the ejector can be removed. Reassemble in reverse order. In assembling the follower spring, the rounded end must contact the lug on the follower. The barrel has a right hand thread, but do not attempt to remove it from the receiver unless you have the proper tools.

Krag Steel and Heat Treatment

According to *Hatcher's Notebook*, Krag barrels were made of Ordnance barrel steel, the same steel used to make 1903 Springfield barrels. The receiver was made from Springfield Armory Class C steel (later known as W.D. 1325), the same steel used in the so-called low-numbered 1903 Springfields. Alloyed with carbon, manganese, silicon, sulphur and phosphorus, it was given a lengthy heat treatment which resulted in the receiver becoming very hard throughout, but having a harder outside surface. The bolt was most likely made of a steel different from that used in the receiver, but it too was thoroughly case-hardened to a considerable depth. After precisely machining and polishing the receiver and bolt, as well as those parts which rubbed together, the result was a very smooth-working action.

Only the single front locking lug holds the bolt closed against the thrust of firing. The guide rib clears the bridge by a few thousandths of an inch, and the base of the bolt handle, which has still more clearance, acts as auxiliary safety lug only. The Danish Krag (chambered for the 8x58R Danish cartridge) and the Norwegian Krag (chambered for the very fine 6.5x 55mm cartridge), while essentially the same as the U.S. Krag, were probably made of better steels and given a better

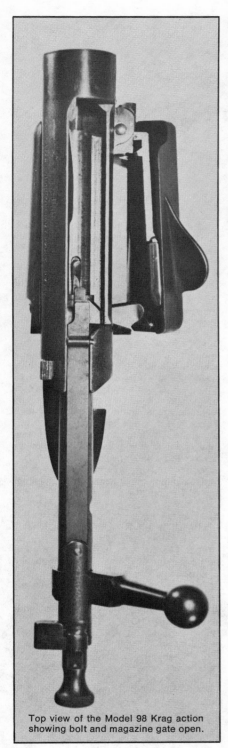

Top view of the Model 98 Krag action showing bolt and magazine gate open.

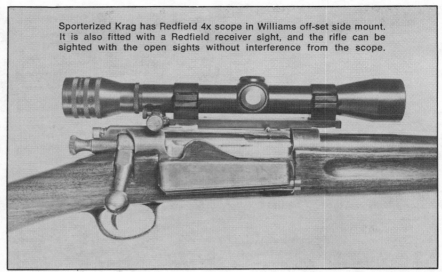

Sporterized Krag has Redfield 4x scope in Williams off-set side mount. It is also fitted with a Redfield receiver sight, and the rifle can be sighted with the open sights without interference from the scope.

heat treatment. They were also made with the guide rib bearing on the receiver bridge, so that these bolts have two locking lugs instead of one. This foreign Krag locking arrangement greatly strengthened the locking system. As a result they could handle the powerful cartridges for which they were chambered. Both are more powerful than the .30-40.

Perhaps because of over-hardening the bolt, or because of improper heat-treatment, and by the fact that only the front lug bore against the receiver, many U.S.

Krag bolts cracked just behind the lug. This was very serious because the guide rib immediately took over the job of locking the bolt. However, cracked bolts should be replaced. I have never seen a cracked Krag receiver, but I have seen a couple of cracked bolts. In both cases I blamed the failure on the shooter. In one instance I believe the shooter was using too heavy handloads; in the other, the action was rebarreled to a cartridge much too powerful for the action. At any rate, the U.S. Krag action would have been considerably stronger had it been made with the guide rib bearing against the receiver. It can be made stronger if the bolt is lapped so the guide rib bears against the receiver equally with the front locking lug. Used only with commercial .30-40 cartridges, however, which are normally factory loaded with breech pressures well under 40,000 psi, or if used with handloads which develop no more pressure than this, then the "as issued" Krag action is sufficiently strong and safe.

At this point it might be interesting to relate what one well-known gunsmith thought of the Krag action.

This man was the late R.F. Sedgley of Philadelphia, best known for his custom 1903 Springfield and Winchester High Wall sporters. Since he was in business when the DCM was releasing Krags, he naturally was called upon to work on them. If my memory serves me right, I recall reading that it was common practice, when a Krag rifle came into his shop, to test fire it first by screwing a .30-06 barrel into the action, and then firing several heavy .30-06 loads through it. I think he had a high regard for the Krag action, and that few of them failed to pass this test. He did not, of course, advocate using this action for more powerful cartridges than the .30-40, since this action will hardly handle any other cartridge through the magazine. He did, however, manage in one way or another to alter the magazine of the Krag to handle the .25-35 cartridge. One such, a fine Sedgley Krag sporter, was once described in *The American Rifleman*. I have no idea of how Sedgley altered the magazine system to

handle this cartridge. I attempted a similar conversion on several occasions but I could never make it work. While Sedgley and other gunsmiths may have thought well of the Krag, many present-day gunsmiths have a very low opinion of them —and some are not hesitant to say so.

Gunsmithing the Krag

Much has been written on gunsmithing the Krag, so I will not go very deeply into this subject. For example, the older gunsmithing books like *Modern Gunsmithing* and *The Modern Gunsmith* contain considerable information on the subject. Also, practically every issue of *The American Rifleman* from the mid-1920s to the late 1940s carried something on this rifle.

As for the availability of Krags for gunsmithing (remodeling, sporterizing, rebarreling, etc.), consider the following: all told, there were about 442,883 Krag rifles and about 63,116 Krag carbines made between 1894 and 1904; practically all of them were disposed of by the military years ago, most of them going to NRA members who bought them through the DCM, but a great number of them went to American Legion posts for parade use. Krag rifles and carbines in very good or excellent condition, and in original, "as issued" state, are now becoming collectors items, so some thoughts should be given before such a gun is altered. I would estimate, however, that at least half of the Krags which were sold through the DCM in the 1920s have since been altered, remodeled or converted in one way or another and such guns rarely have any value to a collector. Such altered Krags are continually being put up for sale, and I'd imagine that most of them only underwent minor remodeling to start with. These guns are still entirely suitable for re-gunsmithing. Separate Krag actions probably are impossible to find today, but an ordinary used and remodeled complete Krag rifle will probably cost no more than a separate action, if one could be found.

Because so many Krag rifles have been remodeled in past years, collectors of military long arms have started another

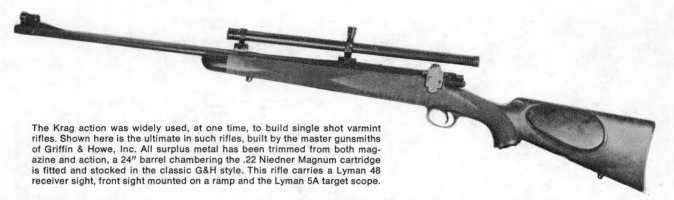

The Krag action was widely used, at one time, to build single shot varmint rifles. Shown here is the ultimate in such rifles, built by the master gunsmiths of Griffin & Howe, Inc. All surplus metal has been trimmed from both magazine and action, a 24″ barrel chambering the .22 Niedner Magnum cartridge is fitted and stocked in the classic G & H style. This rifle carries a Lyman 48 receiver sight, front sight mounted on a ramp and the Lyman 5A target scope.

trend. Beginning collectors often buy a remodeled Krag and then attempt to restore it to its original military configuration by purchasing an issue stock and other parts. Issue Krag stocks, handguards and barrels, however, are hard to come by these days —at least I don't know from whom they are available.

About 15 years ago a friend of mine got about 30 complete Krag rifles from local Legion posts. All but two, which he kept for himself, had completely ruined bores. He decided he wanted $25 each for the others, but he didn't want to box these long rifles for shipment to individual buyers. On my suggestion he advertised Krag actions only at the same price. To our surprise he received many replies, two of them telegrams from prominent eastern gunshops; they wanted every action my friend had—up to 100 or more if he had that many. I could only conclude that there must still have been a heavy demand for custom rifles built on the Krag action.

That an excellent medium-range big game rifle can be built on this action has long been known. For smoothness of operation, for ease of loading, there is no other American bolt action, past or present, that can compare with it.

A number of accessories are still available for remodeling the Krag. Several firms (Fajen, Bishop, and others) can furnish several styles of semi-finished sporter stocks for it. A low scope safety is available from Maynard Buehler, Orinda, Calif. Lyman, Redfield, Williams and some others have various types of iron sights for the Krag, including receiver sights, open rear sights and sight bases, front sight ramp bases and front sights.

Because the Krag ejects the fired cases nearly straight up, mounting a hunting scope low and centrally over the action is not entirely satisfactory. There are, however, several mounts made for, or adaptable to the round Krag receiver. Only a side mount can be used, and the mounts available are made by Weaver, Williams, Buehler, Griffin & Howe, Jaeger, Pachmayr and perhaps a couple others. To avoid ejection interference, the scope should be positioned slightly off-set to the left. This can readily be done with several of these mounts. If the scope must be directly over the bore, than get the mount with rings or base so the scope is mounted somewhat higher than normal over the receiver. Some Krag shooters have fashioned a simple deflector of sheet metal

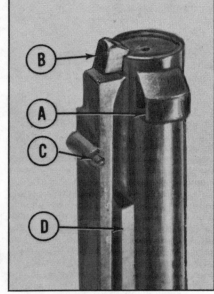

U.S. Krag-Jorgensen bolt head, showing locking lug (A), extractor (B), bolt stop pin (C), and guide rib (D).

to attach to the scope or mount to deflect the ejected cases to the right. Lastly, I see no reason why one of the new long eye-relief scopes cannot be mounted on the barrel, and I see no great problem in mounting the Redfield or Leupold barrel-mount on the Krag barrel.

At this writing (mid-1971) I note from advertisements in *Shotgun News* that at least a couple of firms still have spare parts for the Krag, including bolts. For years Flaigs of Millvale, Penna., have been offering barrels for the Krag, these made from surplus 1903 and 1903A3 Springfield barrels and chambered for the .30-40 cartridge. I've rebarreled a number of Krags myself with Springfield barrels, and they are entirely satisfactory for the purpose. I know one shooter who had the pitted barrel of his Krag rebored and rechambered for a wildcat .35 caliber cartridge based on the .30-40 case with good results.

Other than the above mentioned .35 wildcat, and if the rifle is to remain a repeater, then the only other cartridge choice is the .30-40. There is a popular wildcat cartridge called the .25 Krag (the .30-40 case necked down to .25), but this cartridge is definitely not suitable for the Krag action, and should only be used in the P-14 Enfield action or in one of the

heavy falling-block single shot actions like the Sharps-Borchardt. As I've said before, I know of no method by which the Krag magazine can be altered to handle any cartridge with dimensions much different from the .30-40 case.

The Krag action, however, is suitable for rebarreling to other cartridges, if the rifle is used as a single shot. In years past, a great many .22 Hornet rifles were built on the Krag action. When the .219 Zipper cartridge was first introduced, I built several single shot Krags in this caliber. Other gunsmiths would regularly rebarrel these actions to the .22 Baby Niedner (.32-20 case), .22 R-2 Lovell (.25-20 S.S. case) and .22 Niedner Magnum (rimmed, .25-35 case; rimless, .25 Rem. case). Since the rifle had to be used as a single shot, the common practice was to remove as much of the surplus magazine metal as was possible, and inlet the trimmed and lightened action into a new stock so the scars of removing the metal and remaining magazine-well openings would be concealed.

A classic example of such a conversion and restocking is shown here in a fine Griffin & Howe Krag. This was done in the days when the Krags were both plentiful and cheap, but it still shows what can be done with the Krag if one has the inclination and the skill to do it.

In rebarreling the Krag I certainly recommend enough honing and lapping-in the front locking lug so that the guide rib will contact the receiver equally with the locking lug. Doing this will definitely make the old Krag action a bit stronger, may possibly prevent the bolt from cracking at the front lug area. I believe it was G & H's practice to do this lap-in job on the Krags they rebarreled. But even with the two locking lug system, I still do not consider this action suitable for rebarreling to such cartridges as the .219 Wasp, .219 Improved Zipper, 6mm/ .30-30 and similar hot wildcats. I think that such an action might be suitable for the .222 cartridge, but I prefer the .219 Zipper since it can and does deliver about the same muzzle velocity with the same weight bullets at a much lower breech pressure than the .222.

In fitting the Krag with a sporter stock, an inside barrel band should be used, placing it about three-quarters of the way up the fore-end to hold it against the barrel. I also advise routing out grooves in the stock, inletting to the rear of the magazine and glass bedding this area to evenly

Parts Legend

1. Receiver (side view)
2. Magazine cutoff
3. Magazine cutoff plunger
4. Magazine cutoff plunger spring
5. Sear
6. Sear spring
7. Trigger
8. Trigger pin.
9. Bolt
10. Striker
11. Firing pin
12. Mainspring
13. Bolt sleeve
14. Safety
15. Extractor
16. Extractor rivet
17. Auxiliary extractor spring
18. Bolt stop pin
19. Ejector
20. Ejector pin
21. Magazine cover plate
22. Magazine cover plate screw
23. Magazine cover box
24. Magazine cover box hinge pin
25. Follower arm
26. Follower arm plate
27. Follower arm plate pin
28. Follower arm spring
29. Trigger guard
30. Front trigger guard screw
31. Rear trigger guard screw

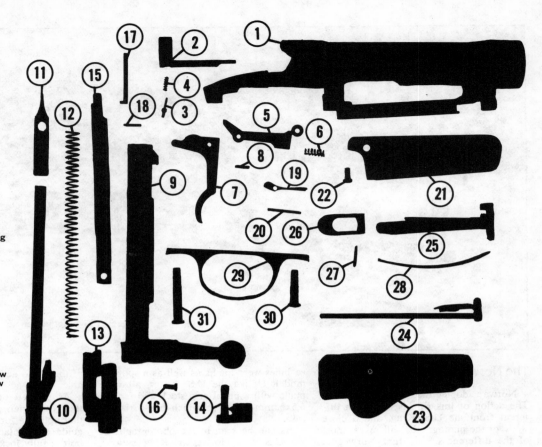

Krag-Jorgensen

Dimensional Specifications

Weight	50 ounces
Over-all	8.312"
Receiver ring dia.	1.30"
Bolt body dia.	.630"
Bolt travel	3.625"
Striker travel	.600"
Bolt face recess:	
Dia.	.555"
Depth	.060"

General Specifications

Type	Turnbolt repeater.
Receiver	One-piece machined steel forging with slotted bridge.
Bolt	One-piece with single forward locking lug. Guide rib on bolt and base of bolt handle act as auxiliary safety lugs.
Ignition	Firing mechanism composed of striker rod with integral cocking piece, separate firing pin and coil mainspring. Cocks on opening.
Magazine	Non-detachable 5-shot horizontal hinged-box type.
Trigger	Non-adjustable, double-stage military type.
Safety	Rotary wing-type built into the bolt sleeve. 180° swing, locking both bolt and striker when in the UP or RIGHT position.
Extractor	Non-rotating bar-type, attached to bolt sleeve, has auxiliary spring.
Bolt stop	Locking lug serves as bolt stop.
Ejector	Pivoting lever positioned in bottom of receiver. Cases eject upward.

distribute the thrust of the recoil. This should prevent the stock from splitting at this point.

The .30-40 Cartridge

Originally known as the "U.S. Caliber .30 Government" or ".30 U.S. Army" cartridge, it was introduced with the Krag in 1892. Today, and for years past, it was most commonly called the .30-40 Krag, or simply the .30-40. The .30-40 designation was given to it many years ago, probably soon after Winchester and other arms makers began chambering some of their sporting rifles for it. For example, the Model 95 Winchester lever action repeater and the Model 1885 Winchester single shot rifle were chambered for the .30-40 as early as 1896. Beginning back in the black powder cartridge era, it was common practice to name metallic rifle cartridges by two sets of digits, as, for instance, the .50-70. The first two figures

roughly represent the caliber, while the last two indicated the amount (in grains) of black powder used. There were other .50 caliber cartridges such as the .50-90 Sharps, .50-100 Winchester and .50-140 Sharps, and the last figures of these cartridges provided a thumb-nail guide to the power of each cartridge by the amount of black powder the case could use. Although the .30-40 Krag cartridge was developed in the smokeless powder era, the "40" in the designation merely indicated that its case had a powder capacity approximately 10 grains more than the .30-30 cartridge, and therefore was comparatively more powerful than the latter.

The .30-40 cartridge would probably have been a very popular one even without the Krag rifle because, long before

Krag rifles and carbines were released for sale, the .30-40 had proved to be quite adequate for hunting most species of North American big game.

For military use it was normally loaded with a full-jacketed, round-nosed 200-gr. bullet, the muzzle velocity 2000 fps. At various times in its long history it was commercially loaded with full-jacketed and soft point bullets of various weights, but mostly with 220- and 180-gr. soft point or some other type of expanding bullet, as it is today. As loaded today, the 180-gr. load develops 2470 fps. while the 220-gr. load is listed as having a muzzle velocity of 2200 fps. This places it between the .300 Savage and the .308; despite its age, the .30-40 is still a remarkable cartridge.

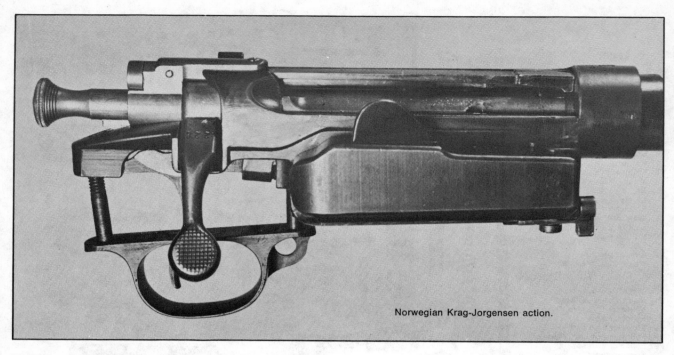

Norwegian Krag-Jorgensen action.

The Norwegian Krag

Norway adopted the Krag rifle in 1894. The action of this rifle is not much different from the U.S. Krag, and a close study of the photographs will reveal most of the differences. The first Norwegian Krags (20,000 of them) were produced for Norway by the great Austrian arms makers in Steyr, and they can be identified by the word **STEYR** stamped on the receiver. The rest of the many Norwegian Krags were made in Norway by the Kongsberg Vapenfabrik, a government-owned arsenal in the town of that name. These rifles can be identified by an ornate letter K, beneath a crown, stamped on the receiver ring, as shown in the illustration. The date (year) of manufacture is normally stamped on the receiver ring and they probably were made as late as 1930. According to the *The Book Of Rifles* by W.H.B. Smith, a few were also made in the late 1940s for target shooting. Various models of the military rifles and carbines were made, as well as a sporting model. Unlike the U.S. Krags, all were made with a pistol grip stock and for the 6.5x55mm cartridge which has a rimless case.

As can be seen in the photographs of the U.S. and Norwegian Krag actions, there are numerous minor outward differences. For example, the safety is different and it is retained in the bolt sleeve with a cross screw; the extractor is retained with a screw and has a near-center auxiliary spring; various parts have different contours such as the magazine gate and receiver, which has a hollow groove milled in the receiver wall. The Norwegian action is several ounces lighter in weight than the U.S. Krag action. Many of the Norwegian Krags have flattened bolt handle knobs, the flattened surfaces checkered. There are also several differences inside the action; for example, the barrel thread is entirely different—it is one of the few rifle actions with a left hand thread. In fact, there are probably no parts of these two actions that are interchangeable.

As pointed out early in this chapter, the Norwegian Krag action is so made that both the forward locking lug and the guide rib contact the receiver when the bolt is fully locked closed. This, plus the fact that most Norwegian Krags were made years after the U.S. Krag was discontinued, makes it almost certain that Norwegian actions were made of a better quality steel, and this steel given a more controlled and uniform heat treatment. All in all, the Norwegian Krag action is superior to the U.S. Krag action, and early Norwegian actions, which reveal most precise machining and finishing, are even smoother in operation than the U.S. counterpart.

Operation of the Norwegian Krag is the same as the U.S. Krag, and the action is loaded in the same way. Many Norwegian Krag rifles were sold on the surplus arms market during the 1950s, so they are fairly common. Fajen and Bishop

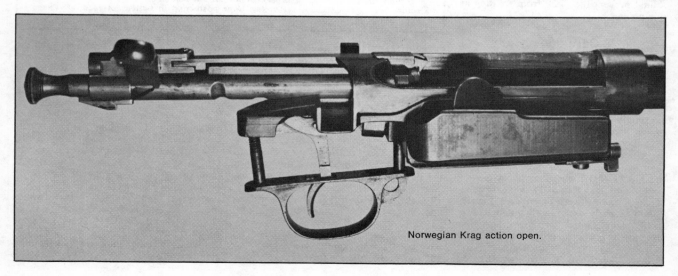

Norwegian Krag action open.

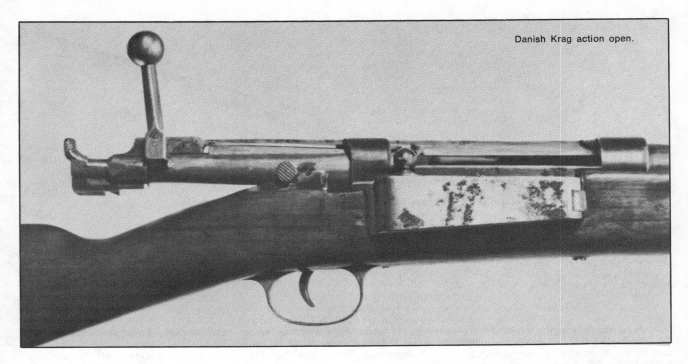

Danish Krag action open.

make several designs of sporting stocks for this rifle. No one makes a replacement safety or trigger. Williams Gun Sight Co., Davison, Mich., makes a special scope mounting plate to fit the hollowed receiver so that the regular Williams side mount can be attached. They also make a receiver sight to fit the rifle.

While I do consider the Norwegian Krag action stronger than the U.S. Krag action, I would limit its use to the standard factory loaded 6.5x55mm Norma cartridge or to handloads which develop somewhat less breech pressure. This action was made for the 6.5x55 cartridge, which it will handle better than any other. Therefore, if rebarreling is required, I advise staying with the original cartridge.

The Danish Krag

As mentioned earlier in this chapter, the Krag-Jorgensen rifle originated in Denmark, and was first adopted as a military weapon by that country in 1889. The various models were made by Gevaerfabriken Kjobenhavn (Copenhagen Arms Manufactory) and Haerens Tojhus (Army Arsenal), and were so-marked on the left side of the receiver. The model designation, as well as the date (year) of manufacture is stamped on the left side of the receiver also.

Several models were made, but the most common one seen in the U.S. is the Model 89 rifle with a 32.75″ barrel. Like the German M88 Commission rifle, the Danish M89 rifle has a thin metal tube over the barrel to serve as a handguard. The rifle weighs about 9.5 pounds and is 52.3″ over-all.

Less common Danish Krags are the M89 infantry carbine with 23.63″ barrel, which has the letter **F** in front of the serial number; the M89 artillery carbine with 24.02″ barrel and the letter **A** proceeding the serial number; the M89 engineer carbine with 23.53″ barrel (with wood handguard) and the letter **I** before the serial number; the M89 cavalry carbine is like the engineer's carbine but has the letter **R** before the serial number; the M1928 sniper's rifle with 26.50″ barrel of heavy weight, globe front and rear sights, and marked with the letters **FSK,** which means

"sniper's rifle;" and the Danish single shot target rifle. This last is similar to the sniper's rifle but is a single shot without magazine cuts in the receiver.

All of these Krags, both rifles and carbines, are chambered for the Danish 8mm (8x58R) rimmed cartridge. The single shot target rifle was chambered for the 6.5x55 Swedish Mauser cartridge.

The Danish Krag repeating action is very similar to the U.S. Krag action except for the following: 1) The magazine cover, hinged near the front, opens by swinging out and forward. It has a checkered knob-type catch on its top rear surface to hold the cover closed and acts as a handle to open it. When open, cartridges are merely rolled into the magazine. 2) The safety is a round, checkered button positioned on the right side of the tang behind the bolt handle. Pressed to the left and swung back the rifle is ready to fire and the bolt can be operated. Swung forward, the safety locks the bolt and sear. It can't be swung forward unless the striker is cocked. 3) The cocking piece has a stubby "hook" with its front curved sur-

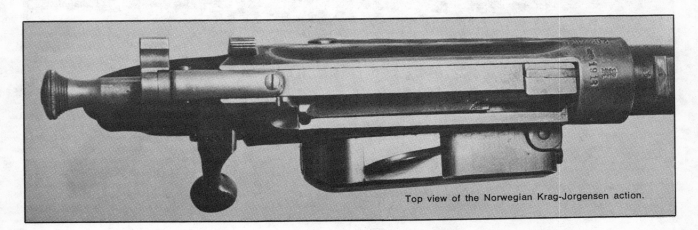

Top view of the Norwegian Krag-Jorgensen action.

Model 1889 Danish Krag rifle.

face checkered. By grasping this hook with the thumb, the striker can be manually cocked or the cocked striker lowered, either to the full down position or to a half-cock position. When in the half-cock position, the safety can be engaged. 4) The ejector is a thin leaf spring mounted in a groove in the bottom of the bolt raceway. 5) The receiver magazine cover or plate is shaped and attached to the receiver differently than other Krags.

Like other Krags, the Danish actions are well made and finished, and are very smooth in operation. The bolt head is recessed and the bolt is disassembled and removed from the receiver just like the U.S. Krag. Unlike the U.S. Krag, but like the Norwegian Krag, the forward locking lug and the guide rib contact the receiver to take up the rearward thrust of firing a cartridge in the chamber. For this reason the Danish action is considered to be a bit stronger and better than the U.S. action.

Here are some dimensional specifications for the Danish Krag repeating action: Receiver diameter, 1.365″; bolt diameter, .700″; bolt travel, 3.710″; striker travel, .500″; bolt face recess diameter, .590″; bolt face recess depth, .060″; magazine length—to handle certain rimmed cartridges no longer than about 3.20″ over-all.

I found the Danish Krag action would accept and feed the .30-40 Krag, .303 British, .348 and .444 Marlin cartridges. However, the bolt face recess is not correct for any one of them; the recess has to be enlarged for the .348, and reduced in some way for the others. Of course, the extractor would also have to be altered a bit.

The Danish Krag single shot target action was made with a bolt face recess to accommodate the 6.5x55 Swedish Mauser cartridge, which has a .480″ case head diameter. It can be considered correct for .30-06 head-sized cartridges. In the early 1960s several firms offered these actions for sale, and they are an excellent choice on which to build a long range target rifle in the 6.5x55 caliber.

Like the other Krags, the Danish action should not be used with cartridges which develop much over 45,000 psi breech pressure. It has the best safety of all the Krags. There is no commercial trigger mechanism made for the Danish Krag, but the same scope mounts suitable for the U.S. Krag are usable on the Danish action.

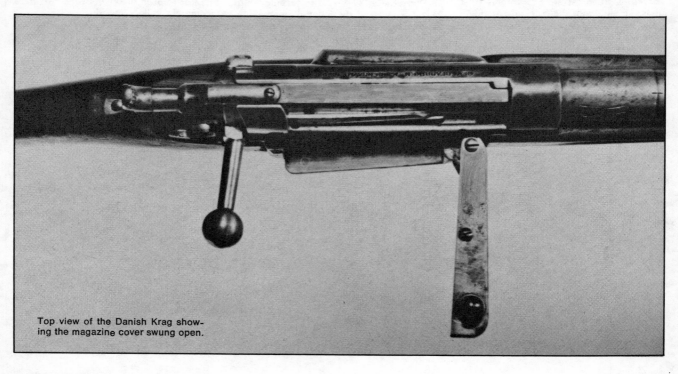

Top view of the Danish Krag showing the magazine cover swung open.

16. 1903, 1903A3 and 1903A4 Springfields

As in the other chapters in this book, my primary intention here is to thoroughly discuss Springfield actions only, i.e., how the actions are made, describing them, listing their strong and weak points, how to remodel them, etc. You may not find here everything you want to know about the history and development of the 1903 Springfield rifle, or learn about the many variations produced. For this information I suggest you obtain one or all of the following books: *The '03 Springfield* by Campbell, *Hatcher's Notebook* by Hatcher and *The Book of the Springfield* by Crossman.

The Spanish-American war of 1898 proved that the 93 Mauser rifle and its 7mm Mauser cartridge were superior to our best service rifle and cartridge then in use, namely the caliber .30-40 Krag-Jorgensen. Immediately after the war the United States began development of a new cartridge rifle. The planning was largely done by boards set up for this purpose, and the work done mostly at the U.S. Springfield Armory, Springfield, Mass., hence the popular name, "Springfield."

Several experimental rifles were tested from 1900 to 1903 before the final version was adopted in 1903, thus the designation of Model 1903 Springfield. Adopted at the same time was a rimless bottlenecked case with the designation of "Caliber .30, Model of 1903," or .30-03 for short. This cartridge was still not the ballistic equal of the 7.9 (8x57mm) Mauser cartridge, with its spitzer bullet, but in 1906 the United States adopted a new and lighter bullet of spitzer or pointed form and the new cartridge was designated the "Caliber .30, Model of 1906," or .30-06 for short. Those Springfield rifles made up to that time were recalled and modified for the new round by refitting the barrel.

The M1903 Action

The Springfield action which emerged in 1903 was sound and compact, a well-designed and well-built turnbolt action having several features copied from the 93 and 98 Mauser actions. The truth is that the United States had to pay Mauser a royalty on each rifle made which resulted in their receiving $200,000 for infringements on the action and stripper clip patents. The 03 Springfield had such Mauser features as the dual-opposed forward locking lugs; non-rotating extractor fastened to the bolt with a collar; staggered-column, non-detachable flush magazine box combined with the trigger guard, and a bolt sleeve which threaded into the rear of the bolt.

The receiver is a one-piece machined steel forging. The front end of the receiver is threaded to accept the barrel shank, which is .734″ long, with a body diameter of .990″, a thread diameter of 1.040″. The threads are square with a pitch of 10 threads to the inch. The breech end of the barrel is funneled as a possible aid to guide cartridges into the chamber when fed from the magazine. The rear inside of the receiver ring is machined to form shoulders against which the locking lugs on the bolt can engage to hold the bolt against the barrel during the thrust of firing.

The bottom of the receiver from the front of the sear to the recoil shoulder is flat. The recoil shoulder is of ample size (about 1.050″ wide and .360″ deep) to prevent rearward movement of the action and barrel in the stock due to recoil. The major part of this flat surface is milled out for the magazine opening. The milling is done so as to leave integral cartridge guide lips in the receiver.

The left receiver wall is smooth with the receiver ring, and is nearly as high as the top of the bolt. The right wall (or rail) is only as high as the bottom of the extractor, which leaves a more than ample receiver opening for loading the magazine.

The receiver bridge is, technically, unslotted since it has a thin raised top to cover or contain the mill cut groove that allows passage of the safety lug on the bolt. This makes the top of the bridge higher than the receiver ring. Clip-charger grooves in the front of the bridge provide a means of loading the magazine with cartridges held in a stripper clip.

The bolt with its integral handle is also a one-piece machined steel forging. The right (or lower) locking lug is solid, while the left (or top) locking lug is slotted for the passage of the ejector. The bolt face is partly recessed for the cartridge head. The recess is undercut to allow cartridges to slip under the extractor hook as they feed up out of the magazine. This prevents double loading because the cartridge being fed into the chamber from the magazine will be extracted and ejected on opening the bolt, even if the bolt is not fully closed on chambering the cartridge.

The bolt handle has a round tapered shank bent down to about a 45° angle and

Illustrated above: The Model 1903 U.S. Springfield rifle, caliber .30-06. This rifle weighs about 8.7 pounds, has a 24″ barrel and is 43.2″ over-all. The full length one-piece stock has a straight grip with finger grooves in the fore-end. Its steel buttplate contains a hinged trapdoor that gives access to the hole within that holds cleaning accessories. The rear sight, adjustable for windage and elevation, is attached to the breech end of the barrel. The one-piece wooden handguard extends forward to the end of the fore-end. The barrel has a groove diameter of .308″, with the 4-groove rifling having a pitch of one turn in 10 inches (right-hand twist).

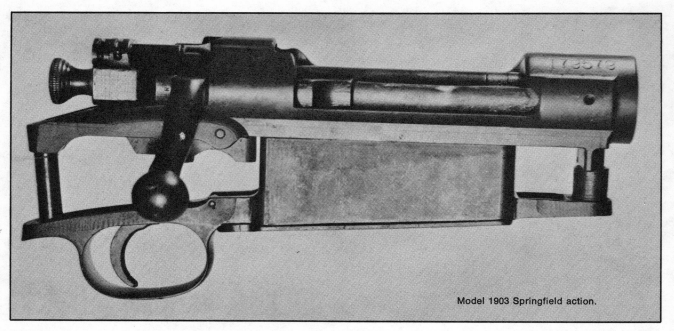

Model 1903 Springfield action.

ends in a round grasping ball. The square base of the bolt handle extends upward, partly over the rear end of the bolt. The front of this raised portion is inclined and imparts the initial camming power to the extractor when the bolt is opened, by contacting and moving against a matching surface milled in the receiver bridge.

The large safety lug is located about 1.25″ ahead of the bolt handle base; when the bolt is closed and locked it is positioned forward of the bridge. This lug is not supposed to contact the bridge; its only function is to hold the bolt in the receiver in the event the receiver ring or the two forward locking lugs should fail. The gap between the safety lug and the receiver should be not less than .004″, although it can be much more than this and not impair the function of the lug.

The long Mauser type spring extractor, which does not rotate with the bolt, is fastened to the bolt by a hooked collar around the bolt engaging a mortise inside the extractor. A lug inside the front end of the extractor rides in a groove cut into the bolt head, which prevents longitudinal movement of the extractor on the bolt. The extractor is made to slip easily over the rim of a cartridge placed in the chamber ahead of the bolt.

The bolt is drilled from the rear to accept the firing mechanism, which consists of the firing pin, striker, mainspring, striker sleeve and bolt sleeve assembly. The bolt sleeve has square threads that turn into the bolt. The round striker rod extends through the bolt sleeve, and the coil mainspring is compressed over it by the striker sleeve, which is in turn held back by the separate firing pin mortised over the front end of the striker rod.

The cocking piece, with its integral cam, is threaded and peened on the end of the striker rod so it cannot loosen or turn, and is flared and knurled so the striker can be manually cocked or uncocked. This feature is of small value except when one might want to re-cock the bolt after a

misfire or hangfire. The extra metal adds weight to the striker, however, and this can be helpful to ignition. The cocking piece, striker rod and separate firing pin of the Springfield action are more or less a hold-over from the U.S. Krag-Jorgensen rifle.

The cocking cam part of the cocking piece extends through a slot in the bolt sleeve and into a raceway in the receiver tang, and then forward into a deep cam notch cut in the rear of the bolt. The striker is cocked on the uplift of the bolt handle.

A small spring and plunger bolt lock fitted into the left side of the bolt sleeve, and engaging in a shallow notch in the bolt when it is open, locks and prevents the bolt sleeve and firing mechanism parts from turning when the bolt is drawn back.

The round stem of the wing safety (another Krag-Jorgensen hold-over) is fitted in a hole lengthwise in the top of the bolt sleeve. The wing, which contains a small spring-loaded plunger, and the stem of the safety are peened together. The plunger rides in a shallow groove cut into the bolt sleeve, providing tension to the safety to keep it in place, and in the ON or OFF positions. The safety is in the OFF or FIRE position when it is to the left. The safety can only be swung over when the action is cocked and bolt closed; the grooves in the safety then line up with matching notches in the top of the cocking piece. When the safety is swung upright or to the intermediate position, only the striker is locked back and the bolt can be opened and closed. When the safety is swung to the far right or SAFE position, both the striker and bolt are locked.

The magazine cutoff is positioned in a recess in the left side of the receiver bridge and is held in place by, and pivots on, a pin lengthwise in the receiver. The cutoff serves a dual purpose; to allow the rifle to be used and loaded as a single shot with a fully loaded magazine, and as a bolt stop to halt the rearward travel of the bolt.

The cutoff contains a small spring-loaded plunger which rides in a shallow groove on the receiver. The groove has three depressions for the three positions to which the cutoff can be pivoted. When the cutoff is up with the word "ON" showing, it is in the normal position to halt the bolt travel and allow the bolt to pick up cartridges from the magazine when it is closed. Swung to the lowest position so that the word "OFF" shows, the rearward travel of the bolt is halted about .375″ short of its normal length of travel, so that the head of the top cartridge in the magazine remains under the bolt head, and cannot be picked up by the bolt when it is closed. When the cutoff is placed in its intermediate position (swung outward), the bolt can be removed from the receiver.

The small ejector is fitted inside the receiver bridge just ahead of the cutoff. It pivots on, and is held in place by a pin through its underside. It does not have a separate spring, but is pivoted so its end is tipped into the ejector slot on the left locking lug by the action of the locking lug against the base of the ejector.

The trigger mechanism is composed of the trigger, sear, sear spring, and trigger and sear pins. The trigger is a standard military double-pull type. The front face of the trigger is curved and grooved.

The trigger guard and the magazine box are milled from a one-piece steel forging. The barrel and action assembly is securely held in the stock by two guard screws through holes (in each end of the trigger guard) which thread into the recoil lug and tang of the receiver. The guard screws have a ¼ x25 thread. The magazine floorplate has lips on each end which engage in matching recesses cut into the guard, and is retained in position by a small spring-actuated catch positioned just behind the magazine box. The floorplate can be quickly detached by depressing the latch with a pointed tool or bullet through a hole in the rear of the plate and sliding it back.

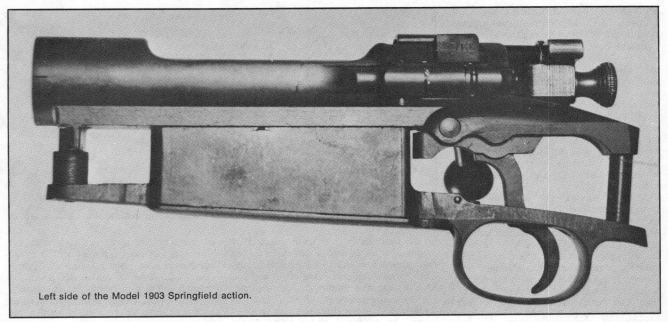

Left side of the Model 1903 Springfield action.

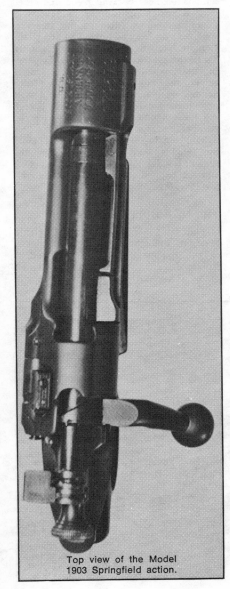

Top view of the Model 1903 Springfield action.

The steel magazine follower is tensioned by a W-shaped flat spring whose ends go into mortises in the floorplate and follower. The ridge on the top left of the follower causes the cartridges to be staggered in the magazine box when it is loaded. The rear end of the follower is squared and prevents blind loading when the magazine is empty by halting the forward travel of the bolt, a sign to the shooter that the magazine is empty.

The 03 actions were made with a small spring and plunger which was called the bolt stop. It was a flat spring with a small round tipped plunger attached to one end. It was positioned under the receiver, in a groove in the rear of the magazine well, with the plunger projecting through a hole into the bottom of the left locking lug raceway. There it contacts, and is depressed by the locking lug, which has two small indentations in its lower surface. With the magazine cutoff in the ON position, and the bolt opened and drawn back, the bolt stop plunger falls into the foremost indentation. With the cutoff in the OFF position the plunger is aligned with the rearmost indentation when the bolt is open. In either case, the intended purpose of the bolt stop was to provide some friction to the bolt when it was drawn back, so that it would not fall forward of its own weight, if the muzzle of the rifle was lowered. It was thought that this would be helpful in single-loading the rifle when the cutoff is in use, since it was likely the muzzle would be lowered so the cartridge could be dropped into the chamber. The bolt stop, however, seemed to interfere with the rapid operation of the bolt, and many owners removed it, as did ordnance repairmen in later years when these rifles were serviced.

Provisions were made in the 03 action to allow powder gases to escape in the event of a pierced or ruptured primer or split case head. A vent hole was provided in the head of the bolt to allow gas to escape into the left locking lug raceway if it entered through the firing pin hole. The size of this hole varied, nor was there generally a hole provided in the receiver ring opposite the hole in the bolt, except in actions made after the mid-1930s. The gases entering the raceway would be directed to the rear and could get into the shooter's face. A gas escape hole was provided, however, through the right side of the receiver ring in line with the extractor slot in the barrel. Generally, a small hole was drilled in the front of the extractor in line with the hole in the receiver. In the event that a cartridge head should split facing the extractor slot, these holes would probably allow enough gases to escape to avoid damaging the extractor or injuring the shooter.

The Mark I M1903 Action

In 1917 Mr. J.D. Pedersen, an arms inventor employed by Remington, developed and patented a small automatic firing device (later known as the Pedersen Device) which replaced the bolt in the 03 Springfield. It fired a special .30-cal. pistol-sized cartridge from a 40-shot magazine. The 03 action had to be slightly modified to use this device. The device was adopted in 1917 and, although many more were ordered, the Remington factory finished only about 65,000 of them before the war ended and the contract was canceled. They were not used and practically all of them were destroyed, along with the 65 million rounds of ammunition made for them. However, as the Pedersen Devices were being made, the Springfield Armory had the job of furnishing 03 rifles to handle them. Apparently, the rifles were not conversions of already manufactured regular 03s. Instead of making the regular rifle, they made the Mark I, since the **MARK I** stamp is included with the regular marking and not added to previously marked receivers. No special serial numbers were assigned to these rifles; they were serial numbered in sequence with the regular 03

Springfields. The modification to the Mark I action consisted of milling an oblong hole in the left receiver wall to provide a cartridge-case ejection port, installing a silghtly different magazine cutoff having a round groove to hold the device in the receiver, and a special sear with an extra lever to function as the disconnector for the automatic firing device. With these modifications the rifle could still be used with its original bolt to fire the .30-06 cartridge. Springfield Armory made approximately 101,775 of the Mark I 03 rifles, all of which, reportedly, were later released when the Pedersen Devices were destroyed in the early 1930s.

Mark I actions, all made after the change to the double heat treatment, are as strong and serviceable as the regular Model 03 double heat treatment actions.

When the Mark I rifles were released for use again as regular rifles, the special cutoff was replaced with a standard one. However, the special sear with the disconnector lever was not always replaced. This sear is as functional as the regular sear. Most of the Mark I rifles were released through the DCM and sold as regular rifles. Except for the oblong hole in the receiver wall, which may be unsightly to some shooters, these actions and rifles are as serviceable as the regular actions and rifles without the hole.

National Match Sporter and Target Actions

Each year, from 1920 to about 1940, Springfield Armory made up a quantity of specially selected 03 rifles to be used in the National Matches. These were called National Match Springfields, but they were not marked as such. Their serial numbers were in sequence with regular 03 rifles. There were various models of these target rifles made, including some with heavy barrels, but it is not our purpose to describe those special barrels here since it is the actions in which we are interested. However, all of these match rifles were fitted with "star-gauged" barrels, which

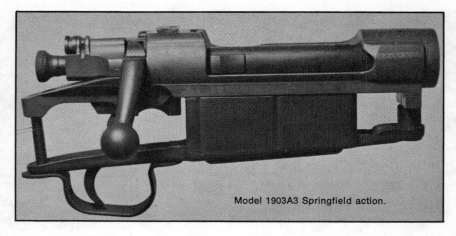

Model 1903A3 Springfield action.

means that the barrels were selected by means of a gauge which determined bore and groove diameter to insure uniformity. The barrels selected were then marked with a star-like stamp on the muzzle. However, it must be noted that not all of the Model 03 rifles fitted with star-gauged barrels are National Match rifles. These barrels were available separately to anyone who wanted one installed on a Springfield rifle. Also, some National Match Springfield rifles were assembled on receivers made by the Rock Island Arsenal and they are so marked.

Briefly, the actions used in making up these match rifles were regular 03 actions, selected for close tolerances between bolt and receiver and for uniform quality. The National Match receivers were Parkerized, the Target and Sporter actions were generally "browned." The locking lug and cocking cam raceways were honed smooth. The bolt and the extractor were polished bright and, in most cases, the serial number stamped on the receiver was etched on the bolt body. The primary extractor cam surfaces, cocking cam surfaces, and locking lug cam surfaces were also honed or burnished very smooth. The contacting sear surfaces and trigger to receiver surfaces were also honed to provide a very smooth and uniform trigger pull. The nose

of the sear was shortened to reduce the final stage of the trigger let-off. The feed ramp was also polished smooth. Everything was done to make the action as smooth and as easy to operate as possible.

Some of the match actions were fitted with a reverse safety. Others were made with a headless cocking piece and fitted with a stiffer mainspring to achieve a faster lock time. Most of the receivers were also drilled and tapped to accept the Lyman No. 48 receiver target sight. In short, these actions were superb. Depending upon when they were made, the receiver and bolts of these National Match actions were made of either the double heat treated carbon steel or nickel steel. All these actions are in the "high serial number" range.

The National Match Model 1903 Springfields were stocked just like the regular Model 1903 rifle, first only with straight gripped stocks, but later on with the Type-C pistol grip stock.

The NRA Sporter

The first Model 1903 Springfield "Sporter" was made at Springfield Armory at the request of, and for, Theodore Roosevelt, then President of the United States. That started a trend that is still

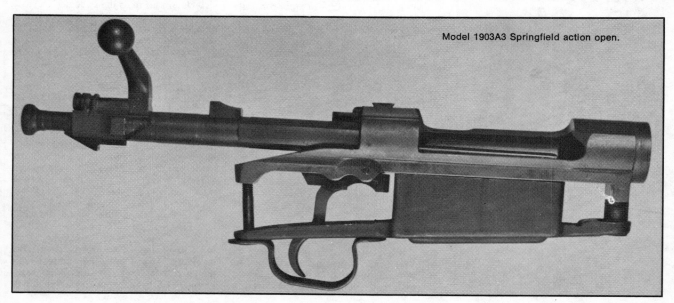

Model 1903A3 Springfield action open.

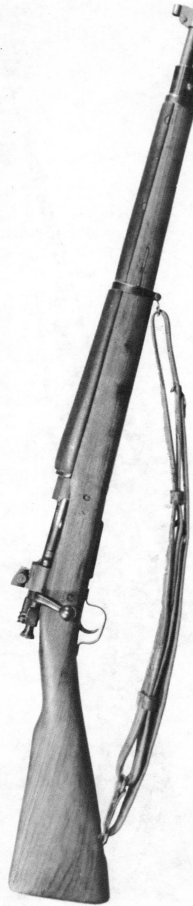

going strong today. It was built on receiver No. 0009 in 1903. There is a full description and drawing of this rifle in the book *The 03 Springfield*. Roosevelt used this rifle on an African hunting trip and liked it. Some of his friends, hearing of this, also wanted Springfield sporters. Somehow, the late Captain E.C. Crossman obtained, about 1911, enough Model 1903 Springfield parts so that 4 sporting rifles could be assembled. The gunsmith work was done by Louis Wundhammer of Los Angeles, Calif. The well-known author Stewart Edward White got one of them.* Both White and Crossman wrote enthusiastically about these rifles, and pretty soon others wanted to purchase the 03 military rifle for sporterizing. As a result of this, in 1910 the Model 1903 Springfield military rifles were made available to members of the National Rifle Association.

In the early 1920s the NRA Sporter was developed and first released for sale to NRA Members through the DCM (Director of Civilian Marksmanship) in 1924. It was officially designated the "U.S. Rifle Cal. .30, Style NRA." (NOTE: Previous to the release of the NRA Sporter, Springfield Armory had developed .22 rimfire rifles based on a modified Model 1903 action. The last version of this rifle was the Model 1922 MII Springfield. It was made with a sporter type stock having a full pistol grip, high comb and a sporter length fore-end with a barrel band. Since these rifles are rimfires, I have not included them in this book, but they are covered in full detail in *The '03 Springfield*.) The NRA Sporter was made up using an action of National Match quality, a star-gauged barrel, fitted with the Model 1922 MII stock and a Lyman No.48S receiver sight. Like the National Match Springfields, they were built on both Springfield Armory and Rock Island Arsenal actions. Many of them were marked on the tang of the guard with the ordnance "flaming bomb" mark, with the letters NRA below it. Only about 7000 of these fine sporters were sold before sales were suspended in 1933.

The NRA Sporters, officially introduced 15 November, 1924, were finished like the National Match 03s as far as the receivers and bolts were concerned, and all were star-gauged. These handsome half-stock Springfields were—in the opinion of many—the finest 03s ever made available to the shooting public.

At Rock Island Arsenal the last receivers were made in about 1920 or pos-

*Mr. White's 03 sporter is now owned by John T. Amber. It is a Rock Island Arsenal specimen, serial number 166,436, and the original barrel is dated February, 1910.

U.S. Model 1903A3 Springfield rifle, caliber .30-06. A World War II modification of the M1903 Springfield, it differs from the 03 mainly in that the rear sight is mounted on the receiver bridge and the trigger guard/magazine is a sheet-metal stamping. The compact 1903A3 aperture rear sight is adjustable for elevtion and windage. The barrel has the same bore specifications as the 03 except that most of them are made with only 2 grooves; however, some were made with 4 or 6 grooves. 1903A3 rifles were made by Remington Arms Co., Ilion, N.Y. and by Smith-Corona Typewriters, Inc.

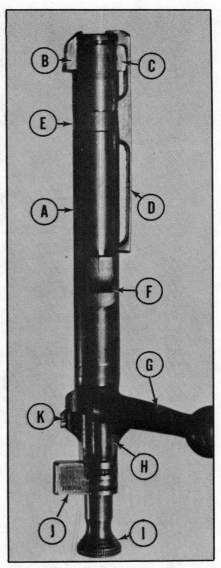

Model 1903 Springfield bolt. (A) bolt body, (B) left (upper) locking lug, (C) right (lower) locking lug, (D) extractor, (E) extractor collar, (F) auxiliary safety lug, (G) bolt handle, (H) bolt sleeve, (I) cocking piece, (J) safety, (K) bolt sleeve lock.

sibly shortly afterwards. Apparently, the last ones made there did not have serial numbers. However, some of these receivers were used in assembling rifles in the Springfield Armory and then given serial numbers. According to *Hatcher's Notebook* the last 03 receiver made at the Springfield Armory was in 1939, serial number 1,532,878. Production of the 03 was resumed again in November, 1941, by Remington Arms Co., in Ilion, N.Y. They produced 348,085 before switching over to the Model 03A3 in May, 1942. Remington began their serial numbering with number 3,000,001.

The Model 1903A3 Action

The "A" in the 03A3 designation means "Alternate," and is thus the third alternate of the 03 rifle. To fill in the gap in the sequence, I should mention the 03A1 and

Close-up of the 1903A3 Springfield action showing a rear scope mount base attached to the male dovetail on the receiver bridge, and an altered bolt handle and low scope-safety installed.

the 03A2 versions, although they have no importance in this chapter since both had the regular 03 action. The 03A1 Springfield rifle is an 03 rifle fitted with a pistol grip stock—there is no difference in the action. The 03A2 Springfield was a standard 03 action and barrel assembly with sights removed and bronze bushings fitted on the barrel, so that the assembly could be mounted in the bore of a tank cannon or artillery pieces for subcaliber practice.

The 03A3 action was a "hurry up" or simplified version of the 03 action. Here is a list of changes found on the 03A3 that distinguish it from the 03 action: 1) a male dovetail base was milled on the receiver bridge for the installation of the rear sight; 2) the trigger guard/magazine box was formed from sheet metal, pressed, folded, and spot welded together; 3) the magazine follower was made from a sheet-metal stamping; 4) some intricate milling cuts on the receiver were omitted, for example, no cuts were made for the bolt stop; 5) some milling cuts were also omitted on the bolt in the final period of manufacture—for example, the safety lug was left a rectangular block and was not milled down in front to match the extractor; 6) the hole in the tang for the rear guard screw was drilled through completely; 7) the gas vent hole in the extractor and in the right side of the receiver were omitted, and instead a large gas vent hole was drilled in the left side of the receiver in line with the gas vent holes in the bolt.

Because of the need to turn out 03A3 actions speedily, previous manufacturing tolerances were increased. As a result of the increases 03A3 actions are much rougher and looser than the 03 actions. This is most noticeable on the outside finish of receiver and bolt. 03A3 bolts are usually very rough, with the bolt body turned to a smaller diameter around the safety lug section than elsewhere, leaving two or more pronounced ridges on the bolt.

The Model 1903A4 Action

The Model 03A4 rifle was made up as a sniper rifle and fitted with a telescope.

An attractive lightweight Springfield hunting rifle from the author's workshop. The remodeled Type C Springfield stock is fitted with a recoil pad and pistol grip cap. The Weaver K-4 scope, mounted in the quick detachable Weaver side mount, places the scope very low over the receiver. The action is fitted with the Numrich speed-lock unit. The 1″ carrying sling is attached with Stith lightweight swivels to studs in the buttstock and barrel. The Type C stock is thick enough through the butt so that a cheekpiece can be left when trimming the stock.

A featherweight (6.5 lbs.) remodeled 1903A3 Springfield sporter rechambered for the .308 Norma Magnum cartridge. The stock is reshaped and trimmed Type C (pistol grip) Springfield stock fitted with a Pachmayr recoil pan and pistol grip cap. Work was done by the author.

It was made by Remington in 1943 and 1944. The 03A4 action is the same as the 03A3, except that the receiver ring and bridge are drilled and tapped with two 8 x 40 holes to accept the Redfield Jr. scope mount base, and the bolt handle shank is altered to clear the eyepiece of the scope.

Low or High Number

Up to 1918 the receivers and bolts of the 03 actions were made of a single heat treated carbon steel. Some of these actions have been known to burst for no accountable reason when fired. At Springfield Armory, beginning with action number 800,000, a new heat treatment method, called the "double heat treatment," was started which resulted in the actions (still made of carbon steel) being much stronger and safer than before. Thus rifles made at the Springfield Armory (all Springfield receivers are marked with location of manufacture) with a serial number above 800,000 are the so-called "high numbered" Springfields, and those with a lower number are the so-called "low numbered" ones.

At Rock Island Arsenal the new double heat treatment was started at about action number 285,507. This is the dividing number between the low- and high numbered actions made at that arsenal.

To repeat, 03 actions made at Springfield numbered below 800,000 and those made at Rock Island numbered under 285,507 are to be considered "low numbered" actions. All others, including the 03s, 03A3s, and 03A4s made by Remington, and the 03A3s made by Smith-Corona are "high numbered" ones. However, all of these "high numbered" actions were not made with the double heat treated carbon steel. A new steel was introduced called "nickel steel" since it contained some nickel.

In the latter part of 1918 at about action number 319,921, Rock Island Arsenal began using the new nickel steel for part of their receiver and bolt production, *but* continued at the same time to make some of these parts from carbon steel. It is thought that the receivers made of nickel steel were stamped with the letters **NS** in front of the receiver ring. However, in rebarreling a number of the Rock Island actions in this serial number range, I have never encountered these letters. It is sometimes possible to guess which steel is used by a file test since the nickel steel is softer and cuts more easily than the double heat treated carbon steel. Actually, there is little difference in regard to action strength, safety and reliability whether an action is made of the double heat treated carbon steel or nickel steel. In my opinion one is as good as the other.

In 1927, at action number 1,275,767, Springfield Armory changed to nickel steel for all subsequent production. The first 03 actions Remington made were of the same nickel steel as that used by Rock Island Arsenal and Springfield Armory. The last of the Remington made 03s, and all of their 03A3s and 03A4s, and the 03A3s made by Smith-Corona, were made of a slightly different nickel steel alloy, one having less nickel, plus some molybdenum.

The low numbered actions which are made of the single heat treated steel are not too desirable, since the receivers are very hard and tend to be brittle. When these receivers fail, instead of stretching or giving, they usually break apart or shatter. The double heat treated carbon steel receivers, however, have a very hard surface with a softer and very tough inner core. The receiver ring on these actions will usually stretch a bit under extreme pressures before they will break. Because of their very hard surface, these actions are usually the easiest to operate, especially if the contacting surfaces of the main moving parts are honed or polished as were the National Match and Sporter actions. The nickel steel actions are probably equally as strong and safe, or more so, than double heat treated carbon steel actions, and under extreme stresses the receiver ring is more apt to stretch and swell than to break apart. However, because the surface is not as hard as carbon steel, nickel steel actions are somewhat "sticky" and the action cannot be operated as easily.

The high numbered Springfield actions are strong—that's a fact. They are suitable for many cartridges which have a normal working pressure up to 55,000 psi. But, how strong and safe are the low numbered 03 actions? This I cannot answer. When made, they were proof tested with loads developing 70,000 psi, and very few failed in this test. Interestingly, many low numbered rifles were kept in service until after 1945, and many of them were rebarreled by various government arsenals during WW II.

Apparently, they were considered safe. The fact is that only a very few of the low numbered actions burst, and some of these for such known causes as a plugged bore. Some experienced gunsmiths feel these actions are safe enough to be used with cartridges that develop up to about 50,000 psi breech pressure, provided the rifle has minimum headspace. As for me, I would limit this action to moderately pressured cartridges like the factory loaded .257 Roberts and 7x57mm Mauser.

Makers, Markings and Serial Numbers

Springfield Armory at Springfield, Mass., manufactured the 03, Mark I and various 03 match rifles from 1903 through 1939 with numbers from 1 to 1,534,878. Not quite this many rifles were actually made, since some of the receivers (the only part of the rifle stamped with a serial number) were used in tests and destroyed, and some were held over for replacement parts. The receiver ring of these rifles was marked:

U.S.
SPRINGFIELD
ARMORY
MODEL 1903
(Serial #)

A fancy restocked 1903 Springfield rifle (photo courtesy of Maynard Buehler).

About 1919 Springfield Armory began making .22 rimfire rifles based on a modified version of the 1903 action. Pictured here is the author's remodeling of the Model 1922 M2 Springfield into a lightweight small game rifle. The 3x Hensoldt scope is carried in a quick-detachable Griffin & Howe side mount.

The Mark I rifles were marked:

U.S.
SPRINGFIELD
ARMORY
MODEL 1903
MARK I
(Serial #)

Some of the 03A2 Springfield receivers (or complete actions or barreled actions) were released into civilian hands, most likely by the arsenals as replacement receivers. These receivers are marked:

U.S.
SPRINGFIELD
ARMORY
MODEL 1903-A2
(Serial #)

Rock Island Arsenal at Rock Island, Ill., manufactured 03 rifles numbered from 1 to 346,779 (for spare parts this arsenal produced receivers numbered over 445,000), from 1904 to 1913, and from 1917 to about 1920. The receiver ring of these rifles was marked as follows:

U.S.
ROCK ISLAND
ARSENAL
MODEL 1903
(Serial #)

The Remington Arms Co., at Ilion, N.Y., made 03 rifles numbered from 3,-000,001 to 3,348,085 from November, 1941 through May, 1942. The receiver ring of these rifles was marked:

U.S.
REMINGTON
MODEL 1903
(Serial #)

Remington 03A3 rifles made from May, 1942 through February, 1944 have serial numbers falling within the following blocks: 3,348,086 to 3,607,999; 3,708,000 to 4,707,999; 4,992,001 to 5,784,000. Not all of these numbers were used, however, and production was halted at about number 4,169,000. Total production probably did not exceed 345,000. The receiver ring of these rifles was marked:

U.S.
REMINGTON
MODEL 03-A3
(Serial #)

Remington 03A4 sniper's rifles made from February, 1943 through March, 1944, have serial numbers falling within the following blocks: 3,407,088 to 3,427,-087; 4,992,001 to 4,997,045; Z4,000,000 to Z4,002,920. Production was stopped before all of these numbers were used. Total production was about 26,653. The 03A4s numbered within the first two blocks were marked on the left side of the receiver ring below the scope mount base:

U.S.
REMINGTON
MODEL 03-A3

The serial number was stamped on the right side of the receiver. The "Z" series were similarly marked, but with the model designation changed to:

MODEL 03-A4

L.C. Smith-Corona Typewriters, Inc., made 03A3s from October, 1942 through February, 1944, with serial numbers within the following blocks: 3,608,000 to 3,-707,999; 4,708,000 to 4,992,000. Production was stopped at rifle number 4,845,-831. The total number produced was about 234,500. The receiver rings were marked:

U.S.
SMITH-CORONA
MODEL 03-A3
(Serial #)

This completes the list of manufacturers who produced the .30-06 Springfield military rifles. In all cases the actual number produced was less than the figures indicate through loss of receivers in tests, etc.

The only other noteworthy markings on these rifles are on the top of the barrel, just behind the front sight. Here the initials of the organization that made the barrel and the month or year of manufacture were stamped. For example, **SA 6-12** means that the barrel was made by Springfield Armory in June, 1912. Barrels made by Remington were marked **RA**, Rock Island barrels were marked **RIA**, Smith-Corona barrels were marked **SC**. Avis Rifle Barrel Co. barrels were marked **AV**, Johnson Automatics barrels are marked **JA**, and Sedgley barrels were marked with an **S** within a circle. The date on the barrel does not necessarily indicate the date of manufacture of the entire rifle, since it was standard practice for arsenals to replace worn barrels with new ones made many years after the receiver.

New Made Springfields

All parts except the receivers have been available for the Springfield from the DCM and other sources for many years. The receiver, the only part carrying the serial number,* was considered the only non-expendable part of these rifles, has never been commercially available. It is only available from the DCM on a replacement basis in exchange for a broken or low numbered receiver. Since WW II, huge quantities of 03 and 03A3 parts have been sold to surplus arms dealers. Within the last few years, 03A3s have been offered for sale, which are apparently assembled from surplus military parts around newly manufactured receivers. I have seen these rifles marked **SANTA FE M-1903A3,** and with the receiver marked:

NATL. ORD.
MODEL 1903A3

and with a serial number over 5,000,000. I have also seen another such rifle marked **NAT. ORD. CO. EL MONTE, CAL.** Of course, such rifles cannot be considered as authentic Springfield military rifles because only Springfield Armory, Rock Island Arsenal, Remington and Smith-Corona made the genuine Springfield, and none of these were numbered over 5,000,-000. I have no reliable information as to the quality or strength of the National Ordnance Company receivers, so I can make no further comments on these rifles at this time.

The receivers are (or were) produced by the National Ordnance Company, P.O. Box 36032, Los Angeles, California 90036. At this writing (1969) these receivers are available from Eastern Arms Corporation, 800 S. Arroyo Parkway, Pasadena, California 91105 ($24.95).

Bolts

The bolt handles of all 03s made up to about 1908 of single heat treated carbon steel, were turned straight down. When the double heat treatment of the bolts and receivers started in 1918, the bolts were made with a slightly swept back handle which placed the grasping ball farther back. Later on, when the receiver and bolts were made of nickel steel, the letters

---

* Aside from National Match, NRA Sporter and M1922 rifles, which carried the serial number on the bolt as well.

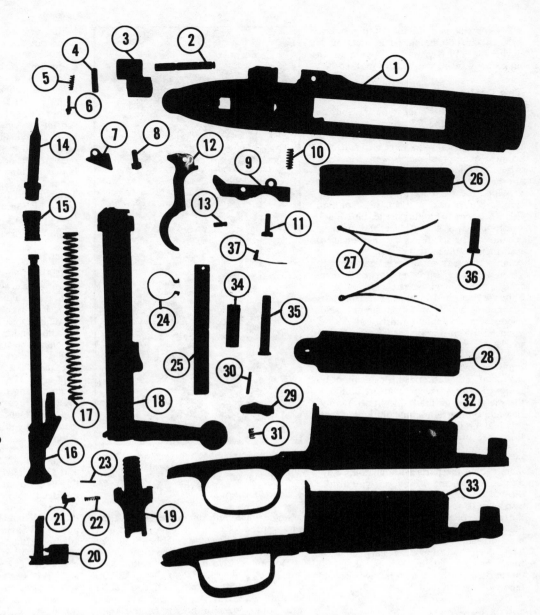

Parts Legend

1. Receiver (top view)
2. Magazine cutoff pin
3. Magazine cutoff
4. Magazine cutoff screw
5. Magazine cutoff plunger spring
6. Magazine cutoff plunger
7. Ejector
8. Ejector pin
9. Sear
10. Sear spring
11. Sear pin
12. Trigger
13. Trigger pin
14. Firing pin
15. Firing pin sleeve
16. Striker
17. Mainspring
18. Bolt
19. Bolt sleeve
20. Safety
21. Bolt sleeve lock plunger
22. Bolt sleeve lock plunger spring
23. Bolt sleeve lock plunger pin
24. Extractor collar
25. Extractor
26. Follower
27. Follower spring
28. Magazine floorplate
29. Floorplate catch
30. Floorplate catch pin
31. Floorplate catch spring
32. Trigger guard/magazine M-1903
33. Trigger guard/magazine M-1903A3
34. Rear guard screw (stock) bushing
35. Rear guard screw
36. Front guard screw
37. Bolt stop

Model 1903 Springfield

Dimensional Specifications*

Weight†	45 oz.
Over-all length	8.562"
Receiver ring dia.	1.305"
Bolt body dia.	.700"
Bolt travel	5.20"
Striker travel	.635"
Guard screw spacing	7.75"
Magazine well opening:	
Length	3.40"
Rear width	.530"
Front width	.560"
Bolt face recess:	
Depth	.055"
Dia.	.485"

*Approximate only, all models, in inches.

†Models 1903A3 & A4 .... 52 oz.

General Specifications

Type	Turnbolt repeater.
Receiver	One-piece machined steel forging with non-slotted bridge. Stripper clip charger guide milled in the bridge.
Bolt	One-piece, with dual-opposed forward locking lugs. A third lug on the bolt acts as a safety lug.
Ignition	Composed of striker, separate firing pin, mainspring and striker sleeve. Cocks on opening the bolt.
Magazine	Staggered column non-detachable box. 5-shot capacity. Detachable floorplate.
Trigger	Curved and grooved. Non-adj., double-stage military type pull.
Safety	Rotary wing-type safety built into bolt sleeve, 180° swing from left to right, locking striker when in upright position, and both striker and bolt when swung to the right.
Extractor	One-piece, non-rotating Mauser spring type, attached to the bolt with a collar.
Magazine cutoff	Rearward bolt travel is halted by the rotary type magazine cutoff on the left rear of receiver when the left locking lug contacts it.
Bolt stop	(See text)
Ejector	Pivoting type housed in left side of receiver bridge.

NS were stamped on top of the square base of the bolt handle. The bolts made during the WW II years, although made of nickel steel, were not usually marked **NS**.

The Parkerized Finish

Until about 1917 most of the outside metal parts of the 03 were browned or blued by various methods. Up to this time most of the metal parts were well finished, so most of the tool marks were removed. After 1917 most of the metal parts were finished by a process called Parkerizing, in which the parts were boiled in a solution of phosphoric acid. In fresh solution this would impart a dull matte, blue-black finish that was wear, glare and rust resistant. As the solution weakened or aged, the metals finished became lighter in color, varying from dark or light greys to greenish shades. In the process of Parkerizing some iron phosphate crystals probably are deposited on the steel. This, plus the etching action of the phosphoric acid, produces a dull matte finish that does a good job of erasing or "covering up" tool marks left on the surface. To some this finish appears to be a film of some sort but it is actually part of the surface of the metal. The Parkerized finish cannot be removed with varnish remover, although the metal can be made bright with some rust and bluing-removing solutions. When this is done the tool marks hidden by the finish are brought out. Therefore, if you like the dull Parkerized finish, but want to refinish it to a blue-black color, then merely blue the parts without doing anything else to them. However, if you dislike the Parkerized finish, whether or not you also want to smooth the metal, then polish the parts, polishing the Parkerized finish off at the same time. The receiver is the most difficult part to polish. If it does not have deep tool marks, a very pleasing finish can be obtained by polishing all the parts smooth except the receiver and then blue everything except the bolt.

Remodeling Tips

If a hunting scope is to be mounted low over the action, and this is the only practical way to mount a scope, it will be necessary to alter the bolt handle so it will clear the scope. I believe this is best done by sawing off the bolt handle and welding on a new forged handle with an electric welder. The shank and base of the bolt is very heavy, and, in my opinion, forging the bolt handle to a low profile is not the way to do the job.

A low mounted scope also requires a different safety. Several commercial low scope safeties are available, and it's much better to install one of these than to attempt to alter the original safety. There are also several commercial fully adjustable single stage triggers available for the Springfields, some of which are made with a side safety. There are numerous other accessories available for the 03, such as a bullet point protector for the magazine, a tang type slide safety, trigger shoes, a quick release floorplate button, trigger attachments to make the double pull trigger into

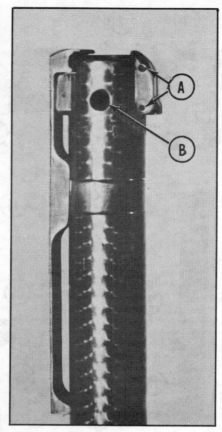

Underside of the 1903 Springfield bolt head showing the two bolt-stop indents (A) in the left locking lug and the single gas escape hole (B).

a single stage pull, one-piece safety firing pins, speed-lock firing pins, speed-lock mainsprings, and a lightweight alloy hinged floorplate guard/magazine assembly.

Do not remove the male dovetail base from the receiver bridge of the 03A3 and A4 actions. Practically all top scope mounts made for this action, and there are about a dozen or more to choose from, require this base to be intact to successfully attach the mount. There are also a couple of aperture sights made to attach to this base, although it would be hard to find a better aperture hunting sight than the original 03A3 rear sight. Other receiver sights made for the 03A3 such as the Lyman, Redfield and Williams sights, have slides which neatly cover the base. However, if you have a 03A3 action with the sight base already removed, you will be restricted to using a side mount if a hunting scope is to be fitted. This is not a drawback since most side mounts are fully as reliable as any top mount.

I also advise against cutting off the flared end of the cocking piece in order to make the striker lighter and speed up the lock time. However, if this is done, it is essential that the striker rod be re-attached permanently to the cocking piece either with a sturdy cross pin or by welding the two parts together. In this case, it would be desirable to install a stiffer speed-lock mainspring.

Installing a one-piece safety firing pin

in the bolt to replace the original two-piece pin does make the action safer to use. However, because these safety one-piece firing pins are quite light they come fitted with a very stiff mainspring. With a headless cocking piece and stiff mainspring, installation of the one-piece safety firing pin unit makes the action much "stiffer" to operate. One of the things I have always liked about the Springfield action, and especially so with the double heat treated and National Match actions, is that opening the bolt after firing a cartridge is quite easy compared to most bolt action rifles. Installing a stiff mainspring spoils this smooth and easy bolt operation. For this reason I still prefer to use the original striker, firing pin and mainspring.

Cartridge Choice

The .30-06 cartridge and the Springfield action were made for each other, but these actions will handle other cartridges equally well. For example, they are ideal for re-barreling to cartridges like the 6mm, .257 Roberts, 7mm, .270, .280, 8mm and .35 Whelen. The unaltered Springfield magazine will also handle shorter cartridges like the .22-250, .220 Swift, .243, .284, .308 and .358. With these cartridges the feeding ramp may be improved by blocking off the rear part of the magazine with a piece of sheet metal riveted or silver soldered in place, and shortening the follower.

Some gunsmiths have modified the Springfield action to handle the long .300 and .375 H&H Magnum cartridges, but this requires removing vital metal from the feed ramp which, as with the 98 Mauser action, weakens the support for the lower locking lug. However, the high numbered Springfield actions certainly are adequate for the modern short magnum cartridges like the .264 and .300 Winchester, 7mm Remington, .358 Norma and .458 Winchester. Altering the action to accept these cartridges requires only that the bolt face be opened up and the extractor hook shortened. Sometimes it will be necessary to smooth the cartridge guide lips in the magazine well to make these short magnum cartridges feed better into the chamber. It is also practicable to rechamber the issue .30-06 barrel to the .300 Winchester Magnum if you want more power than the .30-06 provides. This is much more desirable than rechambering to some so-called "improved" .30-06 cartridge. Incidentally, the issue barrel can also be set back and rechambered for the .308 or rebored for the .35 Whelen cartridge—an excellent big game cartridge.

Springfield actions are entirely unsuitable for such small cartridges as the .222, .222 Magnum and .223 Remington—unless used as a single shot only.

In the past, amateur and professional gunsmiths have used the Springfield actions successfully for building all sorts of rifles. It is most suitable for light- to medium-weight sporting rifles in standard calibers like the .270 and .30-06. It is equally a favorite for building all sorts of varmint rifles, from lightweight combination varmint/deer rifles to medium-

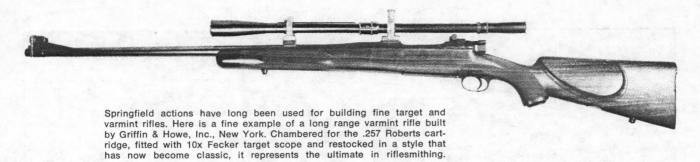

Springfield actions have long been used for building fine target and varmint rifles. Here is a fine example of a long range varmint rifle built by Griffin & Howe, Inc., New York. Chambered for the .257 Roberts cartridge, fitted with 10x Fecker target scope and restocked in a style that has now become classic, it represents the ultimate in riflesmithing.

and heavyweight long range varmint rifles. It has also been a long time favorite with target shooters; made up like the National Match Springfields, or fitted with heavier barrels to be used in the long range matches. There are numerous accessories and all kinds and styles of stocks available to fit the action or rifle; there is no end to what can be done with them. Since Springfield actions are usually only obtainable by buying an entire rifle, and since these rifles are becoming scarcer each year, I suggest sticking with the standard cartridges and with the classic stock styles in remodeling or building up these rifles—especially so if you want the rifle to have a reasonable resale value later. To emphasize this point, the classic rifles that Griffin & Howe and Sedgley used to build on these actions are increasing in value, while many, many thousands of amateurish and odd-ball remodeled Springfield rifles will never be worth more than the action alone—and this provided the action itself has not been ruined.

Take-Down and Assembly

First, make sure the chamber and magazine are empty. To remove bolt: open and close the bolt and place the safety in the upright position; swing the magazine cutoff to its intermediate position and remove bolt from the receiver.

To disassemble bolt: With safety upright depress the bolt sleeve lock plunger and unscrew the firing mechanism from the bolt. With firing mechanism removed, rotate the safety to the left. Grasp the striker sleeve between thumb and forefinger and, while resting the striker knob on a table, pull down on the sleeve until the firing pin can be moved off the striker rod. This done, the striker rod can be removed from the bolt sleeve. Swing the safety up so the plunger in the safety is in line with the shallow slope on the plunger groove and, with a hammer handle, strike the safety to drive it to the rear. Remove the bolt sleeve lock by driving out the small cross pin. Remove the extractor by turning it as far as it will go to the bottom of the bolt and then slide it forward. *Do not remove* the extractor collar unless necessary, since it cannot be easily replaced without deforming it. Reassemble the bolt in reverse order. In reassembling the safety, use a small screwdriver to raise the safety plunger when sliding the safety to its final position.

Turn out the screw in the magazine cutoff and shake out its spring and plunger. Using a small screwdriver blade pull out the magazine cutoff pin. Reassemble in reverse order.

To remove the magazine floorplate, follower and spring, use a pointed tool (or hardball round) through the hole in the rear of the floorplate to depress the floorplate catch; now the floorplate can be slid back and released. Slide the follower off the follower spring and the follower spring out of the floorplate. Reassemble in reverse order with narrow end of the W-spring inserted into the follower.

To remove the stock, first remove the barrel bands and handguard. Turn out the 2 trigger guard screws, lift the barrel and receiver from the stock and pull the trigger guard/magazine from the bottom of the stock. Remove trigger assembly by pushing out the sear and trigger pins. To remove the ejector, drive out its pin from the top (although it has a slotted head, it is not a screw). Reassemble in reverse order.

The barrel is usually screwed very tightly into the receiver; make no attempt to remove it unless the proper tools (barrel vise and action wrench) are available. The rear sight base of the 03 is held in place on the barrel by a small cross pin. This pin is located in the bottom forward part of the base and is hard to find. Drive out this pin and the sight base can be driven forward, off the barrel. The rear sight on the 03A3 is driven on to the dovetail base on the receiver bridge and then staked in place. It is difficult to remove this sight without damaging it, but if it is not to be used again the best way to remove it is to saw through the windage screw to remove the windage base, and then saw crosswise through the base over the center of the dovetail base. Then it is easily slid off.

Comments

I believe that almost everyone would agree that the first-choice Springfield action would be the Springfield Armory-made 03 National Match or the DCM Sporter version made at about the same time. Either will be extremely hard to find! I'd rate the rest in this order: 1) SA 03 of double heat-treated steel; 2) SA 03 of nickel steel; 3) SA 1903 Mark I; 4) RIA 03 of double heat-treated steel; 5) RIA 1903 of nickel steel; 6) Remington 1903; 7) Remington 03A4; 8) Remington 03A3; 9) Smith-Corona 03A3; 10) Low-numbered SA 03 and 11) Low numbered RIA 03.

Given a choice of either the preferred 03 Springfield actions or one of the better models of the 98 Mauser military actions, I tend to favor the Springfield. There are some things I do not like in either

action, but for building a trim easy-to-operate sporting rifle chambered for a cartridge like the 6mm, .270 or .30-06, I'll take the Springfield. My reasons are: the Springfield action is easier to operate for fast repeat shots; less effort is required to lift the bolt handle on opening the action and pushing the handle down on closing the action. Feeding is generally smoother. I like the shape, size and placement of the trigger guard bow better. I also like the Springfield tang better; this feature, plus the slightly lowered angle of the trigger guard bow, allows a trimmer pistol grip to be made. The solid left receiver wall and the absence of a projecting box on the left of the receiver bridge are other features I like. I also prefer the Springfield action over the Mauser 98 for building a target rifle for several of the same reasons. This is not to imply that I think the Springfield action is better than the Mauser action, but as the modern FN action that Browning now uses on their high powered rifles is an improvement over the original Mauser 98 action, so, in some respects, the Springfield action is an improvement over the Mauser.

For use with any of the hot wildcat or belted-head magnum cartridges, I prefer the Mauser over the Springfield because I feel a bit safer behind the latter.

The Springfield action would be a better one if more Mauser features had been copied, including the one-piece safety and firing pin. The Springfield action also would have been better, in my opinion at least, had the safety lug been omitted and its function incorporated with the bolt handle engaging in a notch cut into the tang. This would have allowed a lower receiver bridge.

I've often wondered why Remington did not continue to make Springfield actions after WW II as they did with the 1917 Enfield action after WW I. Certainly the Springfield action has always been more popular and more desirable than the 1917 Enfield action and, had they continued to make Springfield actions of the quality of the old National Match actions, and made them available separately along with assembled rifles of different styles, I believe they would have found a very good market. Instead they introduced the Models 722 and 721 actions which are, to me at least, less desirable than the 03 Springfield action.

The .30-06 Cartridge

Introduced in 1906, the .30-06 (pronounced "thirty-oh-six") cartridge seems to be as popular today as it ever was. At first it proved to be an outstanding mili-

tary cartridge and, not long afterwards, loaded with suitable hunting type bullets, it proved to be one of the finest cartridges for hunting all North American big game. Lastly, loaded with match type bullets and fired in target rifles, it set many long range accuracy records. Now deemed obsolete by most military men for military use, it is at present—and probably will remain forever hence—a most popular and effective hunting cartridge for all thin-skinned big game animals, and as a top contender in any long range match competition. It is the ideal cartridge for the Springfield 1903 actions.

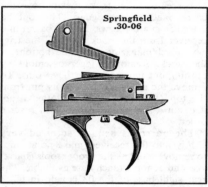

Springfield
.30-06

1903 Mark I Springfield. Note oblong hole in left receiver wall.

At one time Stoeger sold a double set trigger made especially for the 03 Springfield rifle. This trigger is no longer available but a similar mechanism made for 98 Mausers is, and with some modification it can be fitted to the Springfield action.

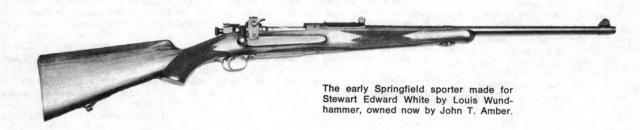

The early Springfield sporter made for Stewart Edward White by Louis Wundhammer, owned now by John T. Amber.

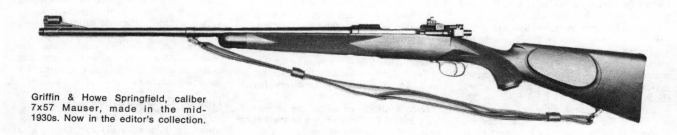

Griffin & Howe Springfield, caliber 7x57 Mauser, made in the mid-1930s. Now in the editor's collection.

17. The Enfields

Part I
1917 U.S. Enfield

PROFESSIONAL and amateur gunsmiths have long been familiar with the Model 1917 Enfield action. It has been used widely in recent years to build custom sporting rifles in both standard .30-06 head-sized rimless and belted-magnum cartridges. A large and rugged action "as issued," it is also a homely one. Fortunately, however, it is receptive to much alteration and remodeling.

When the United States entered WW I in 1917 it was short of rifles, and immediate plans had to be made to acquire more. In 1913 British Ordnance developed a new Mauser type turnbolt action for a .276 caliber rimless cartridge. When England became involved in the war, development work on this cartridge was dropped and the action was modified to handle their standard military round, the .303 British rimmed cartridge. Rather than begin production of this rifle (which was designated the Pattern 1914) in 1914, the British gave contracts to three firms in the United States to make them.

These firms were Winchester, Remington and Eddystone. When the British found that they could produce enough of the older Lee-Enfield rifles they cancelled the contracts in 1916. Thus, at the time the United States entered the war there were three large plants tooled up to make a military rifle. With this in mind, someone (it is believed that Remington initiated this conversion) got busy and redesigned the Pattern 1914 action to handle the .30-06 cartridge. In 1917 new contracts were awarded to these three firms to make the new rifle, officially called the "U.S. Rifle, Cal. .30, Model 1917."

Production Figures

Production of this rifle ended in these plants in November, 1918. According to reliable sources, Winchester produced 545,511, Remington about 545,541 and about 1,181,908 were made at Eddystone, all at an average cost to the government of $26 each. Of the total, perhaps some 80,000 were unassembled rifles to be used for spare parts. These figures reveal that Eddystone made more than Remington and Winchester combined, which accounts for the predominance of the Eddystone make today.

Markings and Serial Numbers

The model designation, manufacturer's name and serial number were stamped on the receiver ring in four lines as follows:

U.S.
MODEL OF 1917
EDDYSTONE
(or WINCHESTER or REMINGTON)
(serial number)

The receiver is the only part serial numbered. Winchester M1917 Enfields were serial numbered from number 1 on, and it is believed this practice was also followed by Remington and Eddystone.

Action Construction

For a military action, the 1917 Enfield was exceptionally well made and finished. Few machine marks can be found under the Parkerized finish. The bolt is made unusually smooth and even, the result a slick-operating action.

The receiver and bolt are machined from 3½% nickel steel forgings, a very strong alloy similar in composition to the nickel steel used in many 1903 Springfield actions.

Most of the receiver bottom is flat. The recoil lug, located at the front of the flat bottom, is about 1⅛" wide and ⅜" deep. The extreme front end of the receiver is round while the rest of the receiver ring is flat on the bottom and round on top. On the right side of the receiver ring there is a raised rectangular portion to strengthen the receiver over the inside mill cut for the extractor. The ⅛" gas-escape vent hole, in the center of this raised portion, is in line with the extractor hook and extractor cut in the barrel. The barrel threads are square. The barrel breech is coned, with part of this funnel edge milled out for the extractor. The front of the bolt breeches nearly against the barrel when the action is closed.

The rear part of the receiver, normally called the bridge, is made to house and protect the folding aperture rear sight. Integral "ears" or "wings" project upward on either side to protect the folding sight components. Although without windage adjustment, this sight was considered one of the best military sights designed up to that time.

The front of the bridge has grooves, these forming a guide for loading the magazine via Springfield 5-shot stripper clips.

The bolt has two large front locking lugs. The right (bottom) lug is solid; the left (top) lug is divided by a narrow slit for the ejector to pass through when the action is opened. The bolt face is partially recessed, surrounding about ⅔rds of the cartridge rim. When the bolt is closed the open, unrecessed segment is toward the left, exactly opposite the gas vent.

Illustrated above: U.S. Model 1917 Enfield rifle, caliber .30-06. This rifle has a 26" barrel, is 46.3" over-all, and weighs about 9.5 pounds. As originally made the M1917 barrels had 5 grooves and a left-hand rifling twist of 1:10". Many 1917s were later fitted with 2- and 4-groove barrels.

The bolt handle has a double bend backward, which positions the hollowed grasping ball about ¾″ back of the base of the bolt. The bolt handle, of the "low" type, need never be altered if the action is to be fitted with a low-mounted scope. When the bolt is closed the heavy base of the bolt handle fits into a deep notch in the receiver, acting as a safety lug. The rear of the bolt handle base does not touch the receiver (which is as it should be), making it a safety lug rather than a third locking lug.

The upper or left end of the bolt handle base is tapered to the rear. When the bolt is opened, it contacts a matching surface inside the receiver bridge, providing positive primary extraction camming power.

The extractor is a long Mauser type attached to the bolt body by a ring in a recess in the body. A narrow lip in the front of the extractor engages a groove cut into the head of the bolt to force the extractor to move longitudinally with it. The extractor is designed to snap over a cartridge rim whether it is chambered via the magazine or singly loaded. Some extractors have a small hole in the hook recess to match the gas escape hole.

The bolt stop follows M98 Mauser design and is positioned on the left rear of the receiver. It is securely held there by a screw through the rear end of the bolt stop and through an integral stud on the receiver. A heavy spring, fitted lengthwise in the bolt stop and rearward over a separate rest, keeps the bolt stop against the receiver. Fitted inside the bolt stop, and held there by the bolt-stop screw, is the ejector. The ejector is made with an integral spring leaf, which provides the tension to move its front end to the right when the bolt is opened. Backward travel of the bolt is halted when its left locking lug comes in contact with that part of the bolt stop which projects through a hole in the receiver. A grasping lip on the front of the bolt stop lets it be swung out for bolt removal.

U.S. Model 1917 Enfield action.

The simple striker mechanism consists of a bolt sleeve threaded into the rear of the bolt, a coil mainspring, a striker (firing pin), and a cocking piece (striker head). The cocking piece is held to the striker by double interrupted rings engaging the two parts. Ordnance specifications called for a firing pin protrusion of not over .068″, and not under .058″ minimum, and a firing-pin hole no larger than .085″.

Two gas-escape holes in the front of the bolt direct escaping gases into the left side locking lug raceway.

Primary striker cocking occurs on raising the bolt handle, when the forward end of the cocking piece engages a shallow cam in the rear of the bolt. Full cocking takes place on the forward travel and closing of the bolt, after it has been fully opened. The shallow cam and the short initial rearward movement given to the striker when the bolt handle is raised are safety features which prevent the action from firing a cartridge unless the bolt is locked sufficiently to hold it closed. The cocking piece is engaged when the bolt is open, also positions and prevents rotation of the bolt sleeve.

The rugged rotary safety, just to the rear of the bolt handle, is built into the tang of the receiver. With the action closed and cocked, tipping the safety lever back locks the striker and bolt. The striker is locked back, and pulled back off the sear, by the end of the safety system engaging a notch cut into the side of the cocking piece. The bolt is locked closed by a pin pushed forward by the safety into a hole in the base of the bolt handle.

The trigger is a common double-stage military type. The long first stage of the pull moves the sear almost all the way off the cocking piece, the final short pull fully releasing it. An added safety feature, built into the sear, is a pin projecting upward through a hole in the receiver. Only when the bolt is fully closed, which places a notch cut into the body of the bolt directly over the pin, can the trigger be pulled to release the striker.

The action is held in the stock by two

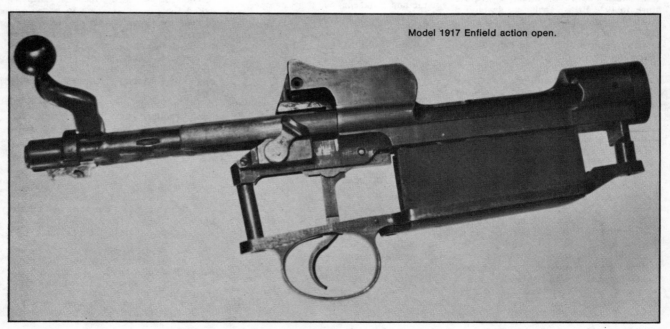

Model 1917 Enfield action open.

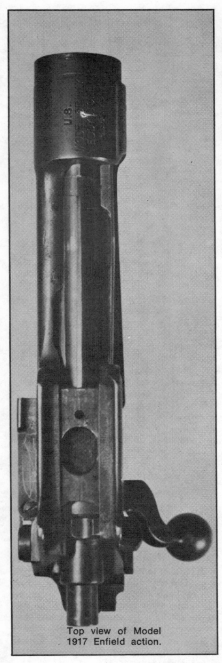

Top view of Model 1917 Enfield action.

Left side view of Model 1917 Enfield action.

guard screws, one at either end of the action, passing through holes in the trigger guard plate. Stock bushings, through which the guard screws pass, provide proper spacing between trigger guard and receiver. The magazine box is a separate unit fabricated by riveting two flat thin pieces of sheet steel, which form the sides, to the thicker ends. The top of the front end projects up into the magazine-opening well to become part of the loading ramp. The magazine box is securely positioned between the trigger guard and receiver, and is partly recessed into these parts. The magazine-well opening in the bottom of the receiver is milled to leave lips for holding the cartridges in place in the magazine. The milled steel floorplate, detachable from the trigger guard, is held in place by projecting lips engaging recesses in the trigger guard, and is secured by a small spring-loaded latch in the guard just to the rear of the magazine box opening. Depressing this latch with a pointed tool, through a hole in the rear of the floorplate, allows the latter to be moved back and released.

The trigger-guard bow is egg shaped, the opening larger in front. The face of the curved trigger is grooved. The milled magazine follower and the follower spring are the conventional Mauser type. The magazine holds 6 cartridges in a staggered column. When the magazine is empty the follower rises in front of the bolt, when the action is opened, preventing the bolt from being closed. All action parts are made of steel; there are no stampings.

Disassembly

To remove bolt, grasp front edge of bolt stop with the thumb, swing it outward, raise bolt handle and pull bolt out. To remove floorplate, insert pointed tool into hole in rear of the plate, depress tool while at same time pulling it to the rear. This releases floorplate, follower spring and follower.

To remove barrel and action from the stock, first remove upper and middle barrel bands and handguard, then remove front and rear guard screws. Lift barrel and receiver from stock, then pull out trigger guard. The barrel is threaded very tightly into the receiver and no attempt should be made to remove it unless proper equipment is on hand.

Disassemble the bolt by grasping the bolt body in the right hand and, with a tool (such as a small screwdriver) in the other hand, pull the cocking piece back, rotating it and the bolt sleeve counterclockwise about ½-turn. Unscrew the bolt sleeve further until cocking piece drops down, then repeat process until the entire striker assembly is removed.

To disassemble the striker mechanism, place the firing pin tip on a hard surface and grasp the bolt sleeve very firmly; pull the bolt sleeve down as far as it will go, then turn the cocking piece ¼-turn in either direction and lift it off.

To remove the extractor turn it on the bolt to cover the gas-escape vents, then push it forward to disengage it from the extractor collar. The collar can then be spread apart and removed from the bolt.

Turn out the bolt stop screw and remove the bolt stop assembly. Push out the sear pin and remove trigger/sear assembly. With a small screwdriver turn out the safety-lock holder screw and remove the holder. Swing the safety back, then pull the safety out, after which the safety lock plunger and spring can be removed. Reassemble in reverse order. In reassembling the safety, first insert the safety lock plunger spring, then the lock plunger into the hole in the receiver. Using a screwdriver, turn the lock plunger so its V surface is in line with the hole, then push the lock plunger forward and, at the same time, firmly grasp the front end of the plunger with a pliers. While holding it, remove the screwdriver, insert the safety and release the pliers.

To assemble the bolt stop, with the bolt forward and the handle raised, lay the action on a bench with the left side up. Position the bolt stop spring rest on the receiver. Insert the ejector in the bolt stop, then insert the bolt stop spring, pressing the hooked end of this spring into the front end of the bolt stop until it is level with the latter. Position the assembled bolt stop in place on the receiver, turning the rest to align the groove for the bolt stop spring. Using a screwdriver handle or similar tool, firmly press the rear end of the bolt stop against the receiver, then insert and turn in the bolt stop screw.

Strong and Weak Points

The only really weak part in this action is the ejector. It is a leaf spring which usually breaks off and leaves the ejector useless. Christy Gun Works, 875 - 57th St., Sacramento, Calif. 95819 makes a reliable replacement for this action. The Christy ejector is fitted with a small coil spring instead of the easily broken flat spring.

Not a design fault, but rather a construction fault, is that some of the 1917 receivers develop hair-line cracks. By no means a common occurrence, it is com-

Close-up of rear part of Model 1917 Enfield action showing how bolt handle forms safety lug by engaging a deep notch in the receiver (arrow).

mon enough to be of some concern to owners of these actions. The cracks usually appear some place around the receiver ring, often starting at the front edge of the receiver and extending rearward in an erratic pattern. Although Winchester and Remington receivers have been found with cracks, the Eddystone-made receivers are by far the most frequent offenders. It is believed that many of these receivers, perhaps, were given a faulty heat treatment, the metal thereby becoming too hard and brittle. Not easily spotted, the cracks are most often detected when the action is polished and reblued. They can often be detected with the naked eye, or by carefully examining the receiver ring with a hand magnifier.

Another good way to detect cracks is to dunk the receiver in gasoline for a moment. If a crack (or cracks) is present the gasoline will seep from it after the rest of the receiver has dried. Cracked receivers are generally not repairable, so they should not be used.

While cracks may well be the result of improper heat treatment, they're most frequently found on receivers from which the original barrel has been removed. Barrels were fitted extremely tight in these actions, some tighter than others. It is possible that some of the receivers cracked when the barrels were originally installed, but I believe most of the cracks occur when the original very tight barrel is removed, for unscrewing a tight barrel puts a lot of strain on the receiver.

The cock-on-closing feature is often considered poor design, but that's a matter of opinion. I've fired many shots through these actions, but I've never found this feature objectionable, certainly not to the point where I would spend time and money to change it.

Others have condemned the long striker fall, the seemingly slow lock time, but again I've had no occasion to complain

about it. The same goes for the double-stage trigger pull which, if one learns to use it, is almost without fault. At any rate, if any of these features are objectionable there are accessories commercially available to change them. Several firms make single-stage trigger mechanisms for this rifle while two firms make speed-lock and cock-on-opening firing mechanisms.

If it is desired to incorporate all these changes then installing the complete Dayton-Traister trigger and speed-lock mechanisms seems to be the best solution. Their address is Rte. 3, Goldie Road, Oak Harbor, Wash. 98277.

Round nosed bullets pose a feeding problem, and many cures have been tried. The simplest method is to install a device, the Tru-Feed Kit, made by Dayton-Traister.

Although I've fired several thousand shots with rifles based on the 1917 Enfield action I never experienced a ruptured case head or primer, which might have allowed powder gases to get into the action. Had a serious rupture occurred I most likely would have got some of this gas in my face, for the design doesn't allow much gas escapage through the action other than towards the rear. Drilling a hole in the left receiver wall, opposite the rear vent hole in the bolt, would have helped. Eliminating the two grooves on the striker shoulder would also have helped stop any gases passing back along the mainspring to escape past the cocking piece, and would instead, tend to deflect the gases out of the vent hole in the bolt at this point. K.E. Clark, 18738 Hwy. 99, Madera, Calif. 93637, offers a clever gas shield cover to install on the bolt sleeve, which is effective in protecting the shooter from powder gases escaping past the cocking piece.

Gunsmithing the 1917 Enfield

Besides installing the above mentioned accessories, the 1917 Enfield action can be "gunsmithed" no end.

Through the years these rifles were available a great many articles were written on their remodeling and conversion, and all of the major gunsmithing books have covered the subject in detail, so I'll just skim over this part.

The unsightly part of this action is the receiver bridge and the protruding sight ears. Removing these ears and rounding the bridge is generally the first thing the amateur gunsmith wants to change. The usual instructions suggest grinding the bridge down to be the same contour as the receiver ring, which is OK—but that still leaves at lot of metal where it is not needed. Top scope mounts for the remodeled 1917 Enfield are usually made for a rear bridge that's the same diameter as the front ring. Be this as it may, I much prefer to grind the bridge down much lower, or to duplicate the bridge on the FN Mauser action, which permits using mounts recommended for that action. At the same time I like to remove all metal directly over the base of the bolt handle, as well as removing metal occupied by

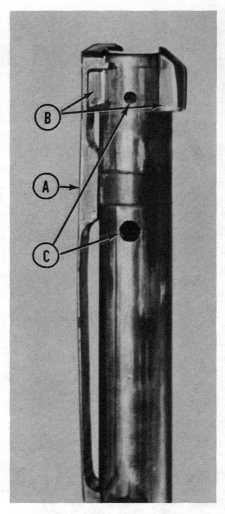

Underside of Model 1917 Enfield bolt showing: (A) extractor, (B) dual-opposed locking lugs, (C) two gas-escape holes.

the bolt stop spring rest, leaving only about a ⅛" metal ledge directly behind the bolt stop. The rear end of the bolt stop spring can be heated and bent down to ride on this ledge after cutting a bit off the end of the spring. All this eliminates considerable weight and the entire action looks much trimmer. The bridge can be further trimmed to eliminate the clip guide slots.

Incidentally, S&K Mfg. Co. (Box 247, Pittsfield, Pa. 16340) makes a mount base (to accommodate Weaver top detachable rings) which can be attached to the unaltered 1917 Enfield receiver. No drilling and tapping is required to attach this base. Although the S&K Insta-Mount base provides a convenient way to mount a hunting scope on this rifle, it is objectionable in that it places the scope very high over the receiver.

If one doesn't like the 1917's "dog leg" bolt handle, it can be heated and straightened out and, with some filing, it can be made to look like the old 720 Remington bolt handle. Or a new bolt handle can be lathe-made and welded on in place of the original.

Another odd feature of this action is the crooked front end of the trigger guard plate; unless this is changed the rifle will

Parts Legend
1917 Enfield

1. Receiver (top view)
2. Bolt-stop spring
3. Bolt stop
4. Bolt-stop spring rest
5. Bolt-stop screw
6. Ejector
7. Safety-plug screw
8. Safety plug
9. Safety
10. Safety-lock plunger
11. Safety-lock plunger spring
12. Trigger spring
13. Sear
14. Trigger pin
15. Trigger
16. Sear pin
17. Bolt
18. Mainspring
19. Firing pin
20. Cocking piece
21. Bolt sleeve
22. Extractor collar
23. Extractor
24. Follower
25. Follower spring
26. Magazine box
27. Trigger guard
28. Floorplate
29. Magazine catch
30. Magazine-catch pin
31. Magazine-catch spring
32. Rear guard-screw
33. Rear stock (guard-screw) bushing
34. Front guard-screw
35. Front stock (guard-screw) bushing

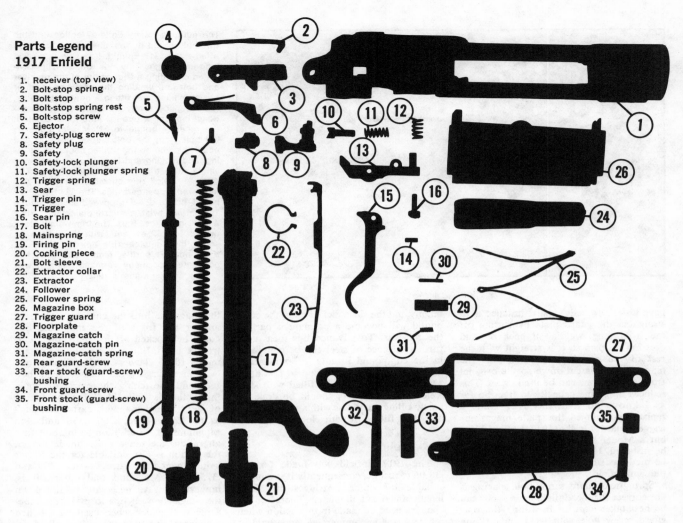

1917 U.S. Enfield

(Uses .30-06 cartridges)

Dimensional Specifications

Weight	58 oz.
Over-all	8.875"
Receiver ring dia.	1.385"
Bolt-body dia.	.695"
Bolt-face recess (partially recessed)	
Depth	.046"
Dia.	.485"
Bolt travel	4.740"
Striker travel	.700"
Guard-screw spacing	8.00"
Magazine-well opening	
Length	3.400"
Rear width	.525"
Front width	.550"

General Specifications

Type	Turnbolt repeater.
Receiver	One-piece machined steel forging with non-slotted bridge. Stripper-clip guide milled in bridge.
Bolt	One-piece with dual-opposed forward locking lugs. Base of bolt handle acts as safety lug. Low-profile bolt handle will clear low-mounted scopes.
Ignition	One-piece firing pin, coil mainspring and cocking piece. Cocks on closing.
Magazine	Staggered-column non-detachable 5-shot box magazine.
Trigger	Detachable floorplate.
Safety	Non-adjustable, double-stage military type pull.
	Right-side rotary type, about 160° swing. Locks striker and bolt when swung rearward.
Extractor	One-piece non-rotating spring type attached to bolt body by a collar.
Bolt stop	Separate, hinged to left rear of receiver. Stops rearward bolt travel by contacting left locking lug.
Ejector	Swinging type in bolt stop housing.

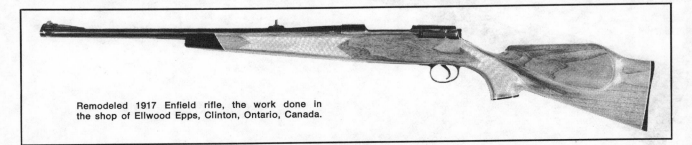

Remodeled 1917 Enfield rifle, the work done in the shop of Ellwood Epps, Clinton, Ontario, Canada.

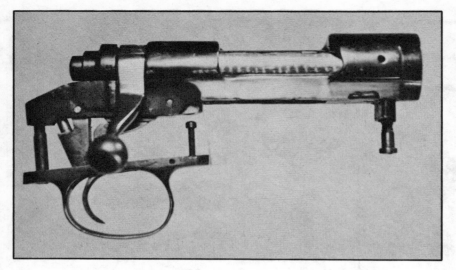

The author's "Baby Enfield" action and the rifle built round it. Yes, this action was once a full-sized 1917 Enfield. It is now just 7.25" long and weighs 2 pounds. Customizing consisted of cutting a section out of the receiver and bolt and welding the sections together again, making and fitting a new bolt handle, removing the safety parts and these alterations: the tang where the safety was located; the receiver bridge to FN Mauser contour; the bolt stop; the bolt sleeve; the bolt and cocking piece so the striker cocks on opening, and making and installing an adjustable single-stage trigger mechanism. Below: The "Baby Enfield" rifle chambered for the .219 Improved Zipper cartridge. The 22" Buhmiller barrel has a .224" groove diameter and a 1:14" rifling twist, a muzzle diameter of .700" and weight 3 lbs., 6 oz. The trim walnut stock weighs just 30 oz. and, with the Lyman 5A scope the complete rifle tips the scales at 8 pounds. This rifle, highly accurate, has accounted for many varmints since it was made in 1942.

have a definite belly. Usual practice is to straighten the guard plate by cutting off the front tang, welding it back on and dressing it down so it is straight with the rest of the guard plate. After this the magazine box is cut down so the original front guard screw can be used again. This reduces magazine capacity to five. So far as I know, no firm has ever made a replacement hinged floorplate/magazine/trigger guard for the 1917 Enfield rifle, but a Model 1903 Springfield guard can be installed. If this is done the stock can be made as slim around the action as on the Springfield.

Springfield guard screw hole-spacing is not correct for the Enfield action, but can be best taken care of by filling the rear guard screw hole with weld and drilling a new hole slightly farther to the rear.

Most Enfield receivers have a deep oblong recess milled in the top of the bridge, rather unsightly looking on a finished sporter. After the sight ears have been removed and the bridge dressed down nearly to the desired point, this recess can be filled. A simple method is to use glass bedding compound dyed blue/black. If the inside of the recess is cleaned thor-

oughly and the sides nicked a bit, the compound will become a permanent part of the receiver. To advance this idea a bit further, a piece of steel can be concealed in the compound in case an extra scope mount screw hole is needed in this area. The recess could also be filled with steel weld; preferably this should be done by partly filling the recess with a piece of steel and then filling in with electric weld.

Rebarreling

The 1917 Enfield was made for the .30-06 cartridge, consequently it is equally suitable for other cartridges of .30-06 length and head diameter. Therefore no changes need be made in this action when rebarreled to commercial and wildcat cartridges such as the 6mm/06, .25-06, 6.5/06, .270, .280, .30-06 Improved, .35 Whelen and .400 Whelen. This action is also most suitable for cartridges slightly shorter than the .30-06, and without any changes it can handle the 6mm, .257 Roberts, 6.5x57, 7x57mm, 8x57mm and 9x57mm.

Even such shorter cartridges as the .243 or .308 will usually feed quite well from

the magazine into the chamber. The rear and/or the front of the magazine box could be blocked off for the shorter cartridges but this is not usually necessary unless 100% flawless feeding is required.

After enlarging the recess in the bolt face and shortening the extractor hook, this action is quite ideal for the family of short belted magnum cartridges, such as the .264, 7mm, .300, .338 and .458 Magnums. If, in addition to the bolt face alteration, the magazine is made longer, this action is also suitable for the longer belted magnum cartridges—the .300 and .375 H&H Magnums and others. It is, however, always necessary to file down the magazine-well lips to make the magazine well wider when used with belted magnums. I've used the 1917 Enfield action for a wide variety of cartridges, from the .22-250 to the .450 Magnum, but because it is a big action I consider it best for such big bore heavy-recoiling cartridges as the .35 Whelen, .338 Magnum and .458 Magnum.

Although it has been nearly 50 years since the two million-plus 1917 actions and rifles were made, they are still very common today and readily available.

Part II
Pattern 14 Enfield

Pattern (P14) 1914 Enfield action made for the .303 British cartridge. Note the two grooves in the side of the magazine box, grooves which produce ridges inside the box, and which are needed for the rimmed .303 British cartridge.

Chronologically this part should precede Part I, on the 1917 Enfield, but since the P-14 action and rifle aren't nearly as important to the average reader I've given them second place.

For a detailed review of the history and development of the British P-14 I suggest readers get *The Lee-Enfield Rifle*, by E.G.B. Reynolds, and read chapter 11.

Briefly, the British became interested about 1910 in adopting a different military cartridge and a new shoulder arm to replace the old .303 British cartridge and the two-piece stocked Lee-Enfield rifle. The cartridge favored was of .276 caliber in a rimless bottle-necked case.

The Small Arms Committee which had supervised development recommended the new rifle be based on a Mauser type turn-bolt action, and made similar to the 1903 Springfield. The trial rifle was developed by Royal Small Arms Factory at Enfield Lock, Middlesex, England. After some testing, in competition with other rifles, the Enfield rifles showed promise. It was decided that 1000 of these rifles be made and thoroughly tested before making any final decision on the rifle or cartridge. This was in 1913, and the arm was named "Rifle, Enfield, Caliber .276, Pattern of 1913."

The 1000 Pattern 13 rifles were manufactured at Enfield and distributed to various British troops for extensive testing. The .276 cartridge did not perform as expected, metal fouling being the major problem. Some minor faults found in the rifle were easily corrected, and after the trials the Enfield plant made up 6 new rifles without these faults. It was now 1914, England had got involved in World War I, so all further experiments and trials of the .276 were dropped.

However, the British had developed a good rifle, and they were in desperate need of many rifles to arm their troops. The British arsenals were still tooled up to make the Lee-Enfield rifles in quantity so it was decided to retain this arm, and have

the new rifles, but chambered for the .303 British cartridge, made elsewhere. It was thus that the British awarded contracts to the three U.S. firms to make the new Enfield. This was in 1914, and the new rifle then became known as the Model (or Pattern) 1914 Enfield.

The three firms were Winchester, Remington and Eddystone. During 1915, 1916 and 1917 Winchester made about 245,866 rifles for England, Eddystone made about 450,000 and Remington probably made more. In March of 1917, shortly before the British contract was canceled, Remington made up to 61,000 P-14 rifles in that one month alone.

The Pattern 14 (P-14) Action

The P-14 Enfield action is essentially like the 1917 Enfield except that it is made to handle the rimmed .303 British cartridge.

Here are the specifications of the P-14 action which differ from the 1917 Enfield action.

Bolt face recess:
    Dia. .... .545"
    Depth .... .60"
Magazine box length..................3.06"
Receiver well opening:
    Length ....3.135"
    Front width .... .555"
    Rear width .... .610"

The parts that are different are the receiver, bolt, magazine box, follower, ejector and extractor.

The P-14 receiver differs in having a wider magazine-well opening, milled to hold and guide the .303 British round. The P-14 bolt has a larger diameter cartridge head recess, and a left locking lug with a rounded front end.

The extractor has a narrow hook and this hook is well beveled so that the extractor will easily slip over the rim of a cartridge that is chambered ahead of the extractor. The P-14 ejector is longer than the Model 1917 ejector, and the P-14 receiver has a longer ejector slot to accommodate it.

The biggest difference between these two actions is in the magazine box and follower. The P-14 magazine box has sides made of heavy gauge sheet metal into which grooves are pressed to form rounded ridges inside. The ridges in the rear of the box guide and hold the cartridges by their rims and in loading the .303 British rounds into the magazine in the normal way their rims slide to the rear of these ridges. The rear ridges as well as the rear wall of the magazine box, angle slightly to the rear, and as more than one cartridge is pressed into the magazine each proceeding cartridge moves back a little so that the rim of the suc-

Remodeled P14 Enfield rifle by Ellwood Epps, Clinton, Ontario, Canada. This rifle is rechambered for the .303 Epps Belted Canadian Magnum cartridge.

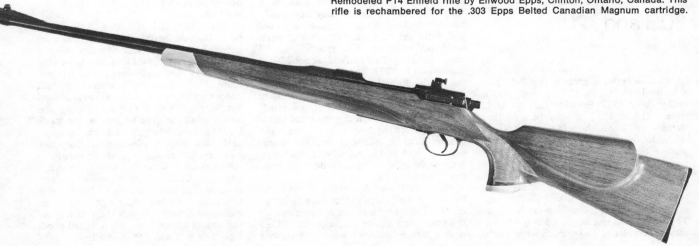

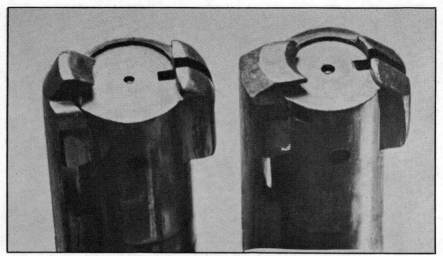

Bolt head of the 1917 (right) and the P14 Enfield (left). Note extractor hook and left locking lug.

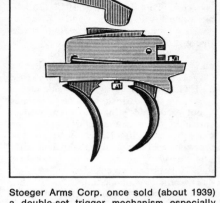

Stoeger Arms Corp. once sold (about 1939) a double-set trigger mechanism especially made for the P14 Enfield 30 and 30S Remington actions.

ceeding one will be ahead of the one below it. This does a lot to help eliminate the problem of incorrect overlapping of the cartridge rims to prevent feeding jams. The rear ridges also hold the cartridges securely in the magazine so that they cannot move forward when the rifle recoils, and thus protecting the points of the bullets. The second ridges are near the center of the magazine box and these merely position and hold the cartridges away from the side walls so that the bullets in the cartridges are pointed to feed correctly.

The P-14 follower has a rib along its left side to stagger the cartridges in the magazine, and this rib is square in back to halt the forward movement of the bolt when the magazine is empty, but it differs from the Model 1917 follower in that its right front groove curves upward to properly guide the last cartridge in the magazine so its bullet will clear the loading ramp as it is fed out.

The P-14 action will handle the .30-40 Krag cartridge as well as the .303 British.

Since it is a very strong action it would be ideal for rebarreling to any wildcat cartridge based on the .303 British or .30-40 Krag case, such as the .22/.303, .22/4000 Krag, .25/.303, .25 Krag, .25 Krag Improved and .35 Krag.

While the P-14 bolt face and extractor are correct for the .300 H&H belted magnum head size, the magazine is too short to handle any of the popular commercial and wildcat cartridges based on this case. However, by substituting the 1917 magazine box and follower it will handle most of these cartridges, and thus be ideal for rebarreling to such short belted magnums as the .264, 7mm, .300, .308 Norma and others. The magazine well and guide lips usually need some work to obtain perfect feeding.

Since the time P.O. Ackley first popularized the "improved" cartridge rechamberings, one which responded favorably to this treatment was the .303 British. After the standard .303 British cases are fire-formed (blown-out) by firing them in the "improved" chamber, careful hand-

loading can result in considerably higher velocity.

There are a number of rifles chambered for the .303 British cartridge, but the P-14 is the only bolt action rifle for which the .303 British Improved rechambering can be recommended since it is a strong action and can safely handle pressures higher than the factory loaded .303 British cartridge normally develops. The "improved" rechambering is a simple job, it offers the handloader more energy and velocity than the factory load can deliver.

P-14 actions are fully as strong and safe as the 1917 Enfield actions and, as with the 1917s, those with the Remington and Winchester names are preferred over the Eddystones. Since the .303 British cartridge has long been very popular in Canada, the P-14s have also been popular there; a great many of them were remodeled and sporterized for big game hunting. The P-14 rifle can be so treated just like the 1917 Enfields, and the illustrations of the Remington Models 30, 30S and 720 show what can be done with either rifle.

Remington 30, 30S and 720

AFTER MAKING a great many P-14 Enfields for Great Britain, and over a half-million 1917 Enfields for the U.S., from 1915 to 1918, it may be said that Remington knew how to make these rifles, for by the end of 1918 they were turning them out at a rate of about 4000 per day. When the contracts for these rifles were canceled—the British contract in June, 1917 and the U.S. contract in Nov. 1918—the many machines Remington had making these rifles were left idle. They were also left holding a huge inventory of completely and semi-finished parts,

probably enough to make up many more thousands of rifles. To save something from this vast operation they apparently decided to keep some of these machines and tools and, with the vast stock of parts on hand, to produce a sporting model based on the 1917 Enfield action. Thus it was that in 1921 Remington introduced the Model 30 high powered sporting rifle.

What Remington did was to modify 1917 barrel and action assembly for sporting use and then fit a conventional lightweight sporter stock to it. The barrel, like the military issue barrel but shortened, was polished and fitted with a band type front sight base to retain a dovetail bead front sight.

The action was slimmed and lightened by milling the bridge to the same diameter as the receiver rings, and straightening the front tang of the trigger guard. Fitted with a simple receiver sight and sporter

stock, this rifle was introduced as the Model 30 High Power, Bolt Action, Sporting Rifle.

The M30 rifle was first made in .30-06 only. Its first barrel, 24″ long, was contoured and tapered just like the military barrel, although it probably was somewhat smaller in diameter through being polished. The stock, of plain American black walnut, was fitted with a curved steel buttplate, grooved to prevent slipping, and had a reinforced toe to prevent the stock from splitting. The stock had an uncapped half-pistol grip, a slim tapered fore-end, with finger grooves, that ended in a schnabel tip. It was fitted with sling swivel eyerings, the front one through the fore-end and threaded into a barrel band. These first rifles were furnished with a Kerr service type canvas or web sling and open-end swivel hooks. The rifle weighed about 8 pounds and was 45″ over-all.

Remington Model 30 Express rifle (photo courtesy Remington Arms Co.).

When first made the M30 was also available in Remington's F Grade. This rifle had an engraved action, finely checkered fancy walnut stock, and was fitted with a foreign made scope in special mounts.

The M30 action is, in every way, practically identical to the military 1917 action except as noted above. The double-stage military trigger mechanism was retained, as well as the bent back bolt handle and the safety. The action, of course, was made to closer tolerances than the military action, and it was well finished, polished and blued. Remington most likely made the barrel and action of the same steels used in making the M1917 rifles, as well as giving the steels the same heat treatment. Remington proof tested these barrels and actions with loads developing 70,000 psi breech pressure.

The rear sight used on the original M30 is most interesting. Its base, dovetailed into the top of the bridge, angles upward to the rear and is grooved to accept a slide with an integral peep disc. Elevation changes are made by moving the slide to the rear. A spring-loaded screw plunger through the base engages in notches in the bottom of the slide; by depressing this plunger to the right the slide can be moved. An additional lock screw in the slide can be tightened to secure the slide even if the plunger is depressed. Windage adjustment was obtained by driving the entire sight to either side in its dovetail slot. This sight was soon discontinued, after which the rifles were fitted with an open sight dovetailed into the barrel band.

After making the M30 for a few years Remington made some changes. Its original skimpy stock was improved by omitting the finger grooves in the fore-end and the comb made a bit higher and thicker. The grip and fore-end of the new stock were checkered and a crossbolt added through the stock to strengthen the wood around the recoil shoulder area. By this time the rifle was dubbed the Model 30 Express. A Model 30 Express Carbine, with 20″ barrel, was also introduced. Up to 1932 both were available only in .30-06 caliber.

The Model 30S

Around 1930 Remington introduced the Model 30S, a special or de luxe version of the M30. It was greatly improved—the stock was much better designed and shaped, wore a steel shotgun type buttplate, had a full pistol grip with cap, a full and high comb better suited for telescope sight use and a fuller fore-end with a rounded tip. Grip and fore-end were checkered. Sights on the 30S were the fine Lyman 48 receiver sight and a gold bead on a band ramp base. No fore-end barrel band was used on the 24″ barrel. Up to 1932 the action was the same as that on the M30, chambering was only for the .30-06, and the double-stage military trigger and the "cock-on-closing" features were kept.

1933 Changes

Some important changes were made in the Model 30S from 1932 to 1933. The Model 30 rifle was designated the Model 30A Standard, the carbine became the Model 30R Carbine and the Model 30S had the word "Special" tacked to it. The most important changes were in the actions, for they were now made to cock on the uplift or opening motion of the bolt, and the trigger was altered to a short, single-stage pull.

On the 30A and 30R the barrel band was retained, the open rear sight fitted into a dovetail slot cut into the band. The fore-end-to-barrel band fastening was eliminated, and Remington described this as a "floating barrel to give maximum accuracy." Finally, several new calibers were added; the 30A and 30R were offered in .25 Rem., .30 Rem., .32 Rem., .35 Rem., 7mm Mauser (7x57) and .30-06. The Model 30 S was made only in .25 Rem., 7mm Mauser and .30-06, the .25 Rem. with a 22″ barrel. In 1934 the .257 Roberts was added to the 30S line-up of calibers. It is believed that a few of these rifles were also chambered for the 7.65 Mauser cartridge. Many of the M30 rifles had barrels with a very short shoulder or reinforce-section; that is, the shoulder contour of the barrel started a short distance from the receiver.

By 1939 the 30A and 30R were available only in .30-06, and again had a barrel band for anchoring the open rear sight. The fore-end was now made fuller and without the schnabel tip. All receivers were now being tapped for a receiver sight, and the 30S was now listed as the 30SL, 30SR or 30SX, depending on whether the rifle was furnished with a Lyman, a Redfield or no rear sight at all. The .25 Rem. caliber was also dropped in the Model 30S.

Model 30 and 30S barrels were usually marked thus, in two lines: **REMINGTON ARMS CO., INC., REMINGTON ILION WORKS, ILION, N.Y. MADE IN U.S.A.** Or: **REMINGTON ARMS COMPANY, INC., SUCCESSOR TO REMINGTON ARMS U.M.C. CO. INC., REMINGTON ILION WORKS, N.Y. U.S.A.**

The left side of the receiver ring may be marked thus, in two lines: **MODEL 30/ EXPRESS,** and the right side thus, also in two lines: **REMINGTON/TRADE MARK.**

The serial number is stamped on the receiver ring, and the caliber designation stamped on the breech end of the barrel.

I have no idea how many of these rifles were made, but they were fairly common in the 1930s. Most of these I've seen were in .30-06 or .257 Roberts caliber. I doubt very much if many were made in .30, .32 or .35 Rem. In the past, many of these rifles were rechambered. For example, the .25 Rem. rifles were often rechambered for the .250-3000 Savage or .257 Roberts, the .257 Roberts to the .25 Niedner (.25-06) or to some wildcat .25 Magnum, the .30 Rem. to .300 Savage or .30-06, the .35 Rem. to .35 Whelen and the .30-06 to the .300 H&H Magnum. In most of these rechamberings some maga-

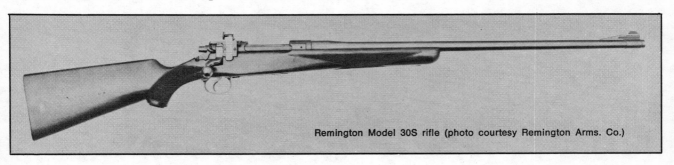

Remington Model 30S rifle (photo courtesy Remington Arms. Co.)

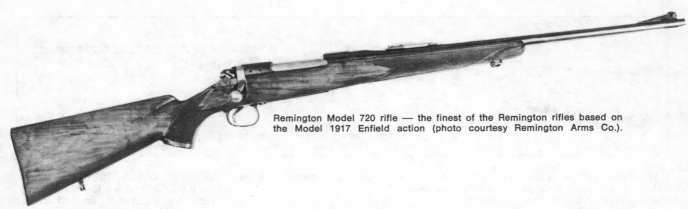

Remington Model 720 rifle — the finest of the Remington rifles based on the Model 1917 Enfield action (photo courtesy Remington Arms Co.).

zine and bolt-head alterations were also necessary to effect proper conversion.

Model 30 and 30S Remington rifles are not too common today, and collectors are beginning to take note of them. However, only rifles in entirely original and very good condition will have any present or future collectors value. Those rifles that don't meet such conditions will continue to be bought, sold, traded and remodeled until they're ruined or worn out.

All Model 30 Remington rifles were discontinued by 1941, replaced by the Model 720 Remington.

The Remington Model 720

The M720 Remington rifle is not well known today. Introduced at the start of WW II, it was continuously listed until 1947, but was probably made in limited numbers the first year or so. It was, most likely, not available at all during the war years. As the 30S had been an improvement over the early M30, the 720 was an improved 30S. The "improvements" were minor, although Remington advertised these to be: 1) Superior stock design of dense walnut having a fluted comb, full pistol grip, slimmer middle section, and semi-beavertail fore-end, with grip and fore-end checkered; 2) Guide rib on the bolt to prevent binding, for smoother and easier bolt operation; 3) Improved bolt handle shape; 4) Short, fast firing-pin travel, and 5) Quick-release floorplate.

Up to the time of this writing I have yet to see a specimen of the Model 720 Remington rifle, so I can't describe action details, how the guide rib is made, etc. The receiver bridge is tapped to accept a receiver sight but not for scope mount bases. Weaver Scopes lists detachable top-mount bases for the 720 (36 rear and 11 front), indicating that the bridge is of the same contour and height as that of the 721, 722 and 700 Remington rifles, which require the same rear base.

The main outward differences of the 720 over its predecessors are two: the bolt handle shank is straight and the bridge is flatter and lower than the receiver ring.

Both features improve the looks of the action. The other readily seen changes are in the shape of the stock, its fluted comb and longer, fuller fore-end, which sets it apart from the 30S. Firing-pin travel was reduced, but only a very small amount. The standard trigger on 720s was the same as on the late Model 30S, but an optional military double-stage trigger was available.

This, the last Remington rifle to be made on the basic 1917 Enfield action, was available in calibers .30-06, .257 Roberts and .270 Winchester. Three basic models were listed: the 720A with 22″ barrel, the 720S with 24″ barrel, and the 720R with 20″ barrel. All were available with open sights; without the open rear sight but fitted with a Lyman, Redfield or Marble-Goss receiver sight, in which case the letter L, R or M followed the regular model designation.

According to *Remington Arms In American History,* by Alden Hatch, the barrel markings are as follows: **Remington Arms Co., Inc., Ilion, N.Y. Made in U.S.A. Pat. No. 2,437,373 - 2,514,981 - other pending.** The caliber is stamped on the left side of the breech section. Hatch also said the rifle was made in .300 H&H Magnum caliber.

The 720 Remington rifles are now collectors items, although they may not become really valuable until many years hence. One rifleman who had seen and handled the 720 called it the "Cadillac" of the Enfields.

Part II
Commercial Turnbolt Rifles and Actions
Past and Present

18. M98 Mauser Sporters

I N THIS CHAPTER I will briefly discuss variations of the M98 action used to build sporting rifles, and review the various sporting rifles made in Europe and Great Britain between the introduction of this action in 1898 and the WW II period. I will also describe, in more detail, two set trigger mechanisms often used in these rifles.

Shortly after Mauser in Oberndorf (Germany) began making military rifles on the M98 action they began making fine sporting rifles on the same action. In due time Mauser also made these actions available to other arms firms in Germany and other countries on the continent, as well as to Great Britain and the United States. As other German firms began manufacturing M98 military rifles, they also started using their own M98 actions for sporting rifles.

A great many firms, besides Mauser, made sporting rifles on the M98 action. In Germany this included such well-known firms as J.P. Sauer & Sohn, Remo, Krieghoff, Merkel, C.G. Haenel, and such lesser known firms as Halger, Vom Hofe, Brenneke and others. Many little-known individual German gunsmiths used both commercial and military M98 actions on which to build a wide array of sporting rifles in many standard and wildcat calibers. Model 98 sporters were also built in Belgium, France, Switzerland, Czechoslovakia and other European countries. In the British Isles practically every well-known gunmaker made sporters on this action, with names like Gibbs, Rigby, Holland & Holland, Westley Richards, Greener, Vickers and others often appearing on these fine rifles. Griffin & Howe, Hoffman, Pachmayr and other American gunmakers also used these actions for building sporters. For many years Stoeger Arms Corp. imported the "original" Mauser Oberndorf actions and rifles, while such firms as Abercrombie & Fitch imported others, including some of the better British-made Mauser rifles. All in

all, there never was, nor is there now, an action more widely used for sporting rifles than the M98 Mauser.

M98 Sporting Actions

Most of the better makes of Mauser sporting rifles were based on actions usually considered "commercial" types, as opposed to those made for a military rifle or reworked from a military action. Even so, the commercial sporting action was essentially the same as the military, and most parts were interchangeable. The commercial action, however, was generally made to closer tolerances, better finished, and smoother in operation. In many cases the commercial actions featured a quick release floorplate or a magazine floorplate hinged to the forward part of the trigger guard.

Mauser sporters were made for a wide variety of cartridges and, for the most part, the standard length action was used —that is, an action 8.75″ long, the same length as the standard M98 military action made for the 8mm Mauser cartridge. This action was made for, or modified to accept, magazine boxes of various lengths to handle cartridges of different lengths. The Mauser firm alone listed 20 different action numbers, most of them the standard action with different magazine lengths. In some cases the magazine depth was increased to handle the fatter cartridges.

Mauser, as well as some others, also made "short" and "long" magnum actions. The true short Mauser actions, about 8.00″ long, are fitted with a magazine of proper length for the various cartridges of 6.5x54mm length or shorter. The "short" military action used on 7mm Mexican Mauser rifles is about 8.50″ long, but I don't know if this action was ever made commercially for sporter use. The magnum, or long action, about 9.25″ long, is intended for cartridges longer than the .30-06. Of course, none of these original Oberndorf or other similar commer-

cial Mauser actions are available today except the standard length FN Mauser action (8.75″) and the Brevex Magnum action (9.50″).

Sporting rifles built on these actions followed several distinct styles or types. I won't describe these in detail, but briefly they're as follows:

European made for European trade (as illustrated) such rifles were quite light, with very slim, tapered barrels about 20″ to 24″ long, and had the typical German "toothpick" stock. Some barrels were round, some part octagonal and round, some full octagonal and some fluted; any of them might have a raised matted rib. The most common open sights were 2- or 3-leaf rear and a bead front sight mounted on a ramp. The walnut stock carried a steel or pressed-horn buttplate and pistol-grip cap (early ones usually had a round-ended grip), a checkered grip, short and slim tapered (usually uncheckered) fore-end which ended in a schnabel tip, small cheekpiece and a thin comb. The lightest of these stocks had raised panels along the receiver sides. Narrow sling swivels were fitted to the buttstock and to the barrel, several inches ahead of the fore-end tip. Double set triggers were quite common, but the rifles could also be had with a single set, single

Illustrated above: A classic German sporting rifle (maker unknown). Based on the military M98 small-ring Mauser action, it has a distinctly German-styled stock of minimum proportions. The checkered buttplate and sunburst pistol grip cap are made of pressed buffalo horn. Note the panels over the action and the small schnabel fore-end tip. The receiver, trigger guard and floorplate are fully engraved and color case hardened. The flat bolt handle is checkered and the action fitted with a double-set trigger mechanism. The very slim, tapered barrel, 24″ long, carries a full length raised matted rib to which the sights are attached. Chambered for the 9x57mm cartridge, it weighs 6½ lbs. (Gilbert Blum collection)

stage or double stage triggers. The carbine styles were usually made with a slim, full-length fore-end finished off with a steel muzzle cap and a clevis-type front sling swivel.

The rifle telescope sight (developed in Europe) was held in the typical and classic "hook" or "claw" type two-piece mounts. These, spanning the bridge and receiver, were quickly detachable. These mounts usually place the scope very high over the receiver but, despite the scope's ready removability, holes or tunnels in the mounts also allowed use of the open sights with the scope in place. In many cases the front scope mount base was dovetailed into the receiver ring rather than being attached with screws or attached to the breech end of the barrel.

European made for British trade: these were similar to the above rifles except the stock was usually made a bit fuller, which did away with the side panels; the front of the fore-end was tipped with ebony or horn and rounded; the fore-end was checkered, and usually sling eyelets or swivel studs were fitted instead of swivels. The British preferred rifles with a plain trigger and round barrel, although the rifles could be ordered with any regularly furnished accessory.

European made for African sportsmen: Mauser—and perhaps some others—made such rifles with very long barrels (about 29″) and with a slim uncapped fore-end that went nearly to the muzzle. This model is not common.

Bavarian style: this sporter variation is distinguished by a larger and longer cheek-piece, made with a pronounced corner. These sporters usually have a slightly fuller stock than most German-made sporters, and a longer fore-end and differently shaped schnabel. These rifles often have a separate shotgun type trigger guard. The bolt handles are often flat or "spooned," or made with a round shank with a grasping ball in the shape of an acorn.

British made: the classic British Mauser bolt action sporting rifle has a round barrel up to about 24″ long, fitted with a multi-leaf "express" type open rear sight and a bead front sight on a ramp base; a dark walnut stock moderately full proportioned with a short, round-ended fore-end, and a standard single stage trigger. The bolt handle is generally conventional, with a round grasping ball; the fore-end is usually tipped with a piece of buffalo horn or ebony, the grip and fore-end checkered. Gaudy decorations like white spacers or contrasting stock inlays are unheard of on these rifles. The front sling swivel stud, or eyelet, is almost always attached to the barrel, ahead of the fore-end tip.

American made: this category is endless but I'll limit it to the better pre-1940 era "classic" types as represented by those rifles made by such notable gunmakers as Hoffman and Griffin & Howe. These rifles were patterned largely after the British-made Mausers, except that the fore-end was usually made longer, and the front sling stud was attached to the fore-end. The general stock lines followed

Engraved action of the Mauser sporter opening this chapter.

British design—straight comb, small- to medium-sized cheekpiece, diamond-shaped checkering panels and a dull oil-type finish. Because it was fuller and had a longer fore-end, the American classic sporter stock weighs about a pound or so more than the typical German toothpick sporter stock, and about a half-pound more than the British. The American classic Mauser sporter was usually fitted with a band-type ramp front sight and a rear receiver sight, and/or with a short hunting scope in a classic detachable side mount like the Griffin & Howe or Jaeger.

The Double Set Trigger

For the great many years that sporting rifles have been built on M98 actions it has been, and still is, normal practice to substitute a different trigger mechanism for the double-stage military trigger. The favorite trigger mechanism used by Mauser, and by most European gunmakers, was the common double set trigger.

The firing mechanism of the M98 action consists of two assemblies: 1) The firing pin, mainspring and cocking piece assembled in the bolt and bolt sleeve; 2) the sear, sear spring, trigger and pin, attached to the bottom rear of the receiver. On closing the bolt the sear, which has a projection extending upward into the cocking piece raceway, holds the cocking piece back against the tension of the mainspring on the firing pin. Normally there is considerable looseness of the bolt in the receiver, which extends to the cocking piece, and to make up for this play, sufficient sear engagement is required on the cocking piece to positively hold the action cocked. The first stage of the military double-stage pull moves the sear almost all of the way off the cocking piece, while the second stage pull, which is shorter and heavier than the first stage, finally disengages the sear from the cocking piece to fire the rifle.

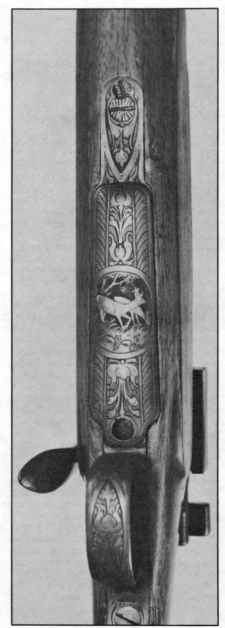

The same Mauser action showing engraving details on the trigger guard and magazine floorplate.

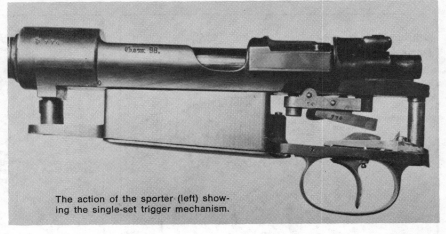

The action of the sporter (left) showing the single-set trigger mechanism.

The double set trigger is merely a miniature hammer and trigger mechanism—an auxiliary lock mechanism which can be adjusted to a very light pull. When fitted to the action it provides a means of tripping the fully engaged sear off the cocking piece.

In the double set trigger mechanism, which gets its name because of its "two trigger" appearance, the rear trigger is actually a "hammer" and the front trigger is the "trigger" to that "hammer." I usually call the rear trigger the "cocking" trigger, for it must be cocked if the set triggers are to be used, and the front trigger the "firing" trigger, since it must be pulled to fire the rifle whether the set mechanism is used or not. Like a hammer on a hammer-type firearm, the rear trigger has its own mainspring to give it power. With the regular trigger in the sear replaced by a short lever, the cocked rear trigger when released strikes the sear lever and causes the sear to disengage from the cocking piece to fire the rifle. The double set trigger is cocked by pulling the rear trigger back under tension of its mainspring until it is caught by the front trigger and held back, and released again by pulling the front trigger. The small screw between the triggers is the adjustment screw, which controls the amount of engagement between the front and rear triggers, and it is possible to adjust the set trigger mechanism to a very short and light trigger pull.

The upper arms of the double triggers are so arranged that either one can contact the sear lever, hence the rifle can be fired in two ways. One, already described, is to cock the mechanism and then release the cocked trigger so it strikes the sear lever. The second way is to merely pull the front trigger back until it releases the sear. Because of the full sear engagement of the sear with the cocking piece, and because the front trigger must of necessity be placed in a poor leverage position with the sear lever, in firing the rifle by this second method the let-off is usually long, creepy and heavy. However, a good dou-

ble set trigger, properly tuned and adjusted, can have an excellent, crisp let-off when unset.

On most of the M98 sporting rifles which were originally fitted with a double set trigger mechanism, the trigger guard was made with an integral housing to accept the set trigger parts. Most other gunmakers, however, when making sporters on this action usually installed a mechanism contained in its own housing, fitting this unit into the regular trigger guard. These units are generally held in place by two small pins.

Double set trigger mechanisms made for the M98 action are still available today (Brownell, Inc., Paul Jaeger, others). Two types are made; those with a flat mainspring are the better of the two, while another has a U-shaped wire mainspring. Installation is not an easy job, but not beyond the ability of the average home gunsmith who can manage a file. (Incidentally, these mechanisms can also be installed in other bolt actions as well, including the 1903 Springfield, 1917 Enfield and M93 to 96 Mauser actions.)

The Single Set Trigger

A "single set" trigger mechanism is a miniature firing mechanism having the same function as a double set trigger, but it has only one visible trigger. They're usually found on combination rifle/shotgun arms, but they were often used on single shot rifles and pistols as well. Their use on bolt action rifles has been somewhat limited, but many European gunsmiths offered the customer a choice of a double or single set trigger on M98-actioned sporters. In most cases the single set trigger was built in a separate housing and installed into the trigger guard via two pins.

The single set trigger is powered by its own mainspring, the mechanism cocked and released by this trigger, with the trigger becoming the "hammer." To "set" or cock the mechanism the trigger is pushed forward with the tip of the thumb until it is cocked; on being released by pulling it back, the trigger, under mainspring tension, snaps back to strike the sear lever. A small screw behind the trigger allows adjustment to a very light pull. The rifle can also be fired in the normal way without setting the trigger.

Typical German M98 sporter (maker unknown) stocked with a full length "Mannlicher" type fore-end and early type stock with uncapped round-end pistol grip. The action is a military M98a, the barrel made by the Spandau arsenal in Berlin. The barrel is 24″ long, the bolt handle is flat, and the trigger is a single set. (Gilbert Blum collection)

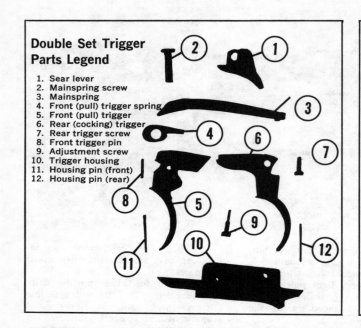

Double Set Trigger Parts Legend

1. Sear lever
2. Mainspring screw
3. Mainspring
4. Front (pull) trigger spring
5. Front (pull) trigger
6. Rear (cocking) trigger
7. Rear trigger screw
8. Front trigger pin
9. Adjustment screw
10. Trigger housing
11. Housing pin (front)
12. Housing pin (rear)

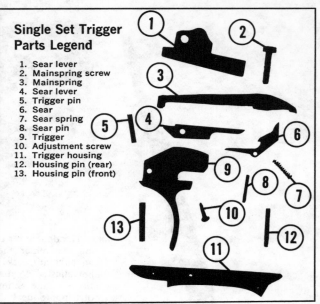

Single Set Trigger Parts Legend

1. Sear lever
2. Mainspring screw
3. Mainspring
4. Sear lever
5. Trigger pin
6. Sear
7. Sear spring
8. Sear pin
9. Trigger
10. Adjustment screw
11. Trigger housing
12. Housing pin (rear)
13. Housing pin (front)

The single set trigger, more intricate and more difficult to make than the DS trigger, is generally not fully as reliable or as trustworthy. The SS trigger cannot usually be adjusted to as light a pull as the DS type. Both are about equally easy to cock and use—provided the shooter is familiar and practiced in their use. The SS trigger is easier and more safely uncocked after having been cocked. Rifles with a SS trigger usually have a better unset trigger pull. This is largely because the SS trigger is placed farther back in the guard, and is easier to reach.

Summary

German sporters are interesting to look at and handle. In suitable calibers they're fine for hunting big game. British style Mausers are excellent for hunting, are generally more comfortable to fire, easier

The two Mauser sporting rifles shown here are excellent examples of German and British gun craftsmanship. The top rifle is a classic Mauser sporter made by J. P. Sauer & Sohn of Suhl, Germany. Its 22″ half-octagon barrel, with raised matted rib, is chambered for the 8x57mm cartridge. The 2¾x Voigtlander scope is carried in typical German detachable claw mounts. Total weight, 8.25 pounds with scope. The bottom rifle is a classic British type sporting rifle made by George Gibbs of London. Chambered for the .404 Nitro-Express, it weighs 9.75 pounds.

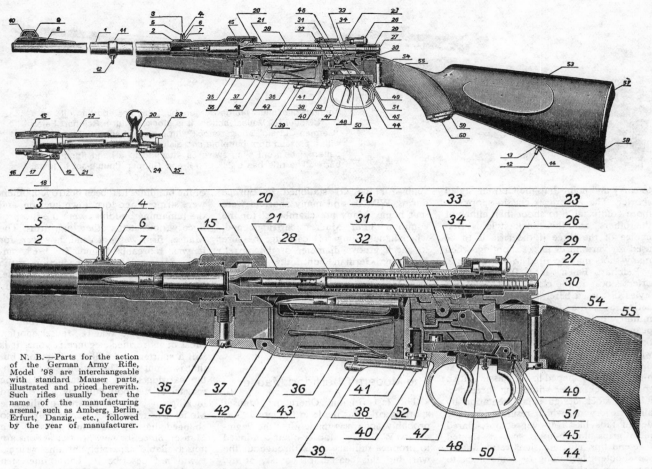

N. B.—Parts for the action of the German Army Rifle, Model '98 are interchangeable with standard Mauser parts, illustrated and priced herewith. Such rifles usually bear the name of the manufacturing arsenal, such as Amberg, Berlin, Erfurt, Danzig, etc., followed by the year of manufacturer.

INDEX OF REPAIR PARTS FOR MAUSER SPORTING RIFLE

		Price				Price				Price
1	Barrel . . . . $25.00 to $40.00		33	Trigger pin	$0.50	64	Bottom plate release spring	$0.50
2	Rear sight base	1.75	34	Sear lever	.80	75	Tangent curve sight base	2.25
3	Standard sight for 100 m	1.75	35	Magazine	10.00	76	Tangent sight leaf	1.75
4	Sight leaf for 200 m	1.00	35a	Magazine for set trigger	10.00	77	Sight slide	1.50
5	Sight leaf for 300 m	1.00	36	Magazine bottom plate	5.00	78	Push button	1.75
6	Sight leaf pin	.25	37	Hinge pin	.50	79	Slide tooth spring	.50
7	Sight leaf spring	.25	38	Magazine lever	1.25	80	Tangent sight leaf spring	.50
8	Front sight block	1.75	39	Locking screw for mag. lever	.25	81	Tangent curve sight base for octagon barrel	2.25
9	Bead sight	1.75	40	Magazine lever screw	.25	81a	Tangent sight complete without base	6.00
10	Sight protector	1.00	41	Locking plate	.75	82	Barrel swivel ring	1.50
11	Swivel ring	1.00	42	Feeder	3.50	83	Wire swivel	.35
12 13 14a	Lower swivel with pin and screw.	1.25	43	Feeder spring	1.25	84	Swivel pin	.10
			44	Set trigger	1.25	85	Stock swivel screw	.50
12 14a	Upper swivel and screw	1.25	45	Set trigger screw	.25	86	Front swivel base with eyelet for octagon barrel	1.50
15a	Receiver	18.50	46	Pull trigger	1.25	87	Front swivel base with stud	1.50
15b	Receiver with telescope fitting . . .	20.00	47	Pull trigger pin	.50	88	Barrel ring with stud	2.50
16	Bolt stop	2.50	48	Pull trigger spring	.50	89	Front swivel base retaining screw.	.75
17	Bolt stop spring	1.75	49	Pull trigger spring screw	.50	90	Washer	.50
18	Ejector	1.25	50	Regulating screw	.50	91	Front sight ramp	3.00
19	Bolt stop screw	.25	51	Set trigger spring	.75	91c	Front sight ramp complete with silver bead sight and sight protector (made in various sizes, see page 19)	5.00
20a	Round bolt	11.50	52	Set trigger spring	2.00			
20b	Flat bolt	12.50	53	Stock . . . . $40.00 and up		92	Barrel swivel ring with ear	2.00
21	Extractor ring	1.75	54	Tube	.50	93	Front swivel for carbine	1.60
22	Extractor	4.00	55	Rear connecting screw	.50	94	Stock rosettes, per pair	.50
23	Bolt plug	6.00	56	Front connecting screw	.50	95	Forend swivel screw	.25
24	Bolt plug stop	1.00	57a	Hard rubber or horn heel plate . .	2.00	96	Steel forend cap for carbine	2.50
25	Bolt plug stop spring	.25	57b	Metal heel plate	2.50	97	Forend cap nut	.25
26	Safety	3.00	57c	Metal heel plate with trap (99-102 complete)	4.00	98	Forend cap screw	.25
27	Firing pin	4.00	58	Heel plate screw	.25	99-102	Steel trap buttplate complete (1 21⁄32 x 5 1⁄16)	6.00
28	Firing pin spring	1.25	59a	Horn grip cap	.50	110	Special take-down cleaning rod . . .	4.50
29	Firing pin nut	3.00	59b	Metal grip cap	.50			
30a	Sear	3.00	60	Grip cap screw	.25			
30b	Sear for trigger	3.00	61	Regulation trigger	2.00			
31	Sear pin	.50	62	Bottom plate release	1.25			
32	Sear spring	.50	63	Bottom plate release screw	.50			

Courtesy Stoeger Arms Corp.

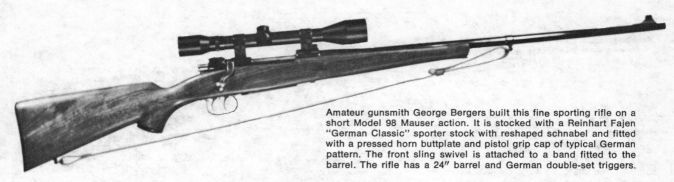

Amateur gunsmith George Bergers built this fine sporting rifle on a short Model 98 Mauser action. It is stocked with a Reinhart Fajen "German Classic" sporter stock with reshaped schnabel and fitted with a pressed horn buttplate and pistol grip cap of typical German pattern. The front sling swivel is attached to a band fitted to the barrel. The rifle has a 24" barrel and German double-set triggers.

to carry and point than the German styled sporter. The American classic sporter is more comfortable to shoot than either of the others, and this stock style is first choice of the three if the rifle is to be used for varmint or target shooting, when many shots may be fired in a short time.

Reinhart Fajen, Inc., Warsaw, Mo., offers stocks in the classic and American styles discussed here. Made for the M98 action, as well as for some other popular military bolt actions, the Fajen "European Special" is a close duplicate of the lightweight German classic sporting stock, while the "Classic Special" patterned after the true American classic sporter stock, may be readily shaped to the classic British sporter stock. After witnessing three decades of stock design experimentation by almost everyone, which resulted in many design fads like roll-over combs, flared pistol grips, thumb-holes, spacers, slanted fore-end tips, etc., etc., it is refreshing to see shooters beginning to come back to the classic designs.

The German sporter was a prized souvenir for the GI stationed in Europe during WW II, and many sporters were sent home. Many are chambered for the common 8mm Mauser cartridge and, when handloading this cartridge be sure to check groove diameter of the barrel, as many German gunsmiths preferred undersized bores. It may be necessary to use .318" 8mm bullets rather than the .323" or "S" bullets. Also, those rifles which have the front scope base deeply dovetailed into the receiver ring should not be subjected to heavy loads, since such receivers have definitely been weakened.

The Modern Oberndorf Mauser

The last original Oberndorf Mauser sporting rifle was made in the late 1930s; probably none was made after the beginning WW II. The Mauser plant continued to produce military arms throughout the war, but this ceased, of course, at the war's end. Then the many thousands of Mauser employees were dispersed. Some of the buildings had been destroyed, others were stripped and torn down later on, and the remaining buildings were used to produce various items other than arms. The Mauser firm was not dead, however, for it was reorganized and, in 1968, announced resumption of production of the Mauser high power turnbolt sporting rifle. The new Mauser sporter is imported by Mauser-Bauer, 34577 Commerce Road, Fraser, Mich. 48026.

This new Mauser is a far cry from the classic pre-World War II Mauser sporter. Most of its former elegance is gone. It is still a sporter, and still a bolt action, but that is about all. The action is a turnbolt, the cartridges are still staggered in the magazine, the bolt still has its forward locking lugs, but all the rest of the true Model 98 features are gone. It is so changed that no one would guess it is a Mauser. Since the new Mauser actions are not available separately at this writing, I will not describe it. Those interested should read the April, 1969, issue of *The American Rifleman.*

Above—Custom rifle built around 1945, maker unknown, on the standard M98 military action. Round, lightweight 24" barrel is a .270, the receiver fitted with claw type scope mount bases. The customized action has a flat bolt handle, quick release floorplate button, shotgun type guard. The extended upper tang carries a sliding safety. Original DS triggers were replaced by an FN single-stage trigger. Receiver, guard and floorplate are engraved. Weight about 7½ lbs.

Below—The latest Mauser-made rifles in conventional turnbolt form are the Models 3000 and 4000. The rifle shown is the M3000, made in several popular sporting calibers. The similar M4000, a varmint rifle, is chambered for the .222 or .223.

19. Mauser 2-Shot Shotgun

NOT TOO MANY years ago I participated in a jackrabbit drive for the sole purpose of getting first-hand information for a magazine article. I don't remember much about the actual hunt except that a small truck load of rabbits was killed by the 75 or so hunters who comprised the group. I remember clearly, however, the wide variety of shotguns these hunters used. Mostly farmers, their shotguns were of every make, model, type and gauge imaginable; from single shots, doubles, pumps and automatics to the "Mauser 2-shot" bolt action—as they are referred to in my section of the country.

I got the chance to see all of their guns as the group assembled for a hot lunch on the grounds of a country school house. A snow fence along the edge of the grounds afforded an excellent stand for the many guns. As the hunters gulped down the hot coffee and doughnuts, I went slowly down the line of guns and, to my amazement, found that about one of every 8 or 10 was a German-made Geha or other make of 2-shot bolt action repeater! I talked to some of the owners of these unusual shotguns and they all insisted their guns were hard hitting and reliable, and that they thought a lot of them, despite the derogatory remarks some noted gun editors had written about them. Some of these guns were marked to assure the user they were indeed hard hitters, for the words **HEART** and **HARD HIT** were pressed into the buttstock.

Their Origin

There were hard times in Germany for a few years, following their defeat in WW I, and the peace treaty forced on them curtailed much of the military arms production on which much of their past economy had been based in good part. They were allowed to make sporting arms which, of course, they continued to do. As I piece the story together, Germany had large quantities of M98 Mauser rifles and/or parts of these rifles on hand, plus facilities to make them. Why not make shotguns from them and dispose of them on the world market at competitive prices? This they did, during the early 1920s, and apparently on a grand scale, if one can judge by the number of guns still around today.

Briefly, the 2-shot Mauser shotgun was made as follows: Starting with an M98 military rifle (or parts), the rifle barrel was removed and discarded. The collar and the locking shoulders in the receiver ring were then bored out from the front and a shotgun barrel fitted. The front of the bolt was bored and a special bolt head fitted. Various other things were then done to the action and magazine so it would accept and handle shotshells, such as installing a shell stop and guide, replacing the magazine follower and ejector, and altering the extractor, magazine and other parts, including remodeling the military stock. The result was a handy, lightweight and low-cost bolt action repeating shotgun.

Description

I have seen many of these German-made M98 rifle-to-shotgun conversions in the last 35 years and, while I've noted a number of variations, they're all about the same as the Geha 12-gauge model pictured here. Most were 12 gauge, the weight about 6 pounds. Some were 16 gauge, and a very few were 20s. All were chambered for 2¾" shells. The steel barrels, usually 26.5" long, were full choked. The magazine held one shell, thus with a cartridge in the chamber one had a 2-shot repeater. The front sight is a brass bead threaded into the muzzle; a small U-groove milled along the top of the receiver ring formed the rear sight. A steel butt-plate, turned-down bolt handle and a single stage trigger pull were also common features. The stocks are usually solid walnut (not laminated or two-piece) cut down from the original military stock and oil finished, with the metal parts polished and blued. The breech end of the barrel is usually stamped with a proof mark and the word **NITRO,** indicating proof testing for smokeless loads. **GERMANY** in small type is usually stamped on the receiver ring.

Most of these I've seen were of the Geha brand, usually having two large brass medallions marked **GEHA,** (one on each side) inletted into the sides of the buttstock. These replaced the original metal firing-pin disassembly tool found in the original military stock. There are supposedly similar shotguns marked **GECO,** a brand name of Gustav Genschow & Co., A.G., formerly of Berlin, but I've never examined one. The only other brand I've seen was the Remo, discussed later in this chapter.

Some Geha-marked guns have the word **BAYARD** stamped under the breech end of the barrel or receiver. Pieper of Belgium made a Bayard automatic pistol, but so far I have no information which would connect this firm with the Geha guns, or even why the word "Bayard" was used.

Action Details

The regular large-ring M98 Mauser military action was used in making these shotgun conversions. Basic features which are unchanged or only slightly so are the trigger and firing mechanism, safety, bolt stop and ejector, extractor and trigger guard.

The front of the bolt is faced off and the firing-pin hole bored out to accept the new shotshell bolt head. The later is machined with a stem to fit into the bored out bolt, its face only slightly larger than

---

Illustrated above: German-made Geha 2-shot shotgun, once available in 12, 16 and 20 gauges. Many were imported and sold in the U.S. after WW I. These shotguns are based on a converted M98 Mauser military action. Those marked Geco are almost the same as the Geha.

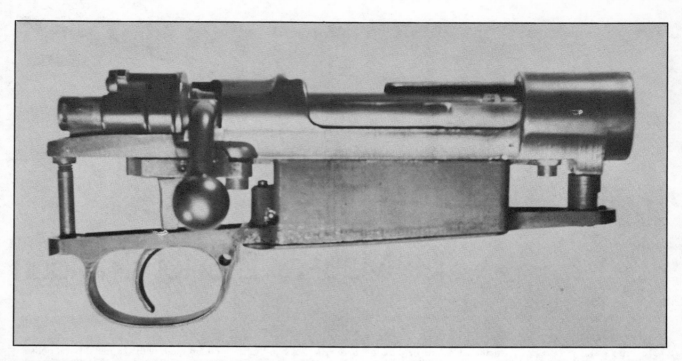

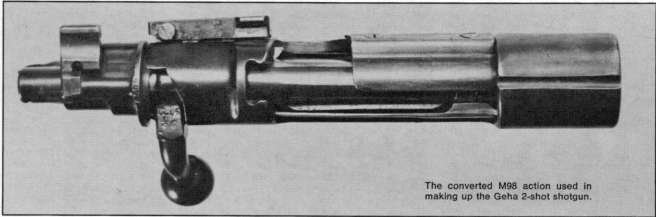

The converted M98 action used in making up the Geha 2-shot shotgun.

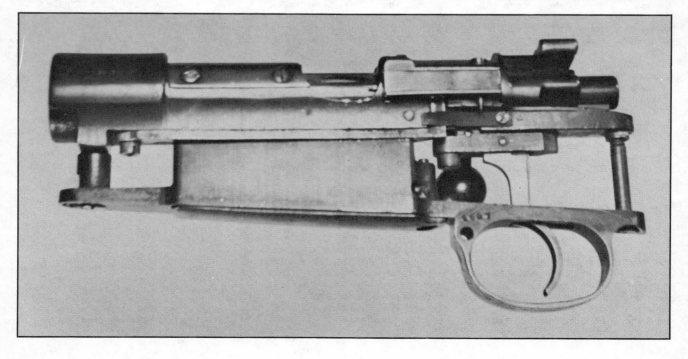

Parts Legend

1. Receiver (top view)
2. Bolt stop
3. Bolt stop screw
4. Bolt stop/Ejector spring
5. Bolt head*
6. Ejector
7. Sear spring
8. Sear pin
9. Sear
10. Trigger
11. Trigger pin
12. Extractor collar
13. Extractor
14. Bolt
15. Firing pin
16. Mainspring
17. Cocking piece
18. Bolt sleeve
19. Bolt sleeve lock
20. Bolt sleeve lock spring
21. Safety
22. Follower
23. Follower spring
24. Trigger guard/magazine
25. Magazine floorplate
26. Floorplate catch
27. Floorplate catch spring
28. Floorplate catch pin
29. Front guard screw
30. Front guard screw lock screw
31. Rear guard screw
32. Rear guard screw lock screw
33. Shell stop*
34. Shell stop screw*
35. Shell guide*
36. Shell guide screws (2)*
37. Shell stop spring*
38. Shell stop spring screw*

*These are the parts added to the M98 Mauser action when it was converted to handle shotshells.

the head of the shotshell to be used. On the left of the removable bolt head a slight forward extension aids in holding the shell in place for proper extraction and ejection. The extractor hook is altered and shortened to a dull V-point which engages a matching V-groove in the right of the bolt head. This holds the bolt head in the bolt. A short extractor hook added to the front of the extractor engages the shotshell rim.

The receiver is bored out from the front to a diameter slightly larger than the bolt head for whatever gauge it is made, and bored rearward to a point about ½″ into the receiver bridge. When made for a 12-gauge shotshell this boring removes almost all of the metal of the collar and locking

shoulder in the receiver ring, as well as considerable metal from the receiver rails and sidewall. Even in the 16- and 20-gauge conversions, enough metal is removed from the locking shoulder areas so that the original forward locking lugs no longer function. This job is taken over by the auxiliary, or safety, lug on the rear of the bolt body engaging its notch in the bottom of the receiver bridge. In the 20-gauge there may be enough metal left in the receiver ring for the locking lugs to gain a little purchase, but in the 12s and 16s the rear safety lug is the only thing which locks and holds the bolt in the receiver when the gun is fired.

A longer ejector replaces the original, and it functions in the same manner.

A new flat-topped sheet metal magazine follower is used, and provision is made so that it cannot be pushed too far down or rise too high to interfere with the bolt. The top left edge of the magazine box is cut away for a long shell stop attached to the underside of the receiver, which pivots on a screw threaded into the receiver ring. The rear end of the shell stop extends through a hole milled in the left of the receiver bridge, and is activated by an inclined mill-cut in the left locking lug when the bolt is drawn entirely back. Only one shell can be pressed into the magazine, and it is retained therein until released by the shell stop.

Another shell stop or guide is provided to halt the upward motion of a shell being

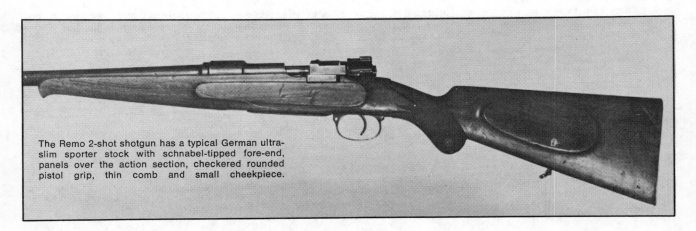

The Remo 2-shot shotgun has a typical German ultra-slim sporter stock with schnabel-tipped fore-end, panels over the action section, checkered rounded pistol grip, thin comb and small cheekpiece.

released from the magazine. This shell stop, a piece of curved sheet metal screwed to the left receiver wall extends over the top of the bolt.

Remo 2-Shot Shotgun

For many years I was not aware of any other Mauser 2-shot shotguns, but then I was shown the Remo shotgun pictured here, and now in the NRA Gun Museum. It is so different from the usual Geha shotgun that I don't believe it to be entirely a conversion, but rather partly or entirely manufactured as a shotgun. As the photographs show, there's the distinctly continental-type sporting rifle stock on the Remo, and the receiver does not appear to be a conversion, either. The shell stop is an integral part of the receiver, not a piece of sheet metal as on the Geha. The rest of the Remo action is more or less the same as the Geha, except for a feature or two that make the action work better. The Remo guns were made by Remo Gewehrfabrik, Gebrüder Rempt of Suhl, Germany. I assume they were also made in the 1920s, perhaps in the 1930s as well, and most likely in 12, 16 and 20 gauge.

Evaluation

I have never heard a good word spoken for the 2-shot Mauser shotguns except by their owners. Most experts generally have a low opinion of them. Mention is always made that only the single safety lug locks the bolt and that if this lug should fail the shooter will get the bolt in his face.

For myself, I have never heard of, or ever seen one of these shotguns in which the locking lug failed — and I know men who have used them for years, firing many heavy duck and rifled slug loads in them. This is not to say that I advise firing these shotguns with heavy loads or even with regular loads, but I cannot imagine the safety lug shearing off. I believe the receiver side rails would break or part first. I've also asked many people well acquainted with these guns if they ever saw one that had failed or blown-up, and none of them had.

The poorest feature of this action is the separate bolt head. Its flange is quite thin and easily broken. The two thin extensions on the left of the flange break off easily, and without them fired cases will not be ejected properly. The bolt head is not positively anchored to the bolt, and it is

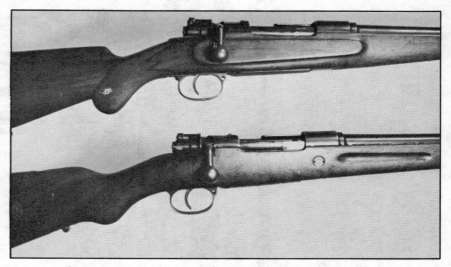

Comparison views of the Remo (top) shotgun with the common Geha.

easily lost if it pops out. Most of these shotguns I've seen for sale lack the bolt head. They are then positively dangerous as they can be fired in this condition, which, incidentally, results in considerable fireworks spurting out of the action! The seller of such a gun has a moral obligation to advise the prospective buyer that the bolt head is missing. I believe some of the stories that have been told about these guns "blowing up" may well have been about guns without the bolt head, not because of some basic failure of the action or barrel.

Comments

A few years ago, before any arms makers had introduced the special rifled slug guns which are so popular today, several hunters talked with me about converting their Gehas into slug guns. One hunter did this by shortening the barrel to 22″, installing a raised rib on the barrel, a front sight on a ramp, a receiver rear sight, and refinishing the stock. It turned out to be a fast-handling, accurate gun.

My ideas along this line go a bit further. I'd want to strengthen the receiver and I would want a low-power scope. I would select the mount and attach it in such a manner that it would greatly strengthen the receiver. For example, by using a one-piece bridge type mount such as the Buehler, and permanently attaching it to the

receiver via screws and silver solder, there would be much less chance that the rear of the receiver would part from the front section. Then, to strengthen the receiver even more, I'd silver solder a strip of steel on the outside of the receiver rails. Since the bolt handle would have to be altered anyway, I would change it so that its base would become a second locking lug, working in a notch cut into the tang. These three things would certainly make this action fully as strong as any of the American-made bolt action shotguns. This done, we can go whole hog by installing a low scope safety, or an adjustable single-stage trigger with side safety, and put the barrel and action into a Bishop or Fajen sporter stock. Of course, I don't believe such a project is at all practical since almost any modern shotgun would be a better choice, but if you want a rifled slug gun to match that Mauser sporter you have, then I see nothing wrong with the idea.

From the above the reader can see that I am not in full accord with the many gun experts who rate these guns as pure junk. I'm not going out on a limb, however, and say that these shotguns are safe to fire — but, as mentioned before, I have never seen one that failed, or ever heard of an authentic case where one failed. Therefore, if you have one of these shotguns, you will have to make up your mind about its safety, whether it is junk or not, or whatever.

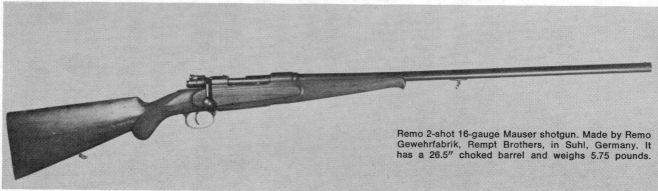

Remo 2-shot 16-gauge Mauser shotgun. Made by Remo Gewehrfabrik, Rempt Brothers, in Suhl, Germany. It has a 26.5″ choked barrel and weighs 5.75 pounds.

20. Mauser Miscellany

Erma .22 Rimfire Conversion Unit

LUGER FANS have long been familiar with the Erma .22 rimfire conversion unit made for that pistol. Not so well known, however, is the .22 Long Rifle conversion unit this firm (Erma-Werke in Germany) made for the M98 rifle. I believe this unit was made in the 1920s and '30s but, although this firm is still in business in West Germany, I don't think they have made this unit since WW II. The conversion unit illustrated here is unmarked (except for serial numbers and proof marks), but I believe, and several other Mauser fans agree with me, that this is the Erma unit.

This, or a similar conversion unit, was also used by the military in Germany for training purposes. It was called the "Model 24 Insert Barrel." It was most likely first made as a single shot, then as a repeater later on. These were probably by Erma.

This conversion unit has the basic mechanical components of a rifle — a complete action and barrel assembly but minus sights, trigger and stock. The action is a turnbolt, the cartridges fed into it from a detachable box magazine. Only the bolt and floorplate/follower assemblies must be removed from the M98 rifle for the unit to be installed. It was made primarily to be used in any 8mm M98 military rifle or carbine having a barrel at least 24" long, but it can also be used in 8mm Mauser sporting rifles with similar length barrels.

The receiver of this unit fits in the receiver of the M98 in place of the regular bolt. The main length of the barrel is only slightly smaller than the land diameter of the 8mm barrel, so it fits snugly in the bore. The breech end of the barrel is the size and shape of the chamber. On the breech end there is a collar and, between this collar and the receiver, there is a two-piece threaded adjustable sleeve arrange-

ment. One part of this sleeve has two lugs which can be rotated to engage in the locking lug recesses in the M98 receiver. When the unit is inserted into the M98 the outer sleeve with its lugs is turned clockwise to engage the lugs in the receiver, then the inner sleeve is turned clockwise to secure the unit in the rifle. Holes are provided in both outer and inner sleeves so that they can be turned with a tool, such as a nail with its point filed off.

The front part of the unit's receiver has two openings; one at the bottom for the magazine, one on the top right for the ejection port. The rear part of the receiver, larger than the main part, is made to fit in the larger opening in the M98 receiver and over the top of the tang. This prevents the entire unit from turning in the receiver. The barrel is attached to the receiver with two cross pins.

The bolt has three main parts; the two-diameter bolt body, which contains the long extractor and separate firing pin; the bolt handle sleeve, which threads into the rear end of the bolt body, and the firing mechanism composed of striker, mainspring, cocking piece, safety and striker nut. A slot is milled in the thick rear part of the receiver for the bolt handle, and a notch cut in this slot for the base of the bolt handle to lock the bolt in the receiver when the bolt is closed. The bolt stop is merely a shoulder in the rear zig-zag slot for the bolt handle.

The cocking piece has a projection which extends through a narrow slot in the bottom of the receiver and into the cocking cam raceway in the M98 receiver to engage the sear. The striker is cocked entirely on the closing motion of the bolt. When the action is cocked, the wing safety can be rotated down to engage over the end of the receiver.

The detachable 5-shot box magazine is well made. The milled follower is guided inside the magazine by its rounded front end moving in a cylindrical guideway built into the front of the magazine. The coil magazine spring is positioned in this

cylinder. The magazine is precisely and securely held in position through a hole in the floorplate, inside of which is attached a sheet metal guide housing. A notched flat spring attached to the right side of the magazine holds the magazine up when the notch engages over the edge of the floorplate. The bottom of the magazine and its release spring project below the magazine floorplate so that it can be easily grasped and removed.

The unit illustrated here is very well made, fitted and finished, and all the major parts are numbered.

To install the unit in an M98 rifle, remove the bolt assembly, floorplate, follower and follower spring. Turn the locking sleeve on the Erma unit so the hole in the rear part of this sleeve is up, then insert the unit into the receiver and barrel as far as it will go. Pull the trigger or open the bolt of the unit so it will stay forward. Now rotate the locking sleeve ¼-turn clockwise until the locking sleeve can be turned. When the locking sleeve is engaged turn the adjustment sleeve clockwise until tight. Install the floorplate, slip in the magazine and the rifle is ready to fire.

I fired the conversion unit shown here at an indoor 50-foot range, using standard velocity .22 Long Rifle ammunition. Taking a fine bead over the crude military sights on the M98a carbine in which this unit was fitted, and with the rear sight elevated to the 600 meter setting, the shots zeroed perfectly in the target. Considering the crude sights, accuracy was quite good, suitable for plinking and small game at close range. The unit functioned perfectly and there were no feeding, ignition or extraction problems.

These Erma conversion units are seldom seen today, but they're an interesting extra for any Mauser rifle collection.

Illustrated above: The model 98 Mauser .22 rimfire conversion unit installed in a WW I M98a carbine. (Gilbert Blum collection).

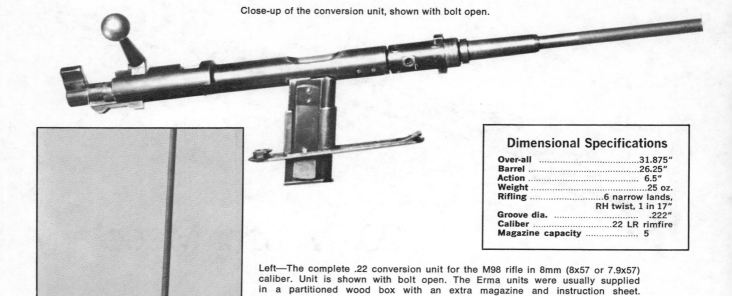

Close-up of the conversion unit, shown with bolt open.

Left—The complete .22 conversion unit for the M98 rifle in 8mm (8x57 or 7.9x57) caliber. Unit is shown with bolt open. The Erma units were usually supplied in a partitioned wood box with an extra magazine and instruction sheet.

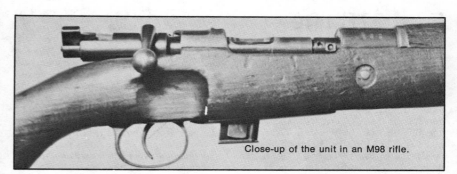

Close-up of the unit in an M98 rifle.

Mauser M98 Breech Cover

ONE OF THE RAREST accessories ever made for the M98 military rifle was a breech cover. During the early part of WW I the Germans discovered that their M98 was not as foolproof as it could have been. The main fault showed up when the rifle was used in all sorts of battle and weather conditions — in mud-filled trenches, on dusty, sand swept battle grounds, or in freezing rain. Then it could become inoperative, or its operation affected, by the entry of foreign material into the action.

Among the several openings in the M98 where foreign material could easily enter, the largest is the thumb notch in the receiver wall, which exposes the left locking lug raceway. This opening is large enough, front and rear, to allow foreign matter to enter the locking lug recess in the front of the receiver and even go inside the bolt, through the two large gas escape holes, and rearward into the bolt stop and ejector openings. Other openings, especially during rain and freezing weather, are the clip guide slot in the bridge, the space between the bolt sleeve and bridge which exposes

both ends of the bolt guide groove, and the space between the extractor and bolt. The problem was evidently considered serious enough to warrant development and manufacture of a breech cover to shield these openings.

Unlike the Type 38 and 99 Arisaka military rifles, whose actions were initially designed for a sliding cover, the M98 action was not so designed, and a cover had to be made to fit it. This was accomplished, as shown in the illustrations. The cover was so constructed that it could be easily attached to the unaltered Gew-98 rifle with the straight bolt handle. Although it was a sort of make-shift affair, the cover did effectively shroud the greater part of the action.

This breech cover consists of two main parts; the cover, and the clip by which the assembly is attached to the rifle. These two parts are attached to each other by a telescoping hinge joint, so the cover will open and close with the bolt.

The clip is made from a piece of wide spring-tempered steel. The top of this clip encircles the exposed top part of the breech end of the barrel, between the rear sight and barrel shoulder, then extends over the left and underside of the fore-end. It is made with enough spring tension so it is not easily unsnapped from the rifle, once it has been pressed into place.

The cover, which is also made of spring-tempered sheet steel, is accurately formed

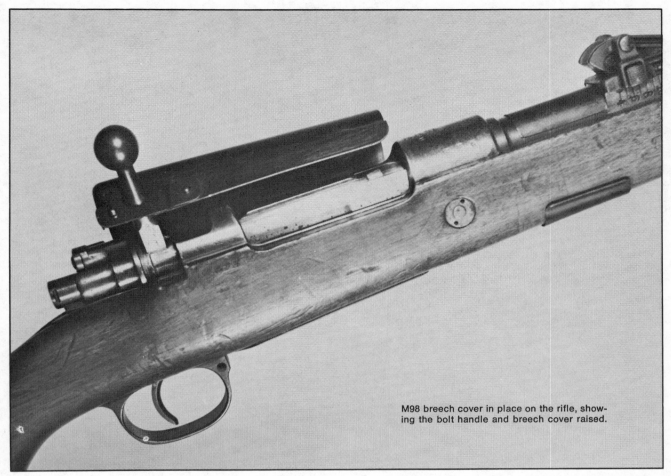

M98 breech cover in place on the rifle, showing the bolt handle and breech cover raised.

to enclose most of the top of the action. It extends from the rear of the receiver ring to just forward of the safety, and is wide enough to cover the top of the receiver ring and run over the edge of the stock. It's wider at the rear to cover the entire bolt stop, bridge, the flared part of the bolt sleeve and the root of the bolt handle. The rear end of the cover is turned inward and cut out to conform to and contact the contoured surface of the bolt sleeve. The rear right side of the cover is notched to fit over the bolt handle, and a simple spring bar latch, fastened at the edge of the cover over the notch, loosely fastens the cover to the bolt handle.

The critical part of the breech cover assembly is the telescopic hinge on the left side. The outer part of this hinge is a steel tube securely fastened to the left of the clip. This tube extends about halfway back on the cover. A long thin spring rod, rolled into the rear left bottom edge of the cover, extends forward into the tube to complete the telescopic hinge, allowing the cover to open and close and slide backward and forward as the bolt is operated.

When the breech cover is in place, and the action closed, it effectively encloses the main part of the action, protecting it against the entrance of foreign material. The cover in no way interferes with the normal operation of the safety, and when the action is open it does not obstruct loading the magazine in any way. On opening the action, however, the cover rises on the bolt handle stem and this makes it necessary for the shooter to grasp only the ball of the bolt when the action is operated.

The breech cover is readily removed by first releasing the bar latch under the bolt handle stem, swinging open the cover and drawing it to the rear to separate it from the clip. The clip can then be removed by pressing the underside of the clip to the left, until it separates from the fore-end.

Apparently the breech covers were not widely used since they are scarce today. Perhaps they were not developed and made early enough to be used before WW I ended, or maybe the cover wasn't entirely successful.

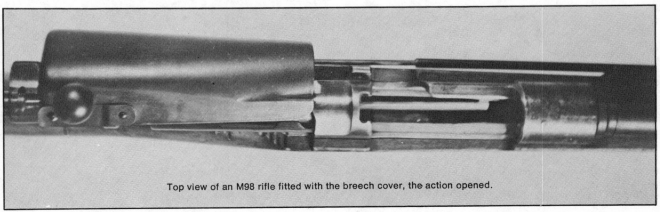

Top view of an M98 rifle fitted with the breech cover, the action opened.

NOTES

21. Modern FN Mausers

FOR A NUMBER of years Stoeger Arms imported genuine Oberndorf made Model 98 actions into the U.S. These were fine actions — no question about that — but they were highly priced. For example, in 1939 Stoeger listed the lowest priced M98 action at $70, while in the same catalog the standard grade complete M70 Winchester rifle was only $61.25. Obviously the customer was paying very dearly for that "Mauser banner" stamped on the receiver. However, by this time Germany was deeply involved in making war, and her arms plants were turning out nothing but military weapons. So, Stoeger had to turn elsewhere.

Fabrique Nationale (FN for short, the same firm which makes Browning pistols, rifles and shotguns) in Liége, Belgium, was and is a very large arms making plant. For many years they had been making various models of Mauser rifles, including many thousands based on the M98. When Stoeger could no longer get original Mausers they turned to FN, and the FN Mauser action was announced in Stoeger's 1941 catalog. Calling it their "Stoeger Peerless Action," it was only $18, unbelievably low, even then.

The Peerless action was nothing other than the standard M98 military action, as made by FN, except that the magazine was made to handle .30-06 length cartridges and the bolt handle was bent down sharply at its root. It was described as being made of high grade steel, properly hardened, well polished and blued, except for the bolt parts which were left bright. It was the large ring type with the thumb slot in the receiver wall, clip-charger guideways in the receiver bridge and the standard double-stage military trigger.

When I received the 1941 Stoeger's catalog, I remember that I quickly ordered one FN action, but my money was refunded. No wonder, for German troops invaded Belgium in May of 1940 and Stoeger's supply was most likely cut off before it started. Stoeger's 1942 catalog did not list these actions.

A couple of years after the close of WW II, the FN 98 actions appeared again. This time it was imported by Firearms International of Washington, D.C. I found the first announcement of it in the November, 1947, issue of *The American Rifleman*. It was called the "1947 FN Mauser" action, but except for its very low profile bolt handle, it was the same as the FN action offered by Stoeger in 1941.

FN Action Improvements

Here was an action that gunsmiths had long been seeking, although it still had a number of features retained from the military action. But, as FI announced in their 1947 ad, changes would be made on it in accordance with the wishes of the American shooter. This was done as will be seen.

In January, 1948, it was announced that the following changes had already been adopted: 1) bolt handle knob partly checkered; 2) trigger changed to a single pull, no-slack let-off; 3) a new type of floorplate quick-release plunger for instant removal; and 4) the thumb slot was eliminated. This last item was the major and most important improvement, since it made the receiver much more rigid.

By May, 1948, the action could be ordered fitted with a double-set trigger mechanism. By fall of 1948 the action was further improved by having a new low scope safety, and the receiver bridge was modified by eliminating the raised portion and the clip-charger slot. Tapping the receiver for a receiver sight and/or a scope mount was also started at this time, though the bridge was not tapped. Up to this time these actions were made for the standard .30-06 length and head-sized cartridges. By the end of 1948 FN barreled actions were offered in .30-06 and .270 calibers, as were complete FN Mauser de luxe rifles and, by the end of 1949, calibers included the .257 Roberts, .250-3000 Savage and .300 Savage. Within a short time two other calibers were added; 7mm Mauser and .220 Swift.

The actions for these different calibers were all alike except that a sheet-metal filler block was fitted in the rear of the magazine box, along with a shortened follower and spring, for the .257 Roberts and the shorter cartridges. The first FN barrels had an unusual "stepped" contour, but this changed in 1952 when the FN smooth-contoured, lightweight barrel was introduced.

The FN Magnum action, introduced early in 1953, was made to handle the then two most popular magnum cartridges, the .300 and .375 H&H Magnums. This "magnum" action was nothing other than the standard .30-06 length FN, but with the magazine box extended in front, the feed ramp altered to accept the 3.60″ long magnum cartridges, and the bolt head and extractor opened up for the head of the belted case. FN engraved actions were also made available at about this time.

An important development in the FN Mauser action came in 1955 when the "bench rest" action was announced. This was a single shot action, the solid bottom receiver minus any magazine-well cuts. The trigger guard was merely made with a long forward strap or tang through which the front guard screw passed. The BR action was made to handle three different sizes of cartridge heads; .222, .30-06 or belted magnum case-head sizes, with the bolt face and extractor altered appropriately.

As soon as the various scope mount makers began standardizing the hole spacing in their mounts, FN began tapping the top of the bridge of all of their actions so that these mounts could be easily and quickly installed.

When new factory cartridges were developed, such as the .243, .308 and .244, the FN line was promptly extended to include them. It was also extended to include the .458, .264, 7mm and .300 Magnums. Then, as some of these cartridges

---

Illustrated above: FN Supreme Mauser rifle.

fell into disfavor with shooters, they were dropped from the FN line-up. At present (1971) FN rifles and barreled actions are available only in the following calibers: .243, .270, 7mm, .308, .30-06, 7mm Magnum, .300 Magnum and .264 Magnum. FN actions alone remain available.

Around 1957 the standard FN action became the FN De luxe action, and a new action was introduced called the Series 300. The new action incorporated the following improvements and changes: a streamlined bolt sleeve, made without the safety; an adjustable, single-stage trigger which included a right-side sliding-tang safety, and an all-steel hinged-floorplate magazine. This was a fine modern action and, within a short time, the "Series 300" name was changed to "FN Supreme." By 1964 the FN De luxe model was dropped, with only the Supreme actions, barreled actions and rifles remaining. To replace the De luxe types a new model was introduced, called the Musketeer, but these actions were not offered separately.

A Quality Action

FN actions are made to the usual exacting FN quality, a quality so outstanding that no one should question it. I don't know what steel is used in the receiver and bolts of these actions, but you can be sure that the best available steel is used, and that the various parts are properly hardened for the work they do. Like the usual M98 military action, the FN receiver depends more on its design for strength than on special steels or heat treatments. The FN receiver is probably made of a top quality, low-carbon steel and surface hardened, which results in a very tough receiver, one that will "give" under extreme stresses but will not shatter. The FN bolt is much harder than the receiver, especially in the area of the locking lugs.

FN actions are finished and furnished in the "white," that is, not blued but with the metal in its natural bright state after machining and polishing. The bolt, bolt sleeve, cocking piece and a few other small parts are usually polished very highly, and need no further polishing. The bolt stop and bolt-stop spring often have a light "heat" blued finish. At first, the receivers were usually finished polished, but the later ones are not completely finished and usually require further polishing before being blued. This also applies to the trigger guard and floorplate, except for the inside of the trigger guard bow which is seldom factory polished at all.

Markings

Every FN action is subjected to a proof test in the Belgian government proof house. Only actions which pass this test are proof marked and sold, with the usual final Belgian proof stamped on the receiver ring. Most FN actions I have observed also have **MADE IN BELGIUM** stamped on the lower part of the receiver. There are usually some inspector's-marks stamped on the bottom of the receiver also.

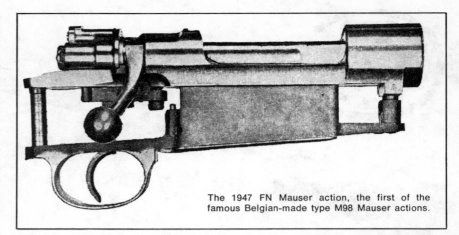
The 1947 FN Mauser action, the first of the famous Belgian-made type M98 Mauser actions.

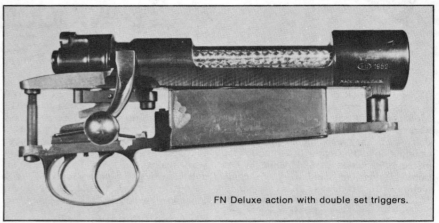
FN Deluxe action with double set triggers.

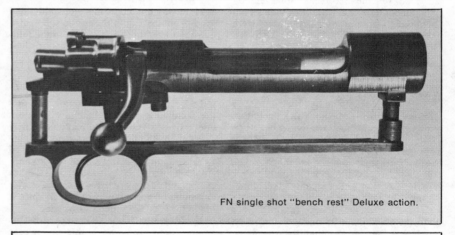
FN single shot "bench rest" Deluxe action.

FN Series 400 or Supreme action.

FN Musketeer sporter.

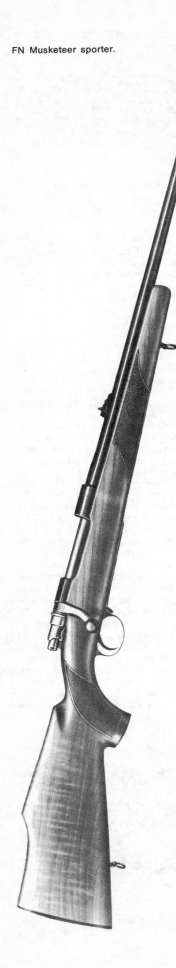

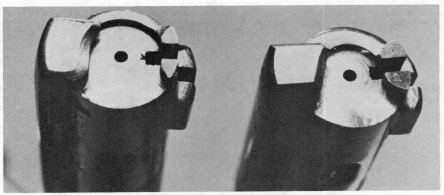

FN Mauser bolt heads: left, .30-06; right, .222.

Early FN Mauser actions usually had the large FN monogram impressed on the receiver ring, as well as having the factory name and address stamped on the left receiver wall. Later on these markings were omitted, with only the letters **FN** within a small circle stamped on the side of the receiver ring. The date (year) of manufacture was also stamped on the early actions.

To my knowledge, the separate FN actions were not serial numbered, nor were the parts of the action numbered in any way.

FN Action Details

The modern FN action is, to describe it briefly, merely a modernized M98 military action. FN had a lot of experience in making the latter type, including .30-06 rifles, and the commercial FN action is a natural result of this activity. Like the military action, the sporting version is perhaps the world's most popular and widely used centerfire turnbolt action.

Apart from the changes previously noted, the FN action has all the basic features of the military action. It has the Mauser "large ring" receiver with the internal collar, the same barrel threads, the same bolt with its two forward locking lugs and the third safety lug, the same bolt guide rib, the same extractor, the

same firing mechanism and the same trigger guard and magazine. The fact is that practically all FN action parts are interchangeable with the standard 98 military action. Current FN actions reveal features that only skilled custom gunsmiths formerly built into military actions. Therefore, to describe in detail the construction and functioning of the FN action would be merely to repeat the information given in the chapter on the Model 98 Mauser action.

When FN actions became available it was no longer sensible to have a military M98 action completely remodeled. This sort of works was, and is now, only practical if you can do the work yourself, or if you don't care what it costs.

FN Action Users

Although several new high power turnbolt actions have been introduced since the advent of the FN action, and other commercial bolt actions have been made available to gunsmiths, the FN action appears to be still the most popular choice for rifle building. One of the first large scale custom rifle makers to adopt the FN action was Roy Weatherby of South Gate, California. They used these actions almost exclusively for their expensive custom rifles in the standard and Weatherby Magnum calibers until 1958, when they

Looking into the front of M98 (left) and FN Mauser receivers. The M98 shows the inside collar cut out for the extractor; typical of all M98 military actions and early FN actions. The FN receiver has the collar cut out in two places, opposite the normal extractor cut-out. This is typical of all late FN actions, including magnum and bench rest types.

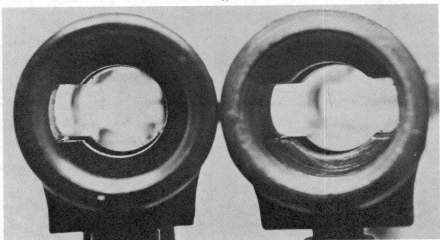

Original 98 Mauser single shot target rifle, chambered for the 8.15x46R cartridge.

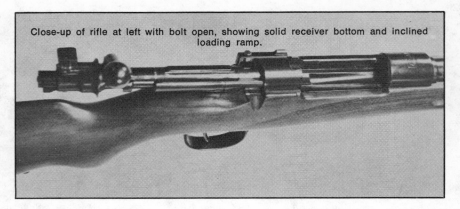

Close-up of rifle at left with bolt open, showing solid receiver bottom and inclined loading ramp.

introduced their own bolt action. That Weatherby chose to use the FN action was probably the very best endorsement that could be given it. The fact that the FN action did not prove entirely satisfactory for some of the very long Weatherby Magnum cartridges was not the fault of the action, as we shall see later.

Other custom rifle makers also adopted the FN action for much of their trade, including such well known names as Paul Jaeger, P.O. Ackley and Keith Stegall. Even more noteworthy is that several large gun-making firms also chose the FN actions on which to build rifles bearing their firm names.

As already mentioned, FN makes rifles on these actions. The Browning firm, which is associated with FN, also makes several fine grades of high power rifles on the slightly modified version of the FN action. A number of other firms made (or are still making) rifles on these actions, including Sako, Parker-Hale, Colt, Marlin, High Standard, Winslow, Harrington & Richardson and others. No bolt action could have a more distinguished endorsement than the wide use of the FN.

Receiver Ring Collar

FN actions were made at first with the full inside collar, just as in the M98 military action, with the collar slotted on the right side for the extractor. At some point FN began to fudge and, thereafter, slotted the collar on the left as well, leaving only partial collars top and bottom. This was done for one reason only—to make milling the left locking lug raceway much easier. I feel this was an unwise move,

and that Paul Mauser would think the same. Although I have no solid evidence to indicate that dividing the collar has affected the strength or safety of the action, I would certainly rather have the collar remain as Mauser designed it.

Trigger and Safety

The original trigger furnished with the FN De luxe actions was nothing more than a double-stage military trigger, modified to a single-stage pull. A poor trigger set-up at best, it would do if one didn't mind a long and heavy pull. Most owners of rifles built on this action soon replaced this poor trigger with one of the several commercial single-stage adjustable triggers on the market, such as the Mashburn, Timney or Jaeger, or with a set trigger.

When the Series 300 or FN Supreme action was announced a new trigger was introduced with it. This was the Sako No. 4 trigger, which is described in detail in the chapter on the Sako actions. This trigger, fitted with a side safety, was used on the Supreme action, and fitted without the safety on the De luxe action.

This trigger underwent unimportant minor changes at first. It had provisions for limited adjustment of weight of pull, and a trigger-stop adjustment, but it was cheaply made, and many proved unsatisfactory. It used a plunger type sear arrangement, which required that it be well lubricated for proper functioning, which caused malfunctions in very cold weather.

The FN De luxe action had the conventional M98 bolt sleeve, which was fitted with a very rugged low scope safety. The safety lever was to the left of the bolt

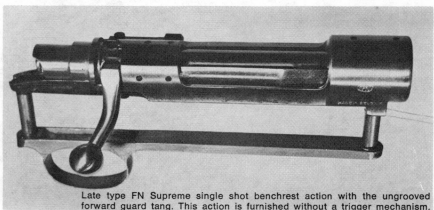

Late type FN Supreme single shot benchrest action with the ungrooved forward guard tang. This action is furnished without a trigger mechanism.

The author's personal long range varmint rifle is based on the FN Deluxe No. 6 single shot benchrest action, with a No. 4 Sako trigger. The 25″ medium-weight Douglas Supreme barrel, rifling twist 1:12″, is chambered for the .244 Remington. The fine curly maple stock is fitted with a Niedner-type checkered steel buttplate and pistol grip cap. The scope is a 1½″ Unertl 16x target scope. This rifle weighs 11.5 pounds and is extremely accurate even with factory 6mm 100-gr loads.

sleeve and, when swung up, the safety locked both sear and bolt. I consider this a very convenient and reliable safety, and preferred it to any other safety ever made for the Mauser action. Most shooters, however, did not like this safety for one reason or another. The Supreme action has a low rounded bolt sleeve minus any provision for a safety, but with the safety built into the trigger mechanism. Early ones had a pivoting type safety lever, later versions had a sliding type lever; both had the serrated button exposed above the stock line on the right of the receiver tang. With the safety to the rear, trigger and bolt would be locked. Because some intricate milling is required on the receiver and bolt for this safety, the No. 4 Sako trigger with the safety cannot be easily installed on the FN De luxe or M98 actions.

FN Action Numbers

Below is a listing of the various numbers of the FN actions as shown in the Firearms International catalog at the time of this writing (1969):

Action No.	For Calibers	Magazine Length
1	30-06, 270, 7 MM, 8 MM, etc.	3⅜″
2	308, 243, 244, etc.	2⅞″
3	22-250, 250, 257	2¾″
4	220 S	2¼″
5	300, 375 MAG.	3⅝″
BR No. 6	222*	—
BR No. 6	30-06*	—
BR No. 6	MAGNUM*	—
7	458, 338, 264, etc.	3⅜″

* Supplied without trigger.

NOTE: all of these actions are the same length (8¾″), since all are based on the same receiver, and all are about the same weight (2¾ lbs.). I'll put down some comments on the different action numbers:

No. 1: The standard or basic action, suitable for all cartridges of .30-06 head-size and approximate length. This is also the action to choose for any of the following cartridges: .240 Weatherby Magnum. .280 Remington. Wildcat cartridges based on the .30-06 size case such as the .25-06, .30-06 Improved and .35 Whelen. The .244, 6mm or .257 Roberts, if these are to be used with long and heavy bullets, in a deep throated chamber.

No. 2: Identical with the No. 1 except for a folded sheet-metal spacer riveted in the rear of the magazine box, along with a shorter magazine follower and follower spring. Use with all .30-06 head-sized cartridges having a length between 2.75″ and 2.875″. Use for the .284 and .358 Winchester cartridges.

No. 3: Same action as No. 2 but with the spacer positioned farther forward, shortening the magazine opening to 2.75″. Use for the .22-250, 6mm International and similar short cartridges of .30-06 head size.

No. 4: Like Nos. 2 and 3 actions except for a sheet metal spacer in *front* of the magazine box, with both rear and front spacers angled slightly to the rear. Since the .220 Swift cartridge has a semi-rimmed head this magazine generally prevents incorrect loading of the magazine so that the rim of one cartridge cannot easily over-ride another. This action is also ideal for the .225 Winchester cartridge.

No. 5: This is the FN Magnum action, the front of the magazine box lengthened and the feed ramp cut to accept the long belted .300 H&H and .375 H&H Magnum cartridges, and with the bolt head and extractor made to handle the belted head magnum case. This is the action formerly used for the long Weatherby Magnum cartridges.

No. 6: This is the single shot Bench Rest action with solid-bottom receiver. The three differ only in bolt head and extractor. The first No. 6 is made for .222 Remington head-sized cartridges, including the .221 Remington Fire Ball, .223 (5.56mm), .222 Magnum, .17 Remington, .17/.223 and 6x47mm. The second one is made with a bolt head and extractor to handle all .30-06 head-sized cartridges, which includes the .220 Swift, .225 Winchester and .284 Winchester. The last BR action is made to handle any of the belted head magnum cartridges or rimmed cartridges of equivalent rim size.

No. 7: Like the No. 1 but bolt head and extractor are made for the belted head magnum cartridge. With the standard .30-06 length magazine, this action is made for such popular short magnums as the .257 Weatherby, .264 Winchester, .270 Weatherby, 7mm Remington, .300 Winchester, .308 Norma, .338 Winchester, .358 Norma and .458 Winchester.

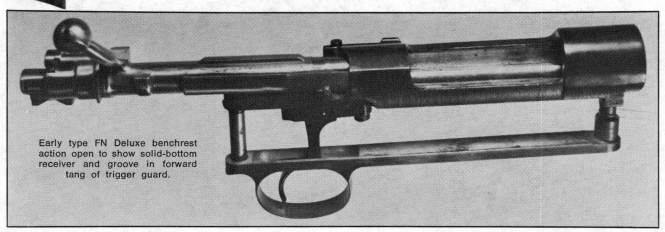

Early type FN Deluxe benchrest action open to show solid-bottom receiver and groove in forward tang of trigger guard.

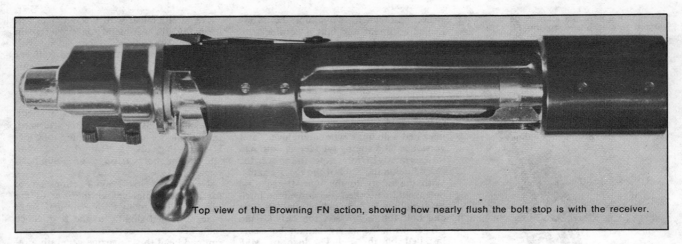
Top view of the Browning FN action, showing how nearly flush the bolt stop is with the receiver.

As noted, the No. 5 is merely the regular FN action opened up to accept H&H Magnum cartridges. In opening the magazine well part of the feed ramp is cut away. The metal in this area is vital in supporting the right (or lower) locking lug, and removing metal from this area weakens the support for the locking lug. How important this is will be examined.

Let us consider the following factors: 1) the upper (or left) locking lug on the M98 and FN bolt is deeply slotted for the ejector, with the result that it has less bearing surface against the receiver than the solid bottom (or right) locking lug. Being slotted, it is not nearly as strong as the bottom lug. 2) in standard FN actions (Nos. 1, 2, 3, 4 & 7) the upper locking recess gives a more massive support to its locking lug than does the lower locking recess to its locking lug because the lower shoulder is partly cut away to form the feed ramp. The result is that the weakest locking lug is more solidly supported by the receiver than the stronger lower locking lug. In the standard action, this support is more than adequate to hold the bolt securely in the receiver against the back thrust of firing the most powerful cartridges. 3) in the No. 5 FN action considerable metal is cut away from the feed ramp to make room for the long magnum cartridges, which weakens the lower locking shoulder even more. Even so, there is still adequate support for the bolt with factory loaded .300 H&H and .375 H&H Magnum cartridges, which normally develop less than 50,000 psi breech pressure. However, with the receiver so modified (and I would also say weakened), and the action used for some higher-pressured cartridge based on the long magnum case, the picture is different.

For example, I used a No. 5 FN action to build a rifle for the .300 H&H Improved Magnum, and the action failed. Its owner fired it quite a bit with heavy, but I do not think excessive, handloads. On a big game hunt he fired a shot at an elk, and then was unable to open the bolt. When he finally got the bolt open he found that the left half of the upper locking lug had cracked off. He wisely did not attempt to fire the rifle after that.

On careful examination of the rifle I concluded that the following took place: on firing the rifle a gradual bolt set-back occurred because of the locking lugs peening into the locking shoulders, and due, I believe, to the minimal support provided by the lower locking shoulder. As the peening quickly increased, the metal of the bottom locking shoulder was further weakened so that the top locking lug was doing most of the work. At this point, and on the final shot, the top lug cracked. Fortunately, the safety lug took over and prevented possible injury to the shooter—even, perhaps, had he fired another shot. However, the receiver and bolt were damaged beyond repair. After this experience, and being told of similar happenings with Weatherby rifles based on this action, I have concluded that the No. 5 FN action is OK for factory-loaded .300 and .375 H&H Magnum cartridges, but it is not suitable for hot Weatherby or similar wildcat cartridges. The FN No. 5 Magnum action is not a true "magnum" action as is the Brevex Magnum, but merely a standard action modified to han-

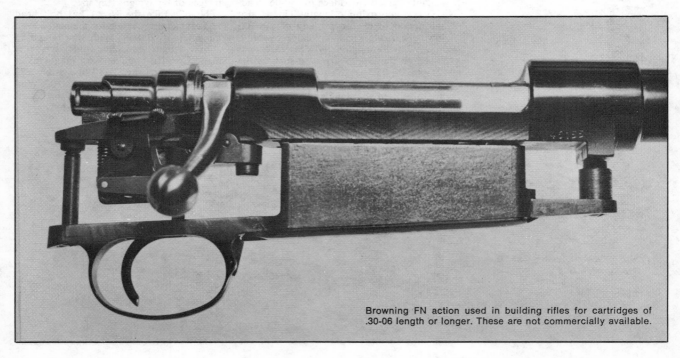
Browning FN action used in building rifles for cartridges of .30-06 length or longer. These are not commercially available.

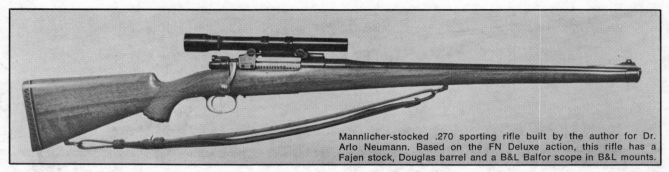

Mannlicher-stocked .270 sporting rifle built by the author for Dr. Arlo Neumann. Based on the FN Deluxe action, this rifle has a Fajen stock, Douglas barrel and a B&L Balfor scope in B&L mounts.

dle H&H Magnum cartridges. I believe the failure described was due entirely to weakening of the lower locking shoulder in the receiver when it was altered. This is also the reason I advise that the M98 military action not be modified in this manner for magnum cartridges too long for the original magazine.

Additional Comments on No. 6

Illustrated here is an original Mauser Oberndorf target rifle chambered for the 8.15x46R cartridge. Known as the *Wehrmannsgewehr* (serviceman's rifle), it is in most respects nearly identical to the regular M98 service rifle with the 29″ barrel. It differs mainly in its chambering, single-shot construction. Instead of opening the receiver bottom for the conventional magazine well, it was left solid. A shallow inclined groove milled in the top of this receiver bottom provides a cartridge loading chute.

Apparently many of these Mauser single shot rifles were brought back to the U.S. by returning GIs after WW II, and any knowledgeable shooter examining this

rifle usually commented that here was "a real action for a varmint or target rifle." Because some shooters knew this, and because bench rest shooters were beefing up M98 actions for their use, Firearms International got the word, and shortly FN made up similar No. 6 actions.

I have a high regard for all of FN Mauser actions, but I have the highest regard for the No. 6 action. I believe it is the strongest Mauser action ever made because the bottom locking lug has the solid support of that wall of steel which forms the receiver bottom. The solid bottom also makes this action very rigid and stiff. It has the strength to support a very heavy, full-floating barrel without the receiver bowing in the middle. The flat bottom receiver makes inletting it into the stock less of a problem. If the shooter wants this action held more securely in the stock than can be provided by the regular front and rear guard screws, an additional screw can be threaded into the receiver bottom.

I consider the FN No. 6 action ideal for building a long range varmint or target rifle, and top caliber choices for the

former would be the 6mm Remington, .240 Weatherby Magnum, .25-06 and .257 Weatherby Magnum; the best long range target calibers would be the 6.5x55 Mauser, .30-06 and .300 Magnum. Serious bench rest shooters say the No. 6 is not quite stiff enough for a "one holer" bench rifle, but for the shooter-held varmint or target rifle I don't believe it can be beaten.

This action, however, has one minor shortcoming. The inside bottom of the receiver is an unbroken, straight shallow groove matching the radius of the bolt. For more convenient loading I believe it should be made with a shallow, inclined loading groove.

I would also welcome the following changes on this action: First, there is no need for an ejector and, with the ejector eliminated, the slot in the left locking lug can be omitted. This would make the No. 6 even stronger than it now is. Secondly, why not eliminate the undercut in the bolt face recess and make it a full diameter recess instead? This would make the action safer. Thirdly, I'd like a small gas-vent hole in the right side of the receiver ring, to coincide with the end of the ex-

Left side of the Browning FN action showing: (A) forked bolt stop/ejector spring, (B) ejector, (C) bolt stop/ejector thumb-piece, (D) sear, (E) trigger, and (F) trigger stop adjustment screw. To remove bolt stop/ejector first take barrel and action from stock. To remove bolt-stop spring, raise its top fork to clear ejector, swing spring down 90° and it can be lifted from receiver; bolt stop/ejector can then be lifted out. The stock must also be removed to adjust trigger-stop screw. To adjust this screw, first loosen lock nut, then turn the screw in or out so the trigger stops the moment the sear is released.

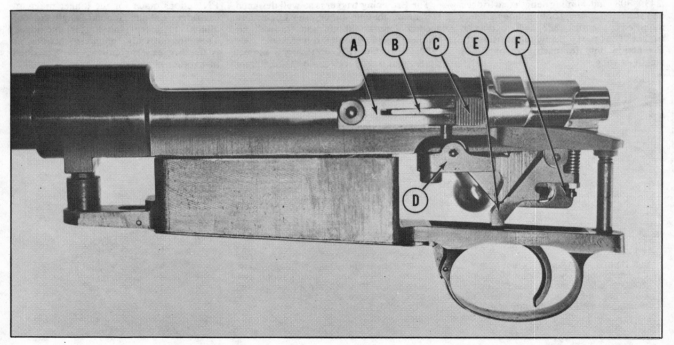

The author built this .300 H&H Improved Magnum rifle on the Series 400 Supreme FN No. 5 action for Mr. Harold Van Zandbergen, who has taken numerous elk, deer and antelope with it, as well as many coyotes and foxes. The 24″ heavy sporter Douglas Timken steel barrel has a 1:10″ rifling twist. The fancy burl walnut stock carries a rosewood fore-end tip, Rex engraved grip cap and Pachmayr recoil pad. The B&L 2½-8x variable scope is in B&L mounts.

tractor, and another larger hole in the left receiver wall opposite the forward vent hole in the bolt body.

Browning FN Action

Browning firearms were — and are — made in the Fabrique Nationale plant in Liége, Belgium, the same plant that makes FN actions. While separate Browning FN actions and barreled actions in the U.S. are not available, I will give a short description of this action because it is slightly different from the regular FN Supreme action.

Browning introduced their first high powered bolt action rifle in 1960. They were chambered for the .243, .270, .308, .30-06, .264 Magnum, .338 Magnum, .458 Magnum, .300 H&H Magnum and .375 H&H Magnum. A few new magnum calibers were added later, among them the 7mm, .300 and .308 Norma. All calibers were built on a modified version of the standard and magnum FN actions. They also dropped a couple of cartridges when, beginning in 1965, they adopted Sako actions for the shorter cartridges in the list above. At present Browning is using the Sako L-579 action for the .22-250, .243, .308 and similar length cartridges, and the Sako L-461 (both actions slightly modified) for the .222 family of cartridges. Thus today Browning is using the FN action only for cartridges of .30-06 length or longer.

The Browning FN action is excellently made and superbly finished, making it the smoothest working, best looking action based on the M98 design made today.

Except for two things—trigger and bolt stop—the Browning FN action is just like, and has the same features as, the regular FN Mauser action. It has the large ring receiver, tapped for scope mounts. The collar inside of the receiver ring is divided, that is, notched out on both left and right sides. The bolt is identical with the FN bolt except the grasping ball is now made round on the Brownings. The magazine is the same, having a hinged floorplate, and either a steel or alloy follower.

As shown in the photos of the Browning FN action the trigger and bolt stop are unlike those on the standard FN action. The trigger, more or less a copy of the Model 70 Winchester, has a sliding tang safety which locks both trigger and bolt when slid back. The trigger spring provides a let-off of about 3 to 3.5 pounds, very short and smooth. Only one adjustment is provided, a trigger stop screw which holds the trigger spring in place; this screw is normally adjusted correctly at the factory.

The Browning trigger is so well designed and made that no other adjustments are needed. One could not ask for a finer, simpler, more reliable trigger.

The Browning FN bolt stop is almost flush with the receiver, quite different

from the regular Mauser bolt-stop box and ejector housing. On the Browning FN action the bolt stop and the ejector pivot together on a pin, these parts fitting into a hole and slot in the left receiver bridge wall. The bolt stop and ejector are held in place and tensioned by a forked spring attached to the action by a stud mortised into the receiver wall. Depressing the flat serrated thumbpiece on the bolt stop allows the bolt to be removed. This appears to be an excellent bolt stop/ejector arrangement and, being nearly flush with the receiver, is a desirable design feature. Neither the trigger/safety mechanism nor the bolt stop/ejector are interchangeable with these parts in any other M98 or FN Mauser actions.

Browning FN actions are serial numbered on the right side of the receiver ring and under the bolt handle stem.

To the best of my knowledge, separate Browning FN turnbolt rifle actions have not been made available in the U.S., but they are in Canada. I found them listed in Ellwood Epps' catalog (Clinton, Ontario, Canada) in the standard and short magnum calibers for $94.50, and in the long belted-magnum calibers for $98.50. As with the FN Magnum action, Browning FN actions made for the longer magnum cartridges are just regular length actions altered to accept the longer cartridges. They are not truly "magnum" actions, as is the Brevex Magnum action, described in another chapter.

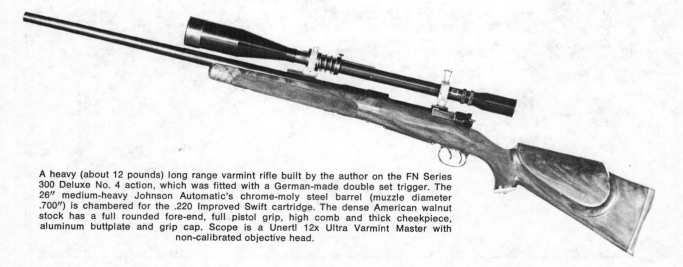

A heavy (about 12 pounds) long range varmint rifle built by the author on the FN Series 300 Deluxe No. 4 action, which was fitted with a German-made double set trigger. The 26″ medium-heavy Johnson Automatic's chrome-moly steel barrel (muzzle diameter .700″) is chambered for the .220 Improved Swift cartridge. The dense American walnut stock has a full rounded fore-end, full pistol grip, high comb and thick cheekpiece, aluminum buttplate and grip cap. Scope is a Unertl 12x Ultra Varmint Master with non-calibrated objective head.

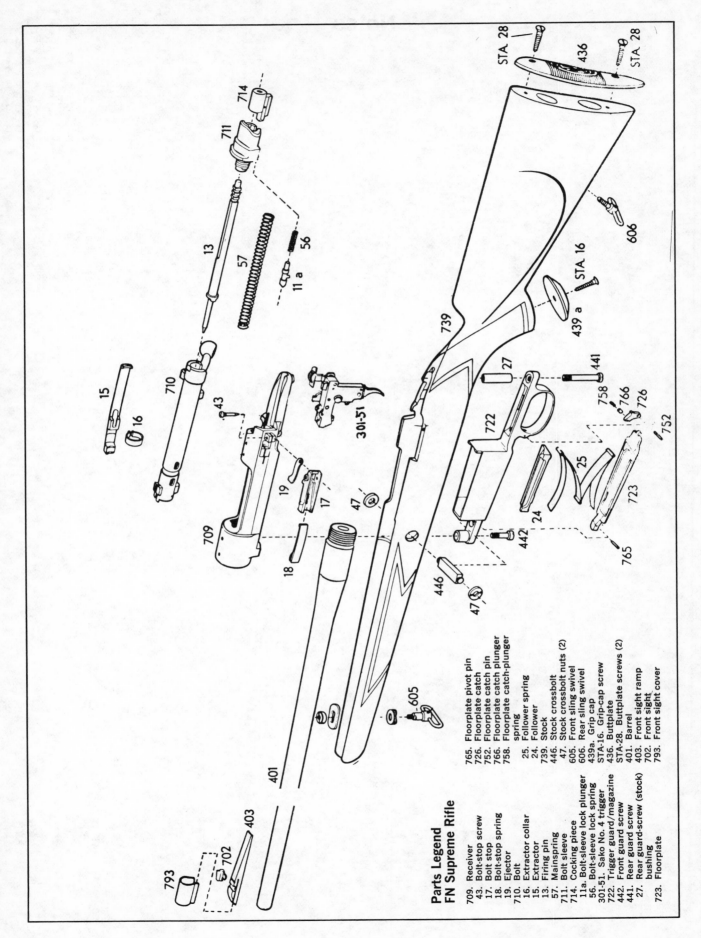

**Parts Legend
FN Supreme Rifle**

709.	Receiver
43.	Bolt-stop screw
17.	Bolt stop
18.	Bolt-stop spring
19.	Ejector
710.	Bolt
16.	Extractor collar
15.	Extractor
13.	Firing pin
57.	Mainspring
711.	Bolt sleeve
714.	Cocking piece
11a.	Bolt-sleeve lock plunger
56.	Bolt-sleeve lock spring
301-51.	Sako No. 4 trigger
722.	Trigger guard/magazine
441.	Front guard screw
27.	Rear guard screw (stock)
723.	Floorplate
765.	Floorplate pivot pin
726.	Floorplate catch
752.	Floorplate catch pin
766.	Floorplate catch plunger
758.	Floorplate catch-plunger spring
25.	Follower spring
24.	Follower
739.	Stock
446.	Stock crossbolt
47.	Stock crossbolt nuts (2)
605.	Front sling swivel
606.	Rear sling swivel
439a.	Grip cap
STA-16.	Grip-cap screw
436.	Buttplate
STA-28.	Buttplate screws (2)
401.	Barrel
403.	Front sight ramp
702.	Front sight
793.	Front sight cover

Notes

I Centurion
II Santa Barbara
III Herter J9, K3
IV Ackley
V Brevex Magnum
VI Mark X

22. Commercial Mausers

Part I
Centurion Mauser

IN 1965 GOLDEN STATE Arms Corp., Calif., introduced a commercial sporting bolt action based on the M98 action design. More precisely, the Centurion action appears to be a direct copy of the now obsolete commercial Firearms International FN De luxe action, except for an alloy hinged floorplate/trigger guard and a slightly different bolt handle.

The Centurion action is readily identified, but only if it is complete and out of the stock. Imprinted on the left wall of the magazine, in three lines, is:

CENTURION (in script)
GOLDEN STATE ARMS CORP.,
PASADENA, CALIF.

The word **SPAIN** is inconspicuously stamped on the left side of the receiver tang, indicating the action was manufactured in Spain. The actions are serial numbered, with the number, preceded by a letter, stamped on the left of the receiver ring. On the Centurion barreled actions the barrel is marked with the caliber designation, plus the single line **PASADENA ARMS CORP., INC.**

The receiver appears to be machined from a die forging. The literature describing the Centurion action, when it was introduced, does not state the type or number of the steel the receiver and bolt are made from, but undoubtedly they are made of a suitable modern steel and properly heat treated.

The receiver is of the large ring type. The collar inside the receiver ring extends entirely around it except for the extractor cut, as in the M98 military action. This is unlike the modern FN Mauser action, whose receiver ring collar is milled out on the left side to match the extractor cut on the right. Because of this the Centurion receiver ring may well be stronger than that of the FN. The Centurion has no thumb slot in the left wall, no clip-charger guides, and the top of the bridge is smooth. Four correctly spaced 6x48 tapped holes, two in the bridge and two in the ring, allow all of the popular scope mounts to be used on this action. The receiver is well machined, with an even, smooth surface.

The bolt is of the standard M98 pattern, but the bolt handle is shaped for the lowest scope mounting possible. All bolt components are M98 copies, except that the bolt sleeve had a groove cut into it for a low scope safety positioned to its left side. The safety locks both striker and bolt when swung upward. The extractor is made so it will easily snap over a cartridge rim when the bolt is closed on a cartridge dropped into the chamber. All bolt parts are well made.

The trigger is practically the same as the original M98 military type except in having only one hump for a single-stage pull instead of two humps for the double-stage pull. The trigger pull is quite long and heavy.

All receiver and bolt parts are of steel, properly machined for a smooth finish and close fit, and given a very good polish. There is no evidence of any welding. The parts were left in the "white" on the actions, but blued on the barreled action.

The trigger guard, with its integral magazine box, is a machined alloy casting. The alloy floorplate is hinged to the guard, its latch in the front of the guard bow. It is released by pressing a button inside the front of the guard bow. The follower is of milled steel, its rear surface sloped to allow closing the bolt on an empty magazine. The alloy parts (guard, floorplate and latch) are anodized black.

Centurion actions were made to handle most popular U.S. centerfire cartridges of .30-06 head size and the short belted magnums.

The actions were all of the same length,

but those intended for shorter cartridges had the rear of the magazine blocked off and fitted with a shorter follower. Thus, actions made for the .243, 6mm, .257 and .308 have a magazine opening (length) of 3.00". Actions for the longer cartridges —.30-06 and short magnum length—have a magazine opening of 3.350", and are unblocked.

Evidently, a great many Centurion actions were made, since the actions, barreled actions and assembled rifles were numerous and sold by many dealers. The few I have examined up to this writing appeared sound and well made, but one .243 would absolutely not feed any cartridge from the magazine except the last one. An isolated instance, perhaps, for others I handled didn't have this problem. I also fear that the latch arrangement of the hinged floorplate is not good; the tiny lip on the floorplate which engages the latch may wear quickly, and then fail to hold the floorplate closed when the magazine is fully loaded.

The Centurion action weighs about 2 lbs. 11 oz. Its general and dimensional specifications are the same as those of the standard M98, including barrel shank and thread specs, disassembly and assembly.

The lowest priced Centurion rifle, the Model 100, has a blind magazine box— that is, no outside magazine floorplate is used, the wood of the stock covering the bottom of the magazine box. Cartridges have to be fed out with the bolt to unload.

Sometime in 1966 or 1967 the Golden State Arms Corp. went out of business. I don't know what happened to their remaining stock, but at this writing various dealers are still offering Centurion actions, barreled actions and rifles, for sale.

Illustrated above: De luxe Centurion rifle in .243 caliber as assembled by Pasadena Arms Corp., Inc., Pasadena, Calif. The scope is a Bushnell 3-9 Banner variable in Weaver top detachable mounts.

I had a letter from one man who said his Centurion receiver and bolt were tested for hardness before having a 7mm Magnum barrel fitted. The gunsmith making the test wrote that he considered the receiver too soft for any magnum cartridge. I don't have much faith in hardness tests for determining whether a given action is safe or not. Other than this, I have not heard any valid complaints about this action. I feel that it is a suitable choice on which to build a big game hunting rifle in the standard calibers. For a varmint or target rifle, or for a rifle which will be fired a lot (especially if it is going to be chambered for a wildcat cartridge), I think it is better to choose an action that has proven satisfactory for hard use, such as the FN Mauser or Sako.

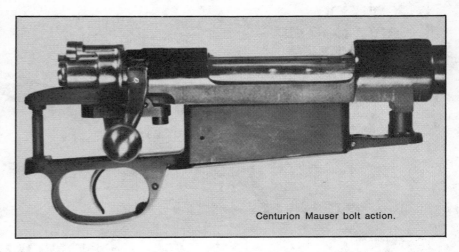
Centurion Mauser bolt action.

Part II Santa Barbara Mauser

I DON'T KNOW what connection there is between the Santa Barbara Mauser action and the Centurion Mauser action (just described), but there must be some link. I say this because the receivers and bolts of these two actions are almost exact duplicates of each other. As mentioned previously, the Centurion receiver itself has no markings by which it can be identified; the only markings it has are the serial number, preceded by a letter and the word SPAIN stamped on the side of the tang. The Santa Barbara receiver is similarly marked, its serial number beginning with the letter Z. There are no markings on the action to indicate it is a "Santa Barbara" action or any other action. Why the name stamping is omitted is beyond me. Santa Barbara actions were first advertised shortly after Golden State Arms went out of business, so I suspect both actions were made by the same manufacturer in Spain. Although I am not sure about this, I have a report which indicates the bolt and receiver parts are made by the Spanish Military Arsenal in La Coruna, Spain. The Santa Barbara action is

being imported by Santa Barbara of America, Ltd., 930 N. Beltline Rd., #132, Irving, Texas 75060.

At this writing Santa Barbara actions with alloy trigger guard are $74.95 for standard calibers, and $84.95 for short magnum calibers. The same actions with a steel trigger guard/magazine are $10 higher. Barreled actions are also available, the barrels made and fitted to the actions by the Small Arms Mfg. Co., Bridgeville, Pa., makers of Star diamond-lapped barrels. (Incidentally, I put a Star barrel on another action and found it gave excellent accuracy.) In standard calibers with alloy trigger guard, the action is $84.95, magnum calibers $94.95. For $10 extra the steel trigger guard/magazine replaces the alloy unit. Calibers available are: .22-250, .243, 6mm, .270, .308, .30-06, 7mm Remington Magnum, and .300, .338 or .458 Winchester Magnums. Santa Barbara actions, barreled actions and complete rifles are distributed by Fajen Mfg. Co., Box 338, Warsaw, Mo. 65355. Complete rifles from Fajen are called "Acra rifles."

The Action

The receiver, bolt and some of the other larger parts appear to me to be investment castings, although I am not sure. There is, however, no valid objection to such castings provided suitable steels are used and the castings finished and properly heat treated. I assume that this is done. Like the Centurion and FN actions, the Santa Barbara is a near carbon copy of the M98 action. The advertising literature describes it as the "Time tested, classic Oberndorf designed rugged Mauser action." Like the FN it is an improvement over the original M98. The thumb notch is omitted, leaving the left receiver wall solid. The stripper-clip guide notch is also left off and the bridge is left smooth.

The receiver has the near-full inside collar, the bolt has the two large gas-vent holes, the slotted left locking lug and the rear safety lug, all basic Mauser features. All receiver and bolt parts are the same as in the Centurion action except for a streamlined bolt sleeve. Since the safety is incorporated with the trigger mechanism, the usual Mauser type safety is eliminated from the bolt sleeve, and it is made smoother in outline by omitting the

The Santa Barbara Mauser trigger mechanism. Built in a cast aluminum housing, this trigger is fully adjustable for weight of pull, take-up (creep or sear engagement) and over-travel. Incorporated with the trigger mechanism is the pivoting type tang safety; pulling it back, locks the sear. There are 4 setscrews in this trigger, each one fitted with lock nuts. Setscrew and lock nut (A) are used only to hold the mechanism against the bottom of the receiver tang. The setscrew is turned in tight, then the lock nut is tightened so the setscrew can't loosen. The stock must be removed before any adjustments can be made. Setscrew (B) adjusts weight of pull. Turning it in (clockwise) increases the weight, and vice versa. Setscrew (C) adjusts trigger over-travel. It is normally set to stop trigger movement the moment the sear is released. The best way to adjust, or set it, is as follows: with the bolt closed and the striker in the fired position, turn the screw in until it is stopped, then back it off about ⅛-turn and tighten the lock nut. Setscrew (D) controls sear engagement. Turning it in (clockwise) reduces engagement and vice versa. It is normally adjusted as follows: with the action closed and striker in the fired position, and after the stop screw (C) has been set, turn the screw in until stopped, then back it off about ⅛-turn and tighten the lock nut. Now, test the trigger by closing the bolt smartly a number of times and, if the striker does not stay cocked each time the bolt is closed there is not enough sear engagement, and/or the weight of pull is too light. (E) is the safety. These instructions also apply to the trigger of the Parker-Hale Super Mauser rifle.

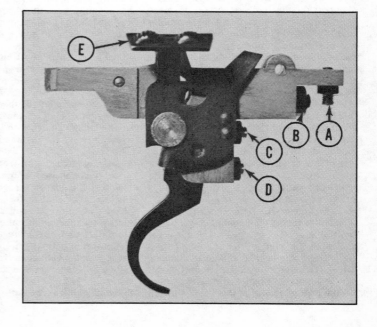

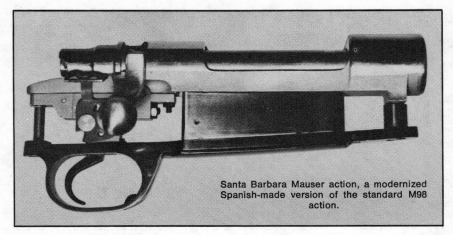

Santa Barbara Mauser action, a modernized Spanish-made version of the standard M98 action.

hole for the safety. The top rear of the bolt sleeve extends over the cocking piece when it is in the fired position, forming a sort of shroud to protect it.

The bolt handle is exactly like the one on the Centurion action, with a very low profile to clear a low-mounted scope.

Offhand, I would say that this action has a stiffer mainspring than used in any of the other commercial M98 type actions.

The trigger mechanism is of the familiar type such as made by Timney, Mashburn and Jaeger. It is fully adjustable and is housed in an alloy casting. The mechanism is attached to the bottom of the receiver by a pin through the regular sear socket and tightened by a setscrew. The finger-piece of the trigger is well curved, grooved and placed well back in the trigger guard bow. It is adjustable for weight of pull, take-up or creep and over-travel. It has a minimum weight-of-pull adjustment of about 2 pounds.

The safety is built into the trigger mechanism. It is a pivoting type, its thumb-piece positioned on the right side of the tang. Pivoting the safety back locks the trigger and bolt. It is convenient to use and quiet in operation. Since it pivots instead of sliding, the stock has to be slightly cut out to the rear of the thumb-piece to give it room to work.

The very long trigger housing extends nearly to the end of the tang, with the rear guard screw passing through a hole in the housing. This leaves very little area for the tang to be solidly bedded into the stock, even if a glass bedding compound is used. For more secure bedding the bottom of the trigger housing at this point should be bedded or "bottomed" into the stock instead.

The steel or alloy trigger guard/magazine units are made with a hinged floorplate, its latch and release button built into the front of the trigger guard bow. The aluminum unit is a one-piece casting, while the steel unit has a sheet-metal magazine box spot welded to the trigger guard plate. The follower is steel in both types.

The magazine box opening is about 3.380″ long, adequate for .30-06 length cartridges and short belted magnums. For the shorter, .308 family of cartridges the magazine has a sheet-metal spacer fitted into the rear of the box to shorten the opening to about 3.00″. The alloy unit is anodized black and the steel unit is polished and blued.

I ordered a Santa Barbara action with the steel trigger guard/magazine from a distributor, and the action I received was generally well made. Although the outside surfaces of all visible parts were well polished, nothing at all was done to the inside surfaces. The bolt was so stiff that it was only with great difficulty that it could be opened and closed. In taking the firing mechanism out of the bolt I could hardly pull the cocking piece back or turn the bolt sleeve. The inside metal surfaces, unpolished, had a frosty appearance, as though nothing had been done to them after manufacture except pickling or sandblasting, at a guess. To make this action work smoothly will take a lot of work, though. The action became noticeably easier to operate after working it a few times. The locking lug raceways, and the locking shoulders, will have to be polished and lapped; bolt sleeve threads will have to be lapped with those inside the bolt. The cocking cam notch in the bolt and the cam raceway in the receiver need to be polished. The inside of the bolt sleeve needs to be smoothed out, and it would be a good idea to smooth the inside of the bolt also. The outside of the bolt needs to be made much smoother. The extractor cam surfaces need to be polished.

Earlier, I mentioned the seemingly very stiff mainspring used in this action; in checking the striker travel, I found it to be .475″ instead of the usual .500″ for most M98 design actions. With the mainspring as stiff as it is, I believe the sear notch could be cut back .100″ to reduce striker travel to .375″. This could easily be done since the safety functions on the trigger sear rather than on the cocking piece.

I have not seen the Santa Barbara alloy trigger guard/magazine unit, but the steel unit on my action was poorly shaped before being polished and blued. The trigger guard bow is slab-sided, heavy, and the edges are square and sharp. On a light rifle, in .270 or larger caliber, the sharp-edged bow could really hash up the middle finger on recoil. The bow should be reworked, the edges tapered off and rounded.

I don't like the flat-head guard screws used on this action. I am going to replace

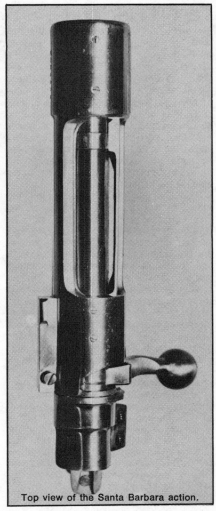

Top view of the Santa Barbara action.

them with the slightly round-head type as made for the FN Mauser action.

With new guard screws and after considerable polishing has been done, I would rate the Santa Barbara Mauser action as a suitable one on which to build a good sporting rifle.

The receiver will accept barrels threaded to M98 barrel shank and thread specifications. The action with alloy guard weighs about 2¾ lbs., while the steel guard version weighs about 3 lbs. It is disassembled and reassembled like the Series 400 FN Mauser action.

The well-known Parker-Hale firm of Birmingham, England, introduced a new high powered sporting rifle in 1967, called the Series 1200 Parker-Hale Super Mauser. The receiver and bolt of this action are also of Spanish manufacture, as well might be the trigger. At any rate, the receiver, bolt and trigger mechanism of the Parker-Hale rifle appear to be identical to those on the Santa Barbara action, and I suspect that both are made in the same factory in Spain.

Since the Parker-Hale Mauser was introduced various gun magazines have reported favorably on it, so if the P-H rifle is to your liking, and if you are skilled enough as an amateur gunsmith, then you can use the Santa Barbara action and build a similar rifle.

Part III Herter J9

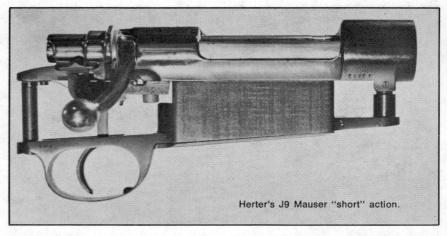

Herter's J9 Mauser "short" action.

IN THE MID-1960s Herter's Inc., Waseca, Minn., began importing a centerfire turnbolt action which appeared to be a very close copy of the FN Mauser De luxe action, except for its bolt stop. Cataloged as the Mark XK3, it was made in Germany, and was described in their 1966 catalog as being an "improved modified Mauser type action." Actually, it was a modified version of the regular M98 large ring action. It was of all steel construction and completely finished, with the receiver and magazine parts blued and the bolt parts left bright.

The Mark XK3 bolt has the usual M98 twin locking lugs, bolt safety lug, long type extractor and guide rib. The bolt handle copied the FN low profile to clear a low-mounted scope. The safety was in the bolt sleeve, its wing toward the left, and it was also low enough to clear a low-mounted scope.

The large ring receiver, tapped for top scope mounts, had the usual M98 collar inside. The trigger was a conventional Mauser military trigger made without the two humps, so it would have a single-stage pull instead of a double-stage let-off. The milled steel combined trigger guard/magazine had a detachable floorplate.

The usual M98 bolt stop was not used on this action; instead, it was fitted with a nearly flush combination bolt stop and ejector. It resembled the bolt stop now used on the Browning FN action described in another chapter. I have only seen one of these actions, and the bolt stop assembly differed from the Browning type in that the bolt-stop spring was attached to the receiver by a screw.

These German-made Herter XK3 actions were listed as being available with magazines for .308 and .30-06 length cartridges, or with the bolt face and extractor made for the short belted magnum cartridges. This action weighed 2 lbs. 9 oz. Undoubtedly, they were marked **Made in Germany.**

I did get to examine a specimen of the Herter's Mark XK3 action at a later date, but this action was marked **Made in Yugoslavia.** It was also marked **HERTER'S M-XK-3.** It also bore a monogram, the overlapped figures **ZCZ** within a circle, the trademark of Zavodi Crvena Zastava, the leading arms manufacturer in Yugoslavia. This probably means that Herter might have had problems in getting the actions made in Germany. The Yugoslavian-made XK3 action I examined had the conventional M98 bolt stop and ejector, a smooth bolt sleeve made without safety, a sliding side-tang safety, and an all-steel trigger guard/magazine with a hinged floorplate. The collar inside the receiver ring is slotted on both sides. There may well have been other versions of the XK3 action, but the two I examined and described above appeared to be very well made.

Herter's 1967 catalog lists still another M98 type action. Called the Mark J9, Herter says it was made for them in Yugoslavia. This action appears to be exactly like the latest J9 action, described below,

except that the top of the receiver ring and bridge are equal in height, flat on top, and with low dovetail grooves on each side (about .770″ wide) to form integral scope mounting bases. I have never examined this action.

(I have a rifle with a similar action, and so marked except for the Herter J9 stamping. This was obtained in Yugoslavia, in .30-06 caliber, and with serial number 48521. The receiver collar is slotted on both sides. I also have one of Herter's XK3 rifles, quite like the one described by de Haas except that the collar in the ring is cut out *only* on the right side. JTA)

Now for the latest Herter's J9 action. The action I received is stamped on the left receiver wall:

MADE IN YUGOSLAVIA

This is preceded by the **ZCZ** within-a-circle trademark. The serial number, stamped on the lower right corner of the receiver ring, would be hidden if the action were in the stock. The last three digits of the serial number are also stamped on the bottom of the bolt handle and on the trigger guard.

The catalog lists three J9 actions; the SSM1 No. 1 for cartridges of .308 length,

Trigger and safety mechanism of Herter's J9 action. Arrow points to the trigger adjustment screw. Turning this screw clockwise reduces sear engagement, shortens trigger pull.

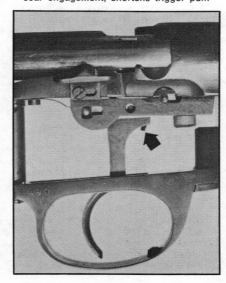

SSM2 No. 2 for those of .30-06 length cartridges and SSM3 No. 3 for short belted magnums. The No. 1 and No. 2 actions are priced at $47.25, the No. 3 at $50.04. J9 barreled actions and complete J9 rifles in various calibers are also available.

Briefly, Herter's J9 action is a modified and modernized version of the large ring M98 actions, made entirely of steel. It has the full receiver collar like the M98, and it is threaded the same. It has the M98 bolt fitted with a low profile bolt handle. It has a solid left wall and a M98 bolt stop and ejector. The bolt sleeve is of the modern FN type, without safety. The trigger guard/magazine box is all-steel and the steel floorplate is hinged. The floorplate latch lies in the front of the trigger guard bow. The trigger follows the M98 military type, but it has a single stage pull. A sheet-metal sliding safety, fitted to the right side of the receiver tang, locks sear and bolt when pulled back.

Here are the specifications of the J9 action I received, which I assume to be the SSM1 No. 1:

Weight	46 oz.
Length	8.50″
Receiver ring dia.	1.408″
Bolt travel	4.40″
Magazine length (inside)	3.215″
Bolt length	6.115″

(The standard M98 bolt is 6.375″ long.)

From the above specifications it can be seen that this action has the same approximate dimensions as the M24 Yugoslavian action described in the chapter "Mauser Model 98." In that chapter I described this action as one having the odd breeching, in that the projecting lips on the left side of the cartridge recess rim are absent, letting the barrel be breeched closer to the bolt. This also required the face of the barrel to be notched for the extractor. All illustrations of the J9 bolt head in Herter's catalogs show it without these lips, and the J9 action I have also has a bolt without these lips. I can only conclude therefore, that the J9 action has a bolt and a receiver that are copies of the M24 Yugoslavian action. Not having had a chance to examine and measure the SSM2 and SSM3 J9 actions, I can only assume that they have a longer magazine to handle .30-06 length cartridges, or are made on the longer regular M98 action and, also fitted with a .30-06 length magazine.

The J9 action I received has a number of faults. The bridge was so poorly machined that it would be very difficult to attach a scope mount base on it level with the front mount base. The top left side of the bridge is not machined down far enough, and the machining that was done is not at all accurate. Such poor and inadequate work is inexcusable.

The surfaces that were polished, which includes almost all outside surfaces, were carelessly done on a soft polishing wheel, leaving the edges rounded and holes dished out. Despite this heavy buffing after initial rough polishing, tool and polishing marks are still present under the high sheen. Parts which should have been left together during the polishing, such as the bolt-stop spring in the bolt stop, were polished separately and all their edges rounded off. The bolt-stop spring also appears to have been bent, and then partially straightened again.

The extractor collar is clamped so tightly around the bolt that the bolt handle can only be raised and lowered with considerable effort. There is a flaw in the metal underneath the base of the bolt handle—a flaw that makes it appear as though the bolt handle was welded onto the bolt.

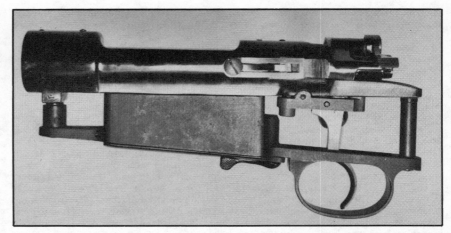

Left side view of the XK3 action showing the nearly flush 5-piece bolt stop. These parts are: bolt stop with its serrated thumbpiece, ejector arm pivoted to the bolt stop on a pin and bolt stop/ejector spring, which is held against the receiver by a screw. This bolt stop is almost the same as that used on the FN Browning turnbolt rifle action.

I view this with suspicion. The trigger is so tight in the sear, and the sear so tight on the receiver, that when the trigger is pulled back it stays there. Certainly, some of these faults can be corrected by the amateur gunsmith, but they should not have been present in the first place. It is the poorest commercial centerfire turnbolt action I have seen. Perhaps not all J9 actions are so poorly made as the one I got, but in making my evaluation of this one, I cannot recommend the J9 action.

Part IV
Ackley Mauser

A COUPLE OF YEARS prior to this writing, Mr. P.O. Ackley, (Box 17347, Salt Lake City, Utah 84117) announced that M98 actions bearing his name would soon be available. Mr. Ackley, one of America's leading gunsmiths, has a very high regard for the M98 action design. He had arranged for a firm in Japan to make his actions, these to be a very close copy of the latest FN Mauser. The most interesting part of the announcement was that a true left-hand Mauser action was to be made, as well as the normal right-hand type. To the best of my knowledge, this was to be the first true commercial left-hand M98 action ever made.

As so frequently happens, good things often fail to last, and such was the case with Ackley's Japanese-made actions. To prepare a story on these actions I got two of them for study, but I also phoned Ackley for additional information. I learned, sadly, that only some 150 of them had been made, 50 of them left-hand

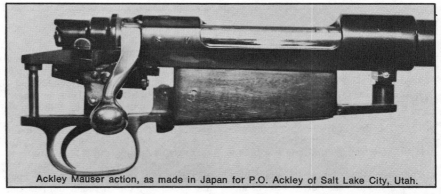

Ackley Mauser action, as made in Japan for P.O. Ackley of Salt Lake City, Utah.

ones, before the Japanese firm making them went bankrupt!

Anyway, since I have two, I'll briefly describe them. First off, they are marked, on the left receiver wall:

P. O. ACKLEY
SALT LAKE CITY, UTAH

The serial number, preceded by **No.**, is stamped on the right side of the receiver ring. The words **MADE IN JAPAN** are stamped on the flat area under the receiver ring. My two actions have 4-digit serial numbers.

To describe the Ackley Mauser action in detail would be to repeat what has already been written about the FN, Centurion and Santa Barbara actions but, as can be seen in the illustrations, the Ackley differs in minor respects. While the FN has a long, slender, swept-back bolt handle, and the Centurion and Santa Barbara have shorter, heavier handles, the Ackley bolt handle is a close copy of the Model

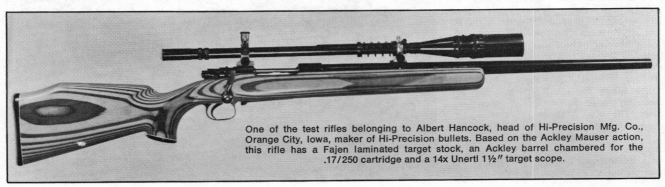

One of the test rifles belonging to Albert Hancock, head of Hi-Precision Mfg. Co., Orange City, Iowa, maker of Hi-Precision bullets. Based on the Ackley Mauser action, this rifle has a Fajen laminated target stock, an Ackley barrel chambered for the .17/250 cartridge and a 14x Unertl 1½″ target scope.

70 Winchester handle. It has a low profile to clear the lowest-mounted scopes, with a stem that is rather heavy and swept back in a double curve, and ending in a pear-shaped grasping ball. This bolt handle shape has become immensely popular, most shooters preferring it over any other. I feel the same way.

The Ackley receiver is tapped for the many popular top mount scope bases and for a receiver sight. Unlike late-type FN actions, the Ackley receiver has the near-full inside collar, slotted only for the extractor. The Ackley action has the smooth, shrouded bolt sleeve of the latest FN.

The Ackley Mauser action is made entirely of steel. The trigger guard and magazine box are a one-piece steel unit. The floorplate is hinged to the front of the magazine box, the latch positioned just forward of the trigger guard bow. The latch button is quite large, making it easy to unlatch with a finger. On one of my Ackley actions the guard bow is neatly narrowed. One of the two has a milled steel follower, the other an alloy one. The magazine box opening is 3.355", long enough to accept the standard and belted magnum cartridge of .30-06 length.

The trigger housing is also made of steel. One action has a trigger adjustable only for weight of pull and sear engagement, while the other one is adjustable for over-travel as well. The safety, part of the trigger mechanism, is the pivoting type with a large serrated button alongside the tang. When tipped back, the sear and bolt are locked.

I don't know how the Ackley receivers were made, or of what kind of steel, but they appear to be machined from forgings rather than from an investment or other type of casting. All the parts appear to be well made and finished. The bolt fits snugly in the receiver and there's a minimum of wobble when the bolt is opened. I tried to put the Ackley bolts in other M98 actions, and the bolts from these actions in the Ackley receiver, but none would interchange. The Ackley bolt body is about .705" in diameter. Both of my Ackley actions were fitted with barrels by Ackley in .17/250 caliber. Both functioned well, although a couple of bugs had to be worked out. It is my understanding that Mr. Ackley is now attempting to have similar actions made elsewhere, and it is hoped that this will be done. There are certainly enough different M98 type actions on the market today, but there is room for another good one, especially a left-handed one.

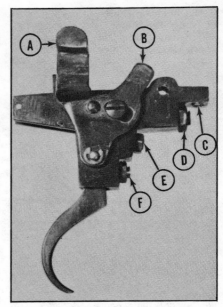

Trigger mechanism of the Japanese-made Ackley Mauser action: (A) safety, (B) bolt lock (part of the safety), (C) tightening screw, (D) weight of pull adjustment screw, (E) trigger stop or over-travel adjustment screw, and (F) sear engagement adjustment screw.

Part V Brevex Magnum Mauser

Made in france and imported into the United States by Tradewinds Inc. (P.O. Box 1191, Tacoma, Washington 98401), the Brevex is the only true magnum Mauser action that has been available to American gunsmiths since before WW II.

The first Mauser magnum action was probably developed shortly after 1900, and most likely it was initially developed in the Mauser plant in Oberndorf, Germany. It came about as a result of employing the standard M98 Mauser action for increasingly larger cartridges.

German and British sportsmen were probably responsible for the magnum when, for economy reasons, they wanted bolt action rifles chambered for large bore cartridges which, ordinarily, were available only in heavy double barreled rifles. These large double rifle cartridges were usually rimmed, but for use in a bolt action rifle a whole new series of similar rimless cartridges was designed. Some of the British cartridges for which the Magnum Mauser action was used are: .404 Rimless Nitro-Express; .416 Rigby; .425 Westley-Richards Magnum; .500 Rimless Jeffery, and .505 Gibbs Rimless Magnum. The calibers just mentioned also indicate some of the prominent British gunmakers using the M98 Magnum Mauser action. Some German cartridges also required the magnum action, but they are not so well known.

Such cartridges not only had large diameter cases and bullets but some of them were nearly 4" over-all. Thus, a longer, larger and stronger action than the standard M98 was needed. The original Mauser magnum action was 9.25" long, made with a very heavy receiver ring, and with a magazine arrangement appropriate to the cartridge to be used. In many cases the magazine box extended below the stock line. Other than this these magnum actions were essentially the same as the regular M98 action. A few of these Mauser-made magnum actions (they were also made by other firms) were used by some American gunsmiths, but not many of them.

The big swing to custom made rifles didn't begin until after the end of WW II, and then almost every amateur and professional gunsmith got into the act. The French-made Brevex Magnum Mauser action was introduced into the U.S. in 1955 to meet a demand for such an action.

Two Brevex magnum actions were originally introduced; the M300 for such common belted magnum cartridges as the .300 and .375 H&H Magnums, and the M400 for the .416 Rigby and its like. Both actions were the same except for the bolt face recess and extractor. Shortly afterward barreled actions in .300 H&H Magnum, .375 H&H Magnum and .416 Rigby were made available.

At this writing the Tradewinds catalog lists only the M400 Brevex Magnum action, its cost $160.

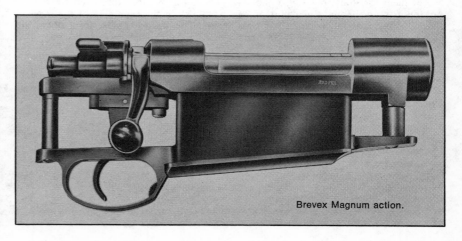

Brevex Magnum action.

Here are the specifications for the M400 Brevex Magnum Mauser action:

Weight	53 oz.
Length	9.25"
Receiver-ring dia.	1.50"
Bolt dia.	.700"
Bolt travel	4.975"
Striker travel	.550"
Magazine length	3.925"
Magazine-well width	.665"
Bolt-face recess.	
(for .416 Rigby cartridge)	
dia.	.590"
depth	.060"
Guard-screw spacing	8.25"
Barrel shank & thread dia.	29x2mm

(1.141" x approx. 12.7 V threads per inch)

Comparing these figures with those for the M98 military action, it isn't hard to visualize the Brevex as being a very large and massive action. According to the importer, the Brevex receiver and bolt are made of chrome-vanadium steel, heat treated for maximum strength and durability. The receiver ring is extra thick and large to give maximum support to the bolt, and to allow a large-diameter barrel shank to be used. The receiver ring has the regular M98 collar, except that it is slotted on both left and right.

The Brevex bolt, necessarily longer than the standard M98 bolt, is otherwise just like it. It does, however, have a gas vent hole in the left side of the receiver, which regular Mausers do not.

The low safety, located in the top of the bolt sleeve permits low scope mounting, as does the low-profile bolt handle. The receiver ring and bridge are tapped for scope mounts. The trigger is of standard M98 pattern, but has only one hump for a single stage let-off. Custom single-stage adjustable triggers made for the M98 can be fitted to the Brevex action. A double-set trigger could also be installed.

The trigger guard/magazine assembly is all steel. The milled guard bow is welded to the very thick-walled magazine box. The welding is well done and doesn't show when the magazine is in the stock. Like

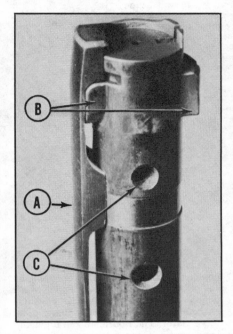

Underneath view of the Brevex Magnum bolt head: (A) extractor, (B) dual-opposed locking lugs, and (C) twin gas-vent holes.

the magnum Mauser actions, the Brevex magazine box is quite deep, this, combined with a heavy and slightly hollowed out floorplate, gives the action a definite belly. The very strong magazine floorplate is hinged to the front of the magazine box, its latch lying in the front of the guard bow.

Although quite expensive, the Brevex magnum action is the one to use if you want to build a classic Mauser rifle for an African hunting trip. The receiver recoil lug is quite large in area, but it alone is not enough to keep the action from setting back into the stock under heavy recoil. Therefore I suggest bedding the recoil shoulder area in fiberglass, fitting another recoil lug to the barrel, about midway in the fore-end, and a cross bolt stock.

The Brevex action received from Tradewinds was well made and finished, but it would need additional polishing before being blued. The word **FRANCE** and the serial number are stamped on the bottom flat of the receiver ring.

Tradewinds told me that Brevex Magnum actions are in very limited supply and deliveries uncertain.

Printed on the box in which this action was packed are the words "Manufactured by BREVEXSURESNES — France." In bold letters on both sides of the box is printed, "Brevex Magnum Action, The only true full sized, commercial MAGNUM ACTION being built in the entire world today." This is no longer true because the Champlin action (described in another chapter) is as large. The Brevex, however, is the only true "Mauser" magnum action made today.

Part VI
Mark X Mauser

IN LATE 1969, Interarms Ltd. (10 Prince St., Alexandria, Va. 22313), announced a new commercial M98 type turn-bolt action, which they designated the Mk X. I obtained one and, printed on the box is "MARK X CUSTOM MAUSER COMMERCIAL ACTION." It is made in Yugoslavia by Zavodi Crvena Zastava.

The Mark X action, based on the original M98 design, has most of the features that made the M98 famous, plus some modern elements which accounts for Interarms describing it as a "custom" action. The literature and advertisements describing the Mark X contain the following statements: "A custom, commercial Mauser action, forged and machined by true craftsmen from the finest high carbon steel." "The Mark X says 'honest craftsmanship' . . . that old-fashioned, almost forgotten concept of real value for money spent," etc. Well, I don't doubt that the

receiver, bolt and some of the other vital parts are made of a quality steel, but I can't go along with that "honest craftsmanship" bit.

Let's see what the Mark X action does have. Based on the standard length (8.75") large ring (approx. 1.40") M98 Mauser receiver, it is threaded to accept the standard M98 type barrels. The bridge is made without a clip-charger guide slot, the left receiver wall un-notched. Receiver ring and bridge are tapped for top scope mount bases, and the right side of the bridge is tapped for a standard receiver sight. Six holes in all, 6x48 size, all holes fitted with plug screws. The bolt is identical to the standard M98 bolt, except for a low bolt handle profile to clear the lowest-mounted scope. The round grasping ball is flat underneath and checkered. The streamlined bolt sleeve, firing pin, mainspring, cocking piece and bolt sleeve lock are like the modern FN M98 action design, including the safety lug feature on the firing pin shoulder. Striker travel is .500". Cocking occurs on the upturn of the bolt handle. The bolt stop and ejector are M98 copies.

The trigger guard/magazine is a one-piece steel unit, the steel floorplate is hinged and its latch positioned in the front of the guard bow. The follower is milled steel. Two types of triggers are available;

Mk X Mauser action (with plain trigger) made in Yugoslavia and imported by Interarms Ltd., 10 Prince St., Alexandria, Va., 22313.

The Mk X adjustable trigger and safety mechanism, showing: (A) sliding thumb safety; (B) rotary safety lock which blocks trigger when the safety is pulled back; (C) weight of pull adjustment screw; (D) safety adjustment screw; (E) trigger stop or over-travel adjustment screw; (F) sear engagement adjustment screw. The bolt lock is an integral part of the heavy sheet-steel safety. Note that all 3 trigger adjustment screws have lock nuts to prevent their accidental turning. To make adjustments the lock nuts must first be loosened, then tightened again afterward. The stock must be removed before any adjustments can be made. To decrease weight of trigger pull turn out (counterclockwise) screw C. About 2 pounds is the lightest pull that can be obtained with safety. To adjust for minimum over-travel: with bolt closed and striker in fired position, turn in (clockwise) screw E all the way, and then back it out ⅛ turn. To obtain minimum safe trigger take-up or sear engagement: with bolt closed and action cocked, turn in (clockwise) screw F until the sear is released, then turn it back ¼-turn. After any adjustments are made test the action by slamming the bolt closed several times; if the striker does not stay cocked while this is done then the sear engagement is too shallow, the weight of pull is too light, or both. This trigger is unusual in that it has an adjustment screw to take up wear in the safety bolt. This screw (D) is threaded into the rotary safety bolt (B) and prevented from easily turning by a small coil spring under its head. As wear develops (this would be indicated if there is trigger movement when the safety is engaged) this screw can be turned in (clockwise) until trigger movement is gone.

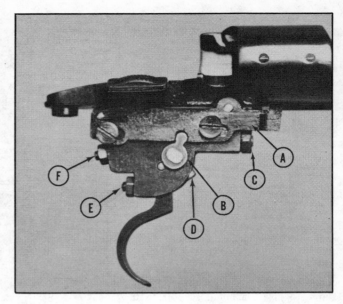

a standard single-stage, non-adjustable trigger not unlike the M98 military trigger, or a fully adjustable single-stage trigger mechanism at extra cost. A sliding side tang safety is standard with either trigger, a safety which locks the bolt and sear when slid back. The complete action weighs about 46 oz. It is of all-steel construction—no alloy or plastic parts are used.

Mark X actions are made to handle 3 family lengths of cartridges; namely, for the long belted magnums the magazine box is slightly over 3.600" long; for the .30-06 class the box is about 3.385" long, and, for such cartridges as the .243, et al, the 3.385" magazine is made shorter through the use of a sheet-metal spacer.

Like the FN receiver, the Mark X action has the collar or shoulder inside the ring slotted on the left side as well as on the right side for the extractor. I believe these actions would be stronger and safer if this collar were unslotted on the left side.

My Mark X action appears to have two fine pinholes on the upper part of the bolt handle shank; to me, as well as to several gun-knowledgeable persons who have seen

the action, these indicate that the bolt handle is welded on. That the bolt handle is actually welded on or not makes little difference, but if it is welded on it should have been so skillfully done that it wouldn't show. The bolt from my action should have been rejected or done over. I have nothing against a welded-on bolt handle (most of my custom rifles have them), but I don't want the weld to show.

Finally, my Mark X action is poorly polished. The floorplate is not level and smooth—it has several flat spots which can be felt and seen, as if extra polishing was done to remove deep tool marks from these places. The floorplate and the guard were polished separately instead of together, leaving the edges of the hinge joint rounded. The bolt stop and the bolt-stop spring were also polished separately on a soft polishing wheel, and their rounded edges certainly look out of place on a "custom" action. A soft wheel must also have been used on the receiver, for the sight-mounting screw holes are dished and edges of the left receiver wall rounded. It is not that the tool marks have not all been removed from the metal surfaces which show when the action is stocked,

or that these surfaces do not have a high polish, but that the polishing was inexpertly done. All major parts except the follower, extractor and the front part of the bolt are blued.

Aside from that, the Mark X action on the whole appears to be well made. The main functional and working parts are mechanically interchangeable with parts from other M98 actions. I consider it a good value for the money. With plain trigger it retails for $59.

The Mark X action is serial numbered, the stamp on the right side of the receiver ring. The **Mark X** designation is stamped on the left side of the ring. There are also numbers stamped on the bottom of the bolt handle stem and on an inside surface of the trigger guard, but on my action these numbers do not match the serial number on the receiver.

Stamped on the left receiver wall in two lines is the following:

ALEXANDRIA INTERARMS
VIRGINIA/ZASTAVA -
YUGOSLAVIA

The **ZCZ** trademark (the letters within a circle) is also stamped on the left receiver wall.

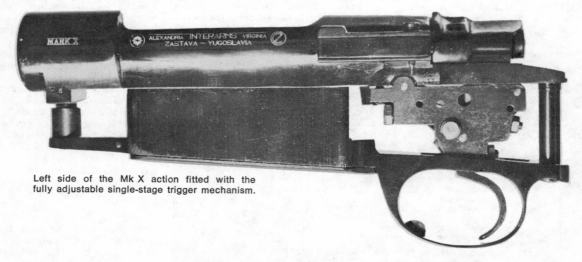

Left side of the Mk X action fitted with the fully adjustable single-stage trigger mechanism.

23. Husqvarna and Smith & Wesson

TRADEWINDS, INC. (P.O. Box 1191, Tacoma, Washington 98401), has been importing the Husqvarna centerfire turn-bolt rifle action since about 1954. Made in Sweden by Husqvarna Vapenfabriks Aktiebolag (HVA for short) in Husk-varna, Sweden until recently,* it is a modified Mauser type action with forward dual locking lugs on the bolt and a staggered-column box magazine with a hinged floor-plate. Well made and finished, it retails today at $80, and it's a good choice on which to build a fine custom made, light-weight sporting rifle.

Since about 1954 Tradewinds has also been importing and selling the HVA bar-reled actions and complete HVA sporting rifles. Barreled actions are now available in calibers .243, .270, 7mm Magnum, .308 and .30-06, although they were previously available as well in several of the more popular European calibers. These units are completely finished, ready to be fitted into a stock.

The complete line of HVA rifles range from the lowest priced Husky at $144.50 to the highest engraved Presentation Grade at $410 in the calibers listed above. These, and their other grades are fine rifles in every sense of the word, and are good values. All have HVA Swedish-made "cold-hammered" barrels.

The HVA has a low-profile bolt handle and a sliding tang safety, both out of the way of a low-mounted scope. The bolt stop is built almost entirely within the receiver. The action is trim, light in weight, clean in outline and smooth in operation. It has proved to be amply strong and safe for the cartridges for which the rifles are chambered.

*Husqvarna actions and rifles are now made at Eskilstuna (Sweden), the site of Swedish military arms making, by a new organization, Viking Sport Arms AB.

The Early HVA Action

Until the early 1960s the HVA action differed somewhat in minor details from the HVA action currently available. Il-lustrated here is an early HVA action which I received in 1955 and on which I later built a very lightweight big game rifle in .270 caliber. Since it is no longer available I'll describe it only briefly.

The markings on the early HVA in-clude the Husqvarna crown trademark and the word **SWEDEN** stamped on the top of the receiver ring. The serial num-ber, proof mark and the word **NITRO** are stamped on the flat on the bottom of the receiver ring.

The trigger guard/magazine assembly was made entirely of steel. The trigger guard bow is part of a magazine plate, and into its magazine hole a sheet-metal magazine box is fitted. Spot welded to the plate in 6 places, the magazine box is 3.385" long. Two HVA actions were then listed by Tradewinds; No. 1 was made for the .257 Roberts, 7mm Mauser and .30-06 length cartridges. No. 2 for the shorter .308 family of cartridges. The latter is identical to the No. 1, including action length and magazine length, but the mag-azine box was made with ribs inside it to hold the shorter cartridges in the rear of the box.

The hinged floorplate latch was a bent, flat-spring affair fitted into the upper front part of the trigger bow. This all-steel action weighs about 44 ounces.

I don't know just when the change from the steel trigger guard/magazine to the alloy assembly was made, but except for this difference, the following description of the HVA action now available applies to the early action as well.

The Late HVA Action

I imagine the Husqvarna action is made of the finest quality, Swedish steel available for the purpose, with all com-ponents properly heat treated. The re-ceiver is slim and smooth in outline, yet ruggedly made. Receiver ring is 1.290" in diameter and 1.750" long. The high and unnotched left wall and the lower right receiver wall extend straight back from the receiver where they connect with the 1.225" long bridge, leaving a receiver opening of slightly over 3". The bridge is the same width as the ring, thus the en-tire left side of the receiver is straight and of the same radius. The top of the bridge is lower than the ring, the general shape and contour the same as the modern FN Mauser action. The receiver ends in a narrow tang, which gives it an over-all length of 8.750". The part of the receiver which shows above the stock line is smoothly and evenly polished. The top of the receiver ring and bridge each have two 6x48 tapped holes for standard scope mounting, plus two 6x48 tapped holes in the right side of the bridge for receiver sight attachment. All of these holes are fitted with plug screws, these having been turned in before the receiver was polished.

The bottom of the receiver is flat except for about .425" at the front of the ring. This flat spot, as well as the heavy recoil lug under the ring, is 1.10" wide. The re-coil lug, about .325" deep, has enough area to prevent recoil from setting the action back into the stock provided it is bedded into the stock properly.

The front end of the ring is inside threaded to accept the barrel shank. There is no inside collar in the ring such as the M98 Mauser action has, so the barrel re-quires a reinforced shoulder to abut against the front of the ring to hold it tightly in place. The breech face of the barrel is flat. Barrel shank specifications

Illustrated above: HVA Imperial lightweight sporting rifle.

are nominally: length — .615"; pitch — V-type, 12 per inch; diameter about .988".

The bolt is of one-piece construction, with the bolt handle made as an integral part of it. The bolt handle has a round tapered stem curved slightly back and out, and ending in a round grasping ball. It has a very low profile so that it will clear the eye-piece of the lowest-mounted scope.

On the extreme forward end of the bolt are the two dual-opposed locking lugs. When the bolt is closed these lugs engage behind heavy shoulders within the rear of the receiver ring, securely locking the bolt. The left (top) locking lug, larger than the right lug, extends forward of the face of the bolt to nearly contact the breech end of the barrel when the action is closed. Neither lug is slotted. The face of the bolt is recessed for the cartridge rim, but this recess is undercut at the bottom as in the M98 Mauser bolt. This allows the head of the cartridge to slip under the extractor hook, on feeding a cartridge from the magazine, to prevent double loading.

As on the M98 bolt, the HVA has an auxiliary, or safety, locking lug on the rear of the bolt body which engages in, but does not bear against, a recess in the bottom of the receiver bridge.

There is a 2.3" long rib on the center of the bolt body and a matching groove under the top of the bridge. This rib guides the bolt as it is operated and prevents the bolt from binding. The extractor is a conventional M98 type, attached to the bolt by a collar in a groove around the bolt. A lip under the front end of the extractor fits in a groove in the bolt head, which prevents longitudinal movement of the extractor. The front of the extractor hook is flat, and quite thin like that of the regular M98 extractor. The surface on the edge of the hook is not angled enough to allow the extractor to snap easily over the rim of a cartridge pushed into the chamber. Like the M98, the HVA action is designed for magazine-fed cartridges.

Initial extraction camming power is ob-

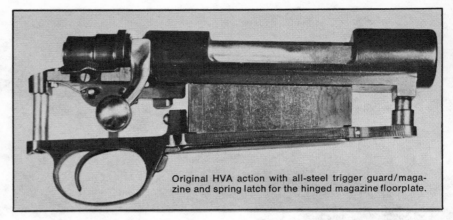

Original HVA action with all-steel trigger guard/magazine and spring latch for the hinged magazine floorplate.

tained by the base of the bolt handle moving across an inclined surface on the rear of the bridge, forcing the bolt and extractor back as the bolt handle is raised. Similar inclined surfaces to the approaches of the locking shoulders in the receiver ring also force the bolt forward when the bolt handle is lowered.

The bolt sleeve threads into the open rear of the bolt. The coil mainspring is compressed between a forward collar on the one-piece firing pin and the bolt sleeve; the rear end of the firing pin is held in place in the bolt sleeve by the cocking piece, which is secured to the firing pin by an interrupted lug arrangement.

The firing pin has a flattened rear section, which rides in a matching hole in the bolt sleeve; this prevents the firing pin rotating. A spring-tensioned, plunger-type bolt sleeve lock fits into the left side of the bolt sleeve and, when the bolt is opened, the end of this plunger slips into a notch in the rear end of the bolt. This prevents the bolt sleeve from turning when the bolt is open.

Like the 98 Mauser bolt, the rear end of the HVA bolt is enlarged to provide thicker metal for the cocking cam notch. The action is cocked on the uplift of the bolt handle.

The trigger mechanism is similar to the conventional military two-hump M98 system but has only one hump, resulting in a single-stage pull. The sear, positioned under the receiver and pivoting on a pin, is tensioned by a coil spring. A projection on the rear end of the sear protrudes through a hole into the cocking cam raceway to contact the cocking piece as the bolt is operated. The trigger pivots on a pin through the sear. The trigger is grooved.

Trigger pull weight is about 5.5 pounds. No adjustment is provided.

The sliding serrated tang safety, at the right side of the tang, is a piece of thin steel fitted along the right side of the sear. There is a groove cut into the bottom of the receiver into which the higher front end of the safety moves, and which projects into the safety locking lug recess.

The safety slides on the sear pin and a screw in oblong holes, and is provided ON and OFF tension by a small spring screwed to the underside of the tang and bearing on a small pin in the safety. A pin through the rear end of the sear projects in an L-shaped slot in the safety. With the action closed and cocked, pulling back on the safety locks both sear and bolt. Pushing the safety forward, exposing the red dot on the rear of the tang, unlocks the sear and bolt. The safety can be put ON when the action is closed and uncocked, but then only the bolt is locked. The safety is

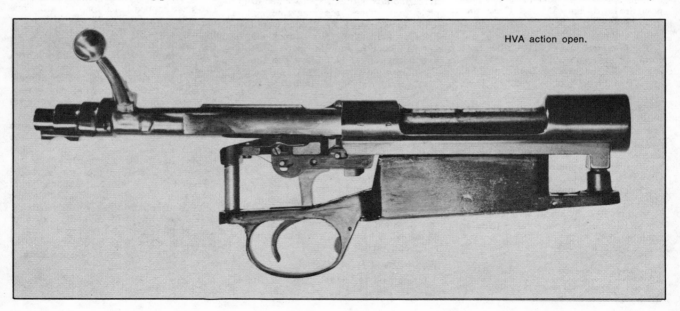

HVA action open.

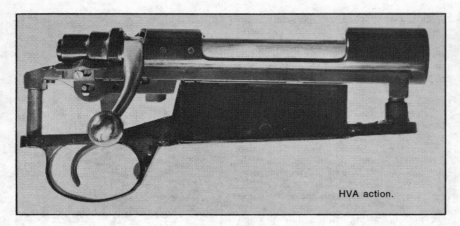

HVA action.

conveniently placed and easy to use. There is no need for an unsightly notch cut into the stock to accommodate the safety. It makes hardly any noise when it is moved from the ON to the OFF (forward) position.

The bolt stop (combined with the ejector) is a thin piece of metal lying in a groove in the left underside of the bridge. It is tensioned and partially held in place by a flat spring screwed to the receiver, with the bolt stop also pivoting on this screw. A serrated button on the bolt stop projects from the receiver and, by depressing this button when the bolt handle is raised, the bolt can be withdrawn. Quite inconspicuous, this button does not stick out far enough on a slim stocked rifle to snag on clothing or brush.

The front part of the bolt stop, which projects into the receiver, has two saw-toothed projections; the front one is the ejector, the other the tooth which stops the bolt.

Two slots are cut into the bolt head; the front slot is cut into the bolt face so the ejector tooth can tip the cartridge case or cartridge, up and to the right, out of the action when the bolt is opened. The rear slot ends in the single gas-vent hole in the bolt. The bolt is stopped when the rear bolt stop tooth contacts this hole.

There is only one gas-escape vent hole in the bolt, and none in the receiver. This hole is located about ½" back from the bolt face and, when the bolt is closed and locked, the hole is positioned to direct the gases into the left locking lug raceway. The left side of the bolt sleeve, flush with the outside of the receiver, would deflect any powder gases outward should any get this far back.

The one-piece magazine box/trigger guard unit is cast in a lightweight alloy, as is the magazine floorplate. Those alloy parts which show are well polished, and the whole unit is anodized black. The floorplate, hinged to the front of the trigger guard on a pin, is released by a spring-loaded lever built into the top front of the guard bow.

One end of the conventional W-shaped follower spring fits into a mortise in the floorplate, the other end in a mortise in the bottom of the machined steel follower. A ridge on the left side of the follower staggers the cartridges in the magazine box. The top of the magazine box fits flush with the bottom of the flat-bottomed receiver.

The magazine-well opening has integral cartridges guide ribs left on each side. The usual ramp on the front of the magazine-well opening guides cartridges into the chamber when they are fed from the magazine by the bolt.

Three HVA actions are available: The 501 is for .30-06 length and head-sized cartridges, the 502 is for .308 and similar-length and head-sized cartridges, and 503 for the belted magnums of .30-06 length. Thus the 501 and 502 are identical except for construction of the magazine walls, and the 501 and 503 are alike except for differences in the bolt-face recess and extractor. All three have magazine boxes of the same length (3.385" inside opening). The No. 502 magazine-box side walls are thicker in front than at the back, and the step-down or ridge left provides a shoulder stop to hold cartridges rearward in the magazine. The shoulder is placed correctly for cartridges of about .243 and .308 body length.

Two sturdy guard screws, through the front and rear ends of the trigger guard/magazine, hold the action securely in the stock. The front guard screw passes through an integral lug on the tang of the trigger guard/magazine. The top of this lug is recessed to fit over a small round stud on the bottom of the recoil lug. This aligns the guard with the receiver. A bushing for the rear guard screw, furnished with HVA actions, is used in the rifles made up by Husqvarna.

Comments

Since the HVA action was first introduced into the U.S. it has been advertised as the "HVA Improved Mauser" and as "The only improved Mauser action designed for lightweight rifles. World famous Swedish steel makes possible an action that is stronger in construction, yet lighter in weight than other Mauser actions." The newly introduced S&W high powered rifle is also built on the HVA action just described and, in the S&W advertising describing this action can be read, among other statements, the following: ". . . Possesses a number of advantages over designs of the military Mauser type." "The striker travel is only half that on rifles of the military Mauser type," and ". . . to cope with the high gas pressures produced by modern ammunition— up to about 50,000 lbs./square inch, as against the former maximum of about 40,000 lbs. . . ." Anyone knowing anything at all about the Mauser system would assume they're referring to the M98 Mauser. I don't think so. I'll explain.

There are only two large arms makers in Sweden; the commercial Husqvarna-firm, making the HVA and other firearms, and the Swedish government arsenal, the Carl Gustafs Gevaersfaktori in Eskilstuna. Husqvarna had made up some rifles on the M98 Mauser action obtained from FN in Belgium, and they'd also made some sporting rifles on the Swedish M96 Mauser action. However, the Carl Gustafs factory—the "Springfield Armory" of Sweden—manufactured many thousands of Mauser military rifles for a period of around 50 years.

The "Mauser" rifles produced at Eskilstuna were the Swedish M94 Mauser carbines and M96 Mauser rifles. Of the original Mauser turnbolt systems, the M98 is without question the best one, but in Sweden it is natural to expect that a "Mauser" there is one they made and used during World Wars I and II, which are the Models 94 and 96. This is borne out by the statement above about the striker travel. The S&W rifles made by Husqvarna have the same actions as the HVA described previously, and their striker travel of .500" is the same as the M98 Mauser. This is exactly half of that of the M96 Swedish Mauser action. Thus, the HVA advertising references to "improved Mauser" means "improved" over the M94 and M96 actions, not to the M98.

Now the M94 and M96 Swedish actions are good and, for a military action, they

Left side of the HVA action.

191

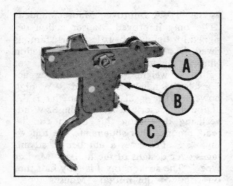

HVA adjustable trigger: (A) weight-of-pull adjustment screw. Pull is made lighter by turning this screw counterclockwise. (B) trigger-stop or over-travel adjustment screw. (C) trigger take-up or sear-adjustment screw.

are extremely well-made and finished. They are certainly strong enough and safe enough to be used with cartridges developing up to about 45,000 psi breech pressure. For details of this action read the chapter entitled "Mauser Models 92, 93, 94, 95 & 96" in this book.

Let's see what HVA copied from the M96 Swedish Mauser and what improvements they made. With some changes they used the receiver which, incidentally is the small ring type. The tang was made a bit wider, the bridge was made without the clip slot and the raised portion, and the thumb groove omitted from the left receiver wall. The same barrel threads are used, the breeching system is the same, with the barrel having a flat face. Except that the left locking lug is not slotted, the locking lugs are the same. The bolt face recess, bolt rib guide and extractor are also the same. The firing mechanism is essentially the same, but the HVA cocking piece is made lighter and the firing pin fall reduced by half making for two improvements over the M96 design. Other HVA improvements are the auxiliary safety lug, the flanged bolt sleeve with its M98 bolt sleeve lock and the low profile bolt handle. The trigger, essentially the same as that on the M98 Mauser, is no improvement.

HVA features which were not copied directly from any other action are the sliding tang safety and the bolt stop/ejector. For sporting use the safety is an improvement, but the bolt stop/ejector is a doubtful one. It is, however, an improvement in that the left locking lug need not be slotted for the ejector, and the bolt stop need not project beyond the edge of the stock line. The bolt stop would be better if it were built heavier.

HVA regressed in designing the gas-escape system. They would have been better off duplicating the venting system used on the M96 action. In addition I also feel there should be a gas-vent hole through the left side of the receiver ring, in line with the vent hole in the HVA bolt, or even two holes, with the second one just to the rear of the barrel face. I also see nothing wrong with a hole through the right side of the receiver ring and a small hole through the end of the extractor. These two or three vent holes would make this action much safer in the event of a serious cartridge head or primer failure. True, such failures are so rare with modern commercial ammunition that one hardly needs to worry about it, but the handloader might want and need more protection.

I also feel that the HVA breeching system would have been stronger and safer had an inside receiver collar been used, as in the M98 action. Still, the HVA breeching is not so much different from that used in the pre-1964 M70 Winchester, and I don't find much fault with it.

As for the HVA standard trigger, I would much rather have the regular two-stage military let-off, for with it the trigger can be a safe one and still have a final release that is short, free of creep and light in weight. It would be just about impossible to obtain a short and moderately light trigger pull with the HVA trigger and still have a safe rifle. Few shooters and hunters today are satisfied with either a heavy, 5 pounds or more, trigger pull or with a double-stage pull, so the only solution to getting a good trigger let-off with the HVA action is to install the Tradewinds adjustable trigger. Priced at $15.95, it is fully adjustable for weight of pull, over-travel and take-up. Easy to install (one hole has to be tapped) it replaces the original trigger and sear and is coupled with the slide safety already on the action.

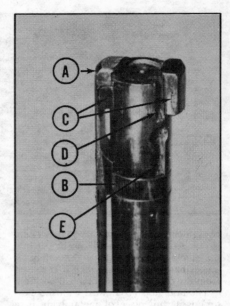

HVA bolt head showing: (A) extractor, (B) extractor collar, (C) locking lugs, (D) ejector slot and (E) gas-vent/bolt-stop hole.

The statement in the S&W literature that the HVA action is made to cope with maximum pressures of 50,000 psi seems odd to me because the factory .270 load develops more than 50,000 psi yet it is one of the cartridges for which their rifles are chambered. Husqvarna also uses this action for the 7mm Magnum, which also develops higher pressure. I believe the HVA action with its solid locking lugs, safety lug and modern steels is suitable for cartridges developing up to some 55,000 psi breech pressure.

There is little question that the HVA is a strong action. Each action, barreled action and rifle is proof tested, probably with proof loads developing up to 70,000 psi. Thus the HVA action would be suitable for all commercial and wildcat cartridges based on .30-06 head-sized cartridges and no longer than 3.375". This would include such cartridges as the .220 Swift, .225 Winchester, .257 Roberts, .284 Winchester, .280 Remington, .358 Winchester and .35 Whelen, besides the many more standard commercial loads.

The HVA action is quite the ideal ac-

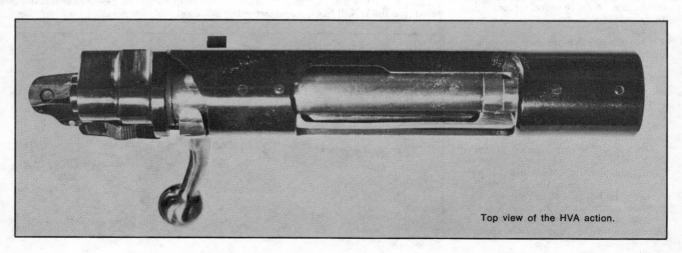

Top view of the HVA action.

Parts Legend

1. Extractor collar
2. Bolt
3. Extractor
4. Firing pin
5. Mainspring
6. Cocking piece
7. Bolt sleeve
8. Bolt-sleeve lock spring
9. Bolt-sleeve lock
10. Bolt stop/ejector
11. Bolt stop/ejector spring
12. Bolt-stop/ejector-spring screw
13. Receiver
14. Safety-spring screw
15. Sear
16. Safety pin
17. Rear guard-screw (stock) bushing
18. Trigger
19. Floorplate latch pin
20. Trigger guard/magazine
21. Floorplate latch spring
22. Rear guard screw
23. Safety spring
24. Sear spring
25. Plug screws (6)
26. Sear pin
27. Trigger pin
28. Safety
29. Safety screw
30. Floorplate latch
31. Floorplate hinge pin
32. Front guard screw
33. Follower
34. Follower spring
35. Magazine floorplate

Husqvarna and Smith & Wesson

Dimensional Specifications

Weight	40 oz.
Receiver length	8.750"
Receiver ring dia.	1.290"
Bolt dia.	.700"
Striker travel	.500"
Bolt travel	4.550"
Bolt face recess	
dia.	.480"
depth	.050"
Magazine well	
length	3.385"
width, rear	.595"
width, front	.550"
Guard-screw spacing	7.187"

General Specifications

Type	Turnbolt repeater.
Receiver	One-piece machined steel. (Early ones were probably machined from a forging, while the late ones are probably made from an investment casting.) Non-slotted bridge. Tapped for scope mounts and receiver sight.
Bolt	One-piece machined steel with dual-opposed forward locking lugs. Safety lug on the rear. Integral low-profile bolt handle.
Ignition	One-piece firing pin powered by coil mainspring. Cocks on opening.
Magazine	Non-detachable staggered-column 5-shot box type. Hinged floor plate. Trigger guard/magazine made of alloy, anodized black.
Trigger	Non-adjustable, single stage pull. Fully adjustable trigger available at extra cost.
Safety	Sliding tang type, locks sear and bolt.
Extractor	Non-rotating Mauser type attached to bolt with a collar.
Magazine cutoff	None provided.
Bolt stop	Positioned in the rear left of the receiver; stops bolt by contacting the gas-vent hole.
Ejector	Part of the bolt stop.

tion for building an ultra lightweight sporter in calibers based on the .30-06 case. It is the lightest action available for this cartridge length, and it would even be possible to trim off another ounce or two by drilling a couple of holes in the bottom of the recoil lug, drilling the desirable extra gas-vent holes in the receiver and bolt, and hollowing out the grasping ball on the bolt handle.

I don't consider the HVA ideal for the shorter .308 family of cartridges. For the lightest and shortest sporting rifle in these calibers the Sako L-579 Forester action is a better choice.

Smith and Wesson Rifles

Smith and Wesson, long known for their quality handguns, entered the rifle field in 1968. Their rifles are based on the exact HVA action I have described here, the only difference being that the S&W trade mark emblem has replaced the HVA seal

on the receiver ring. Except for some slight differences in stock design the S&W HVA rifles are almost the same as the HVA rifles listed by Tradewinds. The higher priced ones have the HVA adjustable trigger. So, if you want to build a rifle like one of Tradewinds' Husqvarna rifles or like the S&W styling, get an HVA action or barreled action from Tradewinds and make your own.

Take-Down and Assembly

Make sure magazine and chamber are empty. To remove the bolt raise the bolt handle and, with the tip of the thumb, hold the bolt stop down and out; now pull the bolt back and out of the receiver. The bolt stop need not be depressed to re-insert the bolt.

To disassemble the bolt grasp the bolt body with one hand and, while depressing the bolt sleeve lock plunger with the thumb of that hand, turn the bolt sleeve counterclockwise so the cocking piece falls into the cocking cam. Then, using a small screwdriver or the like in the other hand, pull the cocking piece back so the bolt sleeve can be turned counterclockwise another turn. Continue turning until the bolt sleeve is unscrewed from the bolt. To disassemble the firing pin assembly grasp the bolt sleeve in one hand and, while resting the firing pin tip on a hard surface, depress the bolt sleeve until the cocking piece can be turned ¼-turn in either direction. The cocking piece can now be lifted off and the firing pin and mainspring separated from the bolt sleeve. Depress the bolt sleeve lock plunger and turn it

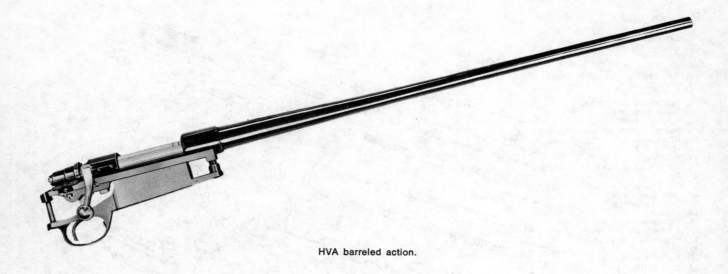

HVA barreled action.

so its retainer stud is released from its groove, after which the bolt sleeve plunger and spring can be removed. Reassemble in reverse order. Remove the extractor by turning it under the bolt and then pushing it forward. Do not remove the extractor collar unless absolutely necessary, as it may be sprung out of shape.

Turn out the front and rear guard screws from the bottom of the rifle and lift the barrel and action from the stock, and the trigger guard/magazine from the bottom of the stock. Drive out the pins from the trigger guard/magazine to remove the floorplate and floorplate latch. Turn out the safety spring screw and remove the safety spring. Drive the sear pin to the left with a drift punch, turn out the safety screw and the safety can be removed. Remove trigger and sear by driving out the sear pin. Turn out the bolt stop spring screw and lift the spring and the bolt stop from the receiver. Reassemble in reverse order.

The barrel is threaded tightly into the receiver (right hand threads) and no attempt should be made to remove it unless you have the proper tools.

Markings

Late model HVA actions have the following stamped on the left receiver wall: HVA ACTION — MADE IN SWEDEN The serial number, proof mark(s) and the word **NITRO** are stamped on the flat under the receiver ring.

Sectional view of the S&W action.

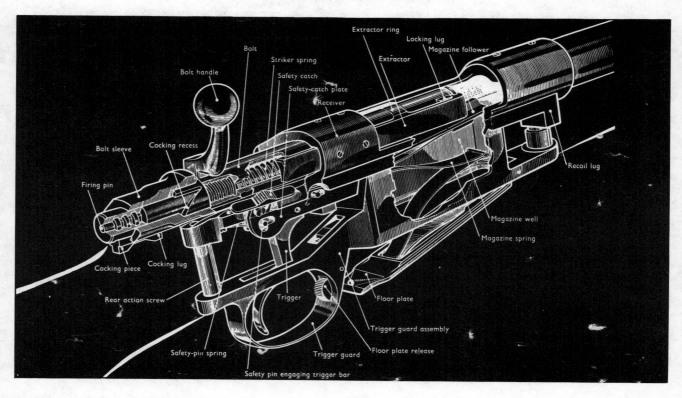

194

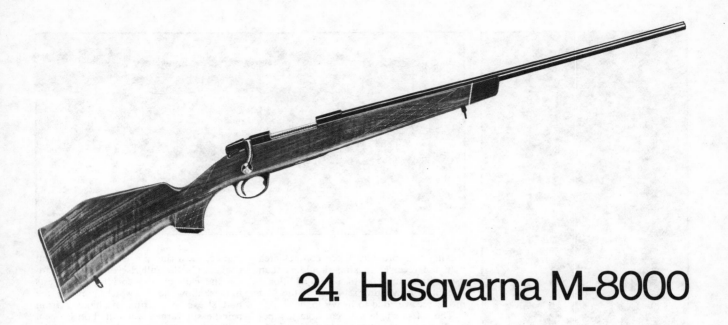

24. Husqvarna M-8000

No sooner had I finished the chapter on Husqvarna actions when an entirely new one was introduced, early in 1969. The Model 8000 HVA rifle action is quite a departure from one described in the preceding chapter. At this writing the "New Husqvarna" action is not available separately, but the importer (Tradewinds, Inc., P.O. Box 1191H, Tacoma, Washington 98401) says these actions will be available by the time this book is in print.

Before describing the new action, I'll cover the Husqvarna rifles built on it. The best one, the M-8000 Imperial, is quite an impressive rifle in every detail. Offered in .270, .30-06, 7mm Magnum and .300 Magnum calibers, this well-made Mauser type turnbolt rifle weighs about 7.5 pounds. The 4-groove lightweight 23.62" barrel has no open sights on it, nor is it tapped for any. The rifle is intended to be used with a scope and the receiver is suitably tapped, as it is also for mounting a receiver sight.

The well-proportioned stock, of select European walnut, is shaped to satisfy the average American shooter, being quite full in the fore-end, grip and comb areas. The fine-grained, well-colored stock is sanded level and smooth, then given a high gloss plastic or varnish type finish. Two panels each of skip-line checkering decorate the sides of the fore-end and pistol grip. The stock has non-detachable sling swivels and a rosewood fore-end tip. The pistol grip cap and buttplate are plastic, with white-line spacers, as has the fore-end tip. Metal parts are beautifully polished and blued, except for the highly polished and jeweled bolt. The anodized alloy floorplate is lightly engraved. This excellently made and finished rifle retails for $285. The M-9000 Crown grade Husqvarna rifle at $212.50, is in every way similar to the Imperial grade, but the stock is a plainer piece of walnut with a semi-gloss finish, and it has open sights.

The HVA M-8000 Action

To make it easier for me to describe, and easier for the reader to follow, and to avoid some repetition, I will compare this new Husqvarna action with the older HVA action described in the preceding chapter.

To begin with, the trigger guard/magazine assembly on both actions is nearly identical, with both of lightweight alloy one-piece construction. The follower spring, follower, and floorplate latch are also the same.

Outwardly the M-8000 receiver is quite similar to that of the early HVA, but it is slightly longer and has a wide and well-rounded tang surface like that on the new M70 Winchester. Underneath, however, there is quite a difference. Except for the recoil lug the bottom of the M-8000 receiver is round. It may be that this receiver is machined from bar stock or from a die forging, or it may be an investment casting. In any case, this would not reflect on the quality or strength of the receiver. It only indicates the Husqvarna has adopted a better method to make a better receiver. The several people I've shown this receiver to all agree that the recoil lug is made integral with the rest of the receiver and, if this is the case, the receiver probably is a modern investment casting.

The barrel, of course, is threaded into the receiver and it has a flat breech face.

The magazine well opening is 3.525" long, though the magazine box has an opening only 3.390" in length. In making the magazine well, cartridge guide lips are left on each side. There are no machine marks on the sides of the well and guide ribs, and the surfaces are unusually smooth and burr free. This is one reason why cartridge feeding is so easy and reliable.

Everything else is a radical departure from the earlier HVA action. The M-8000

action has a number of new design features which modern day rifle shooters seem to demand. These include a set of non-slotted forward locking lugs, a safety lug, recessed bolt face, cock-on-opening, enclosed bolt sleeve, side safety, cocking indicator, adjustable trigger, anti-bind bolt, and a low bolt-handle profile for low-scope mounting.

The fully recessed bolt head is cut away at the rim only for the extractor, the latter held in place and tensioned by a small spring and plunger set into a hole behind it. It is a close copy of the extractor in the Sako L-61 action. The ejector is a spring-loaded plunger fitted into a hole on the edge of the bolt-face recess.

The dual-opposed locking lugs are on the extreme front of the bolt and both are solid. As can be seen in the accompanying photo, the lugs are fantailed in shape or, if you prefer, male dovetail shape. To complement this shape the locking lug guideways in the receiver are milled to a female dovetail form. Thus, as the bolt is opened and closed, with the left locking lug sliding snugly in its guideway, the front of the bolt is guided without binding. There is, in addition, a slight ridge on the lower corner of the right locking lug which slides in a groove cut along the right receiver wall, above the cartridge-guide lip, thus further guiding the front of the bolt.

The result is that the bolt cannot bind no matter how it is operated or by whom —it has to go in a straight line. Finally, the Husqvarna gunmakers finished the contacting surfaces of the bolt and the receiver so well that it is one of the easiest and smoothest actions to operate made today. Since the dovetail shape of the

---

Illustrated above: Model 8000 Imperial Grade Husqvarna sporting rifle, imported by Tradewinds, Inc., of Tacoma, Wash. Available in .270, .30-06, 7mm Magnum and .300 Magnum.

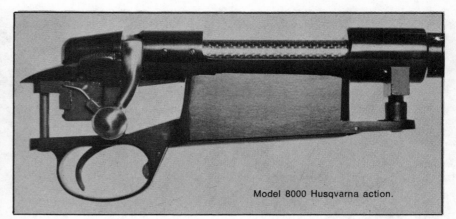

Model 8000 Husqvarna action.

Floorplate engraving. Model 800 Husqvarna rifle.

locking lugs provides more contact area with the receiver locking shoulders than usual, this may be of some additional benefit in preventing set-back of the bolt in the receiver due to heavy loads.

There is a single gas-vent hole just behind and between the locking lugs which, when the bolt is locked, would direct any escaping powder gases into the locking lug recess in the receiver and into the left locking lug raceway. There is no vent hole in the left side of the receiver, but none is needed because the bolt sleeve effectively seals off the rear end of the locking lug raceway so that gases cannot reach the shooter's face.

The M-8000 lacks the separate safety locking lug found on the previous HVA and M98 Mauser bolts. Instead on the M-8000 the bolt handle is the safety lug and the tang of the receiver is notched for it. The bolt handle, made as a separate part, is expertly welded into a slot in the bolt. This, and other short cuts taken in making this action, in no way affect the strength, performance, appearance or reliability of this action—nothing is sacrificed.

The bolt is drilled from the rear to accept the firing pin and coil mainspring. The one-piece firing pin, threaded into the cocking piece, is prevented from turning by a pin through the underside of the cocking piece. A cam on the top of the cocking piece rides a cam surface on the rear of the bolt and, on raising the bolt

handle, the firing pin is drawn back and cocked. On the full rise of the bolt handle the cam on the cocking piece rests in a shallow notch, which prevents the bolt sleeve and firing mechanism from being easily turned when the bolt is open.

The bolt sleeve completely covers the cocking piece. Made with a long stem which fits inside the bolt body, it is held to the latter by an inside groove which engages over a lug on the end of the bolt body. This clever arrangement allows the firing mechanism to be easily removed and replaced. The front of the bolt sleeve is flared outward to seal off the locking lug raceways. Behind these flares it tapers back to a rounded end, making for clean simple lines. In the rounded end there is a small hole and, when the action is cocked, a bright spot on the end of the firing pin can be seen and felt to serve as a cocking indicator.

The trigger, sear and safety mechanism are built into a steel sheet-metal housing attached to the underside of the receiver by a single pin. The sear, pivoting on a pin through the housing, is tensioned by a coil spring. When not cocked the sear acts as the bolt stop. A groove is cut into the bottom of the bolt in which the sear rides, and the bolt is stopped when the front of the sear contacts the end of the groove. Pulling the trigger back hard tips the sear down out of the path of the bolt so that the bolt can be removed. The sear must also be tipped down in replacing

Left side of the Model 8000 Husqvarna action open.

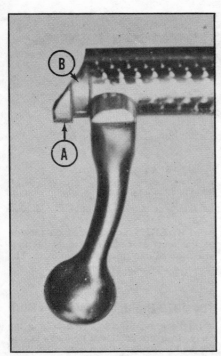

Rear end of the Model 8000 Husqvarna bolt showing: (A) bolt-sleeve retainer lug and (B) cocking-cam surface.

the bolt. The sear is quite wide and rugged, and I believe it will stand up under the punishment of opening the action smartly, something which cannot be said of all actions having a similar bolt-stop system.

The trigger is pivoted on a pin in the bottom of the housing. An arm extends straight up from the trigger, just forward of the front of the sear, where a shallow sear notch engages the trigger when the action is closed. Another arm on the trigger extends backward; between the end on this arm and the housing there is a coil spring backed by a screw. This is the

trigger adjustment screw, and its head is exposed through a hole in the receiver tang. With the bolt removed this screw can be turned clockwise with a small screwdriver to increase the weight of the trigger pull, and vice versa. The total range of adjustment is from about 3 to 6 pounds. The trigger itself, well curved and grooved, is properly positioned in the guard for good control. Trigger travel is a bit longer than necessary, and it overtravels a bit when the sear is released, but neither is objectionable on a hunting rifle.

The safety pivots on the same pin as the trigger. The deeply serrated thumbpiece, extending just over the stock line on the right side of the rounded tang, is easy and convenient to operate. It is virtually noiseless. Pulling the safety back locks the sear and bolt. Pushed forward, a yellow dot in the stock is exposed, indicating the rifle is ready to be fired.

All M-8000 action parts are made of steel except the trigger guard/magazine and floorplate. All exposed steel parts of the receiver and bolt are expertly finished and polished. The surfaces are true, level and very smooth. There are no waves, dished-out holes or rounded edges. Few tool marks can be found anywhere. Bolt operation is very smooth and easy. The bolt handle is well positioned for fast operation of the bolt from any position. The action is clean and smooth in outline. The same scope mounts which fit the earlier HVA action also fit this one.

Take-Down and Assembly

To remove the bolt raise the bolt handle and pull back hard on the trigger; now pull the bolt out. To replace the bolt, the bolt head and locking lugs must be carefully aligned with the bolt and locking lug guideways in the receiver; again pull the trigger to lower the sear and push the bolt home.

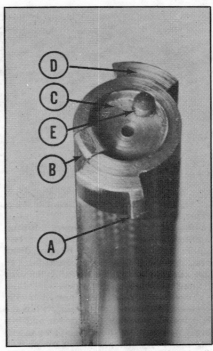

Model 8000 bolt head showing: (A) guide rib on the bottom corner of the right hand locking lug, (B) extractor, (C) bolt-face recess, (D) left locking lug, (E) ejector. Note fantail shape of both locking lugs.

To disassemble the bolt, grasp the bolt body in one hand and turn the bolt sleeve clockwise ½-turn; the bolt sleeve and firing pin can now be removed from the bolt. To replace the firing mechanism in the bolt, align the open bottom of the bolt sleeve with the lug on the rear of the bolt, then push the bolt forward until it can be turned ½-turn clockwise. The firing pin, threaded into the cocking piece, is held from turning by a rolled pin. Although there is no real need for ever

Top view of the rear part of the Model 8000 receiver with bolt removed. Arrow points to the trigger weight-of-pull adjustment screw. Turning this screw counterclockwise reduces pull.

Underside view of the rear end of the Model 8000 bolt showing: (A) flared bolt sleeve, (B) cocking piece, (C) firing-pin retainer pin, (D) bolt handle, (E) groove for bolt stop.

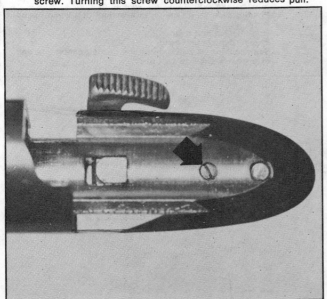

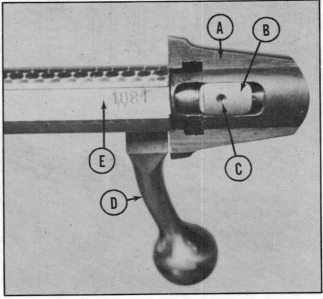

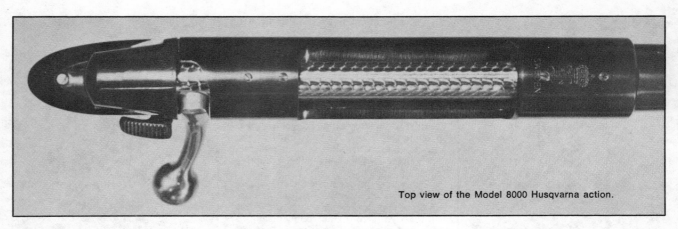

Top view of the Model 8000 Husqvarna action.

removing the firing pin (except for replacement of parts or blueing the bolt sleeve), the firing pin can be turned out after driving the rolled pin in and through the cocking piece, then unscrewing the firing pin.

The extractor can be removed by depressing the extractor plunger within the bolt with a jeweler's screwdriver and lifting it out. Replace the extractor by inserting the spring and plunger in place, then insert the extractor and back it into place. The ejector, held in place by a hollow pin, can be driven out after the extractor has been removed.

To remove the barreled action from the stock turn out the front and rear guard screws, then lift out the barrel and action. Then pull the trigger guard/magazine from the bottom of the stock.

Remove the trigger mechanism by driving out the pin in the very top of the housing which holds the housing to the receiver and pull the mechanism free. Do not disassemble this mechanism unless absolutely necessary, and then do it with utmost care.

Markings

The Husqvarna rifle is marked through a roll stamping on the top middle of the barrel:

HUSQVARNA
VAPENFABRIKS A.B.

This is followed by the caliber designation. The serial number is stamped rather carelessly on the left side of the barrel breech. The last four digits of the serial number are also etched on the bottom of the bolt. A proof mark and the word **NITRO** under it are stamped on the breech—the proof mark is stamped under the receiver also. The Husqvarna trademark and the word **SWEDEN** are stamped on the top of the receiver ring. The trade mark is also molded into the plastic buttplate. The model designation is not stamped on the rifle.

The 1970 Smith and Wesson Rifle

In the previous chapter describing the early Husqvarna action, I pointed out that the Smith & Wesson bolt action rifles introduced in 1968 were built on this action. Now, with the introduction of the new and improved HVA action described in this chapter, the 1970 line of S&W rifles will be based on this new action. Except for the change in the actions, the 1970 S&W rifles will remain about the same. Adopting the new HVA action will improve the S&W rifles.

Dimensional Specifications

Weight	40 ozs.
Length	9.00"
Receiver ring dia.	1.293"
Bolt dia.	.700"
Bolt travel	4.375"
Striker travel	.300"
Bolt face recess:	
depth	.115"
dia. (Standard calibers)	.485"
(Magnum calibers)	.540"
Magazine length	3.390"
Guard-screw spacing	7.75"

General Specifications

Type	Turnbolt repeater.
Receiver	One-piece machined steel with unslotted bridge and integral recoil lug. Tapped for top scope mounts and receiver sight.
Bolt	Machined steel with dual-opposed forward locking lugs. Low profile handle, welded on, serves as safety locking lug.
Ignition	One-piece firing pin powered by coil mainspring. Cocks on the opening. Bolt has 80° swing.
Magazine	Non-detachable 5-shot box type with hinged floorplate. 4-shot for magnum calibers.
Trigger	Single-stage adjustable for weight of pull.
Safety	Pivoting side tang type locks sear and bolt when tipped back.
Extractor	Hook type in bolt head.
Ejector	Plunger type in bolt head.
Bolt stop	Sear doubles as bolt stop; stops bolt by contacting end of a groove cut into bolt body.

Model 9000 Crown Grade Husqvarna rifle.

25. Tradewinds Series 600

IN 1968 Tradewinds Inc. (P.O. Box 1191H, Tacoma, Wash. 98401) began importing a new lightweight bolt action sporting rifle they called the Tradewinds "600." The new rifles (in two versions) are made by Kriegeskorte & Co., Stuttgart-Hedelfingen, West Germany, makers of the well-known Krico brand rifles. The 600S has a standard single-stage trigger and open sights, while the 600K has double set triggers and a barrel without sights. Both have checkered walnut stocks, sling swivels, 23.62″ barrels, and they're made in .222, .222 Magnum, .223, .22-250, .243 and .308. All of the .22 barrels have a rifling twist of one turn in 14″, the .243 has a 1:10″ twist and the .308 a 1:12″ twist. They weigh about 6.75 pounds. At this writing the 600S is $172.50, the 600K $169.50.

Barreled actions are now available in the calibers listed above, the metal parts completely finished and blued, ready to be dropped into a stock. The DS model features double set triggers, while the S model has a standard single-stage trigger. Either is $129.95.

Separate actions are priced at $89.95. Actions for the .222 cartridge family are designated Model 6128; that made for the .308 family, which includes the .22-250, is the Model 6357. Both are available with single-stage or double set trigger mechanisms.

The 600 Action

The 600 receiver appears to be machined from a solid steel bar or from a piece of heavy-walled seamless steel tubing. The receiver ring is larger in diameter than the rest of the receiver, which provides additional metal over the important locking lug area. The flat-faced barrel threads into the receiver ring, the threads of standard V-type, 20 threads per inch. The recoil lug is clamped between the barrel shoulder and the receiver ring. Its lug is ample in size to prevent setback of the action in the stock from recoil provided the lug is properly bedded. The bridge is of smaller diameter than the receiver ring. Both are round and tapped for top scope-mount bases. There is no skimping in the amount of metal left inside the receiver ring for the locking lug support shoulders. Even the bottom one, which forms the loading ramp, is so heavy that it cannot give way under heavy back thrust of the bolt.

The receiver ring is about 1.575″ long, the loading port about 2.560″, and the bridge about 1.175″ long. The left receiver wall, not notched or cut, is amply high and thick to give sufficient rigidity to the receiver to support a free-floating barrel. The bridge area is slotted and notched for passage of the bolt handle, with the notch forming the safety lug.

The bolt body, precision machined from a single piece of steel, has heavy and unslotted dual-opposed locking lugs on its extreme forward end. The approaching corners of these lugs are slightly beveled to engage and move easily over the inclined approaches on the locking lug shoulders, thus forcing the bolt forward as the bolt handle is lowered.

The bolt face is recessed for the cartridge head. The rim of this recess is cut away in one place only, and that for the very narrow extractor. The extractor, fitted into a groove cut into the bolt head, is held in place and tensioned by a spring-loaded plunger set into a hole behind it. The extractor system is not unlike that which Savage/Stevens uses in most of their .22 rimfire repeating rifles. The ejector, a plunger backed by a spring fitted into a hole in the bolt head, is held in place by a rolled pin.

The bolt is open at the rear to accept the firing pin and mainspring. The firing pin is of one-piece design but its front collar, against which the mainspring rests, is a separate part pinned in place by a tempered rolled pin.

The cocking piece, fitted with a black plastic cap, is threaded over the rear end of the firing pin, and is held in place by a heavy hardened pin. Between the cocking piece and the mainspring there is a sleeve with opposing milled flats. There is a square hole milled through the rear of the bolt body to accept the bolt handle. The part of the bolt handle which fits into the bolt is slotted to fit over the milled part of the firing-pin sleeve so that the bolt handle anchors this sleeve and the mainspring tension on the sleeve holds the bolt handle in place.

The rear end of the bolt body is thinner than the rest of the bolt and the cocking piece fits over this portion. Two cocking cam notches are milled in this part, with the hardened cocking piece pin so positioned as to engage these notches. On raising the bolt handle the pin, riding evenly on these cam surfaces, causes the firing pin to be forced back. Above these deep cam surfaces are two small notches, into which the cocking cam pin rests when the action is open; this prevents the cocking piece from being turned.

Two large gas-vent holes in the front of the bolt body will adequately vent off any powder gases which might enter inside the bolt interior through the firing-pin hole from a pierced primer, directing the gases into the left locking-lug raceway.

Behind the bridge the walls are high enough to enclose the entire cocking piece and its plastic cap, these walls having raceways for the bolt locking lugs to pass through. The cocking piece and its plastic cap also have lugs on both sides which fill these raceways. This prevents the cocking piece from turning when the bolt is raised and lowered; at the same time effectively blocking the raceways against the entrance of foreign material and retarding the escape of powder gases should a primer or case head fail.

The bolt handle has a very low profile

Illustrated above: Model 600 Tradewinds varmint rifle.

and its very slim tapered stem, bent slightly back, ends with a round grasping ball. There is a spring-loaded plunger in the base of the bolt handle, and on fully closing the bolt the plunger falls into a shallow detent in the wall of the bridge. This prevents the bolt from falling open when the action is cocked and the safety is not engaged. There is an inclined surface on the rear of the bridge which, on raising the bolt handle, contacts the bolt handle and forces the bolt back to provide the initial extraction camming power.

The Tradewinds 600 action which I received, courtesy of Tradewinds, Inc., was fitted with the double-set trigger mechanism. This mechanism, separate from the trigger, is housed in a sheet-metal box attached to the underside of the receiver by two screws. The side tang safety, pivoted to the right side of this housing, is tensioned in the ON and OFF position by a flat spring which covers the entire right side of the housing. The safety thumb-piece, slightly curved and finely serrated, fits flush against the rear end of the receiver. An arm forward on the safety extends into a groove in the bolt raceway and, with the safety tipped back, the end of this arm engages a notch in the rear of the bolt body, locking the bolt. At the same time the safety locks the sear and rocker (kick-off).

The sear, pivoting inside the housing, is tensioned by a small coil spring. The rocker pivots in the front of the housing on a lever which is, in turn, connected to the sear; pushing up on the end of the rocker, which projects below the housing, causes the sear to be pulled down to release the cocking piece or to allow the bolt to be removed, since the sear also functions as the bolt stop. The front and rear surfaces of the sear which projects into the boltway are square, the rear one being the sear and the front one the bolt stop to contact a square end of a flat spot milled off the bottom of the bolt body.

The steel trigger guard bow itself is machined to form the housing for the double-set trigger mechanism. It is of the common two-trigger type, the triggers pivoting on separate pins running through walls milled in the trigger guard. The front trigger (by which the rifle is fired) is under tension from a small coil spring, while the rear, or cocking trigger, is powered by a heavy elongated-O flat spring. When the rear trigger is pulled back to cock the trigger mechanism it engages a sear notch in the front trigger, holding the rear trigger back under rather heavy spring pressure. Then, to fire the rifle the front trigger is pulled, releasing the rear trigger, which then strikes the rocker to disengage the sear from the cocking piece. A small adjustment screw, exposed between the two triggers, adjusts the pull weight to as light as a few ounces. A hole in the bottom of the guard bow allows insertion of a screwdriver to adjust this screw. Turning this screw clockwise reduces the weight of pull.

The trigger should never be cocked until the moment just before you intend to fire the rifle, and promptly unset if for any

Tradewinds Model 600 short action with double-set trigger.

reason the rifle is not fired. With this rifle the set triggers can be safely unset by engaging the safety and/or raising the bolt handle and pulling the front trigger. The rifle should *never* be carried with the trigger mechanism cocked, for the triggers can be cocked as easily and as quickly after sighting something to shoot at as it is to move the safety to the OFF or FIRE position. It is possible to fire the rifle without cocking the triggers by merely pulling back hard on the front trigger, but the pull is so heavy and rough that it would be difficult to fire the rifle accurately in this manner.

The Tradewinds 600 action with the single-stage trigger mechanism has a conventional trigger in the sear housing in place of the rocker. This trigger is only adjustable for weight of pull, and to make this adjustment the barreled action must first be removed from the stock. The adjustment screw, located at the front of the housing, has a lock nut which must be loosened before the screw can be turned. This rifle has an additional lever at the left of the bridge which depresses the sear for removal of the bolt.

The barreled action is held in the stock by three guard screws threaded into the bottom of the receiver; one through the front of the magazine plate, the others through holes in each end of the guard. Heavy steel stock bushings are provided for these screws, with the rear and center one being partially threaded inside to match the threads on the guard screws, but I have not figured out the reason or purpose of this arrangement. However, when making or fitting a stock to this action the three bushings should be used; especially so the two rear ones, as they will provide the correct spacing between the double-set trigger mechanism and the sear/safety mechanism.

The trigger guard is of milled steel. The magazine plate, a stamped piece of heavy sheet-metal, is held in place at the rear by its fitting into a groove in the guard, and at the front by the front guard screw. A sheet-metal magazine box housing is positioned between the trigger plate and the bottom of the receiver, where it is milled out for the magazine. The magazine catch, fitted to the rear of the magazine plate, is tensioned by a small coil spring.

The simple magazine box is made of

heavy sheet-metal, with the seam welded where the edges come together up front. The bottom of the magazine box has rolled edges which engage over notches crimped in the magazine so that it is easily slipped off for cleaning. It is locked in place by a plate-like plunger fitted under the bottom of the follower spring. The follower spring, W-shaped, has a flat sheet-metal plate riveted on each end. The follower is a sheet-metal stamping. The edges of the rear part of the magazine box opening are curved inward to hold the follower in place, as well as to hold the cartridges in the magazine after they have been inserted.

To load the magazine individual cartridges are pushed down slightly into the front half of the magazine and then slid back under the magazine lips. The magazine, inserted by merely pressing it home, is removed by pushing the magazine latch forward.

Comments

I consider this action an excellent one, with many things about it that I think are very good. The things I don't like are minor, and do not really detract much from the over-all quality of the action or from its performance.

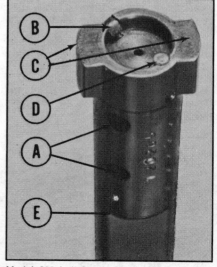

Model 600 bolt head showing: (A) gas-vent holes, (B) extractor, (C) locking lugs, (D) ejector, (E) bolt-stop shoulder.

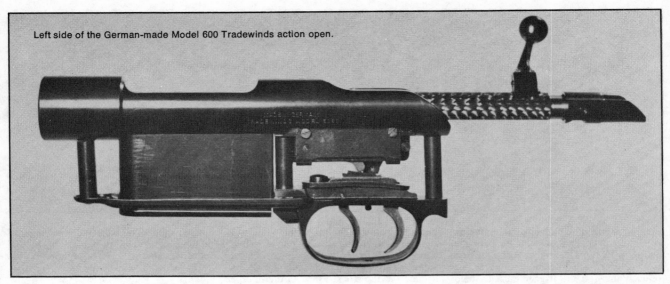

Left side of the German-made Model 600 Tradewinds action open.

I like the heavy receiver ring with its rather large barrel shank thread. I like the solid twin locking lugs and the more than ample amount of metal left in the receiver ring for the locking lug supporting shoulders. Although this action is quite light in weight the strength in the receiver ring and breeching more than adequately support any cartridge for which this action is chambered. Having a recessed bolt face is a good idea, and the bolt of this rifle is large enough in diameter so that the rim around the recess is thick enough to actually support the cartridge rim in the event such support is needed. The ejector is good. That the tip of the extractor does not protrude beyond the bolt face is a good idea because this makes it feasible to fit a flat-faced barrel to the action. I think the extractor will prove adequate, but I'd like to have seen it made about twice its present width or like the extractor in the Sako L-61 action.

Although I think this action has adequate provisions to protect the shooter from escaping powder gases against the rare occurrence of a ruptured case head

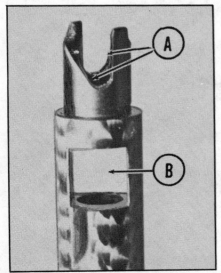

Rear end of the Model 600 bolt showing: (A) twin cocking cams, (B) square hole for bolt handle.

or primer, drilling two small holes in the receiver ring would make it much safer. I would put one hole in the right of the receiver ring, just behind the face of the barrel, and another hole in the left side, just opposite the front gas-vent hole in the bolt. I don't believe there would be any need for the rearmost vent hole in the bolt.

The design and construction of the firing mechanism and the way it is held in the bolt by the bolt handle is very good. The size, shape and placement of the bolt handle is quite pleasing. I very much like the plunger built into the base of the bolt handle — more bolt action rifles should have this feature. The design of the twin cocking cams is excellent. I would prefer something other than plastic used to cap the cocking piece, for in time the plastic may deform or crack.

I think the safety could have been improved in several ways. First, it may be a little too noisy for some hunters as a definite click can be heard when the safety is disengaged. I also believe some will complain that the safety slips too easily under the thumb, and even worse under a gloved thumb; coarser serrations — or better still, two serrated humps — would have taken care of this. Also, if the safety could have been made to slide back and forth instead of pivoting, the unsightly cut in the stock could have been avoided.

The good single-stage trigger mechanism should be the first choice if the rifle is to be used for shooting running game or for big game hunting. Although the trigger pull must of necessity be a bit long, it can be adjusted to a light pull. For the serious varmint shooter I recommend the double-set trigger, which appears to be well made and very rugged. There is plenty of room in the guard to operate this mechanism, and I believe it will stand up under much use.

I like the 600 magazine system, which has some advantages over a non-detachable one. The loaded magazine can be quickly and easily inserted into this rifle, and as quickly removed. A spare loaded magazine can be carried for quick reloading, or a spare magazine with different loads in it may at times be convenient

and desirable. If of the single-column design, as is this one, feeding problems are eliminated because cartridges are fed in a straight line into the chamber. Also, with a single column design less wood has to be cut out of the stock to weaken it at this point. This may be of some advantage in a varmint rifle. The only disadvantage is that the clips are easily lost.

What I like most of all about this German-made action is that it is so well made and finished. Excellent workmanship is evident at every glance. The receiver is beautifully machined, polished and blued. The bolt is perfectly straight and round, highly polished and jeweled. There is no sign of over-polishing, the polished surfaces being perfectly level and without dished-out holes or rounded corners. Most of the other parts are equally well finished. The action operates with ease and smoothness. Lock time is very fast and ignition positive. Some will object to the stamped magazine plate but so little of it shows that it does not detract from the rifle's appearance. All in all, I think highly of this action.

Cartridge Choices

The M6128 "600" action, made for the .222 family of cartridges, would also be ideal for any wildcats based on any one of these cartridges such as the 6x47 and .17/223. The M6357 "600" action made for the .308 cartridge family is equally well-suited for the .243, .308, .358, *et al.* It is also a fine action for the .220 Swift, .22-250, .224 Weatherby, 6mm International (6mm/250), 6mm, .250-3000, .257 Roberts, .284 and other cartridges of .30-06 head size and 2.80" or shorter overall. Either action with the double-set trigger would be excellent for a light- or medium-weight varmint rifle, while the M6357 action, with single-stage trigger, is a fine choice for a light or featherweight big game rifle.

Take-Down and Assembly

To remove the bolt from the plain trigger action, hold the trigger back and, while

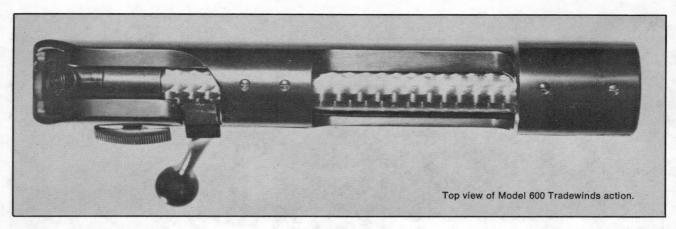

pressing down on the lever on the left side of the receiver, pull the bolt out. On the action with the DS trigger just hold the front trigger back to remove the bolt. To reinsert the bolt the trigger must be held back or the lever depressed.

To disassemble the bolt grasp the bolt body in one hand and the cocking piece in the other, then pull the cocking piece back until it can be turned clockwise. Rotate it ¼-turn or until it falls against the bolt. The bolt handle can then be pulled from the bolt body and the firing mechanism from the bolt. To remove the mainspring drive out the rolled pin from the collar on the front of the firing pin. Reassemble in reverse order. The firing pin is threaded tightly into the cocking piece, and they should not be separated except for replacement of either part, in which case the cocking pin must first be driven out. The plastic cap is pressed on the rear of the cocking piece; there is no need to remove it.

The ejector is removed by driving out its cross pin from the bolt head. Use a sharpened jeweler's screwdriver to remove the extractor by pushing the extractor plunger into the bolt and lifting out the extractor.

To remove the barrel and action from the stock first remove the magazine box. Then turn out the front guard screw and lift the magazine plate up at the front and out of the stock. The magazine catch can then be removed by turning out its screw. Turn out front and rear trigger guard screws and the barreled action can be lifted from the stock. Pinch in the middle of the magazine housing slightly and remove it from the receiver. Turn out the rear and center guard screws all the way and the trigger guard can be removed from the stock. Reassemble in reverse order.

Remove the trigger/sear mechanism by turning out the two screws on the left side of the housing and pull the housing away from the receiver. Do not disassemble this mechanism, or the double-set trigger mechanism, unless absolutely necessary, and then only if you know what it's all about, laying the parts out in the order they are removed so they can be correctly assembled again.

To disassemble the magazine box hold the box upside down and depress the small plunger projecting through a hole in the floorplate with a pointed tool and slide the plate forward and off the box. The plunger plate, follower spring and follower can now be removed. Reassemble in reverse order.

Markings

The Tradewinds 600 action is serial numbered, the number stamped on the bottom right side of the receiver ring and on the bottom front of the bolt body. The following, in two lines, is stamped on the lower left side wall of the receiver:

MADE IN GERMANY

TRADEWINDS MODEL 6357

(or 6128)

All markings are normally covered by the stock.

Conclusion

Just before the completed manuscript of this book was sent to the publisher I heard from Tradewinds that another "600" series rifle had been introduced. Called the Tradewinds Husky, it comes in two action lengths — the short one in .22-250, .243 and .308, its action almost identical to that used on the M600S Tradewinds rifle described earlier in this chapter. The .270 and .30-06 Husky has a longer action than the M600S, but is otherwise about identical to it. It has a magazine box long enough to accept the .270 cartridge, which is normally loaded to 3.340″ over-all. According to Tradewinds the long action will be made available separately, as will a barreled action.

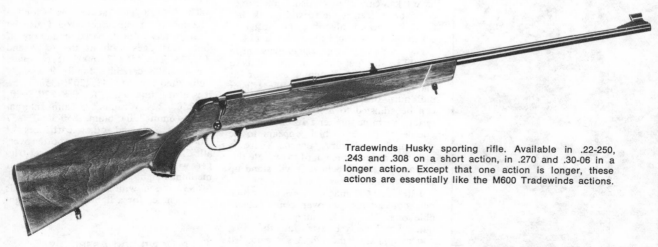

Tradewinds Husky sporting rifle. Available in .22-250, .243 and .308 on a short action, in .270 and .30-06 in a longer action. Except that one action is longer, these actions are essentially like the M600 Tradewinds actions.

Parts Legend

1. Receiver (top view)
2. Sear mechanism
3. Safety
4. Sear housing screws (2)
5. Bolt
6. Bolt handle
7. Firing pin
8. Firing-pin collar
9. Firing-pin collar pin
10. Mainspring
11. Firing-pin sleeve
12. Cocking piece
13. Cocking-piece cap
14. Cocking pin
15. Trigger guard (with double set trigger)
16. Rear guard-screw bushing
17. Center guard-screw bushing
18. Rear trigger-guard screw
19. Center trigger-guard screw
20. Magazine-box plate
21. Magazine-box catch
22. Magazine-catch slide
23. Magazine-catch slide screw
24. Magazine-catch spring
25. Front guard-screw bushing
26. Front guard screw
27. Magazine box
28. Magazine-box floorplate
29. Magazine floorplate retainer
30. Follower spring
31. Follower
32. Magazine-box housing
33. Recoil lug
Not shown:
Extractor
Extractor plunger
Extractor spring
Ejector
Ejector spring
Ejector retainer pin
Bolt-handle plunger
Bolt-handle plunger spring

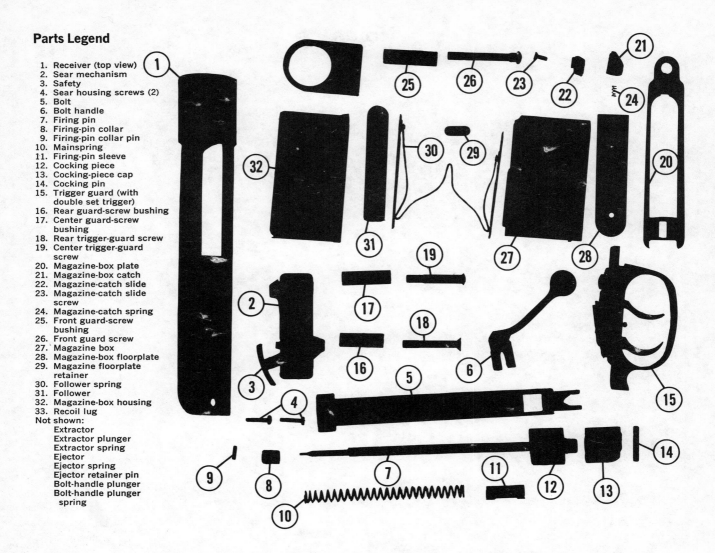

Tradewinds Model 600

Dimensional Specifications

Weight	38 ozs.
Length	7.875"
Receiver ring dia.	1.290"
Bolt dia.	.665"
Bolt travel	3.850"
Striker travel	.360"
Bolt-face recess:	
depth	.135"
dia. (.243 cal.)	.475"
(.222 cal.)	.380"
Magazine length (.243 cal.)	2.820"
(.222 Mag.)	2.290"
Guard-screw spacing	6.75"

General Specifications

Type	Turnbolt repeater.
Receiver	One-piece machined steel. Separate recoil lug fits between barrel and receiver. Non-slotted bridge. Tapped for top scope mounts.
Bolt	One-piece machined steel with detachable handle. Dual-opposed forward locking lugs. Base of low profile handle acts as safety lug.
Ignition	One-piece firing pin powered by coil mainspring. Cocks on opening.
Magazine	Detachable single-column 4-shot box type in .222, 3-shot in the larger calibers.
Trigger	Single-stage, adjustable for pull weight. Optional — double-set trigger.
Safety	Pivoting side tang type locks sear and bolt when tipped back.
Extractor	Hook type in bolt head.
Ejector	Plunger type in bolt head.
Bolt stop	Sear doubles as bolt stop; stops bolt by contacting a shoulder on bolt bottom.

Notes

204

26. The Sako Story

Sako is a relatively new name in the firearms field, especially to American shooters, but it is a name which has become highly respected since the introduction of Sako rifles in the United States. The name derives from Oy Sako AB, Riihimaki, Finland. *The Book of Rifles*, by W.H.B. Smith and J.E. Smith, lists Sako as "O.Y. Sako, A.B., Helsinki," and relates an interesting tale about it. According to this book, the Sako firm is owned outright by the Red Cross of Finland. It is said that this came about shortly after WW II, when Russia began appropriating arms factories in the countries they had occupied. Rather than have the Sako plant fall into Russian hands the Finns talked the Finnish Red Cross into taking complete ownership of the plant. Whatever the circumstances, the Sako people designed and put into production a miniature Mauser type bolt action repeater, for the American market, known as the Sako L-46. Introduced late in 1949, it was imported into this country by Firearms International Corp. (4837 Kirby Hill Rd., Washington, D.C.).*

When shooters began reading about the little L-46 Sako rifle it soon became popular. When gunsmiths learned they could buy the L-46 action separately it really caught on. Then, with a little nudging from the importer, Sako took heed, making a few changes in the action and rifle to better satisfy American tastes. Other changes were made from time to time, and additional actions and rifles introduced to handle a wider variety of cartridges than the two originally introduced in the L-46. The end result is the modern Sako action, which has no peer. The Sako action is synonymous with high quality material and workmanship. In my opinion, Sako actions, as well as the complete Sako rifles, are the finest commercially-made actions and rifles in their price class avail-

able today. They represent a most excellent value for the money.

The several Sako actions introduced to date are the L-46, L-57, L-579, L-61, L-461 and the Bench Rest single shot. I'll describe them in the order of their introduction.

The Sako L-46 Action

When the Sako L-46 action was first introduced it was universally described as a miniature Mauser. Though not a very accurate description, it was a "miniature" action in that it was made especially for the .22 Hornet and .218 Bee cartridges, and a "Mauser" because it had a one-piece bolt with dual-opposed locking lugs up front. However, this thumb-nail sketch does not fully describe this action.

The L-46 one-piece receiver is not unlike that of the Mauser Model 98 action, but it is, of course, shorter and smaller. The receiver ring and bridge are the same diameter, each with integral male tapered-dovetail scope mount bases on top. These base tops, flat and matted, taper narrower to the rear. The bridge dovetail, less wide than the front one, is also used to attach the Sako adjustable receiver rear sight. These integral dovetail bases, providing the very best means of attaching scope mount rings, are a very commendable feature. All Sako bolt actions after the L46 have this feature. Sako always made scope mounting rings to fit their actions and today the rings are available in three heights (low, medium and high), for scopes of 1″ or 26mm diameter, including an extension ring. Sako rings are of split or two-piece type, made of steel, and highly polished and blued to match the finish of the actions.

The bottom of the receiver is flat, with a recoil lug at the front end. The repeating action bottoms are open to accept a magazine box. The loading port on the original L-46 action made for the .22 Hornet and .218 Bee is 1.812″ long. The

rear of the receiver ends in a narrow tang that is grooved to accept the bolt sleeve and the cocking cam lug on the cocking piece.

The front end of the receiver is threaded for the barrel shank. On the original actions the thread was listed as being "Whitworth standard .080 - 16." The breech end of the barrel is flat except for a sloped extractor cut. (See Sako barrel shank specification drawings on pp. 306, 307).

The one-piece bolt machined with utmost precision and highly polished, has dual-opposed locking lugs on the extreme front end. These lugs engage behind shoulders milled inside the receiver ring, securely locking the bolt against the breech end of the barrel. The right (bottom) lug is solid, while the left (top) lug is slotted lengthwise to allow passage of the ejector. The recessed bolt face (about .065″ deep on most models) encloses the entire rim of the cartridge except for the narrow space which the extractor hook occupies.

The spring-steel extractor, long and narrow, fits in a groove milled lengthwise in the front end of the bolt. Part of this groove is a dovetail to hold the extractor in the bolt. A lip under the extractor engages a hole in the bolt head, which prevents the extractor from pulling out, unless the hook end of the extractor is purposely raised.

The bolt handle, at the extreme rear end of the bolt, is made as an integral part of the bolt. The base of the bolt handle forms a heavy collar around the rear end of the bolt. This thick collar around the slender bolt provides extra metal for several functions: 1) to provide a wide surface for the cocking cam notch, to prevent wear and make cocking and raising the bolt handle easier and smoother; 2) to provide metal so that part of this collar

*Sako rifles are now being distributed by Garcia Sporting Arms Corp., 329 Alfred Ave., Teaneck, N.J. 07666.

Illustrated above: Sako L-46 heavy-barreled varmint rifle in .222 Remington caliber, fitted with a Weaver K-6 scope in Sako mount rings. Now obsolete, this model has been replaced by the L-461.

can be formed into a cam matching the slope on the rear of the bridge to supply the primary extraction power; 3) to provide enough metal to seal off the left locking lug raceway.

A notch, cut into the receiver tang for the root of the bolt handle, forms the third or safety lug. The bolt handle is at a right angle to the bolt, its tapered stem ending in a hollow round grasping ball. This ball has a narrow band of checkering around it for better grasping. The top of the stem is so-positioned—and dished out —that it will clear the eyepiece of the lowest-mounted scope.

The Sako bolt has a guide-rib strip as wide and thick as the right locking lug. It is attached to the bolt body by a small spring-steel collar with hooked ends, these engaging a mortise in the underside of the guide rib. A pin through the guide, behind the hooks, prevents the guide from slipping off the ring. The guide rib lies in the space between the bolt handle and right locking lug. In an oblong milled hole in the near center underside of the guide rib is a small steel stop wedge and a small bent leaf spring. When the bolt is closed the guide rib extends a short distance into the right locking lug raceway, in both the receiver ring and bridge; when the bolt is rotated open, a notch, milled in the underside of the bolt body, moves under the stop wedge in the guide rib to halt bolt rotation. This accurately aligns the right locking lug with the guide rib so that the lug cannot hang up on the receiver when the bolt is operated, and prevents the bolt from binding during its rearward and forward travel if undue upward pressure is exerted on the bolt handle. When the bolt is closed, the guide rib also effectively closes the openings of the right lug raceway. All other Sako actions have bolts of similar construction and all are made with the guide rib.

Two gas-escape vent holes are provided in the L-46 action. One is in the left side of the receiver ring at the junction of the head of the bolt and breech face of the barrel. In the rare event of a ruptured case head or primer much of the gases would escape at this point instead of flowing rearward down the left locking lug raceway. The other hole is in the body of the bolt, forward of the shoulder on

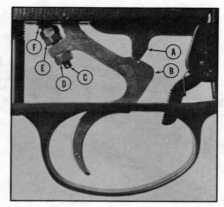

Sako L-46 trigger showing: (A) sear, (B) trigger, (C) trigger stop screw, (D) trigger stop-screw lock nut, (E) trigger-adjustment jam nuts, (F) trigger spring. This trigger is adjustable for weight of pull and over-travel. Instructions for adjusting it are the same as those for the M70 Winchester trigger given in chapter 29.

the firing pin. When the bolt is closed this hole is positioned under the front end of the guide rib, which in turn has a matching hole through it so that any gases getting into the bolt through the firing pin hole will be vented out to the right. All other Sako actions follow this system.

The bolt is drilled from the rear for the one-piece firing pin, a firing-pin design retained in all later Sako action models. The flattened rear end of the firing pin fits a matching hole in the bolt sleeve. This prevents the firing pin from turning. The mainspring, surrounding the firing pin, is compressed between the bolt sleeve and a collar on the front of the pin. The cocking piece is fitted to the rear end of the firing pin on a single interrupted lug or collar. The bolt sleeve has a stem which fits inside the bolt body; it also has a hook extending forward which engages over the collar on the rear of the bolt body to hold the entire firing mechanism in the bolt. Cocking occurs on opening the bolt.

There is no separate bolt sleeve lock, but the bolt sleeve is prevented from turning when the bolt is open by the nose of the cocking piece cam resting in the shallow notch in the rear of the bolt. This system is used in all later Sakos.

The rotary safety is fitted at a right angle through the flat top of the bolt sleeve; rotated to the rear it locks both striker (the striker combines firing pin and cocking piece) and bolt.

A combination "cocked" indicator and bolt lock, fitted into a lengthwise hole in the bolt sleeve, is connected with the safety; with the action closed, when the safety is rotated back to the SAFE position, the safety stem locks the striker back and moves the bolt lock forward to lock the bolt. With the safety swung forward into the FIRE position, the rear end of the bolt lock, which has a red band around it, extends from the rear of the bolt sleeve to indicate the safety is in the FIRE position.

The bolt stop housing, a machined steel box mortised into an opening in the left side of the receiver bridge, is held in place by a setscrew threaded through the housing and into the receiver wall.

The one-piece combined bolt stop/ejector is held in place in the bolt stop housing by—and pivots on—a pin through this housing. It is tensioned by a small coil spring. The bolt is stopped in its rearward travel when the left locking lug contacts the bolt stop. The fired case or cartridge is ejected to the right at the same time when the ejector—merely a thin extension of the bolt stop—projects into the bolt face recess through a groove provided for it through the locking lug. Pressing a serrated button on the bolt stop, which projects outside the housing, allows the bolt to be removed. Roughly the same design of bolt stop/ejector is used on all later models of the Sako actions.

L-46 actions were fitted with a trigger and sear which nearly duplicated those of the M70 Winchester (pre-64) action. The sear, positioned in a groove in the bottom of the receiver tang, is held in place by —and pivots on—a pin. It is tensioned by a coil spring compressed between the receiver and the front end of the sear. The trigger, positioned in the rear of the tang groove, also pivots on a pin. A simple spring, plunger and lock-nut arrangement between the trigger and the end of the tang provides the tension to engage the trigger with the sear; it also provides a means to readily adjust the trigger for weight of pull and over-travel. Like the M70 trigger, this Sako trigger has proven reliable.

When first introduced, and for a few years afterward, the L-46 trigger guard was made from a piece of strap-iron bent into shape. It was suitably machined and polished to match the excellent finish on the exposed parts of the receiver. Slotted oval-head countersunk screws, going through holes in the ends of the guard and threaded into the recoil lug and tang of the receiver, hold the action and barrel securely in the stock. A piece of slotted sheet-metal filled the space in the bottom of the stock around the trigger. A long rectangular hole cut into the front of the guard allowed the box magazine to be inserted and removed; the thin side rails of the opening in the guard are indented enough to permit grasping the magazine with thumb and forefinger. After a couple

Sako L-46 action.

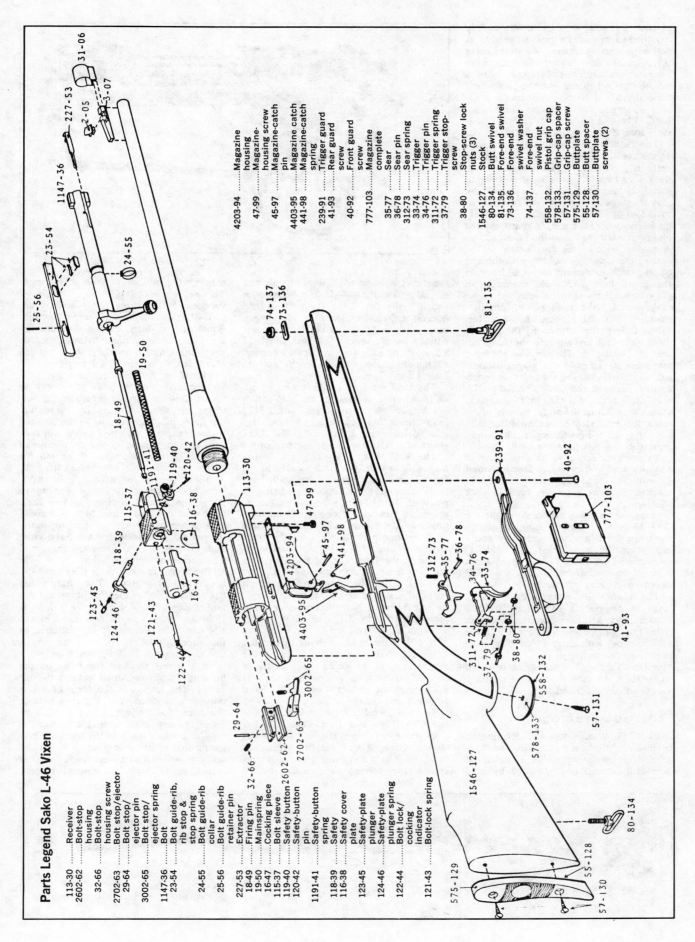

Parts Legend Sako L-46 Vixen

113-30	Receiver
2602-62	Bolt-stop
32-66	Bolt-stop housing
	Bolt-stop housing screw
2702-63	Bolt stop/ejector
29-64	Bolt stop/ejector pin
3002-65	Bolt stop/ejector spring
1147-36	Bolt
23-54	Bolt guide-rib, rib stop & stop spring
24-55	Bolt guide-rib collar
25-56	Bolt guide-rib retainer pin
227-53	Extractor
18-49	Firing pin
19-50	Mainspring
16-47	Cocking piece
115-37	Bolt sleeve
119-40	Safety button
120-42	Safety-button pin
1191-41	Safety-button spring
118-39	Safety
116-38	Safety cover plate
123-45	Safety-plate plunger
124-46	Safety-plate plunger spring
122-44	Bolt lock/cocking indicator
121-43	Bolt-lock spring

4203-94	Magazine housing
47-99	Magazine-housing screw
45-97	Magazine-catch pin
4403-95	Magazine catch
441-98	Magazine-catch spring
239-91	Trigger guard
41-93	Rear guard screw
40-92	Front guard screw
777-103	Magazine complete
35-77	Sear
36-78	Sear pin
312-73	Sear spring
33-74	Trigger
34-76	Trigger pin
311-72	Trigger spring
37-79	Trigger stop-screw
38-80	Stop-screw lock nuts (3)
1546-127	Stock
80-134	Butt swivel
81-135	Fore-end swivel
73-136	Fore-end swivel washer
74-137	Fore-end swivel nut
558-132	Pistol grip cap
578-133	Grip-cap spacer
57-131	Grip-cap screw
575-129	Buttplate
55-128	Butt spacer
57-130	Buttplate screws (2)

207

of years this strap-iron guard was slightly modified to improve its looks somewhat. A real improvement in the L-46 guard came several years later, about when the Sako Forester was introduced (1958) with a machined steel guard. At the same time these machined guards were made available separately so that owners of the older L-46 Vixen rifles could replace their strap-iron guards.

The detachable sheet-metal box magazines used in the L-46 Vixen action were extremely well made. These held 3 cartridges, and could be readily disassembled for cleaning by sliding off the floorplate.

A sheet-metal box-like holder, attached to the underside of the receiver and extending down to the trigger guard, guided and positioned the magazine in the action. A spring-loaded magazine catch in the rear of the magazine holder, with the end of the latch extending into the front of the guard bow, holds the magazine in place and allows it to be removed.

As noted, Sako L-46 rifles were first made only in .22 Hornet and .218 Bee. When Remington introduced the .222 in 1950 Sako quickly adapted the L-46 action to handle it. They made a longer magazine, lengthened the magazine port to 2.125″, and changed the bolt face recess and extractor as required. The Sako .222 was announced in 1951, in the original action with left hand safety. Shortly afterward the bolt sleeve was modified and the safety placed on the right side, where most shooters like to have it.

Before the Sako L-46 actions, barreled actions and rifles were discontinued (about 1963) and replaced by the L-461 models, they were also offered in .222 Magnum.

Adapting the L-46 action to handle the .222 Magnum crowded things a bit, to the degree that a loaded cartridge could not normally be ejected. Incidentally, owners of L-46 rifles in .222 should not have them rechambered for the .222 Magnum—it isn't practicable.

The L-46 rifles were made in three styles; a Sporter, a Mannlicher-stocked sporter and a heavy-barreled Varmint rifle. The Sporter was also made in a De luxe version, with extra fancy stock and engraving on the trigger guard. They were popular rifles, and many shooters hated to see the L-46, with its handy detachable magazine, discontinued.

The Sako L-57 Forester

In 1955 Winchester and Remington each introduced new combination varmint/deer cartridges which were to be heralded, praised and accepted by rifle

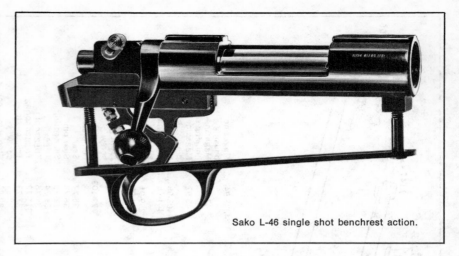

Sako L-46 single shot benchrest action.

shooters the world over. Remington's new cartridge was the .244, while Winchester called theirs the .243. There was great interest in these cartridges from the beginning, and in 1958 Sako offered a new rifle to handle them. This was the L-57 Forester, the action made just long enough to handle these medium-length (up to 2.80″) cartridges.

The L-57 receiver and bolt were essentially the same as those of the L-46 action but longer, with a magazine port 2.812″ long and a non-detachable 5-shot staggered-column magazine box. The L-57 also had a different trigger mechanism.

The L-57 Sako trigger guard had a hinged floorplate, the latch located in the front of the guard bow. It was milled entirely from steel, the exposed parts highly polished. As first made the trigger guard/magazine box was of one-piece construction, but later the magazine box was made as a separate part. It was expertly made from sheet-metal, its bottom partly recessed in the front part of the guard, its top into the receiver magazine well. The follower, also milled from steel, was well polished and had an offset rib to stagger the cartridges in the magazine—for maximum capacity in a minimum of space. The magazine well in the receiver was milled to leave guide rails or lips at the top sides to hold the cartridges in the magazine, and to guide each cartridge into the chamber on closing the bolt. This same magazine system is used in all Sako actions made today.

There were other minor differences between the L-46 and the L-57 actions besides those just listed. The bolt sleeve was slightly changed and the firing pin was threaded into the cocking piece and prevented from turning by a small setscrew

through the bottom of the cocking cam. This same method is used in the latest versions of all three Sako actions described later on. One Firearms International catalog described this threaded firing pin-to-cocking piece arrangement as providing a means to adjust the firing pin protrusion to obtain positive ignition.

Threading the firing pin into the cocking piece is an easy and good way to fasten these two parts together; the setscrew is a suitable means for preventing the firing pin from turning in the cocking piece to prevent a change in the pin protrusion, and it provides a convenient way for the factory to set the firing pin for correct protrusion in assembling the bolt. A much better arrangement, however, would have been to use interrupted lugs to fasten these parts together, as was done in the M98 Mauser and M1917 Enfield actions. Anyway, .055″ is the proper firing-pin tip protrusion for the Sako rifle, and this should be carefully measured when reassembling the Sakos.

The trigger mechanism in the Sako L-57 action was essentially like that which Sako first made for the FN Mauser actions and, except that it lacked the safety, it is almost the same as now used in the FN and Sako actions. It was attached to the underside of the receiver tang by a single cross pin and tightened in place by a setscrew through the front of the housing, which tightened against the receiver. The sear is in the form of a flat plunger positioned vertically in a hole in the rear of the trigger housing, with its upper end extending through a hole in the tang to contact the cocking piece. A coil spring under this sear plunger keeps the sear up, while a small cross pin keeps it from going too high. The trigger is pivoted

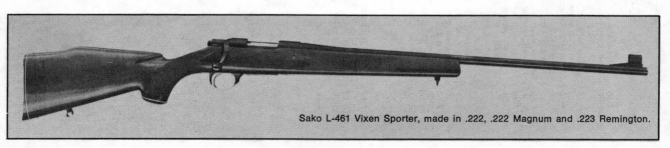

Sako L-461 Vixen Sporter, made in .222, .222 Magnum and .223 Remington.

Parts Legend Sako L-461 Vixen

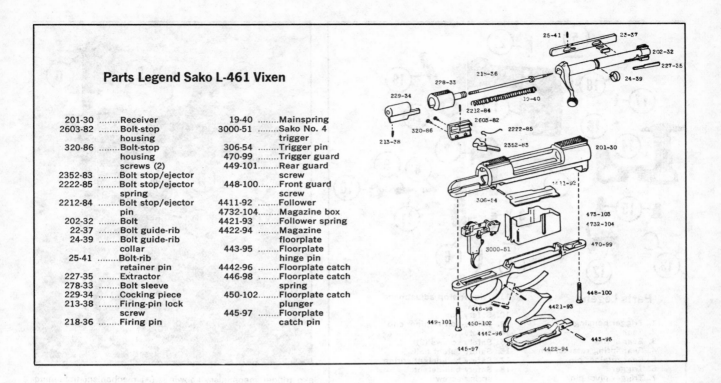

Part No.	Name	Part No.	Name
201-30	Receiver	19-40	Mainspring
2603-82	Bolt-stop housing	3000-51	Sako No. 4 trigger
320-86	Bolt-stop housing screws (2)	306-54	Trigger pin
		470-99	Trigger guard
2352-83	Bolt stop/ejector	449-101	Rear guard screw
2222-85	Bolt stop/ejector spring	448-100	Front guard screw
2212-84	Bolt stop/ejector pin	4411-92	Follower
202-32	Bolt	4732-104	Magazine box
22-37	Bolt guide-rib	4421-93	Follower spring
24-39	Bolt guide-rib collar	4422-94	Magazine floorplate
25-41	Bolt-rib retainer pin	443-95	Floorplate hinge pin
227-35	Extractor	4442-96	Floorplate catch
278-33	Bolt sleeve	446-98	Floorplate catch spring
229-34	Cocking piece	450-102	Floorplate catch plunger
213-38	Firing-pin lock screw	445-97	Floorplate catch pin
218-36	Firing pin		

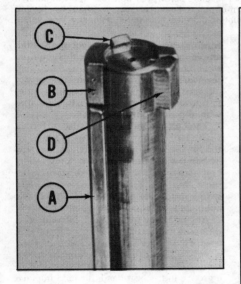

Sako bolt head showing: (A) guide rib, (B) right locking lug, (C) extractor, (D) left locking lug, which is slotted for the ejector.

General Specifications

Type............Turnbolt repeater.

Receiver............One-piece machined steel, unslotted bridge. Integral scope mounting bases on bridge and ring.

Bolt............One-piece with dual-opposed forward locking lugs. The handle base forms the safety lug. Low-profile handle for low scope mounting. L-61 Finnbear bolt has third locking lug at rear of bolt.

Magazine............L-46 action has single column 3- or 6-shot detachable box magazine. All others have non-detachable staggered-column magazine with hinged floorplate. 5-shot in standard calibers. 4-shot in belted magnums.

Trigger............Single-stage, adjustable for weight of pull and over-travel.

Safety............Early L-46 has rotary type on left side of bolt sleeve which locks striker. Late L-46 and L-57 actions have rotary type on right side of bolt sleeve which locks striker and bolt. L-461, L-579 and L-61 actions have side tang safety as part of trigger mechanism locking trigger and bolt.

Extractor............Rotating spring type mortised in bolt head of L-46 & L-461 actions. Other Sako actions have short hook type fitted into bolt head and tensioned by a spring and plunger.

Bolt stop............Mannlicher-type pivoted in a housing attached to left side of receiver. Bolt is stopped by left locking lug containing the bolt stop.

Ejector............Integral with bolt stop.

Ignition............One-piece firing pin powered by coil mainspring. Cocks on opening.

Dimensional Specifications

	L-46	L-461	L-57 & L-579	L-61
Weight (approx.)	32 ozs.	34 ozs.	40 ozs.	44 ozs.
Over-all	7.062"	7.062"	7.375"	8.375"
Receiver ring dia.	1.175"	1.175"	1.300"	1.330"
Body bolt dia.	.553"	.553"	.600"	.685"
Bolt travel	2.925"	3.000"	3.750"	4.635"
Striker travel (approx.)	.243"	.300"	.375"	.360"
Bolt face recess:				
depth	.055"	.055"	.060"	.100"
dia.	.352" (.22 Hornet) .410" (.218 Bee) .380" (.222 & .222 Mag.)	.380	.478–.482"	.478" (.30-06) .537" (Magnum)

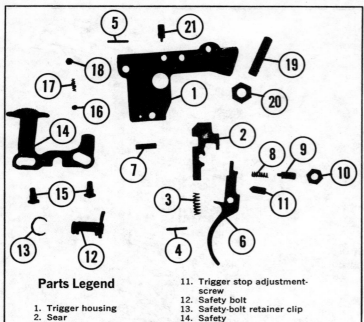

Parts Legend

1. Trigger housing
2. Sear
3. Sear spring
4. Sear-spring retainer pin
5. Sear retainer pin
6. Trigger
7. Trigger pivot-pin
8. Trigger spring
9. Trigger weight-of-pull adjustment screw
10. Trigger adjustment-screw lock nut
11. Trigger stop adjustment-screw
12. Safety bolt
13. Safety-bolt retainer clip
14. Safety
15. Safety screws (2)
16. Safety detent ball
17. Safety ball-detent spring
18. Safety ball-detent spring screw
19. Trigger mechanism tightening screw
20. Tightening-screw lock nut
21. Trigger mechanism-leveling setscrew

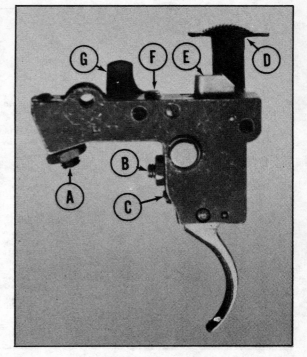

Sako trigger mechanism showing: (A) mechanism tightening screw and lock nut, (B) weight-of-pull adjustment screw and lock nut, (C) trigger stop adjustment screw, (D) safety, (E) sear, (F) trigger leveling screw, (G) bolt lock (part of safety). Limited weight-of-pull adjustment can be had by turning screw (B) counterclockwise for lighter pull, and vice versa.

at the bottom of the housing on a pin. The upper part of the trigger is a sear which engages a matching sear notch in the sear. There are two small setscrews in the front of the lower trigger housing. The upper one holds the trigger spring, and turning it in (for heavier weight of pull) or out provides a limited weight of pull adjustment, from about 3 to 5 pounds. The bottom screw, for over-travel stop adjustment, can be set to stop the trigger the moment the trigger is disengaged from the sear.

L-57 Sako barreled actions and rifles were only made in .243, .244 and .308. The rifles were made in the same 3 styles as the L-46 and in a De luxe Sporter grade as well.

The L-579 Sako Action

In 1960 Sako discontinued the L-57 action, introducing a modified version of it which they called the L-579. The major change was in the bolt sleeve because Sako had adapted this action to accept the Sako No. 4 trigger mechanism with its built-in sliding safety.

The L-579 bolt sleeve is rounded and smooth, with a narrow flat matted surface on top. It is fitted and anchored to the bolt by a small rectangular lug on the otherwise smooth extension on its forward end, which fits into a matching milled hole in the rear of the bolt. This is a very good and simple arrangement for fitting the bolt sleeve to the bolt, af-

fording easy disassembly, yet more than ample in strength. Of course, this required some changes to be made in the bolt and receiver, but these alterations in no way changed anything in the functioning, safety and operation of these parts compared with the discontinued design.

The bolt stop housing was also different. Instead of being mortised in the side of the bridge, as on the L-46 action, the new housing was affixed by two screws. The bolt stop/ejector remained about the same, but was tensioned by a bent-wire spring instead of a coil spring. The L-461 action also used this new system.

At about this time, Sako introduced a different extractor—a close copy of one used by Savage/Stevens in some of their popular .22 rimfire bolt action and automatic rifles. A simple hook type fitted in a groove in the bolt head, it's held in place and tensioned by a spring-loaded plunger set into a hole behind the extractor. The same system, but with a heavier and wider extractor, is used in the L-61 Sako. The L-461, however, has the same extractor used in the L-46.

The No. 4 trigger, similar to the L-57 trigger, is improved and made to include a sliding side-tang safety which, when pulled back, locks the bolt and trigger. Since there are a great many of these triggers in use, I'll describe it in detail.

The housing is a machined steel casting. The flat sear plunger, positioned in a vertical hole in the rear of the housing, is held in place by a small cross pin. It is held upward by a coil spring from below, which is held in place by another small cross pin. The trigger pivots in the bottom

Sako L-579 Forester action. Except for length the L-461 and L-61 are the same as the L-579.

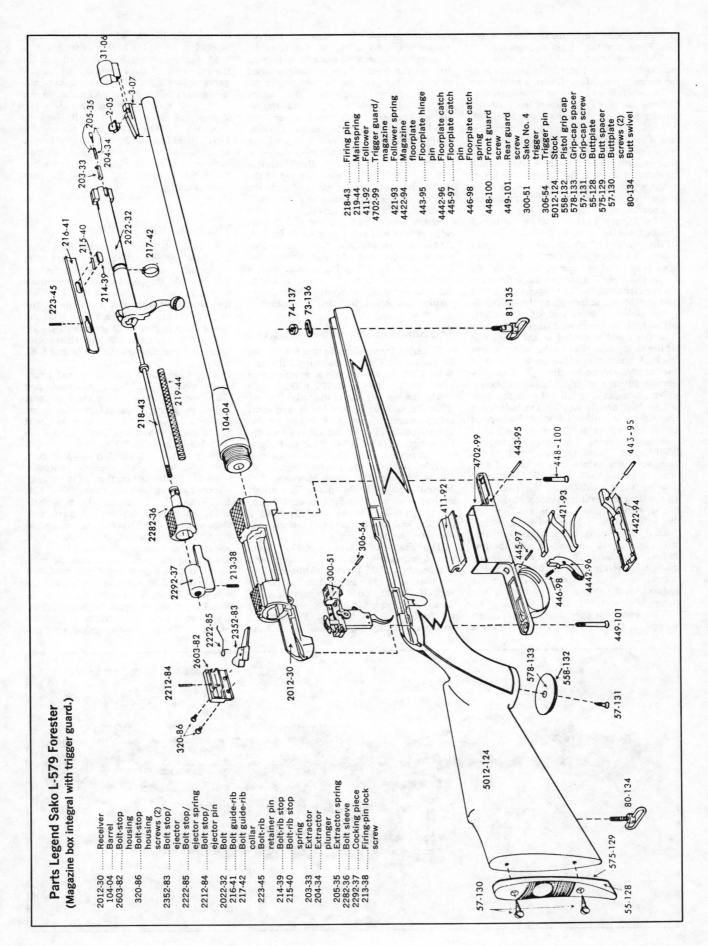

Parts Legend Sako L-579 Forester
(Magazine box integral with trigger guard.)

2012-30	Receiver		218-43	Firing pin
104-04	Barrel		219-44	Mainspring
2603-82	Bolt-stop housing		411-92	Follower
320-86	Bolt-stop housing screws (2)		4702-99	Trigger guard/ magazine
2352-83	Bolt stop/ ejector		421-93	Follower spring
2222-85	Bolt stop/ ejector spring		4422-94	Magazine floorplate
2212-84	Bolt stop/ ejector pin		443-95	Floorplate hinge pin
2022-32	Bolt		4442-96	Floorplate catch
216-41	Bolt guide-rib		445-97	Floorplate catch pin
217-42	Bolt guide-rib collar		446-98	Floorplate catch spring
223-45	Bolt-rib retainer pin		448-100	Front guard screw
214-39	Bolt-rib stop		449-101	Rear guard screw
215-40	Bolt-rib stop spring		300-51	Sako No. 4 trigger
203-33	Extractor		306-54	Trigger pin
204-34	Extractor plunger		5012-124	Stock
205-35	Extractor spring		558-132	Pistol grip cap
2282-36	Bolt sleeve		578-133	Grip-cap spacer
2292-37	Cocking piece		57-131	Grip-cap screw
213-38	Firing-pin lock screw		55-128	Buttplate
			575-129	Butt spacer
			57-130	Buttplate screws (2)
			80-134	Butt swivel

211

of the housing on a much heavier cross pin. The top of the trigger engages a notch in the upper part of the sear when the action is cocked. The trigger is tensioned by a small, but stiff, coil spring held down by a setscrew and lock nut positioned in the top front of the lower part of the trigger housing. A limited weight-of-pull adjustment can be had by turning this screw in (for heavier pull) or out, but only to a safe minimum of about 2.5 pounds. The setscrew just below the weight-of-pull adjustment screw is the trigger over-travel stop, which can be adjusted to stop the trigger the moment the trigger releases the sear.

The rotary safety bolt, positioned through the housing to intersect the top of the trigger and effectively block trigger movement when it is rotated to a given spot, is retained in place by a C-spring clip on its left end. The safety slide is fastened on the right side of the trigger housing by two shouldered screws going through elongated holes at each end of the safety, allowing it to be moved back and forth. The front slot is angled so the front end of the safety also rises as the safety moves back. A short projection on the front of the safety, extending through a narrow groove cut through the bottom of the receiver, engages a notch cut into the base of the bolt handle to lock the bolt when the safety is pulled back. A ball-ended lever, riveted on the right of the safety bolt and engaging a notch in the bottom of the slide, causes the safety bolt to rotate when the safety slide is pushed forward or pulled back. A serrated button on the top of the safety, on the right side of the tang makes it convenient to operate. Tension for the OFF and ON positions for the safety slide is provided by a spring-loaded ball bearing, in the trigger housing, pressing against and falling into shallow holes in the safety. This ball bearing spring plunger is retained in its hole by a setscrew, and it is possible to change the tension on the safety slide by turning this screw in or out.

The entire trigger mechanism is attached to the receiver by a single cross

pin through holes in the upper part of the housing and a lug on the receiver. A long setscrew with lock nut passing through the front of the housing, is used only to tighten the mechanism to the receiver. Another setscrew in the top of the housing, used to adjust the trigger mechanism level with the receiver, can also be used to adjust the amount the sear projects through the receiver and the height of the safety button over the edge of the stock. Normally, this setscrew should be adjusted to leave the top of the trigger housing nearly parallel with the bottom of the receiver when the front tightening screw is tightened.

When first introduced the L-579 barreled actions and rifles were made in .243, .244 and .308 calibers. The .244 caliber was soon dropped. At this writing the L-579 Sako is still going strong, and is available in .22-250, .243 and .308, and in the same three styles; Sporter, Mannlicher carbine and heavy barreled Varminter.

The Sako L-61 Finnbear Action

Firearms International (now taken over by the Garcia Corp.), announced the new Sako L-61 Finnbear rifle a month or so after introducing the L-579 rifles late in 1961. The longest one in the Sako line-up, it handles standard .30-06 length and short belted magnum cartridges. When originally introduced it was also made to handle the longer .300 H&H Magnum cartridges. At the present time Finnbear rifles and barreled actions are available in .270, .30-06, 264 Magnum, 7mm Magnum, .300 Magnum and .338 Magnum. The rifles, available in standard Sporter or De luxe Sporter grades, weigh slightly over 7 pounds and have standard weight 24″ sporter-contoured barrels.

The Finnbear action is 8.375″ long, has a magazine box 3.312″ long and weighs about 2.75 pounds. Although longer than the L-579 action (and as can be seen if the exploded view drawings of these actions are studied) it differs from the L-579 only as follows: 1) The bolt has three locking lugs, as well as the base

of the bolt handle which serves as the safety lug. As on the M98 Mauser bolt, the L-61 Finnbear bolt has its third lug on the rear part of the bolt body, which engages a locking shoulder recess cut into the bottom of the bridge. Again as on the M98, this third lug is only a safety lug and is not in contact with its locking shoulder. 2) The bolt guide rib on the L-61 is held in place by two collars instead of one, and the stop wedge is located between the collars. This rib extends between the front locking lug and the rear safety locking lug.

The L-461 Vixen Action

In 1963-64, Sako redesigned their original L-46 Vixen action. In bolt action repeating rifles the trend was definitely toward the staggered-column magazine with a hinged floorplate, so the L-46 action was fitted with such a system. At the same time they fitted the action with the No. 4 Sako trigger mechanism and safety, and replaced the box-like bolt sleeve with the round one used on the L-579 and L-61 actions.

Sako L-461 barreled actions and rifles, made only in .222, .222 Magnum and .223, are still available in these calibers today. By going to the staggered-column, non-detachable box magazine on this short action more room was available for the .222 Magnum and .223.

Now Sako had—and has—3 distinct sizes and lengths of turnbolt actions— made for 3 different families of cartridges. Except for length and diameter the L-461, L-579 and L-61 actions are essentially alike, all having the same trigger, bolt stop/ejector, bolt sleeve and magazine systems. (See the action specification chart for the dimensional differences.)

I should mention here that some catalogs and books once listed a Sako L-469 rifle. I can find no evidence that there was actually such a model variation, or that this model designation was correct; I suspect it was an incorrect designation of the L-461. At least none of my Fire-

Sako L-579 Forester action open.

Parts Legend Sako L-61 Finnbear

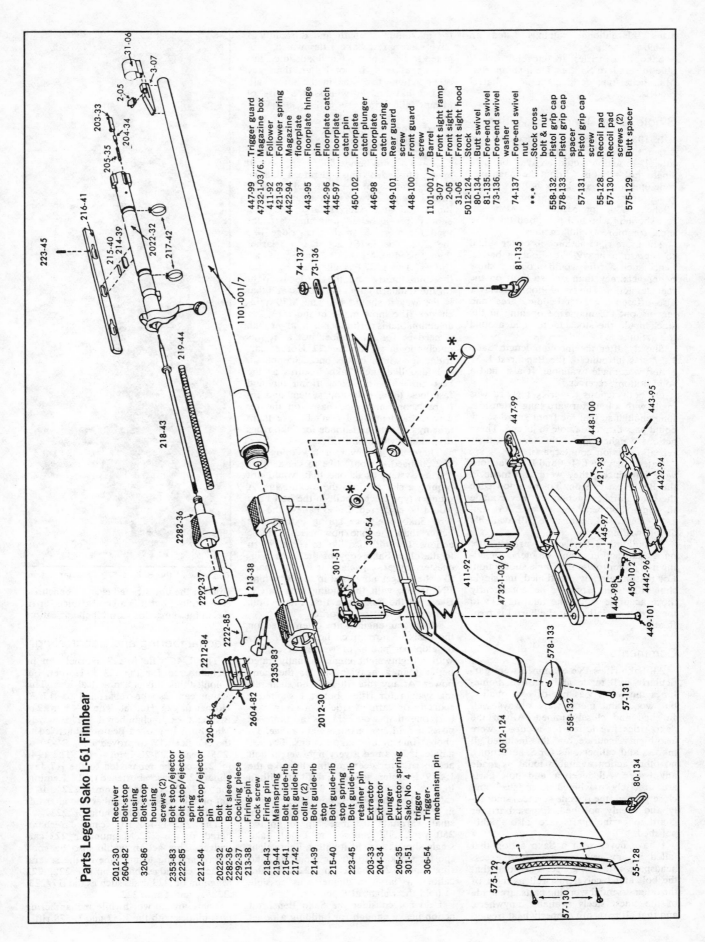

2012-30	Receiver
2604-82	Bolt-stop
320-86	Bolt-stop housing
	Bolt-stop housing
2353-83	Bolt-stop housing screws (2)
2222-85	Bolt stop/ejector
	Bolt stop/ejector spring
2212-84	Bolt stop/ejector pin
2022-32	Bolt
2282-36	Bolt sleeve
2292-37	Cocking piece
213-38	Firing-pin lock screw
218-43	Firing pin
219-44	Mainspring
216-41	Bolt guide-rib
217-42	Bolt guide-rib collar (2)
214-39	Bolt guide-rib
215-40	Bolt guide-rib stop
223-45	Bolt guide-rib stop spring
	Bolt guide-rib retainer pin
203-33	Extractor
204-34	Extractor plunger
205-35	Extractor spring
301-51	Sako No. 4 trigger
306-54	Trigger-mechanism pin

447-99	Trigger guard
4732-1-03/6..	Magazine box
411-92	Follower
421-93	Follower spring
4422-94	Magazine
	Magazine floorplate
443-95	Floorplate hinge pin
4442-96	Floorplate catch
445-97	Floorplate catch pin
450-102	Floorplate catch plunger
446-98	Floorplate catch spring
449-101	Rear guard screw
448-100	Front guard screw
1101-001/7..	Barrel
3-07	Front sight ramp
2-05	Front sight
31-06	Front sight hood
5012-124	Stock
80-134	Butt swivel
81-135	Fore-end swivel
73-136	Fore-end swivel washer
74-137	Fore-end swivel nut
*-**	Stock cross bolt & nut
558-132	Pistol grip cap
578-133	Pistol grip cap spacer
57-131	Pistol grip cap screw
55-128	Recoil pad
57-130	Recoil pad screws (2)
575-129	Butt spacer

arms International catalogs listed an L-469.

Sako L-461 rifles are currently available in standard Sporter, De luxe Sporter, Mannlicher-type carbine and heavy barrel models.

Single Shot Benchrest Action

In 1956-57, to meet the demands of the target shooter, Sako announced that the little L-46 action would be available as a single shot—that is, without the magazine-well opening—leaving the bottom of the receiver solid. They called this the "Benchrest" action because it was benchrest shooters who had pressured them the most for more "rigid" actions.

The more rigid action was better suited to support a heavy, free-floating barrel, hence such a rifle would probably show better accuracy than one so built on the repeater action. The flat-bottomed receiver also offered a greater bedding area, and leaving out the magazine opening in the stock made the stock more rigid around the action.

Shortly after the medium length Sako L-57 was introduced, the Benchrest L-57 action was made available. It also had a solid-bottom receiver.

On both actions the trigger guard was made with a long forward tang extension, long enough so that the front guard screw could pass through a hole in its end. These actions weighed about the same as their repeating action counterparts.

Later when the L-461 and L-579 actions were introduced, they were also made in the Benchrest version. To my knowledge the L-61 Finnbear action was never made in single shot benchrest style. L-461 and L-579 Benchrest actions are still available at this writing.

In building a first class varmint rifle on a Sako action, many shooters, including me, prefer to use the single shot action. For reasons already mentioned, the single shot rifle will probably be consistently more accurate from one hunting trip to the next, especially so if the barrel is free-floating.

Comments

All Sako rifles I've examined were particularly well made and finished. Sometimes the wood was not of best quality, but wood and metal were always well finished and closely joined. All of the Sako rifles I've tested for accuracy were also highly accurate, and this included all models and calibers. As for Sako actions, no other action available today is made any better. All receiver and bolt parts are precisely machined from steel and closely fitted, the outside surfaces smoothly and evenly polished. Exposed trigger guard/magazine parts are also highly polished.

I have never seen a Sako action that failed in any way, or developed excess headspace after long use. I assume that the bolt and receiver, as well as most of the other essential working parts, are made of the finest steels available anywhere, and that all parts are properly heat treated

for maximum strength and durability. I have seen a few Sako rifles which, subjected to firing heavy handloads, took this beating as well, if not better, than any other actions I've seen in the same calibers. I have never witnessed a case of primer failure in these actions, but I believe the shooter would be as fully protected from escaping gases behind the Sako action as behind most other actions.

There are a lot of things I like about the Sako actions beside their being so well made, finished, strong and safe. I like the small diameter of the bolt and receiver, since I see no advantage in an action having a bolt and receiver large and long enough for a belted magnum cartridge used for a much smaller cartridge like the .222. The L-461 action is no larger than it need be for the .222 family of cartridges. The L-579 is also just right for the .308 family and the L-61 just right for the standard larger cartridges, and that is the way it should be. The M70 Winchester rifle, now made in the .222, has an action that is certainly much larger than it need be for this caliber just as it was much too large for the .22 Hornet cartridge for which it was once chambered.

I also like such Sako features as the bolt guide rib, one-piece firing pin and fast lock time, bolt stop system and integral scope mounting bases on the receiver. Incidentally, I don't believe there are any better mounts made for Sako rifles than their own mount rings.

There are, however, a few things I'd like changed. I would like to see another ejector system used, one that would not require a slot cut into the locking lug. A plunger type ejector built in the bolt head would be preferred. I also believe the old type Sako one-piece spring extractor is better than the one now used in these actions. I would also like to see a return to the older Sako copy of the M70 Winchester trigger, especially if it were made like the trigger now used in the Browning FN action, with the sliding tang safety. Even so, the Sako is a first rate action, and one of my top favorites.

Motor car engines are often rated on the basis of how much horsepower they develop per pound of weight of engine, with a lightweight engine usually rated better than a heavier one of the same power. At any rate, there is no such rating system for rifles, but if I wanted a sporting or varmint rifle of a given caliber, one that would be as accurate as possible within a given weight range, I'd choose one of the Sako actions. For example, if I wanted a very lightweight bolt action rifle for deer hunting I'd take the L-579 Forester action and fit it with a lightweight 20″ barrel in .358 Winchester caliber. For the highest possible accuracy in a varmint rifle of 8 pounds for use on small varmints at ranges up to around 250 yards, I'd choose the L-461 Sako single shot action, fit it with a lightweight sporter stock, a 10-power scope in Sako rings and a 22″ barrel in .222 Magnum caliber, as large in diameter as possible to hold the weight at 8 pounds.

I do not consider the Sako Benchrest action heavy enough for building a target

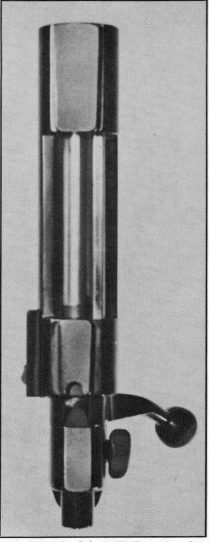

Top view of the Sako L-579 Forester action.

rifle for the unrestricted class of benchrest competition, but it is a good choice for rifles in the sporter or varmint classification.

Rechambering and Rebarreling

The L-46 rifle in .22 Hornet can be rechambered for the .22 K-Hornet, but I don't think this is a practical idea. This action can also be rebarreled to .17/22 Hornet or .25 Hornet. The L-46 in .218 Bee can be rechambered for the .218 Mashburn Improved Bee or rebarreled to the .17 Bee, .17 Improved Bee, .25-20 or .225 Dean (.25-20 Improved). The L-46 in .222 can be rebarreled to the .17 Javelina (.222 case shortened), .17 Remington, .17/222 or 6x47 (6mm/222). It is not practicable to rechamber and alter this rifle in .222 to .222 Magnum or .223.

The .222 L-461 rifle can be rechambered for the .222 Magnum or .223 cartridges. This action would also be good for rebarreling to any one of the several wildcat cartridges based on the .222, .222 Magnum or .223 cases such as the .17/223, .222½, and 6mm/222.

There are no worthwhile rechambering possibilities with the L-57 and L-579 rifles in the calibers for which they're made. However, they are suitable for rebarreling to such cartridges as the .225 Winchester, .250-3000 Savage, 6mm International, .257 Roberts and .358 Winchester.

The L-61 action, made for the .30-06 cartridge, is suitable for rebarreling to almost any cartridges based on the .30-06 head-sized case, including such popular wildcats as the 6mm/06, .25-06 and .35 Whelen. The same action, as made for the belted magnum cases, would be suitable for rebarreling to the .257 Weatherby Magnum and the like.

Other Rifles On Sako Actions

Some commercial arms makers, other than Sako, have built rifles with their own brand name on Sako actions. Marlin was one of the first to do this when they introduced their Model 322 in 1954. This mediumweight rifle, designed for varmint shooting, was built on the Sako L-46 Vixen action, then fitted with a stock and barrel by Marlin. The barrels, of stainless steel, had Marlin's Micro-Groove rifling. These rifles gave exceptional accuracy when new, but according to many reports I've received from owners of these rifles, such accuracy lasted only to some 400-500 shots, after which the bullets began to tip and keyhole. Marlin made these rifles for only a few years, probably not later than 1957.

The Model 52 J.C. Higgins in .222 caliber (sold by Sears Roebuck) was based on the Sako L-46 action.

From about 1957 to 1961, Colt also made rifles on the Sako action. Their rifle, the Coltsman, was based on the Sako L-57 Forester action, and was chambered for .243 or .308 Winchester. Three grades were available, Custom, De luxe and Standard.

Browning was the first commercial arms maker to chamber a rifle for the .22-250 cartridge, the date about 1964. The action and barrel used was the Sako L-579. The action Browning used differed from the standard Sako action only in that the top of the receiver ring and bridge were left round, then tapped for scope mounts. Browning still uses the L-579 for their finely finished bolt action rifles in .22-250, .243 and .308. They also use the L-461

action for their .222 and .222 Magnum rifles.

Harrington and Richardson use a Sako action for their Model 317 Ultra rifles, the L-461. This semi-custom made rifle is chambered for the .223, .17/223 wildcat or the .17 Remington. That these firms chose Sako actions certainly speaks well for the brand.

One manufacturer copied the Sako action. The American Import Company (1167 Mission St., San Francisco, Calif. 94103), imports a bolt action sporter called the Dickson-Howa Golden Bear Model FSD-43. Made in Japan by Howa Machinery, Ltd., the .30-06 rifle has an action that's almost an exact duplicate of the Sako L-61 Finnbear.

Markings

The words **MADE IN FINLAND,** in very small letters, are stamped on all of the Sako receivers, usually on the flat on the lower left side of the receiver ring. The serial number is usually stamped on the left receiver wall as well as on the bottom of the bolt handle. On some Sako actions, the action number and the city where it was made are stamped on the left receiver wall, thus: **SAKO Riihimaki.**

On Sako barreled actions and rifles the name **SAKO** is usually stamped on the breech end of the barrel, along with **MADE IN FINLAND** and the caliber marking.

Take-Down and Assembly

First make sure the chamber and magazine are empty. Remove the magazine from the L-46 models. On all Sakos remove the bolt by raising the bolt handle and drawing the bolt back until stopped. Then depress the bolt stop on the left rear side of the action and pull the bolt free. On all Sakos, to remove barrel and action from the stock, turn out rear and front guard screws in that order. Then carefully remove the trigger guard from the bottom of the stock and lift barrel and action out of the top of the stock. Reassemble in reverse order.

On all Sako models to remove the bolt guide rib drive out the small pin from

the rib just to the rear of the guide rib collar; then, with the rib turned on the bolt between the locking lugs, push or pry it forward about 5/16″. Now, with the bolt held so the rib is down, carefully pull the rib away from the bolt, being most careful not to lose the rib stop and spring. The spring-guide rib collar can then be spread apart and removed from the bolt. Reassemble the guide rib parts in reverse order, proceeding as follows: Holding the bottom of the rib up, insert the rib-stop spring, curved ends down, in the rib-stop recess; then insert the rib stop, groove side down, over the spring. Place the bolt on the rib and, while carefully holding the front end of the rib against the bolt, with equal care raise the rear end and turn the hooked ends of the rib collar under the rib. Use narrow jawed pliers to pinch the collar together so the rib can be pressed entirely against the bolt body. Now slide the rib back and re-insert the retainer pin. Do not force anything.

For Sakos with the long spring extractor, the extractor can be removed as follows: Grasp the bolt firmly in the left hand, bolt head up, extractor to the left. Using a narrow bladed screwdriver in the right hand, place the blade under the extractor hook. Apply pressure to push the hook end of the extractor away from the bolt body and, at the same time, gently pry the screwdriver handle down. When the hook has been raised enough to disengage the lip under the extractor from its recess in the bolt, the extractor will slip forward out of its recess. Reassemble in reverse order.

For Sakos having the latest short extractor, the extractor is removed as follows: Using a small jeweler's screwdriver with sharpened blade, insert the blade between the plunger and the extractor and push the plunger back. While holding the plunger back the extractor probably can be jiggled out of the bolt, or if you have a free finger on the hand holding the bolt it can be used to tip or flip out the extractor. Reassemble by inserting the spring and plunger with notched side of plunger towards the bottom of the extractor recess, depress the plunger fully into its hole with the same tool and then push the extractor into place. Make sure the plunger has properly engaged over the notch of the extractor. The very small extractor parts are easily lost, so work carefully and in a confined area, so that if something goes amiss you'll be able to find the parts.

To remove the firing mechanism from the Sako L-46 and L-59 bolt, proceed as follows: Put the bolt in the receiver and close it; place the safety upright (in the intermediate position) and carefully remove the bolt from the receiver; next, turn the bolt sleeve counterclockwise as far as it will go, and the firing mechanism can be pulled from the bolt. To disassemble the firing mechanism further, rest the firing pin tip on a hardwood surface and, with a firm grasp on the bolt sleeve, compress the mainspring as far as it will go, then turn the cocking piece a ¼-turn in either direction and lift it off. Compressing the mainspring is a two-handed job, so it is best to have someone else handy

Left side view of the Sako Forester action.

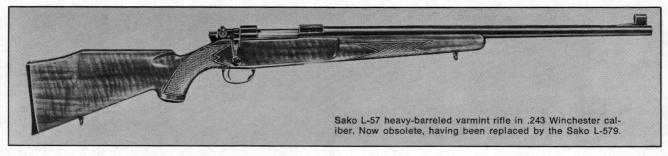

Sako L-57 heavy-barreled varmint rifle in .243 Winchester caliber. Now obsolete, having been replaced by the Sako L-579.

to remove (and later to replace) the cocking piece. The main parts of the mechanism can then be separated.

To remove the safety on the Model L-46 and L-57 proceed as follows: depress the small plunger in the safety cover plate (which is opposite the safety button) and slide the cover plate down and out of the bolt sleeve; remove the safety cover-plate plunger and spring; drive out the small cross pin which holds the safety button on the safety stem, then drive the safety stem out; the cocking indicator can then be removed. Reassemble in reverse order.

To remove the firing mechanism from the L-461, L-579 and L-61 Sako bolts, proceed as follows: remove the bolt from the rifle; grasp the bolt firmly in one hand and, with an equally firm grip on the bolt sleeve, turn the bolt sleeve clockwise until it snaps loose from the bolt. The firing mechanism can then be taken apart by loosening the firing-pin lock screw in the bottom of the cocking piece and turning the firing pin out of the cocking piece. This can be done by hand without tools, although a screwdriver can be used on the head of the firing pin. Reassemble in reverse order. Reassembling the firing mechanism is not easily done because the very stiff mainspring must be compressed. After inserting the bolt sleeve partly in the bolt, grasp the bolt firmly in one hand and the bolt sleeve between the thumb and crooked forefinger of the other hand, and being ready to turn it counterclockwise; with the edge of the bolt sleeve held against the edge of a work bench or hardwood block held in a vise, depress the bolt sleeve into the bolt to full depth, or until it can be turned to lock it. After

this turn the bolt sleeve counterclockwise until the cocking piece falls into the shallow full cock notch in the rear of the bolt. Under no circumstances should the bolt be turned counterclockwise in disassembling it, or clockwise when assembling it; in other words, never turn the bolt sleeve so that the cocking piece falls in the deep cocking notch, for it is then very difficult to turn the bolt sleeve to the cocked position without tools. If, in the assembly of the firing mechanism in the bolt the cocking piece should fall into the cocking notch, then it is best to make a simple tool to turn the bolt sleeve to the cocked position.

Drill a snug ⅞″ hole in a piece of hardwood, notch this hole for the cam on the cocking piece; holding this tool in a vise, insert the bolt sleeve into the hole and raise the bolt handle until the cocking piece is cocked and falls into the shallow cocking notch.

To remove the bolt stop housing on the L-46 action turn out the screw in the front of the housing and slide the housing to the rear. On the other models turn out the two screws below the housing and lift it from the receiver. After the housing is removed the bolt stop pin can be driven out to remove the bolt stop and its spring. Reassemble in reverse order.

To remove the trigger parts on the L-46 merely drive out the trigger and sear pins and all the trigger parts can be lifted free. Remove the trigger mechanism from all the other models by first loosening the setscrew in the front of the trigger housing and then drive out the trigger housing pin.

The barrel is threaded into the receiver (right-hand threads) and is usually set-up

very tightly. Therefore, unless you have the proper tools, which would include a barrel vise and action wrench, do not attempt to remove the barrel from the receiver.

Accessories

Various types and styles of semi-finished and inletted stocks are available from several stock manufacturers for any of the Sako rifles. Although I consider Sako's own scope mounts best for use on Sako actions, other scope mount makers such as Weaver and Redfield also make mount bases which fit over the dovetails on the Sako receiver, and to which their own rings can be attached.

If you want a single-set trigger for the obsolete L-46 Sako, it can be had from Canjar Mfg. Co. (500 E. 45th Ave., Denver, Colo. 80216). If you want a really precision trigger mechanism that is fully adjustable for any of the other Sako rifles, with or without a built-in single-set mechanism, Canjar has them also. Finally, if you need a new barrel for your Sako, or want a barrel of a different size or caliber, you can buy new Sako-made barrel blanks from the importer.* Barrels are rifled by the hammering or cold-swaging process, these barrels are finish turned and pre-chambered. I have used a number of them on various actions other than Sako, (these barrels are unthreaded) and I have found them to be excellent in every way.

---

*Sako rifles and accessories are now being imported by Garcia Sporting Arms Corp., 329 Alfred Ave., Teaneck, N.J. 07666.

Sako L-579 heavy-barreled varmint rifle. The author considers this one of the finest commercial varmint rifles available.

27. Czech Brno Sporting Rifles

I F YOU HAVE a military rifle or action with **CESKOSLOVENSKA ZBRO-JOVKA, A.S. BRNO VZ-24** stamped on the side of the receiver, you own one of the very best Model 98 types ever made. If you have a rifle marked **ZBROJOVKA-BRNO** and **MODEL ZKK,** then you have one of the nicest sporting rifles made in Europe today. Both were made in the city of Brno, Czechoslovakia; the VZs in great numbers from 1924 to 1945, and the ZKKs only in the last few years. The VZs are very common as many of them were sold on the surplus market, but the ZKKs are quite rare in the U.S. because of import restrictions. The rifles, at least, are on sale to some extent in Canada. The VZ action is the same as the standard M98 military action described in another chapter, but the ZKK is quite different.

I don't believe ZKK actions or barreled actions are available anywhere. As this action is so different from any I have seen I'll describe it and the rifle in detail.

History of the Brno Firm

A brief history of the Brno firm is in order since not much is known about it. According to my information, about 1918 some military men took over the Austro-Hungarian armament shop in Brno, naming it the State Armament & Engineering Works. A year later the name was changed to Czechoslovak State Armament Works. Prior to 1924 this firm produced and assembled several thousand Mannlicher rifles and more than 40,000 M98 Mauser type rifles.

In 1924 the firm name was again changed to Ceskoslovenska Zbrojovka A.Z., which translated means Czechoslovakian Arms Factory Ltd. However, it was then more commonly known as the CZ firm. The principal product manufactured was the M24 (or VZ-24) Mauser rifle for Czechoslovakia and several other countries. Various other basic M98 military rifles and carbines were also made

there in large numbers for many countries the world over, including many which Germany used in WW II.

After WW II the firm name was again changed, this time to Zbrojovka Brno (Brno Arms Works), or ZB for short. This was again changed, at least for a short time anyway, to Zbrojovka Brno-Jan (or Jane) Sverma (or Svermy) Works.

In the late 1930s the firm began making a line of fine turnbolt sporting rifles based on the VZ-24 action. After WW II they modified the action considerably and began making an even better sporting rifle called the Model ZG 47. (They also made a short-actioned .22 Hornet bolt rifle*, the Brno ZKM 465.)

For a few years in the late 1940s and early 1950s Brno rifles were imported by Continental Arms Corp. (697 Fifth Ave., New York, N.Y. 10022). I think those few Brno rifles reaching the U.S. in the last 10 years or so, especially the Model ZKK, have been shipped in from a large sports shop, Waffen-Frankonia, of Wurzburg, West Germany. Others came into the U.S. through Canada. In the 1969 Ellwood Epps catalog a "Brno .222 Rem." rifle is listed. No model designation is given and the rifle illustrated does not appear to be a Brno at all. However, it was listed at $169.50, and it most likely is the ZKK 601.

The Brno ZG 47

The "47" probably indicates the date this rifle was introduced. As most often pictured and seen it is generally a typical German-type sporter with a very trim stock and slender barrel. While styles varied the usual ZG 47 has a walnut stock of minimum dimensions, including a very thin comb, small cheekpiece, a

small but well-curved pistol grip and a slim, tapered fore-end ending with a schnabel. Narrow sling swivels screwed into the stock were standard, as were a horn pistol grip cap and buttplate. Grip and fore-end were checkered. The 23.6″ round tapered barrel sported a band ramp front sight with changeable sight blades and a windage-adjustable folding rear sight mounted on a small ramp made integral with the barrel. Later on they were made with a plain German-type stock without cheekpiece and grip cap or with the heavier American-type sporter stocks, the latter having a very pronounced Monte Carlo comb and a full fore-end.

The ZG 47 action was like the basic M98 type but with these "improvements:" 1) receiver ring and bridge have integral scope mounting bases or dovetails, flat on top, with the top of the bridge lower than the ring. The dovetail covered the entire length of the bridge, but the receiver dovetail ended just short of the front edge of the receiver. The Brno-made ZG 47 scope mount was called a "slide-on" type bridge mount with thumbscrew-tightened clamps. An anchor block, provided on the left rear of the base, engaged a matching notch cut into the side of the receiver bridge, preventing the scope and mount from moving forward under recoil. 2) The streamlined bolt sleeve had a rotary-type safety built into its right side. Pivoted upward, the safety locked both striker and bolt, its low position allowing operation with a low-mounted scope. 3) The pear-shaped bolt handle, dropping straight down, is also made so that it can be operated under the low-mounted scope. 4) The all-steel magazine has a hinged floorplate, its latch in the front of the trigger guard bow. 5) Two trigger mechanisms were available; a standard double-set or a single

*The ZKM 465 in .22 Hornet caliber is again available and cataloged. These were seen by me at the Budapest World Exhibition of Hunting in September, 1971.   JTA.

Illustrated above: Czech Brno ZKK 601 rifle chambered for the .222 Remington cartridge. Kesselring mount rings are used here to attach the scope on this rifle.

stage type with a built-in single set trigger.

ZG 47 rifles were available in .270, 7x57mm, 7x64, .30-06, 8x57mm, 8x64S, 9.3x62 and 10.75x68. These well-made rifles are usually highly prized by their owners. They were still listed in the 1964 Waffen-Frankonia catalog, the best grade at $139.50.

The Brno ZKK

I don't know exactly when the Model ZKK Brno rifle was first offered, but probably after 1965. I first read about it in the 1969 issue of the GUN DIGEST.

Illustrated here are the three different ZKK models. The ZKK-600 has the standard length action for cartridges of the 8x57mm to .30-06 length. The ZKK-601, a shorter action, is used for such cartridges as .222, .243 and .308. The ZKK-602, a long or "magnum" action, handles such large cartridges as the .375 H&H Magnum and .404 Jeffery.

Except for action length and calibers, ZKK-600 and ZKK-601 rifles are alike — typical German-type sporting rifles, quite light and trim. The walnut stock without the very thin comb or the schnabel is otherwise typically European, with a small, uncapped pistol grip, and a very slender, short fore-end. The moulded plastic buttplate does not have rounded edges and looks out of place. The checkered panels on the grip and fore-end cover a goodly area, but the checkering was not well done, at least not on the rifle I examined. A plain 1″ sling swivel is screwed into the buttstock; the front swivel is mounted on a barrel band, several inches forward of the fore-end tip. The comb is quite low, about ½″ below the bolt when it is opened, and low enough so that the open sight can be readily used. The 23.6″ slim, round-tapered barrel carries a band-ramp front sight, so made that the blade sight can be easily replaced. The folding leaf rear sight, dovetailed into an integral ramp on the barrel, is adjustable for windage only by driving it over. Flipped up it presents a small-U sighting notch; and when lowered it is out of the way when the rear aperture sight is used.

The rear aperture sight is built into the top flat of the receiver bridge, that is, within the integral scope mount base. Pressed down, it lies entirely within the receiver

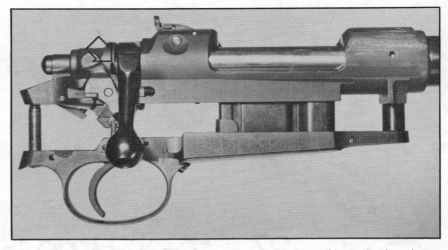

Brno ZKK 601 action. The ZKK 600 and 602 actions are similar to this one but have longer magazine boxes. The action is shown with the peep sight up in sighting position, action cocked, and the safety in the OFF (tipped back) or FIRE position. When the safety is tipped forward it locks the sear and the bolt, the latter being accomplished by the top of the safety engaging over the bolt lock lug (indicated by arrow) on the base of the bolt handle.

bridge, thus is out of the way if the regular open sights or a scope are to be used. Depressing a plunger on the right side of the bridge pops the aperture up into view. A screw in the front of the aperture arm adjusts elevation, while another screw in the aperture arm adjusts windage.

The 601 rifle weighs about 6.75 pounds, the ZKK-600 about 7.

The ZKK-602 rifle, made for really big game cartridges, is heavier, probably going around 8 pounds. Besides having a longer action with a deeper magazine, it is also beefed-up in other areas. The stock has a slightly fuller fore-end, carries a rubber recoil pad, and is reinforced in the recoil lug area by a crossbolt. The 602 rear sight is a 2-leaf express type. Except for these points, and having a barrel proportionally larger, the 602 is just like the 600 and 601 models. It is not furnished with the extra single-set trigger.

The ZKK Brno Action

The ZKK action cannot be described as merely "an improved M98 Mauser" action, for it is much more than that. As we shall see, it does have a couple of M98 features, but it has so many more that are not

Mauser as to make it a distinct action, apart from most other commercial turn-bolt actions made today. We shall also see that the designers copied some features from other modern actions. It also appears to me that it is made entirely by the latest steel fabrication methods, including the investment casting process. The action is of all steel construction which, in this day of lightweight alloys and plastics, is quite a novelty.

The one-piece receiver is a very accurate die forging or an investment casting— I cannot be sure which. Inside the receiver ring the M98 collar is slotted only on the right for the extractor, a good feature that adds strength. The recoil lug, made as an integral part of the receiver ring, has ample bearing surface with the stock to prevent set back. There is no flat surface under the receiver ring, which is regrettable to me since a flat surface here might add years to the life of the stock in preventing the possible splitting of the stock. The receiver ring is about 1.65″ long. The bridge, about 1.50″ long, is built up so its top is level with the raised top of the ring. The ring and bridge tops are flat, becoming integral scope mount bases after grooves are milled in their sides. As mentioned earlier, an excellent and fully adjustable pop-up rear aperture sight is built into the base on the bridge. A deep notch is cut into the left side of the bridge for the anchor block of the Brno scope mount rings.

The high left receiver wall between the ring and bridge is unnotched, though its top half is made thinner to reduce weight. The ejection port opening on the right extends to the bottom of the locking lug raceway. Both walls are greatly strengthened and stiffened by a heavy-walled magazine-box guide or retainer, similar to, but heavier than, the M70 Winchester and M77 Ruger actions. The sides of this box are quite thick and, with the right wall extending back to the safety, they offer a considerable flat surface area for bedding.

Close-up of the Brno ZKK 601 rifle action; scope attached with Kesselring mounts.

Left side of the Brno ZKK 601 action.

Integral cartridge guide lips on either side of the magazine-well opening hold the cartridges in the magazine and guide them into the chamber when the bolt is closed. The loading ramp in front of the magazine-well opening is deep and polished smooth.

The magazine box is made of heavy sheet-metal; pressed, bent and formed into a rigid box. I have had no opportunity to examine all 3 of the new Brno rifles, but I assume that at least 4 different sized boxes are made to handle the 4 families of cartridges for which these rifles are chambered. This would include the short magazine for the .222 cartridge (it is 2.250″ long inside), one for the .243 and .308 (about 2.875″ long), one for the .30-06 family, and the longest one for the .375 H&H Magnum and .404 Jeffery cartridges. In the .30-06 and shorter magazines, grooves are pressed into the sides of the box at the cartridge shoulder junction to hold the cartridges back in the box to prevent battered bullet points as the rifle recoils from firing.

The receiver accepts only the magazine box for the cartridge family for which the action is made, and the cartridge guide lips in the magazine well are made accordingly.

The usual W-shaped follower spring is used with a steel follower, the latter probably an investment casting that's polished very smooth. The unusual thing about it is that the ridge which staggers the cartridges in the magazine is on the right side rather than on the left, as are the followers in most other actions.

The trigger guard is combined with the magazine plate, the magazine box held between this part and the receiver when the rifle is assembled. The floorplate is hinged to the front of the guard plate. A very neat and heavy plunger-type catch in the front top part of the guard bow holds the floorplate closed. Both plates also appear to be investment castings.

Guard screws, going through the ends of the trigger guard plate and threading into the recoil lug and receiver tang, hold the action securely in the stock. Sleeves or bushings are used over each of these

screws to provide the proper spacing between the trigger guard plate and receiver. The ends of the follower spring slip into slots in the floorplate and follower to hold these parts together. Incidentally, the guard screw threads are about .230″ in diameter, their pitch being about 33 threads per inch.

The bolt also appears to be of one-piece construction, the bolt handle an integral part. The dual-opposed locking lugs on the front of the bolt are solid; that is, neither one is slotted or drilled. The bolt face is slightly recessed for the cartridge rim, with this recess undercut at the bottom as on the M98 bolt to allow cartridges to slip under the extractor hook on being fed from the magazine. (This feature largely eliminates the possibility of double loading. In other words, if on feeding a cartridge from the magazine to the chamber the bolt is not entirely closed before it is opened again, the cartridge will be ejected rather than remaining in the chamber. I consider this a desirable feature in a hunting rifle, and more desirable than a fully-recessed bolt head.) The approaches to the locking-lug shoulders inside the receiver ring are beveled and, on rotating the bolt to lock it, the bolt is cammed fully forward.

The low-profile bolt handle will clear a low-mounted scope. Its stem, round and slightly tapered, ends in a pear-shaped grasping ball. The ball is hollow; not just a hole drilled in it, but hollowed out round. The bolt handle is on the very rear end of the bolt, and its base partially encircles the bolt. The under part of this base serves as the third safety locking lug by engaging a matching recess milled into the receiver. The upper part of the base has an angled surface which contacts a matching surface in the bridge when the bolt handle is raised, and this provides the initial extraction power.

The extractor is of the long one-piece

Brno ZKK action open.

non-rotating Mauser type attached to the bolt body by a collar. A lip under the front end of the extractor, engaging a groove cut part way around the bolt head, prevents longitudinal extractor movement. The extractor has enough spring, and room enough to spring, to slip over the rim of a cartridge placed in the chamber ahead of the extractor.

The ejector is a thin piece of steel lying in a slot cut into the bottom of the receiver bridge. It pivots on a pin, tensioned by a small coil spring and plunger. An angled slot is cut into the bolt head, and on opening the bolt the tip of the ejector moves into this slot to eject the cartridge case or cartridge to the right.

The bolt stop is a heavy piece of sheet steel fitted into a slot cut into the bottom left side of the bridge and opening into the left locking lug guideway. Pivoted on the safety pin, it is tensioned by a small but stiff coil spring. The bolt is stopped in its rearward travel when the left locking lug contacts the bolt stop. The rear end of the bolt stop projects out of the receiver just behind the bridge, and by pressing this part forward the bolt stop is tipped down to allow removal of the bolt. The ejector and bolt stop are close copies of the same parts in the old Model 70 action, and there is nothing wrong with these systems.

The firing mechanism is composed of the bolt sleeve, one-piece firing pin, coil mainspring, cocking piece, mainspring retainer nut, mainspring retainer-nut lock and bolt-sleeve disassembly catch and spring. The bolt sleeve, threaded into the rear of the bolt, is bored through for the cocking piece. The cocking piece is semipermanently attached to the firing pin with a cross pin. The stiff coil mainspring is compressed between the stem of the bolt sleeve and the mainspring retainer-nut lock and retainer nut, with this part being threaded on the firing pin. This threaded portion is flattened, and the inside of the lock is made to fit over it so it will not

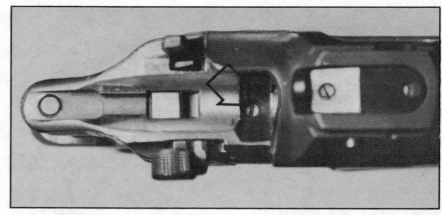

Top view of the rear part of the Brno ZKK action, with bolt removed, showing the location of the trigger adjustment screw within the safety locking lug recess, as indicated by the arrow.

turn. The front of this lock has two small humps which engage in shallow notches in the retainer nut and, with mainspring pressure against the lock, the retainer nut is prevented from turning. A small disassembly catch is built into the left inside of the bolt sleeve, its purpose being to hold the cocking piece back so the firing mechanism can be easily unscrewed from the bolt. After the bolt is removed from the rifle this catch can be engaged to hold the cocking piece back by holding it down while pulling the cocking piece back (see take-down instructions). A cam on the cocking piece engages in a cam notch in the rear of the bolt and, on raising the bolt handle, the striker is cocked. There is no separate bolt-sleeve lock, the bolt sleeve being prevented from turning when the bolt is open by the cocking-piece cam resting in a shallow notch on the rear of the bolt. There is also a small ball bearing in front of the bolt-sleeve disassembly catch-spring which projects through a hole inside the bolt sleeve; when the bolt sleeve is fully in place, and when the bolt handle is raised, this ball engages another small notch in the rear of the bolt, helping to

keep the bolt sleeve from turning. The entire firing mechanism is simple and well-designed, lock time fast and positive. The method of holding the mainspring on the firing pin via a threaded nut is good.

A feature I have not found on any other turnbolt action is the way the cocking piece on the action fits into and slides in a mortise in the tang. A ridge on each side of the cocking-cam arm fits into recessed grooves in the cocking cam raceway. This prevents binding of the cocking piece in the bolt sleeve due to upward pressure from the sear when the action is cocked, as well as limiting up and down play of the cocking piece and bolt.

The standard trigger mechanism, of the single-stage type, is adjustable for weight of pull only. The entire mechanism is comprised of numerous parts and most of them are attached to the receiver. The sear, the part which projects into the cocking-piece cam guideway to hold the striker back, is positioned under the receiver tang; there it pivots on, and is held in place by, a cross pin through the receiver walls. It is held upward by a coil spring held in place under the sear by a small arm, which

Top view of the Brno ZKK action showing: (A) Mauser type extractor, (B) rear aperture sight built into the receiver bridge, (C) bolt lock lug, (D) safety, (E) bolt sleeve, (F) cocking piece, (G) primary-extraction cam surface, (H) windage lock screw, and (I) elevation adjustment screw.

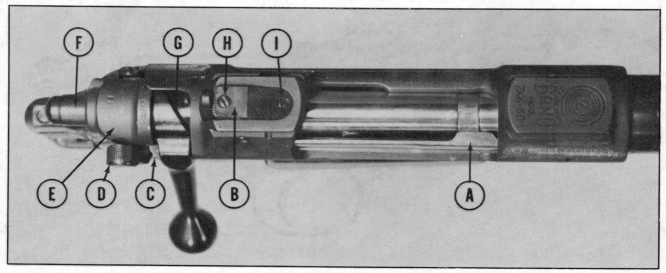

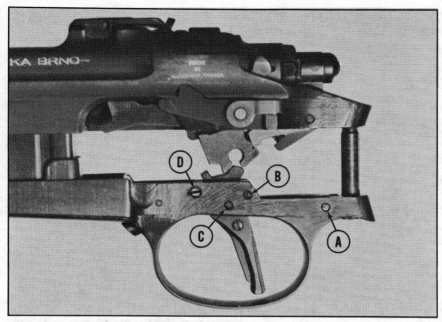

The accessory single-set trigger which is furnished as an extra with the ZKK 600 and 601 rifles. It is shown here in the "un-set" position, and the rifle can be fired in the normal way by merely pulling the trigger back. (A) pin which holds the two set trigger springs in place in the trigger guard, (B) trigger spring stop pin, (C) trigger pivot pin, and (D) set trigger sear pin.

is also held by the sear pin. Forward of the sear is the sear release, which is held in place by, and pivots on, the safety pin. It is tensioned to engage the sear by a coil spring, with the top end of this spring bearing on a small strip of metal; this in turn bears against the notched bottom of the trigger weight-of-pull adjustment screw threaded into the bottom of the receiver. On removing the bolt from the receiver the head of this screw is exposed in the safety lug notch; turning it in (clockwise) increases the weight of pull, and vice versa. A shallow notch on the rear of the sear release engages a sharp corner on the front bottom of the sear to hold the

To fire the ZKK rifle with the single-set trigger it is pushed forward with the tip of the thumb until "set" or cocked, in which position it is shown here. A light touch on the set release lever (A) releases the main set trigger to snap back under tension of the set trigger mainspring to disengage the regular sear release (B) from the sear (C). Also clearly shown in this photograph is the ejector (D), bolt stop (E), bolt disassembly catch (F), and anchor recess for the Brno scope mount (G).

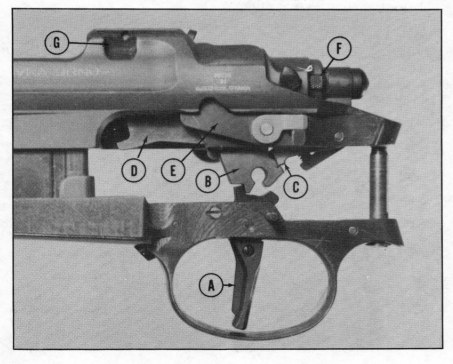

sear up, and the striker back, when the action is closed.

The trigger, which has a well-curved and grooved finger piece, is pivoted on a pin in the trigger guard. A top arm on the trigger extends into a U-notch in the bottom of the sear release and, on pulling the trigger back, the sear release is tipped down to release the sear against the pressure of the mainspring. There is a very slight amount of slack in the trigger, but this is not at all bothersome. Otherwise the trigger pull is short and crisp, and the normal weight of pull can be adjusted from about 2.5 to 4 pounds. This trigger system is standard on all three models of the Brno ZKK. However, an extra single-set trigger accessory unit is furnished with the 600 and 601, and the trigger guards of these two models are set up to accept this unit.

This accessory unit is comprised of a main trigger with a straight finger piece, set trigger lever, release-lever adjustment screw, release-lever spring, release-lever pin, trigger mainspring, trigger tension spring, two hold-down pins, and the release-lever engagement pin, with this last part already fitted in the trigger guard. The set trigger is quite easy to install and it is done as follows: Remove the trigger guard from the stock. Push out the trigger pin, remove the trigger, and replace it with the assembled set trigger. Before inserting the trigger pin, slip the thin spring into the heavy spring and, with the short ends of the springs down, insert the long ends of the springs into the square notch in the rear of the trigger; then depress the bent part of the springs into the trigger guard and insert a pin through the hole provided to hold the springs in place. Now manipulate the trigger by pushing the finger piece forward until the pin can be inserted in the hole over the end of the heavy spring. Then push the trigger down so the trigger pin can be inserted. Turn the adjustment screw in or out as required so that the set trigger can be pushed fully forward so the release lever engages with the release-lever pin in the trigger guard to hold the trigger forward. The screw can then be adjusted so that only a light pull of the release lever will allow the trigger to snap back. Replace the trigger guard in the stock.

The set trigger can be operated in two ways: as a conventional trigger by merely pulling it back, as with the regular trigger. To use as a set trigger push the trigger ahead with the tip of the thumb until it is cocked and stays forward under spring pressure, then fire the rifle by a light touch on the set trigger release lever.

If the rifle is not to be fired after the set trigger has been set, it can be unset again by placing the thumb firmly behind the trigger and releasing the trigger by the forefinger of the same hand. Never set the trigger until just before you are to take a shot, and promptly unset it if the shot is not taken. .

The safety, rugged and positive, is positioned on the right side of the receiver tang directly behind the bolt handle, and is held in place by, and pivots on, a pin.

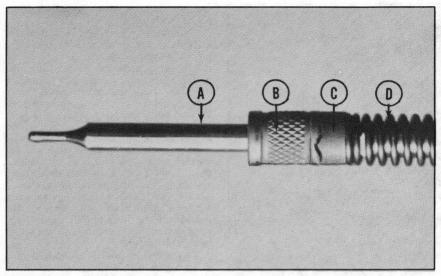

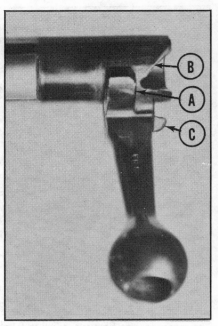

Right—Bottom view of the rear end of the Brno ZKK bolt showing: (A) safety lug, (B) cocking-cam notch, (C) bolt-locking lug. Above—Brno firing pin showing: (A) firing pin, (B) mainspring retainer nut, (C) retainer-nut lock sleeve, (D) mainspring.

It is provided OFF and ON tension by a spring and plunger occupying a slot cut into the side of the receiver, just ahead of the safety. The safety thumbpiece, large and knurled, is convenient in operation. Pulled back, the safety is in the OFF or FIRE position, at which time a red dot is visible in the base of the bolt handle. The bolt can only be operated when the safety is back. When pushed forward, the bolt and sear are locked; by the top of the safety engaging over a projection on the base of the bolt handle and the bottom of the safety engaging over the bottom of the sear and pulling it up slightly. While the safety is convenient to operate and positive, it is not easily operated and makes a distinct click when pulled back, due mostly to the very stiff safety plunger spring. This can be corrected by shortening the spring.

The action is adequately vented in the event of a primer or case head failure. A hole in the right side of the receiver ring coincides with a top corner of the extractor hook. There is a single round vent hole in the bolt body about one inch back of the bolt head, and gases getting inside the bolt would be vented into the left locking lug raceway. There is no flange on the left side of the bolt sleeve to deflect any gases that might escape back through this raceway, so it is no better sealed at this point than the M70 Winchester.

Besides the two guard screws, there is also a fore-end screw to help hold the barrel and action in the stock. This screw threads into a stud fitted in a groove in the enlarged portion of the barrel which forms the rear sight base. The groove for the fore-end stud is milled lengthwise with the barrel, and the stud is made to be a loose fit in it. Thus, on tightening this screw the stud moves to the precise location of the screw. It might also move in the groove as the barrel heats up from firing or if the fore-end should shift through changes in moisture and tempera-

ture. While I think it is a good idea to have a fore-end screw in magnum calibers, I don't see much use for it in the other rifles; but if a screw is used I think the method Brno employs in the ZKK is the best I have seen.

Metal Finish

The Brno ZKK receiver has an unusual finish. To me it seems to have been heavily pickled, sand blasted or Parkerized. At any rate the surface has a matte finish that is greyish in color, contrasting with

Brno ZKK bolt head showing: (A) extractor, (B) right locking lug, (C) undercut bolt-face recess, (D) ejector slot, (E) left locking lug, (F) gas-vent hole, (G) extractor collar.

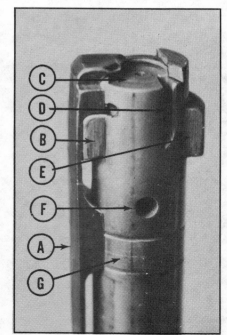

the well-polished blued barrel and the bright bolt and extractor; the effect is quite pleasing. This contrast can be seen in the illustrations. The bolt sleeve, cocking piece, safety, trigger and the bolt stop are finished just like the receiver. The bolt handle is highly polished and blued, as are the trigger guard and floorplate. These parts are smooth, level and well polished, except that on the rifle I had someone forgot to polish the top edge of the extractor. Its action was smooth, easy to operate, and everything functioned perfectly. The boltway inside the receiver was well polished, making for smooth bolt operation. No bolt guide rib is provided, but the bridge is long enough to guide the bolt properly; there is little tendency for the bolt to bind when it is operated.

Comments

There are a few things I don't like about this rifle and a lot of things I do. For my taste the stock is a bit too skimpy, but what I disliked most was the cheap square-edged plastic buttplate. The checkerer could have finished the borders of the checkering much better. If I had anything to do with the design of this rifle I would have made an extra gas-vent hole in the left side of the receiver just behind the inside receiver collar and place the vent hole in the bolt so it would direct gases into the magazine instead of into the left locking lug raceway. I would also have wanted the bottom of the receiver ring flat instead of round. Other than these points the Brno ZKK rifle and action are very much to my liking.

I like the balance and feel of this rifle. On a hunting rifle I like to have the front sling swivel out on the barrel as on this rifle. I don't think any other commercial rifle, made now or ever before, has a better open sight setup than found on this Brno rifle. The rear aperture sight deserves special mention. It not only is a very clever sight, but it is well-designed and con-

Brno ZKK Trigger System

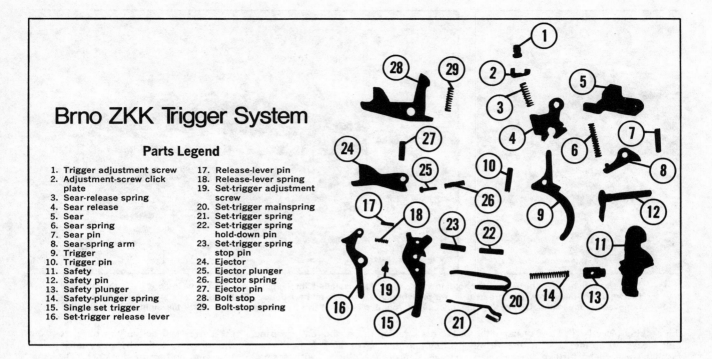

Parts Legend

1. Trigger adjustment screw
2. Adjustment-screw click plate
3. Sear-release spring
4. Sear release
5. Sear
6. Sear spring
7. Sear pin
8. Sear-spring arm
9. Trigger
10. Trigger pin
11. Safety
12. Safety pin
13. Safety plunger
14. Safety-plunger spring
15. Single set trigger
16. Set-trigger release lever
17. Release-lever pin
18. Release-lever spring
19. Set-trigger adjustment screw
20. Set-trigger mainspring
21. Set-trigger spring
22. Set-trigger spring hold-down pin
23. Set-trigger spring stop pin
24. Ejector
25. Ejector plunger
26. Ejector spring
27. Ejector pin
28. Bolt stop
29. Bolt-stop spring

Dimensional Specifications*

Weight (estimated):

Model 601 .... 41 ozs.
Model 600 .... 43 ozs.

Length:

Model 601 .... 8.00"
Model 600 .... 8.625"

Receiver ring width .... 1.340"

Bolt dia. .... .700"

Bolt travel:

Model 601 .... 4.225"
Model 600 ....

Striker travel .... .375"

*No specifications available for the Model 602 action.

General Specifications

Type	Turnbolt repeater.
Receiver	One-piece steel. Integral scope mount bases on the bridge and ring. Pop-up aperture sight built into the bridge.
Bolt	One-piece machined steel with dual-opposed forward locking lugs. Safety lug on the rear of the bolt.
Ignition	One-piece firing pin powered by coil mainspring. Cocks on opening.
Magazine	Non-detachable box magazine with hinged floorplate.
Trigger	Single stage, adjustable for weight of pull. Single set trigger is furnished as an extra.
Safety	Pivoting side tang type locks sear and bolt when tipped forward.
Extractor	Long one-piece non-rotating Mauser type attached to the bolt by a collar.
Bolt stop	Pivoting type positioned in a groove in the bottom of the receiver, stops bolt by contacting the left locking lug.
Ejector	Pivoting type positioned in a groove in receiver bottom.

structed. It is handy and does not interfere with anything. When not in use it is well protected from damage, and when needed it's instantly ready. It is a little package of insurance to a hunter. The shooters I've shown this rifle to have all called this sight a gem.

I don't believe there is another turnbolt action made that has a better, stronger or more positive bolt lock. It is a high contrast to some of the bolt-lock systems used on most of the other centerfire turnbolt actions made today. Few other actions I know of have a better, simpler, or more rugged and reliable trigger and ignition system than this Brno action. I don't think too much of the single-set trigger as Brno has made it, but I find no fault with the standard trigger. I like the long Mauser-type extractor, and on a hunting rifle I like the undercut bolt face recess which prevents double loading better than a fully recessed bolt face.

Brno ZKK Markings

The Brno trademark is the letter **Z** within several concentric circles (meant to represent a view of the interior of a rifled barrel). This emblem, with the words **TRADE MARK** in small capitals, is stamped on the top flat of the receiver ring and on the barrel. On the left side of the receiver is stamped:

— ZBROJOVKA BRNO —

In smaller letters on the side of the bridge in 3 lines is:

MADE
IN
CZECHOSLOVAKIA

The word **BRNO** and the model designation are stamped on the receiver bridge thus:

MOD.
ZKK-600 (or 601 or 602)

The serial number is stamped on the right side of the receiver ring with its last four digits stamped underneath the bolt handle. Stamped on top of the barrel are the words:

ZBROJOVKA BRNO —
CZECHOSLOVAKIA

The caliber is stamped on the breech of the barrel at the top and also on the follower, visible when the action is opened. Current Czechoslovakian proof marks (including the date, as **66**) are stamped on the barrel breech, receiver ring and bolt.

(My ZKK-600 caliber .270 does not have a stamping on the follower, but the bolt sleeve is stamped **SAF** at its front, and **FRE** to the rear. Ed.)

Take-Down and Assembly

First make sure the chamber and magazine are empty. To remove bolt, raise the handle and, while pressing the bolt stop knob fully forward, pull the bolt from the receiver. It can be reinserted without pressing the knob. The safety must be pulled back to remove or replace the bolt.

To take the bolt down press the edge of the cocking piece against the edge of the workbench and, with a firm grip on the bolt, and with a finger depressing the bolt-disassembly catch, pull the cocking piece back until the bolt-disassembly catch holds

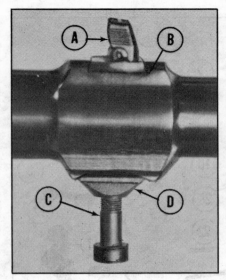 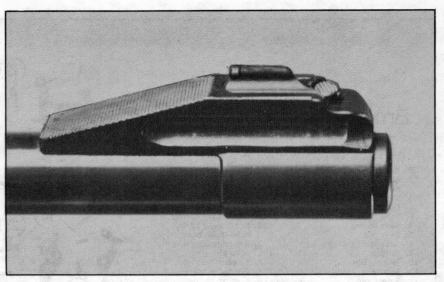

Left—Shown here is the Brno ZKK folding rear sight (A) dovetailed into ramp base (B) made integral with the barrel. Below is fore-end screw (C) threaded into a movable stud (D). See text for details. Right—Brno ZKK band-ramp sight with removabl blade sight. Depressing the checkered round plunger at the front of the ramp allows the sight to be slid out.

the cocking piece back. Now unscrew the bolt sleeve from the bolt. If the firing mechanism is to be further disassembled it will be first necessary to disengage this catch. Do this by placing the firing pin tip on a hard smooth surface and depress the bolt sleeve until the catch is freed. A simple tool must be made to disassemble the firing mechanism. Saw or file a notch about 5/16″ wide and ⅜″ deep in a piece of heavy sheet-metal and place it in a vise with the notch up. Insert the firing pin into this notch at about the second coil back from the front of the mainspring and, while pushing forward on the firing pin to compress the mainspring slightly, unscrew the firing-pin nut from the firing pin; after this the lock ring, mainspring and firing pin can be removed from the bolt sleeve. The cocking-piece catch can then be removed from the bolt sleeve by using a small drift punch and pushing the catch to the inside through a small hole over the catch. Be careful not to lose the very small plunger, spring and ball bearing that are under the catch.

To reassemble, insert the ball bearing, spring and plunger in the hole in the bolt sleeve, depress the plunger with a small punch, and then holding the catch with tweezers, slip it in place. The notched tool you made to disassemble the firing pin parts must also be used to assemble the parts. In assembling the firing pin parts the firing-pin nut must be turned on as far as it will go, but need not be forced tight. Before assembling the firing mechanism in the bolt the cocking piece must be pulled back so the cocking piece catch can be engaged; then, after the bolt sleeve is turned back into the bolt, it is again disengaged so the end of the cocking-piece cam rests in the shallow notch just off the deeper cocking-cam notch.

To remove the extractor lift the hook away from the bolt and push the extractor forward. The extractor collar can be spread apart and removed, but this may spring the collar so that it may not be perfectly round when refitted to the bolt.

To remove the stock turn out fore-end screw, front and rear guard screws; now

the barrel and action can be lifted from the stock and the trigger guard pulled from the bottom of the stock. The magazine box can then be pulled from the receiver and the pins pushed out of the trigger guard to remove the trigger, floorplate and floorplate catch.

Disassemble the safety and sear mechanism as follows: Push out sear pin and remove sear, sear spring and sear-spring arm. Push out the safety pin from right to left. Lift out sear release, sear-release spring and trigger-adjustment click plate. Lift out bolt stop and bolt-stop spring. With a small punch pull safety plunger forward and lift out safety, after which the safety plunger and spring can be removed. With a bent punch push out ejector pin to the left, lift out ejector from the hole behind the ejector. Turn out the trigger adjustment screw. Reassemble all of these parts in reverse order.

The barrel is screwed tightly into the receiver and it should not be removed unless necessary, and then only if proper equipment to do so is at hand.

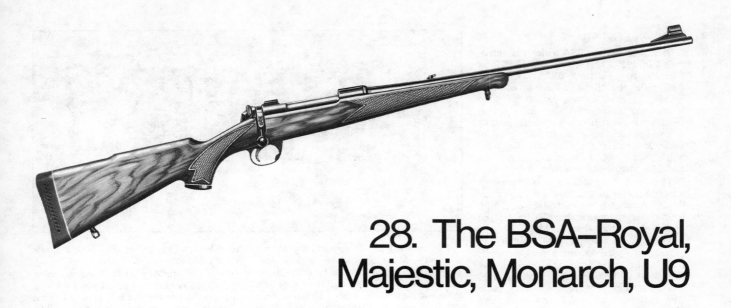

28. The BSA–Royal, Majestic, Monarch, U9

THE BIRMINGHAM Small Arms Co., Ltd., the well-known British gunmakers of Birmingham, England, first displayed an interest in producing a quality bolt action sporting rifle for the American market shortly after the end of WW II. Their U.S. representative at that time was Jack Warwick, who busied himself gathering ideas for the proposed new bolt action on which the rifles were to be made. A prototype action was developed and made, and a rifle assembled on it. It was shown to several gun authorities in the U.S. As expected, some faults and undesirable features were found in this sample rifle and action. Warwick, fortified with suggestions for its further improvement, went back to England.

BSA engineers studied the suggested changes and modified the action accordingly. In 1954 BSA introduced a pilot version of a varmint rifle, to be distributed through Al Freeland (Freeland's Scope Stands) of Rock Island, Ill.

This was the first "Royal Line" rifle to be introduced, though they were not so-named at this time. This was based on a short action, with medium and long actioned rifles to follow, hopefully.

The BSA Short Action

The first BSA modern bolt action centerfire rifle, initially made only for .22 Hornet and .222 Remington cartridges, had a remarkable action in a number of ways. It was short—only long enough to adequately handle the .222 cartridge, which was by that time a highly popular varmint and benchrest target round (my guess is that this action was about 7" long). The receiver was very heavy and massive, its ring 1.350" in diameter, which is larger than the "large ring" M98 Mauser. The bolt, of .700" diameter, had solid dual-opposed forward locking lugs, and the long Mauser-type non-rotating extractor. The breech end of the barrel was counterbored to form a ring or collar to surround the bolt head, the ring slotted for the extractor. The round-knobbed bolt handle (of low scope profile) base formed the third or safety lug, engaging a notch in the tang. The firing mechanism was entirely new, featuring a compact bolt sleeve, two-piece striker/firing pin, and a rotary safety in the bolt sleeve.

This new action also had a staggered-column box magazine, hinged magazine floorplate and an adjustable trigger mechanism that held the bolt stop and ejector. Integral dovetails on the receiver ring and bridge provided anchorage for special Parker-Hale clamp-on scope mount rings. All in all, it was a well-designed and constructed action. Its most notable and impressive feature was the heavy receiver, massive and rigid enough to support a heavy free-floating barrel. Its most obvious fault was the absence, either on the receiver or scope mount rings, of any means to prevent the scope rings from sliding on the straight dovetails. No gas escape holes were provided in the bolt or receiver either.

These original BSA rifles, .22 Hornet or .222, had 24" round tapered barrels fitted with ramp front sights. The very neat stock, of French walnut, had whiteline spacers under the black plastic buttplate and pistol grip cap, a low Monte Carlo comb and forward slanted cheekpiece, straight tapered fore-end, the latter nicely checkered as was the grip. The rifle weighed about 7.5 pounds.

The BSA Medium Action

In 1956, BSA introduced a new rifle with a medium length action. In the interim, some changes and improvements were made which were incorporated into the new medium length action; apparently those short actions made after 1956 also were made with most of these changes. Essentially the new medium action was merely a longer version of the short action, long enough to handle cartridges up to 2.875" over-all. The same heavy receiver was retained, except that it was made longer (again, my guess is that this action was 7.75" long), plus a few other changes. Most important was a hole in the top of the bridge scope-mount dovetail. A matching stud under the rear scope-mount ring engaged this hole to prevent longitudinal movement of the scope mounts from recoil. Instead of the barrel breech being counterbored to shroud the bolt head, the new medium receiver was made with an integral ring or shoulder to surround the bolt head, and against which the barrel abuts. This ring, slotted on the right for the extractor, which greatly strengthens the receiver ring, is a direct copy of the M98 Mauser ring. (While I am quite sure that the first of these medium actions had this feature, I'm also convinced that it was soon dropped in favor of the counterbored barrel—which in effect served the same purpose by enclosing most of the bolt head. At any rate, I believe the integral inside receiver ring feature was dropped before the long BSA action was introduced, which had a counterbored barrel.) Another feature of the new medium action was a guide rib on the bolt body which, when the bolt handle was raised, contacted the left receiver raceway, which helped prevent the bolt from cramping during operation. The action was also made safer via two gas-escape vent holes in the bolt and one in the receiver ring.

The new medium length actioned rifle was originally offered in .257 Roberts, 7mm (7x57) Mauser, .300 Savage and .308 Winchester (7.62 NATO).

General specifications of this rifle match the short action rifle except that the fore-end was more tapered, slimmer, and finished with a schnabel tip. There was also a 3-leaf open rear sight.

Illustrated above: BSA Majestic De luxe rifle.

The Long Action

The long action BSA rifle was introduced in 1957. This action is 8.625″ long over-all. By this time BSA was calling these rifles the "Royal Line." In addition to offering rifles in new calibers suitable to the long action, BSA also introduced a "featherweight rifle," and so designated it. It also appears that at about this time J.L. Galef & Son, Inc. (85 Chambers St., New York, N.Y. 10007) became the importers and U.S. distributors of this line.

The BSA long action was merely a longer version of the medium length action to accommodate cartridges of .30-06 length. Its magazine handles cartridges no longer over-all than 3.375″.

The standard-weight rifles had a 24″ barrel and a receiver with a thick left wall; that is, the left side of the receiver was flush and in line with the receiver ring. The new Featherweight models, made with both medium and long actions, had 22″ slim tapered barrels and receivers on which the left wall, between the bridge and ring, was milled thinner.

In addition to the lighter barrel and receiver, the stock was routed out in places to reduce weight. Lastly an efficient barrel muzzle brake was included. This brake was made by boring out a section of the bore at the muzzle, then cutting several narrow gas-escape slots, one each side of the muzzle, to coincide with the bored-out cage.

The long action standard-weight rifle was available only in .30-06. The long action Featherweight was offered in .270 Winchester, .30-06 and .458 Winchester Magnum; the medium action rifle in .243 and .308. The .458 Magnum rifle weighed about 8.5 pounds, while the same rifle weighed only some 6.25 pounds in the other calibers.

The entire "Royal Line" BSA rifles was discontinued about 1959 and the "Majestic" rifles, with some improved action features, were introduced. Before discussing the latter line, however, I'd like to present a detailed study of the Royal action as made from about 1956 to 1959. Except that the short, medium and long actions are of different length, and that the Featherweight receiver has a thinner side wall, the following description is applicable to all.

Before going into detail I must say I have only thoroughly examined two rifles of the Royal Line; both were lightweight versions in .30-06 caliber, their receivers 8.625″ long.

The "long" BSA Royal line action.

I've never had an opportunity to examine the short or medium actions and, since I have found them to be exceedingly scarce, I've concluded that few rifles on these actions were made. I doubt very much if any of these actions were ever sold separately, although perhaps some were sold in Canada.

The BSA Royal Action

The receiver is precision machined from a solid steel billet. Its bottom is flat, with the recoil lug at the extreme front end. The receiver ring is threaded to accept the large barrel shank, which has right-hand V-type threads.

Except perhaps for a few of the first made, the receiver does not have the M98-type internal ring or collar; instead the breech face of the barrel is counterbored to form a shroud around the bolt head. The rim of this recess is cut away on the right for the extractor. The receiver is not slotted for loading the magazine with a stripper clip.

The bridge is about the same width as the ring. Both, flat on top, are made to form integral dovetail scope-mount bases. The dovetail is about .775″ wide on top and is untapered. A shallow hole, about .200″ in diameter, in the bridge dovetail, takes a stud in the rear scope-mount ring, thus securing the mount against movement caused by recoil. Two tapped holes in the left side of the receiver provide a means to attach a receiver sight.

On the Featherweight models the left wall of the receiver between the ring and bridge is cut down quite thin to reduce weight. On the standard weight model the left side of the receiver is about straight. The loading ramp at the front of the magazine well is made with two shallow

rounded grooves rather than with a single cartridge path.

The bolt follows M98 Mauser design quite closely. Dual-opposed solid locking lugs on the head of the bolt engage behind shoulders cut into the receiver ring. The bolt head is partially recessed for the rim of the cartridge head; part of the left side is built up, its inside recess undercut so the extractor will securely hold the cartridge or case in place for proper extraction and ejection. The long one-piece Mauser-type extractor is held against the bolt by a collar encircling the bolt, with the ends of the collar flanged to engage in a mortise cut in the underside of the extractor. The extractor collar is of two-piece construction and when in place on the bolt the two halves are linked together by a double notch arrangement. This collar is easy to remove and replace without being sprung out of shape. A projection near the head of the extractor engages in a groove cut part way around the bolt head, which prevents longitudinal movement of the extractor.

The bolt handle is at the extreme rear end of the bolt; its base forms a safety lug by engaging a notch cut into the tang. The base of the bolt handle also provides primary extraction power, its beveled surfaces camming against a matching surface on the rear of the bridge. The low bolt handle will clear the lowest-mounted scope.

Adequate gas-escape vents in the bolt and receiver protect the shooter from escaping gases in the event of a ruptured primer or case head. A small hole is provided under the right (lower) locking lug, with a matching hole cut through the left of the receiver ring. This set-up will take care of minor gas escapage around the firing-pin tip. A larger hole, back on the bolt body at the intersection of the main-spring shoulder on the firing pin, will direct additional gases downward into the front of the magazine. There is also a small hole through the head of the extractor to prevent gases from forcing the extractor head outward should gas be directed in its direction. The bolt sleeve is sufficiently flared to the left to seal off the left locking lug raceway should gases escape that far back.

The bolt is made with a semi-guide rib which extends from the extractor collar rearward about 2.6″. When the bolt is

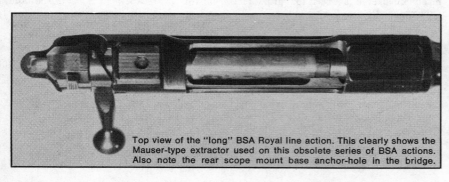

Top view of the "long" BSA Royal line action. This clearly shows the Mauser-type extractor used on this obsolete series of BSA actions. Also note the rear scope mount base anchor-hole in the bridge.

BSA Royal Parts Legend

1. Receiver (top view)
2. Trigger-mechanism group
3. Trigger-housing pin
4. Trigger-housing screw
5. Ejector spring
6. Magazine box
7. Follower
8. Magazine spring
9. Trigger guard
10. Floorplate catch
11. Floorplate catch spring
12. Floorplate catch pin
13. Front trigger-guard screw
14. Floorplate
15. Floorplate hinge plate
16. Floorplate hinge pin
17. Rear trigger-guard screw
18. Front guard screw
19. Bolt
20. Bolt sleeve
21. Safety
22. Safety plunger
23. Safety-plunger spring
24. Striker
25. Mainspring
26. Extractor
27. Extractor collar (2 parts)
28. Firing pin

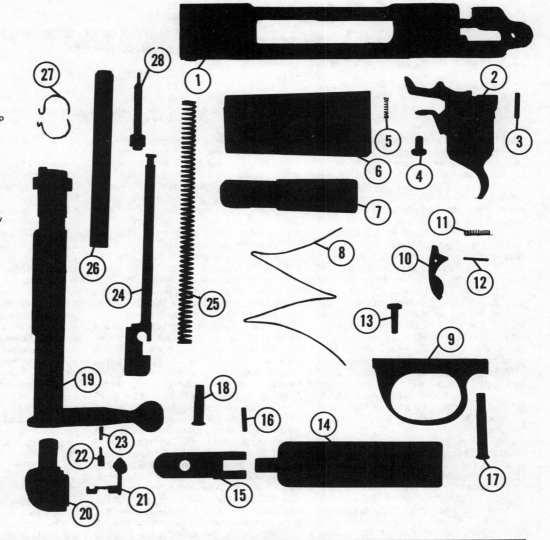

Dimensional Specifications
(long action only)

Weight	38 oz.
Length	8.625"
Receiver ring dia.	1.350"
Bolt dia.	.700"
Bolt travel	4.675"
Striker travel	.300"
Magazine length	3.460"
Bolt face recess	.055"
Guard-screw spacing	8.00"

Dimensional Specifications

Same as for the Royal except:

Action length:	
long	7.75"
medium	7.00"

BSA Royal General Specifications

Type	Turnbolt repeater.
Receiver	One-piece machined steel. Non-slotted bridge. Integral dovetail scope mount bases machined on ring and bridge.
Bolt	One-piece with dual-opposed forward locking lugs. Handle acts as safety lug.
Ignition	Firing mechanism consists of striker, coil mainspring and separate firing pin. Cocks on opening.
Magazine	Staggered-column non-detachable 4-shot box type. Hinged floorplate.
Trigger	Single-stage, adjustable for weight of pull and creep (sear engagement). The grooved trigger can also be adjusted to make a double-stage pull.
Safety	Rotary, in right side of bolt sleeve. UP is the OFF or FIRE position. Tipped back is ON or SAFE locking both striker and bolt.
Extractor	One-piece Mauser-type spring, attached to the bolt by two-piece collar.
Bolt stop	Within the trigger mechanism.
Ejector	Within the trigger mechanism.

BSA Majestic General Specifications

The same as for the Royal except as follows:

Ejector	Spring and plunger type built into bolt head.
Extractor	C-clip type built into the bolt head.

opened the edge of this rib contacts the lower edge of the left locking lug raceway, which prevents the bolt from being turned any further. It also helps prevent any binding of the bolt when the action is operated. The very smooth bolt body is a snug fit in the receiver, and even with the bolt opened and drawn back, very little end play or wobble exists.

The bolt stop, in the top part of the trigger mechanism, pivots on the trigger housing-pin. The front end of the stop projects into the receiver, and under spring tension is pushed up into an oblong notch cut into the bottom of the bolt body, just

forward of the extractor collar when the bolt is opened. When the striker is down, pulling on the trigger causes the bolt stop to remain down so the bolt can then be opened and withdrawn. The bolt stop also locks the bolt closed when the safety is ON by the action of the safety drawing

the striker head off the sear, allowing the sear and bolt stop to rise and allowing the bolt stop to engage the bolt locking notch cut into the rear bottom of the bolt body. The bolt stop also functions as the sear, which function will be discussed later.

The ejector is a thin piece of hardened

BSA caliber .30-06 featherweight model on the Royal line—pre-1959 (long action). This rifle is fitted with a Redfield 4x Bear Cub scope in the excellent Parker-Hale "roll-off" mount rings, which fit the male dovetails milled into the receiver.

steel located in the bottom of the receiver, lying partially in the trigger housing. Held in position on the trigger housing-pin, it is under tension of a small coil spring. The bolt head is slotted to allow the ejector to rise behind the cartridge head on opening the bolt; this bottom slot is slightly to the left of the bolt head. Cartridges/cases are ejected to the right.

The firing mechanism is quite simple. The bolt sleeve threads into the rear of the bolt. The striker fits through the bolt sleeve and the mainspring is compressed over the striker rod between the bolt sleeve and firing pin tip which fits over the end of the striker rod much in the same way as on the Model 1903 Springfield. The flat striker head is an integral part of the striker rod. The rotary wing safety, positioned through the bolt sleeve, engages a milled cut in the striker head. A small spring and plunger lying in a hole in the left side of the bolt sleeve provide tension to hold the safety in place and in the OFF position. The mainspring is quite strong and the striker assembly very light, which makes for fast lock-time and positive ignition. The striker head, engaging a notch in the rear of the bolt, cocks the striker on opening the bolt.

The magazine box is a folded sheet-metal stamping, the ends welded together at the front. The top is gently tapered to fit easily into the magazine well. It is loosely held in place against the receiver by the floorplate. Two vertical ridges, pressed into the sides of the magazine box just forward of the shoulder location of the cartridges, hold the cartridges to the rear of the box and prevent battering of the bullet points from recoil.

The alloy trigger guard bow is the only non-steel part. The floorplate is hinged to the front guard screw plate. A latch, under the tension of a small coil spring and located in a slot in the front of the guard bow, holds the hinged floorplate closed. A screw through the front guard screw plate, threading into the recoil lug, and another through the rear of the guard bow, threading into the receiver tang, securely hold the barrel and action in the stock. Besides the rear guard screw, the guard bow is also held in place in the stock by a screw through the inside of the stock inletting into the front of the guard bow.

The inside of the floorplate and the underside of the milled follower are grooved to accept the ends of the magazine follower spring to hold these parts together.

The Royal Trigger

The trigger mechanism comprises several small parts housed in a sheet-metal box, and this box is attached to the underside of the receiver by a screw and pin. As previously mentioned the ejector and sear, which is also the bolt stop, are fastened in the trigger housing. The ejector is tensioned by a small coil spring. The sear (as it will be called now in describing the trigger mechanism) is supplied upward tension by the trip lever spring, with both the ejector and sear held in place by, and pivoting on, a bushing through holes in the trigger housing. A pin through the ejector and sear bushing helps hold the trigger mechanism to the reciever.

The trip lever, located directly under the sear, pivots on a small pin through the housing. The trip lever is held upward by a small spring, which in turn provides the upward tension to the sear. Pivoting on a pin and tensioned by a spring, the trigger pawl is positioned vertically between the trigger and the trip lever. Notches in the top of the trigger pawl and in the rear end of the trip lever engage each other when the action is cocked, which engagement forms the "sear" in the trigger mechanism itself. The trigger, positioned in the bottom of the trigger housing, pivots on a pin through the housing.

A small but rather sturdy coil spring, backed by an Allen-head setscrew in a hole in the base of the trigger, supplies tension to the trigger as well as providing a means to adjust the weight of pull. A similar setscrew through the top front of the trigger housing can serve to limit the trigger sear engagement, limit the take-up travel of the trigger or, if adjusted to increase trigger travel, the trigger can be adjusted to a double-stage pull. The rear top arm on the trigger contacts a shoulder on the trigger pawl and, when the trigger is pulled, the trigger pawl is tipped forward.

Essentially this is basically a 3- or 4-lever (4 levers if the trigger is counted) self-setting trigger mechanism; the 3 levers merely reduce the very heavy pressure of the mainspring on the striker step-by-step downward through the sear, trip lever and trigger pawl so that the pressure on the trigger sear is only a fraction of that supplied to the striker. In this way a short and *safe* trigger pull can be achieved and still have a firm and positive engagement between sear and striker.

The trigger functions as follows: when the bolt is opened the trip lever spring pushes the trip lever and sear upward, placing the sear in front of the striker head. As the trip lever pivots upward the trigger pawl pivots backward as their sears engage. When the bolt is closed the striker is held back, in turn, by the sear, trip lever and trigger pawl. Then, on pulling the trigger back the trigger pawl is tipped forward, releasing the trip lever, sear and finally the striker.

Turn the trigger weight-of-pull adjustment screw in (clockwise) for a heavier pull, and vice versa. This can be done with an Allen wrench through the guard bow without disassembling the rifle. The trigger-travel adjustment screw can only be reached by removing the barrel and action from the stock. This adjustment is normally set at the factory for a minimum single-stage take-up. However, turning this screw in (clockwise) reduces the take-up, and vice versa. If turned far enough out it alters the trigger to a double-stage pull.

The trigger mechanism is used to disengage the sear (bolt stop) so the bolt can be removed. Here is what takes place: To begin with the bolt must be closed and the striker let down, leaving the sear pivoted below the bolt. To withdraw the bolt the sear must be held down in this position, which is done by pulling back on the trigger firmly and holding it back while the bolt handle is raised and the bolt withdrawn. Pulling the trigger back firmly causes the trigger to tip the trigger pawl forward against the lowered trip lever to hold this lever down. The sear has no separate spring of its own and, if the sear lever is held down by continued firm pressure on the trigger, the sear will remain down of its own weight so the bolt can be removed.

The "long" BSA Royal line action, the bolt open.

Take-Down and Assembly

Make sure the magazine and chamber are unloaded. To remove the bolt raise the handle and pull the bolt back about halfway. Then pull the trigger rearward and, while holding it back, withdraw the bolt.

To remove and disassemble the striker mechanism: With the bolt in the receiver and closed, raise the bolt handle about halfway, place the safety in the SAFE position, then remove the bolt. Being careful not to trip the safety, unscrew the bolt sleeve and firing mechanism from the bolt, then release the safety. Place the bolt sleeve on a table and, firmly grasping the mainspring at the firing pin junction, pull the spring down and slide the firing pin off the striker. Move the striker back in the bolt sleeve, turn the safety down, then pull the safety to the right out of the bolt sleeve. Shake out the small plunger and spring from the bolt sleeve. To reassemble, insert the striker rod in the bolt sleeve and, holding bolt sleeve bottom side up, drop the safety spring and plunger into their hole in the left side of the bolt sleeve. Insert the safety from right to left through the bolt sleeve and, using a small screwdriver, depress the plunger so the safety can be pushed in all the way. Compress the mainspring on the striker rod so the firing pin can be repositioned on it. Insert the mechanism in the bolt and, while pushing down on the bolt sleeve, begin turning it so the threads will catch. On each revolution of the bolt sleeve, as the striker falls into the cocking cam, raise it with a screwdriver so the bolt sleeve can be screwed in another turn. Continue this until the bolt sleeve is against the bolt, stopping it so the striker head rests in the shallow notch above the cocking cam. Remove the extractor by turning it under the bolt and then move it forward. The extractor collar can then be separated and removed.

To remove the barreled action from the stock turn out the front guard screw and remove the magazine floorplate and hinge plate. Then remove the rear guard screw, whereupon the barrel and action can be lifted from the stock. Turn out the front trigger guard screw and the trigger guard can be removed. Reassemble in reverse order. Both guard screws should be turned up tight.

To remove the trigger mechanism, turn out the screw holding the front of the trigger housing to the receiver, then drive out the pin from the top rear of the housing and then the entire assembly can be removed. Do not disassemble the trigger mechanism unless absolutely necessary, and then only if you know what it's all about. Check the position of each part removed, laying them out in sequence so that they can be correctly reassembled.

NOTE: In listing the various BSA action parts I have named them as commonly known in the U.S., not by the names given in BSA literature. For example, the part I call a "firing pin" BSA calls the "striker." Here are some other parts with different U.S. and British names:

BSA Trigger Mechanism

Parts Legend

1. Ejector
2. Trigger housing
3. Trigger-housing pin
4. Trigger-housing screw
5. Sear/ejector bushing
6. Sear (also bolt stop)
7. Ejector spring
8. Sear trip-spring
9. Sear trip
10. Trigger pawl
11. Trigger-pawl spring
12. Trigger-pawl pin
13. Trigger
14. Trigger spring
15. Sear trip-pin
16. Trigger stop-screw
17. Trigger pin
18. Trigger weight-of-pull adjustment screw

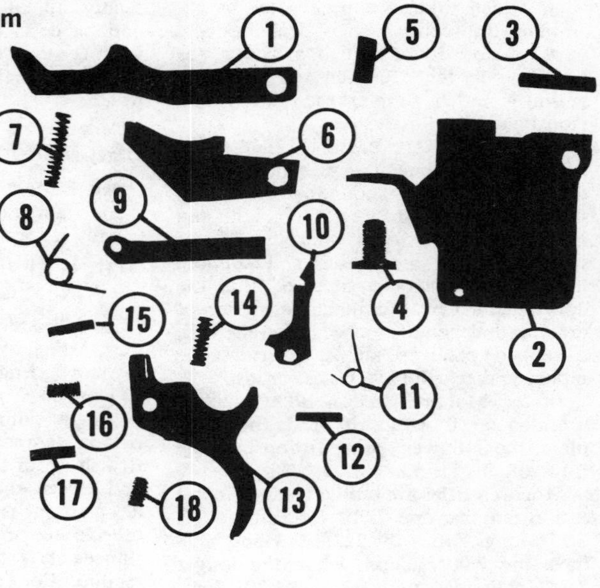

U.S. Name	British Name
Receiver	Body
Striker	Cocking piece
Mainspring	Striker spring
Bolt sleeve	Cocking-piece housing
Magazine floorplate	Bottom plate
Floorplate hinge plate	Bottom-plate hinge piece
Front guard screw	Front body fixing screw
Magazine box	Magazine case
Follower	Magazine platform
Follower spring	Magazine spring
Rear guard screw	Rear body fixing screw
Bolt	Bolt breech

The Majestic BSA Action

An improved BSA turnbolt action was announced late in 1959. The rifles built on this action were called the Majestic. According to Galef catalogs and the "Dope Bag" report on this rifle in the Dec., 1959 issue of *The American Rifleman*, the Majestic action was still being made in the short, medium and long lengths. I am a bit skeptical about this however, and I suspect the "short" action was merely the medium action fitted with a shorter magazine. At any rate, nowhere can I find listed the length of the short action. In my 1962 Parker-Hale catalog the Majestic Featherweight action is listed as made in "two entirely different lengths;" the medium action in calibers .222, .243 and .308, the long action in calibers .270, .30-06 and .458. The long action is listed as being 7.75" long, while the medium action is .700" long. This would seem to indicate that the long 8.625" action was dropped in the Majestic line, and also not used later on in the Monarch line, as we shall see later on. To confuse matters, in the same Parker-Hale catalog the BSA "standard weight" rifle is listed as the Regent Model with short action in .22 Hornet and .222; as the Viscount Model with medium action in .243 and .308; and as the Imperial Model with long action in .30-06 caliber. I know that the long Royal action was 8.625" over-all and here I suspect that the Imperial action was of the same length, that the medium Viscount action was 7.75" long, and the short Regent action only 7.00" long.

In any case, the 1960 improvements or changes to the action consisted of the following:

1) Bolt head, extractor and ejector: to begin with, the Mauser extractor was discarded, as well as the inside collar in the receiver. Instead, the face of the barrel was counterbored for the bolt head. The bolt face is recessed for the cartridge head and the extractor built into the side of the bolt head. The extractor, sort of a C-shaped clip with a hook, slides in a groove cut part way around the bolt head. It is tensioned by a small spring-loaded plunger fitted lengthwise in the bolt. The new plunger-type ejector is also fitted into the bolt head and held in place by a cross pin. The ejector in the trigger mechanism was thereby eliminated, but the rest of the trigger mechanism remained the same.

2) Bolt sleeve: The cocking piece is entirely housed within the bolt sleeve, the latter closed so that the rear of the cocking piece is no longer visible. A small red plastic pin, positioned in a hole in the top of the bolt sleeve, becomes the cocking indicator when it projects out of the bolt sleeve when the action is cocked. The safety is positioned through the bolt sleeve as in the older Royal actions.

The rest of the action remained unchanged, although in the featherweight models the guard and floorplate were made of aluminum.

I don't find the BSA short actioned rifle in .22 Hornet and .222 mentioned any place after about 1962. Apparently the short action was dropped. However, the .222 was again introduced in the BSA line-up.

Latest BSA Monarch Action

I don't know just when the next change was made, but it was probably in 1966 when the safety was omitted from the bolt sleeve and incorporated with the trigger mechanism. It then became a pivoting side safety, located on the right side of the receiver tang. This also required that the trigger mechanism be changed somewhat, which changes can be noted by examining the sectional view drawings and parts photos. Even though a safety was added to it, the Monarch trigger mechanism is much simpler than those previously used.

The final change came in 1968 when BSA began making the receiver without the integral scope mounting bases. Instead, the top of the receiver bridge and ring were made round and tapped for screw-on scope mount bases. I suppose too many shooters complained that the dovetailed receiver limited the choice of mounts that could be used, whereas with a tapped receiver almost every scope mount maker will have bases for it.

In the Monarch action BSA attached a folded sheet-metal strip inside the floorplate, the follower spring fitting into the folds of this strip.

Monarch rifles are built on two different action lengths; one 7.00″ long, the other 7.75″ long. Rifles in .222, .243 and .308 have the 7.00″ action, while the longer 7.75″ action is used for the .270, 7mm Magnum and .30-06 calibers.

I have never seen the separate BSA-marked actions or barreled actions listed for sale, but I have been told that at one time the actions were available in Canada. Note that I said "BSA-marked" actions.

I would also like to point out here that Galef's recent advertisements for BSA rifles indicate that the BSA actions are still being fabricated in the same way today as they were when first introduced. For example, the ad says the receiver goes through 62 separate machine operations before it is finished, and that it is made from a solid steel billet. Another ad says the bolt is entirely machined, also going through 62 separate stages before it is finished. Evidently they have not yet gone to making these parts from investment castings or using some other modern processing methods, techniques being employed today by so many firearms manufacturers.

Before leaving the BSA I must mention the locking system which BSA uses on their centerfire turnbolt actions. In the chapter on Lee-Enfields (BSA made many of these rifles) I noted the fact that the locking surfaces of the bolt and receiver are slightly angled, so that on lowering the bolt handle the bolt is cammed forward a very small amount. Conversely, after firing the rifle, the bolt becomes loose after the handle is raised only slightly. In other words, the bolt never seems to freeze in the locked position after firing. The British-designed Pattern 14 and Model 1917 Enfield actions also use a similar system though not so pronounced. The same system is used in BSA actions—the rear surface of their locking lugs is about 5 degrees off the normal 90-degree angle made with the bolt body. This angle is such that after the locking lugs first engage behind the shoulders in the receiver, as the bolt is fully closed it moves approximately .030″ forward. Thus, as must be done when checking or making a headspace reading of the M1917 Enfield rifles, a true reading can only be had when the bolt is fully down. On practically all of the many other turnbolt actions described in this book the rear locking surface on the bolt lugs are at a 90-degree angle to the bolt or very close to it.

BSA Markings

All BSA rifles I've seen had the firm name stamped on the barrel, in one line, usually as follows:

THE BIRMINGHAM SMALL ARMS CO. LTD. — ENGLAND

(The full address of this firm is: 85 Factory, Marshall Lake Road, Shirley, Birmingham 4, England.)

The BSA trademark — three stacked rifles—is stamped on the receiver. Each rifle is stamped with the usual number of British proof marks on the receiver, bolt and breech end of the barrel. The caliber designation is usually stamped on the breech end of the barrel, and in some instances it is followed by the headspace reading. For example, **.30-06—2.494.** The rifles are serial numbered, the number stamped on the receiver, barrel and bolt.

Herter's U9 Action

Herter's Inc. (Waseca, Minn.), began importing a centerfire high powered turnbolt action about 1965-1966 which they designated the U9 action. U9 barreled actions and complete rifles, assembled by Herter's, were also made available. In every detail the U9 action is identical to the BSA action (except for length) and while nowhere in the long description of this action in Herter's catalog does it mention BSA, it seems almost certain that the U9 actions are made by BSA. At least I am going to assume this to be the case until I have proof otherwise.

Besides being stamped **MADE IN ENGLAND** (in very small letters and shallowly imprinted on the side of the receiver ring), the serial number is stamped on the right lower side of the receiver ring and on the bottom of the bolt handle. British proof marks are also stamped on these actions.

At any rate, when first introduced Herter's U9 action was just like the BSA action being made at the same time. Beginning in 1968, when BSA actions were being made without the integral scope mount bases but with the round topped receiver tapped for scope mounts, Herter's

Herter's U9 trigger and safety mechanism. Arrow indicates location of the trigger weight-of-pull adjustment screw.

also announced that their U9 actions would be similarly made.

At this writing Herter's lists 5 different U9 actions; namely, SSK3055 for the .222, .223 and .222 Magnum cartridges; SSK3042 for such cartridges as the .22-250, .243, 6mm, .257 Roberts, 7mm and .308; SSK3056 for the .284; SSK3043 for the .270 and .30-06 and SSK3057 for such magnums as the .264, 7mm, .300, .338 and .458.

Herter's U9 actions come in two lengths. One, 7.75″ long, is used for cartridges from .222 to .308, while the other one, about 8.50″ long, is used for the .270, .30-06 and the short magnums. Note that Herter's actions are longer than the BSA Monarch actions in the same calibers.

The 3055 U9 action has the shortest magazine box, just long enough for the .222 Magnum, and the magazine well is no longer than the magazine. The bolt is recessed, and the extractor made to handle the .222 head-sized cartridges. The 3042 and 3056 are alike except that the 3056 may have a slightly wider magazine well, and both are like the 3055 except for a longer magazine and a bolt head made to accept the .30-06 head-sized cartridges. The 3043 and 3057 are alike except for a different bolt head, and both are longer than the above 3 actions. Other than that the things just mentioned, and the difference in weight and bolt travel, all 5 of the U9 actions are otherwise essentially the same.

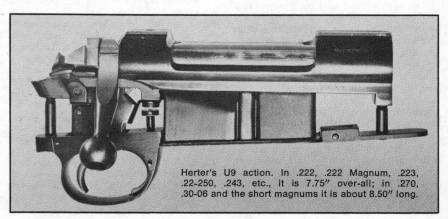

Herter's U9 action. In .222, .222 Magnum, .223, .22-250, .243, etc., it is 7.75″ over-all; in .270, .30-06 and the short magnums it is about 8.50″ long.

Parts Legend
BSA Monarch and Herter's U9

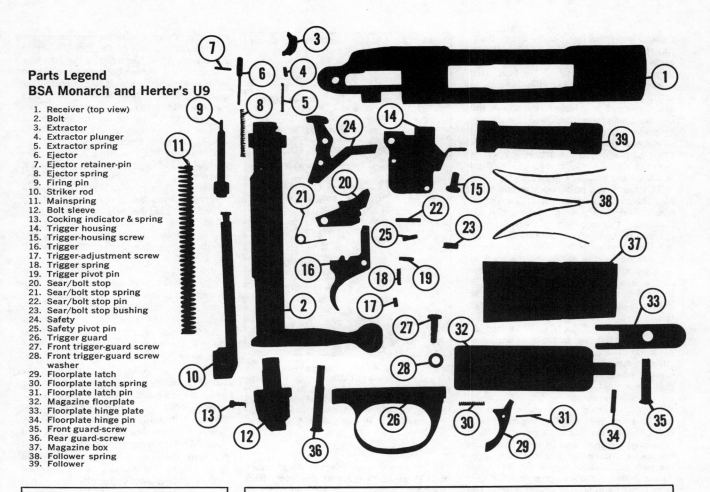

1. Receiver (top view)
2. Bolt
3. Extractor
4. Extractor plunger
5. Extractor spring
6. Ejector
7. Ejector retainer-pin
8. Ejector spring
9. Firing pin
10. Striker rod
11. Mainspring
12. Bolt sleeve
13. Cocking indicator & spring
14. Trigger housing
15. Trigger-housing screw
16. Trigger
17. Trigger-adjustment screw
18. Trigger spring
19. Trigger pivot pin
20. Sear/bolt stop
21. Sear/bolt stop spring
22. Sear/bolt stop pin
23. Sear/bolt stop bushing
24. Safety
25. Safety pivot pin
26. Trigger guard
27. Front trigger-guard screw
28. Front trigger-guard screw washer
29. Floorplate latch
30. Floorplate latch spring
31. Floorplate latch pin
32. Magazine floorplate
33. Floorplate hinge plate
34. Floorplate hinge pin
35. Front guard-screw
36. Rear guard-screw
37. Magazine box
38. Follower spring
39. Follower

Dimensional Specifications

Weight (approx.):
BSA (short) .... 36 oz.
BSA (long) .... 38 oz.
U9 (short) .... 39 oz.
U9 (long) .... 41 oz.

Length:
BSA (short) .... 7.00″
BSA (long) .... 7.75″
U9 (short) .... 7.75″
U9 (long) .... 8.50″

Receiver ring dia. .... 1.355″
Bolt dia. .... .700″
Bolt travel:
U9 (short, .222 Mag.) .... 3.470″
U9 (short, standard) .... 4.185″
U9 (long) .... 4.625″
Striker travel (approx.) .... .365″
Magazine length:
U9 (short, .222 family) ...... 2.350″
U9 (short, .308 family) ...... 3.125″
U9 (long) .... 3.350″
(BSA and Herter's U9 magazines are about the same length.)
Bolt-face recess:
Depth .... .140″
Dia. (.222) .... .350″
(standard) .... .480″
(belted magnum) ...... .540″
Guard-screw spacing:
U9 (short) .... 7.125″
U9 (long) .... 7.875″
BSA (short) .... 6.375″
BSA (long) .... 7.125″

BSA Monarch & Herter's U9
General Specifications

Type	Turnbolt repeater.
Receiver	One-piece machined steel. Non-slotted bridge. Pre-68 models have integral mount bases on the receiver; later models are tapped for scopemounts.
Bolt	One-piece machined steel with dual-opposed forward locking lugs. Handle acts as safety lug.
Ignition	Striker with separate firing pin powered by a coil mainspring. Cocks on opening.
Magazine	Non-detachable staggered-column box type with hinged floorplate. 5-shot capacity for standard calibers, 4-shot for magnums.
Trigger	Single-stage, adjustable for weight of pull.
Safety	Pivoting side tang type, locks trigger and bolt when pulled back.
Extractor	C-clip type fitted on side of bolt head and tensioned by a spring-loaded plunger.
Bolt stop	Sear doubles as bolt stop.
Ejector	Plunger type fitted into bolt head.

The U9 receiver and bolt appear to be entirely machined from solid stock, as I can find no evidence of casting, welding or brazing. I assume that the bolt and receiver, as well as most of the other vital parts of this action, are made of the same quality steel used in the BSA actions. The trigger guard, floorplate and floorplate hinge plate are all made of steel. The follower is aluminum. The lower end of the follower spring fastens in a folded piece of sheet-metal, which is in turn riveted to the floorplate. The magazine box is made of sheet-metal.

The extractor is a sort of horseshoe affair, milled from steel. Part of the side of the bolt head is cut away and a groove cut partly around the bolt head; into this the extractor is fitted, it becoming part of the rim of the bolt face recess. A spring-loaded plunger is located in a hole in the bolt head, its end bearing on an inclined surface on the underside of the extractor; this holds the extractor toward the center of the bolt, allowing the extractor to snap over the cartridge rim when the bolt is closed. The extractor, which appears to be amply strong, cannot be blown out by a defective primer or cartridge head because, with the bolt locked, the extractor is within the counterbore in the face of the barrel. The ejector, also a spring-loaded plunger in the bolt head, is held in place by a cross pin through the left or upper locking lug.

The bolt is like that of the latest BSA bolts in that its two forward locking lugs are unslotted, with the base of the bolt handle acting as the safety lug. The same guide rib is there, which Herter's describes as a "mono-rail." The bolt is drilled from the rear to accept the striker rod with its integral cocking cam head, coil mainspring and separate firing pin which engages over the front end of the striker rod. The one-piece striker housing (better known as the bolt sleeve in the U.S.) is threaded into the rear of the bolt. It is entirely closed except at the bottom. A red plastic rivet and a small coil spring are positioned in a hole in the top of this housing, acting as the cocking indicator by projecting out of the housing when the action is cocked. The housing is prevented from turning when the action is open by the cocking cam, which rests in a shallow notch on the rear of the bolt.

The safety and bolt stops are combined with the trigger mechanism. It is a simpler mechanism than used in earlier BSA actions, but the same as now used in the current BSA Monarch action. The parts are built into a folded sheet-metal housing attached to the bottom of the receiver by a pin and screw. The combination sear and bolt stop is pivoted on a sleeve in the rear of the housing, with the pin which holds the housing in place passing through this sleeve. The sear is tensioned by a bent-wire spring. The trigger, located directly under the sear on a pin, is tensioned by a small coil spring in a hole in the trigger. An Allen-head setscrew in the bottom of this hole allows for weight-of-pull adjustment. Turning this screw counterclockwise reduces the weight of pull. When the action is closed and cocked the trigger holds the sear up, which in turn holds the striker back. When the action is opened the front end of the sear swings up into a groove cut into the bottom of the bolt and thus becomes the bolt stop. There is no adjustment provided for sear engagement and no trigger stop screw. The trigger pull, normally quite short, can be adjusted to as light as 3 pounds.

The safety is a sheet-metal stamping positioned in the trigger housing on a pin, which pin also holds the sear spring. The safety button extends to the edge of the receiver tang and when it is pulled back arms on the safety lock both the trigger and the bolt. The safety is silent and convenient to operate.

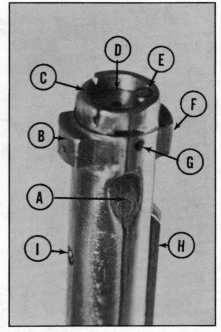

Bolt head of the BSA Monarch and Herter's U9 action, showing: (A) bolt-stop notch, (B) right (bottom) locking lug, (C) extractor, (D) bolt face recess, (E) ejector, (F) left (upper) locking lug, (G) front gas-vent hole, (H) bolt guide-rib, (I) rear gas-vent hole.

Comments

I have only seen about a dozen or so of both Herter's U9 and the latest BSA rifles and actions but, based on this limited observation, the actions on BSA Monarch rifles are made and finished better than the U9 actions. For example, while some tool marks can be found on BSA action parts, many more are plainly visible on the U9 action. Outside BSA parts are much better finished, with much of the U9 surfaces carelessly polished on a soft polishing wheel, leaving the surfaces uneven and the edges rounded. For example, there are lathe tool-marks on the rear of the bolt of the last U9 action I received, while the front of the bolt was over-polished, leaving the bolt out of round in places. The sides of the U9 trigger guard bow were only polished on a belt sander, with many grit lines plainly visible. On my U9 action the outside curved surface of the trigger guard was well polished, and the floorplate latch left in place during the polishing, which is the correct polishing procedure. However, when the action was blued the latch was not removed, nor were these parts properly rinsed afterwards, because the latch spring was caked nearly solid with dried bluing salts.

I also found bluing salts growing out of the barrel shoulder-receiver joint on my U9 action and, on removing the barrel, I discovered that the barrel shank was only partially threaded; the wide unthreaded section near the shoulder was filled with salts, having gotten into this area through the front trigger guard screw hole. If I had not removed the barrel and cleaned the area, those salts would have kept growing out of the joint for several years or more. Also, after removal of the barrel, I discovered that the breech face had not been polished at all—the chamber edge was not even rounded. All in all, the Herter's U9 action I received was poorly finished. Even though this action would probably function OK, and while some of the items mentioned are correctible, there is no excuse for sending out a barreled action with a sharp chamber edge and from which the bluing salts have not been washed.

Despite these criticisms, I consider the U9 action sound and a good value at the price. Herter's 1970 catalog lists the separate U9 actions at $51.75, and barreled actions (with Douglas barrel) at $87.45. Inletted and semi-finished stocks are also available from them priced as low as $10.75.

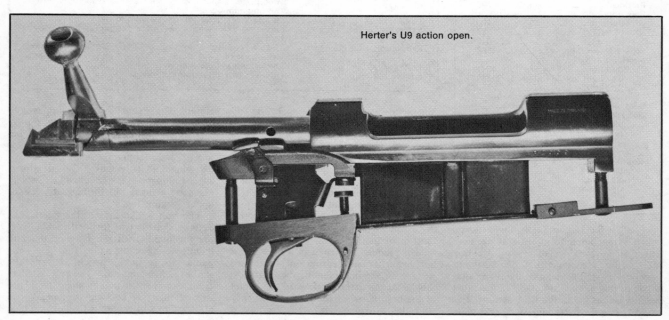

Herter's U9 action open.

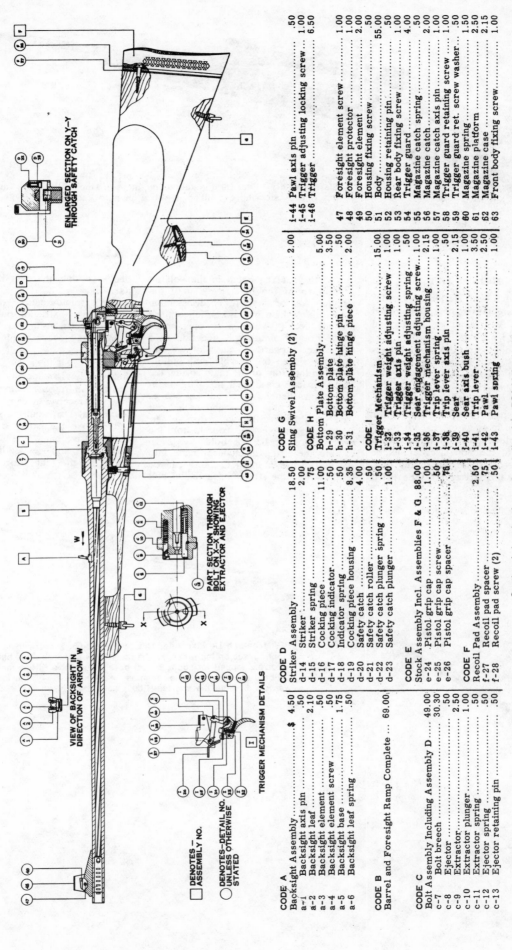

ENLARGED SECTION ON Y—Y THROUGH SAFETY CATCH

PART SECTION THROUGH BOLT ON X—X SHOWING EXTRACTOR AND EJECTOR

VIEW OF BACKSIGHT IN DIRECTION OF ARROW W

TRIGGER MECHANISM DETAILS

□ DENOTES — ASSEMBLY NO.

○ DENOTES—DETAIL NO. UNLESS OTHERWISE STATED

Sectional view drawing and parts list of the BSA Majestic rifle.

CODE A

Backsight Assembly	$	4.50
a–1	Backsight axis pin	.50
a–2	Backsight leaf	2.10
a–3	Backsight element	.50
a–4	Backsight element screw	.50
a–5	Backsight base	1.75
a–6	Backsight leaf spring	.50

CODE B

Barrel and Foresight Ramp Complete		69.00

CODE C

Bolt Assembly Including Assembly D		49.00
c–7	Bolt breech	30.30
c–8	Ejector	.50
c–9	Ejector	2.50
c–10	Extractor plunger	1.00
c–11	Extractor spring	.50
c–12	Ejector spring	.50
c–13	Ejector retaining pin	.50

CODE D

Striker Assembly		18.50
d–14	Striker	2.00
d–15	Striker spring	.75
d–16	Cocking piece	11.00
d–17	Cocking indicator	.50
d–18	Indicator spring	.50
d–19	Cocking piece housing	8.35
d–20	Safety catch	4.00
d–21	Safety catch roller	.50
d–22	Safety catch plunger spring	.50
d–23	Safety catch plunger	1.00

CODE E

Stock Assembly Incl. Assemblies F & G.		88.00
e–24	Pistol grip cap	1.00
e–25	Pistol grip cap screw	.50
e–26	Pistol grip cap spacer	.75

CODE F

Recoil Pad Assembly		2.50
f–27	Recoil pad spacer	.75
f–28	Recoil pad screw (2)	.50

CODE G

Sling Swivel Assembly (2)		2.00

CODE H

Bottom Plate Assembly		5.00
h–29	Bottom plate	3.50
h–30	Bottom plate hinge pin	.50
h–31	Bottom plate hinge piece	2.00

CODE I

Trigger Mechanism		15.00
i–32	Trigger weight adjusting screw	1.00
i–33	Trigger axis pin	1.00
i–34	Trigger weight adjusting spring	.50
i–35	Sear engagement adjusting screw	1.00
i–36	Trigger mechanism housing	2.15
i–37	Trip lever spring	1.00
i–38	Trip lever axis pin	2.15
i–39	Sear	.50
i–40	Sear axis bush	1.50
i–41	Trip lever	3.50
i–42	Pawl	2.50
i–43	Pawl spring	1.00
i–44	Pawl axis pin	.50
i–45	Trigger adjusting locking screw	1.00
i–46	Trigger	6.50
47	Foresight element screw	1.00
48	Foresight protector	1.00
49	Foresight element	2.00
50	Housing fixing screw	.50
51	Body	55.00
52	Housing retaining pin	.50
53	Rear body fixing screw	1.00
54	Trigger guard	4.00
55	Magazine catch spring	1.00
56	Magazine catch	2.00
57	Magazine catch axis pin	1.00
58	Trigger guard retaining screw	1.00
59	Trigger guard ret. screw washer	.50
60	Magazine spring	1.50
61	Magazine platform	2.50
62	Magazine case	2.15
63	Front body fixing screw	1.00

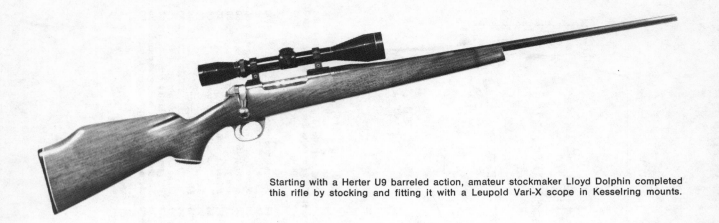

Starting with a Herter U9 barreled action, amateur stockmaker Lloyd Dolphin completed this rifle by stocking and fitting it with a Leupold Vari-X scope in Kesselring mounts.

Take-Down and Assembly

BSA Monarch and Herter's U9 rifles and actions are disassembled/assembled just like the BSA Royal action as described previously except for the following:

To remove the bolt, raise the bolt handle and pull the bolt about halfway back, press forward very hard on the trigger and, while holding this pressure, pull the bolt out.

Because of the very stiff mainspring the firing mechanism is quite difficult to remove and replace in the bolt. To remove the mechanism the bolt sleeve must be turned counterclockwise out of the bolt. In doing this the striker must be lifted out of the cocking notch in the bolt on every turn of the bolt sleeve until the sleeve is free of the bolt. To disassemble the firing mechanism it is helpful to place a small piece of wood in the open space in the bottom of the bolt sleeve to hold the striker forward. Then, while resting the bolt sleeve on a table and pulling down on the front of the main spring, the firing pin can be slipped off. The mainspring can then be removed, the striker tipped in the bolt sleeve and pulled out backward. Reassemble in reverse order, again using the piece of wood to hold the striker forward in the bolt sleeve. In turning the firing mechanism back into the bolt sleeve a small C-clamp can be used to hold the striker back in the bolt sleeve so that the bolt sleeve is easily started.

The extractor can be removed by depressing the extractor plunger with the point of a pen knife and slipping the extractor away from the bolt. To remove the ejector drive out the ejector pin by inserting a small drift punch into the hole through the right locking lug.

After the trigger mechanism is removed from the receiver it can be disassembled as follows: Drive out the safety pivot pin and remove the safety and sear/trigger spring. Drive out the trigger pin and remove trigger and trigger-adjustment spring. Drive out the sear bushing and lift out the sear. Reassemble in reverse order.

BSA Monarch De luxe rifle. This is the pre-68 model with the integral scope mount bases on the receiver. The latest BSA Monarch rifles have round-topped receivers tapped for scope mount bases. Note: this rifle is made in 5 different calibers and on two action lengths. In .270 and .30-06 the long (7.75" action was used, while the shorter (7.00") action was used for .222, .243 and .308.

29. Winchester Models 54 & 70

Part I
Model 54 Winchester

WINCHESTER offered their first high power bolt action rifles in 1925 with the introduction of the Model 54. The action of this rifle was entirely new for Winchester, for they had never before built anything like it—the closest thing to it they had ever made were the Pattern 14 and Model 1917 Enfield actions. Rather than being an entirely new action design, the bolt and receiver of the M54 had features copied from the M98 Mauser and 1903 Springfield actions, though the magazine, trigger, and a few other things were new. Some new and improved design features were also added later on.

Before the M54 was discontinued in 1936 (after about 50,145 had been made), with the introduction of the Model 70 Winchester, several different styles of rifles were made on the M54 action.

There was the standard sporting rifle with 24″ barrel, weight about 7.75 pounds. It had a lightweight stock reminiscent of a skimpy German-style sporter stock, complete with a schnabel fore-end tip but without the cheekpiece. There was also a carbine model with 20″ barrel. Around 1932 some changes were made in the action and a fuller stock introduced, called the NRA Model, along with new calibers and styles. Besides the standard sporter and the carbine, there was also a Super Grade added, plus a Sniper's Model, National Match Model and a Target Model. The following chamberings were offered in the M54 rifles (though not in all models): .22 Hornet (added in 1933), .220 Swift in 1935, .250-3000 in 1931, .257 Roberts in 1936, .270 Winchester 7mm Mauser in 1930, .30-30 in 1928, .30-06 7.65mm Mauser in 1930, and the 9mm Mauser in 1936. The M54 was chambered originally in .30-06 and .270.

The Action

The one-piece receiver was made from the finest high tensile strength steel then available, carefully and precisely machined and properly heat treated to assure maximum strength and safety. The barrel is securely threaded (right-hand V-type threads) into the front of the receiver. The face of the barrel is funneled like that of the 1903 Springfield, the right side notched for the extractor hook. The top of the receiver ring is round, its bottom flat, with a large integral recoil lug on the forward edge. This lug, 1.175″ wide by .435″ deep, has more than ample area to transfer the recoil adequately to the stock without set-back of the receiver.

The bottom center of the receiver is cut away for the magazine opening. Integral cartridge guide-lips are left in each side of the well to hold and direct cartridges from the magazine into the chamber. Additional metal is left on the bottom of the receiver to form a box-like support for the magazine box. This extra metal strengthens the center of the receiver, making it very rigid.

The unslotted receiver bridge is about 1.5″ long, has the same side contour as the receiver ring, but is slightly flattened on top with a shallow matted groove cut lengthwise in it. Between the bridge and the ring the left wall lies about ⅜″ below the height of the receiver ring; the right wall is cut down to the level of the right locking lug raceway, thus offering an ample receiver opening for loading and ejection. Yet plenty of metal is left in the walls to keep the receiver strong. The bored-out receiver ends in a rounded tang much like that of the 1903 Springfield receiver.

The bolt is of one-piece construction, its solid dual-opposed locking lugs on the forward end engaging behind shoulders milled inside the ring. The bolt head is partially recessed for the cartridge rim, the recess cut away at the bottom to allow a cartridge to slip under the extractor hook as it is fed from the magazine. This feature prevents double loading.

The integral bolt handle is at the extreme rear of the bolt body. The square base of the handle projects straight out to the right. The square-to-round tapered bolt handle stem, bent down and swept back, has a pear-shaped grasping knob. A notch is cut into the receiver tang into which the lower part of the bolt handle base fits. This provides the third or safety lug for the bolt.

A cam lug on the rear of the bolt, extending to the left of the bolt handle base, matches a cam surface milled in the left of the receiver bridge. They provide the initial camming power to the extractor when the bolt handle is raised.

On the top center of the bolt body there is a flat sided lug or projection. When the bolt handle is raised to open the action the flat side of this lug contacts the bottom edge of the left locking lug raceway. This lug not only acts to stop the opening rotational movement of the bolt, but also serves as a bolt guide when the bolt is operated.

The non-rotating extractor, of Mauser type, is attached to the bolt with a collar. It has a lip which engages in a groove cut into the bolt head, this preventing longitudinal movement on the bolt head. The extractor hook is quite heavy, its forward face well-beveled so it can easily snap over the rim of a cartridge placed in the chamber ahead of it.

The bolt sleeve threads into the rear of the bolt body, the threads of square type. A small spring and plunger, fitted into the left front edge of the bolt sleeve, lock the bolt sleeve to the bolt to prevent the firing mechanism from turning when the bolt is opened. A small cross pin retains the lock plunger in place. This bolt sleeve lock system is copied from the 1903 Springfield action.

The wing safety, of common Mauser type, fits into the top of the bolt sleeve. The wing engages a ridge on the bolt sleeve, with a notch cut into the top of this ridge so the safety can be removed after

Illustrated above: Model 54 Winchester rifle.

the striker is removed. The stem of the safety, on which the safety rotates, extends forward out of the bolt sleeve to engage a notch cut into the rear of the bolt body. when it is to the right, and in the SAFE or ON position when swung to the left. The striker only is locked when the safety is straight up, while both striker and bolt are locked when the safety is in the ON position. On "improved" 54s a small spring and plunger in the bolt sleeve engage the safety, and the wing of the safety is marked **FIRE** on one side and **SAFE** on the other.

The bolt is drilled from the rear to accept the one-piece firing pin and coil mainspring. The cocking cam is permanently attached to the rear end of the firing pin. The firing pin extends through the bolt sleeve, and the mainspring is compressed over it between the bolt sleeve and a sleeve which locks in a groove on the front of the firing pin rod. The cocking cam extends into a cocking cam notch in the rear of the bolt and, on raising the bolt handle, the firing pin is drawn back to cock the action. On early 54s the striker travel is about ½-inch. In 1932 a "speed-lock" was introduced, cutting this distance about in half. While the M54 was being made, and for a few years afterward, or for as long as parts were available, the early slow-lock could be converted to the speed-lock by replacing the following parts in the early action: sear, firing pin, bolt, mainspring and trigger. The late model also had a firing pin stop screw in the bolt sleeve.

The sear, which also serves as the bolt stop, is positioned in a recess under the rear of the receiver; it is held in place, and pivots on, a pin through the walls of this recess. The sear/bolt stop lug on the rear of the sear projects upward through a hole in the receiver to engage the cocking cam and bolt. Upward tension is supplied by a small sear spring between the receiver and the front of the sear. The trigger, hinged to the sear on a pin, has a double stage let-off. The part of the sear which projects into the bolt well in the receiver engages the cocking cam when the action is opened and closed. Pulling the trigger pulls the sear down to release the striker. A flat and slightly inclined cut in the bottom of the bolt body, starting near its rear end, deepens toward the front of the bolt, where it ends in a hole in the bolt. As the bolt is pulled back it slides over the projection on the sear, and the bolt is stopped when this projection contacts the edge of this hole. This inclined surface and hole are positioned at different spots under the bolt according to the length of the cartridge the action is made for, limiting the bolt travel to no longer than needed. On the bolt made for such long cartridges as the .30-06 and .270, the "stop" hole is near the front half of the bolt, while for the .22 Hornet it is closer to the rear of the bolt. In any case, pulling the trigger back as far as it will go pulls the sear down so the bolt can be removed from the action.

The ejector, a flat piece of metal fitted in a narrow slot cut through the bottom right side of the bridge, is held in place by, and pivots on, a pin, its tension pro-

Model 54 Winchester action.

vided by a small coil spring. On opening the bolt the end of the ejector moved into a groove cut into the head of the bolt, ejecting the cartridges or empty cases upward to the right.

The M54 bolt has a single small gas-vent hole drilled into it at the firing pin tip junction. When the bolt is locked closed this hole would direct any gases escaping through it into the left locking lug raceway. If more gases entered the bolt body through the firing pin hole than could be handled by this small hole, the bolt-stop hole would vent this gas, also into the left raceway. No gas-escape holes were made in the sides of the receiver ring. The bolt sleeve was not flanged enough to deflect any gases rushing rearward down the left raceway, but it sealed this raceway well enough so the gases would be vented out of the thumb notch cut into the top raceway wall, just ahead of the bridge.

The M54 magazine box was of heavy sheet-metal, bent into a rough rectangle to fit the magazine opening in the bottom of the receiver. Magazine boxes for cartridges shorter than the .30-06 and .270 were blocked off with a vertical sheet-metal spacer crimped in place in the rear of the box. These spacers varied in size according to the cartridges used. Magazines made for the .220 Swift and .30-30 cartridges had slanted spacers at rear and front, these to prevent the cartridge rims from overlapping.

The steel followers were made with a ridge on the top left to stagger the cartridges. Different lengths of followers were used for the different magazines. The W-shaped follower spring was held in mortises in the bottom of the follower and in the top of the trigger guard, which formed the magazine cover. Different sizes of follower springs were also made.

The trigger guard, formed from heavy sheet-metal, is combined with the magazine cover or floorplate. A separate plate is inletted into the bottom of the stock through which the trigger projects, with the guard partially inletted into the stock over this plate and magazine box. Three screws, running through holes in the trigger guard and stock and threaded into the receiver, hold the barrel and action securely in the stock.

The .22 Hornet chambering was offered first in the M54 in 1933. Consider-

able changes had to be made so this big bolt action could handle the little Hornet. A special small magazine box, designed to fit inside the regular box, held 5 cartridges in a staggered column. It had a lip or feed chute, extending well forward, which guided the small cartridge into the chamber. The follower spring of the non-detachable Hornet magazine was made of spring wire, the follower of sheet-metal. Loading was done from the top. The head of the .22 Hornet bolt is tapered to fit the funnel in the barrel. A small spring-activated lever, pivoted in a slot in the bottom of the bolt head, pushed the cartridges out of the magazine. The ejectors for Hornet rifles were riveted to the side of the outside magazine box but otherwise functioned just like the regular ejector.

Good and Poor Features

After the M54 rifle had been on the market a few years the general concensus of both experts and shooters was favorable on practically every count. Some corrections and changes were made, along with new styles, so that by 1932 it was considered a very well-made and reliable rifle. Total production of a little over 50,000 units in the 11 years it was on the market indicate that it was not an overly popular rifle, but it must be remembered that there was a depression during much of this time. The M54 was a good "trial" rifle for Winchester, and by the mid-1930s they knew exactly what shooters wanted when they were ready to drop the M54 for a new model.

Here are some of the outstanding good features of the M54 Winchester action. It was a very strong action, its receiver and bolt made of the best steel available and properly heat treated; the breeching system was good; the bolt locking lugs are large and neither one was slotted; the bridge was long enough to guide and support the bolt during operation of the action. No one could ask for a better extractor, and the ejector system proved very good. Design and construction of the firing pin, bolt sleeve and bolt-sleeve lock and magazine were also very good. These good features, however, did not make up for many poor ones.

The poor features were: contour of the bolt handle was so high it interfered with

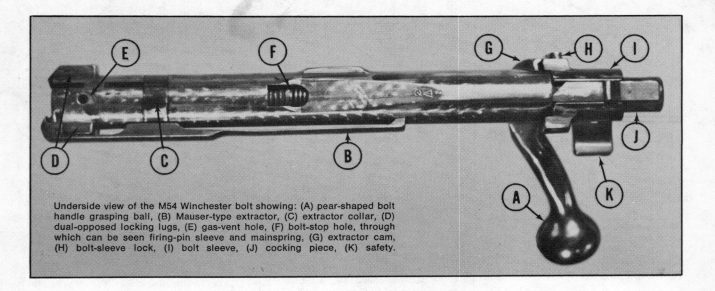

Underside view of the M54 Winchester bolt showing: (A) pear-shaped bolt handle grasping ball, (B) Mauser-type extractor, (C) extractor collar, (D) dual-opposed locking lugs, (E) gas-vent hole, (F) bolt-stop hole, through which can be seen firing-pin sleeve and mainspring, (G) extractor cam, (H) bolt-sleeve lock, (I) bolt sleeve, (J) cocking piece, (K) safety.

mounting a scope low over the receiver; the same was true of the safety, which was not convenient to operate either—even if the scope were mounted high enough to clear it; the bolt stop system was far from good; too much strain was put on the sear if the bolt was operated with any force. Being combined with the sear also limited the trigger design to the conventional military type double pull. Lastly, the sheet-metal trigger guard did not belong on a modern rifle. I could elaborate on these faults, but I suggest you read Part II of this chapter and learn what Winchester did to correct them in the Model 70 action.

Gunsmithing the M54

Model 54 owners almost immediately, in many cases, began sending them to custom gunsmiths for rebuilding or restocking. Griffin & Howe got their share, a firm that really knew what to do to make them into those superb sporting arms, which made the name G&H so well known. Their specialty was restocking, and their classic stock on this rifle did great things for it. Winchester more or less copied the Griffin & Howe classic stock for the Super Grade 54 and, later on, for the Super Grade 70. If the owner wanted a scope on his M54, G&H would alter or install a new low safety, alter the bolt handle to a lower profile, and tap the receiver for their fine double-lever side mount, one that's still made.

Buehler still makes a low scope safety for the old 54 Winchester. Nothing much can be done with the original trigger to modify it, but on special order Canjar, the well-known Denver trigger maker, can furnish a fine single-stage trigger mechanism for the 54. No one makes a milled steel trigger guard for this action, with or without a hinged floorplate. Although I've never done it, in restocking the M54 the M70 trigger guard and hinged floorplate can be used. This would require drilling and tapping a hole for the front guard screw in the bottom flat of the receiver ring.

In altering the bolt handle to a lower profile the best method seems to be to fill in the bottom of the bend with weld and then dress the top of the bend down as required to clear the scope.

For anyone interested in making a simple single-stage trigger for the M54, I am showing (see page 238) details of one I made. I used 3/8" thick tool steel to make the new trigger and sear. The new sear, made to fit in the original sear in place of the original trigger, is held tightly in place by the trigger pin. A hole is tapped in the bottom of the new sear for the sear-engagement adjustment screw. After the new trigger is roughly shaped it is positioned behind the sear and a hole drilled through the receiver and top of the trigger for the trigger-pivot pin. A hole is then made in the top of the trigger for the trigger spring and plunger. I shaped the bottom part of the original trigger and fitted this part in a hole in the bottom of the new trigger, holding it in place with an Allen-head setscrew. After relieving the trigger enough so it can be moved, I then filed the front down to form a notch to hold the sear up. It is necessary to grind the rear corner off of the original sear and polish this surface so the cocking cam can easily slide over when the trigger is pulled. It is also necessary to file or grind some metal from the bottom rear of the bolt body. After fitting and checking that the trigger functions, the new sear and trigger are hardened and tempered and then replaced.

The M54 in .30-30 caliber was not very popular, so not many were made. It was soon discovered that these .30-30 rifles were suitable for rechambering to the .30-40 Krag cartridge, and no doubt a lot of these rifles were so rechambered. About the same time, a number of wildcat cartridges based on the rimmed .219 Zipper, .30-30 and .30-40 cases became popular, and the .30-30 M54 action was used for building rifles for these.

Many M54 rifles in .22 Hornet caliber were also rechambered to the .22 K-Hornet, or converted to handle the .22 R-2

Lovell cartridge, which were extremely popular among wildcatters in the 1930s. Griffin & Howe was one of the first shops to specialize in the conversion to the Lovell cartridge and, later on, to the .222 Remington cartridge. Properly done, these conversions worked out well.

Markings

The M54 Winchester is serial numbered, the number stamped on the right side of the receiver ring. A letter at the end of the serial number indicates a minor change in the mechanism.

The Winchester trademark is stamped on the left receiver wall, thus:

WINCHESTER
—TRADEMARK—

The Winchester firm name and address, model designation and caliber are stamped on the barrel. The Winchester proof mark ($\frac{P}{W}$ within an oval) is stamped on the breech end of the barrel and on the receiver ring. The year of manufacture is often stamped under the barrel, such as **34** indicating 1934.

Comments

Today M54 rifles in original and very good condition are becoming prized collector items. This is especially true for models other than the standard grade sporter, and for any of them in calibers other than .30-06 and .270. Because of this the owner of one of these rifles should take this fact into consideration before altering it in any way, since any changes may affect its future value. Those rifles already altered in some way generally have little collector's value. M54 parts are no longer factory available, so those rifles already altered cannot be readily restored to original condition. Even if you are willing to pay the price of a new M70 for an M54, locating one is going to be difficult since there just don't seem to be many

Winchester
Mod. 54

The double-set trigger mechanism that was once available from Stoeger Arms Corp. for the M54 Winchester.

Dimensional Specifications

Weight	(approx.) 45 oz.
Receiver length	8.750″
Receiver ring dia.	1.340″
Bolt dia.	.695″
Bolt travel (See text)	Varies
Striker travel:	
Early model	.500″
Speedlock model	.350″
Magazine length	3.385″
(spacers provided for cartridges shorter than standard .30-06)	
Bolt-face recess: Dia.	
Standard calibers	.485″
.30-30 caliber	.513″
.22 Hornet	.357″
Depth	.045″
Guard-screw spacing	8.25″

Winchester Model 54 General Specifications

Type	Turnbolt repeater.
Receiver	One-piece machined steel forging. Non-slotted bridge.
Bolt	One-piece, with dual-opposed forward locking lugs. Handle acts as safety lug.
Ignition	One-piece firing pin with integral cocking-cam head. Cocks on opening.
Magazine	Non-detachable staggered-column 5-shot box.
Trigger	Non-adjustable double-stage military type pull.
Safety	Rotary type positioned in the bolt sleeve, 180° swing; locks firing pin and bolt when swung to the left., locks only firing pin when UP, and is in FIRE position when swung to the right.
Extractor	Non-rotating one-piece Mauser-type spring extractor fastened to the bolt by a collar.
Magazine cut-off	None provided.
Bolt stop	Sear acts as the bolt stop, engaging a cut in the bottom of the bolt.
Ejector	Pivoting type, positioned in a groove in the rear of the receiver.

Model 54 Winchester action open.

around for sale. Separate M54 actions were never commercially available.

Operation

To load: place the safety in the INTERMEDIATE (up) or FIRE (left) position; raise the bolt handle and pull the bolt back as far as it will go; place a single cartridge, bullet point forward, in the magazine opening and press it into the magazine with the thumb. Load additional cartridges in the same manner until the magazine is full. If desired, a cartridge can now be dropped into the chamber; press down the cartridges in the magazine so the bolt can be pushed forward over them; close the bolt fully and turn the bolt handle down as far as it will go to lock the cartridge in the chamber. With the safety swung to the left the rifle is ready to be fired by pulling the trigger. If the rifle is to be carried loaded, swing the safety to the right, or SAFE position, which locks the striker and bolt. After firing, raise the bolt handle and pull the bolt back smartly to extract and eject the empty cartridge case. Push the bolt forward to move the topmost cartridge in the magazine into the chamber and, on lowering the bolt handle, the rifle is ready to be fired again. To unload, place the safety in the INTERMEDIATE (up) position and move the bolt fully forward and back, until all the cartridges have been ejected from the action.

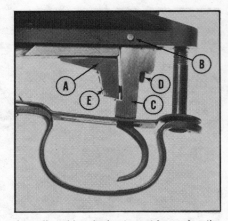

An adjustable single-stage trigger for the M54 Winchester, designed and made by the author. Made of tool steel, part (A) replaces the original trigger and is held in the sear by the original trigger pin. A hole is drilled at (B) for the new trigger (C), which is provided tension by a spring and plunger (D) fitted in a hole in the upper part of the trigger. An Allen-head setscrew (E) in the new sear provides sear-engagement adjustment.

Take-Down and Assembly

First make sure magazine and chamber are empty. To remove the bolt place the safety in the INTERMEDIATE position, raise the bolt handle and pull it back while holding the trigger back as far as it will go; the bolt can now be removed. Remove the firing mechanism by depressing the bolt-sleeve lock on its left, turning the bolt sleeve counterclockwise out of the bolt. To disassemble the firing mechanism remove the firing-pin stop screw from the bolt sleeve, place the firing-pin tip on a hardwood surface and, with a firm grasp on the bolt sleeve, push the bolt sleeve down so the safety can be swung to the right to allow the firing pin to move forward. Now grasp the firing-pin sleeve, pull it back so it can be rotated and released from the firing pin. The firing pin can now be pulled from the bolt sleeve. Swing the safety up and it can be removed. Drive out the very small bolt-sleeve lock pin to remove the bolt-sleeve lock and spring. Reassemble in reverse order.

Turn out and remove the 3 trigger guard screws and the guard (with follower spring and follower attached), and the barreled action can be lifted from the stock. Slip follower off follower spring and the spring off the guard. In reassembling, the narrow end of the spring goes into the follower. Push the magazine box upward out of the stock. Drive out the sear pin and remove sear, sear spring and trigger. Drive out ejector pin to remove ejector and ejector spring. Reassemble in reverse order. The barrel, threaded very tightly into the receiver, should not be removed unless the proper tools are available (barrel vise and action wrench).

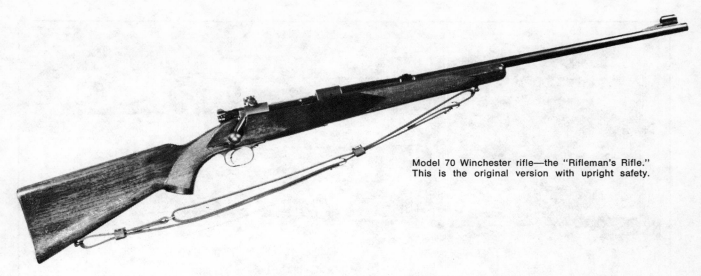

Model 70 Winchester rifle—the "Rifleman's Rifle." This is the original version with upright safety.

Part II
Model 70 Winchester

BY THE EARLY 1930s Winchester had begun quietly to develop a new and improved successor to the M54 action but retaining the best features of the 54. New design features would eliminate the faulty and undesirable aspects. By 1934 Winchester's designers had the new action worked out and ready for manufacture. Because of the depression, perhaps, they decided to postpone its introduction until late 1936.* The new rifle was called the Model 70. As almost every high power rifle shooter knows, the M70 was an instant success. In time it became known as the "Rifleman's Rifle." This very apt title reflects what most shooters and experts think about it.

In 1964 some basic changes were made, and today all Model 70s made between 1936-1964 are known as "old M70s" and are generally referred to as pre-64 70s. The M70 rifles and actions discussed in this part are those made before 1964.

Like the M54, the M70 was made in a number of styles and calibers, though not all of the various styles were chambered for all the cartridges in the following list: .22 Hornet, .220 Swift, .243 (introduced 1955), .250-3000 Savage, .257 Roberts, .264 Magnum (1959), .270, 7mm Mauser, .300 Savage, .30-06, .308 (7.62mm NATO) in 1952, .300 H&H Magnum, .300 Magnum (1963), .338 Magnum (1958), .35 Remington, .358 Winchester (1955), .375 H&H Magnum, and .458 Winchester Magnum (1956). A few M70 rifles were also chambered for the 7.65mm and 9mm Mauser cartridge.

The following different styles were made: Standard rifle with 24″ barrel, Standard carbine with 20″ barrel, Super Grade rifle, Featherweight rifle with 22″ barrel (1952), Target rifle, National Match rifle, Sniper's match rifle, Bull

*Despite the fact that some M70 rifles were delivered in late 1936 (how many is unknown), the Winchester company gives 1937 as the introductory year. See *The American Rifleman* for Nov. and Dec., 1936, for a Dope Bag report on the M70 rifles.　　　　JTA.

Gun, Varmint rifle and the Magnum rifles—Westerner, Alaskan and African. Before 1964 M70 actions and barreled actions were never commercially available.

The M70 Action

The M70 was not really an entirely new action when it was introduced, but rather the basic M54 action redesigned and greatly improved and modified.

Winchester made five major changes on the M54 action to transform it into the M70.

1) Bolt stop: a separate and independent bolt stop is used in the M70 action. It is a flat piece of metal positioned in a slot milled into the left rear of the receiver through the bottom of the left locking lug raceway. It is held in place by, and pivots on, the trigger pin. Tension is provided by a small spring and plunger located at the left rear of the bridge. The rear of the bolt stop projects upward behind the bridge wall, where it can be depressed with the thumb to remove the bolt. The front end of the bolt stop projects up into the left locking lug raceway, halting the bolt in its rearward movement by contacting the locking lug. To limit bolt travel in actions made for cartridges shorter than the .30-06, a bar is fitted to the left of the extractor collar. This bar slides in the locking lug raceway, its front end contacting the locking lug when the bolt handle is raised. On opening the bolt, the bolt stop will contact the rear end of this bar and halt the bolt travel. A short bar (called the bolt stop extension) is used for the .220 Swift to .308 length cartridges, a slightly longer bar for the .250 and .35 Remington cartridges, and the longest bar for the .22 Hornet. The bolt stop is simple, strong, unobtrusive, convenient and easy to operate.

2) Trigger: the M70 has one of the best trigger systems ever made. The sear is located under the receiver in the same manner as the M54 sear, pivoting on a pin and tensioned by a coil spring. The rear part of the sear, which projects into the cocking cam raceway, has a beveled rear surface which contacts a similar sloped surface on the cocking cam when

the action is cocked. The trigger, positioned to the rear of the sear, is held in place by, and pivots on, a pin through the bottom walls of the receiver. Trigger tension is provided by a coil spring fitted over a screw stem between the rear of the trigger and receiver. This screw, threaded into the trigger, has 3 lock nuts which allow the trigger to be adjusted for weight of pull and over-travel. A notch in the front of the trigger matches a projection on the bottom of the sear and, when engaged, holds the sear up against the cocking piece to hold the firing pin back when the action is cocked. The arrangement and the leverages are such that a full sear-to-cocking piece engagement is maintained yet permits a minimum engagement between the trigger and sear, thus achieving a safe, but short and light, trigger let-off. The mechanism is very simple, strong, reliable and foolproof.

Properly adjusted, no shooter need complain about this trigger—it is that good. It is still being used on M70s made today.

3) Safety: the M70 safety is built into the bolt sleeve, its stem fitting into a vertical hole in the right side of the bolt sleeve. Held in place by a small cross pin through the bolt sleeve, it is tensioned by a spring and plunger positioned lengthwise in the top of the bolt sleeve. The hole for this plunger extends forward through the bolt sleeve in line with the rear of the bolt and, when the safety is swung to the SAFE position, the plunger is moved forward to engage in a notch in the bolt, locking it. The two main positions of the safety are SAFE and FIRE, but it can also be placed midway between these positions. When on SAFE the stem of the safety engages the cocking piece, locking both firing pin and bolt. With the safety in the intermediate position the bolt can be operated to unload the magazine, with no danger of the firing pin falling.

On the first M70 actions the safety wing was on top of the bolt sleeve, swinging over a flat surface thereon. Swung far left the safety is in the SAFE position; swung to the rear it is in the FIRE position. This safety was not convenient when a scope was mounted low over the receiver. A new safety, designed later, has a wing along

Original Model 70 Winchester action.

the right side of the bolt sleeve that is easy to operate under any condition; it is in the SAFE position when swung to the rear, and in the FIRE position when swung forward. This fully reliable safety is still being used on the M70 actions made today.

4) Bolt handle: the M70 bolt handle, made to a very low profile, will clear the eyepiece of the lowest-mounted scope that might be affixed. The tang of the receiver is deeply notched to accept the very heavy base of the bolt handle and, though the rear of the base does not contact the rear of the notch, it serves as a safety lug in the event the locking lugs or receiver ring should ever fail. Failure of the receiver, however, is highly unlikely.

5) Magazine: the M70 magazine box, follower and follower spring are the same as those used in the M54, but rather than using a piece of bent sheet-metal for the trigger guard and magazine cover, the M70 has a hinged magazine floorplate and guard milled from steel. The separate guard bow is of steel also. Screws at either end of the guard thread into the bottom of the receiver. An unobtrusive plunger catch is positioned in the front of the guard to hold the floorplate closed; it is depressed to release the floorplate (also milled from steel), which is neatly hinged to a short plate called the magazine cover plate. The front guard screw goes through this plate into the bottom of the receiver ring. When the floorplate is closed it covers a center guard screw as well as covering the entire magazine box. On the Featherweight M70 the guard bow, floorplate and hinge plate were made of an alloy.

The 5 major changes just described greatly improved the action.

By making a separate bolt stop system the extra machining required on the M54 bolt was eliminated. The lower profile of the bolt handle increased the strength of the safety lug it provided. Placing the front guard screw to the rear of the receiver ring, instead of threading it into the recoil lug, strengthened the wood which

supported the lug since this wood is clamped between the bottom of the receiver and the hinge plate.

The receiver, bolt, breeching system, extractor, ejector and firing mechanism proved so reliable in the M54 that hardly any design changes were made in these parts or mechanisms. The M70 receiver is the same length and diameter, and about the same weight, as the M54 receiver. The M70 receiver was always tapped on the left side for a receiver sight. When first brought out only the top of the receiver ring was tapped for a scope mount, but soon afterward the top of the bridge was also tapped. The same barrel shank and thread specifications were used, in fact M54 and M70 barrels are interchangeable. No change was made in the bolt locking arrangement. The same is true of the firing pin, mainspring and firing-pin sleeve. Both models have the same bolt sleeve lock and, except for the modifications for the different safeties used, even the bolt sleeves are similar. In fact, all of these parts are more or less interchangeable in the M54 and M70 actions. The M70 bolt has the same rotational stop lug as on the M54 and the same extractor cam.

Additional gas-vent holes are provided in the M70 bolt and receiver—two in the bolt, a small one near the bolt head, at the junction of the firing pin tip, and a larger one just ahead of the firing-pin sleeve. These allow gases to escape into the left locking lug raceway. If any gas should be expelled into the bolt, and thence into the locking lug raceway, it would flow between and past the bolt body and receiver, as well as being directed rearward down the raceway. The bolt stop and the bolt sleeve could partially stop this flow, but some gas could still escape past the edge of the bolt sleeve and strike the shooter's face. On the M70 rifles chambered for the shorter cartridges (those having a bolt stop extension bar on the extractor collar) the extension bar would cover one or both of the bolt gas-vent holes.

A gas-escape hole through the right side of the M70 receiver ring, opposite the extractor slot in the barrel, allowed any powder gases escaping to the right to be vented through this hole. More on this later.

Only one size receiver and bolt were used for all calibers in the M70 Winchester and, regardless of caliber, all actions were of the same length. Actions made for the .30-06 and .270 have a magazine box with an inside opening length of 3.385″, with the magazine well in the receiver just long enough to receive the magazine box. For cartridges of shorter length, such as the .257 Roberts, .243 and others, the rear of the magazine box is blocked off with a spacer, so the magazine box opening is no longer than needed. Shorter followers and follower springs are then used. The .22 Hornet M70 has a magazine arrangement just like that of the M54 previously described. Model 70 actions made for the long .300 H&H and .375 H&H Magnum calibers have the receiver-well lengthened and the magazine box, follower and spring made accordingly to accept these 3.60″ long cartridges. Regardless of the caliber they were made for, however, M70 receivers were all of the same length.

Early M70 receivers made for such standard calibers as the .30-06 and .270 had a stripper-clip guide milled into the bridge so that cartridges could be loaded from a clip. This feature was dropped later except in the target rifles.

The Featherweight M70

Up to 1952 all M70 actions were of all-steel construction—and of all *milled-steel* construction except for such parts as the sheet-steel magazine box and springs. In 1952, however, the M70 Featherweight rifle was introduced in response to the demand for lighter weight rifles. The weight reduction was achieved by using a very slim 22″ barrel, a trimmer and slimmer stock having an aluminum buttplate, and by making the trigger guard, floorplate and hinge plate of a lightweight aluminum alloy. The standard weight M70, with all-steel parts, was retained until both it and the Featherweight models were dropped in 1964 in favor of the New Model 70.

Except for the 3 aluminum parts, which made the action a few ounces lighter, (these parts were black anodized), the Featherweight action was identical to the standard all-steel action. While many hunters favored the Featherweight model over the standard model, most M70 rifle fans disapproved of the use of non-steel parts, feeling the rifle was "cheapened" thereby. In fact, the anodized finish given these parts did not wear well, and if the rifle was carried a lot the floorplate soon became bright. Also, if bumped hard, the aluminum guard could be easily broken.

Good and Poor Features

Winchester rifle fans, and particularly Winchester 70 fans—and they are legion—stoutly maintain that the pre-1964 M70 action is the best centerfire bolt action ever made, that it has no faults, and that it cannot be improved upon. I'll go along with this up to a certain point.

The M70 actions made before 1964 really has a lot of outstanding features which make it one of the finest, most reliable and strongest bolt actions ever made. In the first place it is made of the finest steels available for the purpose, and the various parts heat treated for maximum strength and durability. It is extremely well made, with all vital parts made to close tolerances and properly finished and fitted. It is easy to operate, and feeding is usually flawless. The M70 action was adopted by a number of wildcat cartridge experimenters for development work with large capacity cartridges, and the actions stood up under this punishment, attesting to its strength.

As mentioned previously the firing mechanism, which includes the trigger, is nearly flawless, and hardly any valid complaints can be leveled against the bolt stop, safety, ejector and extractor systems. The M70 has about the shortest striker travel and about the fastest lock time of any centerfire bolt action I'm aware of, which are features target shooters like. As well known as the M70 rifle has become in the hunting fields, it is equally a favorite on the target range.

The pre-'64 M70 action can also be considered very safe, but I feel that it could easily have been made safer. In discussions with several arms experts and shooters about this action, several of them said that, in case of a cartridge failure when the head of the cartridge cracks or splits, they would rather have been firing some other rifle when this happened than the M70. I have fired many thousands of shots using commercial, military and handloaded ammunition in a variety of centerfire bolt action rifles, but I can recall only two instances of case failure. Both happened when I was firing a Mauser M98 rifle. In both instances a lot of gas blew out of the action, but (I was wearing glasses) hardly any of the gas hit my face. If these had been M54 or M70 rifles I would not have had the protection the Mauser actions afforded me, with their flanged bolt sleeves. The point is, I would consider the M70 action much safer if it had a vent hole in the left side of the receiver as there is in the right side of the receiver ring. I would also prefer to have a flange on the left side of the bolt sleeve, one which extended to the outside of the receiver to deflect outward any gases expelled rearward in the locking lug raceway. I would also want the hole in the left receiver wall opposite the vent hole in the bolt body, and I'd prefer to have both holes well forward, or about ¾" from the bolt head.

In one case reported to me by a gunsmith, whose statement I cannot question, a shooter firing an M70 experienced a severe case-head rupture, probably through an overload or plugged bore. Most of the escaping gases were directed into the left locking lug raceway, and in such volume and force that the bolt-sleeve lock was blown out as the gases rushed past the bolt sleeve. The shooter was injured by the powder gases, but luckily the flying bolt-sleeve lock missed him. This one instance, at least, is enough to convince me that the M70 action would be safer if the bolt sleeve were flanged, and if there were a vent hole in the left side of the receiver.

I have experienced misfires with two M70 rifles I owned and used, but I never really found out what the trouble was. In one rifle I suspected that the misfires were caused by the firing pin not being held back as far as is normal, because the sear-to-trigger surfaces had been honed too much. This resulted in the sear not being held up as high as normal, preventing the sear from holding the firing pin back as much as it should be. The difference was very small, since the safety could still be engaged with some effort, but the difference was enough, I think, to cause frequent misfires. For myself, I would rather have the firing pin travel on the M70 increased by ⅛" to provide an excess of power and momentum to the firing pin for positive ignition under all conditions.

Gunsmithing

The M70 action is one that is seldom gunsmithed, It is, perhaps, the first choice action on which to build a custom sporter or target rifle, but no gunsmithing is necessary unless the caliber is changed or something like that. In fitting a new barrel it should be breeched up so there is some space between the bolt and barrel, leaving some .003" to .005" end play in the bolt. A hole can be drilled in the left receiver ring or wall to provide a gas-escape port on that side. If the rifle is to be rechambered for a longer cartridge, for example from the .257 Roberts to the .25-06, just remove the magazine spacer and install a .30-06 length follower and follower spring. If the action is to be used for a shorter cartridge than the one for which it was made, then reverse the procedure

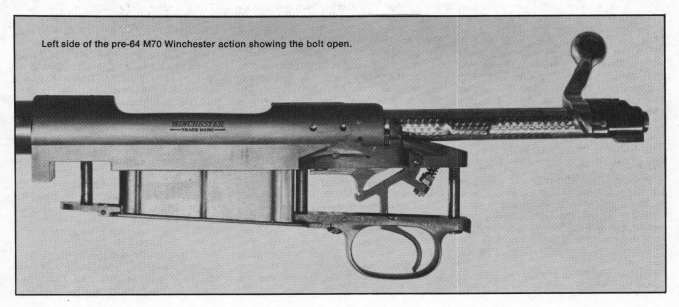

Left side of the pre-64 M70 Winchester action showing the bolt open.

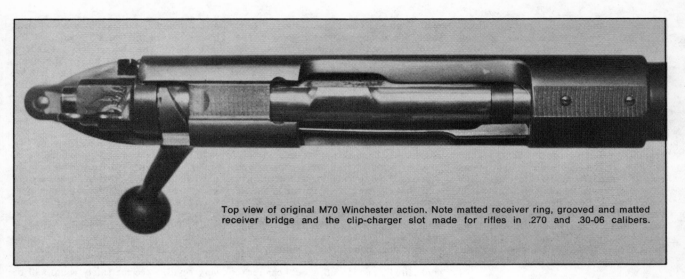

Top view of original M70 Winchester action. Note matted receiver ring, grooved and matted receiver bridge and the clip-charger slot made for rifles in .270 and .30-06 calibers.

by silver soldering or riveting in a magazine spacer and install a shorter follower and spring. I advise against altering the standard .30-06 length receiver to handle the long H&H Magnum cartridges, although there is no objection to using this action for any of the short magnum cartridges. There are numerous rechambering possibilities in the various calibers for this rifle, but since most rechamberings are inadvisable, I will not list them. However, several well-known experimenters in the high velocity field preferred to use the M70 action over any other available.

If you dislike the M70 trigger you can install the fine Canjar trigger mechanism made for this rifle. It is fully adjustable for weight-of-pull, take-up and over-travel, and can be had with a trigger shoe having a built-in single-set trigger. If you want a double-set trigger it is possible to install the regular German set-trigger mechanism as made for the M98 Mauser. Installation instructions can be found in the July, 1962, issue of *The American Rifleman*. p. 37.

I have already mentioned the lack of any gas shield on the bolt sleeve of M70 rifle, old and new. On page 73 in the April, 1964, issue of *The American Rifleman*, instructions are given on how to install a simple Mauser-type gas shield on the M70 bolt sleeve. The outside of the bolt sleeve, just to the rear of its forward flared edge, is fitted with a shield made from a steel washer, silver soldered in place. Why Winchester never incorporated a similar shield for the M70 bolt sleeve I cannot understand; it would have corrected what I consider a fault in the action design.

Take-Down and Assembly (Pre-'64)

Make sure the chamber and magazine are unloaded. Open and close the bolt, place the safety in the intermediate position. To remove the bolt raise the bolt handle and pull the bolt back about halfway, depress the bolt stop on the left rear of the receiver, then pull the bolt all the way out.

To disassemble the bolt depress the bolt-sleeve lock plunger and unscrew the bolt sleeve and firing mechanism. Move the safety to the FIRE position, allowing the firing pin to fall. Grasp the firing-pin sleeve firmly, pulling it back until it can be turned ¼-turn in either direction, then ease it off gently against the strong mainspring pressure. The firing pin can be separated from the bolt sleeve by turning out the firing-pin stop screw from the bolt sleeve. To remove the extractor turn it under the bolt so it covers the gas-vent holes, then push it forward. Reassemble in reverse order. Do not remove the extractor collar unless absolutely necessary.

It is not advisable to remove the safety, but if it must be done proceed as follows: using a small drift punch to drive the safety retainer-pin to the inside of the bolt sleeve, rotate the safety until it can be lifted out; the safety-lock plunger and spring can now be removed; remove the bolt-sleeve lock and spring by driving out the bolt-sleeve retainer pin. Reassemble in reverse order.

To remove the barrel and action from the stock, first turn out the front magazine plate screw, and remove the magazine floorplate and hinge plate. Turn out the fore-end screw. Turn out the rear and front guard bow screws, then pull out the trigger guard bow. Lift the barrel and action out of the stock. Remove the magazine box from the stock. Reassemble in reverse order.

Remove the trigger and bolt stop by driving the trigger pin to the right, removing the bolt stop, bolt-stop plunger and plunger spring first, then drive the trigger pin all the way out to remove the trigger and trigger spring. Drive out the sear pin to remove the sear and sear spring, and drive out the ejector pin to remove the ejector and spring. Reassemble in reverse order.

The barrel is threaded very tightly into the receiver. It should not be removed unless absolutely necessary, and then only if a barrel vise and action wrench are available.

The floorplate can be separated from the hinge plate by driving out the hinge pin. The floorplate release can be removed from the guard by driving out the pin.

The follower can be slipped off the follower spring and the spring slipped off the floorplate. In reassembling, the follower is slipped over the narrow end of the follower spring.

Markings

The M70 Winchester receiver is marked with the firm's special lettering for "Winchester" on the left wall in two lines, thus:

WINCHESTER
—TRADEMARK—

The serial number is stamped on the right side of the receiver ring and etched on the bottom of the bolt body.

The Winchester proof mark (**P** over **W** within a vertical oval) is stamped on the left side of the receiver ring and on the left side of the chamber.

The name and address of the Winchester firm is stamped on the barrel forward of the rear sight. The model (**MODEL 70**) and caliber designations are also stamped on the barrel. The caliber is also stamped on the bottom of the barrel, near the breech, along with the year the rifle was made, thus: **270 42**, which would indicate .270 caliber and 1942.

If you want a pre-'64 M70 action on which to build a rifle you'll have to strip a rifle to get it! In the 1940s and '50s it was no problem to pick up a moderately-priced secondhand M70 and discard all of it except the action. Today, however, these rifles are becoming hard to find, and they're often priced as if they'd been off of the market 25 years or more. Despite this—or maybe because of it—M70s are being hunted down and bought by those who think there is no other bolt action quite so desirable on which to build that dream rifle.

Target shooters seem to have a special preference for this action; I've read that one well-known gunsmith has built over a thousand target rifles on it. It will be hard for anyone to convince my son, Mark, who helped me with this book, that there is a better high power target rifle action than the M70, for the rifle he used in 1966 to win the 1000-yard Leech Cup match at Camp Perry was built on one.

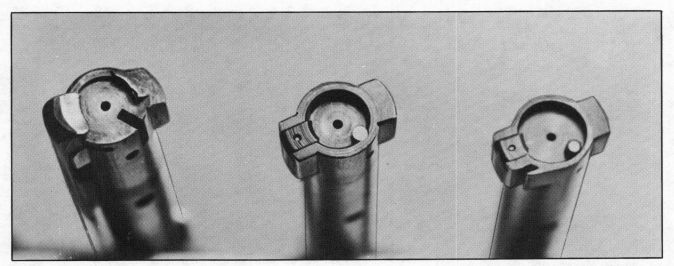

The bolt heads of 3 different M70 Winchesters. On the left is the pre-64 M70 bolt head showing the well-beveled extractor hook and ejector slot. The M54 bolt head is the same. In the center is the bolt head of M70s serial numbered between 700,000 and 866,000. Note the sliding extractor built into the right locking lug (shown on the left in this photo) and the plunger-type ejector. On the right is the bolt head of the latest M70 Winchester, serial numbered over 866,000, showing the anti-bind feature—a groove under the right locking lug.

The 1964 M70

After making the M70 rifle for 27 years, and having made over a half-million of them, Winchester suddenly discontinued it in early 1964 and introduced a "new" M70. This immediately became known as the "New Model 70," while the one dropped became the "pre-'64 Model 70" —designations which M70 fans adopted to distinguish the two. Whatever the reason or reasons for dropping the time-tested old model, M70 fans were seemingly aghast that Winchester could do such a thing. At any rate, early in 1964, and beginning with serial number 700,000 (all M70 Winchester rifles with a serial number below 700,000 are the old or pre-'64 models), the new M70 was put on the market.

The "New Model 70" rifles were quite different from the old. Five different models were introduced: the Standard model with 22″ full-floating barrel in .243, 270, .30-06 and .308; a Magnum model with 24″ barrel in .264, .300, .338 and .375 H&H, all magnums; a Varmint model with 24″ medium-heavy barrel in .243; a Target model with 24″ heavy barrel in .30-06, and the African model with 22″ barrel in .458 Magnum. Introduced with the Standard and Magnum models was a stock with a Monte Carlo cheekpiece, high gloss finish and impressed checkering. The barrels were also new, that is, they were made by the cold-swaged or "hammer-swaged" process. The biggest mechanical change, however, was in the action, and it was these changes that caused M70 shooters to howl.

The 1964 M70 has a receiver longer and somewhat heavier than the old one. The increased length is the result of making the tang longer. The new receiver is not entirely machined—the bottom appears to be an investment casting, although Winchester describes it as being "precision forged," with the forging done in

dies. Beginning with the receiver, it is evident that many short cuts were made to reduce manufacturing costs.

The bolt is made in 3 sections, brazed together. The bolt head, with its heavy unslotted dual-opposed locking lugs, is brazed to the front end of the bolt body cylinder. A plunger-type ejector and its small coil spring fit into a hole at the edge of the bolt-face recess, retained there by a small cross pin. The extractor, a small sliding wedge fitted in a mortise cut into the front of the right locking lug, is tensioned by a small spring and plunger. The bolt face is deeply recessed for the cartridge head, and both locking lugs are flush with the front of the bolt. The breech end of the barrel, no longer coned, has a flat breech face, and is not recessed for the head of the bolt. The barrel boss, which had formerly held the rear open sight and which the fore-end screw entered, was abandoned.

The bolt handle has a short sleeve on its base that is brazed over a turned-down portion of the rear of the bolt-body cylinder. Otherwise the bolt handle and pear-shaped grasping ball are like those on the old M70 action. There is no stop/guide lug on the bolt body as on the old M70 bolt, but the new bolt has the same extractor cam surface. The approaches to the receiver locking-lug shoulders are angled, forcing the bolt forward as the bolt handle is pushed down.

The new bolt sleeve, bolt-sleeve lock and safety are essentially like those used on the old M70, except that the firing-pin stop screw has been eliminated. The end of the bolt sleeve is covered with a metal cap held in place by a cross pin.

The new model firing pin is also different. It has a shorter cocking-cam head and, in addition, it has a lip which projects rearward under the bolt sleeve cap. This lip, serrated and painted red, acts as a cocking indicator which can be felt and seen when the action is cocked. The

mainspring, compressed over the firing pin, is held in place by a washer and a U-shaped retainer collar which lies in a groove in the firing pin.

The bolt stop is the same type as before except that it is tensioned by a wire spring held on the headed trigger pin, instead of the spring-and-plunger arrangement used before. Five different lengths of bolt stops are made for the different cartridge lengths this action can handle. These are the H&H Magnum; .30-06 and short magnum; .308; .22-250 and .222 lengths.

The trigger mechanism of the new M70 is the same as on the old model, except that the curved trigger finger-piece is about double the width of the old trigger.

No changes were made in the magazine, floorplate and trigger guard arrangement except that the guard, floorplate and hinge plate are made of an alloy. Made of some lightweight metal, the follower is riveted to the follower spring in the new M70. The same 3 guard screws are used to hold the action to the stock.

What does this all add up to? The main changes made are these: the method of breeching, with the flat end of the bolt head nearly contacting the flat breech face of the barrel; eliminating the long Mauser-type extractor and its collar, using instead a small and easily-made sliding extractor fitted in the bolt head; eliminating the flat pivot-type ejector, substituting a plunger-type in the bolt head; having a deeply-recessed bolt face so that the cartridge head is fully encircled and supported by a ring of steel; providing a cap for the bolt sleeve to cover the cocking cam head and providing a cocking indicator.

When the new M70 rifles began to appear on the market, virtually everyone familiar with the old M70 expressed disappointment. The new rifle was criticized no end, often by those who had not even seen it. As for me, I waited awhile before making any evaluation of it, but on the

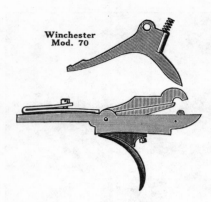

Winchester Mod. 70

Stoeger's single-set trigger that was once available for the M70 Winchester.

whole I thought the new breeching system was an improvement over the old, and I could see nothing at all wrong with the new ejector, bolt-sleeve cap and hammer-forged barrels. I also thought the extractor was adequate. It did not matter to me that the bolt was made in three pieces and brazed together. Of course no one liked the alloy trigger guard and floorplate, and riveting the follower to the follower spring didn't help matters. I also heard complaints that the action was rough, that the bolt was sometimes difficult to operate and had a tendency to bind, and that feeding was not always positive.

The 1968 M70

No doubt the Winchester people heard of all these complaints and more, for some dealers—and gun writers—were very outspoken in their dislike of the new M70. Winchester then set about making some of the needed changes and improvements. This they did when they introduced another "new" Model 70 Winchester early in 1968. Beginning at serial number 866,-000, the following new features and improvements were made:

1) An "anti-bind" feature which positively prevents bolt binding, making rapid operation of the bolt much surer and easier. This was done by adding metal under the right locking lug and cutting a narrow groove through it to separate it from the lug, then making a rib in the right side of the receiver for the anti-bind groove to slide over. This rib extends from the rear of the bridge forward to the inside of the receiver ring, ending at the locking shoulder edge. This rib is also the right cartridge-guide lip of the magazine well. When the bolt handle is raised this anti-bind groove in the bolt head is aligned with the anti-bind rib, engaging it the moment the bolt is drawn back; it stays engaged the full bolt-travel distance. The anti-bind feature holds the bolt in line with the receiver regardless of the tension or pressure put on the bolt handle, so that the bolt will not bind or stick during operation. It's a very effective feature, the bolt being noticeably easier to operate than the bolt in any earlier M70 Winchester. Incidentally, the anti-bind bolt won't fit earlier M70 receivers.

2) The floorplate is made of steel and finished in black-chrome plate, but the guard and the floorplate hinge plate are still made of a lightweight alloy black anodized.

3) The follower, now made of a stainless steel and polished, has short lips underneath for attachment to the follower spring in the customary manner. This follower lists at $7.85 in the 1969 Winchester parts catalog; with the new follower spring it can be installed in the 1964 M70 to replace the riveted follower/follower-spring unit.

About the only other noticeable change made in the 1968 M70 action is that the receiver is polished as opposed to the sand-blast matte finish on previous models.

In 1969 Winchester added a new M70 chambering, the very popular .222 Remington. This was the first time Winchester had chambered any rifle for this cartridge since its introduction by Remington in 1950.

Evaluation

That Winchester decided to go back to the steel floorplate was good news; the finish will last longer, and it can be engraved to last. The new stainless steel follower is also an improvement, and it it should eliminate any feeding problems. However, the most significant and noticeable improvement is the "anti-bind" feature. On receiving my first 1968 Model 70 I saw immediately that the bolt could be more easily operated than either previous 70s. There is no tendency for the bolt to bind or stick on opening or closing, regardless of how the bolt is operated, twisted or pressured.

Model 70 Barreled Actions

To the best of my knowledge Winchester has never made separate M70 actions available, even to qualified gunsmiths. In 1965, however, they did make M70 barreled actions available to anyone. This assembly, completely finished (but without barrel sights) and ready to put into a stock, was made in the same barrel lengths, styles and calibers as their 1964 M70 rifles. This includes the standard sporter barreled action in calibers .22-250, .222 Remington, .225 Winchester, .243, .270, .30-06 and .308; magnum-calibered barreled actions in .264, 7mm Rem., .300 and .338; varmint-barreled actions in .222 Rem., .22-250, .225 Winchester and .243; target-barreled actions in .308 and .30-06 calibers. In 1968 the action of the barreled action assembly included the same changes made in the rifles. At this writing the standard-caliber barreled action lists at $128.95 compared to the complete rifle at $174.95.

Markings

Receivers and barrels of the 1964 and 1968 M70 Winchesters are marked quite similarly to the pre-'64 models.

The M70 Winchester trigger (all models) showing: (A) sear, (B) trigger, (C) trigger-stop screw, (D) trigger-stop screwlock nut, (E) trigger spring jam nuts, (F) trigger spring. See text for details on how to adjust this trigger.

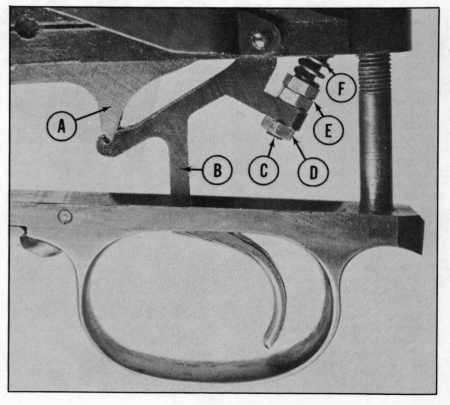

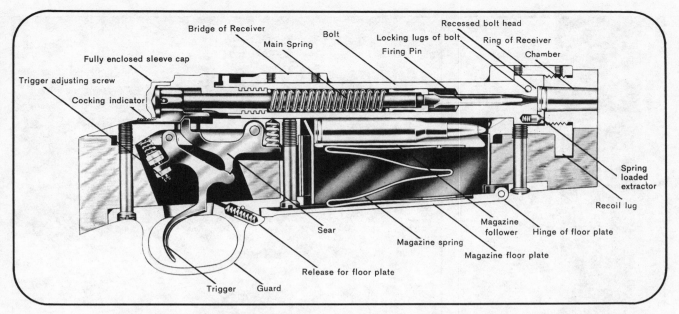

In the above illustration, the rifle has a live shell in the chamber, safety in "fire" position locking the action and bolt handle—ready to fire. The rifle won't fire until bolt is fully turned down. When trigger is pulled—sear releases firing pin which protrudes thru face of bolt and hits primer—exploding the cartridge in chamber.

Action can now be opened by lifting and pulling back on bolt

handle. Lifting motion cocks the firing pin, turns with a camming motion to free the fired case from the chamber. Extractor pulls out fired case, ejecting it sideways. Near end of backward stroke, bolt uncovers fresh cartridge pushed up by spring-loaded magazine follower.

On forward stroke bolt pushes fresh cartridge off follower into chamber—turns down engaging locking lugs—ready to fire.

Sectional view of the post-64 M70 Winchester action.

Serial Numbers

Model 70 Winchesters with a serial number below 700,000 are the "old" model, the pre-'64 version with the long Mauser-type extractor. I have no information as to just how many of these rifles were made, or at what number the serial number was started, or at what number manufacture ended, but manufacture was stopped before the 700,000 number was reached.

The 1964 M70 rifles are all numbered between 700,000 and 866,000, but again I have no information as to how many were made, or at what number their manufacture ceased.

Model 70 rifles with a number above 866,000, and with the letter **G** preceding

the serial number, are the 1968 version with the anti-bind feature, black-chrome floorplate and stainless steel follower.

Take-Down and Assembly (Post-64)

The instructions previously given for the take-down and assembly of the pre-'64 M70 applies to the post-'64 models except for the following: to remove the extractor, the extractor plunger is depressed with a pointed tool and the extractor slid out of its mortise; the ejector is removed by driving out the ejector pin from top to bottom. In removing the extractor and ejector take care to prevent their plungers and springs from flying out and being lost.

To remove the mainspring, the firing pin has to be pulled down to slightly compress the mainspring. The firing pin retainer can then be slipped off of the firing pin. Again, great care should be taken in doing this, as the mainspring is powerful. To remove the firing pin from the bolt sleeve after the mainspring is removed, drive out the bolt sleeve cap pin and pull off the bolt sleeve cap. Reassemble in reverse order.

Dimensional Specifications

Weight .... 48 oz.
    (Featherweight .... 45 oz.)
Receiver length .... 8.750"
    (Post-64, 9.25")
Receiver ring dia. ....1.340"
Bolt dia. .... .695"
Striker travel .... .340"
Bolt travel (see text) ....Varies
Bolt-face recess: Pre-64 models
    (standard calibers) Dia........ .485"
    (magnum calibers) Dia........ .550"
    Depth .... .045"
    Post-64 models
    (standard calibers) Dia........ .485"
    (magnum calibers) Dia. ...... .550"
    Depth .... .110"
Magazine length (.30-06).............3.385"
    (Spacer provided for
      shorter cartridges.)
Magazine length (post-64)............3.60"
    (Spacers provided for
      shorter cartridges.)
Guard-screw spacing ....7.50"

Winchester Model 70 General Specifications

Type	Turnbolt repeater.
Receiver	One-piece machined steel forging. Post-64 receivers are die-forged and machined. Non-slotted bridge. Tapped for scope mounts and receiver sights.
Bolt	One-piece machined steel with dual-opposed forward locking lugs. Handle acts as safety lug. Post-64 bolts are of 3-piece construction, head and bolt handle sections brazed to the body.
Ignition	One-piece firing pin with integral cocking cam head. Powered by coil mainspring. Cocks on opening.
Magazine	Non-detachable staggered-column box type with quick-release hinged floorplate. 5-shot capacity in standard calibers, 4-shot for magnum calibers.
Trigger	Single-stage, adjustable for weight-of-pull and over-travel.
Safety	Three-position rotary type located in the bolt sleeve; locks firing pin and bolt when swung back, locks firing pin when in the intermediate position, and is in FIRE position when forward.
Extractor	One-piece long Mauser-type on pre-64s attached to the bolt by a collar. Post-'64 models have a sliding extractor mounted in the right locking lug.
Magazine cut-off	None provided.
Bolt stop	Pivoting type positioned in a groove at bottom rear of receiver. Stops bolt by contacting left locking lug.
Ejector	Pivoting type in pre-64s positioned in a groove at bottom of the receiver. Post-64 models have plunger-type ejector positioned in bolt head.

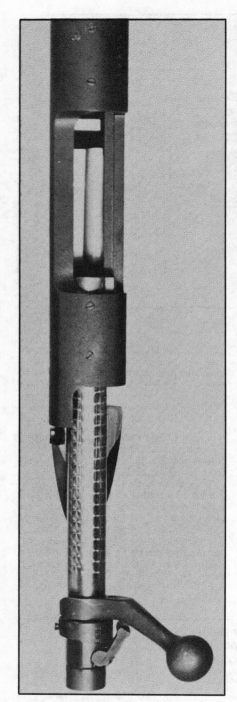

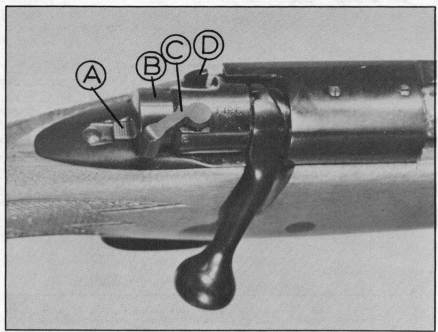

Top view of the rear of the New Model 70 Winchester action, showing: (A) cocking indicator (colored red), (B) bolt-sleeve cap, (C) safety, (D) bolt-stop release button.

Left—Top view of the opened New Model 70 Winchester action. This one, chambered for the .22-250 cartridge, shows the short follower and the top of the front magazine spacer.

Model 70 Trigger Adjustment

This information applies to all M70s. To make any adjustments the barrel and action must be removed from the stock. Only two adjustments can be made readily; weight-of-pull and over-travel. The tools needed are, once the stock is removed: a small screwdriver to turn the stop screw, and two small open-end wrenches to loosen, turn and tighten the lock or jam nuts.

The illustration shows the main parts of the M70 trigger mechanism. Weight of pull is adjusted by first loosening the upper and lower jam nuts; now turn them clockwise to increase the spring tension and weight of pull, and vice versa. As sent from the factory the jam nuts are set for about a 4.5-pound let-off, which is adequately light for a hunting rifle. Many shooters prefer a lighter pull, and one

about as light as 3 pounds can be had. If a lighter pull is wanted it may be necessary to grind off from one-half to one coil of the trigger spring. After the weight-of-pull adjustment has been made the two jam nuts must be tightened together to lock them in place. In any event, if an adjustment has been made to get a lighter pull, the action should be tested to make sure that there is enough trigger-spring tension to insure that the trigger will not slip off the sear when the bolt is slammed home. Test this by closing the bolt very smartly several times on an empty chamber and, if the sear fails to hold (allowing the firing pin to fall) then the trigger pull adjustment is too light.

The other trigger adjustment readily made is the over-travel. Do this by loosening the stop-screw lock nut and turning the stop screw in or out as required. It should be adjusted (and it is usually so-set at the factory) so that the trigger stops the moment the sear breaks from the trigger. This is best done as follows: loosen the lock nut and, with the action cocked, turn in the stop screw about one complete turn, or far enough so that on pulling the trigger the sear will not be released. Now with the action still cocked, and while pulling back on the trigger, slowly turn the stop screw out (counterclockwise) until the sear is released. Now turn the stop screw out at least ¼-turn further so there is sufficient clearance between the sear and trigger, after the sear is released, to prevent the sear from hanging up. After the adjustment is made the lock nut must be tightened to prevent the stop screw from turning.

There is no adjustment for initial trigger take-up or "creep." If there is creep or roughness in the let-off, the pull can be made smooth by carefully honing the trigger-to-sear contact surfaces with a fine hard Arkansas stone. The honing

New Model 70 Winchester action.

Post-64, or New Model 70 Winchester rifle.

should be done very carefully so that the breaking edges are left sharp, the surfaces left flat and without changing the angle of either surface. Trigger travel can be reduced by cutting the sear notch to reduce its depth, but you ought to have an extra trigger on hand before doing so—it is awfully easy to overdo it, and the notch left so shallow the trigger might not hold the sear if the bolt is slammed home. Again, if any honing is done on the sear surfaces, or if the trigger sear notch is cut down, the rapid bolt closing test should be repeated.

M670 and 770 Winchesters

Winchester introduced a lower-priced version of the post-64 M70 in 1966, calling it the Model 670. Offered in standard sporter, magnum and carbine styles in calibers .225, .243, .270, .264 Magnum, .30-06 and .300 Magnum, it had a hardwood stock stained to look like walnut. The main difference between the 670 and

the 70 is in the action: 1) the sheet-metal box magazine, which has a bottom, fits into a recess cut into the stock from the top. The box is thus entirely concealed within the stock, and no floorplate is used. The magazine can only be emptied by running the cartridges through the action. The follower is riveted to the follower spring. 2) A sliding safety is used, the safety button located on the right side of the receiver tang. When pulled back, a lever attached to the safety, and pivoted on the receiver, locks only the trigger so it cannot be pulled. 3) No separate bolt sleeve is used. The bolt sleeve is prevented from turning when the bolt is open by the cocking-piece cam resting in a shallow notch in the rear of the bolt body, as in the M93 and M95 Mauser actions. No bolt sleeve cap is used, the end of the cocking piece projecting through the rear of the bolt sleeve. A red-colored ring on the rear of the cocking piece shows when the action is cocked.

In virtually all other respects the M670 action is just like the post-'64 M70 action,

including trigger, bolt, extractor, ejector, bolt stop and receiver. The receiver is tapped for a receiver sight and top scope mount bases. The serial numbers, stamped on the receiver ring, began with number 100,000. This is a very good action. (In 1971 the Model 670 was offered only in .243 and .30-06. Ed.)

The Model 770

Winchester introduced another version of the M70 in 1969, this one the M770. Priced between the M70 and the M670, it's a sort of cross between the two. It has a walnut stock and bolt like the M70, with the enclosed bolt sleeve, 3-position bolt-sleeve safety and anti-bind device. The trigger is also a copy of the M70. The rest of the rifle is like the M670. The action is a good one. The M770 is available in calibers .222, .22-250, .243, .270, .308, .30-06, and .264, 7mm or .300 Magnum. Separate 670 and 770 actions are not available, nor are barreled actions.

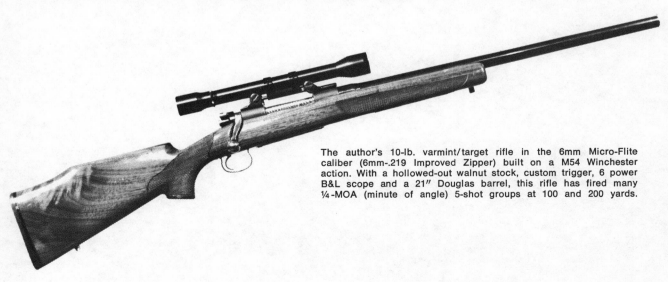

The author's 10-lb. varmint/target rifle in the 6mm Micro-Flite caliber (6mm-.219 Improved Zipper) built on a M54 Winchester action. With a hollowed-out walnut stock, custom trigger, 6 power B&L scope and a 21" Douglas barrel, this rifle has fired many ¼-MOA (minute of angle) 5-shot groups at 100 and 200 yards.

Notes

30. Remington Models
721, 722, 725, 700, 600 & 660

THE MODEL 721 Remington high powered bolt action rifle was introduced in 1948. In describing this new rifle and action in the March, 1948, issue of *The American Rifleman,* the late Julian S. Hatcher flatly stated that it was by far the strongest and safest bolt action produced up to that time. Indeed it was! In this report General Hatcher describes the torture tests to which the Model 721 was subjected. At the time the same tests were made on a high numbered 1903 Springfield, 1917 Enfield and a military 1898 Mauser. The 721 was still going strong long after the Springfield, Mauser and Enfield gave up, in that order. Time has proven Hatcher to have been right for in the more than 20 years following his statement Remington actions based on the Model 721 design are still considered by many firearms experts as being the safest, if not the strongest, actions made today.

Most shooters today are familiar with the 721 and 722 Remington rifles. The 721 was the "long" action (8.75″ length), used for calibers .270, .280, .30-06 and .300 H&H Magnum. Of the several grades made, the lowest was the 721A. The 722 action was the "short" one (7.87″ long), used for rifles in .222 (introduced 1950), .222 Magnum (1958), .244 (1955), .243 (1961), .257 Roberts, .300 Savage, and .308 (1957).

Markings

The 721 and 722 rifles have the name and model designation stamped on the left receiver wall, thusly:

REMINGTON
MODEL 721 (or 722)

The serial number is stamped on the left side of the receiver ring with the same number etched on the underside of the bolt body; the caliber designation is stamped on the left side of the barrel; also stamped on the left side of the barrel, ahead of the rear sight, is:

REMINGTON ARMS CO. INC.
ILION, N.Y.
MADE IN U.S.A.
PATENTS PENDING

or

REMINGTON ARMS CO., INC.
ILION, N.Y.
MADE IN U.S.A.
PATENT NO. 2,473,373:
2,514,981 OTHERS PENDING

The Remington proof mark, the letters **R.E.P.** within an oval, and various inspector's marks, are stamped on the breech end of the barrel.

A Popular Rifle

The 721 and 722 rifles became very popular shortly after they were introduced. There were a number of reasons for this; not least was the fine reviews they got from gunwriters. Word got around quickly that this Remington action was very strong and safe. The price was also right for sales appeal; for example, in 1950 list price of the 722 was $74.95, compared to the 70 Winchester standard grade at $109.50. Of course, the 70s had some features the Remington lacked, but the difference in price favored Remington. I have always considered the 721 and 722 as excellent values for the money. In addition to the free and favorable publicity the Remingtons received, Remington's two new cartridges (the .222 and the .244), which were first introduced in the 722, did more than anything else to popularize the rifle. Few cartridges became so instantly popular as the .222, and the 722 rifle gained the most from this. Hindsight

also indicates that if Remington had introduced the .244 cartridge with the same bullet weights and rifling twist as Winchester used with their .243 cartridge, and/or had chambered the 722 for the .243 immediately, the Remington rifle would have gained an even wider acceptance. I am not going to get into the .243 *vs* .244 controversy here, but for reasons which are quite hard to understand Remington was the loser in the 6mm cartridge race.

The Action

The 721 and 722 actions are alike except for length. The receiver is machined from round-bar stock of the highest quality steel. The recoil lug is a separate part, held between the receiver and the shoulder on the barrel when the barrel is threaded tightly into the receiver. The lug area is ample to hold the barrel and action from setting back in the stock from recoil.

The receiver, threaded at the front to accept the barrel shank, is precisely bored and milled to accept the one-piece bolt with its forward dual-opposed locking lugs. The approaches to the locking shoulders in the receiver ring are beveled, so that on turning the bolt handle down the bolt is forced forward a short distance. The round receiver has the same diameter its entire length. The top of the long bridge is machined nearly flat to reduce weight. Two holes are tapped into the top of the ring and bridge for scope mount bases. Two more holes are in the left side of the bridge for a receiver sight. The bridge is quite long, and the close machining of the inside of the receiver and the outside of the bolt, plus their well-finished, smooth surfaces, makes for a smooth-operating bolt, with a minimum of end wobble when the bolt is open. It also eliminated possible

Illustrated above: Remington 722 in .222 caliber, restocked by the author.

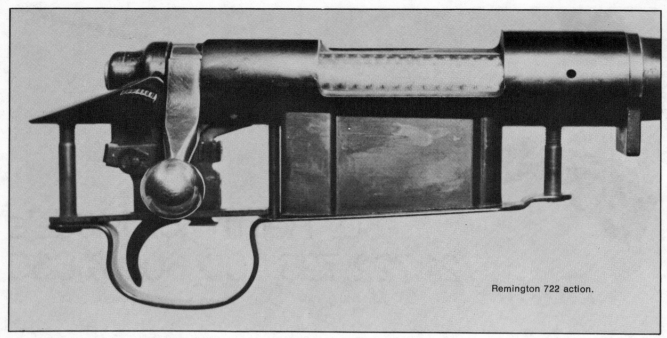

Remington 722 action.

bolt binding when the bolt is operated. The right receiver wall is low enough to leave ample room for loading and unloading the magazine.

To prevent the bolt from binding the right side of the bridge extends forward of the magazine-well opening, yet is back far enough so that the empty cases or loaded cartridges can be ejected properly. Because the bridge is so long a square notch is milled in its top front for easy insertion of cartridges into the magazine. This notch is not a stripper clip guide, however.

The main part of the bolt body is a machined steel cylinder. The bolt head, with the locking lugs, is made as a separate part and then permanently brazed onto the bolt body. The two locking lugs are unslotted, unnotched and undrilled; in other words they are solid. The very low-profile bolt handle, also made as a separate part, is then brazed to the rear of the bolt body. This brazing is so well done that the brazed lines are almost impossible to detect. Fabrication of the bolt in this manner in no way detracts from its appearance or affects its strength. The short rectangular-to-round stemmed bolt handle, ending in a solid round grasping ball, is low enough to clear the eyepiece of the lowest-mounted scope. The right side of the tang is deeply notched for the base of the bolt handle, the bolt handle thus becoming the safety locking lug. Part of the bolt handle base also forms a collar part way around the top of the bolt. This collar has an inclined surface which gives initial extraction power when the bolt handle is raised.

The quality of steel used in making the bolt and receiver (plus the proper heat treatment given to these parts afterward), the heavy solid locking lugs and the bolt-handle safety lug, produce a very strong action. Its strength is complemented by a breeching system which practically seals

a cartridge in the chamber—making these actions about the safest ever constructed. The bolt extends about .150″ ahead of the locking lugs, and the breech face of the barrel is recessed to receive it with a minimum of clearance around its circumference. Further, the face of the bolt head is recessed for the cartridge head. There is about .005″ clearance between the front end of the bolt and the barrel when the bolt is locked. This is needed to prevent the bolt from binding and to facilitate obtaining correct headspace when the barrel is chambered.

The extractor is a thin C-type flat spring clip which has a lip pressed into its inside curve. It fits in a shallow groove cut into the inside of the rim which forms the bolt-face recess. The ejector, a spring-loaded plunger fitted into a hole along the perimeter of the bolt face recess, is held in place by a small cross pin. The ejector prevents the extractor from turning in its recess. When a cartridge is fed from the magazine to the chamber by the bolt, or if a cartridge is dropped into the chamber, on closing the bolt, the extractor snaps over the cartridge rim and the ejector is depressed as the bolt is forced forward when the bolt handle is lowered.

Although the extractor is small, and its lipped hook which engages the cartridge rim is narrow, it gets a good bite on the rim; it seldom fails to pull a fired cartridge from the chamber when the bolt handle is raised. When the bolt is pulled back, no matter how slowly, the spring-loaded ejector will flip the cases to the right and clear of the rifle. Since the extractor is entirely within the bolt-head recess there is no extractor cut in either the bolt head or face of the barrel to break the seal between bolt and barrel.

In the event of a cartridge head failure it is unlikely any powder gases could escape from between the bolt and the barrel, but if any did it would be directed

into the locking-lug recess in the receiver ring and escape through a vent hole in the right side of the receiver. Should any gases enter the firing-pin hole from a pierced primer this gas would largely escape through a vent hole on the left side of the bolt head, it being directed into the locking-lug recess and in the left locking-lug raceway.

The firing mechanism is a simple one. The very stiff coil mainspring is compressed over the lightweight one-piece firing pin between a shoulder on the pin and the bolt sleeve. The rear end of the firing pin extends through the bolt sleeve (listed as the "bolt plug" by the factory) where the firing-pin head is attached to it by a cross pin. The bolt sleeve threads into the rear of the bolt. An extension on the firing-pin head extends forward through a slot in the bolt sleeve to contact the rear of the bolt. Here there is a deep cocking-cam notch which the firing-pin head can move into when the rifle is fired and forced back to cock the action when the bolt handle is raised. There is also a shallow notch into which the end of the firing-pin head rests when the bolt is opened, this preventing the bolt sleeve from turning when the bolt is open as there is no separate bolt-sleeve lock. The extension on the firing-pin head also projects down into a raceway cut into the bottom of the receiver tang so it can contact the sear lever to hold the firing pin back when the action is operated. Lock time is extremely fact, as the total firing pin travel is less than .300″. The ignition is also very positive, and I have never heard of anyone complaining about misfires with these rifles.

The bolt stop is a flat steel stamping fitted in a slot cut under the left locking-lug raceway, with its front end projecting into this raceway to contact the locking lug when the bolt is opened. Held in place and pivoting on a pin, it is tensioned by

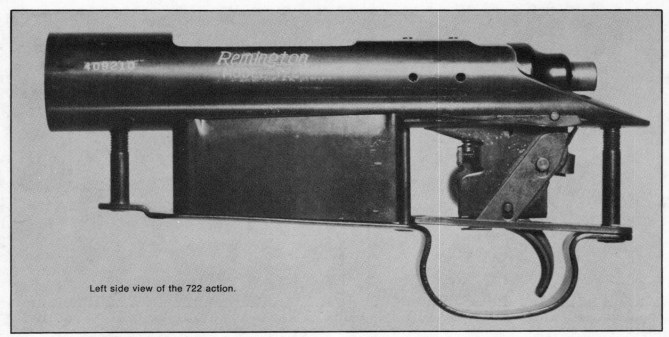

Left side view of the 722 action.

a small coil spring. The bolt-stop release is a bent spring-steel strip of metal sliding on the trigger and safety pivot pins on the left side of the trigger housing, and extends from the top inside of the trigger guard to the rear of the bolt stop. Pushing it up pivots the bolt stop down so the bolt can be removed from the action.

The trigger and safety mechanism are housed in a stamped sheet-metal box attached to the underside of the receiver by the bolt stop and sear pins. The sear is a thin piece of hardened metal positioned in the top right side of the trigger housing and in the trigger-housing opening in the receiver. It pivots on the sear pin in the front of the housing, and is tensioned by a coil spring.

The trigger, positioned in the bottom of the housing, pivots on a pin. A hardened, carefully-ground piece of metal called the trigger connector, fits over the top front of the trigger. The top square edge of this piece, contacting the bottom of the sear to hold it up, releases it when the trigger is pulled. A setscrew, threaded into the front of the trigger housing and contacting the top of the trigger connector, can be adjusted to stop or limit trigger over-travel. Just below this screw is the trigger weight-of-pull adjustment screw, and over its end is the trigger spring. Turning this screw in or out puts more or less tension on the spring, varying the pull weight. Another screw threaded into the rear of the trigger housing adjusts the trigger-sear engagement. All 3 of these screws are normally adjusted at the factory for minimum trigger over-travel, minimum sear engagement to remove creep, and a trigger let-off of about 3.5 to 4 pounds, and then sealed. More on how to adjust the trigger later on.

The safety, a bent steel stamping positioned largely on the right side of the trigger housing, pivots on a pin through the housing. It has a serrated button projecting upward along the right side of the receiver tang, conveniently sited for thumb operation. The front of the safety extends alongside the trigger housing; when the safety is pulled back the front of the safety moves up to engage a notch in the rear of the bolt body to lock the bolt. The safety cam, another strip of metal similar to the sear, lies to the left of the sear and pivots on the sear pin.

A short arm, doubled back on the rear of the safety, reaches into the trigger housing under the safety cam. When the safety button is pulled back (which can be done only when the action is cocked) this arm cams the safety cam up, forcing the firing-pin head back so it is off of the sear. Thus, with the safety pulled back to the SAFE position, the firing pin and bolt are locked. A small ball bearing lies in a hole in the side of the safety; a flat spring fastened on the safety pin tensions the ball to hold the safety in either the SAFE (back) or FIRE (forward) position.

The trigger-guard bow and the magazine floorplate are formed from a single piece of heavy sheet-metal. The top of the bow is enclosed by a narrow plate through which the trigger extends. Three guard screws run through holes in the trigger guard/floorplate, threading into the receiver, hold the barrel and action securely in the stock. The front and rear guard screws are heavy, but the center one, in front of the bow, is lighter. The magazine box, of light sheet-metal, is positioned between the receiver magazine-well opening and the floorplate. The cartridge guide lips are milled in the sides of the receiver-well opening. The ridged follower is also a sheet-metal stamping, while the follower spring is of the usual W-shape. Magazine boxes for .222 and .222 Magnum cartridges have a sheet-metal insert in the rear of the box to hold these shorter cartridges forward; a shorter follower and follower spring are used also, of course.

Good and Poor Features

For Remington to get into the center-fire bolt action rifle market successfully, and stay there, they had to come up with a new and improved action design, and to hold its manufacturing cost down so it could be sold at a lower price than any of its competitors. They did just that with their 721 and 722 rifles. They were, and still are, truly reliable and accurate rifles. The action was well thought out and designed, the entire rifle well constructed. The barrel and action were as good, and in some ways better, than that of any other rifle on the market, while the rest of the rifle was made without frills to keep the cost down.

The 721-722 breeching system — the cartridge head entirely recessed within the bolt face and the head of the bolt recessed in the breech face of the barrel—was the most noteworthy feature which made these actions safe. Making the receiver and bolt out of quality steel, and making the locking lugs large and solid, provided the strength for which these actions became noted. The simple firing mechanism, with its very fast and positive ignition, is another excellent feature. The bolt stop is very good and so is the ejector.

Although made of steel stampings the trigger and safety mechanisms have proven good and reliable, attested to by the fact that essentially the same mechanisms are used in the later 600 and 700 Remington rifles. A more simplified trigger mechanism might have been better, but I can remember repairing only one 722 trigger in the years I was in the gunsmithing business.

While some gunsmiths and shooters didn't like the round-bottomed receiver and the separate recoil lug, I see nothing wrong with the latter system. Locked between the receiver and barrel, it performs its function just as well as if it were part of the receiver, though I'd rather have it

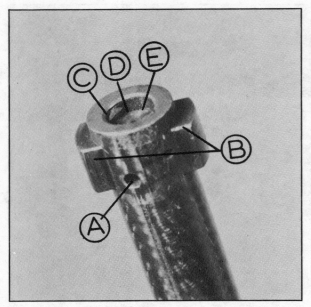

Remington 722 (.222 Remington caliber) bolt head showing: (A) gas-vent hole, (B) twin solid locking lugs, (C) extractor, (D) recessed bolt face, (E) ejector.

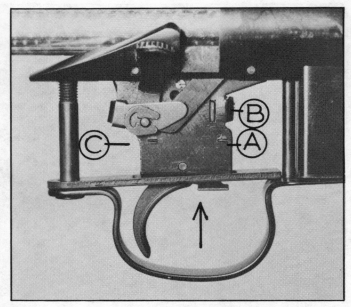

The 721-722 trigger mechanism, showing the location of: (A) weight-of-pull adjustment screw, (B) trigger-stop (over-travel) screw, (C) sear-engagement adjustment screw (see text for details). Arrow points to bolt-stop release.

as a separate piece welded on to the receiver as in the Model 2000 Mauser. A round-bottomed receiver does tend to cause stock splitting if the guard screws are tightened too much, but the use of a glass bedding compound in bedding the action in the stock takes care of this minor complaint.

Many shooters also dislike the stamped trigger guard/floorplate and follower, but they were necessary if Remington was to keep the price down. I never minded these stamped parts myself; the trigger guard/floorplate is heavy enough and shaped so as to be both as rugged and as good looking as can be expected from a stamping. Not long after these rifles came out demand for a hinged floorplate magazine induced Griffin & Howe to make such a guard/magazine for a number of years. Later Remington made a de luxe version of the 721-722, designated the 725, which was made with a hinged floorplate magazine. This magazine could be installed in the 721-722 with a minimum of trouble.

There are a couple of things this action does not have which I think it should. There is one gas-vent hole in the bolt head and one through the right side of the receiver ring, but when the action is closed and locked the vent hole in the bolt is toward the left, where there is no hole in the receiver. I'd like a gas-vent hole through the left of the receiver, in line with the hole in the bolt. I would also have insisted that the bolt sleeve have a small flange on its left side to cover the locking-lug raceway, even with the additional vent hole in the left side of the ring.

I never really liked the very small spring clip extractor, although I never experienced any trouble with it in any of the 721s and 722s I owned or fired. I have had customers bring these rifles in with

a fired case stuck in the chamber, and chunks bit out of the rim by the extractor when the bolt was forced open. In most instances it was a rusted chamber which caused the case to stick, and few extractors in such situations would have pulled the cases out. The point I want to make, however, is that while the bolt head is recessed to fully enclose the head of the cartridge case, the rim of the case is not actually supported in any way. This is because the inside of the rim of the bolt face recess is cut out for the extractor, and cut out deeper than the thickness of the extractor, so that there is enough room for the extractor to move as it snaps over a case rim on closing the bolt. With this type of extractor design there is no way in which the cartridge rim can be supported.

I recall two instances that illustrate what this means. I had fitted a heavy Hart stainless-steel barrel on a 722 action for a friend of mine, chambering it for the .222 Remington cartridge. My friend then sleeved the action and built a bench rest rifle. He was very fussy and a very careful handloader, weighing the powder charges out and putting each charge in a small glass vial so he could quickly and easily reload cases during a match. His most accurate load was not a hot one, and everything went along normally. After firing a couple of hundred rounds of this load, which gave less than ½ minute-of-angle accuracy, one case let go; a lot of powder gases escaped through the rear of the action, spewing his face with gas and brass. Opening the bolt extracted the case easily enough, but it would not eject —nor could the case be removed from the bolt head. He tried twisting the case out with a pair of pliers and, when this didn't work, he used a vise. Failing with this, he brought the bolt to me; I had to use a

lathe and boring tool to turn the head of the case out of the bolt face recess. Expansion of the case against the extractor had broken it, but other than this and the trouble involved, the action was not harmed.

In the second incident the shooter claimed that the cartridge which put his 722 out of order was a factory load. Again it was a .222, and he told me it was mighty fortunate he'd been wearing shooting glasses. The trouble may have been due to a faulty case, but the head of that case had expanded so tightly into the extractor groove that the entire rim around the recess was expanded, so that he could hardly turn the bolt and open it. A gunsmith had bored out the remains of the case head, but the head of the bolt had expanded to such a degree that a new extractor would not fit properly. In this instance, had the bolt head not been recessed within the face of the barrel, the rim of the bolt head might have split. The owner of the rifle then returned it to the factory, where they fitted a new bolt at no charge.

I have never observed or heard of this happening with any of the larger calibers. Apparently the larger cases are stronger, and can take more pressure. It is also a good thing that the heads of the belted magnum cases are strong and seldom expand, for in the 721 there is very little metal in the rim of the bolt-head recess.

A mechanical aspect of this action which I've always been skeptical about is the fastening of the cocking piece to the firing pin by a single small pin. It must be OK, though, for I've never seen or heard of this pin shearing. I've never hesitated to snap or dry fire any of the many centerfire bolt action rifles I have owned, including these Remingtons, and I have yet to see that this has done any harm.

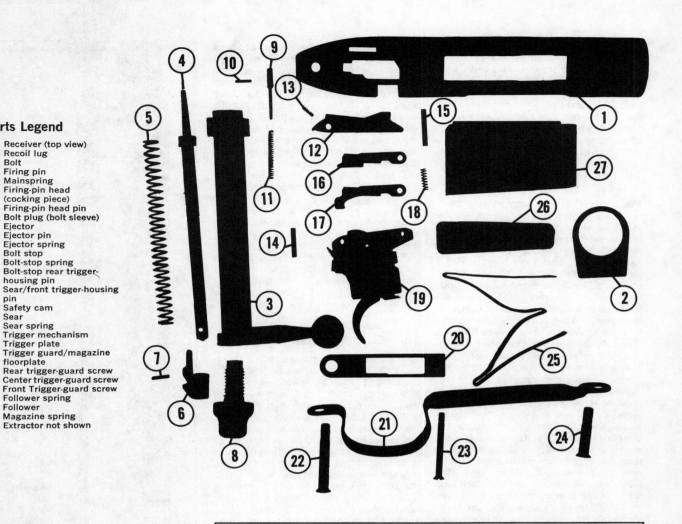

Parts Legend

1. Receiver (top view)
2. Recoil lug
3. Bolt
4. Firing pin
5. Mainspring
6. Firing-pin head (cocking piece)
7. Firing-pin head pin
8. Bolt plug (bolt sleeve)
9. Ejector
10. Ejector pin
11. Ejector spring
12. Bolt stop
13. Bolt-stop spring
14. Bolt-stop rear trigger-housing pin
15. Sear/front trigger-housing pin
16. Safety cam
17. Sear
18. Sear spring
19. Trigger mechanism
20. Trigger plate
21. Trigger guard/magazine floorplate
22. Rear trigger-guard screw
23. Center trigger-guard screw
24. Front Trigger-guard screw
25. Follower spring
26. Follower
27. Magazine spring
    Extractor not shown

Dimensional Specifications

	721	722
Weight	43 oz.	40 oz.
Receiver length	8.750"	8.00"
Receiver ring dia.	1.360"	1.360"
Bolt dia.	.700"	.700"
Striker travel	.285"	.285"
Bolt travel	4.50"	4.00"
(300 H&H)	4.850"	
Guard-screw spacing	7.25"	6.50"
Magazine length	3.350"	2.85"
(Magnum)	3.700"	
Bolt face recess:		
depth	.145"	
dia ....(.222 size)	.385"	
(.30-06)	.480"	
(Magnum)	.540"	

Remington Model 721 & 722 Actions
General Specifications

Type	Turnbolt repeater.
Receiver	Machined from bar-stock steel. One-piece construction except recoil lug is a separate part held between the barrel and receiver. Non-slotted bridge. Tapped for scope mounts and receiver sight.
Bolt	Three-piece construction with low-profile handle brazed on the rear of the body, and the bolt head with dual-opposed locking lugs brazed into the front end. Base of handle acts as safety lug.
Ignition	One-piece firing pin powered by coil mainspring. Cocks on opening.
Magazine	Non-detachable staggered-column 4-shot box type (3-shot for magnum cartridges.) One-piece stamped steel trigger guard and floorplate.
Bolt stop	Pivoting lever type, stops bolt by contacting left locking lug. Release plunger located within guard.
Trigger	Single stage, adjustable for weight-of-pull, take-up and over-travel.
Safety	Pivoting side tang type, locks striker and bolt.
Extractor	Rotating "C" clip spring type, built within the bolt face.
Ejector	Plunger-type built within the bolt head.

The 722 as a Benchrest Action

Almost immediately after the .222 Remington cartridge was introduced it became a favorite with the "benchresters" —target shooters who pit rifles and ammunition against their competitor's by firing from a solid bench and holding the rifles on a rest. This little cartridge soon toppled many previous records, and it is still going strong. These shooters soon discovered, too, that the 722 action was an ideal one on which to build a benchrest rifle. So popular were these actions, that,

for a few years, Remington would sell separate 722 actions to qualified gunsmiths, who would accept the responsibility of fitting a barrel to them. Many benchrest target shooters were amateur or professional gunsmiths, and they soon found that to get the best out of this action a "sleeve" was needed. This could readily be done with the 722 action because of its round receiver. The sleeve, usually made from a piece of seamless steel tubing or heavy-walled steel pipe up to a foot or so in length, was bored or reamed out so that the 722 receiver was

a snug fit inside. The outside of the receiver and the inside of the sleeve were then tinned with solder, and the receiver, up to the bolt-handle notch, was sweated inside one end of the sleeve. At some point, of course, a slot was cut into the sleeve for the trigger housing, and an oblong opening made for the loading port. The barrel was made a bit smaller in diameter than the receiver or the front part of the sleeve (which projected forward of the receiver) was bored out larger than the barrel so that there would be no contact between them. The sleeve was then inletted and glassed into the heavy benchrest stock, being held down with 3 or more screws. Scope mount bases were attached to the top of the sleeve. A sleeve with a wall thickness from 3/16" to 1/4", with the receiver sweated inside, made the receiver a more rigid support for a heavy barrel. It also afforded a perfect means of securing the action and barrel to a stock, and of attaching a scope to the rifle.

Trigger Adjustments

Although the 721-722 trigger mechanism is a rather cheaply made, mass-produced affair with a stamped sheet-metal housing, it is nonetheless reliable. Its 3 screws permit adjustments for weight-of pull, trigger take-up (creep or sear engagement), and over-travel. These screws allow fast factory assembly, so the trigger can be adjusted without any special hand fitting, and also provide some adjustment if the owner wants a lighter or heavier pull. To make any adjustment the barreled action must be removed from the stock. As shown in the illustration, **(A)** locates the weight-of-pull adjustment screw, normally factory set for about 4 pounds. This is usually satisfactory for most shooting, but a lighter pull can be had by turning this screw counterclockwise, or vice versa. The minimum safe pull that can be got is about 2 pounds. Screw **(B)** is the trigger-stop or over-travel adjustment screw, also normally set at the factory to stop the trigger the moment the sear is released. However, it can be re-adjusted thus: with the action cocked, turn this screw in about one turn or so, until pulling the trigger won't release the sear; then, while pulling back on the trigger, turn the screw counterclockwise slowly until the sear is released; it should then be turned further, ever so slightly, so there is ample clearance between sear and trigger when the trigger is pulled; if there is no clearance the sear may not always be released cleanly on pulling the trigger. Screw **(C)** is also adjusted and set at the factory to give a minimum trigger-to-sear engagement for a creep-free let-off, and still have a safe trigger. This screw should *never* be tampered with. To discourage owners from tampering with this screw the factory seals it with wax. However, if it has been tampered with, or the trigger mechanism completely taken apart, the normal adjustment is as follows: turn the screw back (counterclockwise) several turns and close the bolt, leaving the action cocked; then slowly turn this screw in until the sear is released; now turn it back 1/4-turn; adjust the front screw so that it requires a weight of about 3 pounds to release the trigger, and test the action as described elsewhere. If the sear is not released when the bolt is slammed home, then it may be possible to adjust the rear screw to provide less sear engagement; but if the sear is released, it must be backed off further, and/or the weight-of-pull increased.

After making any adjustment, test the trigger thoroughly to make sure it will function properly, and that it is safe. For example, if the trigger-stop screw is ad-

justed the action should be dry-fired several times to make sure the trigger releases the sear cleanly. If it does not, the stop screw **(B)** should be turned out a bit more. After screw **(A)** has been adjusted to obtain a lighter pull, test the action by closing the bolt very smartly several times, checking to see if the striker remains cocked. If the striker does not stay cocked, the trigger pull is too light, and must be made heavier.

Once the factory sealant on the adjustment screws has been broken they usually become quite easy to turn. Therefore, after making any adjustments or after reassembling the trigger, these screws should be sealed again with a drop or two of sealing wax or Loctite.

Finally, if you dislike the Remington trigger or want to replace it, get a Canjar trigger. Precision made, with a full range of adjustments, the Canjar can also be had with a single-set trigger attachment.

Take-Down and Assembly

Make sure the rifle is unloaded. To remove the bolt raise its handle and pull it rearward. Then press upward on the bolt-stop release, located just in front of the trigger, and take the bolt from the receiver.

To disassemble the bolt proceed as follows: grasp the bolt firmly and engage the notch in the firing-pin head over an edge of the workbench; pull the bolt down until a coin can be placed between the bolt sleeve and the firing-pin head to hold the firing pin back; the bolt sleeve can then be turned out of the bolt. If it is necessary to disassemble the firing mechanism further, drive out the small cross pin from the firing-pin head so it can be separated from the firing pin. In driving this pin out, the drift punch will hold the firing-pin head onto the firing pin until the punch is withdrawn. This must be done with caution as the mainspring is very strong. Reassemble in reverse order. To aid in reassembling, drill a 3/16" hole in the side of the workbench in which to insert the firing-pin tip. Finally push the bolt sleeve over the firing pin to compress the mainspring and slip on the firing-pin head, using the drift punch to hold the head in place when the holes are aligned. Then drive in the cross pin, which will push the punch out. Remove the ejector by driving out the small cross pin from the bolt.

A special bent, round-pointed tweezer is required to remove the extractor without damaging it. However, a new extractor can be installed without the use of this tool by carefully pinching the ends of the extractor together until it can be pressed into the bolt-face recess. Be sure to insert the extractor with the sloping side of the extractor hook toward the front.

Remove barrel and action from the stock by turning out the rear, center and front guard screws; lift off the guard, removing follower spring and follower, trigger plate; then lift barrel and action from the stock. The magazine box, which usually remains in the receiver, can then be pulled free. On doing this, note the

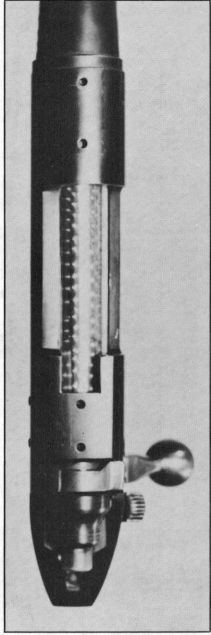

Top view of the 722 action.

position of the box in the receiver so that it can be returned in that position. If the magazine box has a spacer also note its position.

To remove the trigger mechanism and disassemble it proceed as follows: (Caution—this trigger mechanism should not be disassembled unless it has to be repaired or cleaned, and then only if you know how to go about it). Disassembly should be done on a clean workbench, preferably on a white cloth or in a tray; as each part is removed it should be laid down in orderly sequence, so it can be replaced in its proper order and position. Drive out the rear trigger-housing pin, which is also the bolt-stop pin; drop down the rear of the trigger housing, and remove the bolt stop and bolt-stop spring; drive out the front trigger-housing pin,

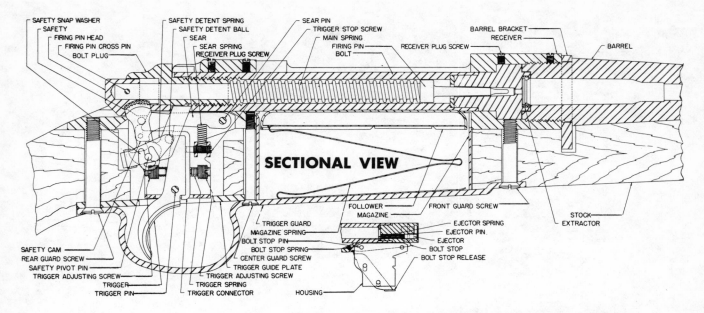

Sectioned action view of the Remington Models 721, 722, 725. The later Model 700, 600 and 660 actions are essentially similar.

which is also the sear pin, and the entire trigger mechanism can be removed from the receiver.

Lift out the sear, safety cam and the sear spring. Push off the safety snap washer from the safety pin and remove the safety-detent spring, safety-detent ball, safety-pivot pin, bolt-stop release and the safety. Be careful not to lose the safety-detent ball bearing. Remove the front and rear trigger-adjustment screws, trigger spring and trigger-stop screw. Drive out the trigger pin and remove trigger and trigger connector.

To reassemble: assemble the trigger connector to the trigger; insert the trigger in the housing and drive in the trigger pin until it is even with the right side of the trigger housing; assemble the trigger spring, front trigger-adjustment screw, rear trigger-adjustment screw and trigger-stop screw (See heading above on trigger adjustments for properly adjusting these screws after the trigger mechanism has been completely assembled and fitted to the receiver.); assemble safety, bolt-stop release, safety-pivot pin, safety-detent ball, safety-detent spring, and safety-pin snap washer; assemble the sear spring, sear and safety cam; assemble trigger housing to the receiver with the sear pin; insert the bolt-stop spring and bolt stop in the receiver and drive the bolt-stop pin in part way; raise up the rear end of the trigger housing until the hole aligns, compress the sear and safety cam, and drive in the bolt-stop pin.

Reassemble the rest of the rifle in reverse order. Turn the front and rear guard screws very tight. If the bolt does not close easily after the rifle has been disassembled and reassembled a few times, and/or if the front guard screw has been tightened over a period of time, this may indicate that the end of this screw is projecting into the receiver and contacting the lower locking lug. In this case, shorten the front guard screw as required.

The barrel is threaded very tightly into the receiver and a special action wrench, as well as a barrel vise, are needed to remove it without damaging the receiver and barrel.

Conclusion

The Remington 721, 722, and the de luxe version of these rifles, the 725, were all discontinued in 1962. A great many of these rifles were made. In years to come many will be offered for sale on the secondhand gun market, and they will become an ever ready source of actions for the amateur and professional gunsmith. If you want a 721 or 722 action, don't waste time looking for a separate action; just look for a used rifle and then strip the rifle for the action. As I have mentioned before in this book, it is usually possible to buy a complete rifle for only a little more than the cost of a separate action alone. It will be a long time before these rifles become collector items, so you need have no concern about stripping the rifle to obtain the action.

The Successors

When the 721, 722 and 725 were discontinued in 1962, Remington brought out the 700 series of high powered rifles. Although the 700s have changed somewhat since that time, their actions, except for the trigger guard and magazine, are still almost identical to the original 721-722 actions. The 700s are still being made in two different lengths, these for medium- and long-length cartridges.

The 700 ADL is made with a blind magazine box, the box inletted into the stock. A black alloy or Nylon trigger guard is used, but there is no magazine floorplate since the magazine box is within the stock. The 700 BDL has a combination trigger guard/magazine box made of an alloy which has a hinged floorplate, with the sheet-metal magazine box fitted between the guard and the receiver. Other than this, the 700 actions are just like the earlier 721-722s, and to give a detailed description of the 700 actions would be to repeat what I have already written about the 721 and 722.

Since 1962, Remington has introduced other rifles and a pistol based on the 722 action. These include the 600 and 660 carbines, and the XP-100 single-shot pistol. All are based on the basic 722 receiver, bolt and trigger mechanism. At this writing, on special order through Remington dealers, 660, 660 Magnum, 700 ADL and 700 BDL barreled actions, in any of the calibers for which Remington chambers these rifles, are available. Separate actions are not available.

Notes

31. Remington Model 788

To offer the sportsman a line of low-cost rifles based on a single turnbolt action, Remington designed and engineered a system that could be used for .22 rimfire cartridges as well as for various centerfire cartridges. Doing this not only facilitated the manufacture of these rifles and held down manufacturing costs, it also enabled the sportsman to buy a rimfire small game rifle and a centerfire varmint and/or big game rifle having similar actions. The entirely new action Remington developed featured multiple rear locking lugs.

Introduced in 1967, the new centerfire rifle was designated the Model 788. It was chambered only for the .222 Remington, .22-250, .30-30 and .44 Magnum cartridges, with the .308 and 6mm added the following year. In 1969 Remington made the 788 available for left-hand operation, but only in .308 and 6mm.

The rifles have a very trim pistol grip stock made of a hardwood finished to look like walnut. The barrels are 24″ long in .222 and .22-250, 22″ long in the other calibers. A post front sight on a ramp is screwed to the barrel, with a screw-adjustable open rear sight fitted over a base rib, the two screwed to the barrel. The rifles weigh about 7 pounds in .44 Magnum, about 7.5 pounds in .222 and .22-250.

Although I do not want to include rimfire bolt actions in this book, it is well to mention the Remington rimfire counterparts to the 788. These are the 580 single shot, the 581 clip repeater, the 582 with tubular magazine, and the 540-X single shot target rifle. All are chambered for the .22 Long Rifle rimfire cartridge, but they'll also handle .22 Shorts and Longs as well. Although lighter in weight (except the 540-X) and smaller in size, the 580 rifles have about the same balance and feel as the 788, with the 581 clip repeater the one most like it. Many hunters find it very desirable to have their centerfire and rimfire rifles based on similar actions

and made nearly alike. When Remington introduced the 788 it did not replace any other existing rifle in their line-up, but with the advent of the 580 rimfires the older 510 and 510-X series (Models 510, 511, 512 and 513) were discontinued.

Reports published on the 788 in the various gun magazines have been enthusiastic. Most of them that I read were very favorable. Almost all of those who tested them found the rifles reliable and accurate. The 788 is undoubtedly the most accurate rifle chambered for the .44 Magnum made today. The 788s in other calibers, including the 6mm, have also proved highly accurate. While the 788 is not much for looks, it performs like a much higher-priced rifle.

The 788 Action

The receiver, machined from a round steel forging, appears to be quite slim, but it is very heavy and rigid. Main wall thickness is slightly over .300″. Because the magazine is a single-column type, and because the ejection port is quite narrow, the receiver is not weakened much by these openings. There is much more metal in the walls of this receiver, on either side of the ejection port, than there is in the 700 Remington receiver. The wall opposite the ejection port is unusually rigid. The receiver is 1.325″ in diameter over its entire length. The magazine well of the 788 in 6mm and .308 is about .635″ wide and about 3.00″ long. The ejection port is about 2.725″ long and .600″ wide. The openings begin at a point about 1.5″ behind the front edge of the receiver. The receiver bridge, which begins at the rear of these openings, is about 2.425″ long. Its length provides a good deal of contact area with the bolt to guide it. It also provides room for the locking-lug recesses. The receivers of the 788 in other calibers vary slightly from the above figures.

The bolt locking lugs are located just over an inch forward of the rear end of

the bolt. There are 9 lugs in all, 3 sets of 3 equally spaced around the bolt body. Each locking lug is about .085″ high and about .150″ thick. Two sets are about .250″ in width, while the third set of 3 is about .350″ wide. These last 3 lugs have the approaching corners angled off so that, on lowering the bolt handle, the bolt is forced fully forward. Three circular grooves, inside the heavy-walled bridge, are divided by milling 3 longitudinal grooves to form the 9 locking-lug shoulders. All of this is done with such precision that all of the lugs bare evenly against the shoulders. With the bridge a solid ring of steel at this point, with two very heavy walls connecting the bridge to the ring, and with the receiver and bolt made of quality alloy steel and properly heat treated, the 788 bolt is locked in the receiver very securely. There is more than enough strength to hold cartridges which develop high breech pressures in the chamber. Locking strength of the 788 action compares favorably to that of the Model 700 Remington, one of the strongest dual-opposed forward locking lug actions made. There is little chance of the 9 locking lugs or the locking shoulders ever shearing off under normal conditions. Incidentally, the total area of the 9 lugs is about .338 square inch, with a locking contact surface of about .191 square inch. The 98 Mauser figures are .493 and .109 respectively. The 3 sets of locking lugs are spaced 120° apart, which results in a bolt rotation of 68°.

The base of the bolt handle is brazed to the bolt body. When the bolt is closed part of this base extends into a deep notch in the side of the receiver, and this could act as a safety lug. The tapered bolt handle stem ends in a pear-shaped hollow grasping ball. The bolt handle will clear a low-mounted scope or one with a very large eyepiece. Primary extraction power

---

Illustrated above: Remington Model 788 rifle.

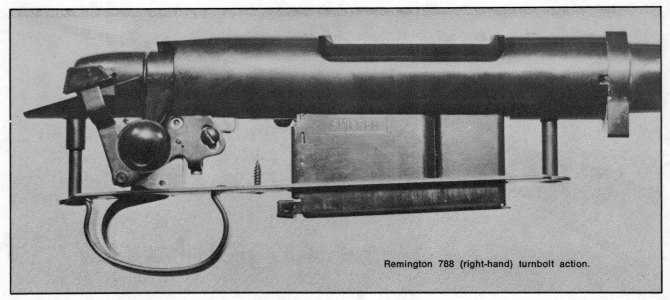

Remington 788 (right-hand) turnbolt action.

is obtained when the bolt handle is raised, its base moving over an inclined surface on the rear of the bridge.

In rimless calibers the 788 bolt is of one-piece construction, the front end counterbored for the cartridge head. The C-spring extractor occupies a groove cut into the rim of this counterbore, and is held in place by a rivet. The ejector, a spring-loaded plunger in the bolt head, is held in place by a small cross pin.

Bolts for rimmed calibers have a separate non-rotating bolt head. A tenon on the rear of this flat-faced bolt head fits into the bolt body, held there by a cross pin which intersects a groove in the tenon. The spring-loaded ejector, located in the bottom of the bolt head, is held in place by a cross pin. This ejector also serves to hold the empty cartridge case against the extractor when the action is opened. The extractor, a long one-piece spring, fits into a slot in the bolt head, its stem extending into the bolt body. The separate bolt head also has a guide pin on its left, which projects into a narrow groove cut into the inside left wall of the receiver. This pin prevents the bolt head from turning when the bolt handle is raised and lowered.

The separate recoil lug is clamped between the barrel and the receiver. The top of this lug extends slightly above the receiver, where it functions as a stop or recoil lug for the scope mount base. The face of the barrel is flat for both rimmed and rimless calibers, although there is a notch cut into the face of the barrel for the extractor of the rimmed cartridge bolt head.

The firing mechanism is simple and well designed. It consists of a one-piece firing pin over which is compressed a coil mainspring between the shoulder on the front of the firing pin and a washer positioned ahead of the firing-pin head (this part is usually called the cocking piece), which is fastened to the rear of the firing pin by a cross pin. The bolt is drilled from the rear to accept the firing mechanism. A hollow cap (called the bolt plug

by the factory, although normally called the bolt sleeve by most everyone else) is threaded into the rear of the bolt. The front end of its threaded stem contacts the washer positioned between the cocking piece and mainspring. This bolt "plug," closed at the rear, would protect the shooter if any powder gases got into the bolt. There are no gas-vent holes in the bolt or receiver. There is a small hole drilled through the side of the bolt sleeve, and a matching hole through the rear of the cocking piece for the insertion of a thin rod when the action is cocked to facilitate removal of the firing mechanism from the bolt. The striker is cocked on the opening of the bolt. The bolt sleeve is prevented from turning when the bolt is open by the nose of the cocking piece resting in a shallow notch in the rear of the bolt. The firing pin and cocking piece are very light; coupled with a very stiff mainspring, lock time is extremely fast.

The trigger/safety/bolt-stop mechanism is built into an aluminum housing, the latter attached to the bottom of the receiver by a cross pin and tightened by a setscrew in the front of the housing. Inside the top rear of the housing is the sear, which projects partially into the cocking-piece raceway in the receiver. Pivoting on a pin in the bottom of the housing is the trigger, which has an arm contacting the sear. A single small coil spring between the sear and the trigger provides tension to both parts. No adjustments are provided, but the normal trigger pull is very short and weight of pull is about 4 pounds. The smooth, well-curved finger-piece of the trigger is properly positioned in the rear of the trigger-guard bow.

The safety pivots on a pin through the bottom of the trigger housing. The large safety button, positioned to the right of the tang above the stock line, is easy and convenient to operate. A spring-loaded plunger in the trigger housing gives the ON and OFF position to the safety. The plunger also locks the trigger when the safety is tipped back, which also locks the bolt. The safety makes very little noise

as it is pushed forward to the OFF or FIRE position, and the safety button is large enough and so shaped that it can be readily moved with a cold or a gloved thumb.

The plunger-type bolt stop, built into the front part of the trigger housing, is a round pin with flattened top. It projects upward into the receiver boltway and into a narrow slot in the bolt. Coil spring around the bolt stop keeps it up. The bolt stop not only halts the rearward travel of the bolt as it contacts the end of the slot, but also guides the bolt and prevents it from turning in the receiver as it is worked back and forth. Part of the sheet-metal safety is bent over to engage a flat spot on the bottom of the bolt stop. Pushing the safety forward as far as it will go depresses the bolt stop so the bolt can be removed.

The trigger-guard bow is a sheet-metal strap, neatly curved to shape. A bent lip on its front end fastens in a hole in the stamped sheet-metal trigger/magazine plate, which the factory calls the floorplate. Guard screws going through the front end of this plate and through the rear of the guard bow hold the barrel and action in the stock. The rear screw, shorter than the front one, threads into a stud attached to the bottom of the receiver tang.

The single-column box magazine, of heavy gauge sheet-steel, is folded to form a box. Its rear top edges, bent slightly inward, form lips to hold the cartridges and follower in the box. The sheet-metal follower has its end bent down to fit inside the box. Below it is a conventional W-shaped follower spring. Magazines for rimless cartridges have ridges pressed into the sides of the box, at the shoulder location of the cartridge it is made for, to hold the cartridges to the rear, thus preventing the bullet points from being damaged when the rifle recoils. Rimmed cartridge magazines have a ridge near the rear end for the rim of the case. This holds all but the top cartridge from sliding forward when the rifle is fired. All magazines for the 6 different cartridges are different, and each one is marked on

Left-side view of the Remington 788 action.

the right side for the cartridge it handles.

A heavy steel bar, screwed to the bottom of the receiver, extends down behind the magazine well. The rear end of the magazine has its walls bent over so that it will slip over this guide bar. A spring release, attached to the rear wall of the magazine box, engages with the bottom of the guide bar to hold the box in place. The magazine box is also guided and held in position by the opening in the trigger/magazine plate and one in the stock. Enough of the box projects below the stock line to let it be easily removed and replaced with two fingers of one hand.

Evaluation

I would much rather evaluate an action or rifle after I have observed it in use for a few years, but in this case I have no hindsight to help me. It must be remembered that the 788 is a low-cost competitive product. In my opinion, however, it is a lot of centerfire rifle for the money.

The only thing I didn't like about the 788 rifle I received was that the barrel/receiver assembly was not properly or sufficiently rinsed after being blued. Bluing salts trapped between the receiver, barrel and recoil lug began "growing" out of these joints. A week after wiping the dried salts off the first time, they had grown again as much as before, seeping out of the joints and the front scope-mount plug screw. There are two notches across the front face of the receiver, for what purpose I do not know, but evidently the salts entered into the barrel-thread area through these notches. It would take considerable rinsing to remove the salt entirely from these confined spaces. The lack of a thorough rinse is also evident by the tacky feel of all of the blued parts of the rifle.

Aside from this, and considering its price, I liked almost everything about this rifle. For hunting game like deer at ranges up to about 150 yards or so, I believe the factory installed sights are entirely adequate. That they are attached with screws

is a good idea for this makes it easy to remove the sights if a scope is to be used, or to install other open sights of another type or make. The idea of providing a recoil lug for the scope mount base, via the recoil lug, is also a good feature. Drilling 8x40 holes in the top of the receiver for scope mount bases instead of the usual and smaller 6x48 holes is also a good idea. I do think another hole ought to have been provided in the bridge for a 4-screw base mounting, or for the installation of a rear target-scope base.

I think the 788 trigger will prove reliable, and I imagine it will satisfy most buyers of this rifle. In time, a fully adjustable commercial trigger may become available for it. This is one rifle that has a safety of adequate size and, so-shaped that it can be positively operated. The action has no separate cocking indicator, but the safety can serve in its place since it can only be moved if the action is cocked. Harnessing the bolt stop to the safety is also a good design idea. As for the bolt stop, I'd like it better if it were larger in diameter, or preferably flattened, which would present more contact area with the bolt-stop slot in the bolt. It wouldn't hurt if this slot were also a bit deeper.

The rimless cartridge extractor doesn't seem very substantial; I think Remington might have done better here by copying the Model 700 extractor. The rimmed cartridge extractor seems good.

I have no objection to the 788's rear-locking-lug system. I see no chance of the thick-walled 788 receiver "stretching" when the rifle is fired; that complaint about such actions is often voiced but has little validity. I don't think the handloader will be in any way limited because of the rear locking lugs.

The magazine is well made, and the arrangement to guide it and hold it in place is good. It is about as easy to insert and remove as any detachable-box magazine rifle I know of, and it can be done with one hand. The only drawback is that magazines will be lost, and there will be

a demand for them long after the 788 is obsolete. I don't particularly like the sheet-metal trigger guard and plate, but for the price one can't ask for more.

I would like to have seen one or two small gas-vent holes in the bolt, either exposed in the ejection port or directed downward into the magazine opening.

All in all, I think it is quite a rifle for the money. At this writing the right-hand 788 is $89.95, the left-hand model $94.95. Separate 788 actions are not available, but the right-hand barreled action in any caliber lists at $73; the left-handed one $77.50. Since Remington barrels are excellent, these barreled actions are good value for the money.

Gunsmithing

The amateur gunsmith will find the 788 a prime object for remodeling and refinishing. Here are some of the things that can be done: the outside metal surfaces can be given a higher polish and reblued; the bolt can be polished and jeweled; the screwed-on sights can be replaced with other sights, or one or both entirely removed; a receiver sight can be installed. A top-mount hunting-type scope can be installed or a target-type varmint scope. In this case the front target-scope base can be placed on the barrel instead of the original rear sight as the screw holes are correctly spaced. One or two holes, however, will have to be tapped in the bridge for the rear target-scope base. The barrel can be shortened to make a carbine out of the rifle. The factory stock can be dolled up, reshaped and refinished to individual tastes. If open sights are to be used the Monte Carlo comb should be cut down. If the barrel is shortened, the fore-end can also be shortened and thinned. Otherwise a plastic or dark-colored wood fore-end tip could be added, as well as a pistol grip cap. The fore-end and pistol grip can be checkered or carved. Several stock firms make several different styles of semi-finished stocks for this rifle so that it can be easily restocked with a piece

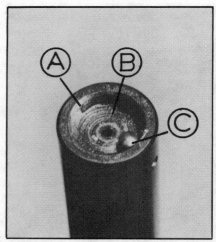

Bolt head of the 788 made for rimless cartridges showing: (A) extractor lip, (B) bolt-face recess, (C) ejector.

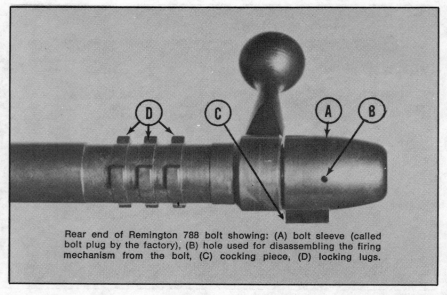

Rear end of Remington 788 bolt showing: (A) bolt sleeve (called bolt plug by the factory), (B) hole used for disassembling the firing mechanism from the bolt, (C) cocking piece, (D) locking lugs.

of wood to your liking. Whether the original factory stock is used or a new stock fitted, I recommend glass-bedding the area around the recoil lug, including the receiver area forward of the magazine to a point about 2″ forward of the barrel lug.

Rechambering & Rebarreling

Most rechambering is no longer practical, but even so it is still being done. Since I have not had the opportunity to examine all of the different calibered 788 factory rifles, I'm not sure about all of the rechambering possibilities at this time.

Two main factors will limit the rechambering and rebarreling possibilities of the 788: 1) the bolt face and extractor of the rimless cartridge bolt cannot be readily changed to accept a cartridge of a head size different from that for which the bolt was made; 2) the magazines cannot readily be altered or lengthened, so the cartridge for which the rifle is to be rechambered or rebarreled must fit the magazine of that rifle—unless the rifle is to be used as a single shot.

Beginning with the 788 in .222, let's see what the possibilities are. The magazine will handle the longer .222 Magnum and .223 Remington cartridges and, since these rounds have the same head size as the .222, this rifle can be rechambered to either the .222 Magnum or .223. The action can also be rebarreled to any wildcat cartridge based on these cases.

There are no rechambering possibilities with the 788 in .22-250. The barrel could be rebored for the 6mm International, but if the magazine is to be used the bullets must be seated deep enough so that loaded cartridges can be inserted therein. This magazine is too short for the .250-3000 Savage cartridge.

The 788 in 6mm could be rechambered for one of the so-called "improved" or sharp-shoulder versions of this cartridge, but I don't consider this practical for the small gain. Some of these, too, may require the barrel to be set back, and the expense of having this done, plus the cost of loading dies, certainly outweighs any improved results one could expect from such a cartridge. The 6mm magazine will handle the .257 Roberts cartridge, so the action could be rebarreled to this caliber.

The .284 Winchester cartridge will just enter this magazine, but it is such a close fit that feeding may not be reliable if the 6mm barrel is rechambered and rebored for it, or the action fitted with a barrel in this caliber.

The magazine of the 788 in .308 will handle .243 and .250-3000 cartridges, and these are about the only rebarreling possibilities. The .358 cartridge binds in the .308 magazine, so reboring or rebarreling to this caliber is not recommended.

The 788 .30-30 offers the most opportunities for rechambering and rebarreling. This rifle would be OK for rechambering to the .30-30 Ackley Improved cartridge. This magazine also handles the following cartridges: .219 Donaldson Wasp; .219 Zipper; .22 Savage Hi-Power; .219 Improved Zipper; .22 Savage Hi-Power Improved; .25-35; .25-35 Improved; 6mm Micro-Flite; .22/.30-30; 6mm/.30-30; .32 Special and .32-40. It won't quite accept the .38-55 cartridge, but except for this, the 788 in .30-30 can be rebarreled to any of these cartridges.

Nothing much can be done with the 788 chambered for the .44 Magnum. One

Dimensional Specifications

Weight (approx.)	40 oz.
Length	8.59″
Receiver dia.	1.325″
Bolt dia.	.700″
Bolt travel	3.220″
Striker travel	.300″
Bolt-face recess:	
depth	.145″
(rimless calibers only)	
Guard-screw spacing	7.062″
Magazine length (inside)	
(.44 Magnum)	1.725″
(.222 Cal.)	2.315″
(.22-250)	2.410″
(.30-30)	2.570″
(6mm & .308)	2.875″

NOTE: Model 788 actions in different calibers do not all have the same specifications as shown above, which were taken from a 6mm action. The .44 Magnum action is a bit shorter and lighter, and actions in other calibers have different bolt travels.

Remington Model 788
General Specifications

Type	Turnbolt repeater.
Receiver	One-piece round steel with non-slotted bridge. Separate recoil lug clamped between receiver and barrel. Tapped for top scope mounts and receiver sights.
Bolt	One-piece for rimless calibers, 2 piece for rimmed. Low-profile bolt handle brazed to body. 9 rear locking lugs. Handle can serve as safety locking lug.
Ignition	One-piece firing pin powered by coil mainspring. Cocks on opening.
Magazine	Detachable single-column 4-shot box type in .222 caliber, 3-shot in other calibers.
Trigger	Non-adjustable single-stage.
Safety	Pivoting side-tang type locks trigger and bolt when tipped back.
Extractor	C-type fitted into bolt-face recess for rimless calibers; long spring-hook type for rimmed calibers.
Ejector	Plunger-type in bolt head.
Bolt stop	Plunger-type into trigger housing fits a slot cut into bolt body. Bolt stop is depressed to release bolt by pushing safety forward.

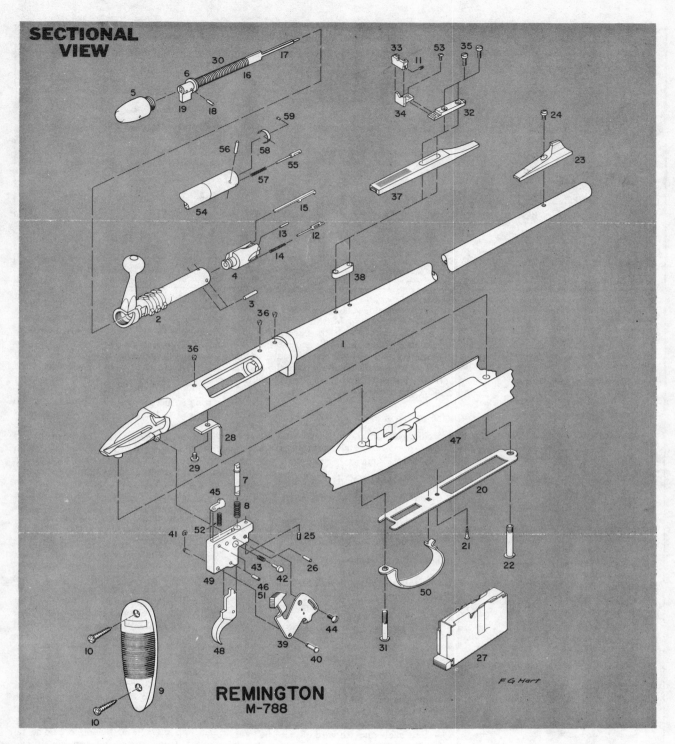

SECTIONAL VIEW

REMINGTON
M-788

F G Hart

Remington Model 788 Parts Legend

1. Barrel assembly (includes barrel, barrel bracket, receiver assembly)
2. Bolt assembly (includes bolt body and bolt handle)
3. Bolt-assembly pin
4. Bolt head assembly (includes bolt head and bolt-head guide pin)
5. Bolt plug
6. Bolt-plug washer
7. Bolt stop
8. Bolt-stop spring
9. Buttplate
10. Buttplate screw
11. Elevation screw
12. Ejector
13. Ejector pin
14. Ejector spring
15. Extractor
16. Firing-pin assembly (includes bolt-plug washer, firing-pin, firing-pin cross pin, firing-pin head, mainspirng)
17. Firing pin
18. Firing-pin cross pin
19. Firing-pin head
20. Floorplate
21. Floorplate screw
22. Front guard screw
23. Front sight
24. Front sight screw
25. Housing-lock screw
26. Housing pin
27. Magazine assembly (includes magazine, magazine release, magazine-release button, magazine follower, magazine spring)
28. Magazine-guide bar
29. Magazine-guide bar screw
30. Mainspring
31. Rear guard screw
32. Rear sight base
33. Rear sight eyepiece
34. Rear sight leaf
35. Rear sight screw
36. Receiver-plug screw
37. Rib (rear sight)
38. Rib spacer (rear sight)
39. Safety assembly (includes safety and safety button)
40. Safety pivot pin
41. Safety pivot-pin retaining washer
42. Safety plunger
43. Safety-plunger spring
44. Safety-retaining screw
45. Sear
46. Sear pin
47. Stock assembly (includes buttplate, buttplate screws (2), stock)
48. Trigger
49. Trigger housing
50. Trigger guard
51. Trigger pin
52. Trigger spring
53. Windage screw

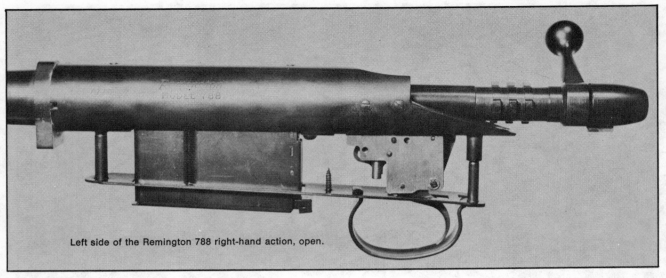

Left side of the Remington 788 right-hand action, open.

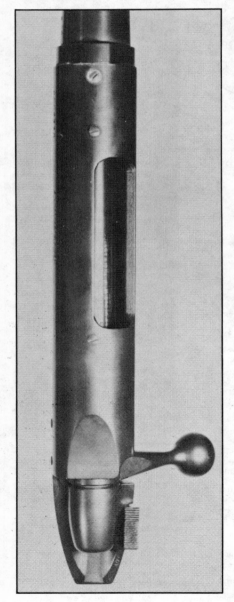

Top view of the right-hand 788 action.

thing is certain, it is not suitable for conversion to the .444 Marlin cartridge. For whatever it is worth, however, the .44 Magnum magazine will accept the .45 Long Colt cartridge. Thus, if you tired of the .44 Magnum you could have the barrel rebored or the action rebarreled to the .45 Long Colt.

Markings

Stamped on the receiver wall in two lines, opposite the ejection port is:

REMINGTON
MODEL 788

In one line, the following is stamped on the barrel:

REMINGTON ARMS CO. INC.,
ILION, N.Y.   MADE IN U.S.A.

The caliber designation is also stamped on the barrel. Various inspection marks are stamped on both sides of the breech end of the barrel, including the Remington proof mark—the letters **REP** within the oval. The serial number is stamped on the left side of the receiver ring.

Take-Down and Assembly

Remove the magazine by grasping the bottom of it between thumb and forefinger, depress the magazine release and pull the magazine from the action. If magazine is loaded, remove cartridges by sliding each one forward. Raise the bolt handle, pull bolt back as far as it will go, push the safety fully forward and the bolt can be pulled from the receiver. The bolt for rimless cartridges can be replaced by merely pushing it back into the receiver. To replace the bolt for rimmed cartridges, first align the ejector with the bolt-stop slot and, holding the bolt so the guide pin in the bolt head is to the left, insert the bolt into the receiver.

To disassemble the bolt proceed as follows: with the bolt in the receiver, locked with the handle down and cocked, insert a close fitting pin, drift or Allen wrench through both holes in the bolt

sleeve **(5)**. Raise bolt handle, remove bolt from receiver, then unscrew bolt sleeve from bolt. To disassemble the firing mechanism further, rest firing-pin tip on the workbench, press down on bolt sleeve and pull out the pin from bolt sleeve. With a drift punch drive out pin **(18)** from cocking piece **(19)**. The mainspring is quite strong so be careful when pulling out the punch after the pin is removed. Reassemble in reverse order. In reassembling the firing mechanism in the bolt, turn it in as far as it will go, remove the pin, then turn the bolt sleeve back until the cocking cam rests in the shallow notch on the rear of the bolt. The bolt can then be inserted into the receiver if firing pin and cocking piece are down (in fired position). In this case use a square-edged tool and pull the cocking piece back, turning the bolt sleeve at the same time until the cocking piece rests in the shallow notch.

The bolt head **(4)** of the rimmed cartridge bolt can be removed by driving out the bolt body cross pin **(3)** and pulling bolt head from the bolt body. This will release the long extractor **(15)**. The ejector of both bolt types can be removed by driving out the ejector pin. Do not remove the rimless extractor except to replace a broken one. Remove it by driving out the extractor pin.

To remove barrel and action from the stock first take out magazine, then turn out front and rear guard screws. Turn out wood screw **(21)** from trigger guard/magazine plate **(20)** and the plate can be removed from stock. To remove trigger mechanism loosen lock screw **(25)** in front of housing and drive out trigger-housing pin **(26)**. Do not disassemble trigger mechanism unless really necessary, and then with care. The barrel is screwed very tightly into the receiver, and it should not be removed unless you have the proper barrel vise and action wrench to do it.

To disassemble magazine press rear of follower down far enough so the front end slips out, then pull follower out. In reassembling, the ends of the follower spring should be toward the front of the magazine box.

32. Savage Model 110 Old and New

THE SAVAGE Arms Corp., formerly of Utica, N.Y. produced several centerfire turnbolt rifles before they introduced the Model 110 Savage early in 1958. These rifles were:

1) The Model 1920 Hi-Power. This was a very lightweight sporting rifle based on a short Mauser-type bolt action with dual-opposed forward locking lugs and a staggered-column non-detachable magazine. Made in .250-3000 and .300 Savage, it was produced from 1920 to about 1929. This very interesting rifle is scarce today because they were not very popular.

2) The Savage Models 40 and 45 Sporters. These were rifles in higher-powered calibers based on an action with locking lugs on a sleeve at the rear of the bolt. They were chambered for the .250-3000, .30-30, .300 Savage and .30-06. They had a detachable single-column 4-shot box magazine, and were made from about 1928 to 1940. Never very popular, they're seldom seen today.

3) The Models 23B, C and D. Introduced in 1933, the 23B was chambered for the .25-20 repeater cartridge, the 23C for the .32-20 and the 23D for the .22 Hornet. Alike except for caliber, these rifles had 25″ barrels, with the receiver an integral part of the barrel. The dual locking lugs were part of a sleeve on the center of the bolt. The bolt handle was also attached to this sleeve. The detachable single-column box magazine held 5 cartridges. The 23B was discontinued about 1945, the 23C and 23D about 1947. Of the 3, the 23D was by far the most popular. There was also the 19H, merely a target type version of the 23D. The 19H, chambered for the .22 Hornet, was made from about 1933 to 1945.

4) The Savage Model 340. Included in this group are the Savage 342, Stevens 322, 325 and the Springfield 840. The first to be introduced was the 325 Stevens in 1948, while the 340 Savage, and its Stevens-Springfield counterparts, are still being made today. These rifles were at vari-

ous times made for the .22 Hornet, .30-30, .222 Remington and .225 Winchester calibers. The Model 340 is now made in .222, .225 and .30-30 calibers only. These were, and are, all low-cost rifles with detachable single-column box magazines. The receiver has a slotted bridge. The bolt is made with a single locking lug up front and another locking lug at the rear, similar to the Krag-Jorgensen action. Because of their low cost these rifles are quite popular.

Since the individual actions were never available separately for any of these obsolete Savage and Stevens centerfire bolt action rifles, and since the action of the 340 Savage and its Stevens counterpart is not now available, these actions will not be covered further in this book.

The Model 110 Savage

Early in 1958 Savage introduced the Model 110 (pronounced "One-ten"), a high power bolt action sporting rifle. Not an unusual rifle as far as the entire rifle was concerned, but inside this action are several features never used before in a bolt action, elements which make this action quite different from any other described in this book. Aside from the several new features, the action is still a "Mauser-type," having a bolt with forward dual-opposed locking lugs and a staggered-column box magazine.

While the Savage 110 action is of novel design and construction, this in itself was not sufficient to induce me to include the action in this book. I'll cover them because these actions are available to the gunsmithing trade.

When, around 1962, Savage announced that they'd make the actions available separately, it was good news for the amateur and professional gunsmith. But what really made this headline news was the offering of two lengths of actions, and that barreled actions, in both lengths, would be available. However, the biggest news was

that separate and barreled actions, in both lengths, would be available in right- or left-hand versions. Nothing like this had ever before been offered—nor even now —at a moderate price.

At this writing, here are the Savage offerings in the Model 110 line of actions and barreled actions:

Actions

110-RA, Right-hand medium-length action only, $64.45

110-RA, Right-hand long-length action only, $64.45

110-RA, Right-hand long action for magnum calibers, $64.45

110-KA, Left-hand action only, same lengths as above, $69.55

Barreled Actions

110-R, Right-hand medium-length barreled action, $89.00

110-R, Right-hand long-length barreled action, $89.00

110-R, Right-hand long-length magnum barreled action, $99.65

110-K, Left-hand medium- or long-barreled action, standard calibers, $93.00

110-K, Left-hand long magnum barreled action, $103.65

(Barreled actions are available in the following calibers: medium-length action—.22-250, .243 and .308; long-length action—.270 and .30-06; long magnum action—.264 Magnum, 7mm Magnum, .300 Magnum and .338 Magnum.)

Since 1958 Savage has offered various models and styles of sporting rifles based on the 110 action. For information on their currently-offered rifles, write to Savage Arms Corp. for their catalog, since it is my intention to discuss only the action.

Illustrated above: Savage 110 MC rifle.

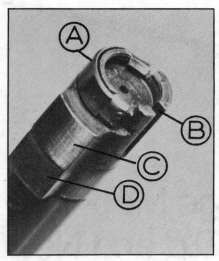

Bolt head of the Savage 110 showing: (A) original C-spring extractor, (B) ejector slot, (C) right locking lug, (D) front baffle.

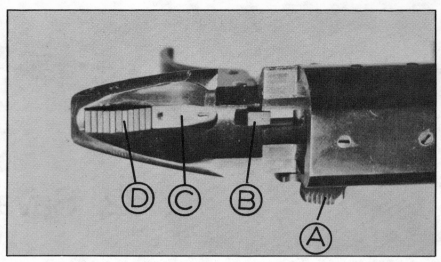

Top view of the rear end of the Savage 110 receiver showing: (A) sear (this part also functions as the bolt stop and cocking indicator), (B) bolt-lock stud (part of the safety), (C) trigger-adjustment-screw cover, (D) safety button.

For several years now Savage has been the U.S. distributor for certain models of rifles produced by J.G. Anschutz GmbH in Ulm/Donau, West Germany. These rifles, in various .22 rimfire sporting and match versions, are sold as Savage/Anschutz rifles. Interestingly, Anschutz also makes a "Continental" type of sporting rifle based on the American-made Savage 110 action; these are listed in the Waffen-Frankonia catalog (a large German sporting goods outlet and manufacturer in Wuerzburg) as the Anschutz-Savage repeating rifle. Made for the European sportsman, it has the regular long right-hand 110 action, but fitted with a German-styled stock and double-set triggers. The stock has a slightly raised Monte Carlo comb, a full pistol grip, and a slim tapered fore-end ending with a schnabel. It has a thick white-line recoil pad, a pistol grip cap with a white spacer, and narrow German-type sling swivels screwed into the stock. This rifle is available in the new 5.6x57 and in the older 7x64 calibers.

This undoubtedly means that the barrels are made in Germany and that Anschutz used only the 110 action, substituting their well-made double-set trigger mechanism and trigger guard for the same parts made by Savage.

The Model 110 Action

The Savage 110 action was designed by the late Nicholas Brewer, who also designed the Savage 340 action. There were several high-power bolt action rifles on the market then, but all were quite difficult to manufacture and therefore rather high priced. For Savage to achieve success in this field, it was necessary that their rifle be made economically enough to let its sale price be lower than similar rifles already available, and yet design an action equal to, or better than, those of other rifles. It is assumed that Brewer was instructed to design the 110 action so that different action lengths could be made easily; it could be made with a left-

hand bolt as well, and be as strong and as safe, or more so, than any bolt action rifle on the market. Brewer did all these things, in the opinion of many firearms experts. In addition, Brewer's action is reliable, easy to operate and easy to disassemble.

The receiver, of chrome-molybdenum steel, probably started out as a piece of seamless tubing. Its front is threaded for the barrel shank, the center milled out to accept the bolt and openings made for the magazine and loading port. The top of the receiver ring and bridge are tapped for scope mount bases, the side of the bridge tapped for a receiver sight.

The receiver ring is about 1.6″ long. The 110 bridge, about 1.5″ long, is longer than in most centerfire turnbolt actions; this extra length gives good support to the bolt when it is drawn back, so that there is a minimum of play or wobble at the end of the bolt. The loading/ejection port is slightly over 3.25″ long on the medium action, about 3.75″ on the long action.

The loading port of most Mauser-type

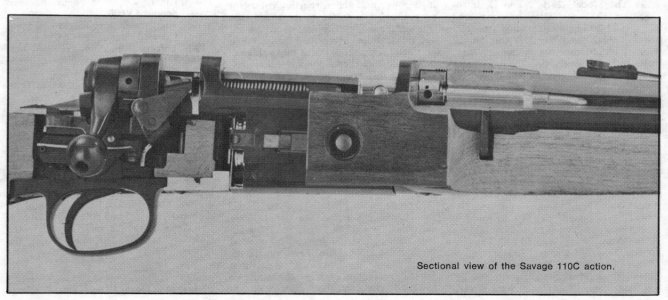

Sectional view of the Savage 110C action.

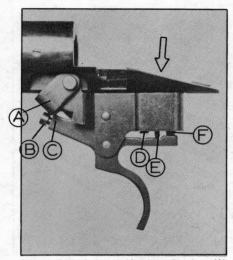

Savage 110 trigger mechanism showing: (A) sear, (B) sear-engagement adjustment screw, (C) sear end of trigger, (D) trigger-stop adjustment screw, (E) trigger-spring plunger (directly under the pull weight adjustment screw, as indicated by arrow), (F) safety stop. See text for complete details on how to adjust this trigger.

turnbolt actions has the right receiver wall cut down to the bottom of the locking-lug raceway, that is, well below the centerline of the bolt. This leaves little metal along the right side of the receiver, next to the loading port. However, flat-bottom receivers made from forgings, such as the M98 Mauser, the 03 Springfield and the M70 Winchester, have the low-cut right wall reinforced at the bottom by the extra metal which forms the flat bottom and magazine support box. Receivers made from round stock lack this extra metal at the bottom, and certain receivers (like the 721 and 722 Remingtons) have only a very thin right wall, if this wall is cut down to the bottom of the lug raceway. On the 110 Savage, however, the wall opposite the high wall is cut down only to the centerline of the bolt. This leaves a reinforcing strip of metal along the locking lug raceway, greatly strengthening the

action, and makes the receiver more rigid and helps guide the bolt. This extra strip of metal on the low wall is an excellent idea. Incidentally, the low right wall of the Ruger 77 receiver is made the same way.

The breech system is unique and good. The 110 barrel has no reinforced shoulder; instead, about 1.5" of the barrel breech is threaded, and screwed onto this is a contoured lock nut. The breech face of the barrel is counterbored for about .250", and into this goes the head of the bolt. The bolt head is also recessed about .135" deep for the cartridge head. The recoil lug, a .150" thick steel stamping is positioned over the barrel shank, between the receiver and barrel lock nut. After the barrel has been chambered and finished it is turned into the receiver. With the bolt in place in the receiver, and a minimum headspace gauge in the chamber, the barrel is turned into the receiver until snug, and then the lock nut is turned tight. This secures the barrel in the receiver and the recoil lug between the receiver and collar. This type of barrel fitting provides an easy and positive way to obtain minimum headspace, and the recessed bolt head and barrel breech completely seal the cartridge in the chamber. The recoil lug is ample to prevent barrel and action set-back in the stock from recoil. The bottom front of the receiver is notched for a projection pressed into one side of the recoil lug; this aligns the lug with the receiver, preventing it from turning when the barrel lock nut is tightened.

The Bolt

The bolt and striker assembly is made of many parts. At first glance it all seems very complicated, but the bolt and striker are made this way for easy mass production and assembly.

All parts are of steel, many of them investment castings. The bolt body is a tube with the cocking-cam notch recess milled into it. The separate bolt head,

with its solid opposed locking lugs, fits into the front end of the bolt body. The C-type spring-clip extractor is fitted over the rim of the bolt head recess on the extreme front end of the bolt head. Lips on the inside ends of the extractor engage grooves cut into each side of the bolt head; these prevent the extractor from being pulled off of the bolt head on extracting a cartridge. When the bolt is closed the extractor is fully within the recess in the barrel face, although there is enough room for the hook end of the extractor to snap over a cartridge rim on closing the bolt. (In 1966 Savage introduced the Model 110C, which has the extractor built into the front face of the bottom locking lug; it is almost an exact copy of the post-1964 Model 70 Winchester extractor.) The ejector is also a spring-loaded plunger built into the bolt head. The 110C locking lugs extend to the very face of the bolt head, which is recessed for the cartridge head, necessitating that the breech end of the barrel be made flat, not recessed. This extractor/ejector system is better than the earlier C-spring system. The new bolt head's retainer-pin hole is drilled at a 90° angle from the old bolt. I have been told by Savage that they now intend to make all 110 actions with this newest locking-lug extractor and ejector. The 110C action also has the detachable box magazine. Up to the time of this writing, at least, separate 110C actions or barreled actions have not been made available.

A clever gas-escape baffle is used on the 110 bolt. A steel piece, shaped much like the locking lugs, is positioned at the rear of the bolt head, between it and the bolt body. A spring-steel friction washer, between this baffle and the bolt body, tensions the baffle. The bolt head and baffle are held in place on the bolt by a retainer pin running through the front of the bolt body. A hole through this pin allows the firing pin to pass; with the firing pin assembled in the bolt this pin cannot be removed. When the bolt is closed and locked, the baffle virtually

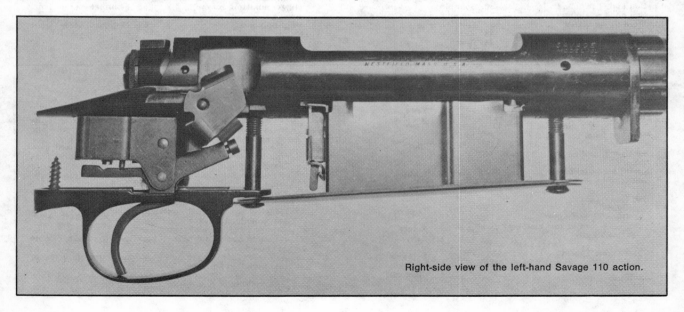

Right-side view of the left-hand Savage 110 action.

Savage Model 110

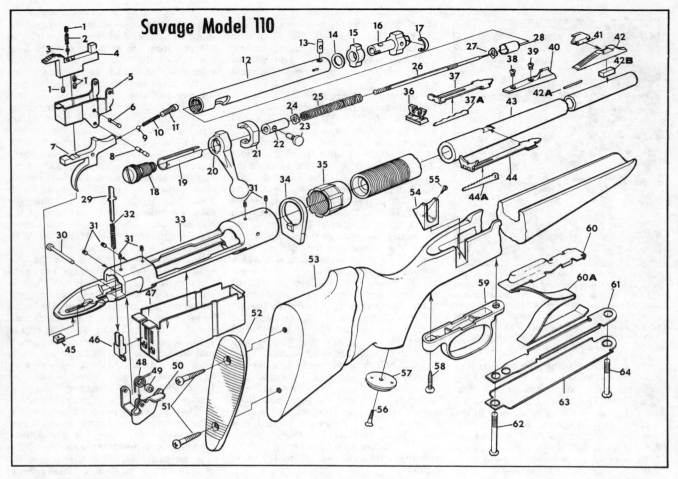

Parts Legend

1. Trigger-pull adjusting screw
2. Trigger spring
3. Trigger-spring plunger
4. Safety
5. Trigger bracket
6. Safety-bearing pin
7. Trigger
8. Trigger pin
9. Steel ball, 5/32"
10. Trigger-pin retaining screw
11. Trigger-engagement adjusting screw
12. Bolt body
13. Bolt-head retaining pin
14. Front-baffle friction washer
15. Front baffle
16. Bolt head
17. Extractor
18. Bolt-assembly screw
19. Cocking-piece sleeve
20. Bolt handle
21. Rear baffle ocmplete
22. Cocking piece
23. Cocking-piece pin
24. Cocking-piece lock washer
25. Mainspring
26. Firing pin
27. Firing-pin stop-nut lock washer
28. Firing-pin stop nut
29. Ejector
30. Sear pin
31. Dummy screw
32. Ejector spring
33. Receiver
34. Recoil lug
35. Barrel-lock nut
36. Rear sight
37. Rear sight and step-high
37A. Rear-sight step
38. Front-sight screw, short
39. Front-sight screw, long
40. Front sight an dscrew
41. Front sight
42. Front sight and base assembly complete
42A. Front-sight pin
42B. Front-sight dovetail block
43. Barrel
44. Rear sight and step
44A. Rear-sight step
45. Trigger-adjusting screw cover
46. Magazine latch
47. Magazine box
48. Sear spring
49. Sear bushing
50. Sear
51. Buttplate screw
52. Buttplate
53. Stock (Monte Carlo)
54. Bolt-handle slot liner
55. Bolt-handle slot-liner screw
56. Pistol-grip cap screw
57. Pistol-grip cap
58. Trigger-guard screw
59. Trigger guard
60. Magazine follower
60A. Magazine spring
61. Floorplate insert
62. Floorplate screw, rear
63. Floorplate
64. Floorplate screw, front

Dimensional Specifications

Weight (Medium-length action) 41 oz.
    (Long action) .... 43 oz.
Receiver length .... 8.750"
    (long action) .... 9.25"
Receiver ring dia. .... 1.380"
Bolt dia. .... .695"
Striker travel (approx.) .... .275"
Bolt travel .... 4.00"
    (long action) .... 4.50"
Bolt-face recess:
    Depth .... .135"
    Dia. ....(standard caliber) .475"
    (magnum caliber) .535"
Magazine length .... 2.85"
    (long action) .... 3.40"
Guard-screw spacing .... 4.525"
    (long action) .... 5.025"

Savage Model 110
General Specifications

Type..Turnbolt repeater.
Receiver..One-piece machine steel. The recoil lug is a separate part. Non-slotted bridge. Tapped for scope mounts and receiver sights.
Bolt...Multi-piece with separate bolt head. Dual-opposed locking lugs on the bolt head, the bolt handle serving as safety lug.
Ignition...One-piece firing pin with detachable cocking piece powered by a coil mainspring. Cocks on opening.
Magazine......................................Non-detachable staggered-column 4-shot box type for standard calibers; 3-shot for magnum.
Trigger..Single-stage type adjustable for pull weight, sear engagement and over-travel.
Safety..Sliding tang type locks trigger and bolt.
Extractor.......................................Rotating spring-clip type on bolt head. (See text for note on new extractor.)
Bolt stop.......................................The sear acts as the bolt stop, contacting right lug of the front bolt baffle.
Ejector..Plunger type positioned at rear of magazine box. (See text for note on new ejector.)

Savage Model 110C

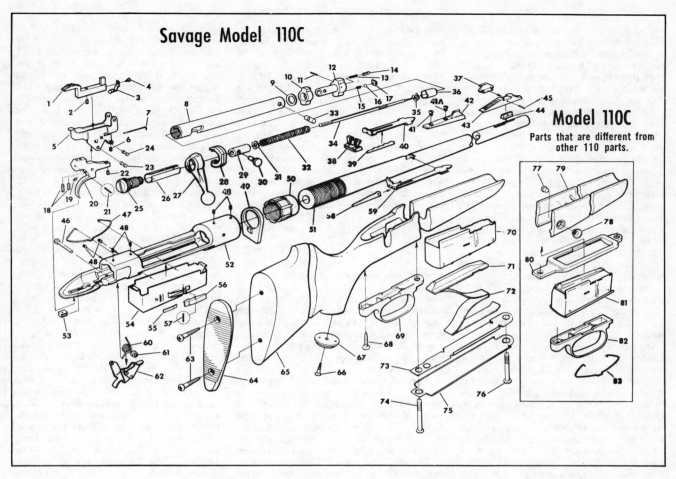

Model 110C
Parts that are different from other 110 parts.

Parts Legend

1. Safety
2. Trigger-pull adjusting screw
3. Safety-detent spring
4. Safety-detent spring screw
5. Trigger bracket
6. Trigger-pull adjusting screw
7. Trigger-pull adjusting spring
8. Bolt body
9. Front-baffle friction washer
10. Front baffle
11. Ejector-retaining pin
12. Bolt head
13. Ejector spring
14. Ejector
15. Extractor spring
16. Steel ball
17. Extractor
18. Trigger-travel adjusting screw

19. Trigger-pin retaining screw
20. Trigger
21. Trigger-spring pin
22. Trigger-engagement adjusting screw
23. Trigger pin
24. Safety-bearing pin
25. Bolt-assembly screw
26. Cocking-piece sleeve
27. Bolt handle
28. Rear baffle
29. Cocking piece
30. Cocking-piece pin
31. Cocking-piece lock washer
32. Mainspring
33. Bolt-head retaining pin
34. Firing pin
35. Firing-pin stop-nut lock washer
36. Firing-pin stop nut
37. Front sight
38. Rear sight (folding)
39. Rear-sight step
40. Rear sight
41. Front-sight screw (short)

41A. Front-sight screw (long)
42. Front sight
43. Front sight and base assembly
44. Front-sight dovetail block
45. Front-sight pin
46. Recoil lug
47. Magazine-retainer spring
48. Dummy screw
49. Recoil lug
50. Barrel lock nut
51. Barrel
52. Receiver
53. Trigger-pull adjusting screw
54. Magazine guide
55. Magazine-latch spring
56. Magazine latch
57. Magazine-latch pin
58. Rear-sight step
59. Rear-sight step
60. Sear spring
61. Sear bushing
62. Sear
63. Buttplate screw

64. Buttplate
65. Stock complete
66. Pistol-grip cap screw
67. Pistol-grip cap
68. Trigger-guard screw
69. Trigger guard
70. Magazine box
71. Magazine follower
72. Magazine box
73. Floorplate insert
74. Floorplate screw, rear
75. Floorplate
76. Floorplate screw, front
77. Magazine-latch button*
78. Escutcheon*
79. Stock complete*
80. Floorplate*
81. Magazine assembly*
82. Trigger guard*
83. Magazine ejector spring*

*Model 110C parts that differ from other 110 parts.

seals off the locking lug raceways in the receiver ring so that escaping gases cannot rush rearward. A large gas-vent hole in the side of the bolt head, and two holes (one in each side of the receiver ring), one of them opposite the bolt head hole, allow all gases to escape harmlessly. The baffle also prevents dirt from entering the open locking-lug raceway, and also serves as a bolt guide when the bolt is opened. This baffle arrangement can be used because the bolt head is detachable. I see no disadvantage in the detachable bolt head.

The bolt handle is also made as a separate part, its base encircling the rear end

of the bolt body. Two projections on the end of the bolt body, fitting matching grooves inside the bolt collar, prevent the bolt handle from turning on the bolt. A solid knurled-headed screw, called the bolt-assembly screw, threads into the rear end of the bolt, holding the bolt handle in place and sealing the bolt. Three ball-bearing plungers under the head of this bolt-assembly screw and notches in the rear of the bolt-handle base, keep the screw from loosening once it has been turned tight. The low-profile bolt handle will clear the eyepiece of a low-mounted scope. The slightly hollowed grasping ball has a knurled ring around it.

Another baffle is fitted on the rear of a bolt body. It is a steel collar, which partly encircles the bolt body, positioned just forward of the bolt-handle base. A ball-bearing plunger holds it in place during the operation of the bolt. It is intended to seal off the two locking-lug raceways at the rear of the receiver, preventing the entrance of foreign material and deflecting any gases that might enter the locking-lug raceway. An inclined projection on one end of the baffle, and a matching inclined surface on the bolt handle base, imparts the initial extractor camming power to the bolt as the handle is raised.

The two lugs, engaging behind shoulders inside the heavy receiver ring, securely lock the cartridge inside the chamber. The root of the bolt handle, engaging a deep notch cut into the tang, serves as the third or auxiliary safety lug.

If the bolt is unique, so is the striker assembly. The one-piece firing pin is very light. The threaded front and rear ends of the firing pin body are milled flat for the length of the threads. The firing-pin stop nut is threaded over the front end; in assembling the firing pin in the bolt at the factory the stop nut is rotated until, when it is resting on the rear of the bolt head, the firing-pin tip protrudes .060″. The rear end of this nut is notched, and a toothed washer fitting over the flattened firing-pin body, and held against the stop nut by the tension of the mainspring, keeps the firing pin from turning and maintains a constant adjustment.

On the rear of the firing pin there is another toothed washer, which cannot turn on the firing pin, and a cocking-piece nut which threads on the firing pin; these hold the coil mainspring captive over the firing pin. The firing pin is given forward tension by a thin steel sleeve, called the cocking-pin sleeve, held in the rear of the bolt body between the bolt-assembly screw and the cocking-piece lock washer forward of the cocking-piece nut. This sleeve, notched at front to match the teeth on the washer, is slotted so the cocking-piece pin can be inserted into the cocking piece. Once assembled the cocking piece cannot turn on the firing pin. In assembling, the cocking piece must be adjusted so that the cocking pin clears the bottom of the cocking cam about 1/64″ when the firing pin is in the fired position. If the cocking pin does not clear the bottom of the cam, it or the cocking-piece nut are likely to be damaged when the rifle is fired; if given too much clearance, the rifle might fire before the bolt is fully closed and locked. When the bolt is in the receiver the large round head of the cocking pin lies and moves within the locking-lug raceway opposite the bolt handle.

The 110 trigger assembly, also quite unusual and clever, does not permit entirely satisfactory adjustments. The trigger mechanism, housed in a heavy folded sheet-metal box, is attached to the bottom of the receiver tang by a long pin, the same pin which holds the sear in place. The trigger is pivoted on a pin in the bottom of the trigger housing. A slotted screw, threading into the front end of the trigger, can be adjusted to limit sear engagement. The safety is above the trigger, sliding in the trigger housing and a groove cut into the tang. Three holes are tapped vertically in the safety. The rear hole contains the setscrew which contacts the trigger when the safety is pulled back to the SAFE position. It is normally satisfactorily adjusted at the factory, but to readjust it the trigger must be removed first. The center hole contains a plunger, spring and setscrew, which provides tension to both safety and trigger, and by which limited adjustment for trigger weight-of-

pull can be got. The hole, exposed in the safety slot in the tang, is normally closed by a small spring cover, which must be lifted off before an adjustment can be made. The front hole contains two set-screws, one to lock the other; these are supposed to be the trigger-stop or over-travel adjustment screws. These screws, usually, are adjustable only from the bottom after removing the trigger, but on some rifles this hole is accessible from the top. A projection on the upper front part of the safety extends into the bolt-way; when the safety is pulled back or engaged this projection moves back into a notch in the base of the bolt handle and locks the bolt. For instructions on how to adjust this trigger see the heading "Trigger Adjustment."

(In 1966, Savage introduced the Model 110C rifle with a detachable box magazine. A new and improved trigger mechanism was also introduced with the 110C and most likely separate 110 actions and barreled actions will be furnished with this trigger. It has more precise adjustments [see the exploded view drawings] but at this writing I haven't had an opportunity to take one apart for detailed study.)

The 110 sear, a marvel of ingenuity, serves a 3-fold function: as sear, bolt stop and cocking indicator. It is a folded piece of tool steel positioned around the front of the trigger housing, pivoting on the pin which holds the housing in place. It is tensioned by a wire spring to keep it forward. One end of this sear, projecting through a slot cut into the bottom of the right locking-lug raceway in the bridge, stops the rearward travel of the bolt by contacting the lug on the front baffle; on closing, the bolt holds the cocking pin back to cock the action. The front end of the trigger, contacting the bottom of the U-shaped sear, holds the sear from

pivoting when the action is cocked. Pulling the trigger releases the sear from the pressure put on it by the cocking pin, allowing the latter to move forward. An adjustment screw on the front end of the trigger limits the trigger/sear engagement. Turning this screw in (clockwise) reduces the sear engagement. The stock has to be removed to make this adjustment. A serrated thumbpiece or button on the right side of the sear projects over the stock line, along the side of the bridge. After pulling the trigger and depressing this button, the sear is pivoted back so the bolt can be removed from the receiver. Cocking the action raises this button; on firing the rifle the button pivots downward, so it also serves as a cocking indicator which can be seen and felt.

The ejector is a plunger fitted to the rear of the magazine box, its flattened end projecting into the receiver. Tensioned by a small coil spring, it's kept in place by a sheet-metal cover held against the magazine box. This cover is called the magazine latch since it also holds the magazine box forward and in place in the receiver. A narrow angled groove is cut into the underside of the bolt head; on opening the bolt the ejector moves into it to flip the cartridge or cartridge case out, up and to one side. The ejector can be easily removed, which may be convenient for the handloader if he prefers to pick the empty cases from the action.

The magazine box is made of a heavy gauge sheet-metal. Its top front and rear edges are bent outward; the box is positioned and held in the magazine-well opening by these lips engaging slots cut into the bottom of the receiver. Cartridges are held in the magazine and guided into the chamber by guide lips milled alongside the magazine-well openings in the receiver.

The cartridges are held in a staggered

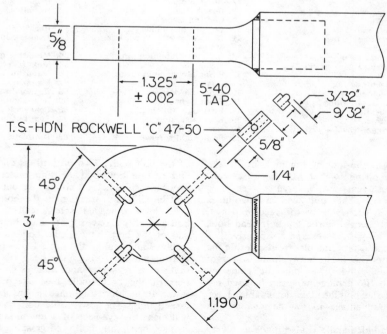

Specifications for making a barrel lock-nut wrench for the Savage 110.

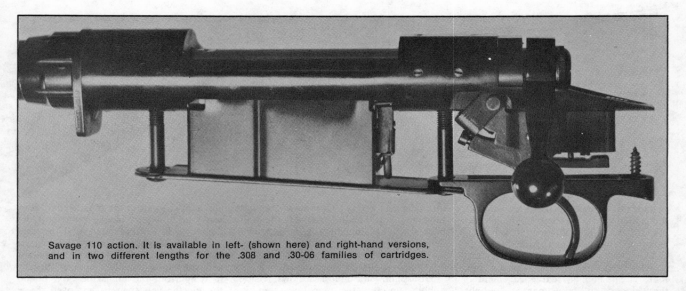

Savage 110 action. It is available in left- (shown here) and right-hand versions, and in two different lengths for the .308 and .30-06 families of cartridges.

position in the magazine box by the stamped-steel magazine follower, which has a rib on its left side. The standard type of W-shaped magazine spring is used. Small vertical ridges, pressed into the sides of the magazine just forward of the cartridge shoulder, hold the cartridges from sliding forward as the rifle recoils, preventing battering of the bullet points. This is a good feature. The magazines in either length action are also made slightly longer than necessary (up to 1/10″), so the handloader can load cartridges to a greater over-all length than factory-loaded cartridges.

The bottom of the magazine is covered by a rounded steel floorplate. Between the two a narrow-ribbed steel insert holds the bottom of the follower spring in place; this prevents undue pressure on the floorplate when the magazine is fully loaded.

The barrel and action assembly is held in the stock by two screws, called floorplate screws. These pass through holes in the ends of the floorplate, the floorplate insert and stock, threading into the receiver in front and rear of the magazine box. The trigger-guard bow, made of a light-weight alloy, is anodized black. The rear floorplate screw goes through a hole in the front end of the trigger guard, while a wood screw holds the rear end in place.

Comments

It should be remembered that the 110 action is made in two lengths, and for either a right- or left-handed shooter. Savage describes these action lengths as Short, Long and Magnum, but there are only two different lengths, best described as the Medium Length 110 and the Long Length 110. The 110 is not made in a true "short" length, say, as compared with the short Sako L-41 action. The medium 110 action handles cartridges of .30-06 head size, whose over-all length is less than 2.80″. The long 110 action, just .750″ longer than the medium-length action, has a magazine long enough to accommodate cartridges of .30-06 length. The so-called "Magnum" action, of the same

length, handles the short belted-head magnum cartridges of .30-06 length, such as the .257 Weatherby, .264 Magnum, 7x61 Sharpe & Hart, 7mm Magnum, et al.

These "3" actions are made for right- or left-hand operation. The left-hand action is not a conversion of the right-hand action, but was originally made that way. Both actions are alike except that some parts, such as the receiver and some bolt parts, are made as mirror images.

No action, of course, will satisfy everyone, and a lot of people find faults with the 110. Some gunsmiths I've talked to like nothing about it. In my opinion it's a very sound action and good value for the money, especially for the left-handed shooter. It certainly is one of the safest turnbolt actions to fire, and there is no question that it is also a very strong action.

The usual criticisms I hear concern the magazine, floorplate, trigger guard, trigger and barrel lock nut. Most people wanting to build a rifle around this action, or those who want to fit a stock to the barreled action, dislike most the alloy trigger guard and the thin stamped floorplate. I'm often asked if a commercial steel trigger guard and hinged floorplate are available for the 110; to the best of my knowledge no such accessory has been made up to now. I have also been asked whether some readily available low-cost steel magazine/trigger guard assembly from some other rifle can be used to replace the original factory parts, and again the answer is "No." Some trigger conscious shooters consider the 110 trigger no good. While there are no commercial replacement triggers available for it, such shooters probably would be dissatisfied with any other trigger. The 110 trigger mechanism is good and it satisfies the demands of most shooters.

As for the barrel lock nut, its use by the factory enables them to keep manufacturing costs down. I dislike the appearance of this sleeve on the barrel of a custom rifle. In fitting a new custom barrel to the 110 action, the lock nut can be discarded, the barrel made with a

shoulder and fitted to the receiver in the same way Remington fits barrels to the 721 and 722 actions. This gives a more pleasing line. The use of the collar also limits the size (diameter) of barrel which can be used. If a barrel larger than 1″ in diameter at the breech is to be used, as in building a target or varmint rifle, the lock nut cannot be used; the barrel must be fitted as in the Remington 721.

A minor objection is the use of a wood screw to hold the rear end of the guard bow in the stock. Some stockmakers discard this screw, using instead a regular long guard screw, tapping a hole for it in the rear end of the receiver, behind the safety. Incidentally, the other guard screws are .250″ in diameter, the thread pitch 28 per inch.

Trigger Adjustments

The accompanying photo shows the various parts of the trigger mechanism. As shipped from the factory the trigger pull is usually quite heavy, often at 5 pounds or more. The location of the trigger weight-of-pull adjustment screw is indicated by the arrow, just forward of the safety button. The thin spring-steel cover can be lifted out with a small wire hook or with a penknife. Before doing this, remove the bolt and pull the safety back. Turning the adjustment screw counterclockwise reduces the pull weight. Only limited adjustment is possible, for turning the screw out too far interferes with operation of the safety. After adjustment, replace the spring cover and test the safety. If it is hard to move forward the adjustment screw has been turned out too far.

Even with the screw turned out as far as possible, trigger pull may still be too heavy to suit many shooters. However, the pull can be made lighter and shorter by adjusting the sear-engagement screw **(B)**. To do this, the barreled action must be removed from the stock. To further lighten the pull, turn this screw in (clockwise). This is best done with a penknife. The lightest pull obtainable is around 3.5

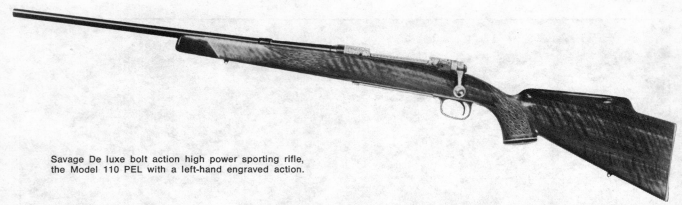

Savage De luxe bolt action high power sporting rifle, the Model 110 PEL with a left-hand engraved action.

pounds. After making these adjustments, the action must be tested to make sure the trigger will hold the striker back everytime the bolt is closed. Make the test by closing the bolt very smartly several times; if the striker falls at any time there is not enough sear engagement or the weight-of-pull adjustment is too light.

If screw (B) has been turned in too much the safety-stop screw (F) may be too far out to allow the safety to be pulled back. In this case, it is necessary to remove the trigger by driving out the trigger pin, and then turning in the safety-stop screw. After reassembling, test the trigger and safety to make sure the trigger cannot be pulled back when the safety is engaged.

Although a trigger stop adjustment is provided (2 setscrews at D), it will be found that the safety-stop also functions as the trigger stop. It is possible, however, to adjust the trigger-stop screws to halt trigger movement the moment the sear breaks. On some 110s this can be done from the top of the safety after removing the adjustment-screw cover, provided two holes are visible. If only one hole is visible, adjustment has to be made underneath, after removing the trigger. In any case, it is hardly worth the bother to make this adjustment since the safety-stop screw does the same thing.

Markings

Model 110 serial numbers are stamped on the receiver ring and etched on the bottom of the bolt. The word **SAVAGE**, and the model designation, e.g., **MODEL 110L**, are also stamped on the receiver ring. Stamped on the receiver wall is:

— SAVAGE ARMS —
WESTFIELD, MASS. U.S.A.

On 110 rifles and barreled actions the caliber designation is stamped on the barrel, along with the Savage proof mark, the letters **SP** within an oval.

The words **PROOF TESTED** are also stamped on the barrel, which means that the rifle was proof tested after the barrel was fitted with regular proof loads (blue-pills) which develop much higher pressures than the commercial loads for any of the cartridges for which this rifle is chambered.

Take-Down and Assembly

Check to see that the chamber and magazine are empty. To remove the bolt raise the bolt handle and pull the bolt back while holding the trigger back and depressing the cocking indicator button. To replace the bolt the trigger must be held back as the bolt is inserted.

Disassemble the bolt as follows: Using a coin, unscrew the rear bolt-assembly screw. The cocking-piece sleeve will come out with it, and it need not be removed from this screw, although it can be spread apart with a screwdriver blade and removed. The bolt handle and the rear baffle can be pulled off the bolt's rear end. Pull out the cocking-piece pin. The firing pin and mainspring assembly can then be dropped out of the bolt. The cocking piece can now be unscrewed from the firing pin, and the cocking-piece lock washer, mainspring and firing-pin-stop lock washer can be removed from the firing pin. The firing-pin stop can also be unscrewed from the front of the firing pin. Unless necessary, the firing-pin-stop lock washer and the firing-pin stop should not be removed. If the firing-pin stop is removed or turned, the stop must be adjusted on reassembly so that the firing pin protrudes about .055″ to .060″ from the face of the bolt head. Reassemble the other parts in reverse order. In reassembling the cocking piece it must be so-adjusted that, when the firing pin is down (in the fired position) the cocking-piece pin clears the notch in the cocking cam by 1/64″. Before the bolt can be inserted into the receiver the firing pin must be cocked. This can be done by pressing the cocking pin against the edge of a workbench and moving it to the cocked position, or by unscrewing the bolt-assembly screw and re-positioning the cocking-piece pin to the cocked position, then turning the bolt-assembly screw back into place.

With the firing pin assembly removed from the bolt, the bolt-head assembly can be removed by pushing out the bolt-head retainer pin with the firing-pin tip. The bolt head can then be pulled off and the front-baffle friction washer and baffle removed. The extractor can be slipped off of the bolt head by lifting up the end opposite the hook until it can be slipped past the bolt head. Reassemble in reverse order. In reassembling the bolt head the ejector slot must be at the bottom.

Remove front and rear floorplate screws, then remove floorplate, floorplate insert, magazine spring and follower from the bottom of the stock, and lift out barrel and action. Remove the trigger-guard bow screw and the bow can be removed from the stock. Reassemble in reverse order.

Remove the magazine by pressing its latch (this part also covers the ejector and spring) toward the receiver, tipping it away from the magazine box; it and the ejector can then be removed. Slide the magazine box to the rear, lifting its front end away from the receiver so it can be pulled forward again and removed. Reassemble in reverse order.

Remove the trigger assembly by pushing out the sear pin, from right to left, then pull the front of the trigger housing away from the receiver until its rear end is unlocked, letting the entire assembly be lifted free. In doing this, and if the rest of the trigger mechanism is to be disassembled, carefully note the position of all parts so they can be correctly assembled again.

The barrel lock nut, set-up very tightly against the recoil lug and receiver, holds the barrel locked in the receiver. To remove the barrel a special wrench (see accompanying drawing) is needed to loosen the lock nut, if the latter is not to be damaged. Once the lock nut is loose the barrel is easily removed.

Savage Model 110 Operation

To load: open the bolt and place a cartridge on the follower; with the thumb push it down and to the rear, into the magazine, until it is retained there; insert additional cartridges in the same manner; with the magazine full, a single cartridge can be slipped into the chamber and, while holding the cartridges down into the magazine so the bolt can pass over them, the bolt closed. The rifle is now ready to be fired by pulling the trigger.

Safety operation: to place the safety on SAFE, slide it back with the thumb; in this position the trigger and bolt are locked. To fire the rifle slide the safety forward as far as it will go, when the letter **F** will show behind the safety button.

Unloading: the chamber and magazine can be unloaded with the safety ON. To do this first slide the safety forward and raise the bolt handle; now slide the safety back to the SAFE position; open and fully close the bolt until the last cartridge has been ejected from the magazine. Always keep the muzzle pointed in a safe direction when loading and unloading the rifle.

33. The Mathieu Left-Hand Action

As a right-handed shooter I never was much interested in left-handed bolt action rifles until the time came when I was forced to change sides; that is, to begin shooting from the left shoulder because of failing sight in my right eye. I then began to understand the problems southpaw shooters faced, and for the first time I realized that there was truly a need for left-hand bolt action rifles. Mossberg had come out with a line of .22 rimfire bolt action rifles during the late 1930s, but it appears now that there was not too much demand for them; they were soon discontinued. Perhaps the first specialty gunmaker to turn out a high-powered turnbolt rifle was R.F. Sedgley of Philadelphia. He is supposed to have made up a few left-hand rifles on the 1903 Springfield, although I have never seen one or ever talked to anyone who has seen one. In the August, 1940, issue of *The American Rifleman* mention is made that Stoeger could also furnish a left-hand Mauser action, but I fail to find any verification of this in any of my Stoeger catalogs, which date back to the mid-1930s.

In the August, 1949, issue of *The American Rifleman* there is a photo of a left-hand 98 Mauser conversion done by Roy Gradle. This was accomplished by fitting a geared bolt handle on the front left side of the bolt sleeve, pivoting it on the bolt sleeve lock, and meshing it with gears cut into the rear of the bolt body. It probably worked, but to me it looks like a flimsy arrangement. Another gunsmith, still in business at this writing, began specializing in converting 721 and 722 Remington actions for left-hand operation. He is Dale M. Guise of Gardners, Pa.

All of these, as well as some others, were conversions of existing right-hand actions; they were not honest-to-gosh left-hand actions. This situation was changed when Mathieu Arms Co. of Oakland, Calif., introduced a quality "true" left-hand turnbolt action around 1950. It was a custom made action, ex-

pensive, and delivery on it was slow, but it was a true lefty action, and a good one.

It was seldom advertised and little has been written about it or its maker. I cannot find it mentioned even once in any of my many gun books, and only once in the last 20 years in *The American Rifleman*. But word got around that it was a good action. It probably received the most publicity from Weatherby, who used it for building those fine Weatherby Magnum rifles for their left-handed customers before the Mark V Weatherby action was introduced in 1958.

Mathieu actions, barreled actions and complete rifles stocked by Fajen were listed in the 1961 Reinhart Fajen, Inc., catalog. The standard action for .30-06 length cartridges listed at $162.50, the magnum at $175.00. Barreled actions were $211.45, while the Fajen-stocked rifle was $277.50.

This is all the information that I have been able to dig up on the Mathieu action. A letter of inquiry to the Mathieu Arms Company was not answered prior to completing this book, so I don't know about their present status. However, when word got out that I was doing a book on centerfire turnbolt actions, I was loaned a magnum Mathieu action by my good friend Dean Miller, the custom gunsmith from St. Onge, South Dakota. Here follows a description of it.

The Mathieu Action

The Mathieu receiver was machined from a solid piece of steel. While not a copy of any other receiver, it does have features of some other actions, which indicate that Mathieu was thoroughly familiar with various turnbolt actions. For example, the barrel shank threads are the same as those in the 1917 Enfield action, the bridge is shaped like that of the 721 Remington,

the bolt-stop housing resembles the cutoff housing on the 1903 Springfield, and the over-all general lines of the receiver, including its recoil lug, flat bottom and tang, are not unlike the 70 Winchester receiver. The 1.5" long receiver ring is round on top, flat on the bottom, with the recoil lug an integral part of this ring. The loading port is about 3.640" long, its right (unnotched) wall enclosing the right locking-lug raceway. The left wall is cut down to the bottom of the left locking-lug raceway. The bridge, about 1.625" long with a flattened, but slightly rounded top, is about 1/16" lower than the ring. The receiver ends with a well rounded tang.

Rearward from the recoil lug, to the rear of the bridge, the bottom of the receiver is flat. The magazine opening is milled out of this flat surface, leaving cartridge guide lips on each side. The extra metal left on the receiver to form the flat bottom provides the needed metal below the receiver walls to give strength and rigidity to the middle of the action. Extra metal is left under the tang to provide walls for the trigger and sear parts.

An extra lump of metal, left on the right side of the bridge to hold the bolt stop, is machined to form a very graceful housing for the very simple bolt stop. I say "simple" because it is merely a thick, notched washer. A slot is cut through the housing into the locking-lug raceway, the bolt stop positioned in it on a pin lengthwise through the housing. A small setscrew holds this pin in place. A small spring and plunger, positioned in the rear of the housing, contact a groove in the bolt stop. The outside edge of the bolt stop is knurled so that it can be rotated with the thumb, and rotating it so its notch is aligned with the lug raceway allows the bolt to

---

Illustrated above: Mathieu left-hand action.

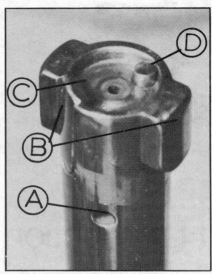

Mathieu bolt head showing: (A) gas-vent hole, (B) dual-opposed locking lugs, (C) extractor and (D) ejector.

be removed. Otherwise the bolt is stopped when the right locking lug contacts the unnotched part of the bolt stop. Although not easily made, the Mathieu bolt stop system is simple, strong and unobtrusive.

The Mathieu bolt body appears to be machined from a solid bar of steel, with the bolt handle base an integral part of the bolt; however, the low-profile bolt handle is welded onto this base. The handle base, by fitting into a deep notch cut into the tang, serves as a safety locking lug. The top part of the bolt handle base has an inclined surface which, contacting a similar cam on the rear of the bridge, provides the initial extractor camming power when the bolt handle is raised.

The dual-opposed locking lugs are on the extreme forward end of the bolt. Neither lug is slotted or drilled, hence not weakened thereby. When the bolt handle is turned down these lugs engage behind ample-sized locking shoulders

within the receiver ring to hold the bolt against the flat-faced barrel. Approaches to the locking-lug shoulders are well-rounded off and, to a lesser extent, so are the locking lugs, thus on lowering the bolt handle the bolt is forced forward about .20". More on this later.

The bolt face is deeply recessed for the cartridge head. The barrel is normally fitted so that when the bolt is closed the front of the bolt comes within .004" of the barrel, thus the cartridge is entirely sealed in the chamber and bolt face recess.

The plunger-type ejector, spring loaded, fits into a hole in the bolt head and is held there by a cross pin. The simple hook-type extractor fits into a groove in the front side of the bolt head; it is held in place, and tensioned by, a spring and plunger set into a hole behind it. The modern Husqvarna Model 8000 action has copied the Mathieu locking, breeching, ejector and extractor systems. Mathieu probably was not the first to use these individual systems, but he probably was one of the first to bring them all together. His system is widely copied today.

There are no gas-vent holes in the receiver ring, but there is a hole in the bolt about an inch back from the bolt face. With the bolt closed this hole appears near the front bottom corner of the loading port. Thus no gases are directed into the right locking-lug raceway, but directly into the open.

Mathieu designed and put together a very interesting firing mechanism, the bolt drilled from the rear to accept it. The square-type threads of the bolt sleeve screw into the rear of the bolt. The cocking piece slides in a recess and slot in the rear part of the bolt sleeve. The rear end of the one-piece firing pin extends into the bolt sleeve and cocking piece, with the coil mainspring compressed over the firing pin and between the bolt sleeve and a shoulder on the front of the firing pin. A groove is cut around the rear end of the firing pin,

over which a split collar is fitted, with the collar in turn recessed into the rear end of the cocking piece. Thus the cocking piece is not solidly attached to the firing pin and the firing pin is free to turn. Forward travel of the firing pin is halted when a shoulder on the front of the pin contacts a shoulder inside the bolt, thus maintaining constant firing-pin protrusion.

A cam notch is cut into the rear of the bolt; on the 90° up-turn of the bolt handle the cam on the cocking piece, which extends into this notch, forces the cocking piece and firing pin (together called the striker) back about .20". Then, after opening and closing the bolt (at which time the cocking cam is placed behind the sear), on lowering the bolt again the striker is cocked another .190" by the action of the bolt being pulled forward as the locking lugs engage the locking shoulders in the receiver. Thus the total striker fall (travel) is about .390". Although the mainspring is very strong and the striker travel short, it takes little effort to raise or lower the bolt handle, at which time cocking occurs.

The left side of the bolt sleeve flares outward to match the top part of the bolt handle (remember, this is a left-hand action) and into this the safety is built. The winged safety lever pivots on a pin held in the bolt sleeve by an Allen head setscrew. A spring and plunger, positioned in another hole in the bolt sleeve, provide ON and OFF tension to the safety, with the plunger also functioning as the bolt lock; when pushed forward it goes into a hole in the rear of the bolt when the safety is tipped up. Also, when tipped up, a cam on the base of the safety is cammed in front of the cocking piece to force it back slightly and hold it back. The safety is low enough to clear the lowest-mounted scope, and its lever is long enough so it is easy and convenient to operate.

The rear part of the bolt sleeve is nicely rounded, with its end threaded,

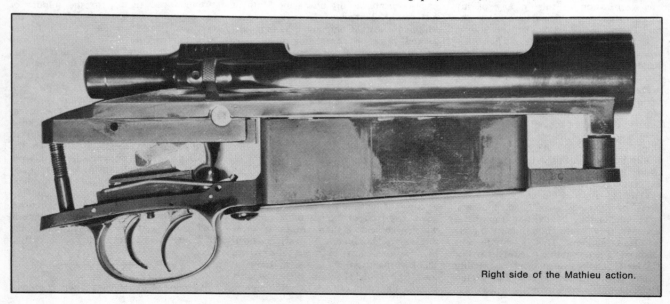

Right side of the Mathieu action.

Parts Legend

1. Receiver (top view)
2. Bolt
3. Mainspring
4. Firing pin
5. Cocking piece
6. Firing-pin collar (2 pieces)
7. Bolt sleeve
8. Bolt-sleeve cap
9. Bolt-sleeve cap-retainer screw
10. Safety
11. Safety pin
12. Safety-pin retainer screw
13. Bolt lock/safety-plunger
14. Bolt lock/safety-plunger spring
15. Bolt lock/safety-plunger, spring retainer screw
16. Bolt stop
17. Bolt-stop pin
18. Bolt-stop pin-retainer screw
19. Bolt-stop plunger-spring screw
20. Bolt-stop plunger spring
21. Bolt-stop plunger
22. Sear (with attached rocker arm)
23. Sear pin
24. Sear spring
25. Trigger guard/magazine
26. Floorplate
27. Floorplate screw
28. Follower spring
29. Follower
30. Front guard screw
31. Rear guard screw
32. Double-set trigger mechanism

Not shown:
    Extractor
    Extractor plunger
    Extractor spring
    Ejector
    Ejector spring
    Ejector retainer pin

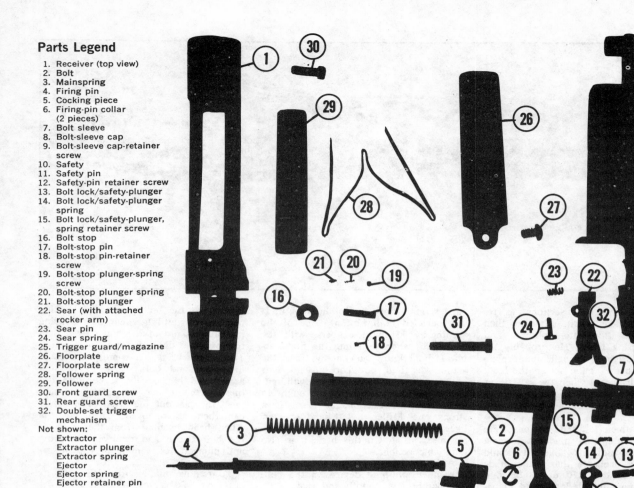

Dimensional Specifications*

Weight	44 oz.
Length	9.00″
Receiver ring dia.	1.307″
Bolt travel	4.950″
Striker travel	.390″
Bolt-face recess:	
Depth	.110″
Guard-screw spacing	8.00″
Magazine length	3.750″

*Mathieu actions were individually made—dimensions may vary. These specifications were taken from an action made for the long belted magnum cartridge.

General Specifications

Type	Turnbolt repeater (left hand).
Receiver	One-piece, machined from solid steel bar stock with integral recoil lug. Non-slotted bridge. Tapped for top scope mounts.
Bolt	One-piece machined steel with dual-opposed solid forward locking lugs. Low-profile bolt handle serves as safety lug.
Ignition	One-piece firing pin powered by coil mainspring. Cocks on up and down movement of the bolt handle.
Magazine	Non-detachable staggered-column 4-shot box type. Detachable floorplate.
Trigger	Commercial single-stage type is usually installed, such as the Jaeger. Anschutz double-set trigger installed on action illustrated.
Safety	Low wing-type built into side of bolt sleeve; when engaged locks striker and bolt.
Extractor	Hook type, built into bolt head.
Ejector	Plunger type, fitted into bolt head.
Bolt stop	Rotary type, built on right receiver wall, stops bolt travel by contacting right locking lug.

over which is screwed a cap. Thus, the bolt sleeve is entirely closed except at the bottom, and no powder gases can escape to the rear. A small setscrew is threaded into the joint between the bolt sleeve and its cap, which prevents the cap from turning.

There is no separate bolt-sleeve lock, as on the 1903 Springfield, but with the nose of the cocking piece resting in a shallow notch in the rear of the bolt, when the bolt is open the bolt sleeve is not easily turned.

So far this action is all, or mostly all "Mathieu." The rest is more or less

"Springfield," which includes the trigger guard/magazine and provisions for a trigger.

The bottom rear of the receiver is machined to accept the regular 1903 Springfield sear and trigger, so any commercial trigger made for the 03 will also fit the Mathieu action. I understand that Mathieu regularly used the Jaeger single-stage trigger in his actions, as the one illustrated here was originally fitted with Jaeger's trigger. This action now has a double-set trigger of modern German (Anschutz) manufacture.

I think the Springfield trigger guard/

magazine unit cannot be beaten for functional reliability or for looks. Probably Mathieu thought the same. At any rate, these units have been readily available in the past. For this reason, as well as the fact that making such a guard/magazine assembly would be about as difficult as making a receiver, Mathieu decided to use this unit. The Mathieu action shown here was made for the long H&H belted Weatherby Magnum cartridge, with a receiver-well opening of 3.750″ in length; the Springfield magazine box was lengthened accordingly by sawing the box in two and

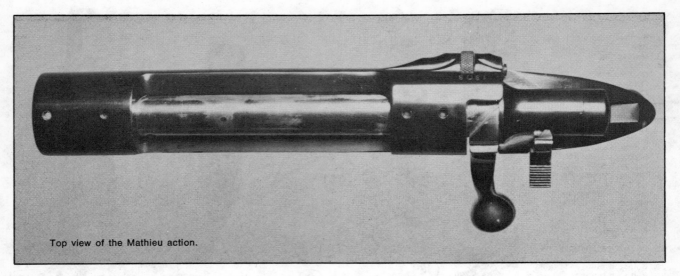

Top view of the Mathieu action.

welding in short wall sections, as required, to make it fit. Mathieu then made a new floorplate, follower and follower spring to fit. He probably retained the original Springfield floorplate latch, but on the action shown the latch had to be discarded when the set trigger mechanism was installed. The plate is now held in place by a round-headed screw.

Since Mathieu left-hand actions were more or less custom made they most certainly are not all alike. It would seem highly probable that if he made an action for the .270 or .30-06 that he'd use an unaltered Springfield magazine and a shorter action. No doubt some design changes were made from the first to his last action. The action shown here is serial numbered **1303** (stamped on the bridge), and I believe it is fairly representative of most of the actions he made.

Comments

I wish I could have examined more than just one Mathieu action, but if I may judge the rest from what I learned about this one, I'd say they are good. This one, certainly, is very well made and, from the very little I've read about other Mathieu actions, they were well made too. This particular action has seen a lot of service, and Dean Miller, its owner, told me he's worn out two

barrels on it since he got hold of it. It was barreled both times to one of the Weatherby Magnum calibers, with the Weatherby shop installing the first barrel. I don't know how many times the action was fired, but there are no signs of heavy use, and it probably will outlast a few more barrels. This ought to prove that this action, at least, is a strong one. Miller, a left-hand shooter, likes this action and never has had any trouble with it. On this basis it is also a reliable action.

Although there is no guide rib or any other anti-bind device on the bolt, its operation is smooth and easy.

Owners of Mathieu left-hand actions, or rifles built on this action, ought to hang on to them because there is no other centerfire turnbolt action quite like it.

Take-Down and Assembly

Make sure the rifle is unloaded. To remove the bolt, tip the safety lever down, rotate the knurled bolt stop clockwise, then raise the bolt handle and pull the bolt from the receiver.

To remove and dismount the firing mechanism unscrew (turn counterclockwise) the bolt sleeve from the bolt. Turn out the small setscrew from the joint between the bolt sleeve and the bolt-sleeve cap, then turn off the cap. Rest the firing pin tip on a smooth hard sur-

face, press the bolt sleeve and cocking piece down until the rear of the firing pin projects out of the bolt sleeve, then remove the divided firing pin collar. This allows firing pin, mainspring, cocking piece and bolt sleeve to be separated. To remove the safety turn out the setscrew under the safety pin and push the pin out the front. The safety can then be removed. Turn out the Allen head bushing from the front of the bolt sleeve and remove the spring and plunger. Reassemble in reverse order.

To remove the ejector, drive out its cross pin. To remove the extractor depress the extractor plunger with the tip of a jeweler's screwdriver, then lift the extractor out.

Turn out the setscrew from the rear of the bolt-stop lug and remove the bolt-stop spring and plunger. Remove the setscrew from the side of the bolt-stop lug, then pull out the bolt-stop pin and bolt stop. Reassemble in reverse order, inserting the bolt stop so the indents are to the rear.

Remove the two guard screws and the barreled action and the trigger guard/magazine can be removed from the stock. The trigger mechanism can then be removed. The barrel is threaded (right-hand threads) very tightly into the receiver; it is not easily removed unless the proper tools are available to do this right.

34. Weatherby Mark V

I DON'T KNOW exactly when I first came across the name of Roy E. Weatherby, but it was in the byline of an article he wrote for one of our popular outdoor magazines in the mid-1940s. At that time I only skimmed over the article, which was about the merits of high-velocity bullets versus slow-moving heavy bullets for hunting. A couple of months later, however, the magazine published some letters critical of Weatherby's article. After reading these I re-read the article and decided to come to the author's defense. I wrote a letter to the editor voicing my support. My letter was not published, but it was forwarded to Weatherby, who promptly acknowledged it and thanked me for siding with him. I was later to learn that, with that article, he touched off a controversy and debate that would be a long time resolving. While there are still many who may disagree, I would say that Weatherby won the decision. Even if he didn't win that argument, he certainly won in every other way. His belief that a light high-velocity bullet has more killing power than a heavy, slow bullet brought him world-wide recognition, respect and wealth.

It was not without a lot of work that he achieved this success. He built his first rifles in a garage, but he now has many others making them for him in one of the world's most up-to-date custom arms factory in South Gate, Calif. His fame derives not so much from his rifles, but from the combination of his very distinctive rifles and their being chambered for a line of magnum cartridges he designed. Ballistics, and especially high-velocity ballistics, were his main interest; that was the theme of his early articles, which appeared in several sporting magazines. He not only knew a lot about ballistics, rifles and hunting, he was also a good writer. Above all, he proved to be a genius at promoting his product—the Weatherby Magnum rifle.

Re-reading Weatherby's article "Back-alley Ballistician," which appeared in the Jan., 1947, issue of *The American Rifleman,* it isn't hard to see why he was successful. This short article gives an insight into his thinking, education, practical knowledge of ballistics and his ability. Since this book is about actions and not about gunmakers, rifles or cartridges, if you want to read more about the Weatherby firm, their rifles and cartridges, I suggest you get the latest Weatherby catalog/book *Tomorrow's Rifles Today*.

After the publicity that resulted from his article, Weatherby began building custom-made rifles, most of them chambered for the .300 Weatherby Magnum cartridge. He used whatever good centerfire turnbolt action he could get, or used the action the customer sent in. These included the 98 Mauser, 1917 Enfield, 70 Winchester and others, including the Schultz & Larsen. Shortly after WW II he began using the FN Mauser actions almost exclusively for the rifles bearing his name. I have read that these actions were especially made for Weatherby by FN, but having seen a number of the early Weatherby rifles built on these actions, I could find nothing "special" about them. All appeared to me to be identical to the FN Mauser actions then being imported by Firearms International, which are described in another chapter.

While FN Mauser actions are good, they were not entirely satisfactory for several of the very hot Weatherby Magnum cartridges, and especially not for the longest cartridges, when the magazine and magazine well had to be made longer and the action weakened in so doing. Weatherby Magnum cartridges were very powerful, and most of them were very hard on both action and barrel. Consequently, while he was developing additional magnum cartridges and experimenting with different barrel steels, he was also looking for a better action. Evidently Weath-

erby decided that if he was to get the action he wanted, he'd have to design it himself, and then have it manufactured. This he did, for in 1958, after having used the FN actions for about a dozen years, he introduced the all-new Weatherby Mark V turnbolt action.

Those riflemen and big game hunters who didn't know before 1958, what the name "Weatherby" meant, quickly learned what it stood for.

Previously, it had stood for extremely high velocity sporting cartridges and expensive custom-made sporting rifles, but afterward it also stood for the world's newest, strongest and safest commercial sporting turnbolt rifle action. Today, of course, the Mark V is no longer the "newest" action, nor is it any stronger and safer than some others now being made, but in 1958, and for a few years afterward, it was exactly that. At that time there was no other turnbolt action quite like it, nor had there been anything made before that was like it. It was designed and built for a specific purpose—to be the strongest and safest, the smoothest in operation and outline possible to make.

Since then a lot has been written about the Weatherby Mark V rifle and action. Even as expert hunters and riflemen disagree sharply on the merits of the Weatherby rifles and the Mark V action. I do not want to get myself involved in this dispute, so I'll describe the action as I see it.

The Mark V Action

The Mark V receiver is made from a one-piece chrome-moly steel forging. After inspection the forging is machined to final dimensions. This probably includes milling, shaping, boring and turning before it is finished. The center of the re-

Illustrated above: Weatherby .300 Magnum Mark V De luxe rifle with 4x Weatherby Imperial scope in Buehler mounts.

ceiver is bored to accept the bolt. The front of the receiver is threaded to take the large barrel shank, its thread diameter 1.160″. The receiver ring is round on top and flat on the bottom. The recoil lug, made as an integral part of the receiver, is positioned just to the rear of the front edge of the receiver. The bottom of the recoil lug, and the flat portion to the rear of it, are the only flat areas on the bottom of the receiver. This seems, however, to be enough area for the receiver to bottom in the stock, and is enough to prevent the stock splitting from a tightly-turned front guard screw. The rest of the receiver is round. The top of the bridge has a different radius and is lower than the ring. The loading/ejection port cut out leaves one wall much higher than the other, depending on whether the action is a right- or left-hand one. Since the Mark V bolt does not have the usual projecting Mauser-type locking lugs, no locking lug raceways are required in the receiver wall. This leaves the high receiver wall very thick, adding to the rigidity of the action.

The Mark V bolt, also of one-piece construction, is machined from a chrome-moly steel forging. The large-diameter bolt (.840″) has the bolt handle on its extreme rear end. The latter is an integral part of the bolt. The base of the bolt handle is quite heavy, but its stem is tapered and slightly sloped back, joining the round and checkered grasping ball. The bolt handle's very low profile will clear the lowest-mounted scope. Initial extraction camming power is obtained on the up-lift of the bolt handle; a sloped surface on the base of the bolt handle moves over a matching surface on the rear of the bridge.

The locking lugs are on the front of the bolt. There are 9 in all, a triple set of 3 to a row. The lugs are formed by reducing the end of the bolt to a smaller diameter, leaving the lugs .360″ high. Six of the lugs are .325″ long, the other 3 about .230″. The interior of the ring, at the rear, has milled-out shoulders for each lug. The ring is not weakened by this milling since the bolt lugs do not project beyond the outside diameter of the bolt body, thus the receiver walls are left thick and solid. The approaching corners of two rows of the lugs are angled off so that, on the down stroke of the bolt handle, the bolt is cammed forward a short distance before it becomes locked in the receiver. There is also a notch in the receiver tang for the bolt handle, which can serve as the safety lug.

The bolt face is counterbored for the cartridge head. The breech end, or face, of the barrel is also counterbored for the head of the bolt—that portion of the bolt head, forward of the first circle of locking lugs, which forms the rim for the cartridge head recess. This rim around the bolt face recess supports the bolt head to fully enclose and effectively seal the cartridge in the chamber.

The Mark V extractor, a small pivoting hook fitting into a groove cut into the bolt head, is held in place by a small cross pin, on which it pivots. It is tensioned by a small coil spring located in a hole under

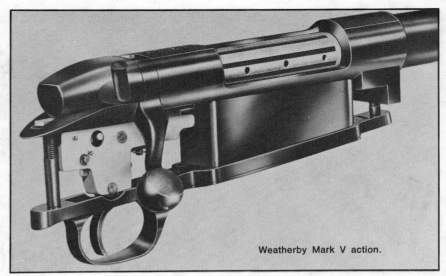

Weatherby Mark V action.

the rear end of the extractor. The front end of the beveled extractor hook, flush with the rim on the bolt head, has enough bevel so that it snaps easily over a cartridge rim when the bolt is closed. The ejector is a plunger, powered by a coil spring, fitted into a hole in the bolt-head face. It is held in place by a small cross pin through the bolt head.

There are 8 evenly-spaced shallow grooves, about ⅛″ wide, milled lengthwise on the bolt body. Evidently the chief purpose of these grooves is to reduce friction between the bolt and receiver. Three ⅛″ gas-vent holes are drilled along the bolt body, so-located that when the action is closed and locked the holes are exposed in the ejection port.

The bolt is drilled from the rear to accept the firing mechanism. This mechanism consists of a one-piece firing pin threaded into the cocking piece, a cocking piece which fits inside the bolt sleeve, a bolt sleeve threaded into the bolt, a coil mainspring, which fits over the firing pin and is compressed between the bolt-sleeve stem and the collar on the front of the firing pin, and a ball bearing, which is fitted into a hole in the bolt-sleeve stem to keep the firing pin from turning.

The one-piece bolt sleeve is entirely closed at the rear. Its top and sides, gently contoured and tapered to the rear, form a very pleasing outline. Only its bottom is open to accept the cocking piece. The cocking piece has a tail extension (as on the post-1964 70 Winchester) which projects back and below the rear end of the bolt sleeve when the action is cocked, providing a cocking indicator. The nose of the cocking piece fits into a cam notch cut into the rear of the bolt, so that on the up-lift of the bolt handle it, and the attached firing pin (together they are called the striker) are cocked. On complete lift-up of the bolt handle the nose of the cocking piece rests in a shallow notch. This prevents the bolt sleeve from being easily turned when the bolt is open.

Proper firing pin tip-protrusion is obtained by turning the firing pin the correct amount in the cocking piece. This adjustment is maintained by a ball bearing

fitted into a hole in the threaded stem of the bolt sleeve. Part of the rear end of the firing-pin stem is milled flat where it contacts the ball bearing; with the ball bearing held down when the bolt sleeve is in place, the firing pin cannot turn.

The safety, built into the side of the bolt sleeve, is a rotary type with a short, serrated lever for its operation. The stem of the safety extends into the bolt sleeve to engage the cocking piece when the safety is tipped back. In a slot cut into the bolt sleeve, in front of the safety, a flat piece of metal serves as the bolt lock. Pivoted on a screw threaded into the bolt sleeve, it is tensioned by a small flat spring attached to it. This spring also serves to hold the safety in place and tension it. When the safety is tipped back it cams the striker back a slight amount and locks it there; at the same time it tips the bolt lock so that the bolt is also locked. When the safety is tipped up and forward a red-colored dot is exposed on the bolt sleeve, indicating that the rifle can be fired.

The trigger mechanism, as well as the bolt stop, is carried in an aluminum and sheet-metal housing, the whole attached to the underside of the receiver by a pin and held tight by a setscrew in the front of the housing. The sear, the front end of which projects into the cocking cam raceway in the receiver, is pivoted on a pin running through the housing, and is tensioned by a small wire spring. Directly underneath it is the trigger, also pivoting on a pin through the housing. Threaded into the front of the housing is the trigger weight-of-pull adjustment screw, with the trigger coil spring positioned between this screw and the trigger. Threaded into the rear of the housing, behind the trigger, is the trigger take-up or sear engagement-adjustment screw.

The bolt stop, a round plunger, fits vertically into a hole in the front part of the trigger housing, its upper end projecting through a hole in the bottom of the receiver. Here its end, projecting into a groove cut into the bolt body, acts to stop the bolt when the end of the groove contacts the bolt stop, to guide and prevent the bolt from turning as the bolt is op-

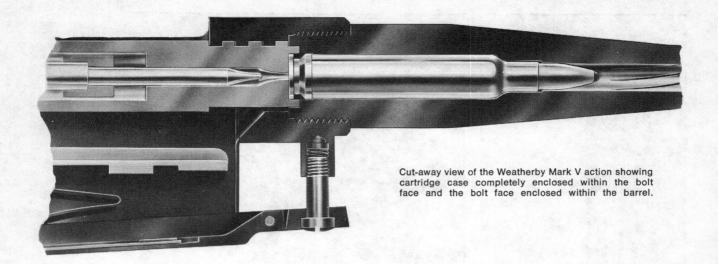

Cut-away view of the Weatherby Mark V action showing cartridge case completely enclosed within the bolt face and the bolt face enclosed within the barrel.

erated. A similar bolt-stop arrangement is also used in the Texas Magnum, Champlin and Remington 788 actions as described in other chapters in this book. In the Mark V action the bolt stop is linked to the trigger by an L-shaped piece of metal; by pulling the trigger back, which pulls the bolt stop plunger down, the bolt can be removed from the receiver. This arrangement makes bolt removal convenient, but it prevented the installation of a trigger-stop adjustment screw, which many riflemen consider desirable.

The separate, sheet-metal magazine box is folded to form and welded at one end. Its top fits into the magazine-well opening in the receiver bottom. The sides of the well are milled to leave cartridge guide ribs in the receiver, but in addition bent lips on the top front part of the magazine box provide additional guides for cartridges fed into the chamber by the bolt.

The barrel and action are securely held in the stock by two guard screws passing through the ends of the guard, these threading into the recoil lug and receiver tang. The magazine box is also held in place by the steel guard, which is not a stamping. The steel floorplate, hinged to the front of the guard, is held closed or released by a simple catch fitted into a slot in the front of the guard bow. The follower has a ridge on one side to stagger the cartridges in the magazine. The ends of the W-shaped follower spring fit into mortises in the floorplate and follower, holding these three parts together.

The Weatherby Mark V action is made entirely of steel. All main working parts of the action are extremely well made, fitted and finished. The bolt fits closely in the receiver, the contacting surfaces between the bolt and receiver level and smooth; the outside of the bolt is highly polished. The bolt and the receiver are heat-treated for maximum strength, as are various other parts, and hardened as required. All outside surfaces are highly polished and blued, except for the bright bolt body and the top of the receiver ring, bridge and bolt sleeve. These are sand-blasted before bluing.

Markings

The serial number is stamped on one side of the receiver ring. Stamped on the other side of the receiver ring is:

MARK V
U.S. PATENT 3,013,355

The name **WEATHERBY,** and the letter **R** within a circle, (name registration mark), are stamped on the receiver wall in bold script.

Take-Down and Assembly

Check to see that chamber and magazine are empty. To disassemble the Weatherby Mark V rifle and action proceed as follows: with the safety in FIRE position, open the bolt and, while pulling back on the trigger as far as it will go, remove bolt from the receiver. To disassemble the bolt grasp the bolt body in the left hand with the bottom side of bolt sleeve up; with a tool (a screwdriver will do) in the right hand, firmly pull the cocking piece back and slip the notch on the side of the cocking piece over the matching notch or shelf on the bolt sleeve. Now grasp the bolt sleeve, bottom side up, and unscrew the bolt body from it—rather than unscrewing the bolt sleeve from the bolt. When unscrewing the bolt from the sleeve, note the ball bearing, located in a slot in the threaded shank of the bolt sleeve; as soon as it is entirely visible, pick the bearing out with tweezers or tap it out. Then unscrew the bolt fully from the bolt sleeve. With a screwdriver, release the cocking piece from the shelf and allow it to move forward. Grasping the bolt sleeve firmly, and using a Crescent wrench on the forward shoulder on the firing pin, unscrew the firing pin slowly from the cocking piece, being careful not to allow the spring to jump out when the firing pin is fully unscrewed. With the firing pin removed, take the cocking piece from the bolt sleeve. To remove the safety unscrew the small bolt-

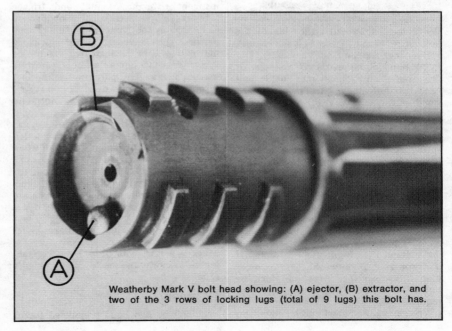

Weatherby Mark V bolt head showing: (A) ejector, (B) extractor, and two of the 3 rows of locking lugs (total of 9 lugs) this bolt has.

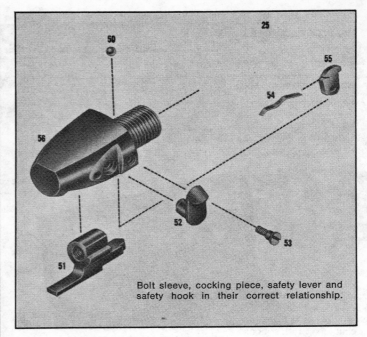

Bolt sleeve, cocking piece, safety lever and safety hook in their correct relationship.

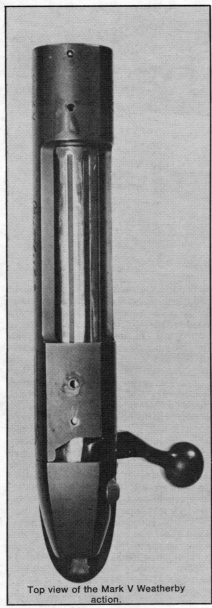

Top view of the Mark V Weatherby action.

sleeve lock screw from the side of the bolt sleeve, remove the bolt-sleeve lock and spring, and pull out the safety.

To remove the extractor and ejector drive out the two small pins in the bolt head that hold these parts in place. The small pins are snugly fitted so a good cylindrical drift punch is needed. With the pins removed, or three-quarters so, the extractor and ejector, also with their springs, can be removed. Reassemble all parts in reverse order.

In assembling the firing pin and firing-pin retainer ball bearing, make sure the flat side of the firing pin coincides with the hole for the ball bearing. Assemble the bolt sleeve in the bolt, then check firing pin protrusion after lowering the cocking piece. Normal protrusion from the bolt face is about .055″ to .060″. If the protrusion is noticeably less or more than this, then the firing pin must be turned in or out of the cocking piece as required.

To remove the barrel and receiver turn out the two guard screws, using a proper fitting screwdriver, then lift out barrel and receiver. Push and pull guard and magazine from the stock. Drive out the hollow pins from the guard to remove the floorplate from floorplate latch.

To remove the trigger mechanism, loosen the setscrew in the extreme front of the trigger housing. Using a proper-sized drift, drive out the pin holding the trigger mechanism to the receiver and remove the trigger unit. Reassemble in reverse order.

It is not advisable to completely disassemble the trigger mechanism, unless absolutely necessary. However, this can be done if great caution is taken.

Trigger Adjustment

The Mark V trigger has only two adjustments; weight of pull and trigger take-up. The pull weight adjustment screw is located in the front of the lower part of the trigger housing; turned clockwise the pull weight is increased, and vice versa. The take-up adjustment screw is located at the rear part of the housing; turning it clockwise decreases sear engagement. This adjustment is normally correctly set at the factory, and it should not be tampered with. If such adjustments are made the rifle should always be tested to make sure the striker will not fall when the bolt is closed smartly. To do this slam the bolt closed several times; if the sear fails to stay cocked at any time, either one or both of the adjustments are too light. There is no over-travel (trigger stop) adjustment.

Incidentally, Canjar now makes a replacement trigger mechanism for the Mark V action, with or without the Canjar side safety or the single-set trigger shoe.

Comments

I don't believe I am prejudiced for or against any particular centerfire turnbolt rifle or action, but being quite conservative I must admit that Weatherby rifles have never appealed to me. I don't like the Weatherby stock, since I dislike white spacers, inlays, slanted fore-end tips, flared pistol grips and skip-line checkering. Put a conservative, classic walnut stock on the Weatherby barreled action and I'd like to have the rifle in my gun cabinet. On the other hand, I very much like the Mark V action, and this is the part of the rifle we're interested in.

The Mark V action is large, long, and heavy, but it is so streamlined that it does not appear to be so. The Mark V action is strong. Some other actions are just as strong, as for example the Texas Magnum and Champlin, but I doubt if any are stronger. The 9 locking lugs offer a lot of locking contact and shear area. Since the receiver ring is not weakened by any deep locking-lug raceway cuts, there is little chance that the receiver will ever fail. According to Weatherby's 1962 catalog the Mark V receiver and bolt are made of SAE 4340 chrome-moly steel. The receiver is hardened to 40-43 Rockwell C, while the bolt is hardened to 50-55 on the same scale. The Weatherby shop proved the strength of the Mark V by subjecting it to numerous torture tests, firing heavy overloads that would have wrecked most other actions.

The Mark V action is also very safe. The shooter firing it can feel safe behind it, and no matter how badly the case head may rupture or the primer leak gas into and around the bolt, there is no chance that any of the gases will strike the shooter. Whatever may happen when the rifle is fired with an accidental overload or with an obstruction in the bore, the cartridge head—limited by the rim of the bolt-face recess—can only expand a very little bit. The only weak point in this rim is the cut for the extractor, but

TOMORROW'S RIFLE TODAY
THE MARK V

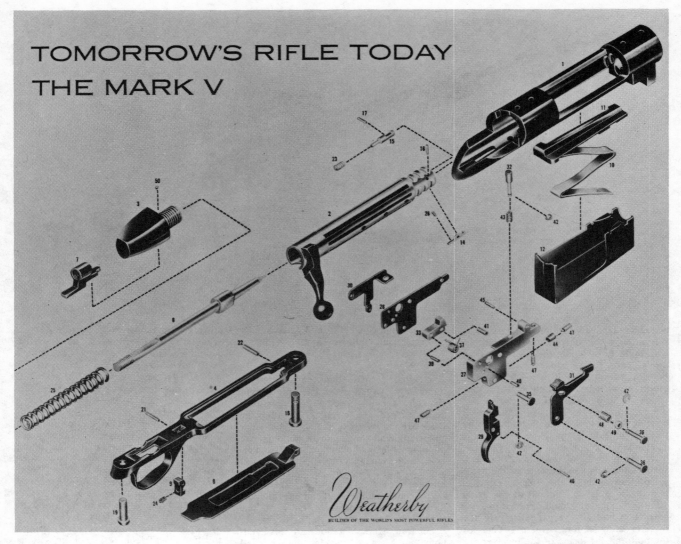

Weatherby
BUILDER OF THE WORLD'S MOST POWERFUL RIFLES

Parts Legend

1. Receiver
2. Bolt
3. Bolt sleeve
4. Trigger guard
6. Firing pin
7. Cocking piece
8. Magazine floorplate
9. Magazine floorplate catch
10. Follower spring
11. Magazine follower
12. Magazine box
14. Extractor
15. Ejector
16. Extractor pin
17. Ejector pin
18. Front trigger-guard screw
19. Rear trigger-guard screw
21. Magazine floorplate release pin
22. Floorplate pin
23. Ejector spring
24. Floorplate-catch spring
25. Firing-pin spring
26. Extractor spring
27. Trigger housing
28. Sideplate
29. Trigger
30. Bolt release
31. Safety lever
32. Bolt stop
33. Sear
35. Bolt-release pin
36. Trigger pin
37. Sear torsion spring
39. Sear pin
40. Sear torsion-spring pin
41. Sear-lock pin
42. Tru-arc ring
43. Bolt-stop spring
44. Trigger spring
45. Trigger-housing pin
46. Trigger-release pin
47. Trigger-adjusting screw
48. Safety return-plunger spring
49. Safety return-plunger
50. Retainer ball
51. Cocking piece
52. Safety lever
53. Screw for safety hook
54 & 55. Safety hook and spring subassembly
56. Bolt sleeve

Dimensional Specifications

Weight (approx.)	36 oz.
Length	9.00"
Receiver dia.	1.342"
Bolt dia.	.840"
Bolt travel	4.50"
Striker travel	.335"
Magazine length	3.750"
Guard-screw spacing	8.125"

Note: The specifications given are for the Mark V Magnum action made for the standard Weatherby Magnum cartridges. The Mark V Varmintmaster action is a scaled-down version of this action and the specifications for it are in the text under the heading of Mark V Varmintmaster action.

General Specifications

Type	Turnbolt repeater.
Receiver	One-piece machined steel forging with non-slotted bridge and integral recoil lug. Tapped for top scope mounts.
Bolt	One-piece machined steel forging with 9 (triple set of 3 lugs in a row) forward locking lugs. Low-profile bolt handle.
Ignition	One-piece firing pin powered by coil mainspring. Cocks on opening.
Magazine	Non-detachable staggered-column box type with hinged floorplate. 2-shot capacity for .378 & .460 WM calibers, 3-shot for the other WM calibers.
Trigger	Single stage, adjustable for weight of pull and take-up.
Safety	Rotary type built into the bolt sleeve, locks striker and bolt when tipped back.
Extractor	Pivoting hook type in bolt head.
Ejector	Plunger type in bolt head.
Bolt stop	Plunger type, fitted into the trigger housing and bottom of receiver, engages groove in the bottom of the bolt. Bolt is released by pulling trigger.

Weatherby Mark V left-hand .300 Weatherby Magnum De luxe rifle with 4x Weatherby Imperial scope in Buehler mounts.

even here expansion is limited because the rim around the barrel-face counterbore will limit how much the extractor can move, and it also supports the rest of the rim around the bolt face. The Mark V breeching system practically seals the cartridge in the chamber. If any gases enter the bolt through the firing pin hole they'll be released through the 3 holes in the side of the bolt.

The Mark V action is easy to operate. The well-placed bolt handle offers convenient grasping and, because of the triple set of locking lugs, the bolt handle has a swing of only 54° instead of the usual 90° for actions with dual-opposed locking lugs. The bolt fits very precisely in the receiver and, as long as the outside of the bolt and the inside of the receiver are kept clean, bolt operation is smooth and easy. If oil and dirt are allowed to accumulate on these surfaces, bolt operation can become sluggish.

When I first examined a Mark V action I was a bit skeptical about the bolt stop. I thought it too small, and I had the idea I could shear it off by opening the bolt very smartly a few times. I tried that a couple of times, but the bolt stop must be made of good stuff—it wouldn't shear. However, while the round-peg bolt stop may be adequate, I think it would be better if it were flat, say 3/16″ wide by 5/16″ long.

About the only thing I don't like about the Mark V action is the tiny safety button. This streamlining business is OK, but it should not include making a safety so small it cannot be easily and conveniently operated under all conditions.

Notes

Weatherby rifles and cartridges are popular the world over. They are expensive and for this reason they are most popular with the wealthy. Because the rifles are very showy, and the Weatherby shop can really make them so, they are popular with show people, potentates, notables and even governors. They are also popular with Asian and African big game hunters. Jack O'Connor, in *The Rifle Book,* estimates that half the hunting parties going on safari have at least one Weatherby Magnum rifle in their arsenal.

Separate Mark V actions are not available, but Mark V barreled action in all Weatherby Magnum calibers (except the .376 and .460) and a couple of standard calibers are. They're offered with right- or left-hand actions (except for the Mark V Varmintmaster, which is made in right-hand only.)

Weatherby does not manufacture Mark V actions. My information is that they're made by J.P. Sauer & Son, in West Germany, a firm once known for their very fine line of shotguns.

Mark V Varmintmaster

The standard Mark V action is unnecessarily large for any cartridge much smaller than .30-06. Even the smallest of the Weatherby Magnum cartridges, such as the .257 WM (it was the smallest Weatherby caliber in 1964) was just too

powerful for the average varmint hunter. Weatherby once offered a .22 centerfire cartridge called the .220 Rocket which was merely an "improved" .220 Swift. It was not very popular and, like the .220 Swift, it has dropped by the wayside. The most recent .22 caliber Weatherby development is the .224 Weatherby Magnum, a cartridge based on a miniature Weatherby belted magnum case. Except for the head it is similar in size to the .225 Winchester case. Weatherby introduced the .224 WM cartridge in a new rifle in 1964, calling it the Weatherby Mark V .224 Varmintmaster.

A scaled-down version of the standard Mark V action, it is only made with a right-hand bolt. Except for size, weight and number of locking lugs, both actions are nearly identical. To give some indication of the differences here are some specifications for the Varmintmaster action:

Weight	32 oz.
Length	7.50″
Bolt travel	3.25″
Receiver dia.	1.100″
Bolt dia.	.709″

Instead of having 9 locking lugs, the Varmintmaster has only six; two in each row of three. Since the .224 WM and the .22-250 don't develop as high breech pressures and back-thrust as do the larger Weatherby Magnum cartridges, the 6 locking lugs are more than ample to securely lock the bolt within the receiver.

In 1968 Weatherby began chambering the Varmintmaster rifle for the very popular .22-250 cartridge as well.

35. Texas Magnum

RANGER ARMS INC. (P.O. Box 704, Gainsville, Texas 76240), introduced an exceedingly fine centerfire turnbolt rifle action in 1967. Its design, construction and workmanship is excellent. Ranger offers several of these actions: a long, a shorter one, a single shot and, best of all, right- or left-hand. All are available separately too, and Ranger also furnishes barreled actions in many popular calibers plus complete custom built rifles in several grades.

Let's see what these are. 1) The Texas Magnum is the long action, about 9″ over-all without recoil lug. Its magazine will accept cartridges of .30-06 length or slightly longer, and it is made for these and short belted-head magnum cartridges. The magazine is not long enough for the .300 or .375 H&H Magnum cartridges. 2) The Maverick action, about 8.375″ long, is made for cartridges of .30-06 head size no longer than about 2.850″. This would include the .308, the 6mm and .284, etc. The Maverick single-shot without magazine or magazine-well, is made for .30-06 head-sized cartridges and also for the .222 family. Any of these is available for right- or left-hand operation. Texas Magnum and Maverick actions are $97.50, the single-shot $149.50.

Design and Construction

Teaxs Magnum (TM) actions are of all-steel construction. The receiver and bolt are machined from solid round bars of SAE 4340 steel, an alloy of chrome, nickel and molybdenum steels. Such parts as the trigger, sear and cocking piece are steel investment castings. The magazine box and trigger housing walls are formed from sheet metal.

The one-piece receiver is round. The receiver ring is about 1.550″ long, its front end threaded for the barrel shank. The barrel shank is 1.00″ in diameter and about .990″ long. The threads are right hand and of standard 60° V-type, 14 threads per inch. The separate recoil lug, clamped between receiver and barrel, is big enough to prevent set-back of the barrel and action in the stock from recoil. A narrow notch at the bottom of the receiver matches a projection on the recoil lug. This aligns the lug with the receiver and keeps it from turning when the barrel is turned into the receiver.

The receiver is precisely bored and reamed for the bolt. The unslotted bridge, about 1.220″ long, is flat on top. Two holes each are tapped into the receiver ring and bridge for scope mounts. The receiver opening, ample in length to facilitate loading and ejection, faces right (or left if the action is a left-handed one). The receiver ends in a rounded tang.

The large diameter (.859″) bolt lugs do not project, and for this reason no lug raceways have to be cut into the receiver. As a consequence the wall opposite the loading port is a solid, curved wall of steel about .225″ thick and nearly 1″ high. Cartridge guide lips are milled in the sides of the magazine-well opening. The magazine wall or rail below the receiver opening is thus left quite thin—not unlike that in the Remington 721 action, but the opposite solid wall in the TM action makes up for it.

The front of the bolt body is turned down, leaving 3 solid locking lugs to engage behind shoulders inside the receiver ring. These lugs are about .085″ thick, the bottom one wider than the other two. The approaching corners of the lugs and shoulders are slightly angled, hence the bolt is cammed forward a short distance when the handle is lowered. Because of the triple locking-lug design bolt rotation to open and close is only 60°.

The bolt face is deeply recessed for the cartridge head. The plunger-type ejector, coil-spring loaded, is held in place in the bolt face by a small cross pin through the bolt. The hooked extractor occupies a groove cut into the outside of the bolt head, held in place there, and pivoting on, another pin through the bolt head. The extractor is powered by a small coil spring. The extractor hook and edge of the bolt face are well beveled so the bolt can easily be closed on a chambered cartridge.

The bolt handle, threaded into the rear of the bolt body, is locked in place by two small Allen-head setscrews. The bolt handle stem is curved back and down, ending in a pear-shaped ball. Its very low profile will clear the lowest-mounted scope.

The very stiff coil mainspring is compressed between a shoulder on the front of the one-piece firing pin and the bolt handle. The rear end of the firing pin projects through the bolt handle; the cocking piece is threaded onto it. Firing pin tip protrusion is adjusted to .055″, then locked by a single Allen-head setscrew, turned in the cocking piece and onto the firing pin. The cocking piece has 3 cocking cams, these engaging 3 notches in the rear of the bolt handle. On raising the bolt handle the action is cocked, the cocking cams moving into the very shallow notches and preventing the bolt shroud and cocking piece from turning when the bolt is opened. The multi-cam arrangement eliminates torque, making it easy to open the bolt. The neatly-shaped steel bolt head shroud threads onto the rear of the bolt handle and entirely covers the cocking piece.

The receiver tang is notched for the bolt handle, which forms the safety lug. Initial extraction camming power is supplied on raising the bolt handle, when the base of the handle moves over an inclined surface on the rear of the bridge.

Texas Magnum actions have a good gas-venting system. There are two holes in the receiver ring (one on each side) and 3 holes in the exposed side of the bolt body. I don't see how any gases could escape through the hole in the bolt handle, but if this occurred the bolt shroud would protect the shooter.

The trigger and bolt stop mechanism

Illustrated above: Right-hand Texas Magnum rifle built by the Ranger Arms Company.

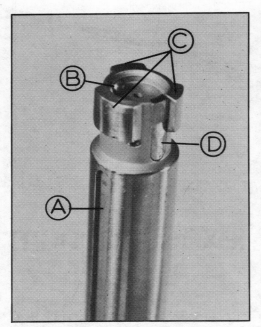

Texas Magnum bolt head showing: (A) bolt-stop groove, (B) ejector, (C) triple locking lugs, (D) extractor.

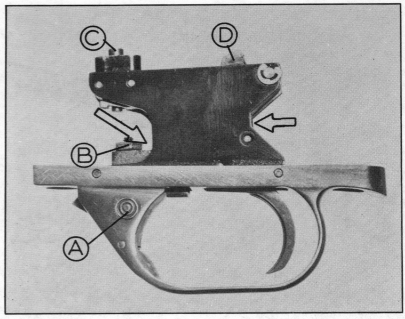

Texas Magnum bolt stop/trigger/safety assembly, showing: (A) cross-bolt safety, (B) safety adjustment screw and lock nut, (C) bolt-stop plunger, (D) sear, (E) bolt-stop release. The long open arrow points to the location of the trigger weight-of-pull adjustment screw; the short arrow points to the sear-engagement adjustment screw.

is built into a separate steel housing, which is in turn attached to the milled steel trigger guard by two pins. The curved and grooved trigger is placed well back in the trigger guard bow. The top of the trigger engages the sear, the latter pivoted in the tip of the housing. The trigger and sear are tensioned by small coil springs. When the action is closed, the sear, which is held up by the trigger, holds the cocking piece back. On pulling the trigger the sear is released to tip down, releasing the firing pin. There is an Allen-head set screw in the rear of the trigger housing by which the trigger-to-sear engagement can be set to provide a short creep-free trigger let-off. There is no adjustment for over-travel. The weight-of-pull adjustment screw is positioned just to the rear of the safety adjustment screw; by turning this Allen-head screw counterclockwise the pull can be made lighter. The trigger mechanism must be removed to make these adjustments.

The safety is a crossbolt built into the top front of the guard bow. The trigger has a forward extension fitted with a setscrew and lock nut, which are in contact with the safety when it is engaged. The trigger and safety are adjusted correctly at the factory but if any change has been made with the trigger adjustment screw then the safety setscrew must be re-set so that no trigger movement is possible when the safety is engaged. On right-hand actions the safety is disengaged by pushing it to the left with the trigger finger and vice versa on left-hand actions. There is no bolt lock. The safety can only be engaged if the action is cocked, thus it can be used as a cocking indicator.

The trigger mechanism, with its attached trigger guard, is held in position against the bottom of the receiver by the rear and center guard screws passing through the guard and threading into the receiver. By this arrangement the trigger mechanism can be removed from the rifle

without taking the barrel and receiver out of the stock.

The action is held in the stock by the front, rear and center guard screws. The front screw passes through a short plate, to which the milled steel floorplate is pinhinged. This hinge plate and the front end of the guard hold the sheet-metal magazine box in place against the bottom of the receiver. The floorplate latch is in the front of the guard bow, its release button inside the bow. One end of the W-shaped flat follower spring fits into lips beneath the milled steel follower; while the other end merely lies within a recess in the floorplate.

The bolt stop is a pin which projects through the bolt raceway into a milled groove in the bottom of the bolt. This pin is supported by the trigger-housing spacer, which is in turn supported by being fitted into a hole in the receiver bottom. The bolt-stop pin is attached to a forked lever (inside the trigger housing) which has an

Texas Magnum left-hand action open.

Texas Magnum left-hand action.

arm that projects down into the guard bow. Pushing this arm up causes the lever to pull the bolt-stop pin down so the bolt can be removed or replaced. The bolt-stop pin also acts as a bolt guide, preventing the bolt from turning as it is operated.

The Single-Shot Action

Made especially for the serious benchrest shooter the Texas Magnum single-shot action will meet their requirements for an action that has a very rigid receiver, one rigid enough to support a heavy free-floating barrel. I would also think it would be a very good action choice for the long range competitive target shooter. Made without a magazine-well opening, the loading port is only wide enough to load the action. Except for the narrow loading port the thick receiver nearly covers the entire bolt. Since no magazine is used the trigger guard is extended forward so that the front guard screw can be fitted through its end. An additional guard screw is also used to hold the action in the stock, this screw positioned about an inch ahead of the center guard screw. About the only other difference in this action is that the ejector has been omitted from the bolt. It is available with bolts made for either the .222 or .30-06 head-sized cartridges.

Comments

There are many things I like about this action, but it has a few things which I believe could be improved upon. The good things first. I think the bolt design is superb. Threading the bolt handle into the bolt body and threading the cocking piece onto the firing pin, and locking these parts with Allen-head setscrews are excellent ideas. Designing the cocking piece with three cams is also a very good idea. The action does not really need the bolt shroud, but putting one on and making it enclose and dress off the rear of the bolt is well executed. I also like the beveled edge of the bolt-face recess rim, the ejector with its smooth end, and I think the extractor is more than adequately strong to do its job. All bolt parts are extremely well made, machined, ground and finished so that all the parts are precisely fitted. The bolt handle is easily raised, and bolt operation is smooth, with no tendency of the bolt to stick or bind.

I like the shape of the trigger guard and the hinged magazine floorplate. The trigger is nicely curved and placed properly in the trigger guard. I find nothing

wrong with the cross bolt safety or its location. The bolt stop is adequate and the bolt-stop release is handily and inconspicuously placed. I believe the trigger mechanism is reliable, and that it should satisfy most shooters.

I've had no opportunity to test the TM action for feeding, but I assume this has been worked out and that feeding is reliable.

This is a fine action, and a very strong and safe one. To quote the Ranger Arms catalog, Texas Magnum actions are made ". . . to hold in excess of 140,000 psi, far beyond standards regularly available in firearms." No action has to withstand such pressures, but if any action will this one will. The 3 locking lug system would be hard to beat, and I doubt if any other action has a better gas-venting system. The thick-walled receiver ring has not been weakened by any deep raceway cuts. This just has to be a strong and safe action.

As a whole I found no real fault with the TM action, but I think there's room for some improvement. For example, on the TM action I had, the sides of the bolt-stop groove were quite wavy. This

Dimensional Specifications

	Long Magnum	Maverick
Weight	48 oz.	46 oz.
Receiver length	9.00"	8.375"
Receiver dia.	1.315"	
Bolt dia.	.860"	
Bolt travel	4.925"	4.30"
Striker travel	.185"	
Bolt-face recess:		
Depth	.125"	
Guard-screw spacing	8.375"	7.75"

NOTE: The Texas Magnum single-shot action is the same as the Maverick except it has no magazine. See text.

General Specifications

Type	Turnbolt repeater.
Receiver	One-piece, machined from round bar stock (SAE-4340 steel). Non-slotted bridge. Separate recoil lug clamped between barrel and receiver. Tapped for top scope mounts.
Bolt	Two-piece type (handle is a separate part) with triple forward locking lugs. Low-profile handle acts as safety lug.
Ignition	One-piece firing pin powered by coil mainspring. Cocks on opening.
Magazine	Non-detachable staggered-column box magazine with hinged floorplate. Capacity: 5-shot for standard calibers, 4-shot for magnum calibers. Single-shot action has no magazine.
Trigger	Single stage, adjustable for take-up and weight of pull.
Safety	Crossbolt safety built into trigger guard, locks trigger only when engaged.
Extractor	Pivoting type in bolt head.
Ejector	Plunger type in bolt head.
Bolt stop	Plunger type in trigger housing, engages a groove in bolt body.

resulted in the only roughness I felt in operating the bolt. This minor fault is easily corrected by honing the sides of this groove smooth.

Some shooters are fussy about triggers. There is no trigger-stop adjustment on this trigger, but one could easily have been installed by just tapping one hole and fitting it with a setscrew. This still can be done very easily.

I don't particularly like the bolt stop. Instead of a round pin I would favor an oblong stop, which would offer more surface on each side to contact the sides of the bolt-stop groove. This would not only be a stronger bolt stop, but a better bolt guide, too.

Now for a thought or two about the trigger mechanism. By having the cross-bolt safety built into the guard bow it is almost necessary that the trigger mechanism also be attached to the guard. If this system is to be used, in which the trigger guard mechanism is not attached to the receiver, then I believe it might be a good idea to use stock bushings for the two guard screws holding the guard in place. If the action parts are properly inletted into the stock, and preferably glass bedded, the trigger mechanism could be removed and replaced without disturbing the sear-cocking piece relationship. I would also want the adjustment screws so-positioned that they could be got at from the outside of the rifle. Personally, in this or any other fine turnbolt action, I prefer a far simpler trigger mechanism. There is hardly a trigger system I haven't used, and of all of them there is scarcely any one more simple, foolproof and reliable than the one used in the Model 70 Winchester. There are dozens of ways to modify this trigger system so that the adjustment screws can be reached from the outside, and I think such a trigger would complement the fine Texas Magnum action.

Markings

The serial number is stamped on the left side of the receiver ring, on the bolt body in the bolt-stop raceway, and on the underside of the bolt handle.

The name **TEXAS MAGNUM** is stamped on the receiver wall, making identification positive.

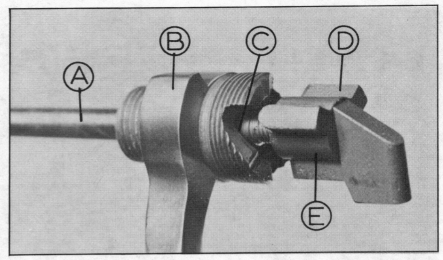

Part of firing mechanism of a Ranger bolt showing: (A) firing pin, (B) bolt handle, which threads into the rear of the bolt body, (C) one of the 3 equally-spaced cocking cam notches on the rear of bolt handle, (D) cocking piece with its 3 cocking cams, (E) firing-pin lock screw.

Take-Down and Assembly

To remove the bolt raise the bolt handle and pull the bolt back. Then press upward on the bolt-stop release, just forward of the trigger, and pull the bolt from the receiver. To replace the bolt insert the bolt into the receiver, press upward on the bolt-stop release so the bolt can slip over the bolt stop; if necessary, turn the bolt a bit until the bolt-stop pin slips into its groove.

To disassemble the bolt and firing mechanism proceed as follows: first remove the two Allen-head setscrews from the rear of the bolt body. Place the bolt body in a padded vise and, with a firm grip on the bolt handle, turn it counter-clockwise out of the bolt body. Next turn out the setscrew from the cocking piece, being careful to confine the parts when the firing pin is completely turned out. After this the bolt shroud can be un-screwed from the bolt handle and the cocking piece removed. Reassemble in reverse order. Before tightening the set-screw in the cocking piece make sure the drilled indent in the threaded end of the firing pin is correctly aligned with the hole for the setscrew, in order to obtain the correct firing pin tip protrusion. Again, in assembling the bolt handle in the bolt make sure the two drilled indents

in the bolt handle align with the setscrew holes in the bolt body. The extractor and ejector can be removed by driving out the pins that hold these parts in the bolt head.

To remove the trigger assembly open the floorplate, turn out the rear and center guard screws, then pull the guard, with attached trigger mechanism, from the stock. The trigger mechanism can be removed from the guard by driving out the two pins holding it in place. These pins, like the other pins in this action, are of the spring-tempered rolled type. The trigger spring is freed when the trigger mechanism is removed from the guard, and take care that it is not lost. Do not disassemble the trigger mechanism unless for a good reason, and then with care. To remove the safety drive out the floorplate latch pin, then remove latch, latch spring, safety plunger and safety. When assembling the trigger mechanism and guard back into place the bolt should be removed from the receiver and the two guard screws tightened. To remove the barrel and action from the stock, first remove the trigger mechanism, then turn out the front guard screw, whereupon the floorplate and hinge can be removed from the stock and the barrel and action lifted out. Reassemble in reverse order.

Custom sporting rifle, based on the left-hand Texas Magnum action, built by gunmaker Dean Miller, St. Onge, South Dakota.

36. Champlin Firearms, Inc.

A NEWCOMER in the field of custom-built sporting rifles is Champlin Firearms Inc. (2931 No. Fourth, P.O. Box 3191, Enid, Okla. 73701). They build their fine rifles on a remarkable turnbolt action produced almost entirely in their shop. The firm was formerly listed as Champlin-Haskins Firearms Inc., but since Mr. Jerry Haskins is no longer with the firm, his name has been dropped. This action was developed around a patent obtained by Mr. Haskins (3,494,216, dated June 17, 1969), which covers the combination rear safety-lug and bolt-guide system—a feature which probably makes this action the strongest and smoothest working sporting rifle action made today.

The two Champlin rifles illustrated are typical examples of the custom-built rifles turned out by Champlin Firearms Inc. Both are stocked in the time-honored classic sporting stock pattern. Strictly made to order, these rifles can be made for most of the large rimless or belted centerfire cartridges, including the very large Weatherby .378 and .460 Magnums. The actions are made only in one length, and only with a right-hand bolt.* Separate Champlin actions are also available.

The Action

The receiver and bolt of this very large and strong all-steel action are machined from 4140 steel bar stock. The receiver was heat-treated to 37 Rockwell on the C scale, the bolt to 45-C. All parts are made of a type of steel best suited to its purpose, and properly heat treated as required for maximum strength, durability and wear prevention.

The receiver is large and massive. It has a flat bottom, flat sides, and is octagonal in shape on top. It is 9.00″ long, 1.265″ wide and 1.285″ deep, not including the integral recoil lug under the receiver ring, which is .375″ deep. Since these receivers were machined one at a time the above

measurements, and other specifications, may vary somewhat. The receiver ring is about 1.70″ long, the bridge about 1.60″ long, with a loading port in between about 3.40″ long. Two holes each are tapped in the top of the bridge and ring for scope mount bases. The receiver ends with a nicely tapered tang, but it is almost entirely covered by the bolt sleeve; only the extreme rear shows when the bolt is closed.

The bolt, also massive, is slightly over 6.00″ long, its major diameter .850″.

To more clearly understand my description of the locking system of the C-H action, the reader should study the illustrations of the bolt. The full bolt diameter is turned down to leave 3 locking lugs on its extreme forward end, each about .415″ wide and .530″ long. About ½-inch to the rear of each of these lugs are 3 equally wide ridges which, as covered by the Haskins patent, provide 3 safety locking lugs, which also function as guide ribs. The inside of the receiver has 3 grooves which accept the ribbed bolt. When the bolt handle is turned down the 3 front lugs engage shoulders in the receiver ring, while the 3 guide ribs engage in front of, but do not contact, shoulders in front of the bridge. The bottom guide rib, however, is grooved for the bolt stop, and it presents only a small area of possible contact with the receiver, thus there are really only two safety lugs at work. The front locking lug system, in fact, is more than adequately strong to hold the bolt in the receiver against the back thrust of any cartridge for which the rifle might be chambered; the safety lugs give an added margin of safety. The bolt is so well secured in the receiver that it would be impossible to drive it back.

The 3.485″ long bolt ribs also guide the bolt in the receiver when it is operated, which is their primary function. This function can best be described by comparing the Champlin action with a couple of others in which a small bolt stop acts

as the bolt guide, namely, the Ranger and the Weatherby Mark V. In both of these actions the round plunger-type bolt stop provides the only bolt guide that prevents the bolt from turning in the receiver. The C-H action has a similar bolt stop, but it functions only to stop the bolt. The C-H guide ribs steady the bolt better than the bolt stop alone could ever do. The ribs also prevent the bolt from binding regardless of how, or from what position, the action is operated, with the result that the Champlin action is smooth and easy to operate. Because of the triple locking-lug arrangement, only about a 60° bolt rotation is required to lock or unlock the Champlin bolt.

The barrel face is flat, as is the bolt face, which nearly contacts it when the bolt is closed. The bolt face is deeply recessed for the cartridge head so that the chambered cartridge is all but completely enclosed. The bolt is so large in diameter that there's a thick rim of metal around the recess, which adequately supports the cartridge head and rim. The spring-loaded plunger-type ejector projects from the recessed bolt face, held in place by a cross pin. The sliding type extractor occupies a mortise cut into the front face of the right locking lug, held in place and tensioned by a coil spring and plunger. The inside edge of the extractor is well beveled, letting it move easily over the rim of a cartridge in the chamber. The extractor is wide enough so that it will not pull through the rim of a cartridge that tends to stick in the chamber. This extractor is not unlike that in the new Model 70 Winchester and Model 110-C Savage actions.

The bolt handle, attached to the heavy rear part of the bolt, has a tapered stem which angles slightly rearward and ends

Illustrated above: Custom-made Champlin rifle stocked in classic form. The action has the bolt-sleeve safety, the scope in the two-piece Buehler mount.

in a round ball. The top of the ball is neatly and finely checkered for better grasping. The bolt handle is low enough to clear the eyepiece of the lowest-mounted scope. The rear side of the bridge is deeply notched for the base of the bolt handle. Although this action certainly does not need another safety lug, the bolt handle could serve this function.

The top of the notch into which the base of the bolt handle fits is sloped slightly rearward; on raising the bolt handle, it contacts this surface and the bolt is cammed back to provide the initial power to the extractor. Each of the 3 locking lugs have their approaching corners cut off so that the bolt is forced forward on the final closing.

The bolt is drilled from the rear to accept the firing mechanism, which is composed chiefly of the one-piece firing pin, coil mainspring, cocking piece and bolt sleeve. The firing pin is threaded into the cocking piece and prevented from turning by a half-moon wedge of metal fitted in a notch cut into the stem of the bolt sleeve, which is in turn threaded into the bolt. This method of keeping the firing pin from turning is better than using a setscrew, as in the Sako and some other actions, since setscrews can work loose. The mainspring is compressed over the firing pin between the bolt-sleeve stem and a C-shaped collar on the front part of the firing pin. The action cocks on lifting the bolt handle, a cam on the rear of the bolt forcing the cocking piece back. The entire firing mechanism and bolt sleeve are prevented from turning when the bolt is opened by the nose of the cocking piece resting in a shallow notch at the rear of the bolt.

The bolt sleeve (called a shroud by the Champlin people) deserves special mention. It is quite large, and octagonal in shape to match the receiver bridge, against which it fits when the action is closed. From the bridge the bolt sleeve tapers gently back to match exactly the contour of the receiver tang, against which the bottom of the bolt sleeve fits closely. It is entirely closed at the rear; only its bottom is open to allow the removal of the cocking piece. The front of

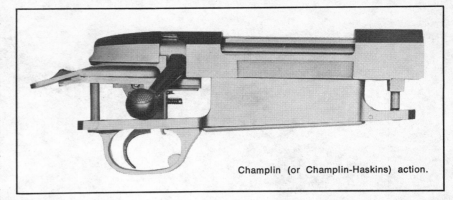

Champlin (or Champlin-Haskins) action.

the bolt sleeve is slightly recessed to fit over the rear end of the bolt. All of this provides maximum protection in the event powder gases should get into the bolt body.

If powder gases should enter the bolt through the firing pin tip hole, there is an adequate oblong hole in the bolt body bottom, about 2″ behind the bolt face, to allow the gases to be directed into the magazine well. Consequently, there are no vent holes exposed on the outside of the action into which dirt or other foreign material can enter.

As previously mentioned, the bolt stop is a round plunger, made as part of the trigger mechanism. It projects upward through a hole in the front part of the trigger housing, through a hole in the bottom of the receiver and into the bolt raceway. The bottom rib of the bolt is grooved for the end of the bolt stop, and the bolt is halted in its rearward travel when the bolt stop contacts the end of this groove. The bolt stop is ample in diameter and hardened, so there is little chance of it being damaged or sheared off when the bolt is opened smartly. It is held up by a small coil spring and can be lowered, to remove the bolt, by a lever which is attached to the left side of the trigger housing. The knurled knob of this lever lies alongside the receiver tang just above the stock line, where it is unobtrusive and convenient to use.

Of the several makes of actions which have similar bolt stops, I believe the

method Champlin uses to depress it for bolt removal is the best. It is entirely independent of the trigger, therefore nothing has to be sacrificed in the trigger mechanism because of it.

The one-piece trigger guard/magazine box is of all milled-steel construction. It is heavily constructed throughout, with thick and smooth walls. In fact, it is not much different from the trigger guard/magazine of the Brevex Magnum Mauser action described in another chapter. The heavy floorplate, hinged to the front tang of the unit, is held closed by a latch fitted in the front of the trigger guard bow. The bottom of the steel follower and the inside of the floorplate are grooved for the ends of the W-shaped follower spring, which holds these 3 parts together. The front and rear ends of the guard are octagonal in shape to complement the top shape of the receiver. The floorplate also has beveled edges to continue the octagonal configuration.

The C-H may be had with a square-backed guard bow, a distinctive feature, or a conventional rounded bow can be ordered. The bow is made narrower from front to back, and the effect is quite pleasing.

The magazine-well opening is milled to leave integral cartridge-guide lips on each side to hold the staggered column of cartridges in the magazine, and to guide each one into the chamber when pushed there by the bolt. The smooth inside surfaces of the well let cartridges be fed smoothly

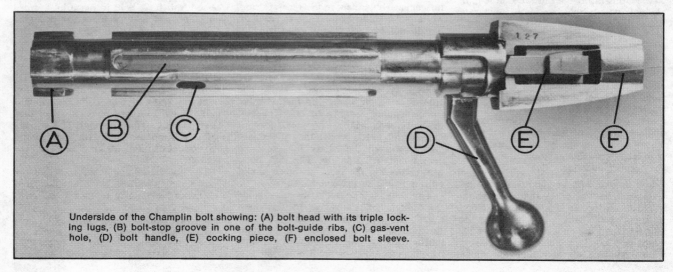

Underside of the Champlin bolt showing: (A) bolt head with its triple locking lugs, (B) bolt-stop groove in one of the bolt-guide ribs, (C) gas-vent hole, (D) bolt handle, (E) cocking piece, (F) enclosed bolt sleeve.

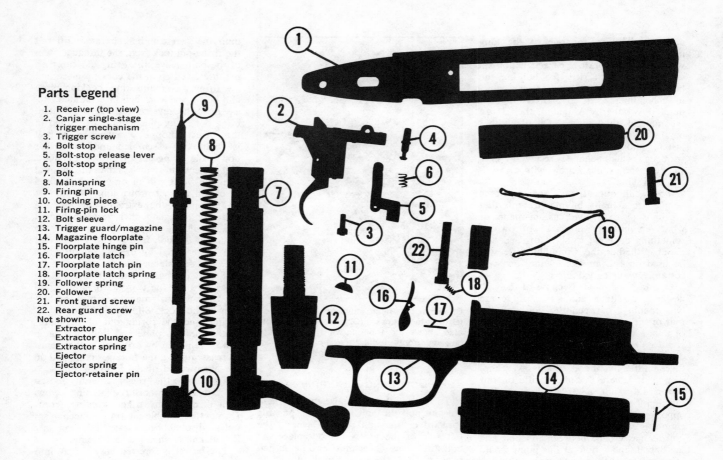

Parts Legend

1. Receiver (top view)
2. Canjar single-stage trigger mechanism
3. Trigger screw
4. Bolt stop
5. Bolt-stop release lever
6. Bolt-stop spring
7. Bolt
8. Mainspring
9. Firing pin
10. Cocking piece
11. Firing-pin lock
12. Bolt sleeve
13. Trigger guard/magazine
14. Magazine floorplate
15. Floorplate hinge pin
16. Floorplate latch
17. Floorplate latch pin
18. Floorplate latch spring
19. Follower spring
20. Follower
21. Front guard screw
22. Rear guard screw

Not shown:
- Extractor
- Extractor plunger
- Extractor spring
- Ejector
- Ejector spring
- Ejector-retainer pin

Dimensional Specifications

Weight	52 oz.
Length	9.00"
Receiver width	1.265"
Bolt dia. (major dia.)	.850"
(body dia.)	.671"
Bolt travel	4.575"
Striker travel	.285"
Bolt-face recess: depth	.135"
Magazine length	3.675"
Magazine-well width	.650"
Guard-screw spacing	7.812"

General Specifications

Type	Turnbolt repeater.
Receiver	One-piece, 4140 steel. Integral recoil lug, non-slotted bridge. Tapped for top scope mounts.
Bolt	One-piece steel bolt with 3 forward locking lugs. Low profile bolt handle. Three guide ribs on bolt also function as safety lugs.
Ignition	One-piece firing pin powered by coil mainspring. Cocks on opening.
Magazine	Non-detachable staggered-column 5-shot box type with hinged floorplate. 4-shot for most magnum calibers.
Trigger	Fully adjustable single-stage type (Canjar).
Safety	Sliding tang type connected to the trigger mechanism. Rotary type at right side of bolt sleeve, locks striker and bolt when tipped back is optional.
Extractor	Sliding type mortised into face of one locking lug.
Ejector	Plunger type in bolt face.
Bolt stop	Plunger type fitted into trigger housing and bottom of the receiver; engages bottom groove in the bolt body.

into the chamber. Made to handle the longest magnum cartridges, Champlin can block off the rear part of the magazine if the customer wants the rifle chambered for a shorter cartridge.

Two Allen-head guard screws passing through each end of the guard and threading into the bottom of the recoil lug and receiver tang, securely hold the barrel and action in the stock.

Champlin uses the very fine Canjar single-stage trigger for their action. This mechanism, with its attached bolt stop, is fastened to the bottom of the receiver by an Allen-head screw and tightened by a setscrew. The trigger is fully adjustable for weight-of-pull, take-up and over-travel. Since the trigger is a Canjar, I assume that Canjar also furnish a single-set mechanism to replace the trigger itself.

Champlin can furnish more than one type of safety. The first is a pivoting type built into the right side of the bolt sleeve. When it is tipped back, it locks both

striker and bolt. The second is a sliding tang type built into an extension of the receiver tang; when it is slid back it locks the trigger mechanism. These two safeties are shown on the two rifles illustrated. The Champlin action illustrated has no safety.

Comments

This is an extremely rugged and strong action, very well made and finished. No other sporting turnbolt action has a stronger or more rigid receiver or a stronger locking system. It is a large and heavy action, and so-made that it will handle the largest magnum cartridge that anyone would want to fire in a shoulder arm. Yet it is not so large and bulky that

it looks out of place on a trim sporting rifle. It is an action that will stand up under hard usage with powerful cartridges. Neat and trim in outline, all parts are well fitted, making it easy and smooth to operate. Lock time is very fast and ignition is positive.

There are other things I like about this action, such as the octagon shape of the receiver and bolt sleeve, the enclosed or shrouded bolt sleeve, the use of the Canjar trigger, and the choice of safeties.

The Champlin action, however, is not one to choose for making a rifle in one of the many standard calibers, and especially not if you want a lightweight rifle. However, it is a most ideal action for building a medium- to heavyweight rifle in one of the belted magnum cartridges, and especially so for one of the long magnum calibers. For example, if you want an easy working, rugged action on which to build a rifle for hunting the largest and most dangerous African game, in such calibers as the .375 H&H Magnum or .460 Weatherby Magnum, then I can recommend this action. On the other hand, if you want a custom made rifle just for show, then the Champlin action, with its octagon-shaped receiver, is as showy as any other action, with or without engraving.

Today, in our affluent society, some people are actually buying firearms that are unusual, expensive, custom made, or whatever, just for the sake of owning something different to show off and talk about. Whether the Champlin rifle will be used or not, anyone owning one will certainly want to exhibit it.

One last comment. Because of the bolt design, with its 3 guide ribs, there are two openings between the bolt and the rear of the receiver ring. In the rare event of a case head rupture much powder gas could enter the locking-lug ways and be directed toward the shooter's face. While there's little likelihood of this ever happening, if I were to build a rifle on this action I'd want a 3/16" hole drilled through the right side of the receiver ring, opposite the extractor. That extractor location is the most likely spot for any powder gas escape between the bolt and the barrel, and a hole at this point would allow much of the gas to escape through it. This is the only thing about this action I don't like. I certainly don't think it a serious fault, but since there is no way to seal these holes, I would want the extra vent hole in the side of the receiver.

Markings

The Champlin actions are serial numbered. The number is stamped on the right side of the receiver ring and on the major working parts. The firm name, **CHAMPLIN FIREARMS INC.** is stamped on the left receiver wall and **U.S. PATENT 3,494,216** will be stamped on the left side of the receiver ring.

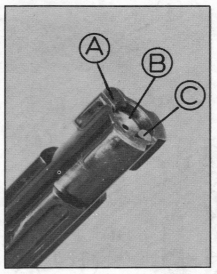

Champlin bolt head showing: (A) extractor, (B) bolt-face recess, (C) ejector. This photo also shows the triple forward locking lugs and the front of the triple bolt-guide ribs, which also serve as safety lugs.

Take-Down and Assembly

To remove the bolt, raise the bolt handle and pull the bolt back while pushing forward on the bolt release lever at the left side of the receiver. To replace the bolt, the release lever must also be pushed forward until the bolt is well started in the receiver.

To disassemble the bolt proceed as follows: grasp the bolt firmly in one hand; with the other hand rotate the bolt sleeve counterclockwise as far as it will go; then, using a screwdriver or some square-edged tool, draw the cocking piece back far enough so the nose of the cocking piece clears the cocking cam and the bolt sleeve can be turned further counterclockwise; rotate the bolt sleeve another turn and repeat the process until the cocking piece no longer prevents the bolt sleeve from being turned; now grasp the bolt sleeve top side up and, holding the bolt level, unscrew the bolt from the bolt sleeve

until the two can be separated; lift out the firing-pin lock from the threaded stem of the bolt sleeve; the firing pin can then be unscrewed from the cocking piece and the firing pin, mainspring, cocking piece and bolt sleeve can then be separated. Reassemble in reverse order. In reassembling the firing pin, it must be turned in the correct amount so that when the bolt is completely assembled and the striker down, the firing-pin tip protrudes .060". If it projects more or less than this amount turn the firing pin in or out as required to obtain correct protrusion.

To remove the extractor depress the extractor plunger with a very small drift punch, sliding the extractor toward the center of the bolt-face recess. The ejector can be removed by driving out its cross pin. Reassemble in reverse order.

To lift the barrel and action from the stock turn out the two guard screws; pull the trigger guard/magazine from the bottom of the stock. Slip the follower off its spring, and the spring out of the floorplate. The floorplate and floorplate latch can be removed by driving out their pins. In reassembling, the follower is slipped on the narrow end of the follower spring.

To remove the trigger assembly loosen the trigger mechanism tightening screw, then turn out the trigger-holding screw. Do not disassemble the trigger mechanism unless absolutely necessary, and then only if you know what you are doing.

The barrel is screwed very tightly into the receiver and no attempt should be made to remove it unless the proper tools are available.

*Since writing the above there have been some minor changes made in the Champlin action. Most of the major action parts are now made of SAE 4140 steel by the investment casting process. The sliding tang safety is now standard. The Canjar trigger mechanism has been improved, and so has the bolt stop, the firing pin, etc. The actions are available in either right- or left-hand versions. The January, 1971 price schedule for actions is as follows, right- or left-hand operation:

Standard Calibers (.30-06 head-size cartridges)	$237.50
Standard Magnum calibers	257.50
.378 and .460 Weatherby Magnum calibers	277.50
Complete Champlin Custom Built rifles start at	890.00

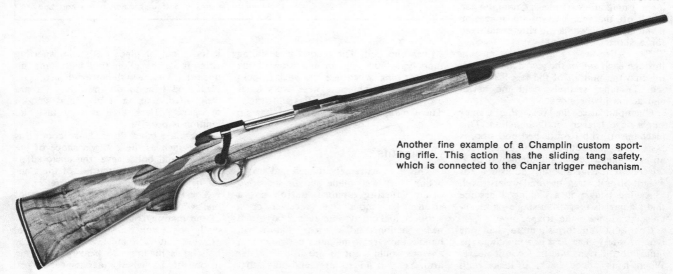

Another fine example of a Champlin custom sporting rifle. This action has the sliding tang safety, which is connected to the Canjar trigger mechanism.

37. Ruger Model 77

B ILL RUGER is a well-known modern gun designer whose creations include the Ruger .22 Automatic pistol, the Single Six and Blackhawk single action revolvers, the Model 10/22 .22 automatic rifle, the Ruger .44 Magnum Carbine and the Number 1 single shot rifle. All are successful, and all are currently manufactured by the firm he heads; Sturm, Ruger & Co. (Southport, Conn. 06490). His latest creation is a very modernized Mauser-type turnbolt centerfire action, around which his firm is building fine "classic" bolt action sporting rifles, originally popularized by Stewart Edward White and E.C. Crossman in the early days of the 03 Springfield. The Ruger bolt action rifle is the Model 77, and without question it will become a leading number in the evergrowing Ruger line-up.

The Model 77 Ranger Rifle

Introduced in 1968, the M77 Ruger rifle today (late 1971) is offered in one grade and in 11 calibers. This list includes the .22-250, 6mm Remington, .243, .308, .284, 6.5 and .350 Remington Magnum; (and in the magnum action .270, .30-06, .25-06 and 7mm Remington Magnum calibers*). Weighing about 6.5 pounds, the M77 has a nicely contoured 22″ sporter-weight barrel, and a classic-patterned American walnut stock that is hand checkered and finished. The stock carries a rubber buttpad, a pistol grip cap containing the Ruger emblem, and sling swivel studs. The 77R, complete with

---

*New Models. In 1970 Ruger announced the Model 77 Varmint rifle in .22-250 caliber. It has a heavy 24″ barrel, tapped for target scope blocks, and has a suggested retail price of $165, including Ruger tip-off scope rings.
In 1971 a new long-action M77 rifle was announced designated the Ruger 77 Magnum. It will initially be available in .25-06, .30-06 and 7mm Rem. Magnum. In the same year Ruger offered the 77 rifles (both action lengths) with rounded-top receivers, contoured to take a wide range of scope bases (Redfield, Conetrol, Buehler, et al). At the same time a redesigned bolt handle was revealed, made a little longer and with a more rounded knob.

Ruger 1″ split scope rings, lists for $165. The 77RS, otherwise the same as the 77R, comes with an open rear sight and a front sight mounted on an English type ramp base, its cost $179.

The 77 Ruger has received many rave reviews from most of the gun authorities and editors since its introduction. Praised are the excellent lines, balance and "feel" of the rifle, its fine "handling" quality. The trim and unadorned classic stock is given much praise. Everyone remarked upon the exceptionally fine accuracy of their test rifles. Few reporters found any fault with the rifle, or desired any changes be made on it or anything added or removed. As for me, I think the Ruger 77 is quite a rifle, but the purpose of this book is not to put down my evaluation of any rifle, but to discuss, describe and evaluate the *action*. While not available at this writing, Ruger 77 barreled actions and separate actions should become available when the production of complete rifles has caught up with demand.

The Model 77 Action

Just as Bill Ruger is a modern gun designer, so is he a proponent of the most modern manufacturing methods and techniques. His aim is to produce the best possible sporting firearms, of superior design at the lowest possible cost, yet without sacrificing strength, reliability and accuracy. This he has done and is doing. Therefore, one of the manufacturing methods he has adopted is the fabricating of the major steel action parts by the investment casting process. This process is too complicated to describe here, but the net result is that many parts can be cast to extremely close tolerances, with only a minimum amount of machining and polishing needed to complete each casting. The process also allows the finest steel alloys to be used, thus the parts are made of the best steels for strength and durability. Before or after finishing, the

steel investment castings can be heat treated as required, the same as if the individual parts were machined from solid stock. To produce the investment castings Ruger built a new facility in New Hampshire.

Castings are generally regarded with suspicion by shooters, as the word "casting" probably reminds them of cast iron or some other form of cheap casting. Years ago the making of precision castings of a quality alloy steel was considered about as impossible as taking a walk on the moon—we know better now! Parts of the Ruger 77 action which are made from investment castings include the receiver, bolt and extractor, all of chrome-molybdenum steel (AISI 4140), with each part properly heat treated. Other small steel action parts are also investment castings, including the scope mount rings. The only non-steel parts are the trigger guard and floorplate, both made of a lightweight alloy.

The 77 action has several unusual and noteworthy design and construction features, these found in no other turnbolt centerfire action. This includes the receiver which, unlike most such actions, is slab sided. That is, the receiver sides are flat, and the effect is pleasing. The receiver bottom is also flat, although the flats are not in the same plane. The receiver ring bottom is entirely flat except for the area taken up by the recoil lug. This affords a large "bottoming" area for the receiver against the stock, an area which, if properly bedded, contributes to the accuracy of the finished rifle. The recoil lug is ample in depth and width to prevent set-back of the barrel and action in the stock from recoil.

To the rear of the receiver-ring flat the bottom plane of the receiver moves up about .250″, with the magazine well opening in it. Extra wide guide lips on each

---

Illustrated above: Standard Ruger Model 77 short action rifle with open sights.

side of this well hold the cartridges in the magazine, guiding them into the chamber when the bolt is closed. A long loading-guide ramp, in the front of the well, leads over the bottom locking-lug shoulder to guide the cartridges upward and out of the magazine into the chamber.

The receiver ring is about 1.725″ long. The loading and ejection port, between the ring and the bridge, is about 2.750″ long, the bridge length about 1.00″. The top of the bridge is about .125″ lower than the ring top, and on each there is an integral flat-topped scope mounting base. In the middle of each side of these bases there is a circular notch. The special Ruger-made scope mount rings are made to clamp very securely on these bases. To prevent the mount rings from sliding on the bases from recoil, a small projection, integral with and rising from each ring, fits into a matching notch cut into the top of the bases. The Ruger mounts, very rugged indeed, are readily detachable.

At this writing the 77 action is made only in one length* and with a right-hand bolt. The left receiver wall is about .775″ high, but though it is channeled out to form the left-locking lug raceway, it is quite heavy and rigid. The receiver wall is unlike most other centerfire turnbolt actions, which have the right wall no higher than the bottom of the right locking lug raceway. The right wall on the Ruger action extends about .250″ higher than this. The extra ridge of metal adds greatly to the strength and rigidity of the receiver. The Savage 110 receiver is made the same way.

The 77 bolt stop is also noteworthy. It is of the 98 Mauser type, in that it is attached to the left rear of the receiver, has a projection extending into the left locking-lug raceway that halts the bolt travel by contacting the left locking lug, and that it is swung outward to release the bolt. It is shaped like the 98 Mauser bolt stop, but is far simpler and more rugged. It is a small rectangular block of steel with a large oblong hole through its rear end. Fitted into this hole is a heavy screw and bushing, with the screw threaded into the receiver. In another hole, length-wise through the bolt stop, a plunger and a very stiff coil spring are fitted. Held in place by a small pin through the front of the bolt stop, the plunger contacts the bolt stop screw and bushing, providing the ten-

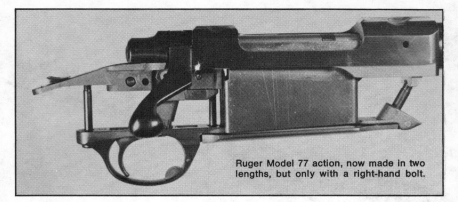

Ruger Model 77 action, now made in two lengths, but only with a right-hand bolt.

sion needed to hold the bolt stop forward, against the receiver; it also allows the front of the bolt stop to be swung away from the receiver to remove the bolt. While the spring holds the bolt stop forward, the oblong hole allows the bolt stop to move back a slight amount against spring tension. This provides a buffer or shock absorber to the bolt when it is opened and drawn back. This lessens the abrupt shock when the bolt is halted, and may help the shooter in speedy operation of the bolt by starting it forward again after it is stopped.

The 77 bolt is of one-piece construction, the bolt handle made as an integral part. Dual-opposed forward locking lugs, engaging shoulders inside the receiver ring, hold the bolt locked in the receiver. Both locking lugs are solid. The left (upper) locking lug, larger than the right one, extends to the forward edge of the bolt, forming part of the rim of the bolt face recess.

The extractor, a long one-piece Mauser type, is attached to the bolt by a collar, which fits into a groove around the bolt body. The extractor doesn't rotate with the bolt. Longitudinal movement of the extractor is prevented by a lip, under the front end of the extractor, engaging a groove cut part way round the bolt head. The well-beveled extractor hook slips easily over a chambered cartridge rim on closing the bolt.

The bolt head is recessed for the head of the cartridge. About half of this recess is .120″ deep, while the other half (over which the extractor hook extends) is only about .030″ deep. Thus, unlike 98 Mauser and pre-64 Winchester 70 bolts, the cart-

ridges are fed into the chamber ahead of the bolt and extractor, thus double loading is possible if the bolt handle is not turned down after a cartridge is chambered.

The ejector, a spring-loaded plunger in the bolt face, is held in place by a cross pin.

The bolt handle has a very low profile to clear the eyepiece of a low-mounted scope. The side of the receiver is deeply notched for the heavy base of the bolt handle, and this forms the safety lug. The flat, but tapered, stem of the bolt handle angles sharply back to place the grasping ball within easy reach of the shooter's hand. The grasping ball is neither round nor pear shaped—it has a shape all its own. While this grasping ball may be satisfactory generally, I don't like the sharp top rear corner of the stem, or its sharp rearward angle.

An angled surface on the base of the bolt handle, which meets a matching surface on the rear left of the receiver bridge, gives the initial camming power to the extractor when the bolt handle is raised; angled corners on the approaches of the locking-lug shoulders provide the power to force the bolt entirely forward when the bolt handle is lowered.

A short projection on the outside center of the 77 bolt, which they call the bolt guide, is not unlike the guide on the pre-64 Winchester 70 bolt. On fully raising the bolt handle the edge of this guide contacts the lower edge of the left locking-lug raceway, stopping further rotation of the bolt. Then, as the bolt is opened, it slides along the raceway until it is out of the receiver entirely. However, this bolt guide does

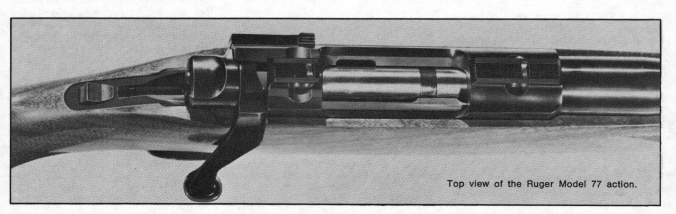

Top view of the Ruger Model 77 action.

little to guide the bolt, and does nothing when the bolt is fully opened.

The bolt is drilled from the rear for the firing mechanism; the latter consists of bolt sleeve, one-piece firing pin, cocking piece and coil mainspring. The cocking piece fits into the rear of the bolt sleeve; the firing pin fits tightly into the cocking piece, secured by a heavy pin. The rear end of the cocking piece can be seen and felt at all times to determine whether the action is cocked or not. There is a deep cocking cam notch on the rear of the bolt into which the nose of the cocking piece engages, and on opening the bolt the striker is cocked. When the bolt is open the nose of the cocking piece rests in a shallow notch on the rear of the bolt, which prevents the bolt sleeve from being easily turned when the bolt is open. Striker travel is very short and fast, which is always desirable.

Ruger has made this a very safe action by providing means for powder gases to escape harmlessly out of the action in the event of a ruptured case head or pierced primer. The vent hole through the right side of the receiver ring, opposite the extractor hook, should take care of most of the powder gases resulting from a case-head failure. One large round hole and two long slots, in the bolt body, directed downward into the magazine box, should take care of gases entering the bolt body through the firing-pin hole. There is little chance that any gases could ever escape back through the bolt sleeve. If any gases got into the left locking-lug raceway they would be deflected outward by the flange on the left side of the bolt sleeve. I think Ruger's idea of having vent holes in the bolt directing gases downward into the magazine is better than having them open into the left locking-lug raceway.

The simple trigger mechanism is fully adjustable for weight-of-pull, take-up and over-travel. The weight-of-pull adjustment setscrew can be adjusted without removing the barrel and action from the stock (see illustration). The take-up and over-

A pair of 1″ split-type scope mount rings are standard equipment with the Model 77 Ruger, included in the price of the rifles and barreled actions. Designed and made by Ruger, they clamp securely on the integral bases milled into the top of the receiver ring and bridge.

travel screws are properly adjusted at the factory so there is no need to adjust them further.

The trigger mechanism is contained in a steel housing, which is fitted in the bottom of the receiver and held in place by a rolled cross pin. The sear pivots on a pin through walls in the bottom of the receiver, and is tensioned by a small coil spring. The long trigger, located directly below the sear, pivots on a pin through the bottom of the trigger housing. The trigger is tensioned by a small coil spring positioned between a setscrew in the bottom of the trigger and a seat on a bracket at the rear of the housing. This setscrew, an Allen-head type, is the weight-of-pull adjustment screw; turning it counterclockwise reduces the weight of pull to as light

as two pounds. The screw can be reached with a bent Allen wrench through the trigger guard bow.

The top part of the trigger is in two parts; the front part or arm engages the safety, the rear arm engages the sear. This rear arm is quite thin and spring tempered. The top of it is honed square and smooth where it contacts a similar surface on the bottom of the sear. There is a hole through this sear arm for a slotted-head adjustment screw, which threads into the safety arm. The bottom of this screw head is notched to match a slight ridge across the edges of the hole in the sear arm; this provides a sort of click effect for the adjustment of this screw, and prevents it from turning after adjustment. Turning this screw in (clockwise) reduces sear engagement. This screw is factory adjusted for minimal safe sear engagement. There is an Allen-head setscrew in front of the hole in which the sear-engagement screw is threaded; after the factory adjustment is made this setscrew is turned against the sear-adjustment screw so that it cannot be turned in farther, as doing so to decrease sear engagement would leave the action unsafe. A hole in the front of the housing, located directly in front of this locking setscrew, is the Allen-head trigger over-travel adjustment screw. It is also correctly adjusted at the factory. This over-travel, or trigger-stop, screw is normally adjusted as follows: with the bolt closed and the striker down, turn the setscrew in as far as it will go, then back it off about ¼-turn.

The 77 has a true sliding tang safety. The receiver tang is made long enough, and slotted, so that a shotgun-type safety button can be positioned in it. The rotary safety shaft (or lock) is located in a hole through the walls in the bottom of the receiver. On the left side of this safety shaft a lever is riveted. A piece of bent wire connects the manual safety button with this lever, so that sliding the button back and forth rotates the safety shaft. A small looped-wire spring,

Left side view of the Ruger Model 77 action opened. Note receiver markings and angled front guard screw.

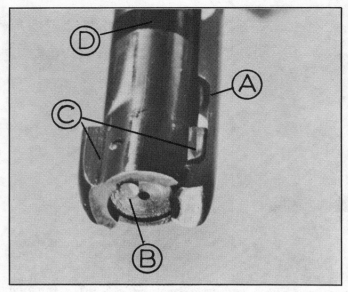

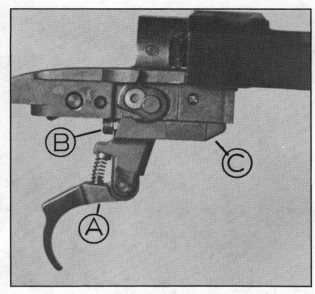

Left—Ruger Model 77 bolt head showing: (A) extractor, (B) ejector, (C) dual-opposed locking lugs, (D) extractor collar. Right—Ruger Model 77 trigger mechanism showing: (A) location of weight-of-pull adjustment screw, (B) sear-engagement adjustment screw, (C) over-travel adjustment screw.

hitched to the lever, provides the ON and OFF tension to the safety. Another lever is attached to the right side of the safety shaft and when the safety button is pulled back the end of this lever rotates up into a slot in the receiver, engaging a notch in the bolt to lock it. The center portion of the safety shaft has a flat spot where it fits between forked arms on top of the trigger; the trigger can only be released when the flat side is aligned with the rear fork, but is locked when the safety shaft is rotated ¼-turn. Design and construction of the various trigger and safety parts are all good, and when the safety is pulled back the trigger and bolt are securely locked. The safety on my Ruger was stiff and quite difficult to engage or disengage, and it would be even more difficult to move with a cold or gloved thumb. I would much rather have a large-buttoned side-tang safety or a bolt sleeve safety—one that can be positively and noiselessly disengaged.

Folded heavy sheet steel forms the magazine box; it is welded together at the rear, and there reinforced by a heavier steel strap. The upper sides of the box are curved slightly inward so that the box will fit into the magazine well in the receiver. Integral projections under the receiver, fore and aft of the magazine well, securely and accurately position and hold the magazine box in place.

The trigger guard bow is a very neat lightweight alloy casting. Screws through holes in each end of the bow, threading into the bottom of the receiver, hold it in place in the stock and help hold the barrel and action in the stock. The front end of the guard bow projects far enough forward to hold the rear of the magazine box in place.

The front of the magazine box is held in place by the floorplate hinge plate. The front guard screw, passing through this plate, threads into the recoil lug on the bottom of the receiver. More on this later. The floorplate is connected to this hinge plate by a pin with the hinge joint on the front end of this plate. Thus the light alloy floorplate covers the head of the front guard screw. A latch in the front top part of the bow holds the floorplate closed. Pressing the serrated button inside the bow allows the floorplate to be swung down for quick unloading. The stainless steel follower is attached to one end of the W-shaped follower spring, the spring's other end fits into a mortise in the floorplate. The Ruger Parts List indicates that a steel trigger guard bow and magazine floorplate can be ordered.

A Ruger-patented feature of the 77 action is the angled front guard screw, which enters the recoil lug at about a 62° angle. This can be clearly seen in the photographs and in the sectional view drawing. The hinge plate, through which this screw passes, has a flat surface at right angles to the screw; on tightening the screw the receiver is not only pulled down into the stock, but is pulled back as well, bringing the rear of the recoil lug in closest contact with the stock. The area under the receiver ring, which includes the recoil lug, is a most vital area in the bedding of the action. Since it is a well-established fact that a constant contact between the rear of the recoil lug and the stock is a factor in obtaining consistent top accuracy, the Ruger angled guard-screw principle is a sound one. That it fulfills this function seems evident, for all test reports on the 77 indicate high accuracy. I don't think, really, that any individual 77 rifle would be any less accurate if it were fitted with a right-angled front guard screw (as all other centerfire turnbolt actions have), but if the Ruger rearward-angled screw helps hold the recoil lug back against the wood, which it does if kept tightened, then I'm all for it. The head of the screw is covered by the front end of the floorplate so there is nothing unsightly about it.

Underside of the Ruger Model 77 bolt showing the 3 large gas-vent holes.

Parts Legend

D-1. Receiver
D-2. Trigger guard
D-3. Barrel
D-4. Stock
D-5. Floorplate
D-6. Floorplate pivot pin
D-7. Floorplate hinge
D-8. Ejector
D-9. Ejector spring
D-10. Bolt
D-11. Firing pin (assembly only, includes firing pin, mainspring, bolt sleeve, cocking piece and cocking-piece pin.)
D-14. Extractor
D-15. Extractor band
D-20. Trigger
D-21. Trigger-pivot pin
D-22. Trigger-adjustment screw (engagement)
D-23. Sear
D-24. Sear spring
D-25. Trigger housing
D-26. Trigger-housing cross pin
D-27. Magazine box
D-30. Magazine follower
D-31. Magazine latch
D-32. Magazine-latch spring
D-33. Magazine spring
D-35. Bolt lock
D-37. Safety spring
D-38. Safety button
D-39. Safety link
D-40. Magazine-latch pin
D-41. Ejector retaining pin
D-42. Sear pivot pin
D-43. Trigger adj. screw (weight of pull)
D-44. Trigger adj. setscrew (over-travel)
D-45. Trigger adj. screw (over-travel)
D-46. Receiver, mounting screw (front)
D-47. Receiver, mounting screw (center)
D-48. Receiver, mounting screw (rear)
D-49. Trigger-return spring
D-51. Trigger-return spring seat
D-53. Bolt stop
D-54. Bolt-stop screw stud
D-55. Bolt-stop stud bushing
D-56. Bolt-stop plunger
D-57. Bolt-stop plunger spring
D-58. Safety shaft assembly
D-59. Bolt-stop plunger spring-retaining pin

D-60. Sight (rear) base only
D-61. Sight base (rear) center screw
D-62. Sight base (rear) rear screw
S-63. Recoil pad
D-67. Sight blade (front)
D-68. Sight (front) plunger
D-69. Sight (front) plunger spring

D-70. Sight base (front) setscrew
D-71. Scope-ring assembly
D-73. Scope-ring nut
D-74. Scope-ring clamp
D-76. Scope-ring screw
D-77. Sight (rear) folding, complete
D-83A. Williams gib lock (sight clamp, rear)

D-83B. Screw for part #D-83A
D-86. Sling swivel front screw with nut
D-87. Sling swivel rear mounting stud
C-96. Pistol-grip cap screw
C-97. Pistol-grip cap
C-107. Pistol-grip cap medallion

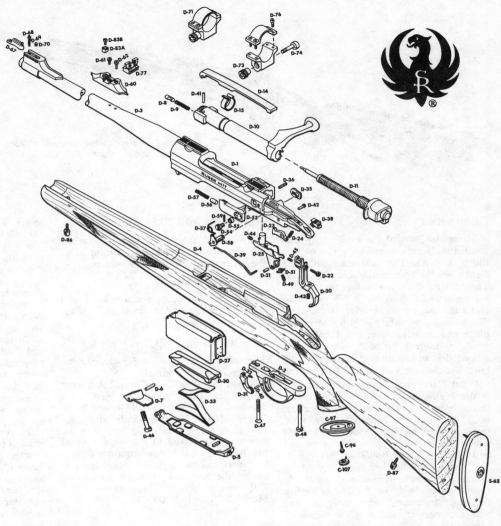

Dimensional Specifications

	Medium Action	Long Action
Weight	40 oz.	42 oz.
Length	9.00″	9.54″
Receiver width	1.315″	1.315″
Bolt dia.	.695″	.695″
Bolt travel	4.140″	4.826″
Striker travel	.281″	.281″
Bolt face recess:		
Depth	.120″	
Dia. (.30-06 head-sized cartridges)	.475″	
(belted magnum cartridges)	.550″	
Magazine length	2.925″	3.380″

General Specifications

Type	Turnbolt repeater.
Receiver	One-piece investment casting of chrome-molybdenum steel. Non-slotted bridge. Integral scope mount bases on ring and bridge, adapted to Ruger mounts.
Bolt	One-piece chrome-molybdenum investment casting with solid dual-opposed forward locking lugs. Base of low-profile bolt handle serves as safety lug. 90° rotation.
Ignition	One-piece firing pin powered by coil mainspring. Cocks on opening.
Magazine	Non-detachable staggered-column 5-shot box type with hinged floorplate.
Trigger	Single-stage type adjustable for weight-of-pull, take-up and over-travel.
Safety	Sliding tang type locks trigger mechanism and bolt when pulled back.
Extractor	Non-rotating one-piece spring Mauser-type fastened to bolt body by a collar.
Ejector	Plunger type in bolt head.
Bolt stop	Mauser type, fitted to left side of bridge, stops bolt by contacting left locking lug.

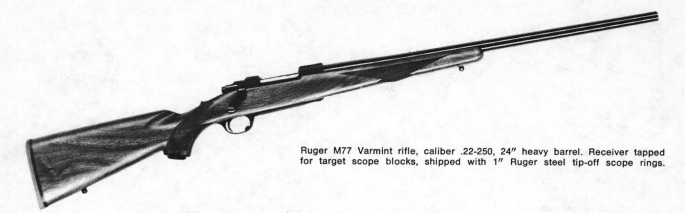

Ruger M77 Varmint rifle, caliber .22-250, 24" heavy barrel. Receiver tapped for target scope blocks, shipped with 1" Ruger steel tip-off scope rings.

Comments

There are several things I really like about the 77 action, and only one or two things I don't. The two main things I dislike are the bolt handle and the safety. The bolt handle stem is too angular for my taste, and I think some will complain about the sharp top rear edge of the stem. The sliding tang safety is in a convenient place and it looks nice, but I believe it would be more functional under all conditions if it was located at the side of the tang, like the safety of the 788 Remington.

What I like most about the 77 action is the Mauser-type extractor. I consider this type much better than the puny claw, hook, sliding or clip-type extractors found in most other modern centerfire turnbolt actions made today. I also like the rugged and buffered Ruger bolt stop very much. The trigger mechanism is to my liking in that it is simple, rugged and adjustable from the outside. I like the idea of having the scope mounting bases made integral with the receiver, and Ruger's system of securing and anchoring the rings to the receiver is without fault. More than ample provisions are made to vent gases harmlessly out of the action, and I like Ruger's idea of having the vent holes in the bolt directed into the magazine rather than into the left locking-lug raceway, as is done with many other bolt action rifles. I think the flat-sided receiver is pleasing, and I like the idea of not cutting the right side of the loading and ejection port down to the bottom of the locking-lug raceway, as the extra ridge of metal left here makes the receiver more rigid.

For further comment on the desirable aspects of the 77 action read my son Mark's chapter, "Ideal Sniper's Rifle," at the back of this book.

Ruger Model 77 Markings

The serial number is stamped on the left flat of the receiver ring. Stamped on the left side of the receiver wall is:

RUGER M77

The Ruger firm name and address is roll stamped on top of the barrel as follows:

STURM, RUGER & CO., SOUTHPORT, CONN. U.S.A.

The caliber designation is stamped on the breech of the barrel.

When the 1968 Gun Control Act went into effect Ruger adopted a new serial numbering system for all Ruger guns. Ruger Model 77 rifles made after this change in serial numbering will have the number 70 prefixed to the regular serial number. When this new digit-prefix system was instituted, serial numbers following the prefix numbers were restarted with number 1, thus: (as example the Model 77 rifle) 70-00001.

Take-Down and Assembly

Make sure the chamber and magazine are unloaded. To remove bolt raise bolt handle and pull bolt back, at the same time swinging the front of the bolt stop away from the receiver; insert a small pin or nail in the hole in the bottom of the cocking piece and unscrew bolt sleeve from bolt. To reassemble, turn bolt sleeve into bolt as far as it will go, then back up until cocking-piece nose rests in shallow notch at rear of the bolt, then remove pin.

It is not necessary to disassemble the firing mechanism unless some part has to be replaced. In this case it might be best to send the entire assembly to the factory. However, it can be disassembled as follows: Rig up some means (a vise or clamp) to compress the mainspring so the pin in the cocking piece is exposed beyond the end of the bolt sleeve, then drive the pin out. Since the mainspring is very strong use great care in releasing the clamp lest you be injured by flying parts or the parts lost. Reassemble in reverse order, and it is absolutely necessary that you use a clamping arrangement.

To remove the extractor raise its front end high enough so it can be pushed forward and slipped off bolt. Do not remove the extractor collar unless necessary because it may be sprung out of shape in so doing. The ejector and ejector spring can be removed by driving out the ejector pin.

To remove the barrel and action from stock, open magazine floorplate, turn out front guard screw, remove floorplate and hinge plate from the stock. Turn out rear and center guard screws, then pull guard bow and magazine box from stock. Lift out barrel and action assembly. Reassemble in reverse order, but tighten angled front guard screw before tightening center and rear guard screws.

To remove bolt stop turn out bolt stop screw stud. It can be reattached by depressing bolt stop plunger with a small screwdriver while turning in the screw stud.

To remove safety button lift out rear end of safety link, then safety link can be removed from safety shaft. To remove safety shaft first remove safety-shaft spring, then pry out Nylon washer from bolt lock with a round tool, then slide off bolt lock. To remove trigger housing (after safety spring is removed) drive out trigger-housing cross pin. Remove the sear and spring by driving out sear pivot pin from left to right. Reassemble in reverse order.

38. Herter's Plinker

THE LITTLE .22 Hornet cartridge has been around since about 1931. During the 1930s and 40s it was a very popular cartridge and several American and foreign rifles were chambered for it. Then along came the .222 Remington in 1950, which created such a stir among varmint shooters that the .22 Hornet was all but forgotten. One by one the American-made .22 Hornet rifles disappeared, including the 54, 70 and 43 Winchesters and the Savage 23D, 19H, 417, 417½, 340 and 219. By 1967 no American-made Hornet rifles were available. The availability of foreign rifles in .22 Hornet caliber was somewhat sporadic but, except during WW II years, it was always possible throughout most of this period to obtain a .22 Hornet by one means or another. Of the foreign-made bolt action .22 Hornet rifles there were two Stoeger imports, the Krico, Brno, Walther, Anschutz, Sako and several lesser-known makes.

Of these the Walther is still available, imported by Interarms Ltd., 10 Prince St., Alexandria, Va. The Walther actions are not available separately. For a few years the Krico Hornet and the original Sako Hornet actions were available, but not for the last 10 years or so. The Krico .22 Hornet action was last offered by Stoegers in 1959, and at that time it was listed at $85. Incidentally, the Tradewinds Model 600 action described in another chapter is an offspring of this Krico action.

I now refer you to the No. 956 Precision Hornet Rifle, from Stoeger's 1934 *Shooter's Bible*. Most knowledgeable arms students can tell at a glance that this was not much of a rifle, and the description of it will fool only a few. In all the years since this rifle was first listed I have seen only one of them, and I can tell you it was a toy. It was no more than a very light boy's rifle, of the type commonly used for .22 rimfire cartridges, merely made over to accept the .22 Hornet cartridge. This brings us to Herter's Model Plinker rifle, the main topic of this chap-

ter, for it too is a "toy" rifle, in my opinion.

During the many years I did rifle-barrel and chambering work I turned down numerous jobs of rebarreling and/or rechambering .22 rimfire rifles to the .22 Hornet or some other .22 centerfire cartridge. Many more were the letters I received asking questions about whether or not this or that low-cost .22 bolt action rifle or action was suitable for the Hornet. My reply was almost always a negative one. I don't know just how well Stoeger's No. 956 Precision Hornet rifle stood up, but I have serious doubts about Herter's Plinker.

For example, if I were asked if a Model D Page-Lewis single-shot bolt action rifle would be suitable for rechambering to the .22 Hornet, my answer would be a positive "NO." Yet that is just about what the maker of the Plinker is doing—using a very weak .22 rimfire action and building Hornet rifles on it. Not only are they using such an action for the .22 Hornet, but for the .222 cartridge as well! Having got a number of letters inquiring about Herter's Model Plinker rifle, I grew curious about it myself. To find out what sort of rifle it is I ordered one, and here it is.

Herter's .22 Hornet Rifle

Listed in Herter's 1970 catalog (Herter's Inc., Waseca, Minn. 56093) as the Model Plinker, this is a single-shot turn-bolt rifle, listed as being available in .22 Hornet or .222 calibers. The rifle I received, in the .22 Hornet caliber, weighs about 4.3 pounds and has a 21″ barrel. The 6-groove barrel has a twist of one turn in 16″, the groove diameter .223″. The barrel, about .630″ in diameter, is not tapered. It is held in the round receiver by a single small cross pin. The simple blade front sight, dovetailed into the barrel, is adjustable for elevation. The receiver top is grooved for common tip-off scope mounts.

The hardwood stock is stained dark,

the inletting done by machine. The barrel and action are held in the stock by a single screw threading into the bottom of the receiver ring. The stock, which has no buttplate, is deeply grooved. It has a full pistol grip and a comb raised so high that it is about impossible to get one's face down low enough to use the open sights. The stock is sanded smooth and given a glossy finish. The rifle is priced at $43.95.

The letters **LUX**, within a diamond, are stamped on the receiver ring. The caliber designation and serial number are stamped on the barrel just forward of the receiver. The words **MADE IN GERMANY** (in small letters and lightly imprinted) are stamped on the left side of the receiver ring. There are no less than three proofmarks on the barrel and receiver!

The Plinker Action

The receiver, .865″ in diameter, is about 5″ long. A 1.5″ opening in the top of the receiver gives access to the chamber.

The one-piece bolt, .587″ in diameter, is recessed for the cartridge head. The bolt handle, which has a bent-down stem and a round grasping ball, fits into a hole in the rear of the bolt. The right rear side of the receiver has an L-shaped slot for the bolt handle to pass and lock into, when the bolt handle is turned down. The back of the slightly enlarged base of the bolt handle is filed flat, this becoming the locking surface against a locking notch in the thin-walled (about .160″ thick) receiver. This locking notch is not very deep, but the bolt handle in this notch is the only thing that locks and holds the bolt in the receiver when the rifle is fired. Neither bolt handle nor receiver are hardened; a file easily cut both parts.

The bolt body, open from the rear,

Illustrated above: The German-made Herter's Plinker rifle, made in .22 Hornet or .222 calibers. Shown fitted with a Savage variable scope.

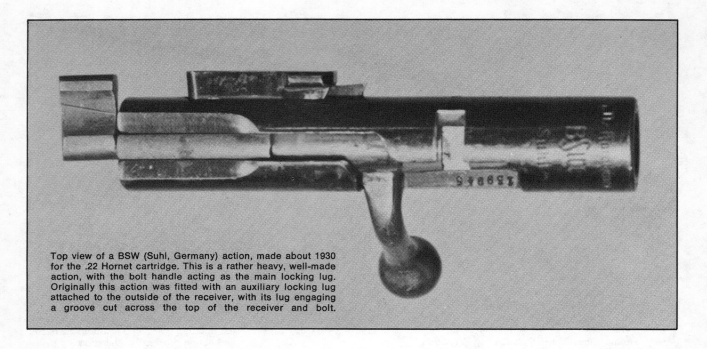

Top view of a BSW (Suhl, Germany) action, made about 1930 for the .22 Hornet cartridge. This is a rather heavy, well-made action, with the bolt handle acting as the main locking lug. Originally this action was fitted with an auxiliary locking lug attached to the outside of the receiver, with its lug engaging a groove cut across the top of the receiver and bolt.

takes the one-piece firing pin and its coil mainspring. A bushing, threaded into the rear of the bolt, compresses the mainspring and holds the firing pin in place. The cocking piece, which fits onto the rear end of the firing pin stem (projecting to the rear of the bolt) is held by a pin. A stud, fitting into the side of the cocking piece, which moves in the bolt handle slot, provides a means to place the rifle on SAFE when the action is cocked. This is done by turning the stud up to engage a shallow notch in the rear of the receiver. The sliding type extractor fits into a slot cut lengthwise in the bottom of the receiver. Its front end half-encircles the cartridge head. The rear end of the extractor, bent upward to engage a groove in the bottom of the bolt, is thus pulled back when the bolt is opened. This type of extractor is found in several different foreign-made .22 rimfire rifles, as well as in the long-obsolete Page-Lewis Model D and Winchester Model 67 rimfire rifles. I don't know how the .222 extractor is made in this rifle, but it probably has a narrow hook which snaps into the extractor groove in the rimless cartridge head.

As in the Page-Lewis rifle, the sear is a long spring fastened to the bottom of the receiver ring by a screw. The trigger is pivoted on the rear end of this spring on a pin. The extractor is normally held in place by this spring. Two projections on this spring extend into the boltway, one forming the sear, the other the bolt stop. When the bolt is closed the rear projection engages forward of the cocking piece, and holds it back as the bolt is moved forward and locked. The trigger has a two-stage let-off, the last stage quite short and light.

The trigger guard is a steel stamping screwed to the bottom of the stock.

Comments

I don't think much of this rifle. Whether it is safe to use remains to be seen. I've already mentioned some very poor features and weak points, such as the pinned-in barrel, the soft thin-walled receiver, and a bolt handle which provides the only locking lug to hold the bolt closed, but there are more. For example, the trigger can be pulled at any time, even if the bolt handle is only very slightly down. The locking notch is not very deep at best and there is nothing to prevent this rifle from being fired even if the bolt handle is not fully closed. More on this later. Also, with the bolt open, if the rifle is held up-side-down and the trigger pulled back, the extractor will fall out. Furthermore, when the bolt is removed the extractor is free to fall out.

The Model 23D Savage, while not having a hardened-steel receiver, nevertheless had two large locking lugs to hold the bolt closed. Yet if this rifle was fired a lot it gradually developed headspace through wear and set-back of the bolt in the receiver.

The Model 43 Winchester receiver was hardened, and its bolt also had twin locking surfaces, but if this rifle was fired a great deal it too would develop excess headspace. I have always considered these two bolt actions as about the minimum for cartridges like the .22 Hornet. However, they had enough of a built-in margin of safety so that they were still usually safe to fire even with considerable excess headspace. I also consider the Model 1922 M-1 and M-2 Springfield actions as being on the minimal side, yet with a marginal safety factor for the .22 Hornet cartridge. At least these rifles could not be fired unless the bolt was locked sufficiently to hold it closed upon firing. Compare these three actions with Herter's Plinker action and it is predictable what is going to happen when the Plinker is fired to any extent. In my opinion the Plinker is an unsafe rifle, in .22 Hornet or .222 caliber, and I cannot recommend it.

Fortunately the bolt in my Plinker rifle locked up very tightly, and some effort was required to fully lower the bolt handle. How long it will remain tight is another question, but I've seen many .22 rimfire rifles, with stronger actions than this one, wear and loosen up to the point where they were positively unsafe to fire. While the action of my Plinker Hornet rifle was still tight my son took it out for a limited range test. I decided against firing factory ammunition in it, but used handloads consisting of 8 grains of #2400 powder behind the 45-gr. .223" Sierra Hornet bullets. This is a moderate load which I've found to be very accurate in a number of different rifles and handguns. Using a 4x Weaver B4 scope, and shooting from a rest, the first 5 shots, after 5 sighting-in shots, grouped within 1.7" at 50 yards. This surprised us. Taking suitable precautions we fired one shot with the bolt handle only halfway down, and the bolt remained in that position. After the shallow locking notch becomes worn, and it surely will if the rifle is fired a few hundred times, firing this rifle with the bolt only half-locked might prove disastrous.

I wish there was a fairly good small turnbolt action available today made for the .22 Hornet cartridge, but there just isn't—not even a surplus military action, readily available today, suitable for making up a trim rifle in the Hornet caliber. I believe there's a market for a good, low-cost single-shot turnbolt action made especially for the Hornet cartridge. For example, an action like the Model 580 Remington, with its 6 rear locking lugs, would be about what I have in mind. Remington could easily make this action to be more than adequate in strength for the Hornet cartridge, and I'm also sure they could make it to sell for less than $30.

39. Ideal Sniper's Rifle

FOR AN ENTIRE YEAR, as an instructor in the Marine scout-sniper school in Vietnam, I had an opportunity—indeed, it was part of my job—to check on the activities of the several platoons of Marine scout-snipers stationed throughout the First Marine Division area around Da Nang and Phu Bai. Besides being an instructor, part of my time was taken up in gathering and keeping records of the kills made, keeping tabs on the sniper rifles, helping the individual snipers keep their rifles properly in order and sighted-in, obtaining replacement rifles and scopes, and doing anything else to aid in the snipers in their work. Thus I had the opportunity to evaluate our present sniper rifle.

The standard sniper rifle now being used by the Marines in Vietnam is the Model 700 Remington. This rifle closely resembles the commercial Model 700 BDL Varmint Special, except that the outside metal parts are Parkerized and the stock has an oil-type finish. It is chambered for the 7.62mm NATO (.308) cartridge. It is equipped with the Redfield 3-9x variable-power scope, in Redfield Jr. mounts, and fitted with the rangefinder reticle. This rifle gave a very good account of itself in the last two years in Vietnam, and it is, almost without question, the best sniper rifle ever issued. However, after having fired, examined and kept tab on a number of these rifles in use in Vietnam, I could not overlook the number of weaknesses that showed up.

The average sportsman owning the counterpart of this sniper rifle, scope and mount, could expect to use it for many years without ever having any trouble with it. But wartime combat conditions are something entirely different. In one year in Vietnam, the sniper rifle may be subjected to more use and abuse (not from the sniper, but from weather and

other conditions) than it would from a lifetime of use by a sportsman. For example, in one month it may be used in an area or during a period that is very hot, dry and dusty. It may next be used in the swampy areas under conditions of rain, mud and high humidity. High elevations present other climatic hazards. Probably the worst hazard occurs when troops are transported in trucks; in the crowded box of a truck the sniper cannot very well cradle his rifle in his lap, and resting it butt down in the hard riding truck certainly does it no good.

Marine snipers are taught to always make the first shot count. That is certainly the most important shot, and it may be the only one he'll get before he is shot at. Since an accurate first shot is so essential, the sniper rifle must be properly sighted-in

---

AUTHOR'S NOTE: This chapter was written by my son, Douglas Mark de Haas, in 1968 shortly after his honorable discharge from the Marine Corps. He practically grew up in my basement gunshop, and he always accompanied me when I went target shooting and hunting. He became very skilled with both shotgun and rifle on game, but especially so with the rifle on moving game and on targets. He spent most of his first 3 years in the Marine Corps as a member of a Marine rifle team, distinguishing himself through his marksmanship. His most important win was the 1000-yard Leech Cup Match at Camp Perry in 1966. The last year of his enlistment was spent in Vietnam as an instructor in the Marine sniper school. His knowledge of turnbolt rifles and his experience qualifies him to write as he does about the sniper rifle.

Frank de Haas

---

and just as importantly, stay zeroed-in for the entire time the sniper is afield.

Even though the Remington 700 sniper rifle is considered the best sniper rifle now in use, I have seen too many of them put out of commission by the weather, a ride in a truck, or by some unavoidable mishap, and not always the fault of the sniper.

A more perfect sniper outfit, in my opinion, would be one more rugged, more weather-proof and above all, more simplified. By "more simplified," I mean a rifle having a minimum of parts and adjustments, with a scope and mount combination more rugged than any commercial scope and mount made today. It should be free of all gadgets and needless adjustments or commercial "sales appeal" refinements, and it should have a minimum number of screws.

The Scope

In my visits with the snipers in my area, I learned that more sniper rifles were put out of action because of scope failure than from all other causes combined. In one such trip, during which I obtained records of some 17 sniper rifles, 10 were out of commission because of some type of scope failure. The result is that I've come to some definite conclusions about a scope for sniper use.

1) The scope should be a fixed power one, and I believe 8x would be ideal. Practically all of the Marine snipers I've talked with set their scopes at the highest power, and leave them so set. Few of them ever had the need to use a lower power. Some of them were set at 7x or 8x because the scopes would be slightly out of focus when set at 9x. Quite often, after

Illustrated above: Sgt. Douglas Mark de Haas, U.S. Marine Corps, sighting-in the Model 700 Remington sniper rifle.

Serving as a Marine Corps Scout/Sniper instructor in Vietnam, the author's son had the opportunity to examine and range test a Model 1891 Russian sniper rifle captured from the Viet Cong. Using captured 7.62mm Russian ammunition, Sgt. de Haas found the rifle very accurate and a weapon to be feared even at a range of 500 yards or more.

a scope was fixed for some time at one setting, it would freeze at that setting. The variable power feature has only been a source of trouble.

2) The scope should have no built-in mechanical rangefinder. While Marine scout-snipers were taught to use the rangefinder, most of them seldom bothered with it in combat. Like the variable power feature, the rangefinder was just another mechanical device that could, and often did, get out of order. For example, the rangefinder post was evidently made of plastic and, if the scope was in a position to let the sun shine into it, or through it, this post would become distorted or "wilt."

3) The scope must be sealed against the entrance of moisture, and must remain so-sealed under all conditions. I heard complaints from several snipers whose scopes had fogged. Elimination of the variable power and rangefinder mechanisms would also do away with the openings in the scope for these devices, and thus eliminate two possible sources of moisture leakage.

4) The elevation and windage adjustment knobs should be made so that they can be grasped and turned by the fingers —at least the elevation knob should be made this way. There should be ½-minute click graduations, with enough tension to let the clicks be felt under any condition, even with cold and numb fingers. There should be well-defined index marks on the turret, and both knobs

should have zero index plates which can be moved and locked after sighting-in. Preferably these index marks on the turret and index plates should be visible from the rear, so that the sniper can check the setting with the rifle in shooting position. In addition, the turn indicators (the arrows with the words UP and RIGHT) should also be on the rear of the turret, and boldly visible to the sniper with the rifle at his shoulder. Thus, if necessary, the sniper can, while in any shooting position, check the elevation and windage settings and reach up and make any adjustments without the use of any tool, and also be sure that he is turning the knob in the right direction if he makes an adjustment. Screw-on caps should be provided to cover both adjustment knobs. It is inevitable, however, that many of these caps will be lost, and some snipers prefer not to have the caps in place when in combat. It would be desirable, therefore, that the turrets and adjustment knobs be so well made and sealed that the caps would not be necessary.

5) The reticle should be permanently centered and etched on glass. In the current sniper scope, reticle failure in the field has put some rifles out of commission. A reticle etched on glass would do away with broken or sagging crosswires, and eliminate possible damage if the scope were placed in such a position as to allow the hot rays of the sun to enter the scope. After much thought and experience in

using different types of reticles, I believe the best reticle would be a medium-fine crosshair, with an additional short crosshair below the main intersection. The main horizontal line should be slightly above the center of the field and the shorter line slightly below center, these spaced to compensate for the difference in trajectory from 500 yards to 1000 yards. This would be an uncomplicated reticle, easy to see through and easy to aim with. The rifle would be sighted-in at 500 yards using the top or main intersection; the lower intersection, or imaginary positions in between, is used for ranges up to 1000 yards. The glass reticle could also be etched with the numerals "500" and "1000" alongside the crossline intersections, but this might well clutter up the view through the scope.

6) The sniper scope should be very strong. For years the manufacturers of hunting scopes have done everything possible to make them light in weight, often sacrificing strength in so doing. There should be no weak points in the construction of the sniper scope, since there is no need for them to be made as lightweight as a hunting scope. The scope tube and objective lens bell should be one piece; the joint between the tube and the bell of the present sniper scope is definitely a weak point. The tube and integral bell can be made of either steel or a lightweight aluminum alloy with a wall thickness of at least twice that of any commercial hunting scope, or thick enough so that there would be little chance of denting, bending or breaking it. The eyepiece bell should have at least a ¾" threaded bearing on the scope tube. The threads should be slightly coarser than on most hunting scopes and, preferably, multi-thread. In addition, the wall of the threaded end of the tube should be thicker than the rest of the wall so that the threads do not weaken the tube. As with the Redfield scope, the eyepiece should not be entirely removable.

7) It has been found that lens caps are a useless accessory; the mechanical ones with flip-open covers soon get out of order and are discarded; the slip-on types are soon lost or discarded by the sniper. Transparent scope caps would also be lost, or would become useless because of scratches from frequent cleaning. After examining many sniper scopes that had been in use for some time, I noticed that the fluoride coating, on both eyepiece and objective lenses, was usually well-scratched or partially removed. This is understandable—the lenses get dirty and the sniper usually has only his shirttail to clean them with. On sighting through these scopes it seemed to me that the damaged coating had affected definition. Therefore, I think that the outside lens of the eyepiece and the objective should be made of hardened glass, and the two outside surfaces left uncoated—although all the other inside lens air-to-glass surfaces should be coated. Unless the coating can be made as hard as the glass underneath, I see little point in coating the outside lens surfaces of sniper scopes.

The Mount

Although the Redfield scope mount is quite well made and rugged, I don't think it's as rugged as a sniper scope mount should be, it requires too much maintenance. For example, the base screws are too small. If these screws become loose (and they often do), or if the sniper or armorer merely wants to check them for tightness, the scope and rings have to be removed first before these screws are accessible. Of course, every time the scope and rings are removed and replaced on the base, the rifle has to be sighted-in again, and each time the scope is removed the front ring becomes looser in its base opening. I see no reason for using a mount of any type with separate rings.

It has frequently happened that, on the sniper's way to, or during a combat mission, his scope and/or mount becomes loose or damaged. When this happens the sniper has an absolutely useless weapon. This can be serious to the sniper as well as to those who depend on him. Snipers, of course, usually go out as 2-man teams, with one of the men armed with the M-16, so they can usually get back to their base to have the sniper rifle put back in order and sighted-in again. Why not use a simple side mount to attach the scope to the rifle, and have a set of simple sights on the rifle as well?

The iron sights I propose would be patterned after the simple and efficient sights used on the M-16. The tip-up 2-aperture leaf of the rear sight should be regulated for the 300 and 600 yard ranges. The base of the rear sight could be made as a separate part, with the sight screwed into the receiver bridge. Preferably, though, the base should be made as an integral part of the receiver. It would have the same windage adjustment as the M-16 sight. The front sight should be mounted on a ramp base silver soldered to the barrel, or otherwise so-attached that it becomes virtually an integral part of the barrel. There should be wings on the ramp to protect the front post sight, which ought to be made with an elevation adjustment like the M-16 sight. Such an iron sight combination with a spacing of about 28″ would allow the sniper to do accurate shooting at moderately long ranges, and to make quick aimed shots at shorter ranges. Most importantly, however, such sights would keep the sniper rifle usable in the event the scope and/or mount were damaged.

For the scope mount I suggest a simple 3-piece (not counting the screws) side mount that would position the scope about 1″ above and ¾″ to the left of the bore. The lower half of the rings would be *integral* with the base. The base should be made as long as possible, say about 5″, and attached to the side of the receiver with 4 heavy coin-slotted screws. The rings should be about ¾″ wide, and the top half of each ring attached with four screws. The mount-base should be designed to give the scope about a 1½″ longitudinal adjustment for eye relief, and so-positioned on the receiver that, with the scope positioned midway in the mount, eye relief will be correct for the average sniper.

I see no objection to the slightly offset position of the scope. With this mount the rings cannot loosen from the base, the scope tube will never be under any torque, and the mounting screws can be checked and tightened without disturbing the scope or anything else. The base should be carefully contoured to contact the receiver evenly, and epoxy used on these contacting surfaces, as well as on the screws, for semi-permanency.

The Rifle

The M700 Remington Sniper rifle has performed well in Vietnam, but there was a major problem with the stock. The stocks were not waterproofed, which caused bedding problems if the fore-end warped to contact the barrel. The armorers solved this by opening up the barrel channel to give at least ⅛″ space between the fore-end sides and the barrel. As originally issued the rifles were not glass bedded. I found many rifles in which the barrel and the receiver had loosened in the stock, or rifles whose guard screws had been tightened so often that the front screw contacted the bolt. I was convinced that glass bedding would largely eliminate these problems and, in my reports, I recommended that this be done. Glass bedding was eventually authorized and the armorers supplied with materials and instructions to do it. The glass bedding did help keep the rifles accurate and in zero, but there were still some other things I thought could be improved on. Since I've already proposed a new scope and mount, as well as iron sights for the sniper rifle, I'm going to propose a new rifle.

1) Barrel: Same length, diameter, weight, same bore and rifling specifications as on the current sniper rifle, but made of the best stainless barrel steel available. This course would assure the finest accuracy possible and would greatly reduce bore and chamber rusting. The finished barrels should be fire tested to eliminate those not capable of minute-of-angle accuracy.

2) Action: I favor one of the pre-64 Winchester M70 type. It should be made no longer than necessary to handle the 7.62mm NATO (.308) National Match cartridge. The receiver bridge should be made to include a base for the aperture rear sight mentioned previously. The left wall of the receiver should be made thicker, or have a ridge for the scope mount base, giving more metal for the mounting screws to thread into. I prefer the one-piece Mauser type extractor used in the old M70s above all other extractor systems because: A) it is, I believe, the strongest extractor made; B) if cartridges are fed from the magazine double loading is prevented; C) the bolt closes easily on a cartridge singly-loaded into the chamber. The M70 trigger mechanism is tops; it is simple, has few parts, is easy to clean and has adequate adjustments. I would favor a 98 Mauser-type bolt sleeve, safety and firing pin over that of the M70 design because the Mauser type is simpler and far easier to disassemble for cleaning. Striker travel should be midway between that of the 98 Mauser and M70 to achieve a faster lock time than in the Mauser, and more positive ignition than the M70 provides. The magazine should have a hinged floorplate, but the latch should be like the one on the current M700 sniper rifle.

3) Stock: This should be the same type, size, shape and weight of the current stock on the M700 Sniper rifle. This stock has proved quite ideal in these respects, but now I'm going to suggest some changes or alternates:

A) First choice—stock made of wood: I prefer wood stocks, but I believe the sniper rifle should be a laminated one, made of ⅛″ layers of hard maple or walnut, joined with waterproof glue. The stock should be made as waterproof as possible, perhaps with polyethylene glycol-1000, and stained a dark color.

B) Second choice—stock made of Nylon or glass fiber-filled polyester plastic. In the long run, the non-wood stock might even be the best choice.

In either case, plastic or wood, the receiver and about 3 inches of the breech end of the barrel should be fiberglass bedded, and the rest of the barrel free floated. There should be a good gap between the barrel and fore-end, at least ⅛″, so that the space can be cleaned by pulling a piece of cloth through it. In either case a ½″ or thicker solid rubber buttplate should be used, and non-revolving sling swivels should be installed. Bases for the swivels could be moulded into the plastic stock. On the wood stock, a butt swivel like that used on the M-1 Garand rifle would be good; the front one could be the type used on the M1903 Springfield. The metal parts should have a Parkerized finish.

The trigger pull should be factory adjusted to release at 3½ to 4 pounds. The rifle should be completely finished at the factory, including glass bedding, the cementing and attaching of the mount to the receiver. This should not be left for the armorer to do.

The only thing the individual sniper should have to do when he gets the rifle is to position the scope in the mount for proper eye relief and sight it in. The rifle described would seldom require any maintenance and, except for the scope turret caps, nothing could come loose or be lost from it. It has a minimum of parts. It would be a "military" rifle in every sense of the word — not a commercial rifle adapted for military use.

Barrel Shank Drawings

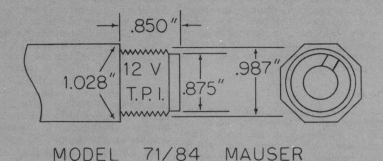

.850"
1.028"
12 V T.P.I.
.875"
.987"

MODEL 71/84 MAUSER

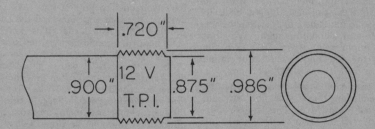

.720"
.900"
12 V T.P.I.
.875"
.986"

GERMAN MODEL 88 COMMISSION

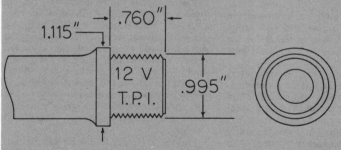

.760"
1.115"
12 V T.P.I.
.995"

MODEL 89 BELGIUM MAUSER

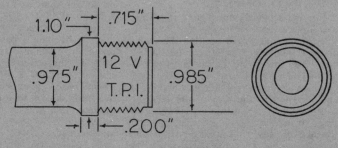

.715"
1.10"
.975"
12 V T.P.I.
.985"
.200"

MODEL 91 ARGENTINA MAUSER

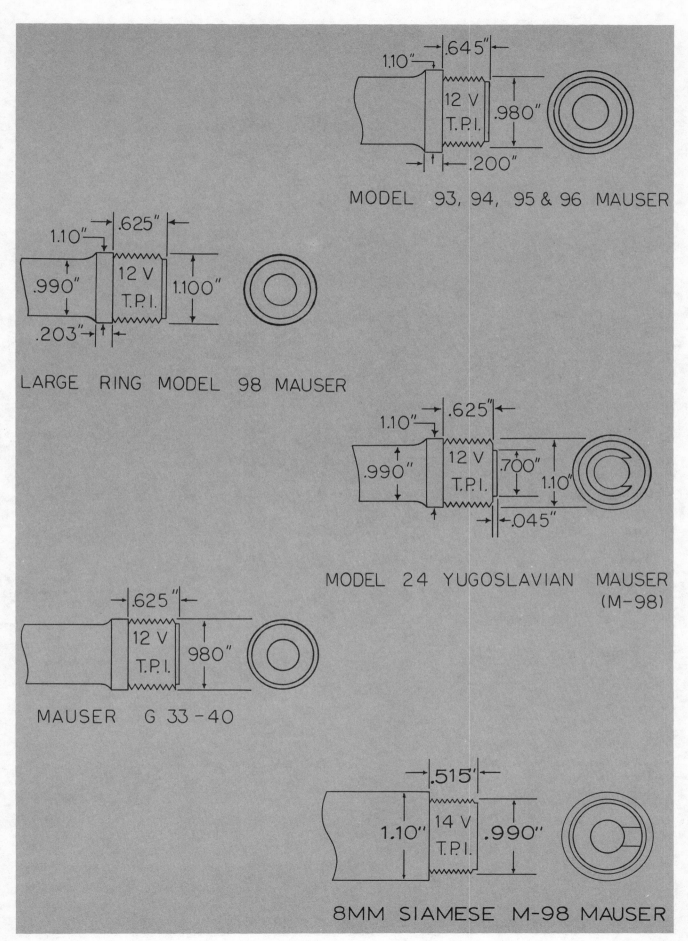

.645"

1.10"

12 V
T.P.I.

.980"

.200"

MODEL   93, 94, 95 & 96 MAUSER

.625"

1.10"

.990"

12 V
T.P.I.

1.100"

.203"

LARGE   RING MODEL 98 MAUSER

.625"

1.10"

.990"

12 V
T.P.I.

.700"

1.10"

.045"

MODEL 24 YUGOSLAVIAN   MAUSER
(M-98)

.625"

12 V
T.P.I.

980"

MAUSER   G 33 - 40

.515'

1.10"

14 V
T.P.I.

.990"

8MM SIAMESE M-98 MAUSER

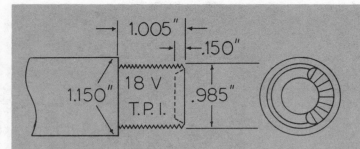

FRENCH BERTHIER 8MM LEBEL CAL.

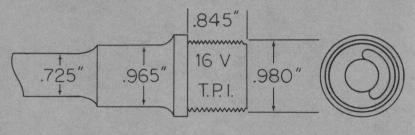

FRENCH MAS M-1936

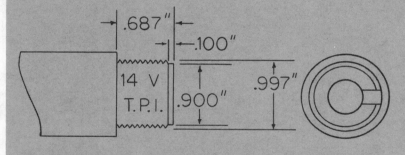

LEE ENFIELD

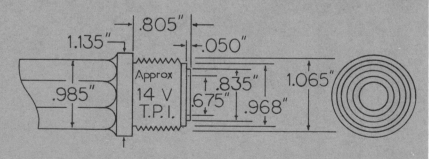

ITALIAN CARCANO

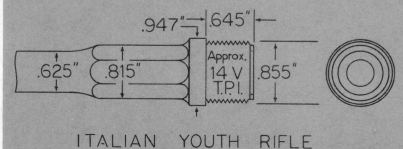

ITALIAN YOUTH RIFLE

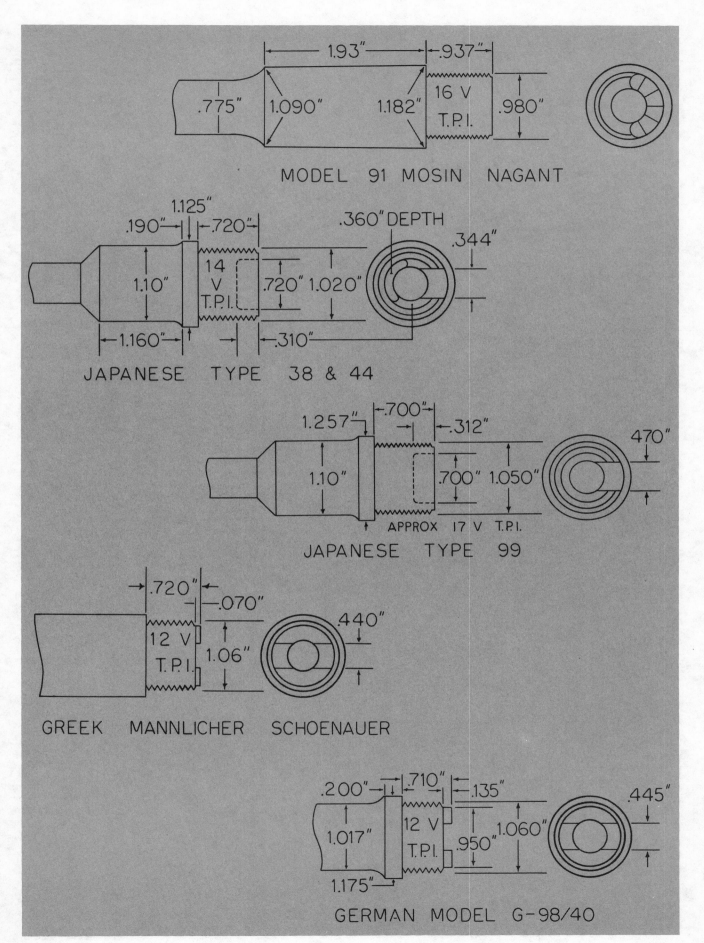

MODEL 91 MOSIN NAGANT

JAPANESE TYPE 38 & 44

JAPANESE TYPE 99

GREEK MANNLICHER SCHOENAUER

GERMAN MODEL G-98/40

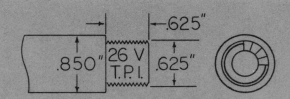

MODEL 1921 SPANISH
DESTROYER CARBINE

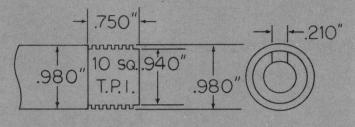

U.S. KRAG JORGENSEN

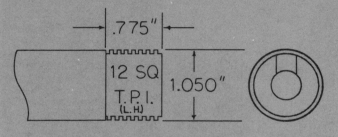

NORWEGIAN KRAG

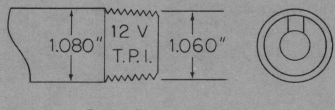

DANISH KRAG

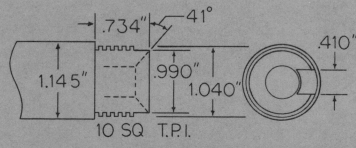

U.S. SPRINGFIELD M-1903, 1903A3-A4

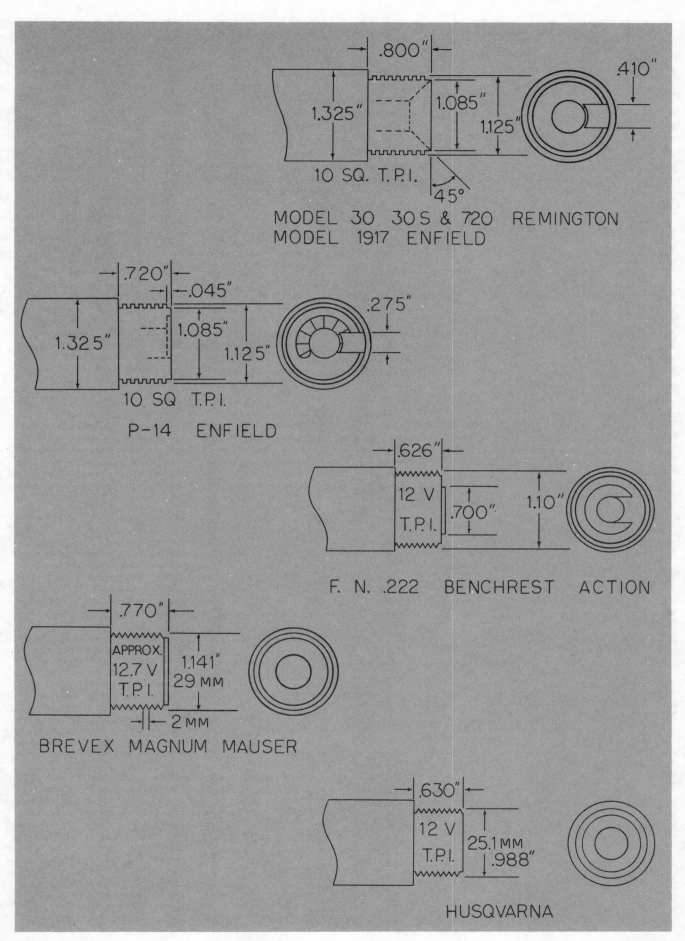

.800"

1.325"

1.085"

1.125"

.410"

10 SQ. T.P.I.

45°

MODEL 30 30 S & 720 REMINGTON
MODEL 1917 ENFIELD

.720"

.045"

1.325"

1.085"

1.125"

.275"

10 SQ T.P.I.

P-14 ENFIELD

.626"

12 V T.P.I.

.700"

1.10"

F. N. .222 BENCHREST ACTION

.770"

APPROX. 12.7 V T.P.I.

1.141"
29 MM

2 MM

BREVEX MAGNUM MAUSER

.630"

12 V T.P.I.

25.1 MM
.988"

HUSQVARNA

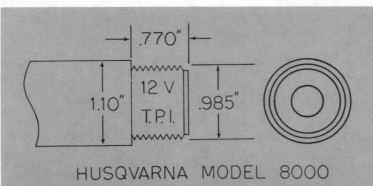

.770"

1.10"   12 V
        T.P.I.

.985"

HUSQVARNA MODEL 8000

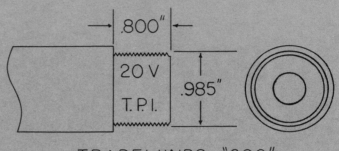

.800"

20 V
T.P.I.

.985"

TRADEWINDS "600"
(KRICO M-600)

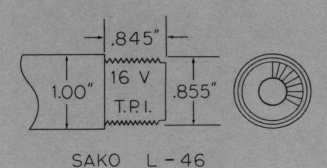

.845"

1.00"   16 V
        T.P.I.

.855"

SAKO   L - 46

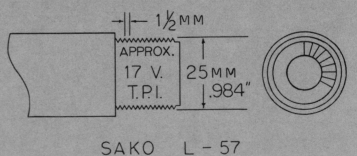

1½ MM

APPROX.
17 V.
T.P.I.

25 MM
.984"

SAKO   L - 57

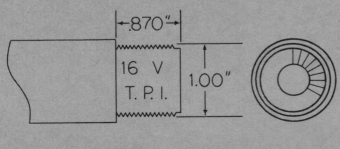

.870"

16 V
T.P.I.

1.00"

SAKO   L - 579

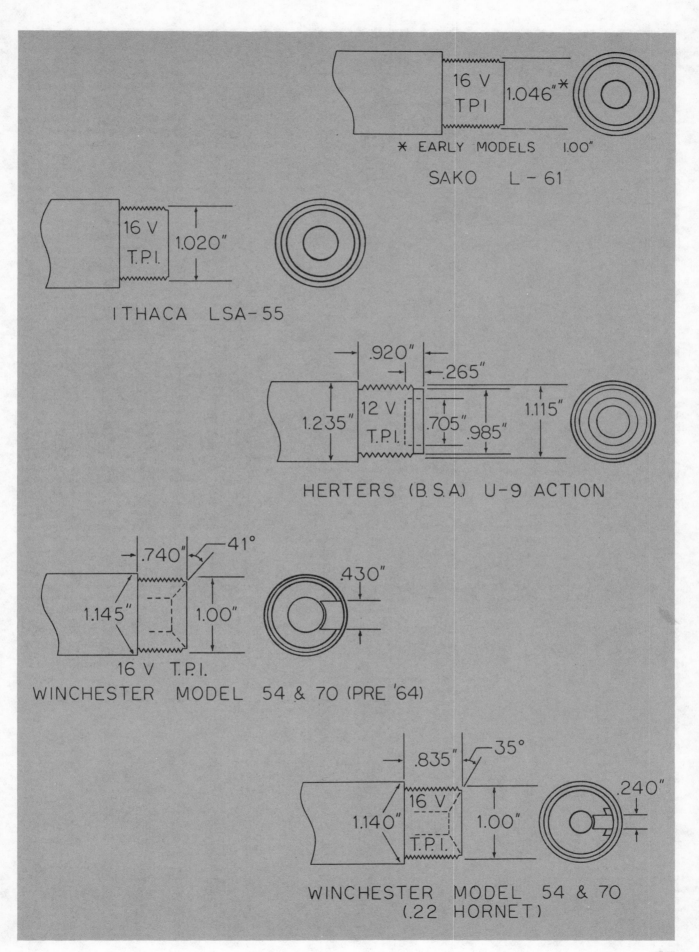

16 V TPI 1.046"*

* EARLY MODELS 1.00"

SAKO   L – 61

16 V T.P.I. 1.020"

ITHACA   LSA-55

.920" .265" 1.115"
1.235" 12 V T.P.I. .705" .985"

HERTERS (B.S.A.) U-9 ACTION

.740" 41°
1.145" 1.00" .430"
16 V T.P.I.

WINCHESTER MODEL 54 & 70 (PRE '64)

.835" 35°
1.140" 16 V 1.00" .240"
T.P.I.

WINCHESTER MODEL 54 & 70
(.22 HORNET)

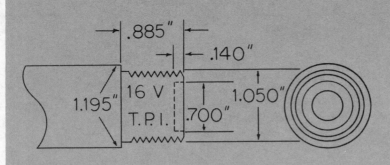

.885″
.140″
1.195″
16 V
T.P.I.
.700″
1.050″

REMINGTON MODEL 721, 722 & 725

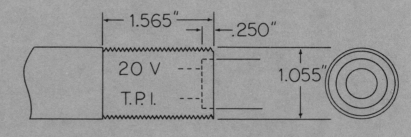

1.565″
.250″
20 V
T.P.I.
1.055″

SAVAGE M-110

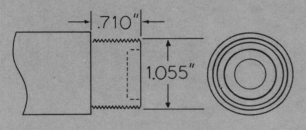

.710″
1.055″

SAVAGE M-110
IF MADE FOR USE WITHOUT
LOCKNUT

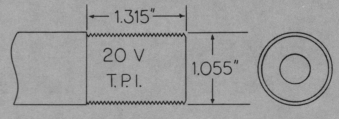

1.315″
20 V
T.P.I.
1.055″

SAVAGE M-110 C

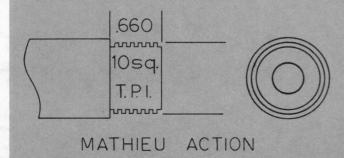

.660
10 sq.
T.P.I.

MATHIEU ACTION

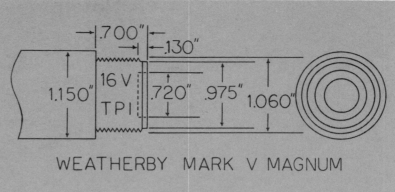

WEATHERBY MARK V MAGNUM

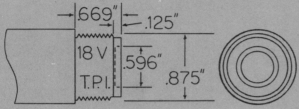

WEATHERBY   MARK   V
VARMINTMASTER

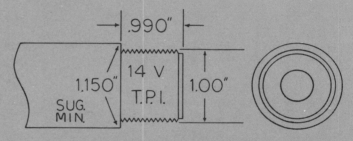

RANGER ARMS TEXAS MAGNUM

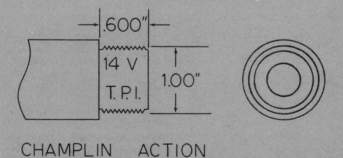

CHAMPLIN   ACTION

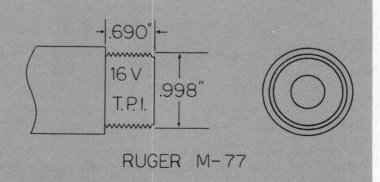

RUGER   M-77

Notes

Appendix

Magazine/Guard Screw Sizes & Threads (tap & die sizes)

Brevex Magnum Mauser 1/4x22
British Lee-Enfield 1/4x26
B.S.A. Monarch 1/4x27
Centurion Mauser M98 . . . . 1/4x22
Champlin 1/4x28
FN M98 Mauser 1/4x22
French Berthier 15/64x26
German M88 Commission 1/4x22
German M98/40 . . . . .275x26
Greek Mannlicher-Schoenauer 1/4x27
Herter J9 and XK3 Mauser 1/4x22
Herter U9 . . . . 1/4x27
Husqvarna 230x26
Husqvarna M8000 . . . . 15/64x26
Italian Carcano 1/4x25
Japanese Arisaka Type 99 . . . . 15/64x34
Japanese Arisaka Type 38 . . . . .228x28 (Tang Screw . . . . 7/32x28)
Mauser M71/84 . . . . 1/4x22 (Front guard screw)
Mauser M91 Argentina 1/4x22
Mauser M93 and M95 . . . . 1/4x22
Mauser M94 and M96 Swedish 1/4x22
Mauser M98 (all models) 1/4x22
Mathieu 1/4x28
Pattern 14 Enfield 1/4x30
Ranger Arms Texas Magnum . . . . 1/4x28 (Center screw . . . . 7/32x28)
Remington M721 and M722 . . . . 1/4x28 (Center screw . . . . 5/32x36)
Remington M700 . . . . 1/4x28
Remington M788 . . . . 1/4x28 (Rear screw . . . . 7/32x28)
Remington M30 . . . . 1/4x30
Ruger M77 . . . . 1/4x28 (Rear & center screw . 3/16x32)
Russian Mosin-Nagant 17/64x32
Santa Barbara M98 Mauser 1/4x22
Sako 15/64x28
Savage M110 . . . . 1/4x28
Springfield, National Ordnance M1903A3 . . . . 1/4x28
Tradewinds M600 . . . . 15/64x34
U.S. Krag-Jorgensen 1/4x25
U.S. M1903 Springfield 1/4x25
U.S. M1917 Enfield 1/4x30
Winchester M54 . . . . 1/4x32
Winchester M70 (all models) 1/4x32

Bibliography

Bibliography of articles pertaining to centerfire turnbolt rifles and actions which appeared in *The American Rifleman* from 1933 through November 1970.

ACTIONS

"HVA Improved Mauser Action"—A Dope Bag Report, April, 1954, p. 72.

"Brevex Magnum Mauser Action"—A Dope Bag Report, Dec., 1955, p. 63.

"FN Mauser Bench-Rest Action"—A Dope Bag Report, Jan., 1956, p. 61.

"Reinforced Action"—A Dope Bag Report, Oct., 1957, p. 66. (Describes a FN Mauser bench rest action fitted with a reinforcing sleeve.)

"Featherweight Sporter"—A Dope Bag Report, June, 1959, p. 56. (Description of the little known Terhaar centerfire turnbolt action.)

"Shilen Actions"—A Dope Bag Report, April, 1962, p. 56. (Illustrating and describing the custom made Shilen single shot bench rest turnbolt action.)

"Texas Magnum Actions"—A Dope Bag Report, Aug., 1967, p. 58.

BARRELS & BARREL FITTING

"The Model 1917 Barrel on The Mauser 98 Action" by F. W. Beckert, July, 1942. (Notes on rebarreling the Model 98 Mauser action.)

"Barrel Removal, Fitting and Chambering," by H. MacFarland, May, 1950. (Detailed information on how to remove, fit and chamber a barrel of a centerfire bolt action rifle.)

"The Versatile Springfield Barrel" by Frank de Haas, Nov., 1963. (Describes what can be done with surplus Model 1903 Springfield barrels.)

BROWNING RIFLES

"Browning Rifles"—A Dope Bag Report, Sept., 1960, p. 58. (Report on the Browning high power rifles based on a modified FN Mauser action.)

"Browning Safari Grade Rifle"—A Dope Bag Report, June, 1965. (Evaluation and test results of the Browning Sako centerfire bolt action rifle.)

B.S.A. RIFLES

"B.S.A. Varmint Rifle"—A Dope Bag Report, Nov., 1954, p. 56. (Information on the BSA bolt action rifle in .222 caliber.)

"B.S.A. Rifle"—A Dope Bag Report, July, 1956, p. 66. (Describes the "medium length" actioned BSA bolt action sporter.)

"B.S.A. Rifles"—A Dope Bag Report, Sept., 1957, p. 72. (Report on the BSA featherweight bolt action sporter.)

"B.S.A. Majestic"—A Dope Bag Report, Dec., 1959. (Describes the British-made BSA turnbolt sporting rifle.)

"B.S.A. Monarch Deluxe Rifle"—A Dope Bag Report, Aug., 1965, p. 69.

BULLPUP RIFLES

"Spoon-Fed Bull Pup" by W. Doering, Dec., 1939. (Describes and illustrates a bullpup type rifle built on the Model 1917 Enfield action.)

"The One and Only Atomizer" by T.K. Lee, Jan., 1942. (Describes a bullpup type rifle in a .22 C.F. wildcat caliber.)

"New Trigger For a Pup" by A. H. Barr, Jan., 1943. (Describes a clever trigger system for a bullpup rifle.)

"Care and Feeding of Bull Pups" by A. H. Barr, April, 1950. (Much information and ideas on bullpup rifle designs, etc.)

"Building the Bull Pup Rifle" by L. H. Brown, May, 1953. (A noted gunsmith tells how to build a centerfire bolt action bullpup rifle.)

"The Bull Pup Again" by M. Kennedy, Oct., 1954. (Dope on scoping, triggering and stocking a bullpup rifle.)

COMMERCIAL RIFLES (Miscellaneous Foreign)

"F.I. Rifles"—A Dope Bag Report, March, 1963. (Evaluation of the Firearms International Musketeer rifle based on the FN Mauser action.)

"Dickson-Howa Rifle"—A Dope Bag Report, July, 1967, p. 68. (Evaluation of the Japanese Golden Bear sporting rifle based on a copy of the Sako Finnbear action.)

"Steyr-Mannlicher SL Rifle"—A Dope Bag Report, March, 1968, p. 47. (Evaluation of the newest Mannlicher rifle.)

"Smith & Wesson Rifles"—A Dope Bag Report, Oct., 1968, p. 92. (Describing the S&W high-powered rifles based on the Husqvarna turnbolt action.)

"Parker-Hale Super"—A Dope Bag Report, July, 1968, p. 56. (Evaluation of the Parker-Hale big game sporting rifle based on a Spanish-made Mauser M98 type action.)

"Ithaca LSA-55 Rifle"—A Dope Bag Report, Aug., 1969, p. 52. (Evaluation of the Finnish-made turnbolt sporting rifle.)

COMMERCIAL RIFLES (Miscellaneous U.S.)

"New Marlin Varmint Rifle"—A Dope Bag Report, Sept., 1954. (Information on the Marlin Model 322 built on the Sako action.)

"J.C. Higgins Rifle"—A Dope Bag Report, July, 1956, p. 72. (Describes the Higgins Model 52 bolt action .222 rifle built on the Sako action.)

"Coltsman Rifles"—A Dope Bag Report, Nov., 1958, p. 72. (Test report on the Colt high powered bolt action rifles based on the Sako and FN Mauser actions.)

"Mossberg Centerfire Rifle" by L. Olson, Aug. 1966. (Special report on the Mossberg Model 800 bolt action rifle.)

"Bolt Action Model 77: In the Ruger Tradition"—NRA Staff, Feb., 1969. (Detailed report on Ruger's bolt action sporting rifle.)

"Fajen Acra Rifle"—A Dope Bag Report, Oct., 1969, p. 92. (Evaluation of the Fajen stocked rifles built on the Santa Barbara Mauser barreled action.)

ENFIELDS (M1914 & M1917)

"Making a Rifle Out of The 1917" by A. Linden, May & June, 1933. (Excellent article on remodeling the M1917 Enfield into a sporter.)

"A Glorified Enfield" by E. H. Whelan, Sept., 1934. (Short piece on remodeling the M1917 Enfield.)

"A Remodeling Job on The '17" by L. K. Shaffer, Sept., 1937. (Short piece on remodeling the M1917 Enfield.)

"Dope Bag Items" by F. C. Ness, May, 1938. (Describes a lightweight remodeled M1917 Enfield.)

"From Enfield to Sporter" by Ness, Lenz, Whelen, Linden, Dec., 1945, Jan., Feb., 1946.

"Model 1917 Sporter"—A Dope Bag item, Feb., 1946. (Notes on remodeling the M1917 Enfield.)

"M17 Knockabout" by L. E. Capek, Oct., 1946. (Describes an easy remodeling project on the M1917 Enfield.)

"Kitchen Mechanic Remodeling" by H. V. Stent, Feb., 1947. (Remodeling the M1917 Enfield.)

"The Ears Have It" by R. Stanley, April, 1947. (Mounting a scope on the "eared" M1917 Enfield action.)

"Enfield Rear Sight Conversion" by A. W. Weiler, April, 1947. (How to put windage adjustment into the issue M1917 Enfield rear sight.)

"An M17 and K43" by L. E. Capek, Oct. 1947. (Mounting a German sniper scope on the M1917 Enfield.)

"Six-Hour Remodeling Job" by H. H. Hill, Jan., 1948. (Simple remodeling of the M1917 Enfield.)

"Another Enfield Conversion" by J. H. Taber, June, 1948.

"Hacksaw Gunsmithing" by J. Howell, May, 1949. (More gunsmithing dope on the M1917 Enfield.)

"Enfield Speed Lock" by R. Heidrich, Feb., 1948. (How to speed up the lock time of the M1917 Enfield.)

"Mount For a German Scope" by H. S. White, Feb., 1951. (Mounting the German ZF-4 scope on the M1917 Enfield.)

"The Big .450" by Hal Stephens, Sept., 1952. (About the .450 Magnum in the M1917 Enfield.)

"U.S. Model 1917 Rifle" by J. M. Triggs, Aug., 1960. (Exploded view drawing and assembly instructions.)

"Remodeling the Enfield Rifle" by M. D. Waite, May, 1962.

"The Pattern 1914 Enfield Rifle" by E. G. B. Reynolds, Sept., 1965. (History and information on the P1914 Enfield.)

FRENCH RIFLES

"The Implements of War (The French Army)" by J. Scofield, Oct., 1940. (Information on French military shoulder arms.)

".22 French Training Rifle" by H. L. Joseph, Nov., 1955. (How the French converted the 1936 MAS rifle in 7.5mm caliber to fire .22 rimfire ammunition.)

"French Model 1936 Rifle" by E. J. Hoffschmidt, March, 1967. (Exploded view drawing and assembly instructions.)

GUNMAKING

"Three Remodeled Rifles" by F. C. Ness, August, 1939. (Describes Lee-Enfields, Lebels and Model 70 Winchesters.)

".300 Magnum Bull Gun"—A Dope Bag Report, Oct., 1940.

"Getting the Gun You Want" by M. G. Holmes, May, 1946. (Notes on building that custom bolt action rifle.)

"This Business of Bolt Handles" by Chas. Golueke, March, 1948. (Complete details on how to alter a bolt handle for a low-mounted scope.)

"That Super Sporter" by M. Holmes, Nov., 1949. (Discussion on building a fine bolt action sporter.)

"Light Hunting Rifles" by L. H. Brown, Sept., 1955. (Notes on making up a lightweight hunting rifle on the M98 action.)

"Lighter and Handier" by P. Autry, June, 1956. (Notes on building a lightweight sporting rifle.)

HARRINGTON & RICHARDSON RIFLES

"H&R Bolt Action Rifle"—A Dope Bag Report, Sept., 1965, p. 70. (Complete test evaluation of the H&R centerfire rifle based on a FN Mauser action.)

"H&R Model 330 Rifle"—A Dope Bag Report, Sept., 1967, p. 82. (Evaluation of a sporting rifle based on the FN Supreme Mauser action.)

HERTER'S RIFLES
"Herter Model U9 Rifle"—A Dope Bag Report, June, 1966, p. 76. (Evaluation of the Herter's rifle based on the BSA bolt action.)

"Herter U9 Super Deluxe Rifle"—A Dope Bag Report, July, 1966, p. 61.

HORNET RIFLES
"Pioneer Work on the Hornet" by Capt. G. A. Woody, Jan., 1933. (Information on converting the M1922 Springfield rifle to .22 Hornet.)

"The Charles Daly Hornet" by F. C. Ness, Aug., 1933. (Short report on this imported bolt action rifle.)

"New Survival Weapon" by G. C. Sullivan, Jan., 1957. (Notes on the MA-1 .22 Hornet survival rifle.)

HUSQVARNA (H.V.A. Tradewinds) (also see Actions)
"Husqvarna Lightweight Rifle"—A Dope Bag Report, June, 1955, p. 66.

"Husqvarna .358"—A Dope Bag Report, Oct., 1960. (Test report on the Husqvarna HVA Rifle in .358 Norma Magnum caliber.)

"Tradewinds 600 Rifle"—A Dope Bag Report, Aug., 1968, p. 50. (Evaluation of a German-made sporting rifle.)

"Husqvarna Model 8000 Rifle"—A Dope Bag Report, May, 1969, p. 52.

ITALIAN RIFLES
"7,000,000 Bayonets" by G. B. Jarrett, June, 1944. (Describes the various Italian military rifles.)

"The Italian Youth Carbine" by B. D. Munhall, May, 1958.

"The Italian Carcano Rifle" by E. J. Hoffschmidt, Aug., 1961. (Exploded view drawing and assembly instructions.)

JAPANESE RIFLES
"The Implements of War (Children Under the Sun)" by J. Scofield, Feb., 1941. (Describes the military arms used by Japan.)

"Japanese Small Arms" by J. S. Diefendorf, July, 1944. (About Japanese military rifles.) Correction on p. 12 in August, 1944 issue.

"Don't Convert Jap Rifles" by W. H. B. Smith, June, 1945.

"Arisaka Ancestry" by M. K. Short, Nov., 1946. (Full details on the Type "I" Japanese military rifle based on the Italian Carcano design action.)

"Arisaka Sporters" by J. V. Gibson & Bob Peel, June, 1949. (Notes on remodeling the Japanese Arisaka rifles.)

"The Quality of Jap Rifles" by L. A. Morgan, Dec., 1950. (Also lists the common markings found on Japanese military rifles and defines them.)

"Handy and Homemade" by H. A. Lind, March, 1954. (Information on how to remodel the Japanese military rifle, including data on making the action cock on opening.)

"Japanese Rifles and Carbines" by M. D. Waite, Feb., 1958. (Excellent article describing and illustrating all Japanese breech-loading military shoulder arms.)

"Bullet Forming"—A Dope Bag item, May, 1959, p. 52. (Amazing story of a 6.5 Japanese rifle chambered for the .30-06 cartridge.)

"Japanese Arisaka Model 1905 6.5mm Carbine" by E. J. Hoffschmidt, June, 1961. (Exploded view drawing and assembly instructions.)

KRAG-JORGENSEN RIFLES
"A Manzanita Stock" by R. M. Broeg, July, 1934. (Notes on remodeling a Krag.)

"A DeLuxe Krag Hornet" by V. A. Coulter, Nov., 1937. (Interesting conversion of the Krag to the Hornet cartridge.)

"The Perennial Krag" by M. Mealy, Jan., 1944. (Notes on remodeling the Krag rifle.)

"The Birth of a Hobby" by H. A. Groesbeck, March, 1945. (Notes on remodeling a Krag.)

"White Collar .30-40" by R. H. Bartlett, May, 1946. (Short notes on remodeling the Krag.)

"Flush Magazine for the Krag," by J. M. Pearson & J. C. Leigh, Apr., 1954. (How to make a flush magazine cover for the .30-40 Krag.)

"The Krag Rifle" by L. Olson, Sept., 1958. (Excellent article describing and illustrating all of the different Krag rifles and carbines.)

"Tyro's Rifle" by T. Henson, Oct., 1945. (More about remodeling the Krag.)

"U.S. Krag" by E. J. Hoffschmidt, Apr., 1960. (Exploded view drawing and assembly instructions.)

"Krag-Jorgensen Rifle" by H. L. Peterson, Dec., 1963. (Brief history of the U.S. Krag rifle.)

LEE-ENFIELD RIFLES
"The Lee-Enfield Rifle," by H. P. Martin, Aug., 1940. (Lengthy article on the Lee-Enfield used during WW I.)

"Britain's Newest Service Rifles" by Wm. Piznak, March, 1948. (Describes the No. 4 & 5 Lee-Enfield rifles.)

"Amazing Old Lady" by H. V. Stent, Aug., 1948. (Praise for the British Lee-Enfield as a hunting rifle.)

"Simple Sporterizing of the Lee-Enfield" by E. H. Harrison, Oct., 1955.

"The Rifle in the British Service" by A. Barker, Apr., May, June, July & Aug., 1956. (Complete history of Great Britain's military rifles with much data on the Lee-Enfields.)

"The .303 Lee-Enfield" by E. H. Harrison, July, 1959. (Thorough study of the British Lee-Enfield rifle.)

"Deluxe Sporterizing the No. 4 Rifle" by M. D. Waite, Aug., 1959. (Complete details.)

"7.62mm No. 4 Rifle"—A Dope Bag Report, Oct., 1962. (Describes the British conversion of the No. 4 rifle in .303 caliber to 7.62mm.)

"Lee-Enfield No. 4 Rifle" by E. J. Hoffschmidt, July, 1963. (Exploded view drawing and assembly instructions.)

"Target Accuracy with the No. 4 Rifle" by E. G. B. Reynolds, June, 1965. (How to completely accurize the No. 4 British Lee-Enfield.)

"Lee-Enfield Rifle No. 1, Mark III" by T. E. Wessel, Sept., 1966. (Exploded view drawing and assembly instructions.)

"Heavier Barrel Adds to British 7.62 Rifle Accuracy" by E. G. B. Reynolds, Oct., 1961. (Details on how the British rework the No. 4 Lee-Enfield for target shooting.)

"Sporterizing the rugged Lee-Enfield" by R. Prusock, Feb., 1970, p. 28.

"BNRA Picks New Enfield for Palma" by E. G. B. Reynolds, April, 1970, p. 8. (Describes the British Enfield Envoy 7.62mm target rifle.)

MANNLICHER RIFLES

"Paging the 6.5" by E. Keith, June, 1950. (Keith on the Mannlicher-Schoenauer rifle and cartridge.)

"Mannlicher Rifles" by L. Olson, Nov., 1959. (Describes all Mannlicher rifles, including the Mannlicher turnbolts.)

"Mannlicher-Schoenauer Rifle" by E. J. Hoffschmidt, Sept., 1963. (Exploded view drawing and assembly instructions.

MAUSER RIFLES (Various Commercial)

"Saive .404 Mauser"—A Dope Bag Report, Sept., 1954, p. 50.

"Dumoulin Carbine"—A Dope Bag Report, July, 1959, p. 57. (Report on the Belgian-made rifle based on the FN Mauser action.)

"Heym Mauser"—A Dope Bag Report, Nov., 1958, p 76. (Test report on these imports.)

"Mauser Model 2000 Rifle"—A Dope Bag Report, April, 1969, p. 52. (Evaluating the new Mauser-built high powered sporting rifle.)

MAUSER RIFLES (Model 98)

"The German War Mauser" by J. P. Gschwind, July, 1936. (Remodeling the M98 Mauser rifle into a sporter.)

"The German Mauser" by W. J. Landen, Sept., 1940. (Discussion on various M98 Mauser military rifles.)

"Veteran in Battle" by L. Olson, Aug. & Sept., 1942. (History of the M98 Mauser rifle.)

"Remodeling the Military Mauser" by M. Holmes, July & Aug., 1946. (Complete details.)

"Save that Mauser Stock" by J. W. Ruzella, Dec., 1948. (Remodeling the M98 Mauser.)

"Slicked-Up Mauser" by P. Barrett, Sept., 1950. (Well-illustrated article on remodeling the M98 Mauser rifle.)

"The Mauser 98 Rifle" by E. J. Hoffschmidt, March, 1955. (Exploded view drawings and assembly instructions.)

"A Floorplate Locking Device" by M. W. Stockel, Nov., 1958. (Instructions for making a hinged floorplate for the M98 Mauser action.)

"Remodeling the Mauser 1898 Rifle" by M. D. Waite, Sept., 1967.

MAUSER RIFLES (Various Sporters)

"A Pair of Custom Built Rifles from Germany" by E. Keith, Jan., 1933. (Describes a fine Mauser sporting rifle.)

"A Good Rifle" by M. Kellerman, Jan., 1935. (Describes a Mauser M98 sporting rifle.)

"The Perfect Hunting Rifle" by H. O. Lokken, Feb., 1937. (Describing a Mauser sporting rifle.)

"A Rival of the .375" by G. F. H. Konig, April, 1941. (Describes a Mauser sporter in 9.3mm caliber.)

"The Magnum Mauser" by P. Autry, April, 1955. (Describes the commercial magnum Mauser rifles and calibers.)

"The Swedish Mauser" by E. J. Hoffschmidt, June, 1962. (Exploded view drawing and assembly instructions on the M98 and 96 Swedish Mauser rifles.)

"Argentina Model 1891 Mauser Rifle" by T. E. Wessel, Aug., 1964. (Exploded view drawing and assembly instructions.)

"Mauser 71/84 Rifle" by E. J. Hoffschmidt, Jan., 1966. (Exploded view drawing and assembly instructions.)

MISCELLANEOUS RIFLES

"A New Design of Bolt-Action Rifle" by R. G. Packard, Apr., 1936. (Describes a very unusual bolt action rifle with unique design features. Of most interest to the arms designer.)

"The Blake Bolt-Action Magazine Rifle" by E. Keith, June, 1936. (Describes this very rare American-made bolt action rifle.)

"Three Venerable Bolt-Action Arms" by E. D. Crabb, Feb., 1941. (Describing the Greene, Prussian Needle and Terry bolt action arms.)

"The Blake .400" by A. H. Tedmon, Jan., 1953. (A history and study of the rare Blake bolt action rifle.)

"Swiss Military Rifles" by H. Grieder, Jan., 1956. (Illustrates and describes all breech-loading Swiss bolt action and straight-pull military rifles, including straight-pull types.)

"Inclined Bolt Rifles" by R. K. Dunham, June, 1958. (Information on experimental bolt action rifles with an inclined bolt.)

"Swedish Small Arms" by W. Piznak, Aug., 1958. (Includes information on Swedish bolt action rifles.)

"Surplus Military Rifles"—NRA Staff, Dec., 1960, Jan., Feb., and March, 1961. (Describes the various most popular surplus military rifles and the cartridges they are chambered for.)

"Dreyse Needle Gun" by H. L. Peterson, Feb., 1964. (Short history of the first military breech-loading bolt action rifle.)

"The Palmer Carbine" by M. B. Peladeau, Aug., 1964. (History and details of the first U.S. breech-loading bolt action military cartridge arm.)

"German Model 98-40 Rifle" by E. J. Hoffschmidt, Aug., 1965. (Exploded view drawing and assembly instructions.)

"Madsen Model 1958 Rifle" by D. Riordan, March, 1969. (Exploded view drawing and assembly instructions.)

"Model 1888 Commission Rifle" by D. Riordan, Nov., 1969. (Exploded view drawing and assembly instructions.)

"Carl Gustaf Model 63 Rifle"—A Dope Bag report, April, 1970. (Covers the Swedish-made 7.62mm match rifle.)

"Ruger Model 77 Varmint Rifle"—A Dope Bag report, Sept., 1970.

"Sportco Appeals with Accuracy and Price" by E. G. B. Reynolds, Sept., 1970. (Details of a 7.62mm turnbolt match rifle made in Australia.)

REMINGTON RIFLES

"Something New" by J. S. Hatcher and A. Barr, March, 1948. (Detailed report on the Model 721 Remington rifle.)

"Remodeling the Remington 721" by W. Campbell, Feb., 1949.

"What's new for '50"—A Dope Bag Report, Feb., 1950. (Contains evaluation reports on the M722 Remington rifle in .222 caliber and .22 Hornet Sako rifle.)

"Remodeling the 722" by G. A. Leyner, Dec., 1952. (Notes on building a lightweight Mannlicher type sporter from a M722 Remington.)

"Minute-of-angle 722" by R. V. Thompson, July, 1954. (Accurizing the M722 Remington rifle.)

"722-721 Southpaw Conversion"A Dope Bag Report, Dec., 1955, p. 62. (A Dale M. Guise left-hand conversion described.)

"Converting Model 722 to .22-250" by W. Dresser, Feb., 1958.

"Remington Model 725"—A Dope Bag Report, Apr., 1958, p. 56.

"Remington 721-722 Rifle" by T. E. Wessel, Sept., 1959. (Exploded view drawing and assembly instructions.)

"Remington Rifles"—A Dope Bag Report, Dec., 1961, p. 76. (Test and evaluation of the M40-X Remington centerfire target rifle.)

"New Remington Rifle"—NRA Staff, Sept., 1962. (Comprehensive Dope Bag Report and evaluation of the M700 Remington rifle.)

"Remington Model 600"—A Dope Bag Report, Apr., 1964, p. 44.

"Remington Model 40X Target Rifle" T. E. Wessel, June, 1964. (Exploded view drawing and assembly instructions.)

"Remington M600 Carbine"—A Dope Bag Report, Apr., 1965, p. 44. (Evaluation of the Remington M600 Magnum Carbine.)

".22-250 Remington"—A Dope Bag Report, June, 1965. (Thorough evaluation of the M700 BDL Remington and the .22-250 cartridge.)

"6.5mm Remington Magnum"—A Dope Bag Report, Aug., 1966, p. 46. (Evaluation of the M600 Remington carbine in 6.5mm Magnum caliber.)

"New Remington Rifles"—A Dope Bag Report, Apr., 1967, p. 46. (Evaluation of the Remington M788 rifle.)

"Remington Varmint Special"—A Dope Bag Report, May, 1967, p. 56. (Evaluation of the M700 Remington Varmint Special rifle.)

"New Remington Carbines"—A Dope Bag Report, May, 1968, p. 57. (Details on the M660 Remington carbines.)

"Latest Remington 700's"—A Dope Bag Report, Sept., 1969, p. 78.

"Remington Left-Hand M788 Rifle"—A Dope Bag Report, Sept., 1969, p. 84.

"Remington offers Bench Rest Rifle"—A Dope Bag Report, Jan., 1970, p. 30.

".25-06 Remington"—A Dope Bag Report, July, 1970. (Detailed test report on the .25-06 M700 BDL rifle.)

"Remington Models 600 & 660" by F. G. Hart, Nov., 1970. (Exploded view drawings and assembly instructions.)

RUSSIAN RIFLES

"A Home-Made Russian Sporter" by E. J. Witzel, Feb., 1934. (Short piece on remodeling the Mosin-Nagant rifle.)

"Under the Red Star—The Russian Rifle" by G. Underhill, Aug., 1941. (Describes the Russian military rifles and training.)

"1891 Mosin-Nagant Rifle" by E. J. Hoffschmidt, Nov., 1958. (Exploded view drawings and assembly instructions.)

SAKO RIFLES

"The Echo of the Sako" by A. Wilson, Oct., 1953. (Notes on the .222 Sako rifle.)

"Sako Heavy-Barrel Rifle"—A Dope Bag Report, Aug., 1954, p. 62.

"Sako Forester"—A Dope Bag Report, Sept., 1958, p. 70. (Test report on the Sako L-57 rifle.)

"Forester Rifles"—A Dope Bag Report, Oct. 1960, p. 66. (Report and evaluation of the Sako L-579 rifle.)

"Sako Finnbear"—A Dope Bag Report, Dec., 1961, p. 81. (Test report on the Sako L-61 rifle.)

SAVAGE RIFLES

"Why not this One?" by F. Merillat, Sept., 1933. (Information on handloading for the M23 Savage in .25-20 caliber.)

"A Real Medium-Game Rifle" by A. M. Crane, July, 1937. (Describing the Savage M23 sporter in .25-20 caliber.)

"New Savage Hi-power Rifles"—A Dope Bag Report, July, 1950, p. 38; May, 1953, p. 64. (Describing the M340 and M342 Savage rifles in .30-30 and .22 Hornet calibers.)

"Savage Model 110 Rifle" by M. D. Waite, Feb., 1958. (Detailed Dope Bag Report.)

"Savage Model 110 MC"—A Dope Bag Report, Oct., 1958.

"Savage Model MCL"—A Dope Bag Report, Jan., 1959, p. 56. (Report on the left-hand M110.)

"Savage Model 110 Rifle" by T. E. Wessel, Sept., 1961. (Exploded view drawing and assembly instructions.)

"Savage-Anschutz M153 Rifle"—A Dope Bag Report, July, 1964, p. 62. (Evaluation of the .222 Anschutz rifle.)

"Savage Model 340-V Rifle"—A Dope Bag Report, May, 1965, p. 74.

"Savage Model 110 MC"—A Dope Bag Report, Aug., 1965, p. 69.

"Savage Model 110C Rifle"—A Dope Bag Report, June, 1966, p. 68. (Evaluation of the M110 with a detachable box magazine.)

"Savage Model 340 Rifle"—A Dope Bag Report, Oct., 1969, p. 95. (Short report on the 1969 version of this low cost rifle.)

"Savage M110 C .25-06 Rifle"—A Dope Bag Report, Aug., 1970.

SCHULTZ & LARSON RIFLES

"Schultz & Larson Rifle"—A Dope Bag Report, Sept., 1955, p. 70.

"Schultz & Larson M-60"—A Dope Bag Report, Dec., 1957.

"Schultz & Larson 65"—A Dope Bag Report, July, 1960, p. 48. (Full details on this interesting Danish rifle.)

"Schultz & Larson 68DL Rifle"—A Dope Bag Report, Aug., 1967, p. 68.

SNIPER RIFLES
"The Jap Military Scope" by C. H. Williams, July, 1944.

"German Sniping Equipment" by R. F. Dunlap, Jan., 1945. (Describes the M98 Mauser sniper rifle.)

"Sniping Rifles" by C. H. Howell, Jr., Apr., May, 1947.

"The No. 4 Rifle Mark 1 (T)" by E. G. B. Reynolds, Nov., 1964.

"U.S. Sniping Rifles" by M. D. Waite, June, 1965. (Among others, describes the Krag, Springfield and Enfield sniping rifles.)

SPRINGFIELD RIFLES
"United States Rifles, Caliber .30" by T. Whelen, Aug., 1934. (Covers various M1903s and the M1917.)

"The Sedgley Short-Action Springfield" by F. T. Chamberlin, Dec., 1934. (Describes a rifle with action shortened for the .250 Savage cartridge.)

"Vacation Echoes" by N. H. Roberts, Jan., 1935. (Describes test firing a Griffin & Howe custom .257 Springfield.)

"New Springfields"—NRA Report, Sept., 1943. (Introducing the M1903A3 and M1903A4 rifles.)

"A .30-06 Pistol" by O. T. Littleton, Apr., 1945. (On making a handgun from the M1903.)

"Death Valley Shots" by D. Lanagan, Apr., 1945. (Story about a .25 Niedner Springfield.)

"DCM Shoppers' Guide" by E. Brown, Apr., 1946. (Notes on Springfield and Enfield rifles then available to NRA members.)

"Guinea Pig Varminter" by M. Holmes, Mar., 1947. (Accuracy experiments on a 1903 Springfield varmint rifle.)

"Springfield Rifles—A Chapter from Hatcher's Notebook" by J. S. Hatcher, Oct., 1947. (History of the M1903.)

"DCM Treasure" by T. B. Gresham, July, Aug., Sept., Oct., Nov., 1948. (Detailed instructions on remodeling M1903 rifles, including stocking.)

"Springfield Patent Troubles" by G. Lyle, Dec., 1949.

"Trigger for your Springfield" by F. F. Berman, July, 1950. (How to make a single stage adjustable trigger for the M1903.)

"Remodeling your Springfield" by C. E. Graves, Oct., 1950. (On remodeling the M1903.)

"A Fallen Springfield" by G. R. Parizek, Nov., 1950. (On making a M1903 into a .410 shotgun.)

".22 Springfield Rifles" by M. D. Waite, July, 1954.

"Remodeling the 03A3 Springfield" by M. D. Waite, Aug., 1957. (Complete information, plus instructions on how to drill and tap the receiver for sights and scope mounts.)

"A Match Rifle from the 03A3" by M. D. Waite, Sept., 1957.

" '03 Firing Pin"—A Dope Bag Report, Jan., 1959, p. 54. (Describes the B-Square one-piece firing pin for the M1903.)

" '03 Conversion Kit"—A Dope Bag Report, March, 1959, p. 57. (Describes the Numrich kit to convert M1903s to .22 rimfire caliber.)

"Sporterizing the Springfield Pistol-Grip Stock" by F. de Haas, Dec., 1962. (How to remodel the Type-C stock.)

"A Free-Rifle from a 1903 Springfield" by C. J. Davis, May, 1963.

"Economy Sporter from the '03A3"—NRA Staff, May, 1964.

"Lightweight Mountain Sheep Rifle" by J. Bryant, Sept., 1970, p. 32. (Making up a lightweight turnbolt sporting rifle.)

STOCKS & STOCKMAKING
"Handicapped Barrels" by H. J. Burkhard, Dec., 1940. (Stocking and bedding a bolt action.)

"Rebedding the Bolt-Actions" by B. Popowski, Sept., 1941. (Tips on bedding the M70 Winchester.)

"Rifle Restocking" by J. Feerick, June, 1943. (How to restock a bolt action starting from a blank.)

"Fundamentals of Gunstock Design" by C. Barker, Feb., 1944. (Sound information on stock design for bolt action rifles.)

"Inletting for Accuracy" by M. Holmes, Feb., 1947. (Finer points on inletting bolt action rifles.)

"Making a Gunstock" by O. V. Stephens, Jr., Nov., 1947. (Design, layout, inletting and finishing.)

"Gunstocks & Accuracy" by C. Taylor & D. A. Robbins, Oct., 1949.

"Laminated Stock Blanks" by J. F. Himes, Jan., 1950.

"Remodeling that Factory Stock" by C. A. Shields, Dec., 1955.

"Stocking the Match Rifle" by R. F. Dunlap, Aug., 1962.

"Stocking Sporter & Varmint Rifles" by M. G. Holmes, Oct., 1962.

"Bedding the Mauser-Type Rifle"—NRA Staff, Mar., 1963.

"Gunstock Design" by A. Guymon, Oct., 1963. (Details of the famous "Guymon" sporter stock.)

"Remodel that Stock to Suit your Taste" by J. Hanson, July, 1970, p. 42. (Tips on remodeling the factory stock on a turnbolt sporting rifle.)

TARGET RIFLES
"Let's Examine the Free Rifle" by R. F. Dunlap, Nov., 1952. (Information on building free rifles on bolt actions.)

"Thoughts on Free-Rifles" by A. E. Cook, Apr., 1956.

"Danish M52 Rifle"—A Dope Bag Report, June, 1957, p. 67. (Covers the M52 .30-06 target rifle.)

"Modern Bench Rest Shooting" by C. H. Hollidge, June, 1962.

"Making a Free-Rifle" by W. B. Vincent, Jan., 1967.

"Rifles for V's at 1000 Yards" by L. F. Moore, July, 1968.

"New Rule Broadens British High-Power Rifle Shooting" by E. H. Harrison, Jan., 1969. (Describes some bolt action target rifles used in England.

TRIGGERS
"Self-Setting Triggers" by F. C. Ness, July, 1939. (Describes the Pike self-setting trigger mechanism for centerfire bolt action rifles.)

"An Adjustable Military Trigger" by A. J. Tiroff, Dec., 1956. (How to modify the common military bolt action trigger so it is adjustable.)

"Winchester Model 70 . . . Set Triggers" by J. E. Gebby, May, 1959. (Notes on a double set trigger for the M70.)

"A Set Trigger for the Model 70" by S. Kol, July, 1962. (How to install a common double set trigger.)

"Set Triggers" by F. de Haas, July, 1963. (Describes several set trigger mechanisms for bolt action rifles, discusses their purpose and use.)

"Sporting Triggers for Military Rifles" by M. D. Waite, March, 1965. (Review of the commercial triggers available.)

WEATHERBY RIFLES

"Weatherby Mark V"—A Dope Bag Report, Nov., 1958, p. 66.

"Weatherby Mark V Rifle" by T. E. Wessel, Apr., 1963. (Exploded view drawing and assembly instructions.)

"Weatherby Varmintmaster"—A Dope Bag Report, July, 1964, p. 72. (Evaluation of the Mark V .224 Weatherby.)

".240 Weatherby Magnum"—A Dope Bag Report, Feb., 1968, p. 50. (Evaluation of the Mark V .240 Weatherby.)

"Weatherby .22-250 Rifle"—A Dope Bag Report, Apr., 1968, p. 51.

"Weatherby Vanguard Rifle"—A Dope Bag Report, Nov., 1970. (Test report on this medium-priced Japanese-made sporting rifle.)

WINCHESTER RIFLES

"The Model 54 Winchester Hornet Rifle" by F. C. Ness, May, 1933.

"The New Model 70 Winchester" by F. C. Ness, Nov., 1936. (First Dope Bag report.)

"A 54 Winchester Conversion" by H. R. Longo, June, 1937. (Converting a .30-30 to .30-40.)

"The Ideal .25 Sporter" by F. C. Ness, June, 1938. (Describing the M70 in .250 caliber.)

"M70 Trigger Corrections" by A. H. Barr, July, 1943. (How to improve the M70 trigger.)

"Two Guns of Verde Valley" by J. Berryman, Apr., 1946. (Story on the Savage 23D Hornet and the M70.)

"Rifle for the Southwest" by E. B. Mann, Jan., 1950. (Making a lightweight sporter of the M70.)

"Three-in-one Rifle" by R. Hutton, Apr., 1950. (Discusses interchangeable stocks on the M70.)

"For the Biggest Game" by J. S. Hatcher, Aug., 1956. (Report on the M70 in .458 Magnum.)

"Winchester Model 70 Rifle" by J. M. Triggs, May, 1962. (Exploded view drawing and assembly instructions.)

"Model 70 Winchester"—A Dope Bag Report, March, 1964, p. 44. (Evaluation of the 1964 version of the M70.)

".225 Winchester"—A Dope Bag Report, Oct., 1964. (Evaluation on the M70 varmint rifle.)

"Winchester Model 670 Rifle"—A Dope Bag Report, July, 1966, p. 54. (Evaluation and test report.)

"Mannlicher-Style M70 Rifle"—A Dope Bag Report, Jan., 1968, p. 55.

"New Winchester Model 70"—A Dope Bag Report, May, 1968, p. 48. (Evaluation of the 1968 rifle.)

"Winchester Model 770 Magnum"—A Dope Bag Report, July, 1970.

"Winchester Model 70 Target Rifle"—A Dope Bag Report, Oct., 1970.

UNCLASSIFIED

"German Arms Codes" by W. H. B. Smith, Apr., 1947.

"Some Interesting Clips" by C. H. Yust, Jr., June, 1960. (Covers many different military rifle cartridge clips.)

"Handling Bolt-Action Centerfire Rifles"—NRA Staff, Oct., 1961. (How to operate, load, fire, field strip the most common bolt action rifles.)

"Bolt Action Operation" by J. F. Kohl, Sept., 1966.

Index

Page number in bold indicates barrel shank drawing